2.0

Alfred Kazin

Alfred Kazin

A Biography

RICHARD M. COOK

Yale University Press   New Haven & London

Designed by James J. Johnson and set in New Caledonia Roman by Keystone Typesetting, Inc.
Printed in the United States of America.

Library of Congress Cataloging-in-Publication Data

Cook, Richard M., 1941–

Alfred Kazin : a biography / Richard M. Cook.

p. cm.

Includes bibliographical references (p.   ) and index.

ISBN 978-0-300-11505-5 (alk. paper)

1. Kazin, Alfred, 1915–1998. 2. American literature—History and criticism—Theory, etc.
3. Criticism—United States—History—20th century. 4. Criticism—United States—History—20th
century. 5. United States—Intellectual life—20th century. 6. Critics—United States—Biography.
I. Title.

PS29.K38A3 2007

809—dc22

[B]

2007019874

A catalogue record for this book is available from the British Library.

The paper in this book meets the guidelines for permanence and durability of the Committee on
Production Guidelines for Book Longevity of the Council on Library Resources.

10 9 8 7 6 5 4 3 2 1

B
KAZIN
ALFRED
C

To Sylvia, Rachel, and Rebecca

Contents

Acknowledgments

I am indebted to many people for help with this book, including, especially, the late Alfred Kazin. He granted me many interviews, helped me obtain copies of his journals, and wrote lengthy letters answering my questions. Since his death in 1998, his widow, Judith Dunford, has been helpful in every imaginable way. Without her cooperation, support, and encouragement, this book would could not have been written. Michael and Cathrael Kazin were both forthcoming and generous with their time, answering my questions about their father and providing me with valuable correspondence. I am grateful to a number of people for granting me interviews and making material available to me: Ann Birstein, Daniel and Pearl Bell, Daniel Aaron, Saul Bellow, Mary Beth McMahon, Morris Dickstein, Jackson Bryer, Irving Kristol, Nathan Glazer, Norman Podhoretz, Daniel Born, Joseph Epstein, Peter Davison, Robert Giroux, Gerald Sorin, Anne Fadiman, Jonathan Rosen, and Louis Menand.

I thank the following for granting me permission to quote from letters to Alfred Kazin: Elizabeth Hardwick, Philip Roth, Herbert Mitgang, Robert Cowley, Marcia Adams, Robert Wojtowicz, Katrin Geller, Peter Stimson Brooks, Betty T. Rahv, Mary Powlesland Commager, and Neil Kosodoy.

I am particularly grateful to Morris Dickstein for reading some of the chapters and offering sound advice. My colleague Joseph Carroll not only read the chapters as they were being written, he reread them and provided critical and moral support when I most needed it.

I owe a very special debt to Isaac Gewirtz, curator of the Henry W. and Albert A. Berg Collection of English and American Literature at the New York Public Library, and to Stephen Crook and Philip Milito, also at the Berg. Their cooperation and help have been indispensable. I also thank Mary Zettwoch, Barbara Hufker, Aziz Atai-Langroudi, and the entire library staff at the University of Missouri–St. Louis for their patience and labors helping me obtain (and retain) necessary material. I very much appreciate the encouragement and support of Barbara Kachur, chair of the English Department at the University of Missouri–St. Louis.

Special thanks also to the following libraries and archives: Beinecke Rare Book and Manuscript Library, Yale University; State Historical Association of Wisconsin; Rare Book and Manuscript Library, Columbia University; Newberry Library, Chicago; Rare Book Room, Smith College Library; Harry Ransome Humanities Research Center, University of Texas at Austin; Bancroft Library, University of California at Berkeley; Seeley G. Mudd Manuscript Library, Princeton University Archives; Brooklyn College Library; the U.S. Library of Congress; and the John Simon Guggenheim Memorial Foundation.

I thank the University of Missouri Research Council and the University of Missouri–St. Louis Research Board for two semesters paid teaching leave that enabled me to move ahead with the writing.

At every point, my wife, Sylvia, has been supportive, patient, and understanding. I am grateful beyond measure for her careful reading, encouragement, and advice.

CHAPTER ONE

Brownsville

The early summers, when I was either too young or we too poor for me to go to camp. The hot afternoons and the tenement women coming back from the market. And then that moment (this it was that always *made* summer: the moment of pause, the enervating season) when mama would say (after hours at the machine), "Oh, it's too hot, too hot!" And I would walk down to [Public School] 66, where the other children would gather to play in the cool basket-ball sweat of the halls downstairs. The fruits on the stand, the jacks on the cool brown floor in the dust, mama in her house dress. Why does this memory seem at once so dim, trivial, and yet so inexpressibly dear to me? Looking back upon it is like opening my mind to everything out of that childhood I've wanted so desperately to lose and can never lose.

—Alfred Kazin, Journal, September 6, 1942

Brownsville is that road which every other road in my life has had to cross," Alfred Kazin wrote in the first pages of his memoir *A Walker in the City* (1951), describing his return to the family flat at 256 Sutter Avenue, where he had been born thirty-six years earlier, on June 5, 1915. He had been leaving and returning and leaving since he was old enough to walk the streets—Blake, Sutter, Dumont, Pitkin—of his neighborhood on the far eastern edge of Brooklyn, the next-to-the-last stop on the subway line, where "they locked up the subway and trolley cars" for the night. He would marry in 1938 and move into a place of his own. His parents would live on in Brownsville until 1957. By then, the Brownsville in which he had grown up—Jewish Brownsville, with its synagogues, butcher shops, and drugstores (the funny-shaped bottles of blue water in the windows)—had largely disappeared. Most of the Jewish residents, once so numerous that to young Alfred's eyes "everyone and everything was Jewish," had left, replaced by blacks and Puerto Ricans. Kazin would continue to return, occasionally as a sightseer, frequently in memory, to tell and retell the story of his beginnings—his mother's kitchen, the terrors of school, his endless walks, his solitary reading, his fascination with the city, "brilliant and unreal" in the distance, his desperation to leave.[1]

The story of Alfred Kazin's Brownsville youth and rapid rise to literary-cultural fame has become part of the larger story (or legend) of notable American successes. At the age of twenty-seven, the son of poor Jewish immigrants—a house painter when there was work and a seamstress who spoke little English—publishes a monumental study of modern American prose that turns him, virtually overnight, into an international authority on American literature. That the book, *On Native Grounds* (1942), documents the democratic impulse in modern American prose when much of the world had fallen under totalitarian tyranny only made the achievement the more significant and the story of its young Jewish-American author the more compelling. What better evidence, what better symbol, of the political-cultural differences between democratic America and Fascist Europe? The twenty-seven-year-old writer—identified by more than one reviewer as a "prodigy" and " the boy wonder of American criticism"—succeeded immediately to the literary editorship of the *New Republic*, a post formerly held by Edmund Wilson and Malcolm Cowley.[2]

More successes would follow. The publication of *A Walker in the City* in 1951 constituted a very different order of achievement, indicating a talent that went beyond the writing of literary criticism and history. A highly evocative, "Proustian" account of Kazin's Brownsville youth, *Walker* would soon be canonized as a central text of American-Jewish writing. In two sequels, *Starting Out in the Thirties* (1965) and *New York Jew* (1978), he would extend his story to tell of "the rise of Alfred Kazin" and more generally that of "the coming of the Jews" into the literary mainstream. "My autobiography will always be most deeply the autobiography of a Jew," he wrote in a 1960s journal entry. Yet Kazin tended to go his own way on Jewish matters, as in other things. Unobservant and largely uninterested in Judaism, he forged his sense of what it meant to be Jewish by exploring (and cultivating) the "inner truth" and "inner estrangements" that he felt as a Jew and an American. Though often grouped with the (mostly Jewish) "New York Intellectuals," who came to prominence in the postwar years, he typically resisted that and all other classifications he believed limited the range of his interests and sympathies. "I was never truly part of *a group.*" He preferred to think of himself as simply "a writer"—an Emersonian thinker-at-large working less in the spirit of the group-minded *Partisan Review* than that of the independent-minded Edmund Wilson, whom he revered and with whom he was frequently compared. In more than a thousand reviews and essays, several books of literary criticism and literary history, and three highly regarded "personal histories," Kazin built and sustained a reputation over sixty years as one of the country's most widely read and influential writer-critics. His death in 1998 was mourned widely as the passing of America's last great "man-of-letters."[3]

Alfred Kazin's rise was not, however, one of uninterrupted advance, clear direction, and unwavering personal assurance. Indeed, for a writer whose public life seemed to move from triumph to triumph, who pronounced with confidence on books, public events, and cultural trends, Kazin was in many ways surprisingly insecure, self-doubting, and self-critical—qualities known to family members and friends, but evident as well in his private journals. "Always conscious of being surprised by my sane, active, responsible *public role,*" he wrote in a 1966 entry, while reflecting on Lionel Trilling's cultural status relative to his own. "When," he asked himself, "would the 'weak' self catch up with me, 'the personal darkness,' the old domestic tradition of pain?" The journals, in which Kazin had been writing since high school, provide a revealing commentary on (and counterpoint to) his public role and apparent success; and frequently their self-questioning, often mordant, speculation leads straight back to "darkest Brownsville," to his parents' "loveless marriage," to his father's "crippling weakness," to his mother's obsessive fears, to his sometimes terrifying loneliness. "My mother had said: Your destiny, ours, is to be weak and sufferers, to deny our strength, to be losers . . . No wonder that I have always referred to *that* tradition in my mind." Brownsville, he believed, was the home of that "weak self" to which he attributed many of his professional and personal (marital) difficulties; but it was also the source, the final source, of his personal aspirations and creative needs. However painful, returning to Brownsville in person and imagination was as essential to his rhythm as a writer, "the push toward home and the pull away again," as it had been in his first adventuring walks into the city.[4]

Family and School

Alfred Kazin's parents, Gita Fagelman and Gedahlia "Charles" Kazin, immigrant Jews from the Minsk area of Poland, had met and married in 1913 in a boarding house on Manhattan's Lower East Side. Shortly afterward, they had moved to 256 Sutter Avenue in Brownsville. Brownsville apartments were plentiful and relatively cheap, enabling the Kazins to rent a four-room flat, which they occupied for the next forty years. At the time, Brownsville was an intensely Jewish world, "the Jerusalem of America," with synagogues on virtually every block. Populated by the largest concentration of Jewish residents in the country after the Lower East Side, it allowed recent immigrants to feel as much at home as possible in a strange, foreign country. Kazin would recall that "living there was like living in a Polish or Russian *shtetl*" and that his neighborhood seemed in many ways an extended family. In fact, many of the neighbors were relatives—aunts, cousins, great-aunts, and uncles. Others were from nearby villages back in *"der heym."* The Dugschitz synagogue, which the Kazins attended, took its name from the town in which his mother had lived in Poland, and many in the congregation were either relatives or old family friends. Alfred would later say that he was forbidden to enter any other of the nearby synagogues: "The little synagogue was 'our' place."[5]

Gita, a stout, plain-looking woman, who in appearance reminded her son of Emma Goldman, had arrived in New York in 1907 at the age of eighteen, accompanied by an older brother. An accomplished seamstress, she quickly found work in the infamous Triangle Shirtwaist Factory on the East Side to which she walked every day from her rented room on Orchard Street. Charles, a shy, handsome man, who passed on his good looks to his son, arrived finally in New York by a more circuitous route. Born in Minsk in 1887, he had moved with his parents to New York in the early 1890s but had returned to Europe with his mother after his father died of tuberculosis. Charles was never able to find any information about his father, whose body was thrown into a mass grave on the Lower East Side. Alfred, who took his grandfather's Hebrew name, Abraham, would later speculate that he had been a pieceworker toting a rented sewing machine through the crowded Lower East Side streets looking for jobs. Alfred also liked to think of his grandfather as a Socialist and labor organizer, "organizing miserable piece workers like himself"—though he admitted he had little hard evidence for his speculations. "The name was everything to me, but the name was pretty much all I had."[6]

Following Abraham's death and her return to Europe, Charles's mother had placed her son in an orphanage, remarried, and raised another family. It was a devastating experience from which Charles never recovered. Alfred would come to see his father as a perennial orphan—abandoned, lonely, bewildered, uncertain about the world, uneasy around the family, always ready to make a quick exit—"the lonesomest man in the world, more like a son than a father." At twenty, however, Charles had been adventurous enough to get himself back to New York, and from there to various jobs around the country. A Jewish immigration society found him work in a potash factory in Albany, New York. He went next to Chicago, where he worked in the stockyards shaking cattle skins free of salt, then, as a stitcher in the Hart, Shaffner, and Marx factory. He eventually landed a job painting boxcars for the Union Pacific Railroad. That job took him around much of the Midwest and eventually to Colorado, where, he told his son, he had been offered a homestead. Kazin would later claim that he owed his fascination with the American Midwest and his love of traveling to his father's wistful descriptions of his travels throughout the American heartland. He recalled challenging him about the homestead. Why hadn't he taken the offer? "Why do we always have to live here [in Brownsville]!" His father's answer was simple: he was lonely and there were no Jewish girls in Colorado. In 1912, five years after he had landed at Ellis Island, Charles returned to New York. There, in an East Side boarding house, he met and married Gita Fagelman, a marriage that Alfred believed sprang less from love than a mutual fear of loneliness. "They had settled on each other in disbelief that anyone else would love them."[7]

Once the couple moved to Brownsville, Gita set up shop in her kitchen, making dresses for relatives, friends, and neighborhood clients. The arrangement suited her skill as a seamstress, her dressmaker's eye for fashion and design, and her extraordinary industriousness. It also allowed her to work at home after her son was born. Though hardly lucrative, the work was reasonably steady. It tided the family over "slack" times when painting jobs were scarce and served as virtually the sole source of family income throughout the Depression. But for all his mother's resourcefulness, life was often hard and frightening. *"Geyst arbeiten?"* Will there be work? was her perennially anxious question after Alfred's father came home from the worker's pool in front of the Municipal Bank on Pitkin Avenue. Like other families in the neighborhood, the Kazins lived in constant fear that the work would stop and they would be evicted. It was not an unfamiliar sight, particularly during the Depression, to see families put out on the street in the rain with all their furniture. Kazin would recall with pride that after one eviction, his mother staged a protest, defied the marshals, rounded up the neighbors, and carried the furniture back into the house.[8]

The Kazin apartment was on the third floor of one of the many non-descript Brownsville tenements. After climbing the stairs, one entered the apartment through a long, unlit hallway, which usually smelled of paint from his father's overalls. At the end of the hall was the icebox. Alfred and his mother regularly filled it with ice blocks from an ice vender two blocks away, carrying the chunks in a towel stretched between them. To the left of the icebox was the door to the kitchen, the largest room in the apartment and "the center of everything." For most of his childhood, the only source of heat was a large black country stove in the kitchen. In winter, the front rooms were closed off, and on cold nights Alfred slept on three chairs arranged in front of the stove, which frequently malfunctioned. He remembered the day the landlord, "an immense, powerfully bearded Jew, named Wishnevski," showed up at the apartment, and after loud mutterings about how he made nothing from such tenants, suddenly with one arm threw the stove over. "My mother screamed. I made a mental vow to kill him when I got just a bit older." In summer the flat could become unbearably hot. Like many other tenement kids, Alfred often slept on the fire escape.[9]

Life at home was concentrated in the kitchen, and the kitchen took its character from his mother, always at work. There, Kazin wrote, "I gained my first picture of life as a white, overheated, starkly lit workshop redolent with Jewish cooking, crowded with women in housedressess, strewn with fashion magazines, patterns, dress material, spools of thread—and at whose center, so lashed to her machine that bolts of energy seemed to dance out of her hands and feet as she worked, my mother stamped the treadle hard against the floor, hard, hard and silently, grimly at war, beat out the first rhythm of the world for me." When Alfred went to bed, his mother would be at the kitchen table working the Singer machine; the first thing he would hear in the morning was the clack of the treadle on the floor. When he returned from school, she would be bent over the wheel, "her hands steering a piece of gauze under the needle with a finesse that always contrasted sharply with her swollen hands and broken nails." Gita Kazin spoke little English and never learned to read it. Alfred spoke to her in English and she replied in Yiddish. Only later did he realize they were speaking different languages—"our bilingualism was so complete." She could read Yiddish newspapers, but rarely did; there was simply no time. Intelligent and extraordinarily resourceful, she kept the family together through force of will, fearful vigilance, and a seemingly unlimited capacity for labor. "It was ourselves she stitched together. I can never remember a time when she was not working. She worked because life was work and anxiety."[10]

Kazin would devote substantial sections of his three autobiographies and dozens of journal entries to his mother. Her strong "intuitive intelligence," industry, and anxious, caring watchfulness, as well as her continual presence at home, made her the dominant force in his childhood, largely eclipsing his reclusive father. Later, he came to believe that she had been too dominant, that their relationship had been too intense, that he had been too dependent, too attentive and responsive to her moods and particularly to her fears. With whatever justice, he attributed his own admittedly anxious, fearful nature (as well as his intelligence and capacity for work) to his "fear-packed, unwearied, obsessive mother." He also came to believe that their relationship adversely affected his later relations with women, particularly his wives. "So much of my moral energy has gone into an awareness of the mother, into courting the mother, into disobeying and even cheating on the mother," he reflected on the verge of his forty-ninth birthday. Was it any wonder that he became a self-admitted "mama's boy," that he saw the important women in his life as mother figures on whom he depended for his sense of well-being and against whose authority he felt he needed to rebel? There were plenty of other reasons for Kazin's marital difficulties—including a roving eye and the availability of women attracted to a successful, handsome writer—but it is also likely, as he repeatedly asserts, that his unusual closeness to and dependence on his mother created needs (and conflicts) that would later complicate his relations with women.[11]

Kazin ascribed much of the intensity of his relations with his mother to her anxious concern for his fragile health and to an apparent lack of affection between his parents—they "never chatted easily together, never went off on outings, never laughed or argued. The life between them was usually silent and quite formal"—and to an imbalance in familial authority. Everything "seems to go back to my mother's strength and my father's weakness" —his mother, the "raging life-force," who kept the family together; his father, the silent one, "the untalented man combined with the superfluous man," "papa whom mama talked down," and whom everybody, family and acquaintances, ignored. Indeed, Charles often seemed a stranger in his own home. Arriving from work, he would wash his paint-stained hands in the sink and retire to the "dining room, where nobody dined" to read the Jewish-American newspaper the *Forward* or simply to sit. After supper he would go back silently to his paper or slip quietly out of the apartment to walk the streets alone "Papa was always looking for an exit."[12]

Charles was not wholly without influence, however. Kazin later wrote that he "grew up between two competing religions—my mother was Orthodox and my father was an orthodox socialist." Although bar mitzvahed at the age of thirteen in the Dugschitz synagogue according to his mother's wishes, he would never become an observant Jew or feel comfortable in a synagogue. The mindless recitation of passages before an old melamed, who slapped Alfred's hands as he stammered his way through the Hebrew, was done wholly "for form's sake." The ritual had little meaning for him then, nor would it ever. His father's Socialism, however, did mean something: "It was not Judaism but the labor movement, with my father's old-fashioned socialism throbbing at the center of it, that made *my* great connection to the outside world." Alfred accompanied his father to Socialist meetings at the Brownsville Labor Lyceum on Sackman Avenue as well as to Saturday night lectures at the *Forward* Building on the Lower East Side. The excursions were a connection with the larger political world and a point of personal contact with his father. They were also exciting trolley rides across Brooklyn into the city: "Plunging into the Lower East Side on a busy Saturday night was something else. There were fitfully glittering arc lights along the narrow, darkly huddled streets, jammed along the curb with pushcarts. I could not get over the shrieks and stabs of light against so much darkness. The crowds furiously alive in the street and some long-congealed deadness in the tenements just behind them." Socialism, the *Forward,* the trips to the East Side and occasionally to a museum or a free concert at the Lewisohn Stadium were opportunities to be alone with his father away from "the raging life-force" back in the kitchen. But they were usually disappointing, his father as silent as ever. "Once the show, the concert, the expedition was over, he had nothing to say."[13]

The family imbalances that troubled Kazin were not uncommon in immigrant households—though the emotional reclusiveness of his "orphan" father may have exaggerated them. Immigrant sons, the historian Arthur Hertzberg has observed, often found their fathers ineffective. Whereas energetic mothers could run the household and do piecework at home, the fathers were unable to support their families with their low-paying jobs and were often at a loss dealing with the outside world. "The immigrant mother became the source of family loyalty for her children because she was their protector," Hertzberg writes. "Her labor helped eke out the family budget and made survival and schooling possible. She raised the sons to achieve what her husband had failed to do." Hutchins Hapgood had noted a similar phenomenon in his account of Jewish immigrant families on New York's Lower East Side in 1902. The father, who in Russia enjoyed the authority of traditional family life, found himself no longer "head of the house" in a society where patriarchal authority was not a given, where the mother took care of household needs and relied increasingly on her son to negotiate outside the family. Kazin later came to believe that his family situation might not have been quite so unusual or "queer" as he had long thought and that his own peculiarities of temperament may have "had more to do with the circumstances of immigrant life and Jewish history than individual psychology." "A great many traits that once struck me as being wholly personal I now [in 1984] see as the marks of a distinct culture." But if the experiences were general, they were no less real, no less personal and painful. Alfred was living his own life, however representative or typical.[14]

Considering the formality, or "aridity," of his parents' relationship—"they were terribly lonely people with little comfort in each other"—Kazin was grateful for the presence of "Cousin Sophie," a boarder during much of his childhood. A cousin of his mother's and several years younger, Sophie worked at the Triangle Factory. She helped pay the rent and occasionally looked after Alfred when he was a toddler. Some of his warmest memories of Brownsville were of trips to Coney Island with Sophie. Sophie, who was anything but silent and formal, brought gossip, friends, and personality into the flat. Unmarried and on the lookout for a husband, she was a creature of shifting moods—at times somber and despairing, at other times "violently gay." To the young Alfred, she suggested an exotic world of romance and love that seemed the farthest thing from the staid lives of his parents. There was a "brooding, dark, sultry arousement" about her that he found exciting. She was at her best when she brought home friends from work. Strumming her mandolin and singing, "she radiated, as if it were warmth from her body, a passionate and angry vividness." Sophie's story ended tragically when she ran off in the thirties with an adventurer who abandoned her in the Midwest. She never recovered from the shock and spent the last twenty years of her life in an asylum in Clarendon, Iowa, recognizing no one. But for most of Alfred's childhood Sophie was a welcome, colorful addition to the sober routine of the Kazin household.

The most exciting visitors to the family kitchen were his Aunt Nechama and her off-again, on-again common-law husband, Berl Heller. Another cousin of his mother from Dugschitz, Nechama was a declared anarchist and principled atheist like her husband—"rebels and idealists of the most unyielding sort." Compared with Kazin's "stiffly proper" family, the Hellers were very dramatic, preaching insurrection and defiance—though smiling Nechama was in person "the gentlest of rebels." His mother called her "*Die susser Nechama,*" the sweet Nechama. Although the Hellers were always breaking up and moving to new apartments, leaving their four children with relatives and friends, Kazin remembers them as the family he had always wanted, their bold outspokenness and eruptive married life wholly unlike the quiet, anxious carefulness of his parents. Nechama would remain a favorite of Kazin's, a lively presence at birthdays and family gatherings and a reminder of the freewheeling radical spirit that had at one time excited parts of the Jewish immigrant community. Kazin gave the eulogy at her funeral in 1979, careful not to mention God or religion.[15]

Kazin's sister, Pearl, was born in 1922. Seven years his junior, Pearl seems not to have played a significant role in his childhood. She does not appear in *A Walker in the City* and is mentioned only briefly in *Starting Out in the Thirties*. Like her brother, she grew up a reader. He later recalled that they had both managed to secure illegal library cards, enabling them to take more than the allowable number of books from the Stone Avenue Library, which, he said, they visited every other day for a new supply. Pearl remembers her older brother, already presuming on his authority in reading matters, dictating her literary choices. She, too, would become a reviewer, critic, and essayist, appearing with some regularity in the *New Leader* and *Commentary* and occasionally in the *Wall Street Journal* and *American Scholar.*[16]

Another mutual interest was music. Pearl played the piano, Alfred the violin. When she was old enough, they played duets. Music was an enthusiasm the entire family shared. In *Walker,* Kazin recalls their joining with Sophie's friends singing Yiddish folksongs and Socialist hymns on Friday evenings before the Sabbath—*"Tzuzamen, tzuzamen, ale tzuzamen!"* The singing, in turn, would lead to his mother's asking him to play part of a Tchaikovsky concerto or *Scheherazade* on the violin. "You could melt their hearts with it; the effect of the violin on almost everyone I knew was uncanny." Kazin had few illusions about his ability, calling himself "a poor but determined violinist." But what he lacked in talent he made up for in enthusiasm for the violin and classical music generally. Concerts and new recordings of favorite pieces and artists would be significant events in his life, discussed (often rhapsodically) in his journals. As an adult he would seek out new partners for duets, sometimes family members and in-laws and sometimes friends, including writer Saul Bellow, *New Yorker* cartoonist Saul Steinberg, and poet and literary critic Allen Tate. In his sixties, Kazin would resume violin lessons, an early passion, which, like so much in his Brownsville life, he refused to abandon.[17]

The violin was also a connection with the world outside his home. Alfred played in the school orchestra, sometimes performing duets with Anne Mattus, a "shining Polish girl" who occasionally invited him to her home, where they played together before her family—a practice that disturbed his mother, who would ask warily, "Are you planning on marrying this *Polyishe?*" Playing in the orchestra, however, was about the only pleasure associated with school, which Kazin remembers as a daily ordeal in fear and loathing. The New York public schools have often been credited with challenging and inspiring determined, able students from immigrant backgrounds. Jewish graduates have been especially grateful for the many dedicated and devoted teachers. "The bulk of the memoirs dealing with the

East Side childhood," Irving Howe wrote in *World of Our Fathers*, "contain warm, sometimes remarkably tender descriptions of the years in school." The public school was respected and honored as a place for learning and advancement. But for Alfred Kazin, learning had nothing to do with it—"only the necessity to succeed" and the terror of failure. Returning to the school yard of Franklin K. Lane High School as an adult, he writes in his memoir, "I went sick with my old fear of it. . . . I felt as if I had been mustered back into the service of those Friday morning 'tests' that were the terror of my childhood."[18]

One source of the terror were the frighteningly high stakes and the shame of failure. He was performing not just for himself, but for his parents. To fail was to let them down; worse, it was to expose and shame them—shame those who already felt ashamed, those who were already cowed by teachers and principals, by schools, the authorities, the system. Shame, Kazin remembers, was general among young Brownsville students (and their parents), and the schools contributed significantly to that shame. As the institutions with early and extended contact with the children of immigrants, schools were expected to take a leading role in facilitating and accelerating their "Americanization." Sympathetically implemented, such a process or directive served a valuable end, instructing students (and their parents) about American institutions and familiarizing them with significant features of American history and culture. Too often, however, Americanization worked to intimidate and shame students for their "un-American," "foreign" ways— particularly when teachers and school officials made little effort to hide their personal distaste for the inflected English and "street" manners of their charges. Norman Podhoretz, a graduate of Brownsville schools, remembers a (favorite!) teacher repeatedly calling him a "filthy little slum child" while scolding him for his (and his family's) terrible taste in clothes. More sensitive than most to the humble circumstances of his family, Kazin remembers being utterly abashed by the schools—feelings epitomized in his vision of "the glacially remote Anglo-Saxon principal, whose very name was King." After flunking arithmetic when he was ten years old, he purchased a small amount of iodine in case he decided to kill himself. "The shame of my nothingness in school, of my family's ineptitude in possibly having to account for it, was more than I could bear."[19]

The pressure did not lessen in the upper grades. "I worked on a hairline between triumph and catastrophe," Kazin recalls his anxiety at the time; and catastrophe was only as far off as a poorly done exam or a behavioral infraction. "Make a bad impression, and you might as well cut your throat." Anything less than perfection risked your being "kept back in the working class forever" or even "fall[ing] into the criminal class itself." The source of the pressure was evident—"the mothers who waited on the stoops every day after three for us to bring home tales of our daily triumphs," parents desperate that their children fulfill their own hopes, redeem the sacrifices they had made, the shame they lived with. "Why the odds should always have felt so narrow I understood only when I realized how little my parents thought of their own lives. It was not for myself alone that I was expected to shine, but for them—to redeem the constant anxiety of their existence. I was the first American child, their offering to the strange new God; I was to be their liberation from the shame of being—what they were."[20]

Not every student felt this kind of pressure or responded to it with the same degree of anxious dread. A Brownsville contemporary, William Poster, remembered that, while sensitive to the opinions of teachers and relatives, he and his neighborhood friends took pride in meeting their low expectations and "ardently desired to be even tougher, dirtier, more ill-mannered, more foul-mouthed, more vicious" than they were regularly accused of being. He further remembered that among his acquaintances (an admittedly tough bunch), there was little desire to "make good," much less go on to college. For Kazin, however, the pressure was real enough, and he was not the only one to feel it. "On coming home from work," another Brownsville native recalled, "the first question the good Brownsville father asked was, 'What happened at school?' And the child had to bring out the test marks and papers." If there were As, the entire family felt they had done well. If there were Bs "the whole house went into mourning." Everyone knew what was at stake: "to Brownsville, school represented a glorious future that would rescue it from want, deprivation and ugliness." What was less appreciated was the anxiety such expectations created in the children.[21]

Alfred was stalked by another, more private, terror at school. He stuttered. His mother also stuttered—evidence, he believed, of the emotional connection between them, particularly the contagious fears that obsessed her. "Showing manners" and "speaking nicely" were central to the school effort to "Americanize" him and his classmates. To fumble around and stammer out some unintelligible answer when called on was instant failure, a humiliation he faced every day. For the most part, he kept silent. When he did find himself on his feet struggling to speak—"the black wooden floor would roll away under my feet, the teacher would frown at me in amazement, and in unbearable loneliness, I would hear behind me the groans and laughter: tuh-tuh-tuh-tuh." Even after he had lost his stammer (once he began to publish at age nineteen), the memories of those terrible moments returned like fresh "gashes." "I think of that day in the Lane annex at high school when I stammered so helplessly in class, and felt everyone looking at me in a pitying but remote circle. I went down to the toilet and standing near the slate-gray walls, wept my heart out." Small wonder school evoked anxiety and dread, that Sunday was ruined by the fears of school on Monday, that "all week long [he] lived for the sound of the dismissal gong at three o'clock on Friday afternoon."[22]

The stammer may also have been a factor in his life outside the classroom—which could also be very lonely. In an interview shortly after the publication of *A Walker in the City*, Kazin said that for the most part he had been a "very lonely and unhappy kid," who suffered from a stammer and sought relief in books. He was also an "abnormally 'sensitive,'" child, "plagued with more than the usual allotment of early disabilities"—including an undescended testicle (later corrected) that worried him and his mother. His sister, Pearl, who shared his passion for books, but none of his handicaps, attests to his largely solitary life. Although he had a few casual friends, he was mostly a "loner," his face usually stuck in a book. A book did not look at you enquiringly, impatiently, pityingly. But neither did a book supply the experiences (and social confidence) that came with chumming around with a close circle of friends or belonging to a gang or joining a "movement." William Poster recalled that gangs were very big in Brownsville in the 1920s and 1930s; and Norman Podhoretz, a proud Brownsville gang member, agreed. Virtually everyone belonged to a gang. A gang brought companionship and social order (of a sort) to one's life; it taught friendship and loyalty; and it provided protection, not so much from members of other gangs, as from the insecurities and "inward anarchy" of youth. "As long has he had sufficient strength to participate, [the gang member] was relieved of some of the worst terrors of childhood," according to Poster. "Inclusion in the gang was absolute."[23]

Alfred belonged to no gang. Nor, despite his political sympathies, did he belong to a "movement"—the (Socialist) political equivalent of a gang. New York writers Irving Howe and Daniel Bell belonged to "the movement," and each remembered it as invaluable to his social and intellectual self-confidence. "The movement," Howe recalled, "eased my loneliness, gave me a feeling of place, indulged me in the belief that I had scaled peaks of comprehension." Bell remembered similar feelings of liberation and belonging. Coming out of the closed immigrant world into a political movement with other kids to argue about political-historical matters, he found that "suddenly the whole world opens up. . . . This is what the socialist movement did for me. It suddenly shows there's a world of ideas, a world of experience," and buddies to share it with. Being part of "the movement" for Bell and Howe meant not only hanging out with comrades, talking politics; it meant speaking in public, frequently on street corners. Bell recalled delivering a Eugene Debs speech as a thirteen-year-old to a gratifyingly receptive street audience. Howe remembered yelling at the top of his lungs to passing crowds—without noticeable effect. But if he persuaded few passersby, he affirmed his connection with the group—a shared experience in a "bonding fraternity" that provided him a "home" in the world and even a hope of changing it.[24]

Though Kazin attended meetings of the Young People's Socialist League and was sympathetic to the interests of "the movement, " he did not participate. He did not speak up at meetings, nor harangue crowds on Pitkin Avenue, where the Socialists competed with the Communists for the hearts and minds of the curious Brownsville public. A halting, stammering response to the latest Communist charge of a Socialist "sellout" would not have served anyone's interest. Instead, he listened; and, as the Socialists' meetings droned on Sunday evenings in the Labor Lyceum, he read—the speeches and the arguments fading to background noise as he settled into *The Portrait of the Artist as a Young Man* or the latest Edmund Wilson book review. With a book in his hand, Kazin learned early the knack of "being with people and yet not being with them"—a condition that suited his "solitary" disposition, but one, he would later acknowledge, that may have entailed lasting personal costs.[25]

It would be difficult to overestimate the importance of reading on Kazin's childhood and early development. "I read walking in the street, to and from the Children's Library on Stone Avenue, on the fire escape and the roof; at every meal when they would let me; read even when I dressed in the morning, propping my book up against the drawers on the bureau as I pulled on my long black stockings." Other successful writers from immigrant backgrounds have testified to their early love of reading, but Kazin's seems exceptional. With few friends and no "movement" or gang or other group activities to occupy him, he turned to books (and writing) for diversion, making a virtue of necessity. "As the years mounted, I was happiest when alone, reading and beginning to note in my school notebook what I thought of the books I was reading." In an important sense Kazin's reading was not escapist, offering, as it did, connections to everything beyond 256 Sutter Avenue—to the past, to "the America my parents would never know," to writers with whom he shared "subterranean channels of sympathy," to "the great world that was anything just out of Brownsville." Yet, together with his practice of writing in a diary, it was a daily temptation to self-preoccupation and "self-withdrawal," a term his later brother-in-law, Daniel Bell, associated with Kazin's childhood tendencies, and a habit that only increased his feelings of solitude and isolation. Was he already repeating the lonely pattern of his father? Years later, he would look back on his early infatuation with books and writing as both a promise and a warning: a promise of his literary future, a warning that "there would be trouble ahead, and that I would pay for this precious solitude."[26]

By his senior year in Franklin K. Lane High School, that promise was showing scattered signs of fulfillment and even provoking a little recognition. Kazin was now associate editor of his high school literary magazine and, if the caption by his picture in his high school yearbook is any indication, known by his classmates for his literary and musical ambitions and his scholarly promise:

> A Galsworthy and a Paderewski
> In vain would he be;
> But methinks that a scholar
> He is more apt to be.

One of his English teachers, Samuel Zisowitz, had recognized his writing talent and had strongly encouraged him to pursue it. Another teacher, Julian Aronson, not only encouraged him, but met with him after school to hear him read from entries in his notebook. Kazin remembers walking around the reservoir in Highland Park listening to the sound of his (un-stammering) voice reading out passages to Aronson from his journal. It seems "the word," so long a "secret ordeal" in school, was opening up possibilities outside the classroom. He was also meeting a few other literary enthusiasts—some of them as shy and socially ill at ease as himself—but who could talk passionately about Keats and Shelley, Blake and Coleridge, Ezra Pound's *Cantos* and T. S. Eliot's *The Waste Land*. His favorite among them was Bernie Davidson ("David" in *A Walker in the City*).

A chemistry student who lived with his cancer-stricken mother in the poorest section of Brownsville, Davidson was not only passionate about literature (especially Blake), he was a committed social activist, who knew his Marx and Lenin and kept himself expertly informed on "the Negro question" in America. (He also knew when the Modern Library books would go on sale at Macy's.) But what most fixed Davidson in Kazin's memory were the visits to his house, down Sutter, past the old basement tinshops, sweatshops, and crumbling, unpainted synagogues to Van Susteren and the border area separating Brownsville from the railroad yards. There, "as far as possible from the *alrightniks* on Eastern Boulevard," in a rotting house, nearly bare of furniture, with the noise of trains shuttling in the yards, Davidson would talk about Marx, Blake, Beethoven, recent accounts of Negro lynchings and the police beating of picketers—his mother "already yellow from the cancer," sitting in one of the few chairs and listening intently. The visits would stay with Kazin as instances of the intense idealism, hope, and fierce class loyalty that were as much a part of his Brownsville youth as the drabness, poverty, and loneliness. Visits to Bernie Davidson's did not lead to the comradely solidarity that Howe and Bell found so rewarding in "the movement." They did, however, appeal to an idealism that transcended the grim, desperate surroundings. More than Davidson's poverty, "more even than the sense of impending death, it was some deep, brave, awful earnestness before life that I always felt there."[27]

Kazin would later speak derisively of the "sticky" idealism and "sentimental universalism" he had absorbed from his family and the Brownsville Socialist milieu. He would also speak of the "violent class prejudice" he traced back to his parents' resentment of the middle-class Jewish "*alrightniks*" making out "all right" on Eastern Boulevard. But while bemused and partly embarrassed by these feelings and their strange persistence, he never successfully suppressed them. "In my youth, our hearts were touched with fire," he would write a few years before his death. "Something in our old poor tenement Jewish life, uplifted by the ideals and energy of the Jewish labor movement and the messianism of our fathers' primitive Bund Social- ism, gave me images of value I have never lost." Nor would he shed his class prejudice, those "social resentments of the rich . . . and other enemies of the good old Jewish proletariat" that were so much his parents' resentments—"a bond that has strangely persisted into the shadow of my death." Those social resentments would prove useful in his autobiographies, particularly in his acid portraits of latter-day *alrightniks* and various notable personalities who had "made it." They did not, however, prevent him from trying to find his own way out of Brownsville, not, to be sure, to the "*alrightnik*" enclaves of Eastern Boulevard, but to the possibilities and satisfactions that he felt awaited him in the "brilliant" city beyond the Brooklyn Bridge.[28]

Though Kazin would later write movingly about the pull back toward Brownsville, Sutter Avenue, and his mother's kitchen, the stronger pull had always been toward the world "beyond"—a talismanic word in his accounts of his Brownsville youth. "Beyond" was the world of books and movies, "where there was nothing to remind me of Brownsville." "Beyond" were the trips into Manhattan Saturday evenings with his father. "Beyond" was America, the America to which he already felt personally and imaginatively connected—the American Midwest described by his father in rare mo- ments of conversation, the America in the pictures hanging in the Ameri- can wing of the Metropolitan Museum—skaters in Central Park, a "red muffler flying in the wind"; crowds circling Union Square; a John Sloan picture of a girl on the deck of a New York ferry boat—the America of Lewis Mumford's *The Brown Decades* with its pictures of the Brooklyn Bridge and the brownstones of Brooklyn Heights from the era of Kazin's parents' arrival. He may have resented the condescension of his teachers toward their Brownsville charges and "the sickening evocation of 'Ameri- canism'—the word itself accusing us of everything we apparently were not." But the resentment did not suppress his growing fascination with the country. Nor, he writes in *Walker*, did it dim the power and the promise he saw in the giant photograph of Theodore Roosevelt hanging in the school assembly hall. "*There* was the other land . . . the new land, that light dancing off the glasses of Theodore Roosevelt." He had read *The Boys' Life of Theodore Roosevelt.* He knew the president had been New York police commissioner, walking the streets of the city. He had looked into *Theodore Roosevelt's Letters to His Children* as though they were written to him. "*There* was America, I thought, the real America, *his* America, where from behind the glass on the wall he watched over us to make sure we did right, thought right, lived right."[29]

One cannot know how much Kazin's detailed descriptions of his early passion for America owe to retrospection. Had he, in fact, gone from room to room in the Met thinking they had painted his city, his country? Had he really imagined that Roosevelt might have written the letters to him? Such specific recollections undoubtedly owe as much to the imagination and the creative demands of art as to the reliability of memory—though Kazin prided himself on his Proustian ability to recall childhood detail. Whatever the accuracy of specific memories, there is no doubting the intensity of his youthful desire to connect with the world beyond Brownsville, a desire fed by books, by trips into the city, by paintings, and by loneliness. Unlike William Poster, who would look back gratefully to the daily adventures and the social advantages of growing up in Brownsville; unlike Norman Podhoretz, who remembers greeting his parents' proposed move from Brownsville with "howls of protest"; unlike Irving Howe and Daniel Bell, who had little interest in moving away from the excitements and protections of "the movement"; Kazin spent much of his mostly unhappy youth yearning for something altogether different, for a life elsewhere, anywhere "just out of Brownsville." It is hardly surprising that he would search out points of personal connection with the country beyond—his father's Midwest, T.D.R.'s New York, the brownstone district of Brooklyn—or that he would treasure those images of New York—skaters in Central Park, the Brooklyn Bridge, the harbor ferries—that depict and sanction his own perceptions and responses to the city. They were describing or painting a city, which from his walks and rides he could already in some sense recognize as his own—"my city, my country."[30]

Kazin would draw on this early passion for an American connection in the writing of his literary history, *On Native Grounds*—one of the more extraordinary personal efforts of connection and possession in American literary scholarship. Looking back on its writing years later, he wrote that he "fell in love with it [American literature] because in a sense this literature was mine—I felt part of it and at home with it. . . . I responded [to the writers and their texts] with intellectual kinship and pleasure. I knew the modulations of their language; I could see their landscapes. And very important, indeed, I shared much of their belief in the ideal freedom and power of the self, in the political and social visions of radical democracy." Sitting in the Franklin K. Lane assembly hall, watching "the light dancing off the glasses of Theodore Roosevelt," he could hardly have been aware of the lasting import of the impressions he was accumulating; he certainly could not have imagined that in ten years he would be on the verge of publishing a breakthrough literary history celebrating America's storied democracy. As late as his junior year in college, he had no intention of becoming a literary critic, much less one concentrating on American literature. (To think of oneself as a specialist in American literature would have been a "confession of mediocrity.") Except for the vague, albeit intense, desire to become a writer and an occasional thought about teaching high school, Kazin had no idea of what profession he might pursue. But the images, landscapes, voices, and especially the personal hope—"the ideal freedom and power of the self"—were in place when the time came—a reservoir of impressions and feelings telling him that "the other land, the new land" was there to be claimed.[31]

CHAPTER TWO

The Thirties
Starting Out

Salvation Would Come by the Word.

—*Starting Out in the Thirties*

In early September 1931, sixteen-year-old Alfred Kazin climbed the long hill from the 137th Street IRT subway exit toward the Gothic spires of City College for his first class as an entering freshman. The ride from Brownsville had taken an hour and a quarter, and the return trip would take at least as long. The ride would have been much shorter to Brooklyn College, recently opened in buildings around Borough Hall, but Kazin had chosen "City." It was "famous, awesome, and severe," accepting only the top 10 or 12 percent of graduating seniors. It also had some notable alumni: Upton Sinclair, Bernard Baruch, Felix Frankfurter, Lewis Mumford, and the philosopher Morris Cohen, currently the most celebrated professor at the college. Kazin knew that he would be in the company of some very intelligent colleagues; he also knew that most of them (85 percent) would be Jewish, commuting from working-class neighborhoods similar to his own. They, too, were attracted by the school's reputation and its free tuition—tuition at Columbia, which restricted Jewish admissions, was six hundred dollars. The only costs at City, which had no ethnic quotas, was the ten-cent round-trip subway fare; twenty cents for food (or a brown bag lunch brought from home); and the price of books, a hardship for many students.[1]

The decision to go to college had not been difficult; he had never thought seriously of not going. For all his fears and frustrations in school, Kazin had proved an earnest and able (mathematics excepted) student. College was the surest route out of Brownsville to a better life. But in the fall of 1931, what that better life might entail was an unanswerable question. The country had not yet reached the depths of the Depression, but conditions were grim and getting worse. The crash of 1929 had not immediately affected working-class families like the Kazins, but the bank failures in 1930 had brought the crisis closer. The closure of New York City's Bank of the United States on December 11, 1930, brought it still closer. Owned and operated by Jews, known by many as the "Pantspressers' Bank," it held the deposits of thousands of Jewish immigrants, many of them attached to the garment industry. Gains in collective bargaining were soon wiped out; workers were being dismissed; piecework and sweatshops of preunion days were coming back. Kazin's mother's clients had less discretionary income to spend on the clothes she made, and by 1931 his father could not find work. "No one who grew up in the Depression has ever recovered from it," Kazin wrote in a 1980 review of Malcolm Cowley's memoir, *The Dream of the Golden Mountains*. "To anyone who grew up in a family where the father was usually looking for work, every image of the thirties is gray, embittered."[2]

Yet the most memorable images Kazin has left us from the thirties are neither gray nor embittered. The dominant feeling that his celebrated memoir of the period, *Starting Out in the Thirties*, conveys is hope—hope tempered with dread to be sure, but hope all the same, hope in the form of personal expectations, but also utopian hope for a radically altered world. The events that were convulsing the country, keeping his father from work and terrifying his mother, were also creating conditions in which a young, would-be writer-radical could feel that his experiences growing up in working-class Brownsville had special pertinence and value. He might even come to feel, as Kazin wrote in his memoir, that there was a connection between his expectations and the direction of history—that "just as I was trying to break through, so history was seeking its appointed consummation."[3]

It is difficult to know how seriously or consistently Kazin entertained such thoughts at the time, particularly in the lonely, bleak years at City College. Hitler's takeover early in 1933 hardly inspired confidence in the direction of history. "The war is coming. I know it," Kazin wrote in his journal in September 1933, adding rather melodramatically, "Such a darkness as will now infect me and my generation would have led him [Christ] to deny his own Heavenly father." Years later, he could still recall the tension, the claustrophobic sense of being trapped in the terrible logic of events. "Sitting in that subway on the way home from City [College] 1934, was like sitting in a gondola immersed below the water, or a plane being shot down with ack, ack guns," he wrote in a 1960 journal entry. "One does not forget such things. The pressure, ye gods, the pressures. No wonder I used to feel, rocking back and forth on my seat, as if I were traveling in no-man's-land." The situation in Europe would grow far more dire; but like other young radicals at the time, Kazin believed, desperately wanted to believe, that the increasingly ominous conditions were preparing the ground for an apocalypse that would usher in a new, more equitable order. "There was the feeling that we were living at the end of the world," Irving Howe recalled, "and in a way we were."[4]

Kazin may have spent the thirties anticipating the coming Socialist revolution; but to follow his progress through that decade is to see that his vision of the future depended at least as much on a growing sense of his own possibilities—his literary ambitions, his developing connections with the publishing world, and his discovery of writers and friends—as on any Marxist theory of a "necessary" future. Indeed, as a young radical and hopeful litterateur out of Brownsville with eyes fixed intently on the world beyond the ghetto, Kazin was not about to entrust his future to any ideology (or ideologue) that would presume to define the meaning of his working-class past or the limits of his expectations. He had too many other interests. He was a Socialist ("as so many Americans are 'Christians'") and a "literary radical," who believed in the revolutionary power of the word. And he was increasingly ambitious—"a starry eyed opportunist" according to Sidney Hook, who met him once in the thirties—trusting that his efforts to "break through" would coincide with "the genius of history."[5]

City College

The breakthrough would have to wait until after City College, however. That long first climb up past Lewisohn Stadium would be followed by many more, "the same bloody exhausting walk," all part of a daily ritual that Kazin would find increasingly onerous and dispiriting. City College would become a legend for the number of eminent figures it graduated during the thirties, including two Nobel laureates (the physicist Robert Hofstadter and the biologist Arthur Kornberg); the future head of the RAND Corporation, Albert Wohlstetter; the actor Zero Mostel; and numerous writers and intellectuals—Nathan Glazer, Irving Howe, Irving Kristol, Bernard Malamud, and Kazin—many of whom would look back fondly on their years there as some of the most valuable and instructive in their lives. Kazin would not be one of them. "I hated City College; it was an hour and more each way from my home in darkest Brownsville, I had to bring lunch from my home, there were no seats in the lunchroom anyway; it was all odorously male, and as I more than hint in the early pages of *Starting Out in the Thirties,* the radical ambience was fanatical, arrogant, quite violent at times, and by no means to my liking." With a few notable exceptions, everything about City College depressed and repelled him, from the two-and-a-half hours he spent on the subway, to the "fanatical" political ambience, to the lackluster teaching. Moreover, with a student body drawn largely from New York's poor Jewish neighborhoods, City offered little change from home. As Alexander Bloom has noted, for most of the students, college was "a continuation of their lives in the ghetto," not, for Kazin at least, a particularly alluring goal at the end of the long subway ride.[6]

What he found most repellent was what other future writers and intellectuals remembered most fondly: the radical politics, particularly as argued by different radical factions in the famous basement alcoves of the college administrative building. Irving Howe recalled that City was a "wonderful place in those years, at least for young radicals," for whom "the real center of life" was the alcoves. "You could walk into the thick brown darkness of Alcove I at almost any time of day or evening and find a convenient argument about . . . the Five-Year Plan in Russia, the theory of permanent revolution, and 'what Marx really meant.'" Years later, Howe noted that the veterans of the alcove wars would feel that "a common tie, more than nostalgia, held them together. It was the memory of the days when we reached for the gift of lucidity and stumbled into the life of the mind." Irving Kristol, another veteran of the alcove wars, agreed. For him, radicalism was not just part of his City College experience, "it was practically the whole of it. If I left City College with a better education than did many students at other and supposedly better colleges, it was because my involvement in radical politics put me in touch with people and ideas that prompted me to read and think and argue with a furious energy." Attending City College at such a time in such an atmosphere, with so many other engaged radical thinkers, Kristol insisted, was "a privileged experience, and I know of no one who participated in it who does not look back upon it with some such sentiment."[7]

Kazin did not participate. He graduated from City College in 1935, before the arrival of Howe (class of 1940), Kristol (1940), and Daniel Bell (1939). But the politics were as charged in the early thirties as they would be later. In the fall of 1931, a vocal core of left-leaning students at City were already making their presence felt. Coming from immigrant, working-class communities that knew something about radical politics, they saw political implications in the deepening depression that would only later become apparent to middle-class students. They also knew something about organizing and protesting. Earlier in the spring, a group of student radicals had staged a loud and successful protest against compulsory ROTC—an action that prompted Frederick Robinson, the school's president, to suspend the student leaders and suppress the Communist-leaning student publication, *Frontiers.* By the time Kazin arrived in the fall, political groups and radical organizations were fully active. The most outspoken radicals were admired as campus leaders. He remembers seeing Albert Wohlstetter, then a "radical program setter," standing in the cafeteria surrounded by disciples, "explaining things in authoritative fashion to someone he clearly regarded as inferior."[8]

Kazin was not impressed by Wohlstetter, nor by his classmate, Milton Hindus, future journalist and author of *Mother Russia* (1943). Kazin once watched Hindus in a paroxysm of political indignation scream and throw a cup of coffee at a disputant. He found the radical politics oppressive and the combative ideological atmosphere of the alcoves stifling. He had no desire to enter this airless arena of "ideologues," where, as Howe would later admit, "politics [was] a function of pure mind, as 'autotelic' as the literary criticism proposed by some theorists a few decades later." Kazin resented the narrowing effect that the radicalism had on the intellectual life of the school, and he was disgusted by the certainty of those who prided themselves as "being 'right' in everything" and pronounced knowingly and contemptuously on the "errors" of those who thought differently. They represented a type of intellectual, "ideologues," as he often referred to them, whom he found difficult to countenance at the time and would find even more repellent in later years.[9]

There were many such "ideologues" on display in the alcoves, but few of them affected Kazin more strongly than Sidney Hook, an alumnus of City College who occasionally returned to talk to the young Communists and who, Kazin remembered, defined the type perfectly. His "never to be forgotten impression" of Hook as he listened to him speak at the Communist "Social Problems" club was that "he was the most ridiculously arrogant, patronizing Communist type I had ever encountered." "And how to explain . . . ," he wrote in 1987, "that from the moment I heard him [Hook] lecture at City College in 1932 (!), I thought of him as the very type of narrow, intolerably conceited, totally relentless 'left' intellectual who helped in the 19th century to prepare so much disaster for the 20th?" Kazin's animus against Hook deepened over the years, especially after he felt Hook "libeled" him in his autobiography. But his distaste and resentment can be traced in no small part to City College and to his discomfort with an intellectual style he found offensively self-assured and wholly incompatible with his own less politically rigorous, more "literary" sensibility. In the coming years Kazin would often look back to the political culture at City College for clues to the "militantly knowing" elitism and ideological stridency of many of the intellectuals who started out on the hard left in the thirties and then turned hard right in later life. "Only a few of us know," he wrote to Daniel Bell about the rise of the neoconservative movement in the 1970s and 1980s, "that some horribly reactionary national policies were actually born, long, long ago, in the violent debates between radicals dominating the City College Alcoves." Ideologues, he often remarked, may change their views, never their temperament, never their confidence that they are "right."[10]

Kazin preferred the quiet of the library or the Great Hall to the hectoring polemics of the alcoves. With its high vaulted ceiling and international display of flags, the Great Hall was a quiet, orderly refuge from the disorder and clamor of the cafeteria and alcoves. The only distraction was a music professor occasionally playing Bach pieces on the organ. Kazin had no close friends at City, though he enjoyed the company of Arnold Roog, who delighted him by writing his term papers on the back of Young Communist League pamphlets. He was also friendly with Louis Redman, with whom he coedited the school's literary magazine. He enjoyed working on the magazine, but gained little recognition for his work. In the thirties "the presiding atmosphere at college was emphatically not literary." "Everything turned on which local brand of salvation-by-Marxism you adhered to." He discovered years later that he and Bernard Malamud were in Theodore Goodman's creative writing class—they both received Bs—and wrote for the same literary magazine, but he did not remember him.[11]

Most of Kazin's friends—Felix Nigro, Eddy Peshkin, and Ben Seligman —were back in Brooklyn. Although Seligman, the future labor economist ("Herschel" in *Starting Out in the Thirties*), attended Brooklyn College, he and Kazin saw each other frequently and would keep up their friendship into the forties. Kazin also knew a few girls back home—there were no women at City College—Trudie Wietz, Sarah White, and Sadie Tolmach. Sadie, the model for the girlfriend mentioned in the Highland Park section of *A Walker in the City*, left the most lasting impression—by dumping him. "Even now, it seems to me, 26 years later," Kazin wrote in 1957, "I shudder with the frightfulness of that summer evening Sadie Tolmach gave me up. I felt that I was dying." Memories of Sadie would keep returning, particularly in moments of lonely panic accompanying the loss of a wife's or lover's affection. "The fright that end [of] summer of 1931, at sixteen, when Sadie ceased to love me," he wrote in 1959; "it was not the loss of a dead one; it was the loss of the world."[12]

Unlike many of the more politically engaged students, Kazin worked hard at his studies, majoring in English and history. Yet he took only modest pleasure in his courses, even that taught by the famous philosophy professor Morris Cohen. A graduate of City College with a Ph.D. from Harvard, Cohen had a reputation for brilliantly dissecting the arguments of his students in what one of them called "a kind of smiling struggle to the death." Kazin was not interested in arguing with his famous teacher. He found Cohen's aggressive, confrontational teaching style "disagreeable" and was repelled by the "showy rationalism he offered as a solution to all life's problems." He was, however, grateful to Cohen for introducing him to the work of George Santayana.[13]

The English instructors were neither disagreeable nor aggressive; they were, with a couple of exceptions, simply uninterested. One exception was Donald Roberts, "a large melancholy man," who taught the English metaphysical poets—George Herbert, Henry Vaughn, and John Donne. Kazin was already familiar with these writers from high school, particularly their meditational poetry. Although bored by the rituals in the Dugschitz synagogue, he had developed an early interest in religious expression, particularly religious verse. He later reasoned that this "private orthodoxy," which puzzled his parents, was another venture into the beyond, another effort "to seek an outlet, a search for some kind of transcendence." The search would continue with varying degrees of intensity the rest of his life, leading him into recurrent reflections on the differing appeal of Christianity and Judaism, prompting his special affection for Emily Dickinson's poetry, and inspiring his last book, *God and the American Writer* (1997). The poetry of the metaphysical poets (particularly George Herbert), with their witty, passionate explorations of religious mysteries, would remain a favorite subject. To the amusement of a future employer, Kazin produced the essays he had written in Roberts's course as evidence he could write book reviews.[14]

Another instructor Kazin remembered fondly was a professor of literary criticism named Bird Stair (whom Irving Howe also remembered as his best English teacher). In an environment that tended to see literature as either irrelevant or "sissy," Stair, a Hoosier of "plain, blunt appearance" whose manner of address resembled "a farmer shouting at cattle," taught his subject as though he believed in it. He not only knew his stuff—Kazin remembers that he was particularly good on Henry James, Virginia Woolf, and the achievements and limits of modernism—he knew how to encourage good critical writing from his students. He found Stair's criticisms daunting and his infrequent praise cause for rejoicing. "You have talent for this sort of thing," Stair wrote on Kazin's last composition (on Johannes Brahms) for his class; "[You] should pursue it." Stair later supported Kazin for a scholarship to Columbia's master's program in history. He did not, however, support him for a 1939 (successful) Guggenheim grant to help him finish *On Native Grounds*. Although Stair praised his former student's "rare gift of expression" and his "brilliant literary journalism," he did not feel he possessed "the scholarship, background, and maturity" necessary for the ambitious project he proposed, adding gratuitously, "These boys are ambitious!" To recommend Kazin for a Guggenheim would, he felt, "lend support to undermining standards of criticism and scholarship." Kazin had no second thoughts about Stair. Looking back half a century later to the unhappy years at City College, he remembers that it was always "a relief to escape into the classes of Bird Stair, the greatest teacher I have known and the man who more than any other led me to discover myself as a writer."[15]

"Roaming"

In the summer of 1934, a year before graduation, Kazin paid a visit to the office of John Chamberlain, the recently hired daily book reviewer at the *New York Times*. The occasion was an essay-review of Chamberlain's on youth and politics during the Depression. Kazin had been reading Chamberlain's essays with interest and some irritation for several weeks; this time, he took exception to the abstract quality of the article, and, as he explains in *Starting Out in the Thirties,* he wanted to set the recent Yale graduate straight on some things—after all, "I was youth, afraid to go home without a job. . . . What does this fellow know about it anyway?" Chamberlain welcomed him—not wholly as a stranger; Kazin had written him earlier of his interest in his pieces—and at the end of a lengthy conversation on all manner of radical and Socialist ideas, he sent Kazin off to Malcolm Cowley at the *New Republic* with a note—"here's an intelligent radical"— and a recommendation that he be given a chance to do some book reviews. His first review appeared in September 1934 when Kazin was nineteen.[16]

Kazin found little time for book reviewing during his final year at City College. In the fall of 1935, however, his reviews began appearing with increasing frequency in the *New Republic,* the *New York Times,* the *New York Herald Tribune: Books*; and V. F. Calverton's *Modern Monthly.* Kazin would later say that book reviewing took him by surprise; while he had always wanted to become a writer, he had never thought seriously about book reviewing and criticism. Yet reviewing made sense at the time. In the thirties, magazines and newspapers were looking for young talent—especially those familiar with the country's straitened financial situation. The job also paid—not well, but more than Kazin was making at the occasional college job writing term papers for "the only rich boy" at City College, working for the National Youth Administration by searching for the names of southerners who had graduated from college before the Civil War, or reading aloud to a blind student. Kazin was himself an avid reader of reviews, especially Edmund Wilson's pieces in the *New Republic*. Finally, reviewing was an extension of his own practice of recording impressions in his journal from his reading. He had been in training for some time.

Reviewing had other advantages. It was an ideal venue for "cultural roaming." An eclectic enterprise almost by definition, freelance reviewing meant constant intellectual variety and change. "You must know everything," wrote Kazin, who was fond of quoting the title of Isaac Babel's short story. "If reading was not indiscriminate and omnivorous, endlessly exploratory, seeking knowledge at every turn and from the most neglected of books as well as the most famous, what was it?" It was a question that many of Kazin's generation would ask in their efforts to shed all taint of provincialism and make themselves both "men of the mind" and "citizens of the world." "Whatever profession we planned to enter," wrote Joseph Freeman of his Williamsburg childhood in *An American Testament: A Narrative of Rebels and Romantics,* "we wanted to know everything. David Abramovitz began to read through the encyclopedia, but quit at 'crustacea.'" Kazin answered the challenge by reviewing. "I suddenly found a way of writing, a form, a path to the outside world." Reviewing was the freedom to explore through reading and writing and out of sheer intellectual curiosity everything from the Russian novel to the Bolshevik Revolution, to Catholic theology, to British fiction, to Jewish folktales, to Scandinavian sagas, to proletarian short stories. It was also the chance to win some public recognition and get paid for it.[17]

Reviewing also entailed some social roaming and establishment of new social connections—with, among others, editors and writers at the *Times* and the *Herald Tribune* as well as the *New Republic.* As "a cause and the center of many causes," the *New Republic* had long held a special appeal for Kazin. Writing for it, he would be participating in a tradition that included Herbert Croly, Walter Lippmann, Van Wyck Brooks, John Dewey, Randolph Bourne, and Edmund Wilson. With Cowley, a friend of Ernest Hemingway and F. Scott Fitzgerald, running "the back of the book," and Brooks, Dewey, and Wilson sending in contributions (Kazin's first review appeared in the same issue with Wilson's first installment of *To the Finland Station*), the *New Republic* offered a young radical the chance to be part of a "society that was not far removed from the old Bohemia of Greenwich Village and Chelsea," a society and an enterprise whose roots in America's radical past seemed to guarantee its influence in the immediate future.[18]

Kazin did not meet Cowley on his first visit. Otis Ferguson, who helped with editing, greeted him in "the parlor," read the note from Chamberlain, laughed, had a talk, and decided to give the young "intelligent radical" a chance. Ferguson, who wrote about jazz and reviewed films, had a talent and temperament in tune with the proletarian temper of the times. Kazin remembers him as "one of the real toughs of the Thirties," who liked to scorn the "cosy, Algonquin lunching" crowd of literary types that had survived into the thirties from more genteel times. "Otis hated them with all the righteous fury of the sans-culotte who feels his hour has come." In his memoir, Kazin describes a visit that Ferguson made to Brownsville for a meal with the Kazin family. Hoping to impress his boss with his proletarian credentials, Kazin invited him home for a glimpse of life in a genuine working-class Jewish family and a meal featuring "exotic" Jewish cuisine. The day was brutally hot, and after the long subway ride through Brooklyn, Kazin and Ferguson climbed to the family third-floor apartment, now sweltering in the August heat. Nervous about entertaining her son's Gentile "boss," Kazin's mother bustled anxiously between stove and table, bearing platters of cabbage and meatballs, chicken and meatloaf, pleading with Ferguson, his cheeks "red with effort," to please *eat something.* His father, slurping his soup and reaching for the meat with his own fork, repeated how much he had always admired the *New Republic* since the days of Herbert Croly—while Cousin Sophie and Pearl stared at their guest wide-eyed and silent. Trying to see things from Ferguson's perspective, Kazin sensed the whole affair was becoming a dreary strain—and, indeed, Ferguson's response on the walk back to the subway seemed to confirm the worst: "What the hell was so exotic about that?" Negotiating between Manhattan and Brownsville was not going to be easy.[19]

In time, Kazin encountered Cowley. "Sail[ing] in after lunch with a tolerant smile on [his] face," Cowley did not make a favorable first impression on Kazin, and the first impression soon hardened into active dislike. The reasons for the bad feelings are unclear. They seem to have come from Kazin's side (Cowley later claimed to have been wholly unaware of them) and to have had their roots in the social divide between the two men, more accurately, in Kazin's painful consciousness of the divide. "As a young reviewer and writer, I was invited everywhere," he would later recall. "I had experiences which made me realize that I was regarded as a Jew." Although he was encouraged and given opportunities, he had the distinct sense of "being watched and judged. It struck me as being a question of *manners*. The general view [was that] Jews were *low*." They were also seen as ambitious, "all the intellectual Jews on the make" (Kazin), all hoping to break into established circles of cultural authority. Leslie Fiedler and Irving Howe (among others) have written about the opportunities the thirties provided to "ambitious young Jew[s] from immigrant backgrounds." Radical politics "allowed them to identify with certain aspects of America" while protesting other aspects of it. Encouraged by the insurgent spirit of the times, "tense with conviction and assurance," they moved into the culture with the released impact of "a tightly gathered spring." Fiedler and Howe were writing largely about Jews their own age, who emerged on the scene in the very late thirties and the forties. Nineteen-year-old Alfred Kazin was there in 1934, stepping into the *New Republic* parlor alone—and he was, indeed, being watched.[20]

Cowley remembered him at nineteen coming out with "a diversity of literary judgments, which he delivered in a heavy Brownsville voice." He also remembered being "amused" by his being so "strenuously on the make," and not being "a sharp or sympathetic observer of the sorrows of others." "These boys are ambitious," as Bird Stair would say. But Kazin was also watching—watching as Cowley "radiated ease and sophistication" handing out review copies to the " 'working-class' writers," never letting "the new writers forget that he had been at Harvard with Dos Passos, had drunk in Paris with Hemingway"; watching as Cowley and the staff made small talk over gin during the deck-tennis games in the back garden, while he (Kazin) struggled "to understand social and intellectual connections" that went beyond his "simple social experience"; watching as the young John Cheever, "a favorite of Cowley's," moved among the guests at Cowley's parties, knowing "exactly what to say to the people he had just met," while Kazin, "an awkward and resentful wallflower from darkest Brownsville," stood quiet or searched desperately for a conversational gambit. Kazin would later claim that Cowley had been "unfailingly snotty" to him when he was "young and unknown" and "unfailingly surly and worse" later on. But he also acknowledged that he envied the "elegance" and "inborn social sense" that he saw in Cowley and Cheever, which reminded him painfully, insultingly, of his own social backwardness. Though he and Cowley would reach a rapprochement in their last years, Kazin would never outlive the "many early humiliations" he suffered in the years of being "watched." Indeed, lingering resentment would provide significant animus to the story he tells in his autobiographies. Nor would he ever get over his perceived lack of social grace, which he attributed at least in part to the lasting "self-conscious proletarian youth" in him. "There is a gift there, a long-bred talent for sociability, that I certainly lack," he wrote to himself in 1986, after watching Rose Styron greet guests at a party. "And it makes me bitter, bitter."[21]

Kazin did not let his fear of social humiliation keep him from seeking out further contacts with writers and radicals, however. In his memoir, he describes a meeting "somewhere in mid-town" with William Saroyan, who was still excited by the success of his short story "The Daring Young Man on the Flying Trapeze." He recalls meeting Nathaniel West and James T. Farrell in a room in the Brevoort Hotel on the day Farrell finished the last of his *Studs Lonigan* trilogy (a meeting that Farrell insisted never occurred). Kazin's favorite place to meet writers, many of them old radicals, was V. F. Calverton's house on Spring Street in Greenwich Village. An independent Socialist with an indiscriminate passion for all things modern and radical, Calverton (George Goetz) came closer than anybody in the thirties to embodying the eclectic, "innocent" spirit of radical dissent that had characterized the Greenwich Village left of the 1910s. He was, according to Daniel Aaron, the "notable contact man of the left," who during the thirties ran "a kind of intellectual brokerage house for revolution." He opened his house and the pages of his magazine, *Modern Monthly,* to any capable writer who believed in the spirit of radical change, personal liberation, and political and cultural dissent. Kazin did editorial work for Calverton, wrote reviews, and attended Calverton's parties.[22]

In *Starting Out in the Thirties,* Kazin describes the mix of guests found at Calverton's affairs: "old Russian Mensheviks and Social Revolutionaries, German Marxists who had known Engels and Bernstein, American Socialists and libertarian anarchists, ex-Communists who had fallen off the train of history . . . old Harvard dissenters, leftover Abolitionists, Tolstoyans, single-taxers, Methodist ministers, Village rebels of 1912, everlasting Socialists and early psychoanalysts." One could overhear Norman Thomas debating with Eugene Lyons, Sidney Hook arguing with Max Eastman. To attend a Calverton affair was to look past current political debates into the rich history of radical thought (and personalities) in the twentieth century.[23]

But did Kazin actually meet these old Menscheviks? Did he, in fact, hear Hook debating Max Eastman? Hook doubted it. In his autobiography, *Out of Step,* he claimed that Kazin "had merely read our exchange." His only memory of Kazin at Calverton's is his interjecting his views into a conversation he (Hook) was having with Calverton. "It was the only time I had been patronized by a political neophyte." Had Kazin really met Farrell in the Brevoort as he claimed, Farrell's denial notwithstanding? Kazin insisted that he had, that Farrell had simply forgotten. Kazin acknowledged that he "stretched the truth occasionally," but "felt no need to invent anything." In his journal (while working on *Starting Out in the Thirties*), however, he insisted that in autobiography, the "presented life" is everything, that "the detail is disposable and movable—fiction under the form of autobiography." Does it matter whether Kazin was telling the literal truth? A strong suspicion that he had invented meetings and events could certainly affect the way we read his account. But had he limited himself strictly to what he had actually seen and heard, he might well have sacrificed some of the fullness and lived immediacy of the thirties experience. Autobiography, Kazin wrote in a 1964 essay for the *Reporter,* while finishing his thirties memoir, inevitably involves "a moral slight-of-hand" with trade-offs between fact and fiction, memory and imagination. What weight should be given to each and whether a proper balance has been achieved is for the wary reader to decide.[24]

"A Talent for This Sort of Thing"

Although he enjoyed the literary-political ambience at the *Modern Monthly* and the *New Republic,* Kazin did most of his reviewing in the thirties for the *New York Herald Tribune: Books* and the *New York Times Book Review.* He particularly enjoyed writing for the Sunday *Books* section of the *Tribune* and for its editor, Irita Van Doren. The wife of Carl Van Doren, the former literary editor of the *Nation,* and the sister-in-law of Mark Van Doren, a literature professor at Columbia, Irita Van Doren was always on the lookout for young talent. One of her finds was Henry Steele Commager when he was a young instructor at New York University in 1928. Kazin was a longer shot when he approached her in the fall of 1935. "A raw City College graduate without academic credentials" (according to *Tribune* historian Richard

Kluger), Kazin had little going for him beyond his enthusiasm and self-confidence. He quickly proved a good bet, however, and in time became one of Van Doren's most valued freelancers. I gave him "the most subtle, thoughtful, and best written novels to review," she wrote to a Guggenheim committee in 1939. He approached "the reading and study of literature with a passion and an intensity that are rare—even a little terrifying." Alfred was equally impressed with Irita—for different reasons. "How I loved Irita, that dazzling bushy hair . . . that air of the 20s flapper . . . Irita and Carl had such style. . . . Of course, they were no great shakes as minds—but how they looked!" His admiration did not prevent his loud complaining when he felt that her editorial decisions "viciously" distorted and "vulgariz[ed]" his reviews, however. The intensity could become a little frightening.[25]

Unlike the *New Republic* and *Modern Monthly*, the *New York Times* and the *Herald Tribune* had no reputation of supporting radical literary and political causes. Throughout much of the 1930s the *Times Book Review* remained under the staid editorial influence of "the careful, hidebound" J. Donald Adams, who disapproved of the leftist "naturalism" of Farrell, Edward Dahlberg, and others. While more open to the literature of immediate social concerns, *Books* remained an organ of the liberal middle class. Kazin, however, felt free in both magazines to review and support new writers, some from minority groups, as well as those writers on the left appearing in more radical magazines and newspapers. It says a good deal about the political climate of the 1930s that these two mainstream papers were prepared to publish reviews on books (including political books) of interest to a young radical like Kazin; it also says something about Kazin's interests and the eclectic, "literary," accommodating nature of his radicalism that he felt comfortable writing for them.[26]

In fact, the reviews suggest that Kazin was happy to write on topics and writers that had little to do with contemporary politics—Elizabethan poetry, the philosophy of William James, British detective novels, German autobiography, contemporary criticism, American immigrant fiction. Religious subjects held a special interest for him, provoking thoughtful reviews of books on Saint Paul, Jesus, and Herod as well as works by the Russian mystic Nicholas Berdyaev and the Catholic theologian Jacques Maritain. However, many of the reviews did relate to current conditions in America and Europe and engaged Kazin's political sympathies (shared by most writers on the left)—enthusiasm for the Loyalist effort in Spain; admiration of cultural heroes of the European left, André Malraux, Luis Aragon, Ignazio Silone, and Maxim Gorky; and approval of the intentions (if not often the execution) of the American proletarian or "strike" novel—"a seismograph of the tremors beneath the social fabric"—and his belief (increasingly a desperate hope) that despite the disasters threatening the world, history was on the side of the people and would ultimately lead to the vindication of the Socialist dream.[27]

But if Kazin's reviews reflect conventional leftist attitudes of the period, they also indicate the kinds of literary/critical concerns that would mark much of his later work. They suggest, for instance, a writer less interested in political (or ideological) issues than in the depiction of ordinary people caught up willy-nilly in historical change. Kazin would later write that the thirties in literature were not so much "the age of the ideologue" as the age "of the plebes, of [the] Jews, Irishmen, Negroes, Armenians, Italians . . . writers brought in from the slums farms and factories . . . those whose struggle was to survive." This was the deeper meaning of the new literary radicalism—a radicalism that consisted less of politics and ideology than of literary enfranchisement. Kazin shared personally in this democratizing tendency in the "starting out" of his writing career. He contributed directly to it with his reviews, helping bring to the attention of a nation apparently willing to listen the voices of people often ignored or forgotten—James T. Farrell's Irish in *Studs Lonigan,* Millen Brand's veterans in *The Heroes* (1936), Sophus Winter's ranchers in *This Passion Never Dies* (1938), Josephine Herbst's farmers in *Rope of Gold* (1939).[28]

Another tendency evident in Kazin's early reviews is his penchant for responding to writers as historical actors and personalities whose moral qualities he closely associates with their literary achievement. Such an impressionistic, biographical approach risks blurring the distinction between writer and work, even turning fiction into a form of autobiography. Yet when done with sensitivity and tact, it can evoke the characteristic qualities of a writer's moral force and style while placing him or her in meaningful relation with other writers of the time. For instance, in his review of Erich Maria Remarque's novel of returning World War I German soldiers, *Three Comrades,* Kazin, after recalling Remarque's reputation from *All Quiet on the Western Front* as a champion of the common soldier, sets him off against other writers of the immediate postwar generation: the disillusioned Hemingway of *The Sun Also Rises,* the British poets of "grave and tearful autobiographies," the Russians with their "robust adventure stories," and the French with their "Dadaist mongrel literature."

> There is little bitterness in Remarque, only an elegiac feeling for things touched in one's youth and never grasped. . . . [His returned soldiers] need money and comfort for solace. They are tired; the long solemn words of accusation mean nothing to them; were they to state their resentment, they would not know whom to blame most. The tingle of being alive seems reward enough. . . . It is the bitter-sweet tang of youth, the slow ebb of an anxious conscience "mixing memory and desire," that one responds to in this book. . . . Nothing sharp, strong, compelling, nothing everlasting, memorable for its anger. But in its place a swift and sometimes cheerful thrust against the threat of aimlessness and death, so simple a tribute to the simplicity of the normal.

What distinguishes this passage (and much of Kazin's criticism) is neither close argument nor precise analysis, but rather its evocation of the "feel" of the book, together with a lyrical and almost mimicking response to the distinctive sensibility of the author. If, in the course of the review, Kazin tends to merge Remarque with his characters, the stoic but always hopeful "little men" (much as we often merge post–World War I Hemingway of *The Sun Also Rises* with his "lost-generation" expatriates), he also brings into focus the special qualities that describe Remarque's "angle of vision" and distinguish his work from that of other postwar writers. Kazin, who took pride in being able to "read the mind behind each book," would refine and extend his biographical-critical skills in *On Native Grounds* with evocative portraits of William Dean Howells, Thorstein Veblen, Theodore Dreiser, Willa Cather, and many others—portraits that remain as vivid today as they were in the forties. As Bird Stair said, he had "a talent for this sort of thing," and he was determined to pursue it.[29]

Another feature of Kazin's early reviews indicating the character (and limits) of his critical temperament is his evident distaste for experimental fiction that concentrates on "subjectivity" and the free play of consciousness to the virtual exclusion of historical-social reality. How, he asked in a review of a James Joyce biography, could a writer of such acute intelligence and sensitivity "live in Paris all through the periodic crises of the last few years without the slightest awareness of Hitler"? In an earlier review of *Finnegans Wake,* after noting Joyce's verbal resourcefulness, he complained that the language not only leaves out history, it abandons "reality" itself. "We begin to feel that his very freedom to say anything has become a compulsion to say nothing. He is not speculating on anything man can possibly know; he has created a world of his own . . . and he has lost his way in it." He says much the same about Kay Boyle's *Death of a Man* and Djuna Barnes's *Nightwood*. Excepting Proust's *À la recherche du temps perdu* and certain novels by William Faulkner, Kazin would take only limited pleasure in experimental or "avant-garde" fiction that explores states of consciousness through techniques often associated with the "modern" movement. Indeed, he had little sympathy for the very notion of an "avant-garde" in literature, a cadre of the initiated who presumed to have "advanced" ideas about art. (He distrusted Trotskyism and Trotskyites for similar antielitist reasons.) While loath to prescribe specific moral and political responsibilities to the writer, Kazin preferred fiction that stayed close to traditional realist conventions, registered the pressures of the "outside" world, and (like his own autobiographies, or "personal histories") moved through private experience into history, engaging the shared public world of people and events.[30]

The thirties, Kazin would later write, were "the years of my apprenticeship, of my basic formation." Writing book reviews constituted a major portion of that apprenticeship. The skills, interests, and habits of response that marked the early reviews—an appetite for new subjects; a curiosity about writers' personalities and careers; a talent for quick, clear summary and vivid "impressionistic" evaluation—would distinguish his criticism from the thirties on. Although he would write in other modes (literary history and autobiography), he would remain an active reviewer until his death, regarded by many as the country's most influential reviewer following Edmund Wilson's turn away from book reviewing in the late forties. Reviewing, Kazin noted more than once, would always be essential to him as a writer, essential "to the excitement that I . . . feel every day in learning something," and essential to his sense of "historical-mindedness." The book review, like the newspaper or magazine in which it appears, is inescapably historical; it is "always a date, an issue, a moment; it is created out of an exacting sense of time and is about time." In a decade of grim fact and growing dread, reviewing marked the opposing, expectant terms of his "starting out"—the anticipation of fresh literary and social discoveries; a small measure of fame; and the hope that he and history were moving in the same direction, that his (and humanity's) "salvation would come by the word."[31]

CHAPTER THREE

The Thirties
On Native Grounds

Writing *On Native Grounds* felt to me—to us—to be a political act. The
country was on the move—we were on the move. *We were learning America.*

—Alfred Kazin, Journal, August 21, 1976

B y 1936, Kazin was reviewing regularly in the *New York Times Book
Review* and the *Books* section of the *Herald Tribune.* Some weeks
he published two reviews in one paper and a review in the other, as
well as pieces under the pseudonym David Tilden. He supplemented his
freelancing with odd jobs—writing the memoirs (from dictation) for a re-
tired British Army colonel, dramatizing episodes from *The Pickwick Papers*
and stories by Edgar Allan Poe for a Brooklyn radio station, and teaching
the occasional evening or summer course at City College. For the moment
at least, living hand-to-mouth felt right. Planning seemed beside the point.
"Most of us did not think seriously about careers," Kazin recalled. "Not
only was there a depression, but we were all quite certain that a war was
coming." History, the linked movement of people and events, not individual decisions, was creating day-to-day reality, moving the world toward
revolution or war.[1]

For all "the bold, persistent experimentation" that Franklin D. Roosevelt had promised in his 1932 presidential campaign, the Depression
ground on. Two years into the New Deal, one in five American workers was
without a job. Kazin's father would remain unemployed for nearly all of the
thirties. Conditions in Europe were becoming desperate and terrifying.
Mussolini and the Fascists controlled Italy and were waging a military

campaign against Ethiopia, attacking a defenseless population with bomb-
ers, flamethrowers and poison gas—foreshadowing the terror that would
later engulf Europe. Two years into his rule, Hitler had destroyed democracy and the rule of law in Germany and was already building concentration camps. In 1936, he remilitarized the Rhineland. How far would he go?
How would France and England respond? And an equally fateful question:
What were the intentions of the Soviet Union, from which were emanating
disturbing reports of political murders and purges?[2]

Kazin read the papers obsessively, talked to friends, and watched history
unfold in the Trans-Lux newsreel theaters in Times Square—where, the
times being what they were, there were only newsreel theaters. A young
radical looking anxiously for signs of things to come, he could still hope that
his future and the direction of events would somehow align, or, as he later
put it, that he would find himself in step with "the surging and unmistakable march of history." He would soon discover, however, that history can
move abruptly, violently, in unexpected directions, crushing hopes, unsettling plans, but also offering undreamed-of opportunities for those with the
talent and the initiative to seize them. Starting out in the revolutionary
thirties, hoping that his efforts at personal liberation would be part of
humanity's liberation, Kazin found his vocation and established his future
in the wartime forties, not as a young radical working for a classless society
but as a young patriot celebrating the democratic values and cultural
achievements of America's past.[3]

Politics and Friends

Part of the excitement of reviewing for Kazin was encountering various
known (or soon-to-be-known) literary and political figures—Malcolm Cowley, Otis Ferguson, V. F. Calverton, Carl and Irita Van Doren, James T.
Farrell, William Saroyan, the old-time radicals at Calverton's parties. But
thirties New York also provided contacts with people his own age, those just
starting out like himself. New York would always be a source of connection
for Kazin—"In New York I make my connections"—and thirties New York,
with its political meetings, rallies, guest lectures, and endless discussions of
radical politics, was especially rich with fresh contacts and connections.
Politics coincided with friendships, and friendships were in part a function

of politics. It made a difference whom one agreed with and argued with. At "City," politics was the hectoring crowd to be avoided in the dingy basement alcoves—loud, combative, smelling of oily sandwiches. In postgraduate New York, politics was new friends, parties, social discoveries.[4]

One new friend with whom Kazin liked to talk politics was William Canning, like himself, a part-time instructor at City. In *Starting Out in the Thirties*, Kazin portrays Canning as "Francis," a Jesuit turned Stalinist, turned "holy informer," who later ratted on his colleagues at the college. Canning was attracted to Jewish radicals—another Canning friend was the young labor activist Moe Foner—and was much impressed with Kazin's wide reading and his regular appearance in the papers. Kazin enjoyed explaining radical thought to him and passing on "heretical books." He occasionally brought Canning home for a meal, where his mother loomed large in his friend's imagination as the proletarian mother who had given her children to the revolution. But Canning's ultimate importance to Kazin (besides being the model of the "holy informer" in his memoir) was his introducing him one afternoon in a Times Square cafeteria to Felice Swados and, through her, to her husband, Richard Hofstadter.[5]

Kazin recalls the meeting in the fall of 1936 vividly. He felt immediately "that something extraordinary" was about to enter his life. A big woman with a round baby face and bangs, Swados ("Harriet" in the memoir) "radiated a hungry self-confidence and an intellectual positiveness" that "charged [the atmosphere] with an excitement that I did not try to account for." Kazin was impressed and not a little intimidated. "I had never met anyone like her. I had never met a *woman* like her." He was impressed in a very different way when he met Hofstadter—"the most charming man I had ever met"—at their apartment at 134 Montague Street in Brooklyn Heights. "Half-Jew" and a one-time "Lutheran choir boy, " Hofstadter, sitting in the single-room flat, "looked marvelous, fresh as a daisy, the all-American blond collegian with crew cut just in from Buffalo with that unmistakable flat accent." He and Swados (the older sister of the novelist Harvey Swados) had met at the University of Buffalo as undergraduates, where they were both active in radical politics. In the fall of 1936, after Swados had taken a master's degree in philosophy at Smith, they had moved to New York and married.[6]

Hofstadter had decided on a career in law. Through his uncle, Samuel

Hofstadter, a state supreme court judge, he had obtained work as an errand boy at the law firm of Irving Kaufman. In the evening he took law courses at New York University. However, he soon discovered he was not really interested in law, and in February 1937, he enrolled as a part-time student in Columbia to pursue a master's degree in history. Swados, meanwhile, had found a position as a researcher at Time Inc. A passionate radical, who scorned the business values of the publications of Henry Luce, she was also extremely ambitious and determined to make her mark professionally, even if on enemy territory. In time she was promoted to write the medicine column for *Time*—a notable achievement as the Luce publications rarely employed female writers.

Kazin was excited by Swados and charmed by her husband, who complimented his wife's authoritative confidence with a quiet, focused "intellectual certainty" and a gift for mimicry. Visiting them in their flat in Brooklyn Heights, two blocks from the New York harbor, he felt that his life had been immeasurably "enlarg[ed]." While Swados tended to "instruct" their friends, Hofstadter "entertained" them with brilliant imitations and humorous stories that broke through his habitual reserve and collapsed his friends on the floor in laughter. Intellectually alert and reflective, "he took things in, he thought them over and waited them out; he let other people take the initiative, but was always more penetrating." Joining Hofstadter, Swados, and their friends in from Buffalo, Kazin was enthralled by the color and excitement that had suddenly entered his life. "The brilliance of this young couple seemed to lie like a fine gold over the staid brownstones of Brooklyn Heights." Years later, he would marvel at the social and intellectual resources forever surfacing in New York, "my 'world city' . . . full of talent, brains, buried treasure." The excitement of discovering treasures like Hofstadter and Swados in Brooklyn Heights in 1936 would be a recurrent New York experience.[7]

The excitement was as political as it was social. There was much to argue over, speculate on, worry about. In July 1936, civil war had broken out in Spain and had become an all-consuming concern. Army generals led by Francisco Franco on the Nationalist right, tacitly supported by the Catholic Church, had begun a military campaign to wrest the government away from the democratically elected Republicans. Although initially unsuccessful, Franco soon began receiving help from Hitler and Mussolini, whose transport ships and airplanes began to tip the balance against the Republicans. France, England, and the United States not only refused to intervene on behalf of the threatened Republic, they embargoed all arms, leaving the Spanish government without the means to defend itself. The intervention of the Soviet Union with tanks and planes on the side of the Republicans halted the Nationalist drive for a time, but Stalin's decision to eradicate all factions on the left and his eventual withdrawal of military aid doomed the Republic. In March 1939, Madrid fell to Franco, and the war was over, leaving five hundred thousand dead out of a population of twenty-five million.

To American liberals and Socialists, the Spanish war was the fight they had been waiting for (and the wound that would never heal)—the day of reckoning between Fascism and the progressive forces of democracy and Socialism. History was moving toward a crisis that would either return the world to the dark ages or usher in the much anticipated Socialist future. Kazin recalled endless hours discussing the war and its implications with Hofstadter and other friends—the role of the anarchists, the contest between the Communists and POUM (Workers' Party of Marxist Unification), the intentions of Stalin, Fascism as "the last resource of the bourgeoisie" before the triumph of Socialism. "It was the great thing in our lives," Kazin recalled. "We [he and Hofstadter] were heart and soul about it." But so was everyone else he knew. He remembered staying up all night with Ben Seligman debating whether to enlist in the American volunteers who fought alongside the Republicans. Forty of Kazin's classmates at City College did enlist with the Lincoln Brigade, and many never returned. The stakes for the world, for the future, could not have been higher, nor the choices more stark—on one side, Franco, Mussolini, Hitler, Fascism; on the other, the elected Spanish Republicans, liberals, Socialists, Communists, and (very important) the writers—"Silone, Malraux, Hemingway, Gide, Rolland, Gorky, Aragon, Picasso, Eluard, Auden, Spender, Barbusse, Dreiser and Farrell." There was little room for neutrals or nuances. Fascism was the enemy; division and hesitation could only "limit maximum resistance to Franco and Hitler."[8]

But if Hitler, Franco, and Mussolini were the enemy, Stalin was not making it easy for those allied with the Communists. Reports from Spain of the Stalinists' efforts to purge the left of anarchists and Socialists left radicals back home wondering about the Soviet Union's intentions. Why intervene on the side of the Republic, then sabotage efforts to defend it? Even more bewildering were the reports of trials coming out of the Soviet Union in which Bolshevik leaders confessed to elaborate crimes of disloyalty and treason against the state. In 1936–1937, old revolutionaries such as Leo Kamenov, Gregory Zinoviev, Karl Radek, and Gregory Piatakov confessed to all charges against them and were quickly executed for conspiring with the enemies of Russia to bring down the Soviet government. Leon Trotsky, who had been expelled from the country and fled to Mexico, was tried and convicted in absentia. Kazin and Hofstadter, who closely followed events in Russia, were familiar with the careers of these revolutionaries. Was it possible that these "prophets in arms" could have turned on the state, made common cause with foreign capitalists and the Gestapo and betrayed Russia for petty personal gain? In *Starting Out in the Thirties*, Kazin wrote that he and his friends were not fooled. He faulted Malcolm Cowley for defending the Moscow trials in the *New Republic* and for siding with the Stalinists, "with whom he identified the future." As for himself and his friends, they found the charges that these men had plotted with the Nazis "absurd and disgusting." "The Moscow Trials completely finished us," he later remarked in an oral history about himself and Hofstadter; "they were phony."[9]

In fact, the trials complicated their feelings about the war and about Stalin, but did not "finish" them. (What finished them was the Hitler-Stalin nonaggression pact on August 23, 1939.) Hofstadter was, in fact, initially convinced of the guilt of the old revolutionaries, though he soon concluded that the charges were "phony" and "frame-ups" and that the trials "are shit." Even then, he was not prepared to repudiate the Communists nor their effort in Spain. In the spring of 1938, he joined the Columbia graduate unit of the Communist Party—"My fundamental reason for joining," he wrote his brother-in-law, Harvey Swados, "is that I don't like capitalism and want to get rid of it. I am tired of talking. I am ashamed of the hours I have spent jawing about the thing." Kazin did not join. But with Hitler in Austria and the Sudetenland, he, too, found himself "more sympathetic to the Communists." "I did not want to dwell on what the Stalinists were doing in Spain. I only wanted to see Fascism destroyed." Although a life-long Socialist, he had grown impatient with endless talk and worrying over scruples. "The Socialists seemed to have only their own virtue. I was tired of virtue, and now wanted to see some action."[10]

Sidney Hook would later challenge Kazin's account of his political views during the thirties, accusing him of reconstructing "his political past to make it fit the prejudices of the current [1960s] literary Establishment." He charged Kazin with presenting himself in *Starting Out in the Thirties* as an "incorruptible radical" who has kept the faith, unlike the "ex-leftists" who have supposedly sold out. He also charged him with misrepresenting himself as an early anti-Stalinist through indignant characterizations of fellow travelers like Cowley who defended the Communists and the Moscow trials. If Kazin thought the trials were wrong, Hook argued, why is he unable to provide any documentation that he felt that way at the time? If he thought Cowley wrong for protecting the Communists, where is the evidence that he opposed Cowley or his views in the 1930s or when he succeeded Cowley as book editor at the *New Republic* in 1942? Indeed, despite pages "which fairly smoke with moral indignation at Communist infamy," Kazin seemed ready to abandon the Socialists for the Stalinists when he self-admittedly wanted "some action."[11]

Although he would privately call Hook's charges a "libel," Kazin did not contest them publicly. It would have been hard to do. There is little in public or personal records to indicate that he opposed the trials or the Communists; and, as Hook notes, Kazin had himself acknowledged his sympathy with the Communists' readiness for "action" as opposed to Democratic Socialism's preoccupation with "virtue." Indeed, he had privately stated his preference in 1934, two years before the Spanish war. "The great difference between Social Democracy and Communism," he had written in his journal at the time,

> is that Social Democracy rests upon ethical, general ideas that are essentially drawn from the tradition of 19th century liberal humanitarianism and that Communism deals with particulars, with the living, seething contemporaneity of contemporary capitalism rather than of a vague general reformism. Communism came out of the maelstrom of the war's politics—it was created not so much, it seems to me, as a development of Lenin's 1903-London theses as of a general impatience with and revolt against the ineffable debacle of democratic Socialism during and after the war. . . . Communism thrives on the offensive—it began with the struggle against debacle reformism and it gains its strength hourly (I am thinking particularly now of the US) through the continual struggle against immediate particular things. It lives within and almost because of action. Communism has method, substance, and form. It lacks the sentimentalism of social-democracy, that particularly opprobrious impediment which

disguises the ineffectuality of endless reformism by poetry of the deep-water variety. Communism in short is a 20th century movement—of the gusto and force of the contemporary weltanschauung. Social-Democracy rather is the expression of the out-moded mold of gentle aspirations and gentle lives. It is a relic of a time when life could be divorced from politics and when the forces of reaction were vulnerable only (it was felt) through the force of argument and rationalistic impetus.

This entry would seem to belie Kazin's assertion in *Starting Out in the Thirties* that his Socialism existed "simply as a moral idea" and "did not require any conscious personal assent or decision on my part" and that he "was remarkably detached from it intellectually." He had apparently thought seriously about the relative merits of Democratic Socialism and Communism and had decided (at least for the moment) that the latter better suited present conditions. Bred in the "maelstrom" of twentieth-century politics, the Communists, unlike the Socialists, knew how to act. They were doing so in the United States "against many immediate particular things." They would do so later when Stalin came to the defense of the Spanish Republic and France, England, and the United States stood aside. And under Stalin they would do so in the war. "More and more," Kazin wrote in 1942, "Stalin is becoming the symbol of the dash, the organization, the Allies long for and need—is he Jeb Stuart or Bedford Forrest—the enemy respected? Or is he the dim vision of the future and the prestige that can make that future?" Kazin, who grew up a good Socialist despising Stalin and the Communists, is as suspicious as ever—but also, for the present, impressed. "Yes, I admire the old bastard as never before."[12]

The thirties, Kazin later acknowledged to his son, Michael, is "so much the skeleton in the closet for all us distinguished professors." Having never joined the Communist Party or signed petitions defending the Moscow trials, Kazin had fewer skeletons to worry about than other thirties veterans —whatever "my brief admiration for totalitarian Socialism." Unlike Edmund Wilson, who in 1932 had written publicly that he "admire[d] the Russian Communist leaders, because they are men of superior brains who have triumphed over the ignorance, the stupidity and the shortsighted selfishness of the mass"; unlike Sidney Hook, who in 1934 published an essay titled "Why I Am a Communist"; and unlike Lionel Trilling and Richard Hofstadter, who either joined the Communist Party or Communist

Front organizations, Kazin, whom Cowley suspected of "expressing safe opinions," never publicly or "officially" supported the Communists. He later acknowledged that he may not have contributed much to the political debate in the thirties, but, he told Eric Glaberson (a graduate student writing a dissertation on Kazin and Irving Howe), "I knew enough not to be a Leninist." If there is no evidence that Kazin opposed the Communists, there is also little public evidence that he supported them.[13]

The lack of evidence may have been because he was playing it safe, as Cowley suspected, holding his political opinions close to his vest. But it is just as likely, as Kazin suggests in his memoir, that, while politics was an integral part of his life in the thirties, he saw himself as essentially a literary person who had "radical" views but was reluctant to identify with any political position or party. "The only reason I escape[d] some of the absolutes (if I did)," he later confided to Matthew Josephson, another thirties veteran, "was that I couldn't get over the discovery of myself as a writer. It was grace." Discovering himself as a writer meant the excitement and public recognition of reviewing for mainstream newspapers. It also meant reflecting on all manner of subjects in the privacy of his diary, where, Emerson-like, he felt no need for consistency—"me and my contradictions"—or sustained argument. There he could try out ideas on the German and English novel, on "the grandiosity" of all "philosophies of history," on the "complex flux and transitoriness of all things," on the solitary independence of the artist, as well as on the relative merits of Democratic Socialism and Communism. If Kazin, the thirties diarist, was more attracted to Communism than the hero of *Starting Out in the Thirties,* he had too many competing interests and ideas to be a party-line Leninist, too many intellectual discoveries and personal expectations to commit to any "absolute." Radical politics, he would later acknowledge, was certainly "very central" to his thinking at the time as well as a point of connection with his friends. But politics was not all-consuming. There was plenty of room for "grace."[14]

Columbia

In the fall of 1937, Kazin enrolled in the master's history program at Columbia—a small gesture toward a possible teaching career. As much as he enjoyed freelance reviewing, he knew it held no promise for the future. He had taught a few courses at City College and thought he had some talent for teaching. With a master's degree he might possibly secure an appointment teaching English, history, or both in college or high school. That Hofstadter was now working for his master's in history at Columbia may also have influenced Kazin's decision. He would have a friend on campus and a ping-pong partner. Kazin was still living with his parents in Brownsville and considered taking a dorm room at Columbia, but he was dissuaded by his mother—a moment of "weakness" he would later regret—and the long daily commute continued.[15]

With one exception—Mark Van Doren's course in "The Long Poem"— Kazin was not excited by his courses at Columbia. Van Doren would become a significant figure in Kazin's life, not because he had a direct effect on his career—as his brother, Carl, and sister-in-law, Irita, had—but because of who he was. To a talented, ambitious, struggling young Jew from "darkest Brownsville" during the Depression, Mark Van Doren—poet, scholar, Columbia luminary, editor of the *Nation*—embodied a scholarly ideal and gentlemanly manner that took much of its appeal from the sheer contrast with the circumstances of Kazin's own life. "As the early winter twilight crept over the Columbia campus, Van Doren's craggy face looked as if he expected the sun to come out because he was teaching Virgil. He was in such pleasant relation to his text, his teaching, his students. . . . He spoke in such accord with the fall of the lines and fall of winter outside, that he embodied all the harmony and smiling charm and love of beauty, which I associated with the writers of every generation and place but my own." The poetry may have been Virgil's, but for Kazin the sweetness and light of those winter afternoons in Philosophy Hall were inseparable from the charm and manner of his illustrious teacher.[16]

Kazin would later look back with some embarrassment on his infatuation with Van Doren—"the pursey little man forever congratulating himself in rhetorical little phrases on the right way to live, the right way to think," he wrote in 1958. "When I think of Van Doren as my beau ideal at all, I have to laugh." At the time, however, Van Doren represented an intellectual manner, a way of life, an easy relationship with the world of learning and culture that a young, intellectually aspiring Jew from the ghetto might well envy and want to emulate. "The Jewish intellectual," Kazin theorized in 1955, "sees the world through a model, usually in the native culture, which he accepts as the norm." Indeed, "I question, given the kind of cultural ambiguity from which so many Jews start, whether it would be possible to sail into this 'foreign' culture completely without a model." Lionel Trilling had Matthew Arnold; Harold Laski had Oliver Wendell Holmes; "I had my model in people like Mark Van Doren." The somewhat sour journal entries about Van Doren do not invalidate Kazin's early impressions or the highly complimentary portraits that would appear in the autobiographies. He admired and continued to admire Van Doren the teacher and the critic and in time came to regard him as a critical ally and friend who shared his old-fashioned belief in "the private reader"—Van Doren's phrase (and book title) for the reader who reads for personal enjoyment unencumbered by the apparatus of the New Criticism. The disclaimers in the diary and the warm public portraits instead reveal the contradictory mix of gratitude and resistance that marked Kazin's (and many of his contemporaries') relations with the native culture. In one form or another, that conflict would engage, puzzle, and trouble him for much of his life—and provoke some of his best writing.[17]

Besides the course with Van Doren, the other significant event in Kazin's year at Columbia was the writing of a master's essay. Under the direction of Professor Eliot Van Kirk Dobbie, Kazin wrote on Edward Gibbon's literary criticism. He chose the topic for the obvious reason that it brought together his interests in history and literature. He also had a good reading knowledge of French, the language in which Gibbon had written his major critical work, *L'Essai sur l'étude de la littérature.* But if Gibbon's literary criticism seemed an ideal subject for a literary critic taking a master's in history, the criticism itself was another matter. Gibbon, Kazin soon discovered, had no interest in literary criticism, classical or contemporary; and when he did turn to literary criticism, as in *L'Essai,* he did so wholly as a historian attempting "to fix the historical limits of a work, to appraise its information, or to check it." He also found that Gibbon was indifferent to the literature of his own time. Although Kazin respected Gibbon's authority as a historian and classicist with a deep appreciation for classical literature—"in an age of neo-classicism, Gibbon was perhaps the lone classicist"—he was dismayed to find how oblivious he was to the contemporary literary scene. "Gibbon knew little of his world and cared less [and] he was even more indifferent to the literature of his time. That is a fact which the student of Gibbon's criticism learns quickly and a little painfully."[18]

Kazin would later acknowledge that he was "no great shakes" at Columbia. He did, however, take some pride in his thesis; and it is, in fact, a lively piece of critical prose (especially for an master's thesis), replete with scholarly discussion and anecdotes drawn from Gibbon's autobiography and journal that help bring the historian into focus. It also contains some blunt observations about Gibbon's writing style. "The *Essai* is difficult, and a good deal of it is inexcusably difficult, for its obscurity in many passages is the result of some of the most fantastically bad writing ever offered to a publisher." Kazin felt he knew something about publishable literary criticism (even in French). The rare readability of a master's thesis evidently impressed Professor Dobbie, who told Kazin that he had sat on the side of the bed reading passages to his wife.[19]

"Write This Book"

After he received his master's degree in history in June 1938, Kazin was as uncertain as ever about his future. His year at Columbia would not have encouraged him to go on for a doctorate, even if he had had the funds to pursue one. Revolution or no revolution, he had begun to think seriously about getting a job, something more secure than freelancing and teaching night classes at City College. That job, however, would be some time coming. In the summer of 1938, Carl Van Doren approached him with the suggestion that he write a critical history of modern American prose to be published by the firm of Reynal and Hitchcock, where Van Doren was an advisor. He had been reading Kazin's pieces in the *Times* and the *Tribune* and had been impressed by his energy, wide reading, and critical intelligence. "You don't need a job," he reportedly told a wary Kazin, who spoke of his worries about the future. "Write this book and you'll have no trouble getting a job." Coming from Carl Van Doren, the suggestion could not be taken lightly. Van Doren had taught American literature at Columbia until 1930 and served as "quarterback" on the pioneering team that had edited the *Cambridge History of American Literature* (1917–21). In numerous articles and books, as well as in his role as literary editor of the *Nation* (1921–1922) and the *Century* (1922–1925), he had been an influential champion of "the younger generation" in American letters and a potent force in raising the profile of American literature inside and outside the academy. One took his advice seriously, and Kazin in the end accepted the challenge to "write this book." He would later call Van Doren's suggestion a "totally unexpected piece of luck" that changed his life and could almost make him believe in divine providence.[20]

Van Doren could encourage Kazin. He could not guarantee success. To abandon all plans of steady employment for the foreseeable future, betting everything on a book whose size and scope (and success) remained to be determined, was a gamble. Kazin decided the risk was worth it, thinking he could do the job in a little over a year's time, which, in fact, took four and a half. He would remember them, however, as some of the happiest of his life—partly because he took such pleasure in the writing. "Of all my books," he wrote in a 1995 preface, "*On Native Grounds* was the easiest to write." "I felt what I have never felt since 1945—that the age was wholly with me, that I was appealing to what Hazlitt called 'the spirit of the age.'" Another source of happiness was his personal life. In the fall of 1938, while at a vacation camp in upstate New York, he had met Natasha Dohn.[21]

Alfred would later try to account for his immediate and powerful attraction to Natasha (or Asya). "She wore blue shorts and an embroidered Russian blouse, and the pert pigtails standing up from her deep black hair were humorous against a delicately olive-colored Russian face that looked Asian in the concentration of its reserve." Much of the appeal came from her Russian aspect, particularly, "the perfection and reserve of that face" and its capacity to lead him "into abysses of nostalgia, into passionate attachment to countries I had never seen and to causes I did not know I believed in." The daughter of Russian Jews, Asya was both exotic and familiar—like everything Kazin associated with Russia in the 1930s. "It did not astonish me to learn that she had been named Natasha, after the heroine of *War and Peace;* that she was a research bacteriologist; that her room was full of Russian cigarette boxes, textbooks of bacteriology, Russian shawls, and pictures of Alexandra Kollantai, Madame Curie and Isadora Duncan." Alfred had fallen in love with a living instance of his "cultural pieties," above all "with that face, that dear Russian face, that commandingly austere and spiritual and world-historical face that had already sacrificed so much for mankind."[22]

Whatever the truth of Kazin's political-cultural explanation, the attraction was real. Two weeks after their meeting (October 1938) they were married in the "fake churchly gloom of the Municipal Chapel" at City Hall with Richard Hofstadter, Felice Swados, and Ben Seligman as witnesses. They moved into a two-room flat at 150 Remsen Street in Brooklyn Heights, around the corner from the Hofstadters. Alfred could not have been happier. "I've always believed in my bad fortune, feared marriage," he wrote a few weeks after the ceremony. "But Asya is like nothing I ever anticipated or even dared to hope for. She's priceless." He was also pleased with the living arrangement, however cramped—one room and a kitchen for fifty dollars a month. Lying on the sofa bed, which had to be made up every night, they could hear the noise from the harbor and the muffled rumble of the Brooklyn traffic—the "sluggishly turning flywheel of the city." Walking down Montague Street, they fronted the harbor, the dark water shimmering with reflected lights and the "great jeweled breast of Manhattan floating" on the surface. And out beyond the warehouses and freighters, "above all and mastering all, the great Brooklyn Bridge itself."[23]

Kazin had long been attracted to this area of the city, the brownstones, the harbor, the bridge. Now he was living there, happily married, in a growing circle of new friends: Felice Swados and Richard Hofstadter (134 Montague Street), Richard Rovere (143 Montague Street), and Bertram and Ella Wolfe (68 Montague Street). Radical politics was the primary topic of discussion, which, according to Rovere, was conducted at a very sophisticated level. Rovere ("Jim" in *Starting Out in the Thirties*) appears in Kazin's memoir as he is splitting with the Communist Party and resigning from his job as a reporter for its official organ, the *New Masses*. Like other refugees from the party, Rovere had "that slightly orphaned look often seen in people after a marriage has broken up." Kazin remembers being struck immediately by Rovere's skeptical intelligence and curiosity (qualities not usually associated with party hacks), which would serve him well in later years when he became a political reporter for the *New Yorker*. He loved hearing from Rovere on the factional infighting and internal machinations of the party. "Do write me and let me know what's new," he wrote Rovere while on a brief vacation to Provincetown in the summer of 1940. "The Trotsky business is horrible. What are people thinking about it in New York? How are the Stalinists behaving? I wish you would keep for me all the available DW [*Daily Worker*] and *New Masses* articles and editorials on the assassination. I'm very anxious to see them."[24]

Rovere, in turn, was impressed by Kazin's knowledge of politics and personalities in the Soviet Union. To Rovere the latter were "spectral figures" with names like Kirov, Bukharin, Zinoviev, Kalinin, and Kamenev. Kazin, however, "knew what they had done, what they had written, what they stood for." Like himself, Kazin had been brought up in Brooklyn, but in a section where names like Kamenev and Zinoviev evoked images as vivid and recognizable as the names Jimmy Walker and Al Smith. Kazin and his friends could talk all evening about events in the Soviet Union "as confidently as if discussing a play they had just seen or a novel they had read," Rovere recalled. "I was not only greatly instructed but shamed into a kind of intellectual responsibility that I had up to then lacked."[25]

None of these friends spoke with more authority than Bertram Wolfe. Indeed, few if any Americans could speak with more authority on Communism. One of the founders of the Communist Party in America in 1919, he had been its foremost theoretician until he had run afoul of Stalin in 1929 and was expelled from the party. Kazin remembers listening to him, "the last of his breed," tell stories of the original Communist International, of John Reed and Angelica Balabanov, of Bukharin and Lunacharsky, and of "the legendary days of the 1920s when the new Communist movement had been led by revolutionary intellectuals" before they were murdered by Stalin. Kazin may also have profited from Wolfe's reflections on the relations of American literature to social and economic change. An early champion (along with Carl Van Doren) of Vernon Parrington's three-volume *Main Currents in American Thought* (two published in 1927, and a posthumous volume in 1930)—a book Kazin called "the inspiration" for his own history—Wolfe regarded Parrington as essential "mental equipment of everyone who would understand American history and the American mind." No other American historian, not even Charles Beard, had a better grasp of "the relation of ideas to class forces and economic development." Wolfe was happy to discuss many things with Kazin—the Moscow trials, the Spanish Civil War, the economic basis of American thought—he had written on all of them. But so were Rovere and Hofstadter and Seligman and all the radical friends who, dropping in at 150 Remsen Street, kept the conversation going. The social-political life that Kazin had missed (or shunned) at

City was now virtually on his doorstep and frequently in his living (and sleeping) room. It was a happy change and contributed to "the constant state of arousement" in which he began serious work on his book.[26]

Alfred remembers starting the book in the fall of 1938 in a mood of "great husbandly contentment," delighted with Asya and excited about his project. He did most of his work in the great reading room (Room 315) of the New York Public Library during its Depression hours: Monday through Saturday, 9 AM to 10 PM, and Sunday, 1 PM to 10 PM "How lucky I was to grow up in the Depression, when my country was poor and there was money for libraries," he would later write about the drastically reduced library hours after the Depression. Asya worked in a hospital laboratory during the day—the only reliable source of family income—before going to Bellevue, where she was pursuing her doctorate on strains of influenza. Theirs, he recalled, was "an intensely scholarly decorous life," interrupted by free concerts at Town Hall and Washington Irving High School, walks along the river, and conversations with friends. Alfred occasionally played duets with Asya's brother, Leon, who also had a flat in the neighborhood. In the summers, they managed to find time and money to take brief vacations, usually to New England, once to Monticello.[27]

But for four and a half years, the library was the center of his life. His accounts of his days in Room 315 have become legendary among those interested in the history of the library. "There was something about the vibrating empty rooms early in the morning—light falling through the great tall windows, the sun burning the smooth tops of the golden tables as if they had been freshly painted—that made me restless with the need to grab up every book, press into every single mind right there on the open shelves." As the tables filled up with "street philosophers, fanatics, advertising agents, the homeless," he came to identify with "this jumpy Depression crowd." "I could feel on my skin the worry of all those people; I could hear day and evening those restless hungry footsteps; I was entangled in the hunger of all those aimless, bewildered, panicky seekers for 'opportunity.'" Working away among such company in the magnificent marble arched room, built in part with money from the estate of the Astor family, Kazin was reminded daily of the age he was beginning to write about, the "amenities" he wanted for his own life, and the democratic impulse he was writing to celebrate. He worked on the book in other places as well—on the kitchen table in Long Island City, where he and Asya moved in 1940; at Province-town in the summer of 1940; and at Yaddo, a writer's colony in Saratoga Springs, during the summer of 1942. But Room 315 was where he did most of his work, and it was the place that he would always associate with the writing of the book.[28]

For the most part he worked alone, but occasionally Hofstadter joined him. After obtaining his master's degree at Columbia in 1938, Hofstadter stayed on for a Ph.D., writing his dissertation, *Social Darwinism in American Thought,* also his first book. After a morning of work, the two friends would break for lunch at a nearby automat, sometimes squeezing in a game of ping-pong at a Times Square pool hall before returning to the golden tables. On Tuesdays, they usually went to a newsreel theater; on other days they simply talked. There was much to talk about—Columbia, the gathering storm in Europe, politics, and now their work. They were both researching America in the late nineteenth century—Hofstadter for his book on Social Darwinism, Kazin for the origins of the "modern" impulse in American prose. "We talked constantly about what each was writing"—money madness in the Gilded Age, growing American power in the late nineteenth century, the building of the Brooklyn Bridge, "the piling up of the immigrant masses" in American cities, the Adams family (Hofstadter accused his friend of overlooking Henry's anti-Semitism because he was a good writer). They talked and argued and read each other's work. "Hofstadter and I were in quest of, forever fascinated by, what Lewis Mumford had called 'the brown decades' of the nineteenth century—years of crude expansion and technical innovation in which *our* America had settled into shape." Though he would write prolifically about life and literature in the twentieth century, Kazin's first love would always be the "brown decades" of nineteenth-century America.[29]

On Native Grounds

Kazin's marriage and daily work routine provided the rhythm and discipline needed to move his book steadily forward. But the discipline of his scholarly life could not protect him from the accelerating events convulsing the world. The four years during which *On Native Grounds* was written (1938–1942) constitute one of the most traumatic periods of the twentieth century. Its more signal events include the conclusion of the Moscow trials in 1938; the Spanish Republic's defeat in the spring of 1939; Hitler's takeover of Austria and the Sudetenland in 1938–1939; the shattering, "inconceivable" Hitler-Stalin nonaggression pact in 1939 in which Stalin made common cause with Hitler, followed nine days later by Germany's invasion of Poland and the beginning of World War II; the fall of France in 1940; and the bombing of Pearl Harbor in 1941, which brought the United States into the war and effectively ended the Depression.[30]

All of these events were shocking, wrenching, fateful. But for Kazin and his radical friends, the nonaggression pact was devastating. Although he had been disgusted by the Moscow trials and unnerved by what he had heard out of Spain, Kazin had assumed that the Soviet Union would maintain the popular front against the spread of Fascism in central Europe. This was his thinking the third week in August 1939 while working on his book at the kitchen table in his Remsen Street flat. The English and the French had sent military missions to Moscow, where, it was assumed, they were finalizing plans for containing Hitler. At noon on August 22, interrupting his work to make a cup of coffee, Kazin turned on the radio to learn that Hitler's foreign minister, Joachim von Ribbentrop, would be traveling to Moscow the next day and that the swastika was already flying over the Moscow airport. No! he shouted at the radio. "It's not true!" "The announcer calmly went on with the details." The pact was signed the next day, with Stalin toasting Hitler's health: "I know how much the German nation owes to its Führer." All the worst fears of those desperate to believe that Stalin would halt Hitler's advance were confirmed. It was now clear that Hitler was not going to be stopped, that Stalin was a murderous betrayer, and that the Communists and Communist press, which supported Stalin's move, were essentially agents of the Soviet Union. The consequence was war. "Stalin had lighted the fuse in Hitler's hand," and the world would be sucked into the explosion.[31]

With a growing sense of the inevitable, Kazin watched Hitler take Poland, then turn to the West—Denmark, Belgium, Holland, Norway, and France. Hitler would be satisfied with nothing less than the destruction of all democratic countries in reach of his planes and U-boats. Like many good Socialists, Kazin initially opposed America's entrance into the war. "We were all Socialists still, and Socialists stayed out of capitalist wars." In

September 1940, he signed a public letter to the *Nation* urging the election of Socialist candidates, Norman Thomas and Maynard Krueger for president and vice president, respectively, as "the only candidates who may be counted upon for unwavering opposition to the forces of reaction, alien-bating, militarist hysteria, and the drive towards war." Shortly afterward, as the Nazis consolidated their hold on Europe and Hitler turned his attention to Russia, Kazin changed his mind. The United States had no choice but to enter the war. Hitler and Fascism were not going to be contained in Central Europe, and what few democracies were left in the world were under threat.[32]

That Kazin was able to complete his five-hundred-page history during such a tumultuous period suggests something about the determination he brought to his task. It also bears out his later claim that he took energy from the movement of history, however turbulent. "The age was with me, the excitement of the thirties [and forties] was in my book and was getting me to write it." With the world in convulsions and modern civilization at the crossroads, to write a book on modern American literature and American democracy was to invest one's task with the urgency of history, to bring to one's efforts a "world-historical sense of purpose." The stakes could not have been higher. "It is clear to me," Kazin wrote in the book's preface, "that we have reached a definite climax in [our] literature, as in so much of our modern liberal culture, and that with a whole civilization in the balance, we may attempt some comprehensive judgment on the formation of our modern American literature." To attempt such a judgment was not only to move with the history but to answer history's demands.[33]

But how to answer history's demands when history was moving so fast? If Kazin found these events stimulating, he also found them profoundly disruptive, upsetting assumptions about the Socialist future, undermining hopes of the literary left, challenging the direction and argument of his book. How to take aim at a moving target from a moving platform and stay on the mark? The answer was to stay as close as possible to the original scheme while making necessary adjustments to the growing wartime nationalism, mindful that an account of the past derives its value from the needs of the present.

Kazin's original plan appears in an application for a (successful) Guggenheim grant submitted in the summer or early fall of 1939. Titled *The*

Years of Promise: Prose in American since 1900, it describes a project
consistent with the thinking of the "Progressive Historians," Charles Beard
and Vernon Parrington, whose vision of American history as an ongoing
struggle of "the people" versus the plutocratic "interests" pervaded American historiography in the 1930s. As the title suggests, it was to be a hopeful
book, tracing the forward movement of the progressive, "militantly democratic" impulse in American letters that got its start in the 1880s and 1890s
and continued into the early 1900s before it was "deflected" by World War
I and the emergence of a postwar literature of Menckenian "supercilious-
ness" and Lost Generation "disillusionment." Kazin proposes to bring the
progressive story up-to-date by showing that after the 1929 crash, writers
returned to the hopeful, insurgent spirit of the prewar period, producing a
literature that instilled new life into the old progressive ideals, inspired
fresh interest in reform, and heralded a new "leftism [that] colored the
fiction, the criticism, drama, even the films." After "the debunkers," "satir-
ists," "escapists," and self-pityers of the 1920s, "the 1930s marked a return
to the sense of responsibility."[34]

Kazin concludes his application with a tribute to Parrington's *Main Currents in American Thought*. "It was Parrington who taught me to regard
American literature as a democratic epic." It was also Parrington who taught
him how to exploit regional differences and partisan struggle ("Western
agrarianism" versus "Eastern capitalism," "Plutocracy and the Working
Man," "the interests" against "the people") for narrative purposes. Yet he
insists that his "critical method" is ultimately quite different from Parrington's. While Parrington subordinated aesthetic considerations to the
interest of ongoing political debate, he (Kazin) would be making the kind of
aesthetic judgments appropriate to literary subjects. "I have never been
able to understand why literary history and criticism should be mutually
exclusive." Kazin would later expand and sharpen his criticism of Parrington
in *On Native Grounds*, following Lionel Trilling's influential denunciation of
Parrington in the *Partisan Review* (1940). "Parrington had his formula,"
Kazin writes in his history, "he had his special notion of what 'history" and
'reality' must be, he had his convenient design. If he could not fit the
individual to the design, he sacrificed him to it."[35]

Whatever his reservations, the book Kazin completed in 1942 relies
heavily on Parrington's "formula," both for its narrative "progressive"

structure and in the deft groupings and counterpointings of writers (naturalists versus "exquisites," Dreiser versus Wharton, Marxist versus New
Criticism, etc.). It is difficult to imagine what *On Native Grounds* would
have been without *Main Currents*. But it also diverges from Parrington and
the progressive model, and not just in its aesthetic judgments. The hopeful,
progressive, politically insurgent history that Parrington had inspired, and
that Kazin had originally intended, turns in the later chapters into something much more uncertain, conflicted, and reflective of the changing attitudes of the period in which it was written—a period that saw the insurgent
spirit of radical politics yield to a war-inspired cultural nationalism increasingly wary of the subversive energies directed at the country's economic and political failings. "Before I came to the end of my book in 1942,"
Kazin wrote in 1982, "the moral bankruptcy of many left-wing writers left
me, though still radical, less convinced of the 'necessary' connection between literature and social criticism." It would have been more accurate to
say that by the time he finished *On Native Grounds*, the political culture of
1942 made the left-wing writers he had been championing seem less perti-
nent to (and possibly destructive of) the ideological needs of wartime
America. The country (and Kazin) needed a very different book than the
one he had first intended to write.[36]

Considering the shifts in ideological intention, one might wonder how he
managed to put together a history that reads so easily, moves so seamlessly,
from writer to writer, chapter to chapter, building steadily toward its coda-
like conclusion. F. O. Matthiessen, whose *American Renaissance* (1941)
was published a year earlier and who knew something about writing literary
history in a period of ideological change, spoke for many in praising the
book's readability, citing Kazin's "comprehensive planning" and "organic"
grasp of the material. Writing twenty years later, R. W. B. Lewis found *On
Native Grounds* as rousing as ever and attributed its compelling forward
motion and "living" quality largely to its "rush of style" and its youthful,
impulsively American energy. More recently, Robert Alter and Morris
Dickstein have credited the cumulative movement of the book to Kazin's
success at linking narrative and evaluation through a series of vivid, evocative portraits in which we see "writer after writer [dispatched] in a stunningly definitive way"[37]

These are perceptive observations. *On Native Grounds* is a carefully planned work (aided by Parrington's example), written in a lively, often exuberant, prose with a novelist's feel for character and event—Kazin once remarked that he began his history much "as one might begin a novel of the past with William Dean Howells arriving in New York, giving up his Boston career, and so on." But style, fluency, narrative finesse, and a flair for portraiture would not in themselves have been sufficient to hold the book together, much less negotiate the shifting ideological terrain encountered in its writing. Kazin also needed a definite story to tell, the story of "the modern," as he calls it, or "the modern spirit"—a concept loose enough to accommodate the various developments and ideals he wanted to elucidate and substantive enough to evoke a strong sense of forward movement. "My subject had to do with the 'modern,'" he wrote in *New York Jew,* with "the modern as democracy; with America itself as the modern; with the end of the nineteenth century as the great preparation." (Walt Whitman had arrived at a similarly expansive definition in *Democratic Vistas.* "I shall use the words America and democracy as convertible terms," he wrote. "Our genius is democratic and modern.") Loose enough for Kazin to stress the qualities he wanted at any particular moment in the narrative, "the modern" stood for America, for the spread of democracy, for intellectual and political insurgency, for artistic experimentation and cultural nationalism. If the modern spirit presented in one section is not quite the same spirit at work in another, they are all part of a larger "modern" movement moving ineluctably forward—with some admittedly serious reversals, including the more militant "left-wing" writing of the thirties he had earlier planned to celebrate and came to regret—all linking past and present in a general celebration of America, American progress, American literature, American democracy.[38]

Kazin also needed a moral-aesthetic framework for evaluating individual authors while registering the advances, retreats, and "deflect[ions]" of "the modern." He is rather loose here as well, proposing in the preface what might be called a personal dialectic that becomes the basis of the judgments to follow. "For me," he writes, "the greatest single fact about our modern American writing [is] our writers' absorption in every last detail of their American world together with their deep and subtle alienation from it." "What interested me was our alienation *on* native grounds—the interwoven story of our need to take up our life on our own grounds, and the irony of our possession." Kazin does not explain what the relation should be between "absorption" and "alienation." But his discussions indicate that, while he valued the acuity of a writer's criticism, a readiness to tell the "harsh, bitter truth" about America, he did not consider "alienation" itself to be an acceptable response. Events and practices, and the capitalist system, might discourage and anger; but the country, its history, its people, its geography and democratic traditions are ultimately indispensable—the grounds of belief on which the most bitter dissensions can (must) find resolution.[39]

Kazin had originally intended to begin his book with the 1900s but soon discovered that to tell his story he needed to go back to the 1880s, to William Dean Howells and "The Opening Struggle for Realism." Kazin had a knack for recapturing the fervor of youthful struggle and early achievement—a talent that would serve him well in his autobiographies. It serves a similar purpose in the book's first (of three) sections, where he depicts the pioneering efforts of Howells as the first stage in the accelerating march of "the modern spirit." Combining truth-telling with social protest with an "elementary nationalism," the "modern" impulse picks up momentum and sweeps all before it—literary naturalists, Chicago realists, cultural progressives, insurgent professors. As in any good story, there are obstructions and reversals—fin de siècle aesthetes, reactionary professors, genteel cultural overseers—but the forward direction is irresistible, while the emergence of major voices such as Frank Norris, Thorstein Veblen, Jack London, and Theodore Dreiser helps shape the zeitgeist and recall the opposing terms of "absorption" and "alienation" marking Kazin's interest in them. Dreiser, who would always inspire Kazin's most deeply sympathetic criticism, offers a particularly compelling mix of absorption and alienation, a writer who understood the cruelties and rewards of American life and accepted them all as a kind of fate—America, the inexorable in human life. Better than any other American writer, Dreiser understood "the bitter patriotism of loving what one knows."[40]

Despite its title, "The Great Liberation (1918–1929)," comprising the book's middle section, does not describe the final triumph of the modern spirit, but rather a standoff between the forces of progress exemplified in the work of Sherwood Anderson, Sinclair Lewis, and Willa Cather and a postwar reaction evident in the cynicism of H. L. Mencken, the preciosity of

James Cabell, the intolerance of the New Humanism, and the "Lost Generation's" "defeatism." In his assessment of this last group (e.e. cummings, F. Scott Fitzgerald, Ernest Hemingway, and John Dos Passos), Kazin saw "a fateful new influence" entering American writing—a new level of "disassociation" and bitterness, an alienation not "on native grounds" but a "detachment from the native traditions [that] now became their own first tradition." Dos Passos, the subject of the book's lengthiest portrait, is Kazin's exemplary case, a writer whose curiosity about America is finally overwhelmed by feelings of alienation and despair. *U.S.A.,* Dos Passos's supreme effort of absorption, is ultimately a monumental expression of dispiriting estrangement. "There are no flags for the spirit in it. . . . It is one of the saddest books ever written by an American."[41]

In his Guggenheim application, Kazin referred to the twenties as having "deflected" the modern spirit before it resumed its progressive advance in the thirties. In *On Native Grounds,* however, the "defeatism" of the twenties marks a direct transition to the thirties, "The Literature of Crisis (1930–1940)." "The tragic 'I' [of the Lost Generation] has become the tragic 'we' of modern society." Instead of staging a healthy rebound to "responsibility" (as Kazin had initially intended to argue), the modern spirit has turned rancorous and sour. We read of novels full of "realistic savagery," of a naturalism turned "explicit, murderous, profane." Once praised for "a lean hard social fiction fit for the thirties," Josephine Herbst is now guilty of "desperate pedestrianism." Others are praised and condemned at the same time. Richard Wright is "honest" in his effort to "represent the sufferings of his race" but guilty of "unconscious slickness" and a "sinister manipulation of terror." James T. Farrell is lauded for a "powerful and vital art" that is also "a perfect example of unconscious . . . philistinism." Leftwing writers—Erskine Caldwell, Edward Dahlberg, and Robert Cantwell —are credited for creating "a moving literature of confession and autobiography" but accused of participating in a "cult of violence" driven by "hysteria" and "necrophilia."[42]

The confusion here is as much Kazin's as his writers'. He did not know how to assess their responses to the times because he no longer knew what to think himself. He recognized these writers as distinct talents but saw them ensnared in the "rancors" of a decade that he had come to regard as "sick." How to separate the writer from the zeitgeist? There are sympathetic discussions of a few writers—John Steinbeck, Henry Miller, Thomas Wolfe, Edmund Wilson—but much of the "The Literature of Crisis" reads today as an expression of the very confusion and violent feeling, the "sadism of the word," that Kazin was deploring, less a guide to the times than a reflection of them. Put somewhat differently, "The Literature of Crisis" is perhaps best understood as a record of personal crisis, a crisis of faith at a time when, he later told Malcolm Cowley, "I was losing my faith in the only religion I ever had." Kazin would spend years evaluating the effect the collapse of revolutionary hopes had on himself and other radicals, including the novelists he now wanted to praise and blame. There was much to be sorted out and much to be salvaged. At the moment, however, there was mostly disappointment, chagrin, uncertainty, and an urgent need to distance himself from a literary decade that had become a painful embarrassment, "a memory," as he later put it, "that everyone wanted to forget."[43]

Kazin betrays very little uncertainty, however, in one area—literary criticism. A practicing critic, he felt he could speak on the subject with authority, and he knew what he wanted to say. American criticism, he argued in the book's most controversial chapter, "Criticism at the Poles," so long the country's "intellectual conscience and intellectual carryall"—tolerant, liberal, curious, and amiable—has been hijacked by ideologues and technicians—Marxists on the left, New Critics on the right. Criticism, "so basic a communication between men," was being turned into ritualized programs following approved "methods" in support of narrow political agendas. The chapter—a mix of shrewd critical observation, sweeping generalizations, and personal attacks, all couched in the rhetoric of broad cultural alarm—put fellow critics on notice that their profession was on the cusp of unsettling changes. While acknowledging that the Marxist threat seemed to have passed, the impact of the New Critics was just beginning as they built up their forces within the universities. Professing to free literature from the noise of history and the vagaries of personality, these "new formalists" proposed that criticism should become an "objective" science. Yet despite claims of disinterestedness, they were, argued Kazin, as ideological as the most militant Marxists. Coming out of the "reactionary" agrarian movement of the South, they articulated an antimodern "modernism" that repudiated the chaos of contemporary democratic life in America, while yearning for the aristocratic grace and feudal order of the antebellum

South—an order that resembled nothing so much as the transcendent unity they believed constituted a genuine work of art.[44]

Reviewers, not surprisingly, took a keen interest in this chapter—the most sustained assault on the New Critics yet to appear. Some were grateful for the warning. Gordon Haight, William York Tindall, Robert Spiller, and Howard Mumford Jones all approved of Kazin's strictures against the politicization of criticism and the ahistoricism or "ivory tower[ism]" of the New Critics. Others—among them Matthiessen, Trilling, and (of all people) twenty-two-year-old Irving Howe—felt that his response was alarmist and the weakest part of the book. Writing under a pseudonym in the *New International,* Howe complained that Kazin had slighted those doing the most to bring "economy, discipline, and technical competence" to criticism "during the age of gushers." New Critic and southerner Cleanth Brooks was understandably incensed. He faulted Kazin for writing faddish literary history "dominated by New York," accused him of not reading the critics he attacked, and (with breathtaking modesty) declared "pathetic" his charge that the New Critics were making inroads in the academy. "I can assure him personally that the new formalists have next to no influence in the universities."[45]

Had Kazin confined his discussion of the thirties to fiction and criticism, he would have concluded his story on a rather discouraging note. Indeed, upon publication, Mark Van Doren sent him a note remarking on the grim state of American letters, provoking a polite response that this is not quite how he (Kazin) saw it. In his review in the *Nation,* Trilling wrote that "it is a good book and a saddening book" about "a literature" which "seems indeed almost to have failed." In fact, *On Native Grounds* concludes with a distinctly encouraging message, thanks to its final chapter, "America! America!"—a groundbreaking discussion of the histories, biographies, WPA guides, and photographic essays that made up the extensive documentary literature of the 1930s.[46]

To be sure, Kazin found much of this work to be of uneven quality. James Agee's *Let Us Now Praise Famous Men* was a genuine literary achievement; many of the histories and biographies were "solid and affectionate." However, a good deal of what he was reading seemed mere "mechanical" journalism. He was also wary of works in which nationalist fervor appeared to overwhelm critical sense—Van Wyck Brooks's most recent books being the most notable examples. But for all his reservations, Kazin saw this literature of "national inventory" as a highly positive development. "So far from being a blind and parochial nationalism, this experience in national self-discovery was largely shaped by the sudden emergence of America as the repository of Western culture in a world overrun by Fascism." Indeed, it arose out of impulses similar to those that had inspired and sustained the writing of his own book—"As we study it [American history], we are making it," he had written in his Guggenheim application. While he did not claim that this "literature of nationhood" represented a major advance of the insurgent "modern spirit" described in earlier chapters, he did see it as promising evidence of a "new historical spirit" in a nation arriving at a fresh valuation of itself. Kazin shared in the revaluation. If he began *On Native Grounds* "feeling radicalism as a spiritual passion," he completed it in profound accord with a country and a culture fighting for survival against an unprecedented kind of barbarism. America, for the present anyway, meant common, not contested, ground.[47]

"The Sudden Invitations, the Florid Compliments and Passionate Attacks"

On Native Grounds was published on October 30, 1942, an event Orville Prescott in the *New York Times* likened to the long-awaited arrival of a major storm, "heralded by flashes of lightning" in advance notices and rumblings of thunder in various scholarly magazines. For the staid world of literary criticism, there was an unusual amount of excitement. Many people in the literary-publishing field were curious about the twenty-something "wunderkind" turning out authoritative reviews in the major newspapers and journals. Excerpts had appeared in the *New Republic* and the *Saturday Review of Literature.* Influential figures in American literary scholarship such as Oscar Cargill had read galley proofs and expressed prepublication enthusiasm. The young Mr. Kazin, Cargill told the editors, was "a gold mine." There was talk of a major revaluation of American literature. Would the five-hundred-page history of American writing meet expectations? The answer, it soon became clear, was that it had. "Now and then," wrote Irwin Edman on page one of the *New York Herald Tribune: Books,* "the publication of a book is not only a literary but a moral event. Not every week brings to attention a first book [by a young author] in almost every sense first rate." Few were as unqualified in their praise as Edman, but many shared his enthusiasm. "Conceived on a grand scale and as not only a history but a moral history," wrote Lionel Trilling in the *Nation*, "it is quite the best and most complete treatment we have of an arduous and difficult subject." Howard Mumford Jones in the *Saturday Review* wrote that Kazin had written the best history of American literature to date. "No one, I think, has been more deft in setting the social scene for the appearance of literature in the successive stages of literary development; and no one has more economically marshaled his writers upon that stage."[48]

The book was praised for its ambition, the energy of its style, its balanced judgments, and above all, its rejection of critical schools and party-line polemics. (Kazin was correct to think that readers wanted to put thirties sectarianism behind them.) The more negative reviews, not surprisingly, came from representatives of the schools and parties he had attacked Cleanth Brooks representing the New Critics, Granville Hicks and Isadore Schneider, the Marxists. Hicks, whom Kazin had called an outdated "little Calvin of the left" in a cruel, patronizing portrait, wrote a measured review challenging Kazin to move beyond name-calling to a more balanced assessment of the hopes as well as the angers of the thirties. Schneider, not so measured, accused Kazin of writing off the progressive impulse in American writing and of pushing critics into extreme positions before taking "a safe squat in the middle." The most disappointing review appeared in the *Partisan Review*. While not exactly negative, the review, written by Fred Dupee, questioned the book's nativist bias and challenged Kazin's critical standards. Kazin thought it "condescending" and "supercilious" and later told Richard Chase that the editors had directed Dupee to "put down" his book. Schneider and Dupee were among the minority, however. Gordon Haight was closer to the consensus: "Kazin has no ax to grind. He belongs to no school or cult, and insists on judging literature in relation to the whole of human life." Several reviewers noted the lack of axes in Kazin's woodshed.[49]

Kazin later claimed that he was "stupefied" by the response, that he was not prepared for such attention—"the sudden invitations, the florid compliments and passionate attacks." Not that he didn't welcome them. Henry Commager wrote to tell him it was "a great book," "the best piece of criticism since Parrington," and asked him to dine at the Century Club.

Lionel Trilling invited him to his home (for the first and last time) to discuss the book and other matters. The eighteenth-century historian Carl Becker wrote to praise his "discriminating good sense"; and Henry Miller, in two lengthy letters, declared himself "amazed" at the accuracy of Kazin's judgment, though he faulted him for not paying more attention to the European influences on American writers. Well after publication, *On Native Grounds* would continue to arouse interest among people eager to meet its young author, many of whom would become important figures in his life (and in his autobiographies)—Edmund Wilson, F. O. Matthiessen, Hannah Arendt, the British historian Denis Brogan, and the English intellectual and radical Harold Laski, to name a few. After reading the book, Laski wrote Kazin's editors that one of the reasons he most wanted to revisit America was to meet the young author, whom he considered "among the six best critical minds America has had since Emerson." Laski and Brogan would be among a number of British writers to befriend Kazin when he visited England during the final months of the war.[50]

If *On Native Grounds* proved a stupefying success in almost every way for its twenty-seven-year-old author, it did not come wholly free of regrets or without cause for future concern. Kazin would repent his harsh treatment of certain writers, especially Richard Wright and Faulkner, whom he had called (among other things) a "calculating terrorist" and a "slick magazine sentimentalist." He would also have reason to regret his intemperate treatment of certain critics. Although his attack on the New Critics did not get him into immediate trouble—Allen Tate wrote him an otherwise civil note saying the remarks about him were "crazy"—he had laid down the gauntlet and declared himself an enemy to an increasingly influential group of writers who would have occasion to take his measure. His harsh treatment of Granville Hicks would have more definite consequences when Kazin later sought a permanent position at Smith College, where Hicks had once taught and had influential friends. It would not be the last time that Kazin's penchant for sharp portraiture would bear bitter fruit.[51]

A very different kind of concern was the book's timing. "*On Native Grounds* came out at just the right time," Kazin would later write. "By 1942 and the war, there was general recognition that a literary period was passed." He was correct. It told the story of a "modern," progressive-radical spirit that emerged in the 1880s and came to an end with the

wartime consensus of the early 1940s. It was the right time to remind a
country at war of the literary achievements and democratic-progressive
impulses that were an essential part of its cultural heritage; but it was also
"the right time" because it was the last possible time. There would be no
repeat performances. After the war, not only was the notion of American
history as progress, as a hopeful, forward movement of "the modern spirit,"
fading into the prewar past; so had the possibility of writing history according to the progressive, Parringtonian formula that Kazin had adapted so
successfully for his book—even as he partly deprecated it. History, he
would say in *Starting Out in the Thirties,* had turned into "a tangle of
meanings"—and with it progressive literary history, which took much of its
meaning from a storyline connecting writers with changing social and economic conditions. The direction of American literary studies, it would soon
become clear, pointed away from Parrington toward F. O. Matthiessen's
thematically structured *American Renaissance* (1941), with its attention to
close analysis and the explanatory possibilities of myth. In his introduction,
Matthiessen wrote that his intention was the "opposite" of Parrington's,
that instead of writing historical narrative elucidating "the liberal tradition," he concentrated on "what these [American] books were as works of
art." In his book, Kazin had sharply criticized Parrington for his "indifference to the problems of art" and for subjecting his writers to his "special
formula," his "convenient design," based on political differences. When,
years later, he would turn again to the writing of literary history, he would
be reminded, much to his bewilderment and frustration, of just how convenient, how indispensable, that formula had been.[52]

If *On Native Grounds,* with its portraits, its "impressionistic" evaluations,
its narrative-historical scheme, was not the future of American literary
studies, it has continued, nonetheless, to serve as a valued guide and lively
introduction to important areas of American literature. Amy Kaplan, Daniel
Borus, and others have credited Kazin's history for doing more than any
other work to keep the subject of American realism alive in the 1940s and
1950s when "myth," "symbol," and "romance" dominated the critical vocabulary. Historians William Stott and Warren Susman characterized Kazin's discussion of documentary literature as "the earliest and shrewdest
account" of that phenomenon and the starting point for all future discussions. Others have been more critical. Where, some would ask, are the

members of the Harlem Renaissance, who contributed so much to the spirit of creative excitement in 1920s New York? Where are the Jews and other ethnic groups, whose fiction Kazin had reviewed positively in the *New York Times* and the *Herald Tribune*? And where are the "plebes," the "writers from the working class, the lower class, the immigrant class, the non-literate class, from Western farms and mills," who Kazin would later write "provided the real excitement of the [thirties] period"? *On Native Grounds* purports to be a book celebrating American democracy, but where are the very different groups that make up that democracy? These are serious omissions, all the more serious, as Alan Wald has pointed out, for the book's illusion of comprehensiveness. Precisely because *On Native Grounds* was such an attractively written, critically energetic book that seemed to "cover" the literature of the time, it helped lead a generation of readers to think the job was done, that the modern tradition was complete.[53]

Had Kazin given more consideration to these different groups, the native grounds of American writing would have appeared more varied, contoured, and richly democratic. But they would also have seemed more fractured and contested at a time when people were eager to subsume group differences in an America united against foreign tyranny. Hitler, Mussolini, and Hirohito, wrote the *New York Times* in 1940, have turned democracy into a fighting faith, "a real dynamic burning creed worth fighting for." In the year of *On Native Ground*'s publication, democracy symbolized an America indivisible in ways it would be difficult to understand decades later. The ethos among virtually all groups was "Americans All"— even if that meant overlooking the ethnic distinctions that would become the focus of multicultural attention in future years. The Jews, who were terrified of Hitler, were no exception. "The wartime vision of American nationalism was basically assimilationist," Arthur Hertzberg wrote in *The Jews in America*. "American Jews needed to feel they were part of America," that its interests were their interests, its traditions, their traditions, and that they would be among the victors.[54]

However harsh its criticism and intemperate its denunciations, for all its dark suggestions about the "nihilism" and "defeatism" in American writing, *On Native Grounds* is a work of assimilation, one of the era's most sustained personal efforts at national "possession." Alienation and protest (Kazin's writers' and his own) were part of his story, part of the act of possession; but possession and belonging were always the guiding motive, and, he notes in an extraordinary 1942 journal entry, central to the joy of the telling:

> Every once in a while, a sentence in a book, a voice heard, will recall for me the fresh instant delight in the sense of being a student of American landscape and culture that I first felt two years ago only after I had begun serious work on the book. The sentence this morning, fresh as a spring wind, comes from Constance Roarke's book on Audubon, on the sudden realization, that his ornithology has the token of a national sense of scale, that like Whitman and the others, he was a great voice of Am. nationality. Yet what it does for me is recall the excitement under which I lived for weeks and weeks early in 1939, when I suddenly realized, and for the first time consciously, that I had a passionate and even professional interest in American culture and literature.
>
> I have never been able to express the pleasure I derive from the conscious study of Americana. When I think of careers like Constance Roarke's or Wm James's or Audubon's or so many others in the American vein—makers and movers and thinkers—great takers of notes—observers in the profoundest sense—I feel happy. I love to think about America, to look at portraits to remember the kind of adventurousness and purity, heroism and *salt,* that the best Americans have always had for me.
>
> Or is it—most obvious supposition—that I am an outsider; and that only for the first American born son of so many thousands of mud-flat Jewish-Polish-Russian generations is this need great, this enquiring so urgent?
>
> Yet the most extraordinary element in all this is something it is difficult, perhaps hazardous, to express; that is, the terrible and graphic loneliness of the great Americans. Thinking about them composes itself, sooner or later, [into] a gallery of extraordinary individuals; yet at bottom they have nothing in common but the almost shattering unavailability, the life strickenness I [find] in each. Each fought his way through life—and through his genius—as if no one had ever fought before. Each one that is, began afresh—began on his own terms—began in a universe that remained, for all practical purposes, his own.[55]

Written in February 1942 as Kazin neared completion of his manuscript, this remarkable entry indicates the personal and vocational passion that he brought to the writing of his book. It also suggests a good deal about his vision of his subject's range and importance—"national sense of scale," "makers and movers and thinkers—great takers of notes—observers in the profoundest sense"—and self-reflectively about his own ambitions to contribute to the "great voice of American nationality." But perhaps the most arresting remarks in the entry are those on his own feelings of isolation, the feelings of the "outsider," son of "so many thousands of mud-flat Jewish-Polish-Russian generations," along with his "hazardous" insight into the "the terrible and graphic loneliness" of American writers. The entry takes us back once again to Kazin's remarks in the preface, that what most interested him in American writers was the contradiction between their "absorption in every last detail of American life" and their equally powerful feelings of "alienation" from America—the outsider and "mud-flat Jew" finding a point of connection with his subject through a shared sense of isolation and "graphic loneliness"—more keenly alert than most to "the irony of our possession."

But it also points ahead to a period when Kazin's (and the country's) immediate needs would seem a little less "urgent," when he could understand the loneliness of American writers from the inside and the outside and could afford to explore more intensively his own and other writers' sense of difference and distance from the country. The success of his book would offer its much anticipated rewards, drawing Kazin, the outsider, into the very center of the nation's culture, a major step in his long journey from Brownsville to Manhattan. It would not, however, assuage recurrent and deepening feelings of loneliness as he moved farther away from his immediate and childhood past. Nor would it clarify his relation to history, which would continue to lurch in unanticipated and baffling directions. If the four years during which Kazin worked on *On Native Grounds* were marked by financial risk and political disappointment, he would remember them as among the least lonely, the most hopeful and happiest of his life.

CHAPTER FOUR

The Break
1942–1945

Open, Disrupted, Ready for Anything.

—*New York Jew*

O ne dreamlike week in 1942," Kazin begins *New York Jew,* "I published my first book, *On Native Grounds,* became an editor at the
New Republic and with my wife, Natasha, moved into a little
apartment on Twenty-fourth and Lex." Riding home in the taxi from the
magazine's "glossy offices" high up in a building at Forty-ninth and Madison, he experienced a "dizzy exaltation mixed with the direst suspicion of
what might happen next." "I loved working in the center of New York and
living in Manhattan. . . . But I missed my solitary days in the Forty-second
Street Library. I was expecting at every moment to be called into the Army,
and I was not prepared for such good fortune."[1]

In fact, things had not happened quite so suddenly. Kazin had been
appointed to the staff of the *New Republic* on July 10, the day before he
finished the final draft of his book. He began work as literary editor on
August 30 and moved into Manhattan shortly thereafter. When his book
appeared on October 30, he had been at the *New Republic* for two months
and had already been offered a job at *Fortune.* Determined to avail himself
of the brightest young talent around, Henry Luce, the publisher of *Time*
and *Fortune,* had sought out the rising star before his book appeared and
offered him one hundred dollars a week, twice his *New Republic* salary.
Kazin had turned him down; he was still learning the job of editor and did

not feel he was ready for *Fortune*—not yet—which did not stop him from
using Luce's offer to boost his salary at the *New Republic* to seventy-five
dollars a week. Luce was willing to wait. "When you have finished with your
apprenticeship on the *New Republic,* come to us," he told Kazin.[2]

But if all the changes did not occur in a single week, they had happened
quickly enough, leaving Kazin exhilarated, expectant, and often uneasy that
in the midst of such a whirl of possibilities his life was moving beyond the
protective borders of his daily routine. After more than four years chained
to a project that had "become the living design of existence" for him, he felt
he had been released into a new life. He was excited to be at the center of
things, constantly meeting new people, learning how to be an editor. But he
worried about where his new life might lead. Would he be able to develop
as a writer amidst such excitement? "I need to be alone again with myself,
[with] whatever it is I may call my writer's mind." He also found himself
subject to disturbing thoughts. "The proud, the beautiful women of New
York," he wrote in a journal entry on the eve of his book's publication,
"dreadful to dream about. For I do dream, continually, and am so ashamed
—but not so ashamed I do not wish to go on dreaming and wanting." The
city of "connections" was also a city of distractions—particularly for a
twenty-seven-year-old, who, having made himself a "prisoner of [his] conscience" for four years, was now "lusting for everything in sight."[3]

Contributing to that restlessness was Kazin's uncertain military status.
Although he had hoped not be drafted until he finished the book, he had
intended to join afterward and had ideas about where he would be most
useful. "When I read of these lectures the Army boys are getting from
soldier-brain instructors," he wrote in a February 1942 entry, "when I think
of what could be done." Would anyone be more qualified to explain the war
and the need to win it? He would not become one of the "soldier-brain
instructors," however. After being turned down twice by the military because of his undescended testicle, he would not again be called to the
induction center. But he would get the opportunity to study and report on
the military's effort to educate soldiers both in the United States and in
England.[4]

The opportunities his book opened for him, his sexual restlessness, and
his uncertain military status all had the effect of making Kazin feel loose,
undefined, and yearning for more—"open, disrupted, ready for anything."

His favorite writer of the moment was William Blake, whose celebration of desire—"I Want! I Want!"—would seem to sanction his own hunger for new experiences, sexual and otherwise. "Those who restrain desire do so because theirs is weak enough to be restrained." Yet, he feared crossing from one life to another with consequences he could not imagine. Years later, he would refer to this period as "the break," marking the end of his early strivings and youthful "innocence"—a period that would prove as crucial to his education as the writing of his first book. That the break, his break, would occur during a historical "break," while Hitler was destroying Europe's Jews, was not lost on Kazin, a troubling coincidence that exacerbated feelings of loss and guilt and deepened his sense that he was moving into an unfamiliar world stripped of "the old invisible connections" on which he had depended (half unconsciously) for security and happiness.[5]

Writers and Bohemians

Kazin had few illusions about his job as literary editor at the *New Republic*—despite the fact that Edmund Wilson and Malcolm Cowley had once held the post. He later remarked that Bruce Bliven, the managing editor at the time—a round, stout, anxious-looking man who reminded Kazin of Oliver Hardy—had hired him because he had never heard of him. Bliven was tired of dealing with literary big shots (like Wilson), who caused trouble. Wilson had attempted an office coup to get Bliven fired, but the owners of the magazine had found out and barred Wilson from its pages. "I am a terrible conspirator," he later admitted to Kazin. Kazin was too young to have a constituency and too inexperienced to know how to hatch plots against the front office. For the brief time that he was in the job, he got on fairly well with Bliven—though he mounted one successful opposition, calling in Cowley for reinforcement when Bliven tried to prevent his publishing Allen Tate's poetry. "If I don't understand these poems," Bliven had asked, "how in hell do you expect our readers to understand them?"[6]

For Kazin, the job's greatest attraction (after the money) was the opportunity to meet writers—on terms more agreeable than when he shared the reviewers' bench back in 1934–1935. Now *he* was being petitioned for reviews; *he* was the editor running interference for Allen Tate, consulting with Philip Rahv, Jacques Barzun, and William Troy over their contributions to a Henry James centenary special he was planning. He enjoyed meeting and formulating impressions of writers like Tate and Lionel Trilling, whom he had read and written about. For one thing, they were always surprising him. At their first meeting, Trilling "astonished" him by reportedly announcing that he would not write anything that would not "promote my reputation." Kazin was much amused by Stark Young, the magazine's drama critic, "the most eccentrically interesting writer on New York theater I ever read." A southerner and a homosexual, who kept trying to seduce Kazin, forty years his junior, Young was "an actor, a flirtatiously genial, oily, subtle man." Kazin liked him. "He was not always at the ready, like the New York intellectuals I knew. He was an actor, a great pretender . . . full of manner and malice, stealthy charm, and sheer pretense," and like his fellow southerner, Allen Tate, "moodier and more sympathetic, than other writers I was meeting for the first time." After a month on the job, Kazin felt that he was losing his fear of people, especially of writers, whose copy he had to wrestle into shape—"How much bad writing there is in the world!"[7]

The *New Republic* was not Kazin's only new venue for meeting writers. During the summer of 1942, he had made his first visit to Yaddo, the writers' colony outside Saratoga Springs, New York. The trip had been arranged with the help of Newton Arvin, a critic of American literature whose work on Hawthorne and Whitman Kazin admired. He had met Arvin through a mutual friend, Howard Nott Doughty, a neighbor when Kazin was living in the Long Island City section of Queens in 1940–1942. Doughty had been at Harvard in the 1920s, where he had helped Varian Fry and Lincoln Kirstein put out *Hound and Horn,* an early journal of American modernism. In the late twenties Doughty obtained a teaching position at Smith College, where Arvin also taught. The two men became lovers and would remain close even after Doughty married and moved to Long Island City. There he taught at the Police Academy and worked on a biography of the historian and distant kinsman Francis Parkman. Kazin would remember Doughty (one of those to whom *On Native Grounds* is dedicated) as "tall, rangy [and] languidly humorous about his descent in the world"—from Harvard to Smith to the Long Island City Police Academy. Doughty liked to talk American literature with Kazin and to tease him about being Jewish, bringing over a bag of oysters on occasion "to see the old-fashioned Jew profaning himself." On one of Arvin's visits Doughty introduced his two friends. They found they had much to say to each other; and on Kazin's inquiry, Arvin offered to secure him a June invitation to Yaddo, where he was currently on the board of directors. Arvin was planning to be there at the same time and hoped to continue the conversation.[8]

Founded by Katherine and Spencer Trask to "maintain a residence and retreat for persons actually and usefully engaged in artistic and creative work," Yaddo had been hosting visiting writers, artists, and musicians since it opened in 1926. "The forty or so acres on which the principal buildings of Yaddo stand," wrote John Cheever in 1986, "have seen more distinguished activity in the arts than any other piece of ground in the English-speaking community and perhaps the world." The ambience was decidedly Victorian: a fifty-five-room mansion—with old sleighs, fountains, thrones, cushions, stained glass, family portraits, candelabra, and heavy chairs—hidden away in a deep pine woods. Guests slept and worked in separate rooms or cabins, where they were assured of solitude and quiet before joining in a common evening meal, after which they could return to their rooms, talk, play ping-pong, or walk into town—a favorite occupation of Kazin's, who loved the walk down Union Avenue, once called by Henry James the most beautiful street in America. Kazin's ostensible reason for the visit was to work on *On Native Grounds*. But curiosity was at least as strong a motive. What was it like to live and work with other writers and artists in a Victorian setting in the woods? The visit more than met expectations—"dazzled by the benevolent splendor of my surroundings and the brilliance of my fellow guests," among them the novelist Michael Seide, the composer David Diamond, the poet Weldon Kees, and Newton Arvin.[9]

There was one sour note: Arvin's response to the last chapters of *On Native Grounds*, which Kazin had given him to read. He had hoped for praise, or at least debate. Arvin offered instead a weak smile and silence, and the silence said everything. Kazin suspected that his bitter attack of the left might be the reason. He would learn nothing from Howard Doughty. That the attack included a patronizing portrait of the "painfully limited" Granville Hicks, an old friend of Arvin's from Smith, did not seem to occur to Kazin. He admitted to being "terribly hurt" by Arvin's response. He would have future cause for regret.[10]

Despite the unsettling encounter with Arvin, Kazin returned from

Yaddo exhilarated. "I learned something at Yaddo—I learned a new solidarity with all the lonely men in the lonely rooms." He would become one
of the "regulars," often visiting twice a year—sometimes for several weeks
at a time, each visit a new opportunity to meet (and renew) acquaintances
with different writers. Flannery O'Connor, Robert Lowell, Elizabeth
Hardwick, Carson McCullers, Josephine Herbst, and Philip Roth would be
among his favorites. Kazin found inspiration in the thought of other writers
working away in their rooms—a "marvelous orchestration of these many
minds at Yaddo, alone in their rooms being creative, [who] nevertheless are
thinking of each other." That it was all occurring in the ambience of late-
nineteenth-century "benevolent splendor" only heightened the spell. With
its Victorian decor—the furniture and the portraits of Spencer Trask and
Katherine looking down on the company—Yaddo suggested a moment
arrested out of a genteel past. It would change little during the forty years
of Kazin's visits. He would sometimes feel that Yaddo was the only permanent fixture in his life.[11]

The writer whom Kazin was most eager to meet would not be found at
Yaddo or the *New Republic*. Kazin had been an Edmund Wilson enthusiast
since high school. He had read him on Joyce, Yeats, Eliot, and Proust at the
kitchen table in Brownsville. He had devoutly followed his dispatches from
around the country during the Depression as well as the chapters pub-
lished in the *New Republic* that would become *To the Finland Station*.
Even when he disagreed with him, he was fascinated. In a 1941 review of
Wilson's *The Wound and the Bow*, Kazin acknowledged that he admired
Wilson's work "so passionately that I sometimes think I would find even his
laundry list interesting." Wilson was an important, reassuring figure for
Kazin. Preserving "an example in a bad time," he wrote in *On Native
Grounds*, Wilson had kept alive the notion that criticism could still be
written as "a great human discipline."[12]

Kazin had sent Wilson a copy of his book, and Wilson had replied that he
would like a meeting when Wilson was next in New York. It took place in
December 1942 and was not a happy occasion. Wilson had just returned
from the *Nation*, which had turned town a writing proposal of his. Exasperated and not feeling particularly generous toward the literary editor of the
magazine from which he had been banned, Wilson seemed "impatient"
with the book. Moreover, "he intimated that anything from the 1890s on

was his own special providence," not that of a young literary upstart. Wilson's wife, Mary McCarthy, who was present at the meeting, was more thorough in her criticism and "went through my faults with great care." The ordeal over, Wilson seemed to relent and walked Kazin partway to the subway, leaving him with a friendly pat on the shoulder after making a point about the cabman's shelter scene in *Ulysses*. Though depressed by the meeting, Kazin had no second thoughts about Wilson. Indeed, as literary criticism turned increasingly academic in the postwar years, Wilson became more than ever the voice of the independent man-of-letters, "going at things exactly in his own way." In time they would become friends. Kazin grew to cherish Wilson's implacable, often cantankerous, personality as much as he did his prose. He was an irresistible "character" to write about, one of Kazin's many "father-figures," and an invaluable source of writerly reassurance. As long as Wilson was out there at work on his next piece, Kazin could feel there was a place for his own efforts.[13]

The *New Republic* was also a point of connection with younger writers, those closer to Kazin's age. Delmore Schwartz, Weldon Kees, William Barrett, Seymour Krim, Melvin Klonsky, Manny Farber, Isaac Rosenfeld, and Saul Bellow were a few of the "young Village poets and philosophers" showing up at the magazine's offices looking for books to review or to exchange gossip. In *New York Jew,* Kazin describes Delmore Schwartz "erupt[ing]" into his office, boiling over in a rush of words, mixing poetry and philosophy in great "gulps of argument." Two years Kazin's senior, Schwartz had already made a mark with his short story "In Dreams Begin Responsibilities" and had favorably impressed T. S. Eliot with his poetry. Kazin was fascinated by the intellectual passion beneath his "familiarly Jewish-frantic manner." Schwartz wrote only one review for Kazin at the *New Republic;* but the two struck up a brief friendship, meeting for lunches at the Jai Lai, a favorite Village restaurant. Later, Kazin would paint a vivid picture of Schwartz's decline into paranoia, a self-destructive "expert in anguish," holed up in "a room that only long practice in disaster could have discovered." At the time, however, Schwartz was witty, brilliant, disarmingly boyish. Kazin did not know that Schwartz was already writing to his friend James Laughlin, the publisher of New Directions Press, calling *On Native Grounds* "dishonest in a dozen important ways" and accusing its author of stealing ideas without acknowledgment. He also fretted that,

because Kazin's book had appeared before his own proposed book of criticism, "Kazin will undoubtedly accuse me of borrowing from him sans
acknowledgment."[14]

Kazin enjoyed Schwartz's company and admired his authority on literary
matters. "No one of my generation . . . knew so well from the inside what
literature was and what a poet should aim at." He never, however, felt close
to him, not in the way he felt toward two other *New Republic* drop-ins:
Isaac Rosenfeld and Saul Bellow. Rosenfeld had arrived in New York from
Chicago in 1941 on a year's fellowship in philosophy at New York University. He had stayed on, writing occasional pieces for the *Partisan Review*
and the *New Republic* while his wife, Vasiliki Sarantakis, supported him,
working for a time as Kazin's secretary. (Rosenfeld would take over as
literary editor when Kazin left.) Once established in the city, the sociable
Rosenfeld began inviting in old friends from Chicago, who soon became
part of a growing circle congregating in his apartment on Barrow Street.
Bellow, a childhood friend of Rosenfeld's, was a frequent visitor to the
sprawling flat—which he liked to call the Ellis Island for Chicagoans. Kazin
was immediately charmed by the mix of informed seriousness and intellectual "playfulness" of the two Chicago friends, who seemed to register the
same impulses to which he was responding—"the issue was always how to
break through."[15]

Young, witty, conversant with the great moderns, Rosenfeld could, reportedly, recite the Grand Inquisitor section of *The Brothers Karamazov*
by heart and play "J. Alfred Prufrock" in Yiddish: *"ikh ver alt, ikh ver alt, un
mayn pupik* [belly-button] *ver me kalt."* Like Kazin, Rosenfeld and Bellow
had gone through a Marxist phase in the thirties and emerged wary of
ideology and concerned with large "existential" questions about life. "The
important thing to stress about Isaac (and Saul)," Kazin later wrote in his
journal, "is that they were naked, lovable, human, without ideology." There
was a quality of freedom, openness, expectation about them, a readiness to
take in what the world had to offer. Bellow liked to quote D. H. Lawrence—
that he wanted no "umbrella" between himself and the sky. Kazin understood. "They were trying to make a stand on existence alone." That the
three of them, sons of immigrant Jews, played musical instruments—Bellow, the violin, and Rosenfeld, the flute—suggested other points of connection that needed no conscious assent. Kazin played duets with both, typ-

ically racing through pieces with Bellow as if to see who would finish first, while playing more deliberately with Rosenfeld (the better musician), who always impressed Kazin by his "impeccable phrasing."[16]

Two writers and searchers hoping to break through, struggling for "an unusual inner freedom," Rosenfeld and Bellow reminded Kazin of himself. "I have never known intellectuals so close to my heart." Yet they were very different. They certainly looked different. Slim and elegant, Bellow possessed "the conscious good looks of a coming celebrity." (He was once contacted by a Hollywood agent who saw his face on a book jacket and thought he could be in films.) By contrast, Rosenfeld was, in the vivid portrait of Village life during the forties by memoirist Janet Richards, "fat and short, with a round, rosy, amused face with sardonic eyes behind twinkly glasses." Bellow once observed that his friend often seemed to be in "disagreement with his own flesh." For Kazin, looks mattered less than the way the men used their sense of freedom. Looking back years after Rosenfeld had been found dead in a basement room of a Chicago apartment house, at a time when Bellow was winning prizes for *Herzog*, Kazin saw the difference in the opposing emphasis each placed on his life and his work. Bellow had used his freedom to advance his talent and to create the exploring voices of his tirelessly reflecting characters. Rosenfeld had used his to experiment with his life. Uncertain about his talent, troubled about his deeper (sexual) intentions, he had looked to writing as he had looked to other interests (including Reichian psychology, complete with orgone box) as a way to try out his life. Bellow was more focused. Although he had not yet published a novel and only a few short stories, Bellow, Kazin wrote in *New York Jew,* "carried around with him a sense of his destiny as a novelist." Walking the New York streets; discoursing on the city, on the war; sizing up D. H. Lawrence, Hemingway, and Melville as rivals at the same game, Bellow "was measuring the world's power to resist *him,* he was putting himself up as a contender."[17]

Bellow would remember things differently. "I didn't have an air of success," he responded when he saw Kazin's portrait. "I felt as weak in the knees as everyone else. I didn't know what the hell I was doing." Kazin's confident young Bellow was undoubtedly a retrospective projection based on the ascendant curve of his friend's later career, as was his portrait of Rosenfeld, the failed, unfulfilled writer—a contrast in success and failure that suited themes he was exploring in *New York Jew*. Yet the tensions between success and failure, between direction and drift, were very much a part of the social-intellectual milieu in which the three friends found themselves in the early forties and were very much on Kazin's mind as he worried about the direction of his own life.[18]

It was wartime, and the eclectic crowd that gathered evenings at Rosenfeld's flat—artists, intellectuals, writers and would-be writers, local Village characters—were not in the war. Some were waiting to be called up; others were just "dangling," like Joseph, the narrator of Bellow's first novel, *Dangling Man*. Cultivating "inner freedom" and "complete emotional 'honesty,'" these wartime bohemians, many of them ex-radicals, argued Nietzsche and Freud and Dostoevsky, issued "urgent existential manifestoes about the absurdity of life," espoused Gandhian quietism, and were not above sexual adventuring as a step toward complete honesty and self-discovery. The notorious Poster brothers, William and Herbert, who had inherited money but chose to live in squalor, led the way in this last area of self-liberation. In celebration of "our animal nature," they practiced public "balling," took no precautions, and kept an abortion fund for emergencies.[19]

Although not a regular member of the group, Kazin visited the Barrow Street flat frequently and was both impressed and unnerved by the choices people were making—more exactly, by their freedom to choose. For the first time, he wrote in his journal, he saw people "dreaming aloud" all day long, "people asking themselves: what *shall* I think? What shall I do with my life, my sex, my fantasies?" After the constrictions of the Depression years, life no longer seemed so determined; one could choose a new direction, a new one every day if one wished—though the chaos in which Rosenfeld surrounded himself suggested that such freedom could lead to breakdown and failure, willed and otherwise—"the Posters in the Village, failures in the mud and darned glad of it, you bet." The will to choose, to follow the impulse of the moment—ecstatic, courageous, thoughtless, even perverse—carried real risks, temptations to new pleasures as well as intimations of disaster, especially for someone habituated to a four year's disciplined routine.[20]

Kazin was also impressed by the intense spiritual and intellectual competitiveness among these dreamers. Not only was there a "bitter rivalry" to be emotionally honest, but to explore the meaning of honesty and freedom as sanctioned by the favored authors of the time—Melville, Blake, Lawrence, Dostoevsky, Nietzsche, Kafka. If Rosenfeld's circle were bohemians, they were, many of them, "armed bohemians," prepared to challenge and debate, to cite and recite chapter and verse from *Moby-Dick, The Marriage of Heaven and Hell, Notes from Underground,* the scriptural texts of the moment. Such intellectual passion could be exhilarating—and intimidating. Seymour Krim, one of the younger members of the circle, recalls the "group of brilliant minds," including Rosenfeld, David Bazelon, Manny Farber, Willie Poster, Milton Klonsky, Bellow, and Kazin, who "roved with barely believable and almost illegal freedom over the entire domain of the thinkable and the utterable." With such a heavy dose of intellectual daring "running wild and demonic through our lusting heads," Krim, who spent time in a mental sanatorium and eventually committed suicide, thought it small wonder that "some of us cracked under the pressure"[21]

Kazin did not crack. He was more than capable of holding his own on the writers then in vogue, especially Melville and Blake, on whom he was planning writing projects. He did, however, take note of "the furious urge to win" among the young, mostly Jewish, intellectuals—their passion for ideas matched by an equal passion for having their say, for gaining the polemical edge over their colleagues. He would later write about "the coming of 'the intellectuals' " in the 1940s, their rise to prominence with "the ascendancy of 'modern literature,' " their hopes for intellectual and literary recognition—and their anxious attention to the *Partisan Review,* the authoritative center of "advanced" thinking on radical politics and modernism. While a number of the younger writers wrote pieces for the *New Republic*—one had to eat, after all—they (like Kazin) recognized that the magazine was not what it had been in the days of Herbert Croly, Walter Lippmann, and Edmund Wilson. By the early forties, it was understood that "the only real magazine was the *Partisan Review.*" That was where you could read T. S. Eliot's latest addition to the *Four Quartets,* George Orwell's "Letter from London," Pablo Picasso on Franco, Sidney Hook on Marxism, and the latest works by Wallace Stevens, Delmore Schwartz, and Saul Bellow. A must-read for all the aspiring Village intellectuals, *Partisan* could, with an approving nod, turn an unknown young writer into the golden boy, the *shoyne boychick,* of the coming generation.[22]

Kazin had closely followed the evolution of the *Partisan Review* since Philip Rahv and William Phillips had wrested it away from the Communists in 1937 and turned it into an "unequivocally independent" magazine of radical politics and avant-garde writing. In *On Native Grounds*, he refers admiringly to *Partisan* articles by Lionel Trilling and Rahv. In 1940, he published his first review (of Van Wyck Brooks's *New England Summer*) in the magazine. *Partisan*, it was clear to Kazin, served a genuine cultural need as a serious magazine dealing with radical politics and modern writing. But it also made him uneasy. "Reading *PR* this morning (a magazine I admire and am indebted to)," he wrote in a 1941 journal entry, adding, perhaps in response to Sidney Hook's latest polemic, that he could not "help but feel how strikingly a certain kind of Marxist disputation has become pure scholasticism." More unsettling was the editors' consistently deprecating attitude toward American literature and culture, which, they repeatedly argued, needed a good dose of "Europeanization" to bring it up to international standards. In his history Kazin had acceded to a number of Rahv's and Trilling's strictures on American writing. He was not, however, prepared to join in a Eurocentric chorus dismissing as "narrow" and "provincial" the nativist impulse in American writing that his book had celebrated. Dupee's "supercilious" *Partisan* review of *On Native Grounds* had led him to suspect that the magazine's editorial offices on Astor Place would never be particularly friendly territory—a suspicion that would deepen over the years. (Daniel Bell recalls Kazin telling him that at a *Partisan* affair he didn't dare go to the bathroom for fear of what would be said about him while he was gone.) Despite his uneasiness, Kazin welcomed the presence and growing influence of the magazine. It was an essential part of the dynamic cultural scene in the New York of the early forties already swelling with the largess of a booming war economy. "There was an unmistakable flow of new life, the sense of creative new direction, an authoritative bold sense of style" he would later write of New York during the war years. The *Partisan Review* was an important contributor to that emerging intellectual style.[23]

Another was the growing presence of brilliant émigrés from Europe. They could be heard at free concerts in high school auditoriums, seen at recently opened art galleries, listened to at lectures at The New School for Social Research, encountered at the *Partisan Review* parties, and bumped into on the street. Kazin recalled the day when he and Rosenfeld ran into Marc Chagall on Fifty-seventh Street. It was Yom Kippur and "I felt a comradely twinge toward a fellow Jew when I remember his speaking Yiddish to us and admitting that though he could not get himself to work on the High High Holy Day, he was sauntering on to Pierre Matisse's gallery for a look (no doubt of his own work)." Chagall was evidently excited by the meeting as well—"I haven't heard so much of the mother tongue since I left Vitebsk!" As Delmore Schwartz remarked famously at the time, "Europe is still the biggest thing in America."[24]

The European intellectual émigrés, many of them Jews, held special value and authority for Kazin and for other New York writers and intellectuals during and after the war years. They were a living connection with European intellectual traditions and articulate witnesses to the disaster that had overtaken their homeland and upended their lives. Their intellectual and artistic efforts were already having (or soon would have) a noticeable effect on the cultural and intellectual life of the country—William Wilder, Otto Preminger, and Peter Lorre on Hollywood; Berthold Brecht on the theater; Theodore Adorno, Leo Strauss, and Max Horkheimer on political science; while Léo Szilárd, Hans Bethe, Edward Teller, and other émigré scientists were developing America's ultimate weapon of war. "The migration to the United States of European intellectuals fleeing fascist tyranny," wrote the historian H. Stuart Hughes in 1975, "has finally become visible as the most important cultural event—or series of events—of the second quarter of the twentieth century." It was also clear that Europe's loss had in every way been America's gain.[25]

For Kazin that gain was largely personal and educational—friendships with Europeans grateful to know a young authority on American literature who "wanted fiercely to learn Europe." The most exciting of these would be with the renowned political scientist Hannah Arendt and her husband, Heinrich Bluecher, both subjects of extended portraits in New York Jew. The longest and most stable (if less publicly celebrated) friendship was with Paolo Milano, a Jewish refugee from Rome, later the chief literary critic of L'Espresso. Fluent in English, French, Spanish, German, and Italian, Milano had found work teaching comparative literature at Queens College in Brooklyn (where Kazin's third wife, Ann Birstein, would have him as an instructor). With his urbane, genial manner, his wide reading, and his European contacts, he was a welcome figure among the Village intellectuals and the Partisan Review cosmopolitans.[26]

Milano soon formed a close friendship with both Kazin and Bellow, who dedicated *Dangling Man* to him. For Kazin, Milano was the quintessential friend-as-instructor, "the first of many 'European' teachers in my life." Under Milano's tutelage he began reading and studying Proust—an education that would prove useful in the writing of *A Walker in the City*. Milano was also a valued cultural go-between, arranging a visit with Berthold Brecht in New York during the war, and introducing Kazin to literary and intellectual figures on his many visits to Italy after the war. The friendship would last forty-five years until Milano's death in 1988, each regularly visiting the other on trips to and from Europe. But it was Paolo of the war years and immediately after, "the faithful friend and teacher," whom Kazin would remember most fondly—"the bright new spirit in the Village," who initiated Kazin's European education and brought so much excitement and presence to his life and the emergent intellectual scene.[27]

"Beautifully Lawless and Outrageous"

In early May 1943, Kazin accepted Henry Luce's offer and moved to *Fortune*. Ensconced in his office high up in Rockefeller Center with an unobstructed view of Queens, he was unsure about his duties beyond coming up with ideas for pieces on American writers and thinkers. After a time he was invited to lunch with Luce in the private dining room for the *Time* executives —"much gloss, tablecloth gentility, etc." He had proposed a piece on the prophetic books in American literature to run in the "philosophy" series Luce was planning. The "Boss" heard him out but had ideas of his own. He wanted to discuss "America and what's wrong with it." Not that Luce planned a serious discussion of the matter in *Fortune*—his idea, rather, was to create a space for think pieces from intellectual stars such as Alfred North Whitehead, Robert Hutchins, Suzanne Langer, and Ernst Cassirer that could be fashioned into a coherent and positive "philosophy" for the country. Kazin left the meeting with mixed impressions. "Shy, vaguely charming, wonderful eyes and beetle-brows," Luce seemed "a puzzled man rather than a stupid one." He concluded, however, that Luce was really "a very negligible man," ardent and intellectually immature, full of "childhood feelings" and the "disputatiousness of a young-college-senior." Luce's interest in American philosophy was—as Kazin had suspected—"a *naive* attempt to bring meaning, purpose into the lives of the business class, buying pro-nouncements on the good life" from notable thinkers.[28]

Kazin had had conflicting views about going to Luce. *Time*, he knew, was "dead cold" when it came to ideals and values. It lived by "cunning, prompt-ness, smartness." *Fortune* had aspirations to seriousness, some talented writers, and could on occasion produce excellent work, but more often it failed to get beyond the essential "vulgarity" of the interests it served, "the theology of the business society." Still, the move had meant a better salary, relief from the demands of editorial work, and the chance to feel he was more than ever part of the brilliant life of the city—something that seemed less and less the case at the *New Republic*. "The whole humming Time-Life Building was somehow a slice of the New York feast at its richest and most intoxicating: a brilliant *center* magnifying everything like the fluorescent tubes in the elevators " Working for Luce might not have the feel Kazin once associated with the *New Republic* of working for a cause at the center of many causes, but it did confirm the impression that he had arrived at the center of American life and belonged there. "It was impossible to feel *oneself* less than brilliantly informed and interesting in the Time-Life Build-ing, so clear was it that the people going to work in those overlighted elevators were there because they deserved to be."[29]

Kazin had another reason for going to *Fortune*. He had hoped for an overseas assignment. He quickly discovered this was not to happen. He also learned Luce was not interested in substantial essays on American prophetic literature. Kazin's "big think piece" on the subject was rejected; Luce told him the American classics were "soft in the head." He was asked instead to do unsigned "trivial" sketches of Simon Bolivar, John Peter Altgeld, and Henry David Thoreau. For all its glitz and centrality, *Fortune* was not working out. In August, Kazin told Richard Rovere he had decided to quit; however, he agreed to stay on when offered the chance to report on the effort of the army's Morale Services Division to educate soldiers on the war. The assignment would take him around the country and, after his rejection by the military, let him feel that he was contributing to the war effort. He also saw it as a step that might eventually get him to England to report on the British program to educate their soldiers. After a preliminary trip to Washington to consult with Pentagon officials, Kazin began a five-week train journey that took him to military bases in Virginia, Maryland,

Illinois, Wisconsin, Colorado, the state of Washington, and California. In early January, he turned in his report, which was promptly rejected for being too critical of the program. A second version was accepted despite the unflattering comparisons Kazin made with the British program. It was the last piece he would write for *Fortune*.[30]

The trip came at a time of personal crisis. In November 1943, he had met Mary Lou Petersen and discovered, as he later put it, "that everything could fall apart in the sight of a young girl with very wide cheekbones standing at an overcrowded party in Greenwich Village." A midwesterner, married to the UCLA historian Hans Meyerhoff, now in the service, Petersen had been in and out of affairs with a number of New York writers and artists. Her partners were either Jewish intellectuals or Europeans (often both), whom, Kazin later told Clive James, she regarded as "her educators." (He also told James of Petersen's approaching Bertrand Russell after a speech and being rebuffed by him. Kazin lacked Russell's powers of resistance—"I sure could have used some easy lessons in the *Principia*.") Attracted by her astonishing good looks and a manner that suggested something "beautifully lawless and outrageous," Alfred introduced himself, got her phone number, and began an affair that would lead to his separation from Asya and a long and traumatic period of personal unhappiness.[31]

Until now a dutiful son and a faithful husband, Kazin would later recall his sense of dread about what he was doing; but he also remembered the passion. Making love to Petersen, he wrote in *New York Jew,* was "one of the true privileges of the human condition." "Just as kissing her induced the sensation of falling, deepening, so being with her spread such a circle of peace, easiness, perfection that I acquired a respect for sex that I had never known before. I was looking at the candlelight behind her head as I thrust my way ahead in her, and I have never felt anything so keen as the vibration that joined me to her, to the candlelight, to the golden helmet in the Rembrandt portrait that shown upon an open picture book on the floor. . . . All that I had carried in silence and secrecy so long, all that I had held against the world—all this burst apart as her body, fully stirred, moving in one sinuous line, heaved up at me when she whispered my name." While the rhythm and diction of this passage strangely echo Melville's climactic account of Captain Ahab's passion against the whale (Kazin had been reading *Moby-Dick* as well as Proust and Blake), it is not hate that Kazin is celebrating here, but a discovered pleasure and sense of release that he had never known before. He was leaving behind his "over-organized," predictable life and adventuring into an uncharted sea of risk—the kind of risk that had so attracted and unsettled him at Rosenfeld's parties.[32]

Kazin would later say that the affair had cut his life in half—"before Mary Lou, after Mary Lou"—and would describe it as his great "fall" from innocence. "The fall of Rome was nothing compared with the 'fall' in the heart of Alfred Kazin," he wrote forty-seven years after the event. Yet "he regrets nothing, especially not the extension of his experience (what a way of putting it) that came with his fall. But to this day (and today I am 75 years of age) he cannot think without a gasp of pain of all it cost him then to be unfaithful to Asya. And what it costs him still." Toting up the costs and benefits of his affair would occupy Kazin for decades. His need to understand his feelings at the time and its significance for his life would be a major concern in his autobiographical writing as well as in his repeated (and largely futile) efforts to write fiction. The only fictional work he ever published, the short story "Going Home" (Harper's, 1946), features a soldier released from psychiatric care deciding not to return to his wife. Over time, Kazin would come to see his "fall" in more general terms. "What happened in the 40s," he wrote in 1964, "was just the beginning of the current sexual sophistication of the Jewish middle class. Everybody of my generation had his orgone box, his [Mary] Lou, his search for fulfillment. There was, God knows, no break, with convention, there was just a freeing of oneself from all those parental attachments and thou shalt nots."[33]

At the time, however, the experience could not have been more personal, exciting, and disruptive. Everything, it seemed, was coming together (or flying apart) at once. In September 1943, a third operation for the undescended testicle had been successful—removing a long-standing source of anxiety and embarrassment. He had begun an affair, the consequences of which were unclear; and now (in November), he was traveling about the country with possible future trips in the works. He had applied for a fellowship to study the Blake Illuminations at the Huntington Library in Pasadena, California, and for a Rockefeller grant to take him to England. Things were opening up in unexpected ways. Even the war was turning around. The Allies had beaten back Rommel in North Africa and were scoring victories in Italy. The Russians had routed the Germans in Stalingrad. There were new bombing offenses against Germany. Traveling nights on the train, Kazin read what newspapers he could find, listened to briefings, interviewed the recruits and their instructors, and felt that his life had veered into strange, uncertain territory. "I was in a state of perfect contradiction, gravely conscious that I had done it at last, and feeling so far-flung that *I* was the smoke following the train."[34]

Back in New York in January 1944, he had a better sense of the contradictions and consequences. Wanting Mary Lou as much as ever, Alfred moved out of his flat with Asya—her face "calm, stolid, full of compassionate contempt"—and into that of Isaac Rosenfeld, who was away at the time. Making love to Mary Lou was everything he had imagined. She seemed the embodiment of the lawless pleasure, drift, and uncertainty he was letting into his own life. Indifferent to money, clothes, position, and her own future, she often said she would "end in a closet." She desired only to be "educated" by brilliant intellectuals and to make love. Listening to Alfred or Paul Goodman or any other "brilliant" intellectual, she would suddenly break into a smile of "transcendent self-discovery." Alfred talked God and Whitehead and Melville and Blake and Tolstoy to her. He remembers her turning white with pleasure when she heard him quote Tolstoy that "God is the name of my desire."[35]

He was impressed by her passion for "education" and mystified by her readiness to "face absolutely nothing." But he was growing increasingly uneasy. If the chaos in which Mary Lou lived had been a welcome change to his overorganized life—"a bullet going through walls"—it offered nothing for the future. He had no intentions of marrying his already married lover and was not prepared to go back to Asya. But neither was he prepared for the emotional desolation that increasingly overtook him following their separation. After a month on Barrow Street he moved into a "miserable" room in the Albert Hotel; and suddenly "everything was falling apart. . . . There was no light, no habit, no naturalness to my day." Walking the New York streets, eating alone in cafeterias, he found himself taking notice of the lonely souls of the city, particularly the homosexuals, who reminded him of himself—"homeless, intellectual, desperate . . . intimates of that nameless despair in the heart which is like a great sweeping fog."[36]

On February 29, he resigned from *Fortune,* having learned he had received a Huntington fellowship as well as a grant from the Rockefeller

Foundation to study the education of soldiers in England. Soon after, he received an invitation to teach at Black Mountain College in Asheville, North Carolina, in the fall. He did not know when he might secure passage to England and accepted the Black Mountain offer contingent on his still being in the country. He was free to continue his adventure into the world "beyond"—though he was increasingly uncertain whether he could cope with such freedom.

"As Bad as Any Nazi"

During the spring of 1944, hoping to bring some emotional order to his life, Kazin began seeing a psychoanalyst, Janet Rioch. Rioch quickly concluded that many of Kazin's difficulties stemmed from "a deficiency in 'interpersonal' relations" that was particularly acute with women—a deficiency she traced back to early family relations. Intelligent and personally sympathetic, Rioch (both of whose parents had been Protestant missionaries in India) was the ideal psychiatrist for Kazin. Wary of dogma, Freudian and otherwise, impatient with theories that did not yield practical results, she looked for imbalances in her patients' relationships with their parents that might have led to defensive, "neurotic" adaptations that became a source of continuing unhappiness. Effective treatment depended on creating a relationship in which patients felt free to "transfer" their feelings about one or both parents to the analyst, whose sympathy and understanding encouraged the recovery of repressed feelings and unrealized possibilities of the self. It was a "method" or "treatment" on which Rioch had published a seminal article in 1943 and one to which Kazin enthusiastically and gratefully responded. He would remain Rioch's patient—sometimes seeing her three times a week—until she moved away from New York in the early 1960s. He later claimed that without her he would never have written *A Walker in the City.*[37]

Rioch helped Kazin understand a few things immediately. His current unhappiness arose in part out of his tendency to reject women who loved him and his inability to cope with the loss of what he had been taking for granted. Faced with "the loss of something I had in my own mind discounted, or something that had simply become habitual and necessary," he felt mortally threatened and fell into a despairing panic. Rioch indicated that his recurring sense of threat could be traced to his mother's "profound anxieties" over him as a sickly child. Under the stress of her obsessive fears, he became "consciously and excessively aware of life's hazardousness" and developed a crippling anxiety of which his childhood stammer was the most obvious symptom. In time, Rioch led him to confront "the great hostility" he felt toward his dominant mother, whom he "wanted to demote" and to escape, but whom he continued to "believe in unswervingly" and who commanded his loyalty out of ingrained emotional habits as well as out of pity "for the poor immigrants without English in a strange land."[38]

While alleviating some of the confusion and pain, Kazin's better understanding of the source of his conflicted relations with women did not lead to their quick resolution. Nor did it mitigate feelings of loss or pangs of guilt. "Mama stares at me as if she no longer knew me. 'What happened? How could it have happened? What did you do? What did you do?'" He had plunged into a affair with Mary Lou Petersen knowing it would change his life. That had been part of the appeal—the "wild longing in my heart to move on and be changed." But moving on meant leaving behind, abandoning, Asya, family, and at some level not fully understood, the Jews now being murdered in Europe. "The sex thing was related to the Jewish thing," Kazin would later say of his affair and the "shock" that followed. "The Jewish religion is really a family religion, it's ancestor worship. Breaking up the family—which is what happens with these things—it's breaking up the Tradition." It would be some time before Alfred would work through the full implications of what he had done; meanwhile, he felt that he had committed a grievous "sin," and not just against Asya. Seeking a "larger and larger experience" of the world, he darkly suspected that he was betraying and possibly losing what he did not yet know how to value. "It was now early 1944," he recalled his feelings at the time, "and I was out of it, consumed with guilt. . . . I was as bad as any Nazi."[39]

That the fate of Europe's Jews as well as Jewish matters at home were very much on Alfred's mind at the time of his break with Asya is apparent from his journals and from two short pieces published early in 1944. In the first of these, "In Every Voice, in Every Ban," Kazin reprints and discusses a suicide note by the Polish Bund leader Shmuel Ziegelboym, who had been living in exile in London. Addressing himself to the president of Poland, the Polish people, and "the conscience of the world," Ziegelboym took note of the murder of more than three million Polish Jews by the Germans and the continuing slaughter of those still alive, all occurring under "the passive observation" of the rest of the world. He wrote that he belonged with the victims in their mass graves and that by his death he wanted to express his "strongest protest against the inactivity with which the world is looking on and permitting the extermination of my people."[40]

Kazin had found the note in a May 1943 *New York Times* and had held onto it, hoping to reach a point where he could "write thoughtfully" about its contents. His piece, when it appeared in the *New Republic* in January 1944, indicates that he was still searching for an appropriate response. After asserting that Ziegelboym had killed himself out of despair over the "terrible . . . break in human solidarity" evident in the destruction of the Jews, Kazin insisted that suicide solved nothing. Neither did focusing on the plight of the Jews—"I do not speak here of the massacre of the Jews, for there is nothing to say that has not already been said." Instead he spoke of "our contemporary self-disgust" and "humiliation" and attacked a range of targets—the "optimism" of the liberals, the cynicism of the "reactionaries," the "indifference" of governments and "the fascism . . . deep within all of us." Kazin had taken the title of his piece, " 'In Every Voice, in Every Ban,' " from Blake's poem "London"; and like the poem, the essay can be read as a cry against "the mind-forged manacles" that chain the human spirit in ignorance and prejudice. But the image from Blake is of uncertain value in identifying the welter of confused, half-suppressed feelings—anger, outrage, despair, and guilt—erupting in the piece.[41]

One of only a handful of essays by an American Jew about the fate of European Jews to be published in the American mainstream press during the war, Kazin's piece provoked limited response. But the few who did respond were grateful. His future brother-in-law, Daniel Bell, wrote that he was "struck so deeply" by it that he could concentrate on nothing until he sent Kazin a note. Lewis Mumford wrote that its "warning deserves to be graven deep on all of us." Archibald MacLeish referred (unaccountably) to its "perfect and agonizing precision." Saul Bellow (who was working on *The Victim* at the time) praised its "unsentimentality" and the "*feelings*" that went into it—"I am primarily concerned with feelings, it was the *feeling* of your piece that took me." To read "In Every Voice, in Every Ban" today is to be struck by the intensity of its feeling but also by its incoherence. There was simply no orderly coming to terms with what was happening—not even with select passages from William Blake on the suffering children of London.[42]

Kazin had known of the threat to the Jews since the 1930s. In 1937, he reviewed Robert Gessner's descriptions of the condition of Germany's Jews in *Some of My Best Friends Are Jews,* concluding his review with the warning that without an immediate solution the present situation may well "end in collective death." By September 1942, it was clear to him and those who were interested that the systematic destruction of Europe's Jews was under way. "They are killing us off in Europe," he wrote in his journal at the time. "They are killing us by the thousands from the Rhine to the Volga. The blood of the Jews is like the vapor in the air that Faustus saw when the Devil claimed his due; but no one claims us but death." Three months later, Varian Fry, a friend of Kazin's who had spent the early war years in France rescuing Jews from the Gestapo, had documented the slaughter of 2 million Polish Jews in a lengthy piece in the *New Republic.* Barring direct intervention by the Allies, he warned that European Jewry faced annihilation. Thus, it may have come as a blow, but hardly a surprise, to read Ziegelboym's claim in May 1943 that 3.5 million Jews had already been killed in Poland—"if it is true, comprehensible, it must be believed," Kazin reasoned. That he felt the need to respond somehow, anyhow—if only to express outrage and frustration, guilt and shame—speaks to the desperate seriousness of his concern. That he had not yet found an adequate or even a coherent mode of response is of less significance than the force of his "feelings," which, as Bellow indicated, eloquently carry the message.[43]

"'In Every Voice, in Every Ban'" appeared in the *New Republic* on January 10, 1944. In February, the *Contemporary Jewish Record* published Kazin's and other responses to a survey of Jewish-American writers younger than forty. The editors wanted to learn the extent to which they considered their "Jewish heritage" an influence on their work and whether "the revival of anti-Semitism" had affected their writing. The editors apparently hoped that in view of what was occurring in Europe the young writers would ally themselves more closely with Jewish concerns. If so, they were disappointed. Though Delmore Schwartz stated that being Jewish "has been nothing but an ever-growing good to me," the prevailing sentiment was that their Jewish background had been of little use to them as writers. Lionel

Trilling claimed that he knew of no writer in English "who has added one micromillimetre to his stature by 'realizing his Jewishness,'" though he knew of some "who have curtailed their promise by trying to heighten their Jewish consciousness." Clement Greenberg wondered what kind of sustenance could possibly come from an American-Jewish culture that was so "restrictedly and suffocatingly middle-class."[44]

Kazin shared the sentiments of the majority. He wanted no part of a "parochialism" that cut Jews off from the wider world of literature and learning. He detested "the dreary middle-class chauvinism" of an American-Jewish community that wanted nothing more than to be safe in their "Babbitt-warrens." And he was dismissive of the contributions of Jews to American culture. Where, he asked, can one find a Jewish novel comparable to James T. Farrell's *Studs Lonigan* or Dreiser's *Sister Carrie*? He also warned against misinterpreting the sentiments coming out of the immigrant Jewish community. "I think it is about time we stopped confusing the experience of being an immigrant, or an immigrant's son, with the experience of being Jewish." Though he acknowledged that it was not always easy to separate the two, one had to try. As a writer who found spiritual sustenance in Melville, Blake, the prophet Amos, and Scholem Aleichem, Kazin thought it essential "to follow what I believed in, not that which would merely move me through associations or naive community feelings." But he also acknowledged the difficulty of repressing such feelings. Though he found "chauvinism no more attractive in Jews than in anyone else," he knew the cause and would "always feel it." In a sense he was like "many another American" in that he had "to make [his] own culture." But he was also "an American Jew," caught in an "unhappy limbo"—"neither lost in what he thinks his ancestors had, nor found in what he wants." "Who is he? What is Jewish in him?"[45]

Kazin's response is in some respects the least coherent of the lot, replete with contradictory feelings and unanswered questions and thus, arguably, the most interesting and suggestive. Although he would apparently have liked to solve questions of faith, identity, and culture through a conscious choice of who he was and what writers he most admired—the Hebrew prophets, Blake, Emerson, and Melville—he understood there were areas of association and sympathy, "feelings," over which he had little conscious control but which he also refused to deny. In time, he would find less reason to challenge or repress these unrepressible feelings, "the old invisible connections" tying him to family, neighborhood, ancestors. That shift in sentiment would reflect a gradual reappraisal among many of the New York writers of their Jewishness and of American-Jewish culture, a reappraisal prompted in no small part by the accumulating images and growing psychic effect of the Holocaust. "Because of the Holocaust," because "the Holocaust would not go away," Kazin later remarked, "I became much more consciously Jewish." In early 1944, however, he was not at all sure what to think or feel about his Jewishness, nor about the destruction of Europe's Jews. Alfred sensed that by leaving Asya he had violated the sanctity of the "Jewish family" and was somehow complicit with the horrors occurring in Europe. But he saw no way of resolving his feelings or of ridding himself of his loneliness and guilt. And he soon discovered there was no going back.[46]

Wartime Travels

On June 6, 1944, D-Day, Kazin arrived in Pasadena, California, on a two-month fellowship at the Huntington Library. On the way he had stopped for a weekend in Santa Fe, New Mexico, where, he reported to Richard Rovere, he wandered about "with my mouth open in wonder," enchanted by "that lovely old Spanish-Indian village and the hills beyond." "Something real has been kept alive" there, he told Rovere. In contrast, Southern California was "a proliferation of pure material impulses. It's as if insects were milling around the sea-wall, having flung themselves against the last barrier." Pasadena struck him as a "palatial Westchester," and Hollywood Boulevard was simply "indescribable." He stayed in a faculty residence center on the campus of Cal Tech and spent most mornings at the Huntington, where he viewed the Blake *Illuminations* and dutifully looked through the manuscripts—all under the eyes of a uniformed guard toting a gun.[47]

Blake had long been one of Kazin's special writers—"when I think of writing, I think always of Blake and Tolstoy," he had written in his journal while working on the final chapters of *On Native Grounds*. Pascal Covici, an editor at the Viking Press, had learned of his interest and offered him three hundred dollars to edit *The Portable Blake*. Kazin had jumped at the chance. He regarded Blake, the romantic visionary who had lived through the anticipation and disappointment of a revolution (in France), as "a man peculiarly of our time"—an unabashed writer-revolutionary from the working class determined to assault the barriers to human freedom with the "absolute energy" of the creative will. That Blake denounced all constricting habits of thought, the "mind-forged manacles," while preaching the sanctity of desire, especially sexual desire, also exerted a strong appeal. Kazin would not finish work on *The Portable Blake* until after the war. In the meantime he read, reread, and taught Blake (at Black Mountain College), always keeping a poem or two in his wallet—"a talisman and a medal of light."[48]

Kazin's sessions at the Huntington took only part of his time. Much of the rest was spent exploring Southern California, including the movie lots, where, he boasted to Rovere, he was asked by the actor who played Uncle John in *The Grapes of Wrath* whether he (Kazin) had been offered a part yet. In the thirties he had met some members of the Group Theater, who had since moved to Hollywood where they were now making films—the "Hollywood liberals" who would later be hounded by the House Un-American Activities Committee (HUAC) for their Communist affiliations. He looked up Sylvia Sidney, who, along with Stella Adler and her "kindly modest husband" Harold Clurman, showed him the sights in and around Hollywood. He was invited to a private screening of a film, where he sat between actor and fellow Brownsville native John Garfield and Thomas Mann, who struck him "as unbending, tight-lipped, and severe as a Prussian field marshall." One of his more memorable afternoons was spent on Clifford Odets's patio with Odets and the Irish actor Barry Fitzgerald, looking out over the Hollywood ravines, listening to Brahms on a Capehart phonograph *"that turned the records over."*[49]

But the treasures of the Huntington and the excitements of Hollywood could not keep Alfred's mind off the divisions that had opened up in his life. Four days after his arrival, in a panic of loneliness, he called Asya—a phone call that went nowhere and only reminded him of the difficulties he had created for himself. A trip to San Francisco brought little relief. He would later recall his state of mind (only half ironically)—"O help me, he cried to the mute inglorious passersby, I've left my wife to sleep with Mary Lou, and the pain of having no solid real world under foot any more is too much. . . . O help me, you, god, for having dared say fuck it to the old life." He would look back on his 1944 summer stay in California as one of the unhappiest

periods of his adult life. He was living "in the country of separation"—
separation from the war, separation from Asya and Mary Lou, separation
(alienation) from the California scene: "Hell—Pasadena in the summer of
1944; sprinklers forever turning on the lawn, everyone smiling, flowers,
sun, even dust . . . The emptiness, the void, the panic void of those streets in
Pasadena in 1944."[50]

Back East in late August, he accompanied Mary Lou on a trip to Monhe-
gan Island off the coast of Maine. The trip was pointless and painful. He
knew the affair was over and that he was subjecting her to further unnecessary hurt. "I have thought only of my own progress," he wrote in his journal
at the time. "And in the end there has been no progress, for in my lifelong
terror, in my never-ending anxieties, I have lived only for myself, so that
now I am left only with myself." Loneliness and self-recrimination did not
lead back to Asya, however, who was not prepared to let bygones be bygones; but rather to Provincetown, where in a spasm of nostalgia Alfred
retraced his earlier walks with Asya and stayed in the room the two of them
had rented during the summer of 1940. It was all quite childish and self-
indulgent—returning in grief to the scene of lost innocence—a pattern with
possibilities for the future autobiographer, however.[51]

Having failed to secure passage to England, Kazin spent the fall semester at Black Mountain, an alternative college in the Blue Ridge Mountains
of western North Carolina. Founded in the thirties by a renegade classical
scholar from Rollins College, Black Mountain sought to bring together
artists, writers, dancers, architects, and composers in an environment
where they could do their work and instruct and inspire interested students. The school achieved its highest reputation in the forties when it
numbered among its faculty the poets Charles Olson and Robert Creeley,
the futurist Buckminster Fuller, the dancer Merce Cunningham, the Bau-
haus painter and architect Josef Albers, and the musicologist Edward Lo-
winsky. Kazin arrived in the fall of 1944, just as the drama critic Eric
Bentley was leaving. Kazin had visited the school earlier and thought it
might be a pleasant place to start work on a book. The pay was minimal,
fifteen dollars a month, and the instructors had to do chores along with the
students. The setting, however, was spectacular, particularly in the fall, and
he was happy to get back to teaching.

He taught classes on Blake and Melville and the book of Job, which quickly became the most popular at the school. In his history of Black Mountain, Martin Duberman writes that as "an available male and a literary 'celebrity,'" Kazin "became something of a lion." His teaching format was traditional, lecture and discussion, but "Kazin's impassioned manner wasn't." "He was a kind of evangelist for Melville and Blake—a Jewish evangelist, something akin, as one student of his put it, to 'the Holy Schlemiel,' rhapsodizing eloquently one minute, playing the inept joker the next, mixing gossip, profundity, calculated impetuosity and exhortations into such a staccato, stammering, sometimes testy brew, that his students, or at least those with literary aspirations and a taste for the histrionic, left class intoxicated, 'drunken and reeling.'" Kazin's enthusiasm for his subjects did not extend to the intellectual character of the college or the preparedness of the students. He later told Duberman that he had "no respect for what went on educationally at Black Mountain" and could not believe that someone might have been "turned out of that place who was not an intellectual nebbish." Nor did he find Black Mountain a conducive environment for writing, despite a suggestive entry in his journal on beginning a book about childhood and modern literature, a "history of personal history and of the idea of personal history." "If you were a serious writer," he concluded, "Black Mountain could be in many ways a very half-assed place."[52]

Whatever its drawbacks, Black Mountain had a salutary effect on Alfred. Although one entry mentions an aborted effort to contact Asya—"she will not even speak to me"—the journals contain few laments of loneliness and despair over the disconnected quality of his life. "Black Mountain has been the first real home I've had in a year," he wrote in a December entry. "I have been happy here and a workman again." The beauty of the setting—"primitive, magnificent country"—made a daily impression; and the students, despite their educational deficiencies, were memorable. "To this day when I think of Black Mountain, I always think of individual stories," he told Duberman. "It was like a gallery of the higher neuroticism. . . . They were idiosyncratic, crazy, wonderful in certain ways. There wasn't a dull or banal person there." Before leaving Asheville, he submitted a piece to the *New Republic* on a folkdance festival in town that gave a taste of the local culture. The week before Thanksgiving, he received news from the Rockefeller Foundation that he would be sailing to England in January or February.[53]

"A Blitz People"

On February 11, 1945, Kazin boarded the SS *Hart Crane* in New York harbor, and the next day in a convoy of fifty-three ships he began a fifteen-day journey across the North Atlantic to Liverpool. Crowded into the ship's "hospital" with a Franciscan friar, a Protestant clergyman, a radio engineer, and piles of bedpans that crashed about in the North Atlantic gales, Kazin found the journey an ordeal and took what consolation he could from reading W. H. Prescott's *History of the Conquest of Mexico* and collections of Sherlock Holmes stories. He had waited three years to get nearer the war and was prepared to put up with inconvenience and discomfort.

In the seven months he was in Europe, Kazin never got very close to the war. The Battle of the Bulge in the Ardennes Forest had occurred in December 1944, and by the end of January 1945 the Allies had regrouped and crushed the last serious German offensive of the war. The troops were moving steadily eastward, and bombing raids were being conducted regularly over Berlin. On February 4, Roosevelt, Churchill, and Stalin met at Yalta in the Crimea to discuss the final phase of the war. Kazin did, however, get close to wartime England: close enough to hear and feel the V-2s exploding randomly and unnervingly in the streets and parks of London, to see the thousands of people sleeping in the subway stations of the West End, to gaze at the spotlights playing above the mounds of antiaircraft guns in Hyde Park, and to learn a good deal about the English people during wartime.

Housed in billets in Great Cumberland Place for visiting Americans, Kazin went about in the freezing, damp, drizzling weather—"cold all the way and all the time"—collecting material on the education of soldiers. Dressed in woolen long underwear under his clothes and a waterproof, a flashlight always at hand for the blackout, he searched for the right bus and tube stop that would take him to the day's assignment. Whatever London might have been, it was now a city that seemed largely in ruins. Kazin breathed in the icy rain and coal dust, surveying the damage—collapsing houses, smashed churches, "splintered statues of bewigged judges and ancient public men"—half conscious of the constant overhead thrum of airplanes on their way east. His mission was to observe and report on the education of soldiers and war workers in England. He had also agreed to give talks and lead discussions on America and American literature for the Office of War Information. The two assignments took him to military barracks, first-aid stations, firehouses and into working-class neighborhoods around London. He also traveled to other English cities, where he talked with soldiers and workers about their education and their future after the war.[54]

Adult education had played a role in English working-class life from the early 1800s. On his first trip to England, Ralph Waldo Emerson spoke to the workingmen's college in London and noted the "pathetically noble effort of English scholars to educate their humbler brethren." In 1919, it began to receive substantial government funding (employing T. S. Eliot among others) for the instruction of adults and workers in "liberal studies." With the beginning of World War II, the program was redirected to the education of soldiers and those working in the war industries; at the same time, its instructional agenda was broadened to include economic and social concerns among a population anxious to learn what postwar England would do for them. Kazin knew something about the program from his research for his *Fortune* article on America's efforts to educate its soldiers. In that piece he had indicated the superiority of the British effort, which unlike the American encouraged discussion of all aspects of British life, not just the war. While American soldiers were watching war movies and having the news read to them, British troops, encouraged by their officers, were discussing, among other things, the class structure of British society, educational reform, and Sir William Beveridge's 1942 plan to ensure complete social security to all British citizens in the postwar years.[55]

Kazin arrived in England predisposed to think well of its soldier education movement and was not disappointed. In part, the credit went to the program, the officers, and the participants. A leader of one group told him that adult education in England now played the role that religion once did for the people. But the war itself and the nature of British society were also important. Whereas the coming of the war in America had relegated the class struggle of the thirties to a memory, the war in Britain "took the roof off," exposing the different classes to each other as nothing in Britain's history had done before. With the buildings in the East End flattened and thousands of homeless people living in the streets and makeshift shelters, one saw not only misery and want, but "a social bitterness dangerous to ignore," a "long, smoldering rebelliousness" that threatened the unity of the country. There seemed little choice, Kazin quoted from the authorities: the country had decided "to go left with the troops."[56]

Listening to the ongoing discussion and remembering England's historic role in provoking a literature of class struggle and social thought, Kazin felt a resurgence of class feeling—"the old passion of English socialism, of working class struggle and affirmation." But he also understood that what made Socialism in England particularly attractive and plausible at the moment was that the war had not only taken the roof off, it had shown its inhabitants that with the help of the government they could live cooperatively in the same house for the benefit and security of all. Under such conditions, revolutionary abstractions and utopian dreams were neither relevant nor useful. What was important, Kazin stressed repeatedly in his one-hundred-page Rockefeller report, was the sense of a shared community with long memories and habituated roles. It was as if the whole country were "a vast orchestra in which people crowded the podium and the concertmaster's desk, while others were always braying out of turn, but that everyone was part of the ensemble, knew what set music was being played and where *he* came in. Smugness was less apparent than snugness." Or to use a favorite metaphor of George Orwell's, England was a family, though frequently "a family with the wrong members in control."[57]

Like earlier American literary visitors to England—Emerson, Henry James, Henry Adams—Kazin was keen to fathom the "character" of the English. Unlike his predecessors he had a chance to see them in highly extraordinary circumstances, a population deprived and weary and under attack for four years. What he found was resilience, patience, stubbornness, astonishing modesty—"You simply do not put yourself forward"—and a curious suspiciousness about Americans, whom they knew by daily contact with the hundreds of thousands of GIs stationed in their country. Above all, he was impressed by their decency and toughness—"What was wonderful in Britain [during the war] was the sheer direct humanness and goodness of so many. And the English rough irony, absence of crap—gallows humor of Blitz people—of people in trouble." But a "Blitz people" who refused to yield to the blitz—"Where else in this world at war would I have had the bliss of hearing Kathleen Ferrier sing Handel and Gluck in a war factory to hundreds of workers joyously massed together at lunch to hear her?" Or of listening to Myra Hess, bundled against the cold, play Schubert in the National Gallery (stripped of its paintings) for the crowd that had waited more than an hour in line to hear her? Or even the joy of listening to the hymn singers in Hyde Park on a Sunday evening—"the blotched faces of the prematurely old, lower-middle-class Englishwomen, singing with such clarity and sweetness, such practiced contrapuntal sense, that it suddenly seemed to me the greatest proof one could ask for of the rightness of such devotion." A stiff-necked "hidebound" tribe, snobbish and "superior," riven by a "raging class struggle," the English were none-theless a unified people—and in wartime, "what a people." So "solidly together to preserve their existence that [it] moves me every time I find myself in the middle of them."⁵⁸

Kazin (again like his predecessors) was eager to meet and form impres-sions of those literary and intellectual luminaries who were willing to see him. His official responsibilities as reporter and lecturer put him in touch with many; the success of his book accompanied by a letter from Henry Moe of the Guggenheim Foundation secured introductions to others; par-ties and occasions held by new friends like the sociologist David Glass and his wife, Ruth, were another source of contacts. And one contact, one interview, tended to lead to another—"the great chain, the network of names"; he jotted them down in his diary: D. W. Brogan, Chaim Raphael, Alva Myrdal, Kingsley Martin, Graham Greene, T. S. Eliot, A. W. Dent, Harold Laski, Stephen Spender, Maurice Erdman, Russia's Count "Orlov," Cyril Connolly, Edwin Muir, etc., etc. The one person he most wanted to meet, however, who had said he would be glad to speak to any reader of the *Partisan Review*, George Orwell, was on the Continent reporting for the *Observer.*

Some meetings were more memorable than others. He had been anx-ious about meeting T. S. Eliot, fearing Eliot would be aloof and unforth-coming—"impenetrably courteous." In fact, he "was extremely kind, gen-tle, spoke very slowly and hesitatingly, livened up a bit when I pushed the conversation to literary topics. . . . He looks like a very sensitive question mark—long, winding, and bent; gives the impression that his sensibility is in his long curling nose and astonishing hands." Kazin traveled to Cam-bridge to meet the brilliant historian Denis Brogan, who had reviewed *On Native Grounds* favorably in the *Times Literary Supplement*. Brogan took him on a quick tour of the colleges and to a meal at high table, maintaining a rapid-fire commentary on all subjects European and American. "His quickness of mind absolutely amazing: a photo-electric cell with violent, accurate and perhaps shallow illuminations." Kazin later did a BBC discussion with Brogan, who, swigging from a bottle of Scotch, showed that he knew more about America than any American.[59]

Labour Party chairman and theoretician Harold Laski, who had also been impressed by *On Native Grounds*, invited Kazin to one of his dinner parties at his half-destroyed house in Addison Bridge Place. There, Kazin had the chance to see another Englishman display his vast knowledge of America—and to witness Laski's legendary talent for name-dropping. At one point in the conversation Laski interrupted himself to refer to "my old friend, *Frank* Roosevelt." (Kazin would later compare impressions of Laski with Edmund Wilson, who had found him more sympathetic, but an embarrassing fibber.) Kazin's meeting with Graham Greene was less happy. They had met at a party and then gone out for drinks at a pub; but what began as a friendly excursion and chat soon degenerated (in Kazin's view) to Greene's simply staring at him—"his taking me in, as [if] I weren't supposed to know the professional exam of me American Jewish features going on. Quite rude, Graham, after that friendly rush to the beer." This and other incidents (Brogan also seemed put off by his Jewish looks) suggested to the sensitive American that he was not simply the American observer abroad, but the American *Jew*—"Jew and American investigator, the outsider among all these fluted voices."[60]

Of all the English writers Kazin met, the one he liked most was the Scottish poet, critic, autobiographer, and translator Edwin Muir. Muir, who served as representative of the British Cultural Counsel in Edinburgh, had invited Kazin to Edinburgh to deliver an address on American poetry. A native of the Orkney Islands, Muir, and his family, had been forced to move from a remote peasant life on the islands to Glasgow when Muir was fourteen. Kazin saw in Muir a quality of "transparency," "a seriousness of mind and a personal humility" virtually "unknown to Americans." He also found great literary intelligence and cultural sophistication, startling in a person of his background. With little formal education, Muir had educated himself in modern literatures, traveled widely on the Continent, and published some excellent poetry and criticism. In 1930, he and his wife, Willa, had produced the first English translation of Franz Kafka's *The Castle*, followed in 1937 by *The Trial*, soon to become a canonical, even scriptural, work of the postwar years. (Kazin read it for the first time immediately after his visit.) By the early 1950s, Muir had gained international recognition as a poet and in 1955–1956 would deliver the Charles Eliot Norton lectures at Harvard.[61]

On May 7, 1945, Germany surrendered to the Allies, and on May 8, the European war was declared officially over. Kazin continued to interview people, give talks, and conduct discussions on American literature. He had come to enjoy his role as cultural ambassador, one he would happily reassume many times in the future. On July 10, through an arrangement with the Guggenheim Foundation, he flew to Paris to give a series of talks on American literature to the *Quinzaine Anglo-Americanine,* a congress of French professors of English. Once settled in the Hotel Astor, he went out to see the town. Paris reminded him of a World's Fair—the holiday mood and the look everywhere of a bazaar, the booths along the avenues selling trinkets and tickets to the national lottery. The main attraction was the *"Crimes Hitleriens* at *le Grand Palais,"* which displayed an array of Nazi atrocities. In one room was a huge photograph of a corpse found on the grounds of a concentration camp, "his skeletal arm outstretched like Christ on the Cross." Shortly before midnight on the third night, Kazin joined a group of people on the way to the Arc de Triomphe for a vigil honoring those who died for the liberation. The arch was lit up and an enormous flag hung from the top. Masses of people were packed along the Champs-Elysées. After speeches honoring the war dead, the "Marsellaise" was sung and cannons fired off at regular intervals. Kazin found the ceremony "overwhelming." The war really was over.[62]

He remained in Paris until August 2, giving lectures, walking the streets, buying the occasional book. His talks were well received. America and American literature had become hot topics. "Europe was crazy to learn the latest American writers," Kazin wrote, and "I wanted fiercely to learn Europe." In a speech to a group of literary GIs, Albert Camus declared his passion for Faulkner: "I love Faulkner because I too am a Southerner. I love the dust and the heat." The French were interested in other American writers as well. Kazin later told F. O. Matthiessen that the French he met in 1945 thought Melville as "important and symbolically central to Europeans as he is to us." He left France sensing a convergence of French and American literary sensibilities. In appreciation of his talks, the French professors presented him with a copy of Pascal's *Pensées,* whose passages on "the abyss"—"*Le silence éternel de ces espaces infinis m'effraye!*"—were a favorite of Kazin's and reminded him of *Moby-Dick.*[63]

He returned to an England now governed by the Labour Party. On July 26, the English had gone to the polls and handed Labour an absolute majority, with 61 percent of servicemen and servicewomen voting Labour. T. S. Eliot had voted Labour! Labour was ecstatic and the Tories appalled. "But this is terrible," a Tory woman was reported saying when she heard the results. "*They've* elected a Labour Government and *the country* will never stand for that." Kazin was not surprised. His travels and public discussions over the past months had convinced him that most people in England wanted the social programs Labour had promised. The war had shown what the government could do when it chose to act, and many felt they needed the government as much now as during the war. Kazin also saw (or thought he saw) in Labour's victory a hopeful sign for a Socialist future. Labour would show that Socialism was a practical not an ideological matter, a limited means for finite ends, a technical necessity rather than a utopian dream. He acknowledged that the United States was perhaps too prosperous at the moment to turn to Socialist means. But he saw a trend. "A large portion of the world has gone and is going socialist in one form or another," he wrote in his Rockefeller report. "In all countries [socialism] represents the first great movement, in the line of democracy, to advance the thesis that the state is responsible for the welfare of all its citizens."[64]

When Kazin boarded the *Queen Mary* (now serving as a troop ship) in mid-August for New York, he had a companion, Caroline Bookman, the daughter of Judith Wertheim Bookman and Dr. Arthur Bookman of Seventieth and Madison in New York City. They had met outside an army post office on Duke Street earlier in the summer where Alfred had been standing in line hoping for a letter from Asya. Caroline, who worked for Public Opinion Surveys, was directly behind him; they were soon seeing each other. He did not know how seriously to take the relationship. He intended to look up Asya as soon as he was back in New York, hoping there was something left to salvage. But Caroline, who spoke little, was persuasive. "She communicated by signs and wonders, deep looks, by the flush that suddenly rushed up her face, by a whole switchboard of colors flashing signals from her skin, by the amazing luster of her brilliant black hair." And, for the moment, he was happy to be persuaded.[65]

The last days in London had been hot, sultry, lazy—people relaxing in the parks, reading the papers, napping in their penny chairs, just looking out. Kazin saw one couple having intercourse under a mackintosh as others walked politely by, saying nothing. No V-2s or fire alarms, no news from the front, no anxious waiting. "The long winter was over." The war in Europe was over and by August 17, the war in the Pacific as well. But for many the pain, horror, and incomprehension would continue and deepen. In April, Kazin had read the famous news brief in the *London Times* reporting on the liberation of the concentration camp of Bergen-Belsen. "It is my duty to describe something beyond the imagination of mankind." Later, in a Piccadilly movie house he had watched a newsreel from the camp. "Sticks in black-and-white prison garb leaned on a wire, staring dreamily at the camera; other sticks shuffled about, or sat vaguely on the ground, next to an enormous pile of bodies, piled up like cordwood, from which protruded legs, arms, heads." Belsen, it turned out, was one of the better camps. There were far worse in the east—Treblinka, Maidenek, Auschwitz. Back home he would learn of relatives murdered—his mother's sister, Schaene, shot by the Nazis in front of her house. It would take time to absorb what had happened. What was clear, and would become clearer over the years, was that there had been a break, a break in his own life and a break in history—and that the costs remained to be counted.[66]

CHAPTER FIVE

After the Apocalypse
1945–1950

The twelve years of Hitler, 1933–1945, were the years of my apprenticeship, of my basic formation. During those twelve years Hitler and Stalin were the prime builders of the new totalitarian system and the destroyers, at the same time, of the myth that politics could be the saving force and prime interest of my generation. The drama of those twelve years, ending in Hitler's defeat, was the painful last struggle for survival, and when it was over, one could only look back, "after the apocalypse," as if the intensity and world scope of that struggle had left a permanent barrier between the two periods. After 1945, one picked oneself up, blinking in a little daze, to look at the world with entirely new eyes.

—Alfred Kazin, Journal, May 20, 1964

K azin arrived in New York on the *Queen Mary* at the end of August 1945, wondering what he was coming back to. Where would he live? Would Asya agree to a fresh start? How would postwar New York (and America) feel? He quickly discovered that much had changed but that some things remained the same—Asya would not have him back. He could not find a room, boarding with his parents and friends before finding a "ramshackle" flat in Brooklyn Heights. It was too soon to tell about jobs and the economy, but New York seemed to be full of people with money to spend and few places to stay. Politically, the relief was palpable. The war was over. The world had rid itself of two murderous regimes. One had a sense of living "after the apocalypse." "Americans," wrote the historian Allen Nevins, "suddenly seemed to stand, as the war closed, beholding a new heaven and a new earth." Kazin shared in the hopes for a fresh start, a new beginning. He would later look back nostalgically to those "gloriously expectant days right after the war" when it seemed a "new time" was in the making. There would be much in the immediate postwar years to warrant such hope, including new possibilities in his writing and developing relations with the dark-haired beauty he had met in London. But there was also cause for concern. The new heaven described by Nevins would soon fill with darkening clouds—the Soviets' refusal to leave Poland and the Baltics, the possibility of a Communist coup in Greece, Churchill's "iron curtain" speech, the 1947 Truman Doctrine meant to "scare hell" out of Congress and the American people, the 1948 Communist takeover of Czechoslovakia. Had the defeat of one totalitarian regime provided opportunity for another? The trend soon seemed unmistakable. Americans would be spending the years of peace preparing for war.[1]

The threat posed by Soviet Communism stirred feelings of alarm that would pervade American politics and culture for more than three decades. Kazin understood the sense of urgency. He had long since lost hope that Stalin could be trusted. He believed that all necessary measures must be taken to contain Russia's territorial ambitions and to check the predations of the totalitarian state. But he also believed, strongly believed, that "just to be anti-Stalinist is not enough." He worried that an obsessive focus on Stalinism would absorb other social concerns while pushing the political culture sharply to the right. "I feel the reaction in America creeping around me like the blast of a cold wind," he wrote in a February 1947 journal entry. That wind would blow colder as the decade progressed, freezing discussion, threatening dissenters with exposure, forcing all but the most daring and reckless to take cover.[2]

For Kazin and others of his generation, living and writing after the apocalypse meant a narrowing of political hopes and an increased attention to the self—a period of "crisis and conversion," to use Mark Shechner's phrase characterizing the moral change among thirties radicals "after the revolution." This was not necessarily bad for literature or the self. "Ideology crumbled, personality bloomed," Irving Howe wrote of the New York Jewish intellectuals who, "unmoored" from politics, began turning inward for inspiration. But the process was painful, and there were no guarantees. "I shiver inwardly with shame and anger when I think of the barren solitude, politically, into which so many of us have been thrown since the

Moscow trials, the Nazi-Soviet pact, the war," Kazin wrote in a journal entry. "What all of us lack more than anything else is a political solvent for our ideas." Writing *On Native Grounds,* he had felt buoyed along by the political energies of the moment. "The age was with me, the excitement of the thirties was in my book and getting me to write it." Now he would have to look elsewhere—to the city, to memory, to himself—for the kind of inspiration and momentum he had once taken (for granted) from history. It would be a long, uncertain search.[3]

Pineapple Street and Park Avenue

Kazin would later say that renting the third-floor, two-room apartment at 91 Pineapple Street in Brooklyn Heights was a "clutch at my old innocence"— the narrow streets, the sounds from the harbor, the Brooklyn Bridge, all reminding him of his happily married days with Asya. In fact, it was more an act of necessity. There was nothing else available at a price he could afford. He had heard of the place from Saul Bellow, who knew the tenant-landlord, Arthur Lidov. A painter suddenly in the money, Lidov had moved to the country and was happy to let the flat to Kazin, complete with paintings of "emaciated rabbis standing behind barbed wire in Nazi camps [and] skeletal young maidens drooping under the contempt of Nazi guards." Kazin moved in and removed "the bad, sick" pictures. But he could not fix the dilapidated condition of the building, which still smelled of smoke from an old fire; nor could he muffle the footsteps of Mr. Ramirez, the Puerto Rican carpenter, who lived on the other side of his bedroom wall and wakened him every morning as he walked down the hall, sounding "like the long backward roll of the surf." One asset was a skylight that flooded the apartment with light during the day. Despite the problems—"the wearing out, the rusting out, the decay"—Kazin kept renewing the lease through 1952, staying in it between two marriages, subletting it to his sister and numerous friends, and always returning—his closest thing to a "postwar home."[4]

It took some time for him to understand that home was not to include Asya. Since their break in 1943, Alfred had repeatedly asked for another chance. She had repeatedly refused, and by the fall of 1945, he knew his suit was hopeless: "Standing under the skylight—and weeping. Preparing to shave at the urinous sink and weeping." He knew he had lost something valuable in Asya, whose love, patience, and generosity had meant a great deal to him in the early years of their marriage. Janet Rioch, his analyst, had been right. He had taken Asya's love and support for granted, discovering too late how much he wanted and needed her. In a final gesture of generosity, Asya agreed to have their marriage annulled, thereby saving him from a "disgraceful divorce." Asya, he would later say, "makes all things possible."[5]

But there were other possibilities. Returning to his apartment one evening in October, Alfred found Carol Bookman waiting on the steps, as collected and attractive as ever. He was soon seeing her regularly—going out to dinner, attending cultural events, making love in her flat at Fifty-fifth off Fifth Avenue. He marveled at her quiet, confident, easy manner, so different from the charged uncertainty and volubility of the Jews with whom he had grown up. Carol, who like himself had been previously married, seemed unbelievably free of "all Jewish anxieties"—a quality he attributed to her privileged background. Shuttling between the winding streets in Brooklyn Heights with its crumbling brownstones and his dates with Carol in booming Manhattan, bristling with new steel and aluminum towers, he grew sensitive to the historical changes overtaking the city and to the peculiarities of his own situation, the Brownsville native caught between "triumphant, glossy" postwar New York and his ancient, decaying Brooklyn "home"—every day, a journey of contrasting impressions and historical associations to be stored for the future.[6]

Meanwhile, he had to make a living. During an extended visit to Yaddo in November, he finished the Rockefeller report on the education of soldiers. A section of it was published in *Twice a Year*. The rest was buried in the Rockefeller Foundation files. He read manuscripts for Houghton Mifflin. He signed up to write a "Letter from America" column with the Swedish magazine *Bonniers Litterara Magasin* and sold book reviews to the *New York Times Book Review* and the *New Republic*. One of these was a front-page essay-review for the *Times* (January 7, 1946) of Dostoevsky's shorter fiction.

Kazin had been reading and discussing Dostoevsky with friends since the war years. After the war the Russian writer had come to seem more relevant than ever, "a master-critic of our civilization." Kazin, however, was of two minds about Dostoevsky and his current popularity. He admired his "merciless" eye for human weakness and his tough-minded skepticism about historical progress, particularly his anticipation of totalitarianism. But he recoiled from his demand for religious absolutes and wondered about the unrelieved focus on human degeneracy at a time when "a sense of guilt is so ripe and universal that it is the freshest device of innocence." "Sin," "guilt," "anxiety" were becoming favorite terms among writers and intellectuals in "the deep human winter" that had set in after the disillusionments of the thirties. Karl Marx, as Arthur Schlesinger put it, had been displaced by Reinhold Niebuhr, the "neo-orthodox" theologian, with his "devastating Christian polemic" against human self-sufficiency and the "the whole idea of salvation through history." While Kazin acknowledged the need to face the painful truths encountered in Dostoevsky (and Niebuhr), he was not convinced that the new preoccupation with human depravity and historical failure led to a more viable view of the future or of humanity's possibilities—even in a postapocalyptic "era of the disappointed." While taking a stand on one's disillusionment was an understandable response to recent events, it had the potential to create ideological blind spots as distorting as a programmatically hopeful liberalism. The Dostoevsky piece was one of a number of (public and private) minority reports that Kazin would lodge against the deepening spiritual-political pessimism of the postwar years.[7]

The last week of March, Alfred sent off the completed *Portable Blake* to Viking. He had worked on it so long he did not know whether it was any good and was simply relieved to have done with it—"My affair with Blake was really becoming a scandal." Now he could think about the future. "Is it really going to be a new time? How wonderful it would be not to look back anymore, not to have the familiar stabbing regrets about Asya." Relations with Carol suggested that a new time might well be at hand. He felt increasingly at ease around her for all her quiet, undemonstrative manner. He was sure enough of his feelings to propose an August visit to Cape Cod, where memories of times with Asya still lingered.[8]

Before that, he was off to a six-week teaching stint at the University of Minnesota. In September 1945, the chair of the English Department, Joseph Warren Beach, had written to Henry Moe at the Guggenheim Foundation asking about Kazin and whether he might be interested in teaching at Minnesota. The university was in the process of establishing notable graduate and undergraduate programs in American studies, and

Kazin seemed an obvious candidate for a faculty position. Kazin was not interested in moving to Minnesota, however, though he was happy to teach during the summer.

His first impressions on arriving in Minneapolis in late June were not encouraging. "The room is small, the people are dull and strange. I feel suffocated in this narrow atmosphere." Two weeks later, things looked better. The students were hard working, interested, and well prepared—unlike the neurotics and misfits at Black Mountain. In a July "Letter from America" to *Bonniers,* he wrote that he was "exhilarated" by his experiences at Minnesota, where "Swedish names and folkways are as thick as blueberries in the field." Calling himself a "hardened New Yorker," he marveled at the "equanimity" of his students, many of them farmers' children, and the earnestness with which they read Melville, Kafka, Rimbaud, Strindberg. "Here all thoughts are possible." This would be the first of a number of teaching and lecture visits to the University of Minnesota. He would also make frequent teaching trips to the universities of Iowa, Michigan, and Notre Dame. He enjoyed visiting and teaching in the Midwest, which he often called "The Peaceable Kingdom" after Edward Hicks's famous painting of a harmonious animal scene signifying American innocence. But, despite tempting offers, it would remain a nice place to visit, not one in which this "hardened New Yorker" chose to settle down.[9]

Back East in August, Alfred and Carol went to the Cape. He had worried that returning to places he and Asya had visited in 1940 might be painful, but walking the shore and trekking to the inland ponds was as pleasant as ever. The past seemed to be passed. He worked on a few poems (never published) and prepared a review of Edmund Wilson's *Memoirs of Hecate County* for the *Partisan Review.*

The book had been making headlines and provoking lawsuits. It contained some graphic sex scenes, and Wilson was hoping for a *succès de scandale.* Kazin was unimpressed. He found *Memoirs* schematic, repetitious, and lacking in the novel's most important quality, "a novelist's respect for experience." As for the accounts of fornication, Kazin thought them "really pathetic." He had been hurt by Wilson's "snooty" response to *On Native Grounds,* and one might wonder about the intensity of the review's animus. But the criticism does not come across as petty or vengeful. As warm as ever in praise of Wilson's criticism, Kazin insisted that it is Wilson's critical intelligence and high literary standards that make *Memoirs* so disappointing—that, and its all-pervading "misanthropy." There is, he complains, an "unrelieved personal bitterness" throughout the book that repels hope, turns all relations sour, and reminds one of Melville's "distorted parable," *The Confidence Man,* another failed novel by a superior talent.[10]

Wilson's "pessimism" would, in fact, be the subject of Kazin's most consistent complaint against his literary hero in the immediate and more distant future. There is no critic he admired more, he told Wilson in a 1950 letter, no critic whom he read with "such instinctive sympathy, pleasure, and admiration," which he is why he found the "calamitousness" in his novel and in recent articles so upsetting. Reading Wilson's recent work, he too often had the "feeling that everything has gone to rack and ruin, that the younger generation has never known what it is to have any fun in life, that the great power machines, the slick ass magazines, the totalitarian parties, etc, etc, have frozen us all hard into a situation from which there is no relief and no appeal." That Wilson's recent work was contributing to the increasingly "fashionable" postrevolutionary, postliberal pessimism of the times struck Kazin as particularly regrettable.[11]

Kazin returned from the Cape wondering what to do with himself professionally. With the Blake finished, he had no major writing projects in the works nor any prospects for a job. In early October he enquired about a teaching position in Columbia's English Department. The chair, Oscar Campbell, a "bright-faced twinkling, twinkling little man," seemed hopeful, but nothing came of it. Later in the month he submitted an application for a renewal of his Guggenheim fellowship to do "a study in American literature centered around the work of Herman Melville, to be called *The Western Island.*" Melville's literary stock had been rising steadily in recent years in part because his subversive intelligence seemed to foreshadow the current "existentialist" challenge to all received opinion and settled assumptions. Noting that Melville shared with Kafka and Camus an "'existentialist' conception of man as a stranger on the island of his own being," Kazin proposed to show that Melville was not only our "contemporary," but that he was describing America itself as an "island" apart—a country where writers created their own truths in lonely confrontation with an alien wilderness. Kazin did not indicate when he might complete this project, which, in fact, did not appear until 1984, much deferred and revised as *An*

American Procession. Indeed, when he submitted the application in late October 1946, he was already working on another project that would occupy the largest amount of his writing time for the next four years.[12]

In August, he had accepted an assignment from *Harper's Bazaar* to collaborate with the French photographer Henri Cartier-Bresson on a photographic essay of the Brooklyn Bridge. The bridge and its immediate environs were familiar territory to Kazin. But walking over it and through the surrounding neighborhoods with Cartier-Bresson—"I take his kind of picture in my mind"—while researching its history and rereading Hart Crane and Whitman, he began to see possibilities for something more substantial than a magazine piece—a work that might tap into talents other than those of a literary critic. Kazin had been chafing at the creative limits of literary criticism for some time. "When I write criticism," he had written in his journal while finishing *On Native Grounds*, "I feel as if only a quarter of my mind—and too much of my strength—were going into it." He had had hopes for fiction. But by the end of the war he had published only one short story and had no further plans in that area. The bridge suggested a very different mode that would draw on his daily jottings in his diary—a private meditation, not unlike Thoreau's *Walden*—a "personal journal," he told Van Wyck Brooks, "based on the inner world of a man walking in the streets"—a "spiritual autobiography" describing "one man's relations to certain problems, memories, institutions as they are pressed in on his consciousness walking about New York." In mid-November he visited Yaddo, his head full of plans, returning six days later with an outline and the beginnings of a rough draft. He tried unsuccessfully to enlist Cartier-Bresson in the project. But he had made up his mind; he was going to do the book, with or without the photographer. And he already had a title, *A Walker in the City.* On January 4, 1947, he wrote to Allen Tate and reneged on a Faulkner article he had promised, explaining that he was writing a book that he "simply must finish by summer," when he expected to go abroad.[13]

It is doubtful that Kazin honestly expected to finish by the summer. He had too many other claims on his time. The most pressing was a series of talks he had contracted to give at the John L. Elliot Institute for Adult Education. This meant working up or revising lectures on Malraux, Kafka, Dostoevsky, D. H. Lawrence, Blake, and Melville. As Carol Bookman, her mother, and her friends would be attending, he felt he had to take special care with the preparations. In the end, he was pleased with the results. He believed he was becoming a proficient lecturer and no longer feared the return of his childhood stammer. He was particularly happy when his father showed up for his Blake lecture. "We had coffee together afterwards, and then, two amiable acquaintances, went to the subway. Always it is I [who] feel[s] like the father, and he is my oldest boy. Always deeply touched by his faith and pride in me, the *naches* [the joy Jewish parents derive from their children]."[14]

Kazin was also writing reviews, the most ambitious, a front-page review-essay on Kafka for the April 13, 1947, issue of the *New York Herald Tribune: Books*. Kafka, who had been on his mind since his 1945 Edinburgh meeting with Edwin Muir (Kafka's translator), had become a major figure in postwar culture. Kafka's evocation of unspecified guilt and his disturbing, "Kafkaesque" depictions of victimization by an unaccountable, impersonal "totalitarian" bureaucracy seemed uncannily prophetic of present conditions. Kazin appreciated Kafka's visionary gift, much as he did Dostoevsky's. The primary interest of Kafka for Kazin, however, was his genius for conveying "metaphysical anguish" without dissolving the world into myth and symbols. In the introduction to *The Portable Blake,* Kazin writes that Blake, revolted by the brutal exploitation and inhuman ugliness of industrial England, "imagines a world equal to his heart's desire" and turns his imaginings into "an absolute personal myth," defying reason and the evidence of the senses. Kafka makes no concession to desire. He will not "let himself off, and hence us as we read him." While similar to Blake in the cryptic simplicities of his style, he renders with "scrupulous accuracy" the "actuality" of this world, never suggesting we can transcend its horrors with myth, symbols, or doctrine. "The religious ache" in Kafka derives not from otherworldly revelations to be interpreted according to some "higher theology," but from his embrace of this world and its inherent mysteriousness. Like Emily Dickinson, another Kazin favorite, Kafka conveys powerful religious feeling without making claims on the supernatural.[15]

One consequence of the Kafka piece was a note from Hannah Arendt, whom Kazin had met the previous fall at a *Commentary* dinner. Seated next to her, he had been impressed and excited, or as he later put it, "enthralled, by no means unerotically." "Darkly handsome, bountifully interested in everything, this forty year old German refugee with a strong accent and such intelligence—thinking positively cascades out of her in waves." They promised to meet soon for further conversation. The promise went unfulfilled until she read his "excellent review" in the *Herald Tribune* and sent him a note reminding him of their date. Kazin was happy to arrange a meeting—"I am a sucker for this kind of advanced European mind"—the first of many in a friendship that he would come to regard as among the most important of his life.[16]

When not preparing lectures or writing reviews, Alfred spent his mornings pushing his "Walker" book forward with painful slowness in his light-bathed, smoky-smelling Pineapple Street flat. He usually spent the rest of the day in the city—an occasional lunch with his sister, Pearl, who served on the editorial staff of *Harper's Bazaar;* a cocktail party at Houghton Mifflin (for Henry Wallace), "the strangest collection of big shots and literary cocktailers"; an afternoon with Carol at the Bronx Zoo, featuring the lion, "so full of gravity and intelligence and a kind of heavy forbearance of his own captivity"; a party at Chaim Raphael's, a friend from the British Information Service—"very nice but dull." Movies were a favorite pastime for both Carol and Alfred, as were concerts at Carnegie Hall and the New York Philharmonic.[17]

In fact, concerts and recitals were more than a pastime for Kazin. Classical music had always been a special passion. Although a "poor violinist" with only "the most rudimentary technical knowledge," he was, as he often noted, a powerful "echo," responding (in his journals) to performances and recordings with an intensity that all but compensated for his lack of technical knowledge: "Listening to [pianist] Kurt Applebaum play Beethoven . . . I understood what Plato meant, what I had guessed so long—that music does drive us mad"; after an evening of Schubert—there is "no music so personal, none which seems with such exquisite pathos to confront the abyss"; Bach ("The Easter Cantata")—"the sheer triumph stands at the crest of the universe radiant with the sound of trumpets: Christ is risen!"; Mozart as therapy—"I thought I would break down [from the "strain" of an evening with the family]—when completely, out of memory, I began to sing arias from Mozart operas, and sang and sang. I could not bear to leave off singing, until I was quieter to myself." Postwar New York offered countless opportunities to hear classical music performed by the world's most accomplished artists, and Alfred (and Carol) took full advantage of the offerings—sometimes attending two or more concerts or recitals a day. "I need music the first thing in the morning, and the last thing at night," and through much of the day—"there is always music playing in my head. I am my own unbelievable jukebox and Muzak system." Not the least of New York's long-term attractions for Kazin was the predictable availability of good music.[18]

Frequently an afternoon concert or movie ended at Schrafts, where Alfred and Carol joined her mother to discuss the New York cultural scene. Judith Bookman née Wertheim (one of New York's prominent manufacturing and banking families) was interested in culture and intellectuals, particularly European intellectuals. "Rosy, bouncy" Judith, she cheered each of them on indiscriminately, "whether A contradicts B, or whether C is the enemy of D." Her husband, Arthur Bookman, a distinguished physician and pioneer in diabetes, had interests that did not overlap Kazin's, and there was little conversation between them—"a very canny . . . private old man." Like many descendants of German Jews who immigrated in the mid-nineteenth century, Carol's parents were assimilated Jews. Michael Kazin recalled his surprise as a child to come across his grandparents' marriage license—in Hebrew. "It shocked me because I had never seen anything in Hebrew around their house, or any acknowledgment that in any way they were Jews in any religious sense." When the Bookmans and the Wertheims (great-aunts, uncles, cousins) got together at Christmas, they celebrated as though it were their holiday. "They could have been named Cook or Butler," Michael said. "I still know more Christmas carols than I know Jewish songs."[19]

Kazin had grown up in a very different milieu, celebrating Holy Days with Yiddish and Socialist folksongs. Like other Jews of Polish-Russian extraction, the Kazins tended to regard their German cousins with a defensive uneasiness tinged with resentment. Although New York's German-Jewish population had contributed significantly to the welfare of the "Russian" Jews in the years of heaviest immigration, relations between the two groups had always been strained, the "Germans" fearing the "un-American ways" of the "wild Asiatics," the Russians resenting the snobbishness and patronizing manner of the Germans. Acutely conscious of the social differences between them, Alfred recalled that dinners at the Bookmans' at Seventieth and Madison could sometimes be a trial—not least for Carol, who was painfully aware of the gulf separating her family and her lover from "darkest Brownsville," struggling to suppress his "violent class prejudice."[20]

· Whatever the class differences and moments of social awkwardness, the courtship continued. By early spring of 1947, Carol and Alfred had decided on a wedding date, May 23, to be followed by a honeymoon in Italy. She was passionate about Italy, which she had visited as a student before the war. He was excited by the prospect of living and writing abroad—vowing to work conscientiously on *Walker*. On April 8, he learned that the Guggenheim Foundation had renewed his fellowship of twenty-five hundred dollars for *The Western Island*. This, together with Carol's resources and the strength of the postwar American dollar, would enable them to live several months in Italy in reasonable comfort.

Europe

On May 29, the Kazins set sail on the *Sobieski*, a Polish ship bound for Genoa. Alfred was relaxed, happy, expectant. He spent "the long lazy days" on deck studying Italian grammar, reading, and discussing Italy with Carol and her friend Mario Salvadori. Born in Rome in 1907, driven from Italy by the Fascists, Salvadori, whom Kazin found "wonderfully bright and engaging," would serve as their guide in the early stages of their visit. (He would later serve as a guide or counselor to their marriage and eventually become Carol's husband.) On June 5, Kazin celebrated his birthday onboard ship. "Hard to believe that I am already 32—hard to believe that I am married, going to Europe and that I am not alone anymore. The contrast with other birthdays these last years very sharp." It was going to be "a new time" after all.[21]

After a brief tour of Genoa, the Kazins boarded a bus to Florence. Racing up and down narrow mountain roads, Kazin was stunned by the beauty of the landscape and appalled by the ruins left by the Allied bombing. Once in Florence, he found it impossible to put down all his impressions, "so insistent is the demand on my attention, on my historical sense, on my sense of the city's beauty." He was determined to record as much as possible, both for his own benefit and for a piece he had agreed to do on postwar Italy for the *Partisan Review*. The editors (and the State Department) were worried about political conditions in Italy.[22]

The cause for worry was the growing influence of European Communism among workers and certain leading European intellectuals. Stalin, it
was feared, might achieve at the ballot box (or perhaps by a coup) what he
would not attempt with his armies. In March, President Harry S Truman,
alarmed by developments in economically devastated Europe and citing a
possible Communist coup in Greece, had addressed a joint session of Congress, warning that the United States must take immediate steps "to support free peoples who are resisting attempted subjection by armed minorities or by outside pressure." The speech, outlining the Truman Doctrine,
clarified the stakes and obligations. If precautions were not taken to contain Soviet ambitions, totalitarianism might once again establish itself in
Western Europe, dashing hopes for a democratic Europe, perhaps leading
to a new war.[23]

Italy was to hold the first national election since the war, and a Communist
victory seemed a real possibility. Kazin was to register his impressions and
report back. A few days after his arrival in Florence, he listened to the Social
Democrat Pietro Nenni address a crowd in the Piazza del Signoria. If Nenni
were elected, it was suspected that he would surrender the Italian Socialist
Party to the Communists. Kazin understood the stakes but had difficulty
keeping his mind on politics. "If one tired of Nenni or the meeting, one
could regale oneself with the Palace, the centerpiece of Neptune, and the
reproduction of Michelangelo's David which stands before the door of the
Palace." It was a taste of things to come. Postwar politics were important to
Kazin, but so were many other things, and he was not prepared to let
Communism or the fear of Communism distract him from the interests and
the beauty he was discovering daily in Italy. (Thanks largely to American
financial aid to the competing political parties, Nenni was defeated.)[24]

While in Florence, Kazin looked up a friend of Paolo Milano, Ramy
Alexander, a consultant for UNESCO on the reconstruction of museums
and art damaged during the war. Alexander had a car and was happy to
drive the Kazins around the Florentine countryside, including a visit to
Bernard Berenson's nearby villa, I Tatti. Berenson was not at home, but
Leo Stein, Gertrude Stein's brother, who was staying there, showed them
around. Kazin thought the villa "very beautiful, very!" The pictures were
"excellent," the library "magnificent," though he was put off by the "fin-
icky" rightness of everything—"the last word in connoisseurship as a per-

sonal principle." Leo Stein fascinated him, particularly his resentment of his sister. "After all these years, the bitterness rankled, keeping him young." Kazin would meet Berenson in Rome in October.[25]

A few days later, Alexander drove them to Rome, where the Kazins settled down for some serious sightseeing. Alfred was enchanted with everything—"the warm evening hush of the Roman Street, a lovely statue set in the wall like an altar, the sight of three pretty girls walking arm in arm down the street, made a picture of such loveliness." But he worried about his unfinished book, about the casual routine he was falling into; and he worried about his worrying—"not to be so prudent and so everlastingly careful." Rome showed "a very great portion of human experience [that is] new to me. I must give myself to it more—not worry about the unfinished book . . . the unplanned days. Like all neurotics I am an incurable bourgeois." He also worried about his marriage, about Carol's being so "utterly self contained, so entirely undemonstrative." He acknowledged his exaggerated need for shows of affection, but he couldn't help himself. He wanted more, expected more; and he feared that he was "imprisoning" himself in a relationship whose meaning was apparent to his "mind," but not at all to his "heart." Was the problem Carol's "idiosyncrasy" or his own "ridiculous" yearning for affection? Was there really a problem at all? If he was an "incurable bourgeois," he could also be an emotionally demanding husband.[26]

On July 15, Kazin boarded a train to Salzburg, Austria, to participate in a six-week seminar in American studies. The Salzburg Seminar, as it came to be called, was the brainchild of Clemens Heller. A resourceful Harvard graduate student from Vienna, Heller believed it was the right moment to bring European students together to hear American faculty talk on various aspects of American life and culture. Working through family connections in Austria, Heller secured the use of the picturesque Leopoldskron Castle in Salzburg, home of Mozart's patron and nemesis, the archbishop of Salzburg and the future setting for the movie *The Sound of Music*. With the help of Harvard friends, Heller had scouted up funds and persuaded a prestigious American faculty to lead seminars (without pay) for ninety-seven students recruited from seventeen European countries. Among those who agreed to attend were the sociologists Margaret Mead and Lyman Bryson, economists Wassily Leontieff and Walt Rostow, and American literary scholars F. O.

Matthiessen and Kazin. Other preeminent figures, including Mario Praz and Gaetano Salvemini, agreed to make presentations.

Following Matthiessen's suggestion, Heller had sought out Kazin in February and persuaded him to participate. Once there, after an "unforgettable" journey in "a shot-up, gutted, blackened piece of ex-Nazi rolling stock," Kazin was quickly caught up in the pioneering spirit of the enterprise. For someone determined to learn Europe, the seminar offered a crash course in European types, disparate war experiences, and population displacement—a White Russian who had grown up in Yugoslavia; a Hungarian DP (displaced person) working for the American army; a Romanian Jew whose mother had been shot before her eyes; a Communist Czech who liked to sing Russian revolutionary hymns; a Spanish Republican who had fought in the civil war; and a former member of the Nazi Africa Korps, getting his Ph.D. in history at the University of Vienna—whom Kazin found the most interesting student of the group. He had expected the seminar to be "a strange experience," but not of its becoming "such a tableau of postwar Europe."[27]

He and Matthiessen lectured on American literature, which, in presenting "the very stuff of American life" (according to Margaret Mead), proved ideal for the seminar. Matthiessen began with Emerson. Kazin followed with *Walden,* which he presented as a "concrete" embodiment of the issues raised by "The American Scholar." Kazin next turned to *Leaves of Grass* to express the buoyant, expansive element in American romanticism, while Matthiessen explored "the tragic strain" in Hawthorne. Both lectured on Melville: Matthiessen on *Moby-Dick,* Kazin on *Billy Budd.* Both also discussed Dreiser's *Sister Carrie,* a Kazin favorite, and an author on whom Matthiessen was writing a book. Matthiessen closed out the nineteenth century with a discussion of Henry James's *Portrait of a Lady,* a performance Kazin found amazing. "To hear him open up, in the grand salon that is our lecture hall here, on the intricate beauty of *The Portrait of a Lady,* and this to an audience of spellbound Europeans hanging on every word, so much had his tension communicated itself to everyone in the room, was to be present at something remarkable." Margaret Mead found listening to both men remarkable. It is impossible to overstate the "impact of the lectures on American writing," she later reported. "They communicated the sense of a living literature, and of a culture to which self-criticism is a necessary condition of life." She and the students had much to appreciate—they were watching arguably the two foremost authorities on American writing weave their very different talents and approaches into a sustained critical discussion of the country's literature.[28]

For all their cooperation, Kazin found Matthiessen a tricky personality to work with—"Subtle st[r]ains of life with F.O.M.," he wrote in his journal at the time: "a lovely little, gentle scholar-man with more rivalry to me than I would have expected and full of odd little strokes of malice. A man I like or could like very much, if he would let me, let himself . . . essentially a teacher, and a very good one." Kazin would later object strenuously to Matthiessen's politics, which he thought sentimental, wrong-headed, and naive; but for a seminar intended to advance a sense of shared humanistic values among very different people, many of them former enemies, he seemed the perfect teacher-leader. "In listening to Matthiessen talk on Eliot, I had an unforgettable experience of the kind of cultural solidarity that can arise in a group when the lecturer unites it by his conviction and creative emotion." Kenneth Lynn, a Harvard student attending the seminar, agreed. It was, he felt, Matthiessen's finest moment as a teacher "talking out of his American heart in the heart of Europe."[29]

Kazin was not as pleased with Salzburg itself. The city's elaborate cultural display, complete with concerts by Jewish musicians, struck him as overdone, phony, and grotesquely oblivious to its recent Nazi past—a past still very much present if one walked a dusty road out of town to the local DP camp, once a Gestapo prison and now housing several hundred Jewish refugees. What did Yehudi Menuhin playing Mendelssohn or Otto Klemperer conducting Mahler at the Festspielhaus have to do with them? "Went to the DP camp with V. [Vida Ginsburg] and Carl Kaysen—oh misery, oh Jewish brothers," Kazin wrote in a journal entry after the visit.

> We climbed over the fence of the DP camp; I climbed back into East Europe, and we Americans gave out our chocolate bars and bobby pins and razor blades and listened sympathetically to a 28-year-old woman, looking anywhere older than that, telling again the old incredible story of the war. . . . Twenty four of them in a room the size of my bedroom here, just a little larger. A concentration camp of a room, wooden slats—dirty, unkempt, food in pails or sizzling on little burners. Copies of Yiddish newspapers from NY (packages from relatives?) all around; sick people; ten children or so . . . A woman who might have

stepped out of Sutter Avenue—so much so that looking at her, and the *Day* on the table, I almost forgot that I was in a DP camp. [Another woman in a] black dress was bitter, humorous, proud: I loved her spunk; her face cracked with inexpressible, useless defiance. Everybody has gone home now, she said; only we are left; only we have no home to go to. You American Jews, she said, you American Jews—do something!

After this confrontation, the cultural show of Salzburg could seem obscenely beside the point.[30]

The seminar concluded the last week in August, and Kazin was surprised by how well things had gone. The "free communication between individuals" had, he believed, been the primary goal. "How far did we get in the seminar?" he asked himself in his journal. Farther than he had imagined. Essential to that communication had been the willingness of the Americans to talk openly and critically about America's problems and on occasion to let down their political guard—which Kazin (to his later regret) did one evening when he led an informal group in the singing of the old Socialist hymn the *Internationale*. He would return to the seminar in later years (which survived a covert investigation by army intelligence for political unreliability). By then, the faculty were paid and accommodations much improved, but the élan was not the same. Like many others, Kazin felt he had been part of a pioneering adventure in democracy—the Marshall Plan in American culture, it would often be called.[31]

Back in Rome, the Kazins rented a bungalow on the grounds of the French Academy just off the Borghese Gardens. It would be five months before they returned to New York; and Alfred was determined to saturate himself in the beauty and history of the city, while pushing ahead with his book. He had more success with the former than the latter. Every day seemed to bring unexpected discoveries of the beauties of Rome and new frustrations with his book. "Worked badly this morning." "Got nowhere this morning over my perplexity." "Wrote the same passage over and over again." In October, he sent off a section to Reynal and Hitchcock to be published in a limited eighteen-page edition for distribution among friends as a "New Year's Greeting." He hoped the effort would build some momentum. But he was not happy with the results and stood wavering in the post office before finally mailing it. An account of an early-morning walk in Brooklyn Heights, when "for once the city belongs entirely to him who walks in it," the piece was published as *The Open Street.* An introductory note states that the completed book would be published in the fall of 1948—three years before its actual appearance.[32]

In the evenings Kazin socialized with friends and new acquaintances—Mac Goodman, a friend from home with whom he liked to discuss Italian culture and politics; Frances Keene, Carol's college teacher of Italian, who would become a well-known translator and a reviewer for the *Nation;* and Eleanor Clark, a writer (and future wife of Robert Penn Warren), who like himself was on a Guggenheim fellowship. Clark was there to write a novel but composed instead a series of sketches of Roman life that would become the popular classic *Rome and a Villa.* One of Kazin's more memorable evenings was spent with Carlo Levi, an anti-Fascist novelist, whom he had reviewed favorably before leaving New York, and Ignazio Silone, a hero of his since the thirties. Kazin was delighted with Levi—"wonderful to be with; looks like either a benign old Roman or a sturdy Jewish grandmother. Marvelous confluence of the Italian and the Jew." Silone was another matter—silent, unresponsive, almost surly. Kazin met them both at an outdoor Roman café—on one side Levi, all exuberance and personality, nodding at everyone, telling jokes, flirting openly with Carol, the "hearty Italian personality" soon to become a Communist senator; on the other side, Silone, "a great disappointment—mulish, ungiving sort of man," his face buried in his plate of food. But it was not Silone, the raconteur, who interested Kazin. At nineteen, he had read *Fontamara* and was deeply moved by Silone's commitment to the poor and oppressed. He was "not a Marxist like other Marxists." Now a Socialist deputy in the Parliament, he carried on his fight for the poor as a legislator and journalist. "The Silone I loved was to be found not in a crazy quilt evening [at an outdoor Roman café], but in his work, with its scruples, its awkward tenderness, and its humor."[33]

In October, Bernard Berenson, "a master of receiving visitors," received Kazin at the Hassler Hotel. In *New York Jew* Kazin paints a vivid picture of the great connoisseur—the self-made "Jewish aristocrat" who had turned himself into a piece of art—"this perfectly composed picture of Olympian detachment, as finely put together as his great library." Berenson was happy to deliver his views on virtually every subject Kazin proposed, including the "confused" and "cloacal" Henry Miller. "He slowly and ostentatiously pronounced 'clo-a-cal' in a way that made me see all the refuse coming up from the bottom of the Tiber and gathering itself into the works of Henry Miller." A journal entry immediately after the meeting is more generous. There, Kazin marvels at the "wonderful lucidity and delicacy of perception in everything [Berenson] said."[34]

Two "travel" essays would come from Kazin's seven-month trip abroad: "Salzburg: Seminar in the Ruins: A Report on the European State of Mind" for *Commentary* and "From an Italian Journal" for the *Partisan Review*. He was particularly happy with the latter—"one of the few things" in which "I got all my tone and feelings in." The piece is notable for its loving, almost rhapsodic, enthusiasm for Italy, particularly the distinctive mix of politics, culture, and history that Kazin found so attractive in Rome. While concerned (like his *Partisan* editors) with the growing Communist influence in Italian politics, he understood that politics takes its moral color from the character of the country. The Communists were certainly a presence in Italy. But mediated through complex historical associations and the shifting debates among different parties and known figures in literature and the arts, Communism was part of a political-cultural mix in which it was not always easy (or sensible) to make exact distinctions. In a society where a conservative literary luminary such as Benedetto Croce voted to award the nation's highest literary award to the Communist Antonio Gramsci, it was difficult to see the struggle between Communism and anti-Communism, however important, as the culture's defining concern. What Kazin discovered talking with his friends; reading Gramsci, Levi, and Silone; walking the city streets trying to make sense of the multilayered social-cultural past, was a prospect where politics merges with personality, literature, history, and art—one of many interrelated concerns occupying the consciousness of the country. While such a compounded political-cultural perspective might seem confusing, even ominous, to someone determined to define "positions" and sort out friends and enemies, it also made conversation possible and interesting (if unpredictable), while keeping relations fluid and mostly civil. It was a perspective that Kazin would find increasingly and depressingly absent back home.[35]

Cold War New York

"I hate to leave Italy. I haven't the words to express my love for it," Alfred wrote in an early December journal entry about his coming departure. "I want to go home—God knows why!" He had reason to wonder. He would be returning to a city where he had no job, no place to live, and an unfinished book that wasn't moving, with a wife now several months pregnant. After he spent a night in quarantine in New York harbor, the harsh light of the early January morning of 1948 reminded him of what he had been missing—the pounding rush of the traffic, the underground rumble and screech of the subways, "the violent quality of people's energy and the brutal cop pushing the Italian woman back on the curb."[36]

After living briefly with Carol's parents at 33 East Seventieth Street, the Kazins took over a temporary sublet at 727 Park Avenue from a Russian pianist friend of Carol's. Despite the provisional nature of the arrangement, Alfred moved in with a sense of relief. Talking with Carol after their first dinner in their new home, he suddenly felt that he was "no longer living on the margin" and that he owed much of his happiness to his wife. In the months since their marriage, he had learned how very different they were, temperamentally and intellectually—so much so that he sometimes felt he was "calling to her across a great gulf." But he also recognized reserves of strength—"her deep solidity, her naturalness, her humor and irony."[37]

With the living arrangements solved for the moment, he began looking for work. He met with Clara Meyer, dean of the New School about a possible course in the fall on Whitman and Melville. He contacted Oscar Campbell again about a possible opening at Columbia and asked Matthiessen for a recommendation. Matthiessen wrote back saying he would tell Campbell that "any university would be lucky" to get him as a teacher. He also told Kazin he was working on a manuscript of the Salzburg experience that would interest him. Like the previous two applications to Columbia, this one went nowhere—a pattern that Kazin came to believe could be laid at the door of Lionel Trilling, "who would never have wanted me, another Jew at Columbia." There were other job possibilities. Bard College was thinking of offering him a position, as was the University of Minnesota. But he wasn't interested. Saul Bellow, teaching at Minnesota at the time, wrote that there was "universal lamentation" when he turned the university down. But Kazin did not want to leave New York, especially while working on *Walker*. Lacking a permanent post, he hoped to make do (barely) teaching at the New School and writing freelance reviews. He had been there before.[38]

In February, Kazin learned he would no longer be doing editorial work for Houghton Mifflin. But other options were opening up. Harcourt Brace, which had bought Reynal and Hitchcock, hired him as an editorial scout, a position that would provide a steady if limited income for the immediate future. He also agreed to serve as a (paid) panel member on a new literary program, *Invitation to Learning,* broadcast by the radio station WCBS. The half-hour program consisted of three prominent scholar-critics discussing the work of an important writer. Mindful of his childhood stammer, Kazin was initially apprehensive when he sat down at his first taped session in May 1948 with host Lyman Bryson and Jonathan Daniels to discuss Ellen Glasgow's *Barren Ground.* But the session went well, and the one-time stammerer, though "exhausted by the accumulated tension" of the debate, joked that he was on the way to becoming an "intellectual performer." He would be a frequent guest and occasional host until the show ended in the late fifties. The format suited his literary intelligence—his reviewer's capacity to sum up and evaluate a book succinctly, to place it historically, to make telling comparisons with other works and authors. Reading through the transcripts today, one is astonished by the intensity of literary passion and high level of learning broadcast on a commercial radio program.[39]

Another promising offer came in the spring from William Shawn of the *New Yorker.* Would he care to review books for the magazine? Kazin shared the view among many of his generation that the *New Yorker* was not intellectually serious, that its literary interests did not extend beyond the bland expectations of the educated suburban housewife. The running joke was that it most admired writers who could write "by not saying things." Still, it paid well and had a large national following. That Edmund Wilson had been publishing in it suggested a certain level of intellectual respectability. In fact, Wilson strongly encouraged Kazin to write for it. The staff, he said, were sticklers for clarity, and this could help him with "his most serious flaw"—"precision with language." Though Kazin would never feel "relaxed" working for Shawn, he would write reviews for the magazine into the mid-fifties.[40]

A few minutes after midnight, on June 6, 1948, Michael Kazin was born. His parents had disagreed over the name. Carol had wanted Peter, but Alfred argued successfully for a Jewish name, "Michael, from the Hebrew *Mik-ha-el* 'who is like God.'" The birth came as a great relief—a tangible achievement. Alfred might be stymied by his book, but he could at least father a son. "Except for the baby I have no sense of direction or the peacefulness that comes with having done something." The birth had certainly made his parents and the Bookman household very happy: "Isn't it wonderful to have a son! Isn't it wonderful!" Alfred agreed that it was wonderful, too, but he had no idea how the three of them were to live (and work) in the minuscule sublet they were now occupying, or what effect the new family situation would have on his writing. He would soon have other worries as well.[41]

In his note about the Columbia recommendation, Matthiessen had told Kazin he was working on a book, *From the Heart of Europe,* describing his summer experience in Europe. In May, Kazin saw the proofs and was "surprised and pleased" by Matthiessen's "courage." But he was also worried. In the book, Matthiessen wrote of him leading the singing of the *Internationale* at Schloss Leopoldskron. "Did he have to put that in and so little else? Carol jokes that I may not be able to get a passport. It would be horrible if some reactionary jackasses could get me that way." Kazin would have more cause for concern when the book appeared in the summer and he had read it more carefully. Where he had earlier seen "courage," he was now "sickened" by "compromises and bad faith." After attacking economic injustice in America, the Truman Doctrine, and the Henry Luce publications, Matthiessen had pulled his punches with the Soviet Union and had badly misrepresented the political situation in Czechoslovakia, which he had visited after leaving Salzburg. His Czech friends, he wrote, neither feared nor had reason to fear the Soviet Union and were far more alarmed by American attitudes and intentions. Shortly before the book's publication, a Communist minority backed by the security forces seized power in Czechoslovakia, banished all competing parties, and allied the country with the Soviet Union. Matthiessen declined to revise his account and claimed that the American media and the Truman Doctrine "bear a grave responsibility" for having aggravated tensions to the point at which the Communists felt that Socialism was threatened. This was a strange argument. One could sympathize with Matthiessen's views about Luce and the aggressiveness of Truman's foreign policy, but there was no excuse for not calling a coup a coup, a brutal suppression of democratic freedoms. Matthiessen's failure to do so made his book, with all its talk of "community" and "understanding," seem a sentimental piece of propaganda, an act of bad faith.[42]

If Kazin was disgusted by Matthiessen's bad faith, he was moved to near panic with what followed. In October, the *Partisan Review* published a review of the book in which Irving Howe, making full use of his polemical skills, denounced Matthiessen for his "sentimental fellow-traveling," including in the attack a portrait of Kazin leading "a gang of future cultural commissars" in the singing of the *Internationale*. By the fall of 1948, Matthiessen had become a controversial national figure. A strong supporter of Henry Wallace (FDR's former vice president), he had made one of the nominating speeches endorsing Wallace's campaign for the presidency at the Progressive Party convention on July 22 in Philadelphia. The Truman administration, the CIO (Congress of Industrial Organizations), the ADA (Americans for Democratic Action), and the *Partisan* editors had repeatedly denounced the Progressives as a front for the Communists and Wallace as their willing dupe. Matthiessen, a leading literary intellectual, "the most distinguished literary fellow-traveler in this country," according to Howe, was seen lending intellectual and academic prestige to a policy of appeasement. The *Partisan* editors told Howe to give Matthiessen "the works." He had obliged, and, with the editors' evident approval, included Kazin in the attack.[43]

Frightened and angry, Kazin wrote a long letter to the magazine (which he later withdrew), complaining that Howe had identified him with political views that he did not hold—and that Howe knew he did not hold them. He accused him of libeling the Salzburg faculty (among them Gaetano Salvemini, Margaret Mead, and Mario Praz) and the students who came from all over Europe representing all political persuasions. Howe's characterization of the seminar as "a gang of future commissars" showed that he continued to practice "the best adjectival Bolshevik prose" when not writing book reviews for Henry Luce's *Time*. Howe, who undoubtedly saw Kazin's letter before it was withdrawn, immediately wrote him a personal apology and reminded him that he had reviewed *On Native Grounds* favorably (though he had done so under an alias). He also published a letter in the *Partisan* retracting his charge against Kazin: "Since I know that Kazin, as an anti-Stalinist, rejects [Matthiessen's] views, I wish to state that I regret exceedingly any embarrassment or harm my unqualified reference to his role at Salzburg may have played." Kazin was not appeased—then or ever. Howe had shown an impulse for the political jugular that Kazin knew all too well from the thirties and now associated with the "PR [*Partisan Re-*

view] boys." Though he and Howe shared roughly the same political views, often found themselves on the same panels, and eventually became colleagues in the English Department at the City University of New York, Kazin would continue to see him as an unreconstructed "ideologue," ready for the next political fight—the hardened, eager veteran of the City College alcove wars.[44]

Kazin also wrote to Matthiessen accusing him of harboring feelings of "hostility" toward himself and denouncing "the spirit of hatred" that suffused his book. Stunned and hurt, Matthiessen replied that he had only the warmest feelings for Kazin, thought the feeling was mutual, and was sorry for any personal difficulties his book might have caused. He also told him that he had recently put his name forward as someone the Harvard English Department might think of hiring for a visiting professorship (visiting professors sometimes became permanent professors). Kazin wrote back immediately, lamenting the "wasteful misunderstanding" between them. He said that he regretted the charge he made in the letter as soon as he had sent it, but that Matthiessen had no idea "how much the whole business has been used to plague me." He explained that, though they both shared Socialist sympathies, he as a Socialist had long resented the Communists, while Matthiessen saw Socialism as "a moral choice of solidarity with another class." He concluded by attacking "the stale ex-Commies of PR" who "have been knocked out of all generosity and faith by the furious internecine struggles within the radical movement" and by declaring that he was "opposed both to Communism and 'anti-Communism.' "[45]

Though a relatively contained affair, the Howe-Matthiessen-Kazin dispute was a sign of where things were heading. One needed to be careful, to check one's impulses—no more singing the *Internationale* in mixed company. Will they confiscate my passport? Have I given ammunition to the reactionaries? Was the FBI watching? (In fact, the FBI had already opened a file on Kazin, prompted by an article on March 7, 1946, in the *New York Times* stating that he and others—Maxwell Stewart, Elizabeth Ames, Agnes Smedley, Eric Severeid, and Theodore White—had sent a letter to Chiang Kai-shek protesting the arrest, imprisonment, and death of Yang Chao, an editor and employee of the Office of War Information.) Cold war politics were beginning to narrow options. Which side are you on? "A vote for Nixon," declared the would-be freshman congressman from California in

1946, "is a vote against the Communist-dominated PAC [Political Action Committee]" of the Democratic Party "with its gigantic slush fund." Campaigning in Minnesota in 1948, Democrat Hubert Humphrey announced that if he had "to choose between being called a Red-baiter and traitor, I'll be a Red-baiter." But was it necessary to chose? Some, including Kazin, had hoped otherwise, holding out for a "third-camp," "opposed both to Communism and anti-Communism."[46]

The best known of those looking for a third way was Dwight Macdonald, a writer Kazin admired (some of the time) but never much liked. In 1943, Macdonald, who had been on the editorial board of the *Partisan Review*, broke with the magazine to begin his own journal, *Politics*, which he edited and funded and for which he wrote much of the copy. A staunch anti-Stalinist with Marxist sympathies, Macdonald argued, in the words of his biographer, Michael Wreszin, that "a third-camp socialist revolution [was] absolutely necessary to save the Western world from advancing totalitarianism." He saw his magazine as an organ for anti-Stalinist radicals who rejected the injustices of capitalism and the belligerent ambitions of both the East and the West. Reading through back copies in 1958, Kazin remembered how grateful he had been for a journal that refused to excuse Soviet behavior or to defend America's growing militarism on the grounds of political "realism." He had also been grateful to learn early in 1948 that Macdonald, Mary McCarthy, the Italian writer Nicola Chiaromonte, and others were resisting the movement into armed camps by proposing the formation of Europe-America groups to provide material and moral support to European intellectuals caught between Euro-Stalinism and American power.[47]

Kazin attended the first meeting in March and volunteered to work with McCarthy in writing a charter. In it they declared their "solidarity" with intellectuals in Europe, who like themselves were feeling increasingly isolated and powerless "in the face of the extreme polarity of Soviet and American power." While stating that Stalinism is "the main enemy in Europe today," they rejected any identification with American capitalism and "oppose[d] the social and economic and racial inequities this system perpetuates." In lending what support they could to European intellectuals, they were, they repeatedly insisted, "individuals and intellectuals, independent of the State Department and of any other official agency."[48]

The Europe-America groups initiative soon began to founder, however, as high-minded aspirations yielded to cold war realities, specifically to the efforts of the "PR boys" to redirect its idealism along more politically "responsible" lines. Philip Rahv hosted the May meeting and packed it with *Partisan* people who challenged its third-camp intentions and vague humanistic goals. There was deep skepticism about the "principles of internationalism [and] of distributive economic justice," which seemed too close to "neutralism" and smacked of "fellow-traveling." Moreover, it was discovered that the original draft of the charter had been substantially rewritten by Sidney Hook, then in Paris and in contact with Chiaromonte—one of Hook's additions: "we consider the destruction of the Soviet regime (not Russia) as a precondition for peace." McCarthy was discouraged, and Kazin, frustrated and angry. He found the meeting "utterly useless," concluding that "Rahv is a commissar out of a job and Macdonald an utter fool." Still, he continued to attend meetings until the venture folded at the end of the year and to read *Politics* until Macdonald gave it over in 1949. For all his impatience with Macdonald's "smart-alecky writing" and "boring" negativism, Kazin respected him for avoiding the paranoid nationalism of the recently "obsessed" patriots and for his "unashamedly ethical attacks on political realism." But by 1949 it was difficult to find an anti-Stalinist willing to support a "third camp." As for Macdonald, he soon announced his decision to "choose the West."[49]

Outsider/Insider

In early July 1948, the Kazins moved "baby, baggage, books and all" into "the Hill Farm," a country residence of the Bookmans in Solebury, Pennsylvania, not far from New Hope—a popular Bucks County artistic community on the Delaware River. Hoping the move might shake loose the book, Kazin set up shop in a loft over the tool house, where his only distraction was the birds roosting in the beams above his trestle desk. He typically worked until early afternoon and then went for a walk on Solebury Road, occasionally running into Lewis Mumford, who lived nearby. He also took frequent trips into the city to see publishers, to drop off reviews at the *Tribune* or the *New Yorker*, to appear on *Invitation to Learning*, and to visit friends. He found the trips into the city trying—and tempting. "The blousy half-nakedness of the girls in the streets, with that peculiar languor of summer, the faint drops of sweat on their lips, drove me crazy with desire." He resisted, but he wasn't sure why or for how long. "What part of this was 'honor,' what part my love for C., what part mere cowardice, and worse than cowardice, superstition?"[50]

By summer's end, the book had barely moved. Kazin's most significant achievements were a piece on André Gide's *Journals* for the *New Yorker* and a *Herald Tribune* review of Thomas Mann's *Doctor Faustus*. Mann wrote thanking him for his "beautiful appreciation" and for restoring his faith in the "intellectual level of the American literary critique," though he objected to Kazin's interpreting the hero, Adrian Leverkuhn, as an allegorical figure of Germany. Kazin was also moving ahead with an omnibus piece, "The Mindless Young Militants," for *Commentary* on American war novels. But all this counted for little beside his stalled book, and now he had to look for a new apartment and prepare lectures on Melville and Whitman for his New School course.[51]

Although too distracted to prepare as carefully as he liked, he assembled a two-semester course on American literature that apparently went over well with at least one student. "I like this guy because he is excited," wrote Jack Kerouac in his diary after talking with Kazin following one class. "He stumbles about, chatting away, almost getting run over by trucks, eager, stuttering, proud, a little piqued at this world, which makes him cast furtive looks out of the corner of his eye. Calls me 'John.'" Kerouac, who wrote a paper for the course, "Whitman: A Prophet of the Sexual Revolution," remembers how "marvelously" Kazin "'blew' on Whitman, Melville, Twain, Thoreau, Emerson"—marvelously enough to persuade him that Kazin might look favorably on a novel he was just finishing. Kazin was sufficiently impressed by *The Town and the City* (1950) to send a note of recommendation to Robert Giroux, editor at Harcourt. He would be far less enthusiastic about Kerouac's later "spontaneous" efforts, *On the Road* and *Doctor Sax*, "scribbled swiftly," Kerouac told him, "in a toilet in Mexico City in 1952." Kerouac's "verbal violence," Kazin later wrote of *On the Road* (which had become a best seller by 1958), cannot hide the fact that he "writes not so much *about* things as about the search for things to write about."[52]

In November, the Kazins moved into another small sublet at 415 Central

Park West. Alfred disliked it intensely. They were eating with other people's silverware; he had no room of his own (with a door) to write in; and the wallpaper in the bedroom with its view of the lakes of Killarney sickened him "with its irrelevance." The book, the pokey apartment, the lack of a steady income—all left him feeling helpless, frustrated, angry. "If you want to know what it is like to be . . . making a living at teaching in New York" without a job, he wrote to Richard Chase, who taught American literature a Columbia, "I can tell you what it is really like." Carol bore the brunt of his unhappiness, and he knew it. "Story of a marriage here between a frustrated writer and his wife: the writer acting out on his wife all he has not found in his life to work and therefore condemning the marriage as well." But there was also some good news. In April the Harvard English Department offered him a visiting lectureship for the coming fall. Although Matthiessen advised him that such openings do not turn up often, Kazin turned it down. Teaching at Harvard would mean putting off the book—perhaps forever. In May, he learned that he had been awarded a one-thousand-dollar grant from the National Institute of Arts and Letters, enabling him to take a leave from teaching at the New School to concentrate on the book.[53]

In fact, he was making progress—in attitude and conception, if not in the number of finished pages. Kazin had conceived of his project as a meditation based on walks through various neighborhoods of New York—a spiritual travelogue told in "images of solitude that embrace the world by defining the distance between it and the walking man." But excerpts from *The Open Street* and journal entries suggest someone less interested in embracing the world than in protecting himself from it—"My theme," he had written in 1947, "the assault on personality, the struggle for the safe guarding of personality." "My theme more than ever," he wrote in the summer of 1948, "the alienation of man from present institutions." The stress on "self"-protection and the need to cultivate an "alienated" solitary stance were consistent with a deepening concern about the "totalitarian" threat to the self and the postwar mood of radical individualism ("existentialism") that had replaced radical politics in New York intellectual circles. They were also consistent with Kazin's interest in Melville and other American interpreters of "man's separateness on earth," as well as with his own preoccupation with solitude and loneliness. But they were also frustrating his efforts to understand his deeper, more complex relations with the city.

Partly the problem was "literary." He was seeing the city through writers' eyes other than his own. He was still too much the critic, he later said of his difficulties, "with a critic's weakness for ideas." He had not found a way to get himself into the book. But it was also attitudinal. The "theme" of alienation was trapping him in a self-pitying rhetoric of complaint. "Walking along Amsterdam . . . I felt my mind crushed by the inexpressible anarchic rot."[54]

By the fall, however, there were signs of change. "Walking in the street as usual, between boredom and fatalism," he wrote in an October 1949 journal entry, "I nevertheless realize to the depths of my being something I have so rarely admitted to myself—that I am grounded in this city, these streets, among these people, as a matter of course, without even the possibility of hypothetical denial." New York might look like a spiritual wasteland, but, as he seemed to have forgotten in his stress on the alien city, it was also his home; he was part of it—not just *in* the city, but *of* it, with no possibility of denial. He continued to find the alien and ugly on his walks— "the pile, the rubbishy pile: the refuse of commercialism strewn along the streets." But he was also increasingly alert to the personal and the transcendent, the deeper, unspoken sources of his attachment. "Along the River Road. Picking up the old life as I go, walking parallel to the river, I feel that I march along side my hidden genius, who sleeps in the river at my side. How slowly and gently he paces me, leading me on. At night the towers are hooded, and in the faint light up from the boats in the river and the lights from the other side, they hulk over the bridge. When you start from the Brooklyn side in the misty rain, you see—first and last—the towers over the bay. Their gray is luminescent despite the mist, concentrated by the mist. They gleam over the bay, pyramids and watchtowers, the first and the last things here."[55]

Another development was beginning to play into his evolving conception of the book—changing attitudes toward Jews and Jewishness. In the 1944 "Under Forty" symposium, Kazin had said that being a Jew in America did not entail "being part of any meaningful Jewish life or culture," and he firmly rejected the parochialism that singled out Jewish life in America as a special area of cultural interest. He knew there were talented Jewish writers in America, but, as he noted in a later essay, they were "boxed in mentally" by "the poverty and hopelessness of their upbringing." By the late forties, however, as the economy continued to grow and prospering Jews were abandoning the ghetto in droves, want and despair seemed less appropriate responses to circumstances than pride, ambivalence, nostalgia, and a more challenging engagement with the surrounding culture—attitudes that suggested new areas of interest and new stories to tell for writers describing their experiences as Jews and Americans.[56]

The Holocaust, or rather the persisting and intensifying accounts of the Holocaust, also contributed to changing attitudes toward Jewishness. The enormity of the crime had been working its way into the consciousness and unconsciousness of Jewish writers since the war. "We do not understand what happened to the Jews of Europe, and perhaps we never will," wrote Kazin's friend Isaac Rosenfeld in 1948. "Here is the 'extreme' situation, beyond all extremes—incomprehensible, unattainable to reason." Initially, the New York writers had said little about the Holocaust, the horror of which defied comprehension. Instead, as Alexander Bloom has shown, they began to talk to each other about their Jewishness. History had left them little choice. "We could no longer escape the conviction that, blessing or curse, Jewishness was an integral part of our life," Irving Howe would later remark. At the time, Howe and Daniel Bell wrote autobiographical essays describing their ambivalence and "uneasiness" as Jews, Americans, and intellectuals—never satisfyingly at home in any camp. Saul Bellow in *The Victim* (1948) takes up the question of Jewish guilt and deals obliquely with issues raised by the tragedy (anti-Semitism and Jewish victimization). If the Holocaust remained a subject too "extreme" to approach directly, Jewishness and Jewish matters were subjects that Jewish writers and intellectuals were increasingly willing, even eager, to discuss. And many non-Jews in a post-Hitler, increasingly philo-Semitic America seemed ready to listen.[57]

No one understood this better than Elliot Cohen, the editor of *Commentary;* and no journal did more to argue the centrality of Jewish concerns and their vital connection with postwar America. Cohen, who had become editor in 1945, was determined that *Commentary* not be seen as "narrow, sectarian, provincial" in the way many had viewed its predecessor, the *Contemporary Jewish Record.* In a series of editorial essays that bear a surprising resemblance to the prophetic cultural nationalism of Walt Whitman, Van Wyck Brooks, and Randolph Bourne, Cohen predicted (correctly it turned out) that *Commentary* marked the emergence of a Jewish-American cultural renaissance that would thrive through "the most open association" with "the native and foreign born groups among whom we live." The arrival of this vibrant, new Jewish-American culture could not be "blueprinted" or subjected to "principled criteria." Rather, it would rise "spontaneously from the minds and hearts of men." "We have talked of and hoped for a cultural pluralism in American life. Is it too much to ask for a cultural pluralism in Jewish thinking and culture too?"[58]

A Jewish critic-intellectual, an authority on modern and American writing, Kazin was precisely the kind of writer Cohen wanted in his magazine, and Kazin was happy to contribute. He was personally pleased with the magazine—"'the people of the book' have become the people of the magazine." It paid reasonably well. He approved of its heterodox editorial policy —though he bridled at Cohen's editorial meddling. He "simply can't let any piece alone after he has bought it." Its intellectual level was impressive. Whatever one thought of individual articles, the magazine raised the kinds of issues he wanted discussed—Jewishness versus Judaism, Israel and the Diaspora, Jews and modernism, Jewish-American writers and the immigrant past. *Commentary* not only took these and other controversial subjects seriously, it encouraged their vigorous debate, typically leaving matters unresolved and in dispute—all of which suggested to Kazin that his own unsettled and heterodox views on Jewishness might meet with an interested reception were he to raise them in his accounts of his walks about the city.[59]

Another issue on the minds of Jewish writers (including Kazin's) in postwar America was anti-Semitism—not so much in American life, where quotas and old barriers seemed to be coming down, as in the literary culture. In February 1949, a committee of literary luminaries, W. H. Auden, Robert Lowell, Allen Tate, and T. S. Eliot, voted to give the prestigious Bollingen Award for poetry to the unreconstructed Fascist and notorious anti-Semite Ezra Pound. The action stunned many in the Jewish literary community and raised painful questions about the attitudes of their Gentile colleagues. (Karl Shapiro, the only Jew on the selection committee, voted against Pound.) Angry letters defending and denouncing the decision appeared in the *Partisan Review,* the *Saturday Review,* and *Commentary.* Clement Greenberg wrote that the decision to award the prize to

Pound left him "physically afraid." But the issues raised by the award went beyond Pound's anti-Semitism. In a provocative *Commentary* essay—"What Can We Do about Fagin?"—Leslie Fiedler asked whether it was not time for Jews to acknowledge the virulent strain of anti-Semitism running through English literature. "In the light of Dachau," how are Jews to feel about a literature that, from Chaucer's "Prioress's Tale" to Shakespeare's Shylock, to Dickens's Fagin, to Pound's *Cantos,* is rife with unflattering, even vicious, portraits of Jews? Fiedler added that the "moderns" posed a particularly painful problem. After Hitler, how to respond to Eliot's "Bleistein with a cigar," to Hemingway's nasty portrait of Robert Cohn in *The Sun Also Rises,* to Pound's vicious slander? Is it not time "to admit that Western culture is basically hostile to us as Jews?" "What response can we make to a culture in which so terrible and perilous a myth of ourselves is inextricably involved?"[60]

Recognizing the seriousness of the issue, *Commentary* solicited views from its contributors. Most acknowledged the problem but agreed with Lionel Trilling that it would be a mistake to make too much of anti-Semitism, which he claimed was an "accidental" rather than an "essential" characteristic of our literary tradition. Kazin was less sanguine. He shared Fiedler's apparent dismay, but went further, noting that the writers who most interest Jewish intellectuals were precisely those who say the worst things about Jews—"the nasty ones, the clever modern ones—a Dostoevsky, a Henry James, a Henry Adams, an André Gide, a Santayana, a Cummings, a Céline, an Eliot, a Pound. How we love them, though they love us not." Indeed, Kazin argues, what Jewish intellectuals value in these modern writers—their troubled status as modern exiles—is exactly what the modernists hate about Jews. However, "If we [Jews] wrote of Pound as he writes of us, who would pass judgment on anyone and give him the prize?"[61]

Kazin's response, as Alexander Bloom noted, "struck the central chord" in the debate. Not only are Jews isolated in Western culture, they are despised because they symbolize better than anyone else the qualities of isolation, alienation, and exile that "the moderns" hate in themselves and in modern life. But if Kazin was the only one to deal fully with the ironies of the Jews' predicament, he was not happy with his response. "How awful, how shameful," he wrote in a journal entry, "is the self-pity and theatrical isolation of the contribution of mine to the *Commentary* symposium."

Far from being a stranger in the Anglo-American literary tradition, I am morally at the very center of it. I [may] not belong to the "official party," and thank
God that I do not; I am rather a sentinel of the truly universal experience and
far, far closer to the central moral problems in modern literature by reason of
my being a Jew, than I can possibly say . . . I realize more deeply than ever
before that so many of the cultural fixtures I mechanically equate with pain,
are, in truth, sources of very deep pleasure and enrichment to me—America
itself in the larger sense and myself as a Jew. What has always kept me from
affirming my positive affirmation for them more clearly, is my fear that if I did,
I would be false to my inner estrangements, to my untiring awareness of the
rift at the heart of our culture.[62]

Kazin's second thoughts about his *Commentary* response nicely encap-
sulate the outsider/insider paradox that Jewish writers faced in America.
He was gratified to be an outsider (a Jew in America), which placed him at
the center of the moral problems (alienation, estrangement, exile) that
marked the modern condition. He felt he could speak with personal authority from within the culture, much as he felt he had done fifteen years
earlier in the writing of *On Native Grounds*. There, Alfred Kazin, the
"outsider," "the first American-born son of so many thousands of mud-flat,
Jewish-Polish-Russian generations," had turned himself into an outsider/
insider through an act of imaginative sympathy with other "alienated"
American writers based on a shared sense of dispossession that ironically
brought him inside the tradition. "This literature was mine—I felt part of it
and at home with it." What he dared not let himself forget either out of
"self-pity" or by "mechanically" equating the fixtures of contemporary culture with pain, were the "pleasure and enrichment" that derived from the
ironies and contradictions of his being a Jew and an American—a condition
that would yield more discoveries as he worked (or lurched) toward the
final version of *A Walker in the City*.[63]

"A Profoundly Anti-Liberal and Anti-Intellectual Tyranny"

By the end of the 1940s writers and intellectuals seemed increasingly eager
to debate all manner of issues pertaining to Jews and Jewishness. No similar
sense of freedom existed on political matters, however, where fear, suspicion, and intolerance seemed to grow weekly. People believed they were

being watched—with good reason. In November 1948, another item had been added to Kazin's FBI file—a clipping from the *Newark Evening News* listing him (along with Alexander Meikeljohn, Lewis Mumford, and Norman Thomas) as a member of the James Kutcher Civil Rights Committee. A Purple Heart veteran and double amputee, Kutcher had been dismissed from his job at the Veterans Administration because of his membership in the Socialist Workers Party, one of several hundred groups included on the attorney general's list of subversive organizations. Kazin told Kutcher, who won his case against dismissal in 1959, that he disagreed with Kutcher's political views but was "indignant" that he should lose his job for them.[64]

He had other opportunities for indignation. On March 1, 1949, the poet Robert Lowell, on the verge of a nervous breakdown, joined with three other Yaddo guests—Elizabeth Hardwick, Flannery O'Connor, and the composer Edward Meisel—to request that the Yaddo directors fire the executive director, Elizabeth Ames, for harboring an alleged Communist sympathizer and Soviet agent, Agnes Smedley. In February, the army had issued a MacArthur report citing Smedley, a correspondent who had done work in China and the Soviet Union, as a likely traitor. Within days the army withdrew the charges, but suspicions had been aroused. The FBI sent agents to Yaddo to interview Ames and the guests, and Lowell quickly convinced himself that under Ames's leadership the place had been turned into a den of Communist spies and subversives. In his charge to the board, Lowell called Yaddo a "body" and Ames "a diseased organ, chronically poisoning the whole system." He warned that he had "influential friends in the world of culture" and would be informing them of the conditions at Yaddo. Elizabeth Hardwick, meanwhile, warned potential guests to stay away. One of these, Dwight Macdonald, who had been planning a visit, immediately informed Ames that he would not be coming and expressed outrage that Yaddo had become a "center for pro-Soviet propaganda."[65]

Kazin, Eleanor Clark, and a few other Yaddo regulars were appalled by the charges. They knew Ames was no subversive. They also knew of the unbalanced emotional state of Lowell, whose sickness, according to one observer, "required a conspiracy." A letter-writing campaign was organized with a petition to rebut the charges against Ames, calling them "thoroughly foolish and nasty . . . a perfect example of the use of innuendo and personal disparagement in lieu of evidence." The board quickly dismissed all charges and kept Ames on as director. Kazin was relieved but disgusted, not only with Lowell and his cohorts, but with others who knew Ames was innocent but had refused to write letters, explaining that they " 'could not take the risk.' " "The artist under political stress," he later wrote in *New York Jew,* "was an unforgettable picture of limitless self-regard."[66]

By 1949, the stress was real enough. The Communist coup in Czechoslovakia in the spring of 1948 had been followed in June by the Berlin blockade. In Asia, the Chinese Red Army under Mao Ze Dong had consolidated gains in the north and was marching into Manchuria with the forces of Chiang Kai-shek in full retreat. Driven by events abroad and provoked by HUAC investigations of Communist subversion at home (including headline trials of the "Hollywood Ten," of alleged traitor Alger Hiss, and of the eleven top officials of the Communist Party), anti-Communism dominated the country's political discourse as well as the attention of many intellectuals. In March 1949, Sidney Hook, leading a select army of prominent anti-Stalinists, organized a conference and rally to counter (and subvert) the famous Waldorf Conference to promote peace and understanding between America and the Soviet Union. Kazin was not asked to join. Hook later attributed Kazin's notable absence to the fact that he was not enough of "a big shot." Kazin said Hook didn't consider him anti-Communist enough. In fact, it is doubtful Kazin would have participated had Hook asked him personally to do so. He had never enjoyed direct political confrontation, whether staged in the ballrooms of the Waldorf Astoria or the alcoves of City College.[67]

But if Kazin shied away from public political debate, he was willing on occasion to talk politics in a book review or critical essay. In August 1949, he agreed to do a piece for the *Partisan Review* on Richard Chase's *Herman Melville: A Critical Study.* The editors had discussed the book with him, and he sensed an opportunity (far preferable to shouting from the back of a hotel ballroom) to explain what was troubling him about the current political-cultural scene. At the center of his discontent was the trend among intellectuals, many of them former radicals, to make Stalinism (particularly liberals' susceptibility to Stalinism) the centerpiece of their thinking on virtually all subjects—including literature. Kazin was himself an anti-Stalinist; he believed that Soviet-style Communism represented a serious threat to human freedom; and he supported a "realistic" foreign policy that would check the expansionist ambitions of the Soviet Union. He also acknowledged that in the past certain liberals and progressives had been too willing to overlook the threat of Stalinism. However, he did not believe that "realism" toward the Soviet Union called for a repudiation of one's liberal beliefs and values (and associations), or that anti-Communism could be translated into a literary-critical-cultural program for interpreting and evaluating writers and works—which is what he saw happening in Chase's book on Melville.

Chase said as much himself. "My purpose," he stated in the preface, "is to contribute a book on Melville to a movement which may be described (once again) as the 'new liberalism.' " He then aligned Melville's characters with key concepts of the "new liberalism." Ishmael is "young America—the revolutionary nation"; Ahab is "the progressive American," sure of the righteousness of his own motives; Pierre is "the well meaning idealist," disarmed by "our liberal-democratic thought"; and so on. Kazin, who had a keen eye for the absurdities of academic method run amok and little patience with criticism that ignored the distinctively personal-creative interests of the writer, had fun ridiculing Chase's reductive symbology, noting that the only figure not allegorized in the tendentious scheme was the reader as "The Chastened American Liberal Who Has Turned His Back on Stalinism and Progressivism." Titled "Melville as Scripture," the piece indicated what happens when literature is used to inculcate doctrine—an ideological reduction that Kazin saw occurring in the culture at large as the "new liberalism" became the most intellectually respectable form of anti-Communism.[68]

Chase's book was one example. Lionel Trilling's 1946 attack on Theodore Dreiser was another. There, Trilling argued that the liberals' "doctrinaire indulgence" of Dreiser reflected the same "intellectual vulgarity" to be found in Dreiser's anti-Semitism and his decision to join the Communist Party. (Trilling would achieve his greatest influence as a scourge of the old liberalism with the publication of *The Liberal Imagination* in 1951, a collection of essays, a number of which link liberalism with Stalinism.) In 1949, Arthur Schlesinger's *The Vital Center* (cited in Kazin's piece) represented the most complete statement of the "new liberalism" to date. Drawing on the thinking of Reinhold Niebuhr, Schlesinger argued that recent history—totalitarianism, Fascism, "the degeneration of the Soviet Union" —had (or should have) taught a lesson in moral realism that acknowledged humanity's capacity for evil and the illusoriness of nineteenth-century "liberal" theories of progress. He was particularly critical of liberals for embracing theories of human perfectibility and failing to anticipate or effectively confront "the totalitarians of the left," who had fed off long habits of "official optimism" and a blind trust in human goodwill.[69]

Kazin did not wholly disagree with this. "Chastened" like many other thirties radicals, he acknowledged that the liberal left (including himself) had placed too much hope in the automatic progress of society, "the sweep of history." But he also rejected the "'guilty' apocalyptic morality" that had been seeping into the consciences of American intellectuals since the war. If, as Schlesinger complained, an "official optimism" had set the tone for political-cultural discourse in the thirties, that optimism, Kazin believed, had been overtaken by an equally "official," or "party-line," pessimism that evaluated people, politics, and literature by its own grim formulas. He rejected the claims of Chase, Trilling, Schlesinger, and others to a higher order of wisdom that dismisses as "sentimental," "soft headed," and "shallow" more hopeful views of human possibility. And he resented "the lesser evil" argument scornfully directed by the "new liberals" at "'utopians and wailers'" who in their protest against inequities in American society were thought insufficiently mindful of how much worse things always are in the Soviet Union. "Not to be taken in by the 'realists,'" Kazin had written in a journal entry of April 2, 1947. "Not to surrender to life construed only as politics. Life does not end because there are bad and hopeless days; life will survive even this totalitarian ice age. Always and always to hold out for cardinal values. And to live by them, whatever 'they' say, whoever 'they' are at the moment. Against all policies of the lesser evil, in one's life as in one's politics; against all pessimism glossed as social interpretation; against all theories which begin by fitting our human universe to their iron measures."[70]

It would be some time before life would wrench free of the iron measures of politics. Following up on the 1949 Waldorf Conference, *Life* magazine, citing the threat of international Communism and the propagandistic efforts of the Kremlin, ran a two-page spread featuring pictures of prominent intellectuals whom the publisher, Henry Luce, felt were soft on Communism—"a rogues gallery of American leftists," as Kazin later called it—that included Albert Einstein, Leonard Bernstein, Arthur Miller, Thomas Mann, Frank Lloyd Wright, and Kazin's teacher and friend, Mark Van

Doren. The fear and suspicion deepened on August 5, when the State
Department announced that China had fallen to the Red Army, and deepened further in September, when the administration reported to a frightened public that the Russians had detonated an atomic bomb. On January
21, 1950, Alger Hiss, whose trials had been making headlines for more than
a year, was convicted of perjury. Three weeks later the junior senator from
Wisconsin, Joseph McCarthy, delivered a speech to the Women's Republican Club of Wheeling, West Virginia, announcing that he had a list of 205
members of the Communist Party who "were still working and shaping the
policy of the State Department." The cold wind Kazin had felt three years
earlier had turned into a gale.[71]

On April 19, 1950, he notified Sol Levitas, managing editor of the *New
Leader,* that he was backing out of a promised book review. He did not want
to appear in the magazine. Founded in 1928 as an official publication of the
Socialist Party, the *New Leader* had a long history of supporting Socialist
and labor causes. Kazin, who knew many of its contributors, including its
former editor (and his future brother-in-law) Daniel Bell, was a frequent
reader and very occasional contributor. Though not as politically minded as
most of its writers, he respected the magazine, not least for its longtime
principled struggle against Communism. But by 1950, that struggle, in
Kazin's view, had turned irresponsible and vicious. Instead of exerting the
intellectual discipline one might have expected from a respected journal of
political opinion, it was joining McCarthy and the red-baiters of HUAC,
attacking indiscriminately Communists, fellow travelers, liberals—or, indeed, anyone who dared to disagree with its writers. Kazin cited a recent
front-page article backing McCarthy's attack on Judge Dorothy Kenyon for
having allegedly been "connected with fellow-traveling causes." It was, he
said, but one of many pieces "lump[ing] together Stalinism, FDR, the
mildest liberalism" with the clear and "revolt[ing]" implication that all pose
equally serious threats to the nation's security. "These are ticklish times for
American intellectuals," he concluded. "I ask myself every day *where* this
intellectual reign of terror is going to end. . . . I seriously and thoroughly
believe that important as it is to fight Stalinism tooth and nail, the deep
suspicion in this country of all social ideals . . . [is] leading us into a profoundly anti-liberal and anti-intellectual tyranny. I have never in my life
seen so many people afraid to express an idea that may possibly be inter-

preted 'the wrong way.' This sort of thing has to be fought, right here, not just the Stalinists." The letter was not published, and it is doubtful Kazin intended it to be. He had no desire to engage in public polemics with the *New Leader*. He may also have worried that it would be interpreted "the wrong way." In the same April 1, 1950, issue attacking Judge Kenyon, the *New Leader* included a letter titled "Why We Write for the *New Leader*," signed by Arthur Schlesinger, Reinhold Niebuhr, Sidney Hook, and Alfred Kazin, supporting the magazine as "America's leading periodical." Whatever his private reservations about the magazine's red-baiting during these "ticklish times," Kazin was proud to back it in public.[72]

CHAPTER SIX

A Walker in the City

Yet as I walk those familiarly choked streets at dusk and see the old women sitting in front of the tenements, past and present become each other's faces: I am back where I began.

—*A Walker in the City*

Writing can be a frighteningly uncertain activity. How does a writer like Kazin find his way into a book he thinks he wants to write? How does he know when he has found his true subject, his right voice, the proper approach? The uncertainties are more daunting if he is attempting something new, drawing on untested talents with few obvious models or precedents. By the fall of 1949, Kazin had been working on his New York book for three years and was feeling as lost and desperate as ever. After a second summer working in the tool shed at Solebury, he had a completed draft. But reading it over with much "fear and trembling" he despaired. Except for a short segment, nothing sounded right. The exception was an account of a childhood conversation with a Mrs. Solovey, who lived on the first floor of his family's Brownsville tenement. In September he took the excerpt to the *New Yorker* offices to see whether Shawn was interested. "I was sweating so profusely that I could not stand his looking at me, and fled as soon as I could"—a painful replay of earlier meetings with Cowley at the *New Republic*. Shawn turned it down. It appeared in the January issue of *Commentary* as "The Woman Downstairs." Nothing else in the manuscript seemed to work, and Kazin was beginning to think there might be no solution.[1]

Eight months later, all had changed. The once wavering book was on track; Kazin believed (correctly) that he had found his true subject and that he had worked out the proper method to treat it. What had happened? Why had everything suddenly fallen into place? One can cite different reasons. Kazin's personal life had undergone a shock that had shaken him emotionally but also (he believed) allowed him to tap into "self-suppressed" creative energies. Prevailing cultural winds were blowing in a direction that suggested there might be receptive readers for a very different kind of narrative from the one he had originally planned. He was also looking to different models for precedent and guidance in the use of literary talents he had not known he possessed. In the end his patience, his uncompromising criticism of his own work, and his determination to write something that was "emotionally authentic" paid off. He produced a book very different from his groundbreaking *On Native Grounds* but in its own way as impressive. During the more than fifty years since its publication, *A Walker in the City* has become the most popular and widely read of Kazin's books, "a classic account of the first American-born generation," "a central text of Jewish-American writing."[2]

"Living a Lie"

If any single event precipitated the changes in Kazin's life and work in 1950, it was a visit to Yaddo in the late fall of 1949. Supported by the one-thousand-dollar grant from the National Institute of Arts and Letters, he had taken the semester off from the New School to concentrate on the book; and in early November, frustrated with distractions at home, he boarded the train to Saratoga Springs and Yaddo—there to "be impaled on nothing but my work." But there were new distractions. During the day he worked diligently on the book, but in the evening he was much diverted by the presence of two women who were about to enter his life in important ways—Jean Garrigue, a thirty-seven-year-old poet, and Josephine Herbst, a fifty-seven-year-old novelist whose works Kazin had reviewed in the thirties. The two women had just met at Yaddo. Lonely and at a low ebb in their different careers, Garrigue and Herbst were finding in each other qualities and needs that would lead to an intense if not always happy relationship lasting until Herbst's death in 1969. Yaddo that November, according to Eleanor Langer, Herbst's biographer, was an opening moment of resurgent "romantic" excitement for both of them: "a brilliant and passionate younger woman momentarily forlorn and an ostensibly serene older one offering wisdom from a seemingly endless well." Kazin was attracted to both for different reasons, and they to him.[3]

He had been wrestling with his desire for other women for some time and worrying that his unsatisfied needs might be responsible for his difficulties with *Walker*. Arriving at Yaddo, he could not keep his mind off a young woman on the train, "not all attractive," who nonetheless excited him and provoked him to further reflections on the connection between his "erotic ache" and the fact that he had "been so impotent on the book." Whether the connection was valid or a rationalization, Kazin was soon working on the book in the day and making love to Jean Garrigue at night. A talented, ambitious poet, Garrigue was a passionate and emotionally demanding lover as well as a lesbian, a fact that Kazin felt enhanced her sexual attractiveness. He would remember her as a "difficult, delicious lady . . . whose claim on life was so angry and aggrieved for all her sexy silkiness." She would remember him from Yaddo and a few sexual encounters in New York as a faithless lover from whom she had hoped for something better. "I alternate," she later wrote him, "between hating your memory thoroughly —but this is too human—and throwing cold stones over it that it may be obliterated. But I do remember." Although their affair was short, they would remain in touch, largely out of mutual concern for Josephine Herbst.[4]

Kazin's interest in Herbst was not sexual, but generational, cultural, even, to a degree, filial. A once prominent figure in the twenties and thirties and a friend of Hemingway and Dos Passos, she had reported on the International Congress of Revolutionary Writers in Kharkov in 1922, the Paris café scene in 1924 (where she met Hemingway and her husband John Herrmann), the peasant guerilla movement in Cuba in 1934, the resistance efforts in Berlin in 1935, and the conditions in Madrid during the Spanish Civil War. She used impressions garnered from her travels as well as from her Iowa childhood to produce five novels, which together with hundreds of essays and articles constitute an extensive personal record of the period between the wars. Her reputation did not survive the war years, however. Divorced, without any immediate family, her Depression-era novels long out of print, she lived alone in a farmhouse in Erwinna, Pennsylvania, making occasional visits to Yaddo and New York, her friendships with literary and political luminaries now largely a memory.

Herbst had reason to be resentful of Kazin, who, after praising her novels in his early reviews, had disparaged their "desperate pedestrianism" in *On Native Grounds,* a book that helped bury the proletarian fiction of the thirties. However, she quickly put aside whatever resentment she may have felt when the young, handsome writer sought her out at Yaddo, told her how much her writing had meant to him early in his career, and declared himself still a "revolutionary" who shared her radical values. This was not empty talk. Kazin, like others of his generation, including Saul Bellow, who also befriended Herbst, recognized in the fiery fighter for social justice some of the literary excitement and political idealism that had flourished in the intrawar years. To radicals and idealists like Bellow and Kazin, "trapped in the fifties," she was, Eleanor Langer wrote, "a treasure from an earlier period," a "vivid embodiment of a life lived according to principle"—or as Kazin put it in his 1969 memorial, an unmistakable instance of the "burning old-fashioned American idealism . . . that was the gift of the Middle West to so many writers of her generation." As the friend and confidant of many writers, she was also someone to whom he felt he could turn if and when he needed sympathy and support.[5]

Kazin returned to New York as frustrated as ever. "I keep on wanting two things—the family, and freedom of sexual exploration; 'security,' and the elementary rights of my complicated, sensual, and propulsive nature." He was, he felt, "the fool of virtue," lost and crying "to be saved from the fierce hungry sharks of his own nature." And he was increasingly convinced that until he reached some "new understanding," some resolution to his conflicting needs, he would not be able to move ahead with "the *Walker.*" In early January, the tension that had been building around work, family, and his sexual needs erupted in an angry dispute with Carol that broke far beyond the boundaries of their usual disagreements. Alfred knew immediately that something had snapped. "It's bad, very bad—I feel sick in every bone," he wrote to Josephine Herbst, hoping that she would remember him kindly—"and now I really need a friend." His marriage, he explained, "has gone on the rocks," and "two people are walking up and down in this house with an awful coldness between them, and a child to worry about, and in each the memory of another failure in marriage behind them." Alfred blamed himself, his "harsh angry words" uttered "in protest" against Carol—"a wonderful and very mature gal." And he was alarmed about the immediate future, fearing that he would soon be alone again. "It is about this aloneness that I am writing," he told Herbst, and the feeling that he had "just been expelled from everything." The letter is a cry, almost a child's cry, for help, sympathy, reassurance against approaching desolation.[6]

He and Carol did not separate immediately; but by early February, the direction of events was clear. Their lease of the sublet was ending, and Carol was seeking an apartment of her own. "And so begins," Kazin wrote to Herbst, "that long travail . . . in which for the sake of the child, one goes on having relations with the other, in the merest, formalist, coldest sense, and one hopes against hope that it will work out, while deep in one's heart there is this knowledge that there's no reaching the other." Whether or how much Kazin genuinely hoped that things would work out would not be clear for some time. One moment, he was exulting in his freedom "to stand alone, to love where I please and whom I please." The next, he was hoping things might be patched up. Writing long letters to Herbst and to Garrigue, whom he looked forward to seeing soon in New York, helped keep his spirits up. Talking with friends also helped—Chaim and Diana Raphael, "who brought me back to life" after an initial period of shock; Monroe Engel, a young editor friend at Viking Press; and Mario Salvadori, the Kazins' one-time guide to Italy and confidant of Carol. Salvadori was especially helpful, "a diviner," who "sees things with an eerie clarity . . . a wonderful reader of people." "More than the others it was Salvadori who made [me] look squarely at the hopeless truth of my relations with Carol, and away, with new love and hope for myself." On March 6, Alfred moved out of their apartment into a sublet at 339 East Fifty-eighth Street.[7]

If Salvadori was Kazin's "diviner," Heinrich Bluecher was his "reality instructor," a favorite phrase Kazin picked up from Saul Bellow indicating someone who had authority in areas where one most needed it—though there was no telling how authoritative that authority might be. Bluecher was Hannah Arendt's husband, and by 1950, both had become important people (and instructors) in Kazin's life. He left vivid accounts of their marriage in New York Jew and A Lifetime Burning in Every Moment—"the most passionate seminar I would ever witness between a man and a woman living together." Arendt, a Jewish refugee from Hitler's Germany, a director of Jewish Cultural Reconstruction, and an editor at Schocken Books, typically set the intellectual agenda in their household seminars (attended by selected guests), which in the late forties were often on anti-Semitism, the decline of the nation-state, the concentration camps, and the origins of totalitarianism. Kazin remembers the excitement and sense of reassurance he felt listening to Arendt explain the camps, the emergence of the superfluous man, racism and "the break" in modern thought—all in the shabby apartment she and Bluecher rented across from "the unenterable enemy territory that was Morningside Park." Listening to her line up her authorities—"she quoted, quoted, quoted," from Spinoza, Nietzsche, Marx, Duns Scotus, Montesquieu—he felt that he could see signs of intellectual and spiritual order rising out of the chaos and horrors that had overtaken the modern world. At a time when history had seemingly overwhelmed mind, Arendt was determined to use mind, her mind and the greatest minds, whose words were always at her fingertips, to understand and reconnect with history. "She gave her friends—writers so various as Robert Lowell, Randall Jarrell, Mary McCarthy, the Jewish historian, Salo Baron—intellectual courage before the moral terror that the war had willed to us." History may have been made (or broken) in Munich, in Berlin, in Warsaw, in the camps; but Kazin felt he was watching it take new shape in the formation of *The Origins of Totalitarianism* in a run-down apartment on West Ninety-fifth Street "secured by two locks and a pole." He contributed by listening, responding, editing ("Englishing") the manuscript of her book and procuring a publisher for it.[8]

Bluecher, a German and a veteran of World War I, was part of the conversation, "growling his thought out as if he were still on the battlefield—against wrong-headed philosophers." A Protestant from a working-class background, he had joined the Sparticist League after the war and developed considerable skill as an orator campaigning (unsuccessfully) for the German Communists. With only a patchy formal education, Bluecher had read widely and intensively in philosophy and political science during the twenties while familiarizing himself with Berlin's artistic scene. With the rise of the National Socialists he had fled to Paris, where he met Arendt and began the long-running "seminar" about politics and philosophy that would mark their married life. Despite differences in formal education—Arendt had studied philosophy at Marburg with Martin Heidegger (with whom she had had an intense if brief romantic affair) and completed a doctorate on St. Augustine at Heidelberg under Karl Jaspers—Bluecher proved an ideal intellectual companion for Arendt. She credited him with invaluable contributions to *The Origins of Totalitarianism,* which she referred to as "our book." Outside observers, however, noting that Bluecher never wrote anything for publication, saw things differently. Diana Trilling, according to David Laskin, claimed that Arendt kept Bluecher "chained to her bedpost so he would always be there when she needed him." "Hannah pretended Blücher was her intellectual equal, but he wasn't," insisted Lionel Abel. "He was a nobody." Kazin was more generous. "Heinrich was her partner. There was no tension between them over their intellectual standing or accomplishments. They did not compete with each other. It was not a typical American marriage." He remembers Bluecher as "unstoppably *mental,*" "shouting philosophy at you in the sweetest kind of way." Kazin later helped Bluecher get a teaching post at the New School where he proved a "vehement" success.[9]

Bluecher saw himself as a spiritual advisor to his friends. "Since priests are no longer in the picture," he wrote to Arendt while he was counseling the Kazins, he was happy to extend sympathy and advice, as one of those "metaphysical psychologists versed in human nature." Both Kazins sought him out. Alfred would later recall that Carol had been impressed with Bluecher's "exalted common sense" on the subject of their disintegrating marriage. She found him a "practical lawgiver." As for himself, Kazin thought him "an inspired madman of sorts." In fact, the journals indicate that he depended heavily on Bluecher. At a time "when the world I took for granted has vanished under my feet," an afternoon of "glorious and strengthening talk" with Bluecher could be fortifying. He had never felt "so close to anyone" and had "never been so conscious of his irrevocable quality." Bluecher was sensible, supportive, understanding. "He is what I need most now in this period of violent change." Bluecher's letters to Arendt, in Europe at the time, indicate that Kazin needed the support. Bluecher felt that he had shielded Kazin from the shock of Carol's decision to separate, and even "squeezed out of him the fact that he's somewhat relieved" by convincing him (shrewdly) that his writing had been "enhanced" by the separation. Although initially "quite hysterical," Alfred got hold of himself and declared he wanted a fresh start. "He's well on his way to forgetting his past, hates his *self-pity,* doesn't want to be sentimental anymore, connects with his friends." Bluecher believed (and argued) that the Kazins' best option was to separate for a time so they could look at things more clearly "in an unpoisoned atmosphere." Alfred eventually agreed, thinking he might win Carol back "when he was in a better state," an outcome Bluecher thought unlikely.[10]

Bluecher was obviously pleased that he had been able to help with the Kazin "case," one of a number he was currently working on. But he was uncertain how long-lasting that help would prove and thought there might well be trouble later. He also saw something uncertain and childish in Kazin's behavior—"hysterical," desperate for consolation and protection. In an earlier letter he mentioned that Kazin was very unhappy that he had not heard from Arendt. "He's aching for a letter from you. (What a nice, and yet so feminine boy! Carol rebuked him, but he grumbled on, even if assuaged, and somewhat strangely.)" It was an impression shared in some degree by Arendt as well, who also referred to him as "that boy." She, too, saw difficulties ahead, but she also considered him a valued friend. "As everyone knows," she wrote to Bluecher after learning of Kazin's complaints, "once I make friends with a person, that's that." Kazin agreed. "The moment you entered her flat she tried, as it were to hold you. . . . a passionate and anxious friend."[11]

Bluecher was right. Carol wanted a clean break, and Alfred had little choice but to agree. Soon he was searching for his own flat. He tried to put a good face on the situation. He might "want to run home to [his] nonexistent mama," he wrote Herbst, but there was no point crying about the inevitable; and while he could not wholly suppress his bitterness with Carol, he had to admire her "dignity and courage." She was not playing it safe, and neither was he. "I will see it through." Nor, he told Herbst, would his troubles keep him from working. He had written a review of John Hersey's *The Wall* for the *New Yorker,* "all through the crisis," and was now preparing a long piece on the New York theater scene for *Commentary.* Kazin took pride in his capacity to lose himself in his writing "The hell with all my aches and pains! I can work anytime I please!" His future wife, Judith Dunford, would later agree. Not only could he write anytime, but anywhere. All he needed was paper, pen, and a place to sit down. Of course, a readiness to work does not guarantee good work or sound judgment. His review in the *New York Times* of a Melville biography by Newton Arvin was both enthusiastic and convincing. *Herman Melville* won the National Book Award in 1951. In contrast, his gushing review of *The Wall,* John Hersey's fictionalized diary of Noach Levinson's account of the destruction of the Warsaw ghetto was as sentimental as the book is dull and pious; while his indiscriminate attack for *Commentary* on *all* aspects of the New York theater—plays, actors, audience, even the seats—makes one wonder why he agreed to write on the theater at all. With the exception of the *Walker*, he was, he told Herbst, "strangely unconcerned about the fate of [his] writing" during this time and wanted only to write to people and especially to her.[12]

Kazin did write regularly and fervently to Herbst, but he also wrote ambiguously and dishonestly. "I have just discovered you and love you very much. Don't be alarmed, for I really mean it: i.e., I'd like you to remember that this man loves you, and that you can count on him. . . . I don't feel one whit 'younger' than you, only much less harmonious." "They don't make the female sex like you anymore." It is not surprising that such suggestive language led Herbst to propose in the return letter that she move in with Kazin—a proposal he immediately rejected. Nor should he have been "bewildered and shocked," as he says he was, to receive a note from her when they were both at Yaddo in March apologizing for "resisting" him. It is not clear what happened on that visit, but Herbst had apparently read or misread a sexual motive into Kazin's words and behavior and felt the need to "explain" why things had not developed as she thought they might. Startled, he wrote back that her note "shows such a misunderstanding of what I feel about you that I'm bewildered and shocked that you should even need to 'explain' things to me." Their relationship, he insisted, did not depend on "fornication" but on the "love" and "understanding" he believed existed between them. But he also wrote that "as soon as it is easy and natural, and without self-consciousness about Yaddo, I will go into you—anytime, with great pleasure and ease." He concluded that it was impossible to know what will happen in the future—"perhaps we will be 'lovers' in the physical sense, certainly I want us to be," but whatever happens, "the bond between us is one of the greatest things I have known and ever will know."[13]

Nothing in Kazin's journals indicates any sexual interest in Herbst. He saw her as a "sick," "frightened" older woman, her body "sapped" by age and worry, her whole demeanor suggesting "a kind of inner panic almost a queer hypnotic disintegration." He cared for her, respected her, felt sorry for her, worried about her condition and future, "so broke, bent and backward in many ways"; but he never expressed a hint of sexual interest—which is not to say it never crossed his mind. Do these letters, at best ambiguous, at worst deliberately misleading, mean that he was playing with the affections and expectations of a lonely, vulnerable woman, fifteen years his senior, who was yearning for intimacy with an admiring, younger writer? To a degree they do—they can be very painful reading. But they also leave little doubt that Kazin did "love" Herbst—at least in the sense that he depended heavily, even abjectly, on her emotional support at a time of profound personal uncertainty and that he was genuinely grateful for her kindness and understanding. "If only you know how much you have done for me, and have kept me in life. . . . you would know that whatever happens to us individually, or with each other, we will always be close to one another." As his emotional needs became less acute over the coming months, the weekly, sometimes daily, letters and cards to "Josie" became less frequent and lost much of their urgency. But they did continue—for eighteen years until her death—often mentioning a recent success, sometimes looking forward to an upcoming meeting, always concerned for her health and future writing prospects. Her letters to him, filled with colorful material from her life—"incomparable letters, the kind of letters people never even think of writing anymore"— were equally warm and attentive to his welfare and happiness. Whatever the misunderstandings and sexual miscues of the first months, there was a lasting bond between them. Each of their lives was richer for it.[14]

On May 24, Alfred wrote Herbst that he and Carol had agreed to separate permanently. He had picked up Carol the night before after her work and taken her out for drinks. It was their third wedding anniversary, and he had bought her a present "at ridiculous expense," hoping somehow that the occasion might change things, that they might even get back together. It didn't happen. "There I was off again, protesting a love I do not really feel, not *that* kind of love anyway, and being as bitter and generally hysterical as I could. God, I was a sight." He was not sure why he thought he might change Carol's mind or even whether he wanted to save the marriage. Perhaps it was "only some last desperate sentimental wish to hold on, to try to break down that indifference." Carol, however, made it clear that it was over, and Alfred agreed. "We had no business ever getting married, and she's right as hell insisting on our remoteness now. But she's a fine girl. We are getting a divorce."[15]

There was another piece of news in the letter. A week earlier, he had had a "brainstorm" and was now revamping *Walker* from start to finish, basing the whole thing on his Brownsville childhood. "The walks into the city are now the explorations of the world away from that early restricted life." And this time, he was sure he had it right. After all the false starts, he had found the right voice at last. "The whole book is simple and sings." He knew there would be difficulties ahead. Reliving the past would be painful, opening up "old sores and wounds." But he was confident, even exultant. Moreover, he knew, or thought he knew, the source of the sudden revelation—the break with Carol. "I married three years ago, stifling the doubts and protests in my heart," he told Herbst. "And three years later, I realize that the book I worked on all that time was self-suppressed and forlorn and without my true and characteristic spring because I was living a lie." Now he could write a book that drew on his true feelings and his love for his "own sort of people."[16]

The split with Carol may well have precipitated the "brainstorm." A shock to one's personal life can open creative possibilities, especially if the writer feels suddenly liberated. But there were other considerations, most notably the growing interest among readers, especially among *Commentary* and *Partisan* readers, in the ghetto life that many of them had left behind. In the 1930s, he had written dismissively of "the prose-poets of the tenements" (Michael Gold, Isadore Schneider, Henry Roth, Meyer Levin), whose imaginations had been cramped, "boxed in mentally," by the life of the ghetto. Now that it was being abandoned and repopulated by other groups, the Jewish ghetto was attracting fresh attention and some nostalgia. In the fall of 1949, Saul Bellow had published a rousing piece in *Partisan Review* describing the adventures of one Augie March, a child of the tenements, whose vitality and canny independence (and enterprising grandmother) turned a small corner of the Chicago ghetto into the perfect place for launching a "free style" American career. Other pieces, many of them sketches of the old neighborhoods, were appearing regularly in the section of *Commentary* titled "From the American Scene," pieces that editor Elliot Cohen claimed were "nearest the heart of the magazine's purpose." Gratified by the positive responses to his own contribution, "The Woman Downstairs," Kazin was alert to the possibilities. Released from Park Avenue, the Bookmans and Wertheims, the whole upper-crust social world where he had always felt an alien, he had good reason to believe that his creative interests and the times favored an imaginative return to his Brooklyn roots, to his "own sort of people."[17]

In fact, it did seem that by June Alfred had turned a corner—emotionally and creatively. Dealing with Carol over the divorce and custody rights could still throw him into periods of panic and depression. But they were relatively short-lived as long as he stayed with "the revelation" that had led him to recast his book, rescuing it "from the jaws of despondency." All he needed to do was keep his "eye on the ball," he told Herbst. "In my work, alone, now, is my being."[18]

Other things were also falling into place. Earlier in the spring he had sent a copy of his *Portable Blake* to Edmund Wilson, and in May he received a letter back. Wilson liked it, thought Kazin's introduction "the best thing of yours I have read," and declared that the first part on Blake and Beethoven was "brilliant." He had also enjoyed "The Woman Downstairs" in *Commentary* and wondered whether Kazin knew what *"solovey"* meant in Russian. (Mrs. Solovey, nightingale in Russian, was the name of the woman downstairs.) Kazin was very pleased. It was especially gratifying to get a positive response to the Blake book, which, to his great irritation, had gone largely unnoticed when it appeared in the spring of 1947. He responded by telling Wilson he was happy to get his letter and that despite Wilson's "snooty" views of his history and the pessimism he (Kazin) sensed in *Memoirs of Hecate County,* he very much wanted to be in touch with him. Wilson replied immediately that he was not really pessimistic, only "dissatisfied" with a number of things and that he would soon be sending him material that was much more cheerful. He also hoped he might see Kazin later in the summer. It was an important exchange. After Wilson's dismissal of *On Native Grounds* and his (Kazin's) harsh critique of *Memoirs,* Kazin was not sure what the two of them had to talk about. But apparently, Wilson wanted to continue the conversation.[19]

On July 7, Kazin left New York and joined Hannah Arendt and Heinrich Bluecher at Manomet on Cape Cod for a two-week working vacation. Rose Feitelson, a friend of Arendt, who had been helping to edit the totalitarian book, was also there. Kazin wrote in the mornings and spent much of the rest of the day editing Arendt's book. He took the job seriously. In March he had paid a visit to Van Wyck Brooks in Bridgewater, Connecticut, to

discuss possible difficulties with "Englishing" Arendt's text. Kazin thought
Brooks a fine prose stylist and wanted him to look over some of his efforts
with Arendt's prose (which Brooks approved). Kazin also found time for his
favorite activity on the Cape—walking. He was particularly fond of a hike to
a nearby bluff from which he could look down at the shore, a view which,
he told Herbst, put him in mind "of a kind of classic American landscape,
the sea, the sand, the up-rolled trowsers, as Whitman would still have
spelled it, the rawness of the land everywhere in sight." Manomet also
provided occasion for a brief affair with Rose Feitelson, whom he would
remember fondly for her demanding passion. "Fuck me hard!" Rebound-
ing from the break with Carol, Alfred had hopes the affair might turn into
something permanent.[20]

He returned to New York on July 20 to appear on an *Invitation to
Learning* discussion of *King Lear* before flying to Minneapolis for another
six-week teaching stint. He spent the summer session comfortably housed
in a faculty member's home who was away for the summer—"a most select
neighborhood," he wrote Herbst, and "very dull." But the study where he
worked had a grand view of the Mississippi; and he was, as before, impressed by the seriousness of the students, even if many of them looked
alike—the "not so young women in porous purple dresses who wear rimless
glasses and carry enormous gray notebooks." The Midwest "niceness" in
the faculty lunchroom could get "a little thick," and there were always the
young scholars eager not to be shown up "by the effete East." More upsetting were recurrent thoughts of Carol and Michael, which made him feel
"so lonely, so damned lonely, all of a sudden." But he could always return to
the book. "What has kept me going most of these last few months has been
the recovery of my book and the recognition and my realization of all sorts
of new powers, for writing."[21]

The going would get tougher when he returned to New York at the end
of August and had to deal directly with Carol over divorce and visitation
issues. He knew the marriage was over, had known it for months; divorce
proceedings were moving steadily forward; still, he found it hard to accept
the loss, or to "give up this bitterness that she has ceased to love me." He
also discovered that whatever hopes he might have had about Rose Feitelson were going nowhere. She was not interested. Meanwhile, he was carrying on an unsatisfying, impromptu affair with a "Marian K—," whose apart-

ment was "full of diddley diddley things, so girlish I did not know whether it made me laugh or suffocated." He was "worried, worried stiff" by how much he wanted her, knowing there was no future in it. "Josie" was again proving his most reliable source of support. Returning from a visit to Herbst's home in Erwinna, he marveled at her emotional directness and intuitive understanding. "She is inexpressibly precious and rare for one can depend on her as on so few for absolute spontaneity, goodness, considerateness." But he worried about her physical and mental stamina. Years of living alone, brooding over her earlier failed marriage, had, he felt, sapped her resilience. "Josie is a tragedy of the writer *qua* writer, especially of the woman writer who is almost too nice, too decent, too womanly, without a sufficiently combative, asserting intelligence to find her complete balance as a woman or as a writer." Just how prepared he was to embrace a more "combative, asserting intelligence" in a woman was another issue—one that he would have reason to ponder in the months and years after his introduction three weeks later to Ann Birstein.[22]

The meeting took place on October 13 at the apartment of Elizabeth Stiles, an editor at Dodd Mead Publishers. The publishing house had recently published Birstein's novel *Star of Glass*, after awarding it a prize as the best novel written by a college student. Birstein, who had graduated with honors from Queens College in 1948 and done graduate work at the Kenyon School of English, had recently decided to forego graduate school to pursue a career as a novelist. Stiles was unhappy that *Star of Glass* was not getting more attention and thought it might be helpful to introduce her to an influential critic who was also a friend.

Kazin would later recall Birstein that evening as a "blond wise-cracker who comes on like show-business." She remembers him in her memoir, *What I Saw at the Fair*, as "scary" and rude. After remarking that she had "nice legs," he pushed away her book when it was presented to him, asking whether this was "the first novel that was panned in *Commentary*." She had heard that he was "humorless and hypochrondriacal," and the characterization matched her impressions. Moreover, at thirty-five, he seemed "pretty old. His dark hair was close cropped, his nose was large . . . and his eyes, though a piercing light hazel green, were Oriental in shape." Still, she was impressed. If not exactly "handsome," he was very "authoritative." Except for his pocketing her cigarettes and talking so fast she could barely understand him, her most vivid impression of the evening was their ride home in a shared taxi where they were repeatedly being thrown together in the back seat—an experience they both later claimed to have enjoyed.[23]

Ann Birstein's father was the rabbi of an Orthodox synagogue on West Forty-seventh Street in Manhattan. Known as the Actor's Temple, it served the needs of the local congregation but also opened its doors to Broadway actors and impresarios, including, among many others, Eddie Cantor and Sophie Tucker. Ann had grown up where visits from actors and celebrities were part of the daily routine, and she enjoyed joining in their jokes and repartee. Impressed by her liveliness, wit, and good looks, Alfred called her the next day, and they were soon seeing each other. Ann recalls that after their first session of love-making, he had proposed marriage (which she declined) and then read passages to her from the book he was writing—an autobiography ("at his age!") about his childhood, about his mother's kitchen, about his father scrubbing his hands after returning from a day's work painting, about the sights and smells of Brownsville. "I'd never heard anything like it. . . . It was singular, a masterpiece. That naked man in the maroon paisley bathrobe is reading me a masterpiece."[24]

At the end of October, Kazin took the train to Saratoga Springs. He was having trouble with the final section of the book and thought a stay at Yaddo might help. It did not; and despite the company of the poet Elizabeth Bishop, whom he very much liked, he cut short the visit and returned to the city. Birstein may also have figured in his early return; he had been writing her letters and reading her novel (the story of a less-than-pious rabbi), about which he was polite, if unenthusiastic. Alfred's divorce, a continuing source of unhappiness for him, was now in its last stages; and it was a relief to be able to talk to Ann about the proceedings, and the book—something he would never have thought of doing with Carol. Ann was proving an enthusiastic and meticulous reader, offering useful advice in matters of style and syntax. They spent hours going over passages in an all-night cafeteria on Lexington Avenue and Fifty-ninth Street. By early December he was over the hump with the last section, just as his Fifty-eighth Street sublet was up. On December 15 he moved back into his old Pineapple Street flat and three days later flew to Key West for a vacation—taking along the manuscript.

A week later Birstein joined him. They stayed in the seedy Overseas

Hotel where Hemingway used to stay; drank at the bars where Hemingway drank; walked on the beach; went over the manuscript; and visited with Kazin's editor from Harcourt, Denver Lindley, and his wife, Frances, who were there on vacation. With a letter of introduction from Josephine Herbst, Kazin had made the acquaintance of Hemingway's former wife, Pauline, who maintained "a magnificent establishment" on Whitehead Street and threw lavish parties for the resident literati. Ann was impressed. "This was *literary*, not fancy schmancy Florida, authentic, the real thing, Caribbean." To top off the "Caribbean" experience, Alfred and Ann took a quick trip to Havana, stopping in Miami Beach on the way back to see her parents, who seemed happy enough with her new "boyfriend."[25]

Back in New York, Kazin settled in at Pineapple Street to finish the manuscript, warming his feet with a space heater against the drafts leaking in around the windows. Things were coming to an end. On January 18, 1951, he and Carol met in court to complete the divorce. In February he journeyed to Harvard to deliver a paper on Faulkner, where he also read a section of *Walker* to a group that included Archibald MacLeish and Thornton Wilder. In the subsequent conversation, it became clear to Kazin that "Wilder understood everything instantly." Indeed, the whole Harvard experience had been "glorious," and he wondered, hoped, some future appointment might be in the offing. The second week of March he turned the finished manuscript over to Denver Lindley—four and a half years since he had walked the Brooklyn Bridge with Cartier-Bresson, a long slog for a slim book; but he had no regrets.[26]

"The Passage Through"

In his "brainstorm" note to Josephine Herbst on May 24, Kazin had stated that he had completely revamped his book and had decided to base everything on his Brownsville childhood, on "explorations of the world away from that early restricted life." In a later account of how he wrote the book, "The Past Breaks Out," Kazin indicated that the action he finally settled on was more complicated, that the exploratory trips beyond Brownsville were invariably followed by return trips home, which, in turn, led to new flights abroad—"the push toward home and the pull away again." In other words, restlessness—"this constant state of division, even of flagrant contradiction between wanting the enclosure of home *and* the open city"—was the "key" to his book. Nor did the restlessness end once Kazin moved away. The book opens with the writer's returning to Brownsville again, now an adult, to "go over the whole route," to revisit the sites of his childhood—the school, the synagogue, Pitkin Avenue, his mother's kitchen—the need to leave leading ineluctably to the impulse to return. "This conflict has never ended for me."[27]

That conflict, Kazin also explains in "The Past Breaks Out," entails more than physical restlessness. While writing the book, he came to understand that contradictions, conflicted feelings, unanswered questions were central to his Brownsville experience. Indeed, virtually every site he revisits provokes conflicted impressions and responses—"an instant rage . . . mixed with dread and some unexpected tenderness" that he feels exiting the subway; a rushed feeling of protectiveness and fear when entering his mother's kitchen, where he is reminded of both the Sabbath meal and his learning of the Belsen concentration camp at the end of the war. The contradictions typically raise troubling questions, many of them about his Jewishness. "Was being a Jew the same as living in Brownsville?" "Were there really Jews who lived beyond Brownsville?" "Why had I always to think of insider and outsider?" Can a Jew be enthralled by Yeshua (Jesus) and passages from the New Testament? In his response to the 1944 "Under Forty" symposium, Kazin had asked whether it was "about time we stopped confusing the experience of being an immigrant or an immigrant's son with the experience of being Jewish." "Who is he?" he asks of the assimilating American Jew. "What is Jewish in him? What does he believe?" The confusion and questions had continued. Looking back in 1987 on the composition of *Walker*, Kazin realized "it came to me more and more that there was no intellectual solution to my long search for the meaning of Jewishness."[28]

But if *Walker* is a restless story of conflicted impressions, doubts, and questions, it is also a story of discoveries. In a particularly insightful and convincing review, Leslie Fiedler wrote that "in the end," the book is "the account of a series of illuminations, strung on the strand of reminiscence, the evocation of deep intuitive experiences of unity" with others, with God, with nature and himself. Such moments of illumination or transcendence are not infrequent in the American writer's encounter with nature—Thoreau's Walden, Twain's Mississippi, Melville's Pacific Ocean. But, Fiedler argues, Kazin has shown that they are equally part of the nation's urban experience, including that of the immigrant ghetto. Indeed, emerging out of the drab, homely ordinariness, the "seediness and squalor" of the Brownsville setting, such moments bring to transcendence an added quality of "redemption." Fiedler does not cite specific instances but one might well be Kazin's description of his mother, who, while preparing supper, suddenly interrupts her unending labors to look out the window into the street below. "I see her now, perched against the window sill, with her face against the glass, her eyes almost asleep in enjoyment just as she starts up with the guilty cry—'What foolishness is this in me!'—and goes to the stove to prepare supper for us: a moment, only a moment, watching the evening crowd of women gathering at the grocery for fresh bread and milk. But between my mother's pent-up face at the window and the winter sun dying in the fabrics—'Alfred, see how beautiful!'—she has drawn for me one single line of sentience."

A defining moment for mother and son—she, looking into the street below, he, registering her response—suggesting a capacity for aesthetic pleasure she feels she must reject, but which he clearly sees as redemptive, evidence of a sensitivity to life that for the moment eclipses the anxieties that afflict her. Kazin describes other such discoveries often while walking or reading, each indicating a heightened responsiveness to the impressions and possibilities of his Brownsville life. What gives this moment its unusual power and pathos is his success in recording both the unspoken sympathy that exists between himself and his mother and the implied differences that divide them. It would be the privilege of the children, not the parents, to tell just "how beautiful" it was.[29]

A very different but equally telling moment of illumination occurs in the book's last chapter, "The Passage Through," describing a walk with a girlfriend to Highland Park. The school year had just ended, with two teachers encouraging the young man in his aspirations as a writer, and he is excited about the future. After looking out from the heights past the row of white crosses in the cemetery and the roofs of Brooklyn to the Manhattan skyline, the couple turn toward home. "The lampposts winked steadily from Jamaica Avenue, and the YMCA's enormous sign glowed and died and glowed again. Somewhere in the deadness of the park the water gurgled in the fountains. In the warmth and stillness a yearning dry and sharp as salt rose in me. Far away a whistle hooted; far away girls went round and round the path laughing. When we went home, taking the road past the cemetery, with the lights of Jamaica Avenue spread out before us, it was hard to think of them as something apart, they were searching out so many new things in me."

These concluding sentences recall the book's epigraph—"the glories strung like beads on my smallest sights and hearing—on the walk in the street, and the passage over the river"—from "Crossing Brooklyn Ferry," Whitman's tribute to the wonders of the New York scene. Like Whitman's "appearances," the sights and sounds of the city create both a setting and a state of mind that for the moment dissolve and transcend the contradictions, ambiguities, and doubts—Whitman's "dark patches" and "abrupt questionings"—always latent in the images and memories of Kazin's Brownsville life.[30]

But Proust also comes to mind—the sights, sounds, tastes, and smells of childhood, "the new things" stored in the young man's memory now recovered by the older writer in the process of composition. Kazin, who had recently been rereading Proust, would later describe "the creative rapture" that seized the novelist when he discovered his gift for turning recovered images and events into art. It was an experience that Kazin, "intoxicated with the sensual Proustian memory," felt that he, too, had had in the writing of *Walker*. "Forging those images, one out of another, all sealed in memory, I had the joy of dealing with things in themselves, with what, for once, demanded no interpretation, no exchange into something else." The hopeful young man, walking home from Highland Park watching the lights on Jamaica Avenue, could not have been more excited by the possibilities ahead than the older writer rejoicing in his recently discovered powers of re-creation. Writing *A Walker in the City* was also part of "the passage through," another important step in the continuing success story, the rise, of Alfred Kazin.[31]

"A Singular and Beautiful Work"

Thornton Wilder may have "understood everything" at the Harvard reading from *Walker*, but Kazin was not sure others would. Josephine Herbst, who unsettled him by calling the book a novel, obviously did not. (He told her it was "a poem in four movements"; he also called it a "sonata.") However, the reviews following publication on October 29, 1951, indicate that most did understand—and approved. Irwin Edman, in a front-page review in the *New York Times Book Review,* wrote that *A Walker in the City* was sensually alive sometimes to the aching point and emotionally intense to the degree of passionate pain." Charles Rolo, in the *Atlantic Monthly,* said that it was clearly a book written out of "deep necessity," "a small beautiful memoir . . . which transcends the particularity of its subject." Brendan Gill of the *New Yorker* called it "a singular and beautiful work . . . a small book, and an immense achievement." Leslie Fiedler, as indicated, saw *Walker* as a moving struggle for "redemption" and evidence that the experiences of the urban Jew were moving into the American literary mainstream, that American literature had traveled a "long way from Walden Pond to Brownsville."[32]

Not all the reviews were positive. Mistaking Kazin's use of the Proustian memory for narrative confusion, the Harvard historian Oscar Handlin faulted the book for an "ambiguity of perspective" that conflates the impressions of the present with those of the past. Others, David Daiches (*Commentary*) and Morris Freedman (*Chicago Jewish Forum*), acknowledged the beauty of the work but took exception to Kazin's heterodox views of Judaism. Daiches, a rabbi's son, thought Kazin "excessively vulnerable to his own religious discoveries" and complained that his apostrophe to Jesus at one point was the "one piece of sentimentality in an otherwise restrained book." Kazin, who was deeply attracted to the Jewish Jesus, "Yeshua . . . the very embodiment of everything I had waited so long to hear from a Jew," and who acknowledged reading parts of the New Testament with "excitement and shame," had expected this criticism; but, he insisted, it was precisely "the ambiguity and long ache of being a Jew" that made him feel most intensely a Jew.[33]

There were also personal notes of approval. "You make all the sights and sounds and smells and tastes of Brownsville immediately palpable," wrote his one-time neighbor from Solebury, Lewis Mumford. Nothing had given him such pleasure since reading the opening chapters of Proust's first volume. "Perhaps, Dear Kazin, you are a novelist and a poet, even more than a critic." Coming from the writer and urbanologist whose *Brown Decades* Kazin claimed had been a major inspiration for *On Native Grounds,* this was high praise; as was a note from Van Wyck Brooks, whom Kazin had long thought one of the finest prose stylists in America. "You are an artist . . . in the tradition of Turgenev," Brooks told Kazin. "You convey a magical feeling of both wonder and discovery." *Walker* "is a book like no other autobiography." Edmund Wilson, who earlier had praised "The Woman Downstairs," was also enthusiastic. Both Mumford and Brooks expressed the strong hope that Kazin would follow up with more autobiographical works.[34]

In his letter Mumford predicted that *Walker* "would have as long a life" as Proust's novel. Whether or not it has the staying power of *À la recherche*, the book has remained a popular work that has never been out of print. One reason for its popularity (aside from intrinsic literary merit) is its representation of an important moment in Jewish-American history. The sociologist Marshall Sklare has declared *Walker* invaluable to an understanding of the immigrant Jewish community in America. It is "the best . . . the most interesting" account of "the Jewish street," better than anything in the novels of Saul Bellow, Bernard Malamud, and Philip Roth. Kazin "has tremendous antennae; he is out all the time—very perceptive." Historians Irving Howe, Abraham Sachar, and Alexander Bloom have all cited *Walker* for its useful portrayal of the ambiguities and problems that young Jewish intellectuals from the immigrant community faced. While grateful for the attention, Kazin was not altogether happy about the uses being made of the book. To his French publisher, he declared himself "very distressed" that it was so often read as a historical work and a "sociological document." He particularly resented Howe's reservations (in *World of Our Fathers*) about its historical accuracy. "Imagine taking a book like mine, so obviously 'constructed,' based on images, a conscious and deliberate literary work in every way, and hinting that the experience behind it was different!" Of course it was different, "*so* different I had to write *A Walker in the City* to forget the difference, to wipe out the pain and insignificance of so much behind it."[35]

Whatever their reasons, readers continue to embrace the book, now regarded as a canonical text in American-Jewish writing, "one of the few original texts to have come out of the immigrant experience," according to Theodore Solotaroff. At a time when large numbers of American Jews were leaving or had already left the urban ghetto, *Walker* provided a look back at what had been a way of life for generations of immigrant Jewish families. In an evocative language of personal feeling Kazin had given voice to the conflicts and contradictions, the yearnings and fears that had been part of the experience of Jewish children making their way from Brownsville, the

South Bronx, and other immigrant urban neighborhoods into the main-stream of American life. If his first book was a work of acculturation that helped to consolidate a modern tradition in American writing, *A Walker in the City* is a work that extended the boundaries of that tradition, as more writers like himself began staking their own claims on native grounds.[36]

CHAPTER SEVEN

Living in the Fifties

1951–1958

I feel I do not belong to any of it.

—Alfred Kazin, Journal, January 27, 1955

W hen he handed over the manuscript of *A Walker in the City* to Denver Lindley in mid-April 1951, Alfred Kazin sensed a new life in the offing. "What lovely days, with my Walker finished at last and Europe ahead—with Ann." Not everything was joyous, however. The divorce from Carol had left a bitterness that would color and distort his memories of his "stupid" "loveless life" with her. He had also lost the chance for "normal" daily relations with his son. Thinking about future absences from Michael, he felt "a tight band of ice" forming around him and "a kind of fatality." But while mourning his life with Michael, he was hopeful, even ecstatic, about life with Ann Birstein. "How I recognize my love," he mused after a February visit with her to Lindley's: "That when I look at her face it should seem to me so amazingly beautiful that I should wonder that all others looking upon it do not feel the same thing."[1]

Birstein had been awarded a Fulbright scholarship to Paris (beginning in the fall) to research a book on American expatriates. She planned to go over in the spring, and Kazin decided to join her. He was scheduled to teach at the Salzburg Seminar in July and August. In the intervening weeks they could explore France and Italy together. "Daydreams were coming true all over the place," Ann recalled. Alfred remembered feeling as "giddy" as Ann. "There was a lightness to our days. . . . We swept past many invisible doors of air." He was not sure where things were heading. He was not ready to remarry, but he was increasingly convinced that his future lay with Ann, that she would be both lover and the kind of writer's companion he had not found with Carol.[2]

Much in the coming months and years would warrant excitement and hope. Though twelve years younger than Kazin, Birstein was a lively companion for him. She not only shared his literary interests, she was herself something of a literary character and inspiration—Zelda to his Scott, lightning fast in her repartee, full of unexpected insight, mercurial and often bewildering in her response. Life with Ann, he was confident, would be very different from that with the "statuesque philistine" who had recently divorced him. Moreover, her enthusiasm for A Walker in the City suggested he could depend on her support for future projects. He had plans for a number—The Western Island, for which he had received his 1946 Guggenheim fellowship; a collection of meditations from his journal; a short story, "The Girl," based on a wartime London encounter; and possibly another autobiographical work. A Walker in the City indicated talent in that area. The future seemed rich in creative as well as personal possibilities.[3]

Yet, as they both later acknowledged, there was something unreal, even fantastic, about their expectations as they boarded the Île de France on May 22, 1951. "It was all just as in the movies," she recalled, or like the owl and the pussycat in Edward Lear's poem—sailing away for a year and day in a beautiful pea-green boat. (Their term of endearment for each other, taken from the poem, was "pussy" and occasionally "pussoo.") Life, it soon became clear, would not always be a free-wheeling vacation abroad—with or without honey and plenty of money. Indeed, for most of the fifties, life for Alfred and Ann would be lived at home in America, much of it in rural New England, where romantic hopes yielded to domestic duties and creative aspiration to growing uncertainty and frustration.[4]

Many of the difficulties were personal. What makes writers stimulating companions may not make them ideal marriage partners and parents. But the times also took their toll. The fifties were not happy years for women trying to pursue independent careers—as writers or anything else. Birstein remembers her dismay listening to presidential candidate Adlai Stevenson tell the graduating class at Smith that he could think of no more worthy vocation for women than "the humble role of housewife." Less concerned with domestic trends, Kazin despaired of the ongoing moral and political retrenchment in the culture at large. The anti-Communist paranoia that had alarmed him in the forties continued to spread and deepen, while the "torpor" in the country's creative-intellectual life—"this desolately thin, self-satisfied, utterly dry culture"—left him yearning wistfully for the passion, belief, and solidarity of years past. "Whatever the thirties came to, there was a feeling of having one's beliefs shared." Although widely respected in the intellectual community and increasingly sought after as a critic, Kazin felt intellectually and spiritually stranded throughout much of the decade—"I feel I do not belong to any of it." This sense of isolation fed into his writing, particularly his essays on American writers (some of his very best) and his plans for *The Western Island.* It would, however, prove a frustrating, uncertain muse to live with, one that could provoke short bursts of inspired writing but only wavering support for the sustained effort needed to finish books.[9]

Europe and Back

If, in retrospect, there was something unreal about their European trip, it does seem to have been a genuinely happy time for Alfred and Ann. From Paris, he wrote Hannah Arendt that he was having the time of his life, that they could not stop walking or looking until fatigue forced them into bed. At Arendt's suggestion, they booked two "attic" rooms in the Hotel Lutitia on the Left Bank offering a view of the gabled roofs and chimney pots of Paris. It was Ann's first trip abroad, and Alfred enjoyed taking her to the streets, squares, and cafés he remembered from his 1945 visit. They toured art galleries with the art historian Robert Rosenblum, an acquaintance of Kazin's; had lunch with another friend, the essayist Stanley Geist, and his wife Eileen; and attended a Sunday afternoon soiree at the home of Harold Kaplan and his wife. Kaplan had arrived in Paris with Kazin in the days following the armistice and stayed on as an advisor to the newly founded UNESCO. Currently an officer in the U.S. Information Agency, "Kappy" entertained lavishly in his huge living room that served as a meeting place for French intellectuals and any of the *Partisan Review* people who happened to be in town. Visiting the Kaplans would become a regular feature of Kazin's visits to Paris.

He and Ann took trips to the Lascaux cave to see the Paleolithic drawings, to Aix-en-Provence to see the Cezanne landscape, and to Chartres and Mont-Saint-Michel. Eighteen years earlier, Alfred had read Henry Adams's *Mont Saint Michel and Chartres* in the history reading room of City College. Now, following "in a straight line of expectancy" to the sites themselves, he felt that he better understood the "union of all forces converging to a common unconscious end" that had inspired Adams's work. The last week of June, they left for Italy—Venice, Pisa, Siena, Florence and Rome—with a side trip to the Italian Alps, where at the Hotel Alberto Internazionale they went over proofs for the *Walker*. Ann was astonished that Alfred knew so many people: the Geists and the Kaplans in Paris; the director Harold Clurman and his actress wife, Stella Adler, in Florence; Kermit Lansner, the professor and editor of *Art News* and his artist wife Fay, also in Florence; the poet and critic Horace Gregory in Pompey; writers Alberto Moravia and Ignazio Silone in Rome. Knowing little Italian, she was often at a loss with Alfred's Italian friends and acquaintances, while he, knowing only some-what more, plunged confidently ahead, assured that his ebullience and the Italians' tolerance for error would carry him through. Italy, he declared, is not at all like France—"No French person ever understands my French."[6]

In mid-July he took the train to Salzburg. Ann would follow three weeks later when he found her a room at a farmhouse "with squawking things in the yard and a huge snarling watchdog." Salzburg was not such a happy time. After the pioneering adventure of 1947, the now smoothly running seminar seemed tame. The aura of political urgency had dissipated before the routinely academic. Kazin enjoyed the teaching; the students were intelligent and interested. But the young American academics, he wrote Arendt, are "awfully pallid," and there is a cloying emphasis on "niceness" and "human relationships." The presence of Henry Steele Commager helped some. They had first met in 1945 when Commager had invited Kazin to the *Century* to discuss *On Native Grounds*, a book he then praised lavishly in his classic study *The American Mind*. Kazin found Commager a reassuring figure, a scholar and man of letters who never lost faith in the "old-fashioned" liberalism that it pleased so many to distrust during the cold war years. The two men would remain good friends (and for a brief time colleagues at Amherst) until Commager's death in 1998. But despite the presence of Commager and the Yale historian R. W. B. "Dick" Lewis, whom Kazin also liked, the seminar remained a pale reflection of its original self. "Ugh," he wrote Arendt. "I've outworn this."[7]

On September 10, Alfred left for America, going back to a semester's teaching at the New School, to Pineapple Street, and to a "strange new life" without Ann. He was sure he was in love with her, and he hoped to return to Europe in the spring of the following year, possibly as a visiting professor. Back in New York, he suffered the usual bouts of loneliness but was reassured by Ann's letters. He in turn reassured her of his intention to return. He had plenty to keep him busy—his novel course at the New School (in which Ann's sister, Julia, was a student), taping broadcasts for *Invitation to Learning*, reading manuscripts for Harcourt, writing reviews for the *New Yorker*. In December, he traveled to Northampton to give a reading at Smith from *A Walker in the City* and to visit with friends Daniel Aaron and Robert Gorham Davis. There was talk of a position—possibly a Neilson visiting professorship.[8]

The high points (socially) of this waiting period were with Hannah Arendt. Kazin had been attracted to her "commanding," passionate intelligence since their first meeting at the *Commentary* dinner in 1947. Journal entries from the present period indicate that the attraction was more than intellectual. "I'm not in love with her, just adore her as a human being, with all my heart," he wrote after a dinner with her and her friend Alexander Korye. Following a trip with Arendt and Bluecher to the country, he declared her "the [most] conclusively *human* creature I have ever known." Holding her arm in the subway, he "blushed with pleasure all over, could have kissed her there, felt more love touching her than I'd felt in ages." Whatever the quality of the attraction, and he acknowledged it was not "unerotic," Arendt was not interested in a sexual relationship—neither with him, nor, according to her biographer, Elisabeth Young-Bruehl, with anyone other than Bluecher. Still, his feelings for her—"the woman I love most"—did not portend easy relations when Ann was back on the scene.[9]

Nor was it a good sign that he was carrying on sexual liaisons with two women—Vivienne Koch and Celia Koron. He was not happy about these affairs, believing them to be signs of weakness—not so much of the flesh as of character. He saw the one with Koch, who irritated and bored him, as "miserable, petty and really sordid . . . a sickness in every part of my body and spirit." He was less disturbed by his relations with Koron, whom he had met at Isaac Rosenfeld's apartment and who seemed to grow as "a human being" the more he saw her. He confessed his affairs to Ann and asked for forgiveness—but would later resume relations with both women. The affairs did not appear to affect his feelings for Ann, who was now hinting about marriage in her letters. By February 1952, Alfred had decided to marry her. "I am striking out for life at last. . . . I am not going to shirk my happiness."[10]

During his five-month sojourn in New York, Kazin did little serious work on his proposed books. Nor with one exception did he put in a major effort on his reviews. The exception was a piece on Simone Weil's *The Need for Roots*, an assignment he had requested but found unexpectedly difficult to complete. Kazin had first heard of Weil when Dwight Macdonald published her famous essay on *The Iliad* in *Politics* in 1945. Since then, her life, death, and writings had made her a legendary figure among many intellectuals and religious thinkers in France and America. A brilliant French Jew with deep Christian-Catholic sympathies, a graduate of the École Normale Supérieure, Weil had taught school, worked in factories, and joined the Republicans in Spain in 1936 before leaving for the United States and then England, where, it was alleged, she had died of malnutrition, refusing to eat more than was allowed the French under occupation. When a collection of her letters and notebooks were published as *Waiting for God* in 1951, Kazin was astonished by their religious intensity and particularly by her views on Christianity, which brought into fresh focus many of his own heterodox religious feelings. Sensing a spiritual kinship, amounting, he said in his journal, to virtual "identification," he requested an assignment from the *New Yorker* to review *The Need for Roots*.[11]

The essay was short and added little to what others had already said. It was, however, a important piece for Kazin to write. Not only did it give him the opportunity to sort through his feelings about Weil (including the error of his earlier "identification" with her—"You are not Simone Weil!"), it helped him locate what he believed was a significant connection between religious feeling and his as yet unwritten book, *The Western Island*. Reflecting on her statement that "attention is the highest form of prayer," Kazin wrote that what Weil "sought more than anything else was a loving attentiveness to all the living world that would lift man above the natural loneliness of existence." Though he had not yet formulated a clear argument for his book, he was certain that it would focus on American writers' efforts to apprehend through love and wonder the promising, strange new world that was America—a process of solitary religious and creative meditation that, at least in Kazin's mind, bore an important resemblance to Weil's "waiting for God."[12]

Kazin arrived back in Paris at the end of February. He had been offered a position as *Gastprofessor für Amerikanistik* at the University of Cologne to begin in May, and he would soon learn he had been appointed to a Fulbright seminar in American studies to be held during July and August at Cambridge University. He was also scheduled to give lectures at the American embassy in Paris and in Munich. It was, he noted, a good time for Americanists abroad. After centuries of looking to Europe for enlightenment, Americans were now "the teachers" and Europeans "the earnest students and dutiful inquirers." Alfred and Ann continued to explore Paris; they saw old friends, visited Simone Weil's parents (who were more interested in Ann than in talking about their daughter), and planned for the future. They wanted to marry in Paris. But the legal difficulties were proving insurmountable, and they wondered, with some misgiving, whether Germany might be a possibility.[13]

Hannah Arendt arrived at the end of March—"in a great burst of train steam like Mephisto," according to Birstein, who was not particularly happy to see her. She knew how much her husband-to-be admired Arendt, whose picture was displayed prominently in his room. He once told Birstein that he could not love her if she did not like Arendt. (He also told her he could not love her if she were not a writer.) She was disturbed by his deference to Arendt and came to resent what she believed was Arendt's dismissive attitude toward her. But if she was irritated, she apparently hid it well. Arendt wrote to Bluecher that Birstein was "extremely charming" and that she was giving the marriage her blessing, though she noted a disturbing imbalance in the relationship and wondered about difficulties ahead. "That child is really frightened of him [Kazin]," and he—"always the same story, moody and unpredictable. I really like her very much, she really loves that boy."[14]

Birstein would later write bitterly of Arendt's attitude and manner during the weeks they spent together in Europe. In her autobiography and in a short story, "When the Wind Blew," she describes Arendt ("Erika Hauptman") as officious, patronizing, and ill-mannered, laying down the law on everything from sex to parenting to hotels, peremptorily dismissing other people's views, and interrupting conversation with "a horribly familiar hoarse barking laugh that made my blood run cold." While it undoubtedly took some time before Birstein's early impressions hardened into this harsh characterization, it is also likely that she sensed quickly that Arendt was a rival for her fiancé's affection and attention and that Arendt would never take her very seriously. Later events would reinforce initial impressions— impressions of a dismissive hauteur and "purposeful rudeness" shared by the wives of other intellectuals whom Arendt befriended. "Year after year Hannah made believe that I did not exist even when we were a few feet apart, staring into each other's faces," Diana Trilling complained. "But Hannah was attracted to Lionel . . . and was therefore . . . resentful of me."[15]

On April 22, Kazin gave his address at the American embassy—on Europe's role in recognizing and advancing American poetry—which, according to Arendt, made us "all very proud and pleased." The following week he left for Cologne. He rented an apartment at the end of the trolley line and commuted to the university through miles of destroyed buildings and piles of rubble, "block after block after block, the same squashed houses with their insides open to the street." Kazin's impressions of postwar Europe had come largely from Italy and France, both relatively intact (architecturally) after the war. Germany was different. The war was visible everywhere, in the bombed-out streets and buildings as well as in the smashed bodies of the people. "The lame, the halt and the blind of Germany. Everywhere I go in this wounded and accursed land, I see the tell-tale glove hiding the stumps of amputated hands." And though his students seemed "amazingly like nineteen-year-old undergraduates in Minneapolis, Cambridge and Washington Square," he could never forget that he was living in the land of Hitler, that behind "the smiling deference," "the heavy good manners," "the infernal correctness," any number of the professionals he met and worked with had once been Nazis—"under the nodding, bobbing smile of the civilized man, the deep blood-ties of race."[16]

Keeping the recent past out of mind did not become easier when Ann joined him at the end of May. Germany was as "horrible" as she expected. "Everyone on the street looked lumpen, gross and suspicious, men with heavy jowls and big paunches, women with elastics under their chins to hold their hats in place." Nor did Arendt's reassurances help when she later joined them. Alfred had earlier asked her to come to Cologne to help them arrange the marriage and to serve as a witness. But the German bureaucracy proved as difficult as the French. In the end, he and Ann took the train to Basel, Switzerland, where the rules were less strict. They married on June 26, their witnesses, a clerk from the hotel and an official from the American consulate. Alfred was ecstatic—"My glorious wedding day. My great unbelievable gift. Tonight my spear is tipped with fire." Less exciting was the prospect of returning to Cologne to finish out the semester—and, according to Arendt, Kazin left for England before the semester was over. It is "really terrible," she reported to Bluecher. "More so, because he (I just found this out) did the same thing last year in Salzburg. That boy is going to cause us much worry."[17]

Cambridge—"dear beautiful Cambridge—more beautiful than ever"— did seem a better site for a honeymoon than bombed-out Cologne. Kazin had not been back since the war, and his responses to London, Cambridge, and the English were tinged with the memory of those cold, grim, lonely days when he trudged between the billets and tube stops and his day's assignment. England had changed—"shining with postwar paint and polish"—but so had he, now happily married and confident enough to be amused by the British manner and speech, "by the authority of their style," by "their tense assertiveness of place and background in every syllable." Whatever its achievements, the Labour government had not destroyed the British sense of class, which at the Fulbright seminar on American studies displayed itself in a cool disdain toward "all things American." Quick to notice signs of "snootiness," Kazin observed "the fascinated dislike" with which certain young dons discussed America and listened in amazement to the "silky insults" delivered in the opening address by Allan Pryce-Jones, the editor of the *Times Literary Supplement*. What was all the fuss about? the editor seemed to be asking. Did the Americans really think they had anything much to tell the British? If the United States wanted to fund conferences in which Americans lectured England about America, well and good; but this hardly entitled them to unqualified thanks. "We will astonish the world" laughed one don to Kazin, "by our ingratitude."[18]

Looking back on the occasion, the English Americanist Marcus Cunliffe did not think the English "were quite so bad" as Kazin indicated. Yet there was no denying the "patronizing" tone of Pryce-Jones's address or the condescension with which various British historians inside and outside the conference regarded the new interest in American studies. "Oh, so that's your racket," the Oxford historian A. J. P. Taylor remarked to Cunliffe on learning that he was in American studies. "You teach American . . . *history?* Is there any?" was another familiar response. Cunliffe needed little convincing that "the British *did* condescend to the United States." But he also knew, as did the sherry-sipping dons at high table, that the emergence of the United States as the preeminent military and fiscal power in a postwar world entailed cultural consequences. However much (or little) Europeans may have thought about American history and institutions before the war, they had little choice but to pay attention now. The Fulbright seminar was the first of many such "jamborees" to come, many of them hosted by English universities. Funded by the American government and allied foundations, they represented an invasion very different from that of the war years when the London streets were crowded with free-spending GIs. The barbarians were now within the gates, within the university common rooms, striking at the heart of England's spiritual-cultural life. Professorships in American literature and history were being established, and soon American studies programs would be flourishing at the universities of Sussex, East Anglia, and Keele.[19]

Kazin was alert to the resentment and to the historical moment of which he was gratefully a part—"Nothing like working your way through Europe on the strength of *On Native Grounds!*" And he happily shared in a vision that placed America at the center of things, even at the end point of history. "How much we Americans look at our country from the point of view of *all* history," he reflected after returning from a session of lectures. "Henry Commager this morning, rattling off the names of the continents and proportionate weights of the other ages: all avenues leading up to this spotlighted center: us." Although this put the matter somewhat personally, it was hardly a new idea, the notion that America represented a special providence, an ideal, or "brave new world," toward which history (and geography) was pointing. "O my America! my new-found-land," had long had a place in the mind and imagination of Europe, as it had in the writings of American religious and literary prophets: John Winthrop, Emerson, Thoreau, Whitman. Listening to Commager, Allen Nevins, John Hope Frank-

lin, and Cambridge's own Denis Brogan expound on the origins and qualities of "the American character" and "the American mind" in the King's
College lecture halls, it was clear to Kazin that the subject was more exciting
and relevant than ever. It was time to get on with *The Western Island*.[20]

"The Literary Profession—What a Misnomer, What a Horror"

Kazin returned to New York full of ideas and enthusiasm for his book. The
problem was staying focused amid the swirling "lava" of American life and
the daily assault of the city. "After six golden months abroad, NY is a shock,"
he wrote to Bernard Malamud. "Nothing that ever hurt you before, here,
ever goes away." One thing that never seemed to go away was housing, or
the lack of it. He still had his Pineapple Street flat; more run-down and
smellier than ever—though Ann's sister had tried to spruce it up with a pink
shag rug for the bathroom and a toilet seat cover, which Alfred immediately
ripped off and threw out the window. He and Ann decided they had to
move; they stayed there at night and prowled the Upper West Side during
the day, finally settling on an apartment at 545 111th Street just off Riverside Drive. Compared with his previous flats, the 111th Street flat was
roomy, large enough for him to have a separate study. Instead of walks over
Brooklyn Bridge and along Brooklyn Heights, he could stroll along the
Hudson, occasionally crossing over the George Washington Bridge to the
Palisades.[21]

Although not large, the apartment could accommodate small parties,
and Ann liked to entertain. She had already met many of Alfred's friends:
Isaac Rosenfeld; Richard Hofstadter, now teaching at Columbia, and his
second wife Beatrice; Chaim and Jacqueline Raphael; Robert Lowell; Randall Jarrell. A favorite was Saul Bellow. Bellow was at Princeton working for
the creative writing program (while finishing *The Adventures of Augie
March*) and frequently came into the city. Birstein thought him funny,
charming, and stunningly good looking—"the ultimate beautiful Jewish
intellectual incarnate." She enjoyed walking with him along the river and
occasionally playing ping-pong in a parlor on Riverside Drive. She also
liked Alfred's friend Harold Rosenberg. "A big guy [six foot three], with a
big black mustache and a big stiff leg [surgically fused]," Rosenberg, who
came from an earlier generation of intellectuals, was an impressive figure

in any social gathering. "Harold, the old-fashioned man," Alfred wrote in his journal after one party; "face of the silent movies, tall in a way that fathers used to be. . . . With his hooked nose over his paternal moustache, his forthrightness, his delight in stating *his* case first, Harold gives me an acute case of nostalgia." Rosenberg was apparently struck by Kazin's manner as well, which, he told Hannah Arendt, resembled "in walk and posture an arrogant camel."[22]

Another Birstein favorite was Alfred's sister, Pearl. A junior editor at *Harper's Bazaar*, Pearl wrote reviews for *Commentary*, the *New Leader*, and other journals and seemed to know all the trendy literary people in the city, including the young author Truman Capote, whom she had visited at his vacation home in Taormina, Sicily. In 1950 Pearl had carried on a passionate affair with the Welsh poet Dylan Thomas. She was very sharp about people and books—"a female Alfred with the same Asian eyes and impressive intellect," according to Birstein, "but much kindlier in manner."[23]

Alfred had been initially reluctant to meet and socialize with Ann's family. Wary of rabbis since he was a child, he now had one as a father-in-law. But he quickly came to like Rabbi Birstein; and the rabbi approved of him, proud to have a noted intellectual as a son-in-law. Berel Birstein had immigrated to America from Brest-Litovsk when he was a young man and spent his early years in Atlanta and Denver as a fund-raiser for Jewish organizations. He obtained his first parish in Canarsie, Brooklyn, before settling in Manhattan as the rabbi of an Orthodox synagogue on Forty-seventh Street in Manhattan. Kazin remembered him as "tiny, clean-shaven, agile, immensely intelligent, sharp witted and sad." Visiting the Birsteins in their apartment on Fifty-fourth off Seventh Avenue was a very different experience from visiting the Bookman's apartment on Madison and Seventieth. In the latter, the word "Jew" was never heard. "Here [on Fifty-fourth Street] everything is *Jew, Jew, Jew*, wherever you look and whatever you heard." On one wall a Marc Chagall picture of a rabbi in a prayer shawl; on another a Yiddish mother "over there" reading a letter from America; plaques everywhere acknowledging the rabbi's leadership and good works.[24]

The new apartment, the socializing, the high cost of living in New York— Birstein did not yet have a job—together with alimony and child-care payments for Michael, all contributed to the "shock" of Kazin's return. Teaching his Monday evening course at the New School, reading manuscripts for

Harcourt, and writing reviews for the *New Yorker* defrayed immediate expenses but provided little beyond the essentials, and no security. Kazin was used to the hustle needed to stay afloat in literary New York, but he sometimes chafed at the worry and the constant need for self-promotion. "The literary profession—what a misnomer, what a horror. This very profession (of faith) to which I entrust my life (for by that I mean my thinking) is also a mad scramble for social prestige *and* a job. So that at every point (but obviously most on Sunday night, before the treadmill gets me back), I oscillate between the native purity, the relative selflessness of my inner thoughts—and this splinterey, tormented, boring, boring attempt to get things by my profession—my name on this list, my bank account full." Hoping to get his name on one more list, he wrote in October to Edmund Wilson, who he heard was in charge of the Christian Gauss Seminar at Princeton, asking about the possibilities of an appointment. He thought there might be interest in "a strange tome" he was working on to be called *The Western Island.* Wilson, who was giving a series of lectures at the Gauss Seminar in November and December, was not in charge of future appointments, and nothing came of the request. (Kazin would be offered a Gauss lectureship in the fall of 1961.) On December 4, he wrote to Henry Moe at the Guggenheim Foundation, wondering about a third crack at a grant. He was hesitant to ask. His 1947 Guggenheim renewal had been for the still-unfinished *Western Island,* and now he was asking for another one; but, he told Moe, he was getting a little desperate, and he promised the book would be "nothing less" than an examination of America "as virtually a creation of the Western World, the greatest in history." In the end he decided against applying. In fact, Kazin's circumstances may not have been quite so exigent as his letter to Moe indicated. On December 16, he informed Morton Zabel at the University of Chicago that he could not accept a summer position there because he was the recipient of a summer fellowship at the Indiana School of Letters and was to be offered a visiting lectureship at Harvard in the fall. He did, however, ask to be kept in mind for possible future appointments.[25]

Another (not wholly unexpected) "shock" greeting him back in America was the political scene. "Coming home," he wrote in his first journal entry after arrival—"All the scoundrels talking about *atheistical* Communism. Hour of the opportunists"—specifically Senator Richard Nixon stating that under Adlai Stevenson the country could expect four more years of "wishy washy" treatment of Communism. There would be many entries reacting to the red scare of the early fifties, including one quoting a Patricia Blunk in the *Progressive* (April 1953): "I think [a Communist] is someone who does-n't believe in another country's lord." It is not clear what Kazin intended to do with these items. A few would appear in *New York Jew.* For the moment they documented the ominous strangeness of the times and reminded him of how little he was doing about it. "George S. Kaufman dropped from a television program for having made a quip about the commercialism of 'Silent Night,'" he wrote in his journal in December 1952: "God, almighty, I ask myself every day when I look at the papers—am I a coward for not fighting all the time and in every way against this stinking fog of orthodoxy creeping over the country." He did write to Irving Mansfield of CBS television to say "how disgraceful and cowardly" he considered Kaufman's discharge. Beyond that, he had no idea what to do. He would later confide to Bellow that the only way he knew to fight back was to continue with his work—"it is not by abstract clarifying of the position that we will ever conquer the stultification of the present, but by an achievement."[26]

He was more willing to enter the fray when he believed that politics was misrepresenting a writer he respected. He had earlier highlighted the absurdities in Richard Chase's attempt to turn Melville into a propagandist for the "new liberal" scripture. In the fall of 1952, he stepped into the breach once again, agreeing to write an introduction to a collection of essays on Theodore Dreiser—a writer whose reputation had plummeted with the postwar repudiation of the socially conscious literature of the thirties. The introduction and the book represent a rare intervention on the side of American realism (and Dreiser) at a time when formalist criticism was deploring the "clumsy" writing associated with realist fiction and the political culture was still recoiling from the "leftist" tendencies found in writers like Dreiser and James T. Farrell. Kazin worried that a new "genteel uninvolvement" was taking root in American writing. "Literary people" enjoying the "cosy prosperity" of "post-Communist, post-Marxist" America did not want to be reminded of the poverty, fear, and lust for power that Dreiser had depicted in American life. These are the realities "we should like to leave behind" in our increasingly self-satisfied, middle-class lives, "this prig's paradise . . . the best of all possible worlds."[27]

The essay is also noteworthy as Kazin's first public challenge to Lionel Trilling, Dreiser's most influential detractor. In a 1946 essay in the *Nation,* "Reality in America," republished in *The Liberal Imagination,* Trilling had attacked Dreiser for anti-Semitism, "intellectual vulgarity," and "showy nihilism." His real target, however, as Kazin noted, was not Dreiser, in whose novels he took little interest, but Dreiser's "liberal" defenders. The latter, Trilling argued, had demonstrated a "doctrinaire indulgence" toward all of Dreiser's faults because he, unlike Henry James, seemed to speak for the "realities" in American life invoked for progressive causes. Trilling acknowledged that by opposing Dreiser to James he was deploying writers "at the dark and bloody crossroads where literature and politics meet"; but, he insisted, it is "not a matter of free choice" whether one goes there or not. Kazin disagreed. Does it make sense, he asked, for a literary critic to evaluate writers—Dreiser, James, whomever—according to the politics of their supporters? "What happens whenever we convert a writer into a symbol is that we lose the writer himself." Responsible criticism does not confuse writers with political positions, much less the politics of their supporters. Trilling was not writing about Dreiser; he was using him for the wholly extraliterary purpose of reeducating the liberal class.[28]

Though Trilling makes no reference to the "new liberalism" celebrated by his Columbia colleague Richard Chase, he was obviously writing out of the same felt need to repudiate the old liberalism for its "naivete" and especially for its alleged failure to purge itself of Communist sympathizers and sympathies. If in the process, Dreiser's novels were reduced to anti-Semitic tracts, much as Melville's fiction had been turned into new liberal "scripture," this apparently was a price worth paying to correct and discipline the defenders of a suspect literary past. While Kazin realized he was bucking the trend and saw little chance of dispersing "the stinking fog of orthodoxy" creeping over the country, he could at least object when the opportunity presented itself. He could also refuse to participate. On May 7, 1953, he wrote to Irving Kristol declining to contribute to *Encounter,* a publication of the anti-Communist Congress for Cultural Freedom (secretly funded by the CIA) that Kristol was then editing. Kazin had been reading Kristol's and Sidney Hook's justifications for revoking the civil liberties of Communists and other alleged subversives, and he was wary. "You must understand," he told Kristol, "that I have very grave doubts

Alfred Kazin's mother, Gita Fagelman Kazin
(Courtesy of the Berg Collection and Judith Dunford)

Young Alfred posed on
a pony (Courtesy of the
Berg Collection and Judith
Dunford)

Alfred Kazin being held by a friend (Courtesy
of the Berg Collection and Judith Dunford)

KANTROWITZ, LEON
He is taking a course in
"How to Become A Lady Killer".
Vice-President of Annex Dramatic Club.
C. C. N. Y.

KANTROWITZ, SIMON
Here's a lad who's full of ambitions,
We hope he accomplishes all of his missions.
G. O.

KAPLAN, IRVING
*Member of English Book Squad, Varsity
Basketball, Hockey Squad, Senior Basketball
Team.*
Harvard College

KAPLOWITZ, JOSEPH
As an actor he has secured his fame,
But is known as the most conceited in Lane.
*Capt. of Hockey Team, Lane Follies, Choco-
late Soldier, H. M. S. Pinafore.*
N. Y. U.

KARESS, ISIDORE
Hair of blond,
Eyes of blue;
Boys like you,
Lane has but few.
*Varsity Basketball, Senior Class Baseball
Team.*
C. C. N. Y.

KATZ, MARTIN
Who are you?
What have you done?
Help me so I
Can write a pun.
G. O.

KATZ, THEODORE
In class you always look so cozy,
Does that account for your being nosy?
Sec. to Miss Vergason.
C. C. N. Y.

KAUFMAN, ABRAHAM
He plays a mean game of soccer.
Forum.
Brooklyn College

KAZIN, ALFRED
A Galsworthy and a Paderewski
In vain would he be;
But methinks that a scholar
He is more apt to be.
*Arista, Pre. Forum, Associate Editor of Mir-
ror, Orchestra, Librarian.*
C. C. N. Y.

KESSELMAN, YETTA
Yetta may be small,
But how her voice can fill a hall!
Typist for Year Book.
C. C. N. Y.

KOCH, AUGUST
Wake up, "Little Boy Blue;"
Time won't wait for you.
G. O.

KOLETTY, MARION
"Who are you looking for"?
"Oh, Marion's in the candy store."
*Sec. to Mr. Wolfe, Pres. and Sec. of Glee Club,
Pinafore, Lane Follies, Chocolate Soldier.*

[28]

Page from the 1931 Franklin K. Lane High School (Brooklyn, New York)
yearbook showing the graduation portraits of Alfred Kazin and classmates
(Courtesy of Judith Dunford)

City College of New York, 1930s (Courtesy of CCNY Archives)

City College library, 1930. Kazin studied here and in the Great Hall.
(Courtesy of CCNY Archives)

Kazin's City College graduation
picture, 1935 (Courtesy of the
CCNY Archives)

Henry Steele Commager (left) and Alfred Kazin with an unidentified
woman, Leopoldkron's Schloss, Salzburg Seminar, 1951
(Courtesy of the Berg Collection and Judith Dunford)

Alfred Kazin in New York City, ca. 1952
(Courtesy of the Berg Collection and Judith Dunford)

Hannah Arendt and Heinrich Bluecher, ca. 1950. Arendt and Bluecher were friends of Kazin in the late forties and fifties. (Reprinted by permission of Georges Borchardt, Inc., on behalf of the Estate of Hannah Arendt)

Alfred Kazin, Michael Kazin, and Ann Birstein at Cape Cod, 1955
(Courtesy of the Berg Collection and Judith Dunford)

Michael Kazin and other famous-name freshmen at Harvard University, 1966. From left: Michael Kazin, Michael Bundy (son of Assistant Secretary of State William Bundy), Arthur Kempton (son of columnist Murray Kempton), Thomas Saltonstall (son of John L. Saltonstall Jr., of the Massachusetts Saltonstalls), Roy Campenella Jr. (son of the former Dodgers star), and Andrew Schlesinger (son of historian Arthur M. Schlesinger Jr.). (Reprinted from the *New York Times*, Sam Faulk photographer)

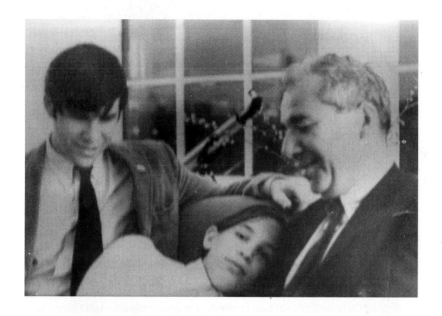

Michael Kazin, Cathrael (Kate) Kazin, and Alfred Kazin, in Alfred's New York apartment, 1967 (Courtesy of the Berg Collection and Judith Dunford)

Alfred Kazin in Palo Alto, California, in 1978
(Photo by, and used courtesy of, Judith Dunford)

Judith Dunford and Alfred Kazin on their wedding day, 1983
(Courtesy of Judith Dunford)

Alfred Kazin lecturing in 1986
(Courtesy of the Berg Collection and Judith Dunford)

Alfred Kazin with his sister, Pearl Kazin Bell, in 1987
(Courtesy of the Berg Collection and Judith Dunford)

Judith Dunford, Alfred Kazin, and Louis Auchincloss visiting Russia in
1990 (Courtesy of the Berg Collection and Judith Dunford)

Alfred Kazin with his son Michael
and grandson Daniel, 1991
(Courtesy of the Berg Collection
and Judith Dunford)

Alfred Kazin at his home in Roxbury, Connecticut, 1994
(Courtesy of Judith Dunford)

about the magazine, and that I won't undertake to write for it, unless I'm sure that it's not going to be dominated by the point of view you expressed in your civil liberties articles, which scared the hell out of me." Whether out of conviction or for other reasons, Kazin never wrote for *Encounter*, one of very few prominent anti-Stalinist intellectuals not to appear in its pages.[29]

The upcoming Indiana and Harvard appointments relieved Kazin of his more immediate financial worries, but he knew each would entail distractions and significant expenditures of time—preparing lectures, working with students, socializing with colleagues—not spent on *The Western Island*. Determined to make progress on his book before these new responsibilities overtook him, he tried to carve out a period each morning for writing. But he found it hard going. "Utterly appalled by how much . . . there is to do in addition to *the* book," he wrote in a March 1953 journal entry: the James review, the Dreiser essay, reading for Harcourt, studying Donne for his next week's radio broadcast, preparing his New School lectures. But he refused to cut back. "I will do my Island book, and I will teach . . . I will have it all," he told himself, though he admitted to Herbst in April that the book was proving "a tough nut to crack" and he was barely inching his way into it.[30]

New York was itself a distraction, a city of distractions, particularly for someone having trouble getting on with the job. There were parties and dinners with friends, appointments with editors and publishers, unexpected encounters (running into Saul Bellow outside the Museum of Modern Art and retiring for drinks), an afternoon spent with Pearl and Dylan Thomas, whom she brought around for a visit—"a charmer, but so stupid with drink, it was impossible to talk with him." Then there were the *Partisan Review* get-togethers—sometimes quite interesting (depending on whom one talked to), at other time times, an ordeal. For the wives, who were typically dumped at the door to fend for themselves, they were almost always an ordeal. Ann Birstein recalls sitting alone one grim evening when *Partisan* editor William Barrett approached her from a group that had been glancing in her direction to ask whether he could look at the part in her hair to see if she was a natural blond. "We were not gentlemen—or ladies," *Partisan* editor William Phillips later acknowledged. Diana Trilling agreed, adding that the *Review* parties were "torturing affairs for any woman who attended them as a marital appendage rather than in her own right." Kazin was himself often bored and disgusted by it all. "The minute you enter the house, see the drinks laid out, the first conversational gambit given, you know it all in advance," he wrote in a June 1953 journal entry. "A competitive, soused-up intellectual is a mockery of the arts and the religious man's vision—he comes in always walking in shoes that are too large for him, he talks by habit, he lives in a routine. You never know with these people whether you are talking criticism or gossip. I'm sick to death of all this talk, self-perpetuating, competitive talk"—though (he admits in another entry) he could be as combative in "the tactics in self-advancement and self-assertiveness" as the next guy.[31]

Kazin spent July teaching at the Indiana School of Letters in Bloomington, where everything was "bleak"—the Courthouse Square, the long ride from Indianapolis, even "these farmers and hillbillies com[ing] to town in the hot moist noon." It was his first and last summer at Bloomington. In August, he and Ann escaped to Wellfleet on Cape Cod. There were only a few people there, nothing like "la plage des intellectuels" that would descend on "Joan's Beach" in future years. But Alfred was content. He liked the quiet and the chance to work on his book and prepare himself for Harvard —which he anticipated with some misgiving.

In May he had gone to Boston to look for an apartment and meet with colleagues; he had left anxious and depressed—resentful that he did not have an academic post, but also frightened of what one might do to him. After a "miserable" time making conversation with Howard Mumford Jones and Perry Miller, he worried that "com[ing] too close to academics" he might lose his "innermost self," and even his will to write. Would his personality accommodate academic habits and niceties? Was he assimilable? Did he want to be? Would he have written A Walker in the City as a professor? Would Fitzgerald have written The Great Gatsby? These and similar unsettling questions would soon provoke a searching and timely essay, "The Writer and the University." Would the benefits outweigh the costs as the evolving, expanding American university found ways to attract and accommodate (and tame?) writers, novelists, and poets? Kazin believed writers deserved whatever support they could get, but he wondered whether the academy ultimately served their creative interests.[32]

Whatever uneasiness Alfred may have felt about Harvard dissipated once he and Ann moved into 17 Chestnut Street on Beacon Hill in September. (They arrived in a hearse commandeered by the well-connected Rabbi Birstein, who insisted they travel in something large enough to carry themselves and their belongings.) Reveling in the historical ambience of Beacon Hill and the prospect of teaching at Harvard, Kazin walked the cobblestone streets, thinking he had at last entered one of the "old villages . . . of purely imaginative memory" that he had stored away in his childhood dreams. Now that dream appeared to be coming true. Suddenly everything, including the book, seemed possible—"so full of projects and plans and ideas and people walking through my life and my utter joy and confidence in being here. . . [I] decided not to pick and choose, to make the day heavy with false decisions, but to do *everything*." Contributing to his excitement were the glittering social occasions. One week he was dining at the Leontieffs, where he had a long talk with the eminent Austrian scholar-critic Erich Heller—"a man I like so much and am so attracted to." A week later he was attending an affair at Zelman Cowen's, where he discussed Beethoven with Isaiah Berlin, a discussion he continued when they met later at a dinner party at Arthur and Marion Schlesinger's. He and Birstein socialized also with a number of Harvard faculty, including Walter Jackson Bate, Howard Mumford Jones, and Benjamin Kaplan of the Law School (later justice on the Massachusetts Supreme Judicial Court) and his wife, the writer Felicia Lamport. Both Kaplan and Lamport would become lasting friends of Kazin and Birstein, to be visited on return trips to Boston. Alfred was impressed by virtually everyone and everything he encountered at Harvard: the intellectual eagerness of his students, the cultural opportunities offered by Boston and Cambridge, "the fine social intelligence" of the people he was meeting—so unlike the "graspingness" and "assertiveness" he was used to back in New York. Ann was equally enthusiastic. "We loved Harvard, we loved Boston, we loved being social lions, and could have gone on that way forever."[33]

Unfortunately, it all ended at the close of the semester in January—with no indication of a future appointment. Years later, Kazin learned from Harry Levin, who had been head of the English Department at the time, that he had been seriously considered for a permanent position (and strongly supported by Levin) but that his name had not appeared on the final roster of candidates. Even without the nod toward the future, Kazin was grateful. He found he could be happy in an academic environment and hold his own with some very bright students. One of these, the writer Theodore "Ed" Hoagland, would become a good friend—though Kazin remembered him from Harvard largely for his "frightful stammer, the worst I ever encountered." Another reason why Kazin was not terribly concerned about the immediate future was that he had recently learned of his appointment to the William Allan Neilson professorship at Smith for the 1954–1955 school year, a prestigious post for writers and scholars of distinction currently held by W. H. Auden.[34]

One thing the Harvard experience did not do was advance the writing of *The Western Island.* Kazin thought a good deal about the book while preparing classes on Emerson, Thoreau, Whitman, and Twain. But the ideas remained ideas, scattered notes and journal entries. Moreover, his decision not to make decisions, but to do *"everything,"* suggested a restlessness hardly conducive to the kind of sustained and focused effort that finishes books. Indeed, by spring his attention had shifted to a different book, *The Love of Women,* an autobiographical effort that would describe the various women in his life. He was sure he needed to write such a book but uncertain how to proceed, and he was getting little encouragement from his wife. Initially confused about his intentions, she grew increasingly uneasy with his passion "to praise God's plenty in women, to praise human freedom and love and desire," as he put it after an argument. After Ann's unqualified enthusiasm for *Walker,* Alfred was surprised and "resentful" of her attitude toward this new project.[35]

There was another point of discord. Ann was finding it increasingly difficult to accept her husband's special relationship with Hannah Arendt. Mindful of his ultimatum that "I can't love you if you don't like her" (Arendt), she had put up with Arendt's "bossy" behavior and personal slights in Europe. Back in New York, she had accompanied Alfred to evenings at Arendt and Bluecher's home, where the guests sat in a semicircle, "a circle of iron," with Arendt at the center dispensing wisdom. When Ann occasionally offered an opinion, Arendt typically laughed it off—"Little one, what do you know?" It was an insupportable situation for Ann that reached a new level of insult and outrage at an Institute of Arts and Letters ceremony in early May. Arendt, there to receive an award, met Alfred and Ann at the door, told her to go sit in the balcony with Rose Feitelson, and led him down the aisle to sit with her in the front row. Ann went to the balcony as told; then, furious that Arendt would presume to escort her husband away while ordering her to the balcony (to sit with his former girlfriend!), she left the building alone and rode the subway home. When she confronted him, Alfred apologized, then called Arendt to tell her that she had hurt Ann's feelings. Arendt hung up on him. He would later look back on the episode as the beginning of "the end of a beautiful friendship."[36]

Alfred and Ann had planned to go to Europe for the summer but then decided they could work better at home. She recently had had a short story, "Stab Me," published in the *New Yorker* and was working on a novel. In July they rented a cottage in Wellfleet. This time there was plenty of company, including Saul Bellow and his son Gregory, the Schlesingers, Philip Rahv, James Wechsler, Harry Levin, Mary McCarthy, and Daniel Aaron, among others. Edmund Wilson had just left for his ancestral home in Talcottville, New York—fearful the summer visitors would "frustrate and tempt" him. There was much partying and much worrying about not being invited to parties. McCarthy, famously alert to the nuances of social situations, wrote to Arendt, "Your value is continually being called into question; you shiver at all the social slights, even from people you don't care for." Kazin was one of the people she didn't much care for; still, she was shocked when he "cut . . . [her] dead" one afternoon for no apparent reason. She later learned the snub was in response to some blighting comments she had made about the decor of Kazin and Birstein's New York apartment. Never a personal favorite of Kazin, McCarthy would later figure as the subject of one of his harsher portraits.[37]

Smith

"This is a *nice* quiet world," Kazin wrote to Edmund Wilson in mid-September after moving into the guest apartment overlooking Paradise Pond in Northampton. "Not many writers around, God knows, but to battle-weary New Yorkers, serene, 'rustic,' quiet." To Sylvia Plath, a senior writing him up for the *Smith Alumnae Quarterly,* he confided that he and Birstein were "enchanted by Northampton" and that their view overlooking Paradise Pond was truly "paradisiacal." He was looking forward excitedly to his year as Neilson Professor. He liked and respected a number of people at Smith—Daniel Aaron, Newton Arvin, Robert Gorham Davis in the English Department—and would soon become friends with Sidney Monas in Russian history and Edgar Wind in philosophy and art. To be sure, Northampton was not Cambridge, and "the nervous gentilities" of the small college world could make conversation difficult. "It is impossible to talk to these people," Kazin complained after a strained evening with Arvin and Elizabeth Drew. "In fact, I do all the talking, and they listen to me with a snotty little smirk on their faces." But he found the overall atmosphere congenial. He liked the teaching: a course on literary masterpieces from Homer to Tolstoy and a short-story writing course. And he very much appreciated the look of the students—"lovely young pullets in shorts and red socks riding on their bicycles." As the honored Neilson Professor, he was the cock-of-the-walk at this women's college. "Smith girls" are so lucky, gushed *Mademoiselle,* they "can pedal from Pulitzer prize–winning Oliver Larkin's beloved course in American art to critic and writer Alfred Kazin's twentieth century American novel course."[38]

One of the responsibilities of the Neilson professorship was to deliver two public lectures, one in the fall and one in the spring. In his fall lecture, "The Opera House at Parma: Stendhal and the Image of Italy," Kazin reflected on Stendhal's and his own preference for Italy over France. At the time, he was hoping to write a book on Stendhal, Mozart, and Italy, a project he abandoned for lack of the necessary musical expertise. (This did not keep him from breaking into Mozart arias on the street, after sex, and, to relieve the strain, after difficult occasions with his family.) He also delivered a public lecture, "The Age of Harmlessness," at neighboring Mount Holyoke College in October. Reiterating his complaint in the Dreiser introduction against the new genteelism and the present embarrassment with American realist fiction, Kazin pointed to another sign of the times: the middle-class blandness of fiction in the *New Yorker*. It is unclear whether Birstein, a recent contributor, was present to hear *New Yorker* short stories dismissed as "quick, portable, sellable, readable and disposable." One eager listener who did attend was Judith Schwartz, a Holyoke student on scholarship from the Bronx who felt she had "just heard the most brilliant man" and wanted her New York accent back. Twenty-nine years later, she would marry him.[39]

Kazin was not just being polite when he told Sylvia Plath that he was enchanted with Northampton and Smith. He was very happy to be there and let it be known he hoped to stay on. He was a popular teacher; he liked most of his colleagues; and he brought national attention to the school. Thus, he was shocked to learn in mid-November that he would not be asked to return. "I was prepared to be 'happy' here, forever" he wrote in his journal. It was a hard blow. He had been unaware of anything wrong— though Ann had warned him—and he had fallen in love with "the physical quietness and general ambience" of Northampton. He came to believe that Newton Arvin had been responsible for the decision, that he was still angry over Kazin's attack on his friend, Granville Hicks, in *On Native Grounds*. Perhaps Arvin saw him as untrustworthy, even as a bully. He had certainly sensed Arvin's coolness, found him difficult to talk with, but had not suspected that he would oppose his appointment, much less sway others to his view.[40]

The situation at home was also becoming difficult. Ann was one month pregnant and miserable with nausea, and Alfred was fearful. "Last night I felt so awful I thought I would die, and Ann came to bed weeping, weeping, weeping." There had been fights, fights and reconciliations, and more fights, "a whole solid day spent fighting with Pussy, then going to movies with Pussy, then fucking with Pussy." The pattern had been developing for some time—the fury, then the passion; yelling, fighting, then sex and reconciliation. This had not occurred in his earlier marriages, and he did not understand what was happening. Did the sex depend on the violent reversals of feeling? He only knew that the rush of feeling left him in "awe" with a "delicious" sense of "the most passionate screaming inner closeness." Moody and often conflicted in his own feelings, he was startled by Ann's extreme mood swings, which, combined with a "slam-bang, swashbuckling expressiveness," could make him feel as though he were married to a Saul Bellow character in extremis—brilliant, shrewd, desperate, angry, loving, and half-hysterical. He had had hints of these qualities earlier but was only now sensing their range and intensity. What he could not fathom was where it all might be leading.[41]

Though he was living and teaching in rural New England, Kazin had not lost touch with New York. He returned every few weeks to visit his parents, to tape another session of *Invitation to Learning*, to meet with friends. He usually stayed in the apartment on 111th Street, which he had leased to Pearl, who shared it with Sonya Tschabaschov, Saul Bellow's girlfriend.

During an October visit, Kazin passed another milestone: he made the first of many appearances on television. Speaking without a script on *Moby-Dick* on the high-brow program *Camera Three,* he was amazed by his fluency and poise—"chattering away in a composed and business like way . . . What has been locked up in me so long, I thought in wonder . . . is now broadcast alive to millions." Jack Kerouac, who always seemed to be catching Kazin in a command performance (as well as looking for critical approval, this time for *Doctor Sax*), sent in a fan's note—"you were as great as ever you were at the New School, which I hope doesn't sound like flattery and [is] intended to be only a tribute to your unselfconsciousness before the camera millions." In fact, it *was* extraordinary that the boy who once stammered incoherently in front of his classmates was now talking easily and expertly before television's "millions."[42]

Another person Kazin sometimes met on his visits to New York was Celia Koron. He was not proud of this and felt that he had "betrayed my dear Puss," but he believed he needed "relief from the pressures" of home. And, typically, he felt guilty about feeling guilty. "I would rather sleep with somebody else because I really want to, than not do it out of fear of 'God.' I am sick and tired of playing tag with myself, of feeling guilty, of dodging my self-inflicted accusations. I want to unroll, to power out, to *be,* to *be,* simply to *be.*"[43]

The Smith decision against keeping Kazin was not only a shock, it was cause for alarm. He did not see how they were going to make it. Apparently the scramble would have to continue—freelancing, applying for grants, hustling up visiting professorships, getting his name on lists. He asked Bellow, now teaching at Bard College, whether there might be a place for him there. But he was soon weighing another option. In early December, Charles Cole, president of Amherst College, contacted him about a possible professorship in their American studies program. Kazin was interested, but also uncertain. Amherst was one of the best small colleges in the country, and it had an established American Studies Department. However, he would he housed in an English Department with a faculty he did not know. And he would be teaching only men—not an appealing prospect. On the other hand, he would be able to stay in a region whose natural surroundings he had grown to love and that suited his literary (and writing) interests. "I feel terribly wealthy and lucky just to be in this part of the country," he wrote in his journal when contemplating the move to Amherst. "Is not the secret of this 19th century American writing I love really its grasp of rhyme and colors from nature? The sea, the leaves, the ponds, the forest."[44]

Ann did not feel so lucky. She would be trapped in the role of faculty wife in a small town away from family and friends, among people she did not know; and she would be looking after a newborn. Alfred could get away to the office, the classroom, the library. Where was she to go? And with the baby, would she have the time and energy to write? But the baby also argued for Amherst. They needed something more secure than what Alfred's catch-as-catch-can New York hustle could provide. He accepted Cole's offer in January—$9,600 per year, two courses each semester—but not without reservations. "I will not lie to you," he wrote Henry Nash Smith. "I am unused to all this."[45]

Kazin did not let the Smith decision sour him on his last semester there as Neilson Professor. "Trembling with the joy of being alive here," he wrote to Arendt in March and confessed that he had "fallen madly in love with trees." He had even been skating on the river. He was also having fun in the classroom, more at ease teaching a class in American fiction than he had been swatting up the *Iliad* and the *Inferno;* and he had some very good students, including Sylvia Plath and her friend Jane Truslow, both taking his course in advanced expository prose. In addition to his teaching, Kazin was busy with preparations for a public colloquium to be hosted by the college on "The American Novel at Mid-Century" (March 3–4) at which he, as Neilson Professor, would give the keynote address. Hoping to make the colloquium a lively affair that would engage the issues raised in his earlier talk on the "harmlessness" of American fiction, he invited Brendan Gill and William Maxwell of the *New Yorker* as well as Saul Bellow, whose *Adventures of Augie March* had recently been savaged in a *New Yorker* review by Anthony West.[46]

Kazin led off with an address titled "The Novel and the Unknown," attacking the faint-heartedness of the contemporary novel more concerned with "art," "style," and "correctness" (typified by *New Yorker* fiction) than a risky probing of the unknown. Predictably, Gill and Maxwell took strong exception to Kazin's comments. They accused him of creating a "straw man," the novelist who tries to write "a novel of style" without substance, and of blaming novelists rather than encouraging them. Did Alfred Kazin really think that critics should be prescribing the right subjects for novelists to write about? Gill needled him personally, declaring that novelists are often useful critics, but that it is a rare critic who can write a good novel. Still smarting from the West review, Bellow sided with Kazin, warning of a growing "fastidiousness" in contemporary culture—though, with three novels to his credit, he may not have been pleased to hear his friend speak so generally and dismissively of recent fiction. (Ralph Ellison, whose *Invisible Man* had won the 1953 National Book Award and had accompanied Bellow to the colloquium, may also have had reservations.) The audience was evidently pleased by the spirited interchange, which one reviewer of the proceedings called an up-to-date "battle of the books." After the public debate, the battle moved to a private party, where, according to Birstein, matters took a domestic turn, with Maxwell praising her latest novel, *The Troublemaker*, and her husband, unable to work up enthusiasm, giving "an almost painfully embarrassed shrug."[47]

While gratified by the lively, even festive, quality of the colloquium, Kazin took the issues seriously. The participants, he insisted in his closing remarks, were not speaking merely about the strengths and weaknesses of recent fiction; they were describing the character of the age—an age in which the creative-intellectual will seemed (to him at least) to have settled for far too little. He had made a similar point in his Mount Holyoke address and would make it again in the postscript he was then writing for a 1955 paperback edition of *On Native Grounds*. There, backed by his account of the modern American literary achievement, he argued that disillusionment with the radical hopes of the thirties and a corrosive skepticism about humanity's moral and imaginative will after the war had led to a general failure of literary-intellectual nerve. Where "our early 20th century fiction seemed to carry the whole weight of society," current fiction "exquisitely studi[es] personal problems alone." "Contemporary novelists do not criticize the world they live in and have no thought of changing it; they merely live in it, as fish do in the sea, and keep their own counsel."[48]

Writing the short postscript proved to be an unexpectedly difficult "ordeal" for Kazin. Puzzling over his hesitations, he realized he had been afraid of looking "ridiculous" by encouraging writers to take a more expansive view of the possibilities of their art and to engage more forcefully and idealistically with the larger social, political world. He sensed that he was increasingly out of step with the times and had been for a while. In a 1948 essay on the critic Paul Rosenfeld, he had observed that "reactionary" trends on the political-social scene were coincident with a spreading "fear of the humanistic moral passion that is still the great heritage of our romantic and democratic past." Apparently, the collapse of thirties radicalism, the totalitarian menace, and the deepening cold war were to be accompanied by a general suspicion of all "liberal," "progressive," "revolutionary" writers, ideas, and heroes. Shelley, Emerson, and Whitman (as well as Dreiser) were to be swept out along with Marx, Lenin, and the American Communist Party. The situation had hardly improved by the mid-fifties. One risked feeling absurd and hopelessly out-of-date as well as "naive" and "immature" citing, much less celebrating, the idealistic, "romantic," and often revolutionary impulses that had figured importantly in much of the great literature and art of the past 150 years. It seemed to Kazin that truth now "consist[ed] in saying no" to anyone fool enough to say "yes," and wisdom meant refusing to be duped about the darker motives behind all idealistic aspiration. "To stand up and to shout as one could for these old generous ideas and ideals, for all these things so easily condemned these days as 'sentimentality,'" had become an unnerving experience. Sensing uneasily (and correctly) that he had been overtaken by a profound paradigmatic shift in cultural attitudes and taste, Kazin had come to feel very much alone. "I do not belong to any of it."[49]

Perhaps out of resentment at feeling marginalized, he had accepted a summer assignment from the *New Republic* to review Leslie Fiedler's *An End to Innocence.* A collection of essays drawn from the *Partisan Review, Commentary,* and *Encounter* republished, Kazin notes, "with the particular encouragement of leading members of the American Committee of Cultural Freedom," Fiedler's book attacked American liberals for their reluctance to face up to the fact that they had been "wrong, drastically wrong, about the most important political fact of our time"—the true character of the Soviet Union. Citing verdicts against Alger Hiss and the Rosenbergs, Fiedler declared that it was time for liberals (including himself) to admit to their lost innocence and acknowledge that the "buffoons and bullies" and political opportunists had been right all along, "damnably right." Kazin did not quarrel over the Hiss and Rosenberg verdicts, or even challenge Fiedler's defense of the McCarthy and the HUAC investigations. Instead, he asked, what was served by this drumbeat by one-time radicals condemning the errors of the past? What was served by such paroxysms of "new liberal" guilt (now growing old), aside from the exhibitionist pleasure of people like Fiedler and Whittaker Chambers preening themselves on "courageous" public confessions of misplaced beliefs and shameful gullibility? For Kazin it was an old story: former believers (Communists like Chambers and Sidney Hook, Trotskyites like Fiedler) turning their disillusionment into a new article of faith that was as aggressively intolerant as their earlier convictions. Meanwhile, the real casualty of this disenchanted "realism" was belief itself, belief in human aspiration and "moral passion," in "the old generous ideas and ideals" that had inspired writers and thinkers in the past and whose espousal had come to seem hopelessly belated and ultimately "ridiculous."[50]

Fiedler was an easy target—a "bright," "brash," "shrewd" young man, obviously on the make, displaying the "sad wisdom" of the chastened radical, riding a "fashionable thesis" as far as it would take him. But disposing of Fiedler did not solve the problem of belief. In October, reflecting on his friend Richard Hofstadter's recently published The Age of Reform, Kazin felt more dispirited than ever. A critical study of the progressive-populist tradition whose values had inspired many of the writers celebrated in On Native Grounds, The Age of Reform was anything but brash. Kazin found it all too persuasive, "brilliant and realistic and true." "Who can quarrel with Dick about the silly populists?" But if Hofstadter's book was measured and well reasoned where Fiedler's was strident and posturing, it, too, in Kazin's opinion, was spiritually disheartening—"no values, no real values, no conscious values." As such, it was of a piece with the whole "post-liberal move of my generation . . . from Trilling up and down; it is not that the particular point they are making is ever wrong. What is wrong is the whole careful, saving, prudential point of view—they are always within the circle of what they are criticizing."[51]

What was wrong, of course, was that they were no longer radicals, no longer angry and defiant. It was difficult, perhaps impossible, for former radicals, now advancing comfortably in their careers, to stay alienated and "fighting." Nor, Kazin admitted, were they alone. "I [too] have graduated from suffering," he wrote a few months later. "I have joined the great middle-class world of daily self satisfaction—What has happened is the story of America. The 'success story' for America does blunt and dampen all one's fires by its belief in happiness and fulfillment. All those fat Jews— Jason Epstein and my own Richard H[ofstadter], all the Beichmans and Cultural Freedom overseers—all this represents the death not merely of 'alienation' but of the vital, fiercely hungry intelligence. . . . We wanted to get out of Brownsville, the steerage, and we got into the 'American' business." Bemused by the shifts in the political-cultural climate, Kazin began reflecting on yet another possible project, an "American orthodoxy book" that would describe the ideological temperament and historical changes shaping his generation—"a passing generation," a "delayed generation," a "baffled generation," he would variously call it, "a generation brought up on ideas of radicalism, of freedom and independence and revolutionary militancy, brought down to a period more or less statist, 'big,' bureaucratic, reactionary." It would be about the intellectuals, about New York, about the ex-left, "about Fiedlerism, Hookism, and Trillingism, about everything I know and have been a part of." This was a project he was sure he could handle. "I have it, all of it, inside me." As with most of his book ideas, it would take time and assume many shapes before actually appearing—in two books, *Starting Out in the Thirties* (1965) and *New York Jew* (1978). In the meantime it would provide some direction to his creative plans and a way of accounting for changes occurring in himself and his relations to once-radical friends and the now increasingly remote radical past.[52]

Amherst

On August 29, 1955, Alfred, Ann, and two-month-old Cathrael (Kate) Kazin (named after a favorite uncle of Ann's) drove fifteen miles northeast from Paradise Pond to Amherst, where they unloaded their meager assortment of furniture into the large, twelve-room, college-owned house with an extended porch at 155 Woodside Avenue. Kate would spend the next two years of her life a couple of blocks from where Emily Dickinson had spent her first years—in a town that to her parents appeared little larger than when Dickinson's father had been the college treasurer. Amherst, Kazin wrote in his diary on the day of arrival, is "one long, long street. You just get out on the street, start walking and trust to luck." With its "washed down" appearance, the street, Pleasant Street, seemed of a piece with the "almost convent-regular quality" Kazin detected in the Amherst people. Nature relieved the monotony—the giant copper beach in the yard, the Pelham Hills on the horizon, the fields and nearby woods, the Connecticut River, "the changing shades and weight of the weather." "Nature was a daily event," Kazin would later write of Emily Dickinson's Amherst. It and family sexual liaisons had helped sustain her and her family in this "tribal village." Whether they could sustain the Kazins was another matter.[53]

Kazin had accepted the Amherst position with some reluctance. He did not relish teaching at a men's college. He had hated City College with its "odorously male" and politically aggressive student body. Whether or not Amherst men were less odorous, they seemed far less politically and intellectually engaged—"the way [they] lie back in their seats as if they were 106 and just recovering from coronary thrombosis," "the dry belchy look" of the languorous, bored, and entitled. Kazin would remain unimpressed by his Amherst students, who did not strike him as "serious." Jackson Bryer, one of Kazin's more serious students, remembers him as "quite cynical." "I know you won't do this reading. But here is the assignment anyway," was Kazin's usual class manner. There were a scattering of foreign exchange students whom he "played to" as more serious than the rest, while the few Jews and other minorities, who might have livened things up, stayed invisible. Peter Schrag, a Jewish alumnus, has written that attending Amherst in the fifties "required that one abandon blackness or his Jewishness and become as much as possible a WASP." Kazin was acutely conscious of the gulf between himself and the student body, and no more so in than in his course "American Problems." "The little stinkers," he wrote after reading a set of term papers on immigration, were all for immigration provided it aided the cold war effort, provided it was "good for us." What has not occurred to "these young shits" "is that America as an idea, as a civilization, is founded on the very idea of immigration, on the idea of a world-civilization and a world frontier." Cold war "realism," it seems, was not confined to politicians, "new liberal" critics, and revisionist historians.[54]

Kazin was as unimpressed with the Amherst faculty as he was with the students—the "marble-like puffiness one sees in the faces of Amherst men grown middle-age professors." He felt a special aversion to the members of the English Department, "which dislikes me as much as I dislike the English Department." In *On Native Grounds,* he had warned of the New Criticism's move into the academy. He now found himself in the midst of what he had dreaded—a crusading insistence on reading texts "objectively" through close attention to language and formal structures. How, he asked himself in exasperation after a faculty meeting, was one to keep alive a passion for literature "surrounded by these braying voices, these noises, these nothings 'objectively' addressing themselves to their new-critical shit and straw?" Over the summer, he had written a piece for the *Atlantic Monthly* on the growing number of "writers" in the American universities and declared it not necessarily a bad thing. Writers had to make a living. But he warned that the rewards and subtle pressures, the "recognition and acceptance," offered to the writer "may be actually harmful," for "they can distract and deceive and soften him up." Apparently, Kazin was not softened up. "I feel sick to my stomach this morning after seeing these nothings," he wrote in his journal after the English Department Christmas party. "To have to stoop every time one talks. To be everlastingly conscious of the puzzled or disapproving expression on their little faces: Academic rot and rottenness."[55]

His dismissive contempt was recognized and resented. The news got back to him that he was rude and condescending, that he took himself too seriously. "Who the hell do you think *you* are?" was the look on many faces. He occasionally wondered if this had been a factor in the Smith decision. Was he too insistent on his moral authority? Daniel Aaron later recalled that Kazin's penchant for moral grandstanding had upset a number of people at Smith. But he was unapologetic. "I do take myself seriously as a writer and do feel important to myself and other people." He had a few friends at Amherst—Joseph Epstein in the Philosophy Department, Benjamin DeMott (a writer) in the English Department. He continued to see a good deal of his friend Sidney Monas, assistant professor of Russian history at Smith—"Sidney, who at least is always Sidney, and whom I love; alone of all the people I meet every day here." Alfred and Ann occasionally entertained Robert Frost, who held a chair at Amherst and sometimes gave a reading or talk. Frost interested him, a species from an earlier, tougher generation, like Edmund Wilson, a nineteenth-century man "who dominated the twentieth by having grown up with that ancient ferocious self-assertion"—and never a hint of "objectivity."[56]

For all his irritation with the students and faculty, Kazin was not unhappy at Amherst. If the students exasperated him, he enjoyed lecturing on material that interested him to classes that usually filled. If the town was boring, it was also charming, "charming and boring," the emphasis shifting depending on his mood. If there were few people to talk to, he always had his work and "need not look for conversation where there isn't any." Ann, however, was deeply unhappy. With the baby she felt more trapped than ever and despaired of finding time and energy for her writing. She took little comfort in the company or the attitude of other faculty wives who "were vocal about dedicating their lives to husband, house, baby and cooking." Her unhappiness met with resentment from Alfred, whom she claimed did not understand her complaints. Why was she complaining when other wives were glad to type their husbands' manuscripts? In fact, he did understand. Ann wanted (and demanded) exactly what he wanted, the freedom to get on with her work without interference. He understood and he feared for the future. He had been uneasy with Carol because she was temperamentally different from him, had little grasp of his interests and enthusiasms. Now he was married to a woman who understood him all too well. "Great God, what security have I got living with a temperament just like mine. What security have I ever had, *will* I ever have, with a mind like mine and a wife like mine?" Perhaps, the answer was to stop thinking of Ann as a "wife" in the family sense, to go back to "the only kind of wife one has ever been for me, as a comrade and lover, and fellow-writer." But this ignored the facts—the baby, household duties and responsibilities. "I cannot relieve her of being a mother, and my situation with her is based on my outrage that she should not accept all this gladly." There was no solution, and the unhappiness would continue.[57]

The nearest thing to a personal solution for Kazin was to stay busy and keep the assignments coming. In the fall, he arranged with Houghton Mifflin to write an introduction to the Riverside edition of *Moby-Dick*. He was also negotiating with Seymour Lawrence, editor of the *Atlantic Monthly*, to write regularly for that publication. (Though he would do a couple more reviews for the *New Yorker*, the Smith colloquium effectively concluded that eight-year relationship. Without a word being said, Kazin assumed he had been "dismissed.") He had originally hoped to publish a version of "The Age of Harmlessness" in the *Atlantic*, but in the end substituted "The

Writer and the University," which appeared in October. Lawrence liked it and wondered whether Kazin would do a follow-up on the spread of the New Criticism. Kazin was willing—"I am surrounded by the new criticism on every side here"—and persuaded Lawrence to pay $100 over their "top price" ($250) for it. But again, in a switch that would become routine in his dealings with the *Atlantic,* he submitted the *Moby-Dick* introduction instead—which Lawrence agreed to publish.[58]

Alfred was busy with other work in the winter and spring of 1956—a review-essay on Ernest Jones's biography of Freud for the *Times;* a review (very negative) of Nelson Algren's *A Walk on the Wild Side,* also for the *Times;* a piece on Sholom Aleichem for the *American Scholar* (his first); a review of J. F. Powers's *The Presence of Grace* for the *New Republic;* and preparations for two appearances on *Invitation to Learning* on George Eliot's *Adam Bede* and Henry James's *The American Scene.* Although the work engaged and excited him, it failed to keep domestic strife at bay. Ann resented that she had to spend time and energy looking after the baby and doing household matters while her husband was free (or freer) to get on with his work. The disapproval he sensed in his colleagues' faces—"Just who the hell do you think *you* are?"—was unmistakable in the laughter and snorts of dismissal to any allusion made at 155 Woodside about the tasks before him. Alfred was well aware of the difficulties under which Ann worked and knew that he would go crazy if their situations were reversed. He also sensed professional rivalry—her refusal to do him "housewifely kindnesses," her "determination to show, by not serving me, that I am not [more] important than she." He had been aware of similar responses in his sister, but, where Pearl had shied away from open hostility, "Ann has more guts, and fights solidly to make sure I will not get above myself, that all things will be equal between us." Hoping that some time off and a possible change of venue might improve things, Kazin approached President Cole in March for a year's leave of absence. Cole gave him half a year, but not until the fall of 1957. In the meantime, Kazin accepted a summer Fulbright to teach in Nice. Perhaps a return trip to France would bring back better times.[59]

They spent the last week of June in Paris, visiting with the Geists and with Ralph and Fanny Ellison, who were in town. In early July, they moved into an apartment in Nice with the baby and realized immediately that they had made a mistake. Another pretty town in a pretty area—they could see the sea from their balcony—but domestic, self-contained, and for the Kazins "the death of our spirit." "We look at them, we are always outside them," Alfred wrote of provincial towns—Nice, Aix-en-Provence, Amherst. Nice was as bad as Amherst, with no babysitters, no help, no one Ann could talk to, no way to get out at night—a replay of the "jailhouse conditions" back home, and a forecast of things to come. After the conclusion of his duties in Nice, they took a quick trip to Oslo and Stockholm, where Kazin delivered a public lecture and met the Jewish poet and German refugee Nelly Sachs. They spent a few days in London, where they visited with the writer and Cambridge fellow C. P. Snow, and on September 10, boarded the *Île de France,* dreading what lay ahead.[60]

Henry Steele Commager, whom President Cole had lured away from Columbia, arrived on the Amherst campus in the fall of 1956, leading Alfred to hope that with the lively, gregarious Commager family in the neighborhood, his unhappy wife would find the social atmosphere of small-town Amherst a little more to her liking. But Ann, her face as "mutinous and despairing" as ever, was unmoved; and in November she made it clear that this was her last year at Amherst—even if she had to leave without him. Kazin was not surprised; though he suspected that the difficulties between them went deeper than Amherst. Still, he agreed that life there had become impossible for the two of them. Moreover, New York might be just what he needed for his book projects. He complained in his journal that he had lost his "writer's way" at Smith and Amherst, that the "machinery" and "easy rhythm" of college life had left him too comfortable, that he was no longer "fighting." New York could be "a decided clearing of soul."[61]

Attributing a lack of progress to the "easy rhythm" of college life was a useful attitude for someone preparing to leave it. A more serious concern, a "besetting weakness," was Kazin's admitted inability to stay with a subject. "I am devoured by so many interests, I cannot help responding to so many calls on my imagination"—as well as to offers and requests from magazines and journals. Like an undisciplined child (or habituated reviewer with a promiscuous intelligence) Kazin felt he had "to have it all," to explore and write up every subject that interested him—and get paid for it. But he also believed that in his writing, "as in everything else, the rule is to follow the tug of one's reins," to go where he felt he had to go at any moment, without sorting through every option, without knowing where it all would come out.[62]

He certainly did not know where or when *The Western Island* would come out. He had been worrying over this project for ten years since his 1946 Guggenheim application proposing a book focused primarily on Herman Melville. The topic had since broadened into a study of "America as an idea, a hope, a symbol for the ages," which would include discussions of a dozen writers. Determined to tap into feelings of hope, fear, and wonder from his immigrant background, Kazin wanted to bring a sense of personal urgency to the writing. He certainly did not want to compete with the "academic" books on American literature now appearing—Henry Nash Smith's *Virgin Land* (1950), Perry Miller's *The New England Mind* (1953), Charles Feidelson's *Symbolism and American Literature* (1953), R. W. B. Lewis's *The American Adam* (1955), and Richard Chase's *The American Novel and Its Tradition* (1956). Such books, he complained, always go to "the scheme, to the 'intellectual' rather than to the felt." He wanted the excitement, impact, and risk of a more personal, more "emotional," encounter. "There is a kind of explosion, true, but one can sort out the pieces. The boat rocks, one shivers trying to adjust oneself to the force of the blow, but one is in the direct path of life. These damned schemers and finaglers are always looking for subjects, for things to write about . . . The 'naive,' the feeling man exposes himself directly to the subject."[63]

But how to structure such a book or control its parameters? The difficulty with writing an intensely personal book of criticism, making oneself the measure of everything, is the absence of any "objective" way to limit and organize one's material. "I am constantly trying to put everything I am and everything I think into a book, and it takes me years to realize just what I can make a book of." Carl Van Doren had given him his subject when he had written *On Native Grounds*, and he had had a tradition of progressive history (primarily Parrington) to provide him with a means of selection and a dramatic structure. Now, in the fall of 1956, he was on his own with lots of ideas—"I constantly fall into the trap of the 'good idea'"—but with no plan that could move him forward. He still wanted to write the book. He sensed a genuine spiritual kinship with its writers, these "sensitive, solitary brooders and fantasts." He believed he understood from the inside their "long loneliness," "their sense of themselves as queers and different ones in a violently expansive society." But he had yet to arrive at a "scheme" or even a sufficiently formulated vision that would organize his sympathies and insights into a coherent pattern or narrative.[64]

Alfred submitted his resignation the last week of January 1957. It was agreed that he would be on paid leave in the fall and come back for a final term during the winter of 1958. The die was cast; but if he had expected the decision would bring peace at home, he was disappointed. Ann had learned of his continuing affair(s) in New York and, angry and bitter, was threatening one of her own. The fights continued, the two of them now sleeping in separate beds, "breathing defiance." Ann spoke of divorce, and Alfred wondered whether that might be the solution—"when I think of the eternity possibly spent under this tense regime." Their marital difficulties, he later recalled, had become common knowledge in the community—the shouts and screaming, the crash of upended tables and thrown dishes— rude (if welcome) distractions to the "immense long-suspended quietness" of domestic Amherst.[65]

In the midst of this trouble Kazin found some relief working with Daniel Aaron on an anthology of Emerson's writing (for Houghton Mifflin) drawn largely from Emerson's journals. In the introduction, Kazin, who spoke with some authority on the subject, takes note of Emerson's "genius at catching life's quickness," of recording that "flash" of insight that can occur when thought is freed to pursue its own ends—"uncalculated and head long and indiscriminate." The journal entry, Kazin argued, was "fundamental" to Emerson's thought. Though he made his living delivering lectures and publishing essays, it was the original journal entry, "the dry reflection," "the spontaneous epigram," where Emerson "met life with the greatest possible directness."[66]

Kazin was also working on a critical essay of Faulkner's *Light in August.* He had long been embarrassed by his treatment of Faulkner in *On Native Grounds,* where he had "badly underestimated" the writer he now believed to be "the last American of great vision." To produce a major interpretive essay on a novel central to Faulkner's achievement would go some ways toward righting an old wrong. He also believed he might be able to use Faulkner to exemplify and illuminate a central concern of *The Western Island.* The essay, "The Stillness of *Light in August,*" is arguably Kazin's strongest interpretive piece. In it he draws on a variety of personal interests —the moral effect of the American landscape, the fear and the reality of isolation in American life, the nature of Christian compassion, and the role of meditation ("brooding reflection") in American writing—to illuminate a wide range of effects and qualities in the novel. Reading the essay (which Philip Rahv claimed was "the best analysis of *Light in August* I have ever seen—and not only of the novel specifically, but of Faulkner's creative psychology in general"), one watches a critic alert to all aspects of the subject—the style, the themes, the quality of mind at work in the text. Yet Kazin keeps his topic in focus—the stillness he sees at the heart of the novel in the silent figure of Joe Christmas—"the most solitary character in American fiction," who in his suffering evokes our "spiritual" attention and compassion. Christmas is castrated and murdered by a crazed racist in an act of "immolation" that leads Faulkner (and Kazin) into a meditative reverie of pity and terror that suggests Greek tragedy, but that has obvious overtones of the crucifixion as well.[67]

Though written on a twentieth-century novel, the Faulkner essay draws on Kazin's reflections on the isolation and solitude he associated most closely with the nineteenth-century writers Melville, Emerson, and Thoreau, who were to be the leading figures in his still unwritten *The Western Island*. It had been fifteen years since his journal entry noting "the terrible and graphic loneliness of the great Americans" and more than a decade since his Guggenheim proposal for a book on Melville focusing on the "'existentialist' conception of man as a stranger on the island of his own being." During these years, Kazin had published numerous essays and reviews highlighting solitude, isolation, loneliness as the central experiences in American life and the keys to the American literary imagination; but except for the republication (and indifferent reception) of a number of essays collected in *The Inmost Leaf* (1955), he had no book to answer for his long-hoped-for and much delayed study, nor any clear plans for one—a fact he found exasperating and on occasion humiliating. "What a long time between books," Irving Howe (author of four books during the fifties) had exclaimed when introducing him for a talk at Brandeis University in the spring of 1956. The words would echo in his dreams: "How little Kazin produces! What a long time between books!"[68]

Feeling he had to do something, but unsure of just what, Kazin began talking to Seymour Lawrence about moving from Harcourt Brace to Atlantic–Little, Brown. He had been with Harcourt since it had bought out Reynal and Hitchcock in the forties, and he was fond of his Harcourt editor, Denver Lindley. But while supportive and patient, Lindley tended to let writers steer their own course and move at their own pace; Kazin felt he needed someone more directly involved in the books he was working on. After some discussion, Lawrence invited him to send him a bill of particulars. On May 21, Kazin laid out the details in a letter that seemed as much a warning as a hopeful proposal.

He explained that he owed Harcourt an advance of $1,118.27 on his unwritten book on American writers, *The Western Island,* whose "nature" remained "highly indeterminate." He was also working on an autobiography, *The Love of Women,* that he saw as a "sequel" to *A Walker in the City.* Other projects included *In Praise of Diaspora,* a book on "Jewish writers and Jewish history"; a book compiled from his journals; a small book on Edmund Wilson; and a "textbook" collection of essays compiled by Ann Birstein and himself, which he thought should remain with Harcourt. There were other unnamed projects (including the "orthodoxy book")— "many ideas." But he did not want to "delude" anyone about his productivity. "I very badly need some direct encouragement and stimulus for my many (mental) projects, and I honestly feel you provide this for me much better than Denver does." But, he warned, "I can be a hell of a problem to a publisher because of my slowness and faintness of heart." Lawrence took the risk, agreeing to cover the advance for *The Western Island,* and in July, Kazin wrote to Lindley requesting an official release. His instincts were right. Seymour "Sam" Lawrence proved to be the engaged and attentive editor he needed; as was his successor at the press, Peter Davison. Kazin would publish three books with Atlantic-Little, Brown (though not *The Western Island*): *Contemporaries* (1962), *Starting Out in the Thirties* (1965), and *Bright Book of Life* (1973).[69]

"New York, New York!"

With his tenure at Amherst ending, "the mad scramble" to make a living in New York would soon resume again. The immediate future looked promising. Kazin had been awarded a Berg professorship at New York University for the fall semester that would supplement his paid leave from Amherst. He was also lining up magazine assignments. His new relationship with Atlantic-Little, Brown would, he believed, lead to increased opportunities to write for the *Atlantic.* Over the summer, he would write two excellent

pieces for it—"Dry, Light and Hard Expressions," a discussion of the epi-
grammatic qualities of Emerson's prose; and "The Posthumous Life of
Dylan Thomas." (He found it interesting to be writing the piece during a
visit by Pearl, given her affair with the poet.) He also hoped to arrange something with Max Ascoli, publisher of the *Reporter.* Finally, there were the
Guggenheim and Bollingen foundations to petition—all part of the "splinterey, tormented, boring, boring, attempt to get things by my profession."[70]

The Kazins spent their Cape Cod vacation the last of June at Waquoit,
where they rented a house with Sidney and Carol Monas. Still angry with
Alfred for his infidelities, Ann began an affair with Sidney. "You've had your
fun in the past, why shouldn't I," Kazin remembered her saying. He was
angry, but hardly surprised; and thinking of Celia Koron, he wondered
about the "defections" awaiting them in New York. But Ann was not
through. The affair over, she wrote it up as a short story, "Love among the
Dunes," showed it to her husband, and began sending it out to magazines. In
it, Sidney ("Charlie") is "quick and authoritative," with a voice "absolutely
wonderful, deep, masculine, energetic," "everything a man should be,"
while the cuckolded husband is "poor miserable Max," "a lump on the
beach," who likes reading Thomas Carlyle and reciting Matthew Arnold's
"Dover Beach"—"a hopelessly distracted academic fossil," as its target later
put it. The affair ended the friendship with Sidney (whom Alfred called a
"schlemiel" in *A Lifetime Burning in Every Moment*). Published in the
Mediterranean Review (1971) and in the collection *Summer Situations*
(1972), the story was Birstein's most aggressive statement to date that she
had her own resources, was not to be taken for granted, and was moving to
the city fully armed. Kazin who "winced" at the "brutal" treatment of Max,
dismissed it as a work "of one of these literary females who sucks our
blood."[71]

The first week of September the Kazins moved into an apartment at 110
Riverside Drive. Alfred would be in New York until January and then
return to Amherst to teach his final semester; Ann and Kate would remain
in the city. They were ecstatic to be back—"percolating inside with excitement, can't stop bubbling. It's New York again, New York, New York!"
Kazin recalled that Kate, then two years old, was standing up in the back
seat waving to passing cars as they entered the city. When asked to sit down,
she reportedly said she couldn't: "I feel married to everybody." Ann was

particularly pleased to be back on home turf. After reflecting on the pleasures of pushing Kate's stroller past friendly doormen and Jewish shopkeepers rather than Amherst lawns, she published "The City Mouse" in
Mademoiselle, describing the advantages of bringing up children in the city.
Alfred was relieved by Ann's change of mood but knew their troubles were
not over. "The sadness of those first days in Nice, of the two long years at
Amherst, is now with us here," he wrote after fighting with Ann about Kate
three days following the move. "Why can't we simply be the bad, bad, anti-
social unadjusted and 'criminal' parents that we dare not admit to being?"
Even allowing for the self-dramatizing hyperbole that typically accompanied Kazin's mood swings, there was cause for concern. To what extent
was Kate to become a pawn in her parents' ongoing fight for time, freedom,
recognition, and advantage?[72]

Busy with family and friends and his classes at NYU, Kazin did little
writing in the fall. At a crossroads in his teaching career, he was also contemplating changes in his long-range writing plans. He had worked out a
new outline for *The Western Island* in August, but got no further. "The old
electric urgency" was gone. Indeed, he questioned whether the project still
made sense, either on its own merits or measured by personal needs. His
original notion of the American writer in solitary contemplation—"the
lonely transcendental heart . . . poised on an empty rock looking out to sea"
or into the interior of the continent—seemed less and less tenable. He also
wondered whether basing everything on his *personal* relation with his
writers ignored some important differences. One could be attracted to the
passion and conviction of the lonely prophets of the nineteenth century,
but could one really regard them as contemporary soul mates, spiritual
comrades-in-arms? They were, after all, writers from a different age,
"lonely, wayfaring men *in* their time," living in and overtaken by history.
This argument had been brought home with special force after the publication of *The Inmost Leaf* (1955), a collection of his essays from the forties
and early fifties.[73]

The book had received generally positive, if limited, attention. However,
two of the reviewers, Leo Marx (*New Republic*) and Hans Meyerhoff (*Partisan Review*), had complained that Kazin's exclusive focus on the creative
psychology, or what Melville had called "the inmost leaf," of his writers
tended to isolate them from the real world of events. "Reading Mr. Kazin,"

wrote Meyerhoff (Mary Lou Petersen's husband!), "one often feels as if the great literary rebels were only fighting an inner struggle over the success or failure of their artistic visions and aspirations, as if there were no enemies abroad." He also noted that *The Inmost Leaf* largely ignored the American scene after World War II and that Kazin seemed content to look back to his writers without taking due account of different historical conditions. While Kazin found it "odd" to be taken to task by his former mistress's husband, he could not dismiss the thrust of his critique. One could make too much of a writer's (or one's own) "lonely integrity," particularly at a time when, as he had repeatedly complained, writers seemed notably disengaged from history and public life. The more he thought about it, the more convinced he became that he needed to reengage history, to direct more of his attention to contemporary matters—and the more *The Western Island* seemed a project whose time had passed.[74]

Persuaded that he wanted (and needed) to involve himself more directly with the contemporary literary scene, Kazin contacted Max Ascoli at the *Reporter.* He knew Ascoli from the New School, where Ascoli had been a teacher and a dean. An Italian anti-Fascist who fled Italy in the thirties, Ascoli had founded the *Reporter* in 1948 (with money from the Sears and Roebuck Rosenwald family, into which he had married) and had sought out Kazin for advice. Kazin had encouraged him in the project and had contributed an article to its first issue. But preoccupied with *Walker* and writing for the *New Yorker,* he did not become a regular contributor. In the fall of 1957, no longer writing for the *New Yorker* and lacking a steady income, Kazin indicated his availability to Ascoli and was soon contributing essays— roughly one a month—largely on contemporary literary and cultural matters, essays he hoped might lead to a book on contemporary fiction.

With an eye on the latter, he submitted project (book) proposals in early January 1958 to the Guggenheim and Bollingen foundations. Tentatively titled *The Twenties and After,* the book would describe the difficulties contemporary writers faced trying to find their own voices in a period still dominated by the great "moderns." While acknowledging the achievements of the latter, Kazin argued that their influence and the assumptions associated with their study, now codified by the New Criticism, made it difficult for other kinds of writing to get a serious hearing. It was as if "the modern" had become the only tradition, setting the standards by which all

future literature was to be judged. Much of the thinking in Kazin's proposals reprises his attacks on the academic New Critics and his critique of
the "harmlessness" of recent fiction. What was new was his decision to
dedicate himself "wholly to the service of contemporary literature." *The
Twenties and After* was not to be an elegy for past achievement but a
sympathetic "description of what the contemporary situation is really like
for writers"—"from a writer's point of view."[75]

Kazin's stated intentions in his Guggenheim and Bollingen applications
(both of which were funded) correlated nicely with his anticipated work for
the *Reporter.* They also coincided with the move back to New York, which
he now saw as a move from a timeless world of nature, the seasons, trees and
fields to the crowded, ever-changing life of the city. Walking the streets,
looking for an apartment in August, he was at first appalled by the changes
he was seeing, especially "the whole Latin-American, dark Cuban-night
side of NY" with its "vomit-making bodegas" encroaching on the Upper
West Side. It was as if "the stony land, the uninhabited island" of *The
Western Island,* had disappeared into "the slag-heap of nations." But weaving among the garbage cans on Columbus Avenue, watching "the Puerto
Ricans sitting on the steps of those flaking Brownstones—color of caked
shit," he realized it was time "to come to grips with the *realness* of America
. . . the full concentrated force of the living moment, the present hour."
Returning to New York, he was returning to history, contemporary history,
to Whitman's "teeming nation of nations" and "the joy of being toss'd [once
again] in the brave turmoil of these times."[76]

CHAPTER EIGHT

The Writer in the World
Part 1
1958–1963

It is not to favor the ideal self over the world, or the world over the self, but to
bring the self back into the world as its natural home.

—Alfred Kazin, Journal, May 2, 1959

In mid-January 1958, Kazin moved into an apartment in Northampton
next door to Daniel Aaron. He had a semester's work to do at Amherst,
and he was not happy to be back. Nor was he pleased with the news
from New York. Oscar Cargill, the head of the New York University English Department, had led Kazin to believe he might be hired permanently.
This, he discovered in late December, was not to be. Kazin told Josephine
Herbst that Cargill had "gotten so emotional about me after my great
success there that he had written an article denouncing me for some trade
journal of English professors." Cargill did denounce Kazin (along with
Cleanth Brooks and John Crowe Ransom!) in *College English*, not for his
"success" but for turning out "facile" essays rather than solid scholarship.
Cargill, who had praised *On Native Grounds* in a reader's report as "one of
the best critical books ever written in America" and called its author "a gold
mine," now labeled him one of "the masters of reviewermanship," even
suggesting that his more recent work lacked "manliness." This was not the
kind of person one elevated to "securest positions."[1]

Lacking such a position, Alfred would have to depend on his "facile"
essays. Anticipating the uncertainty and the hassle, knowing what "a long

hard pull it [will] be all around," he wrote to Henry Nash Smith about a possible position at Berkeley and even asked Heinrich Bluecher about openings at Bard. He did not want to leave New York yet again, and he doubted Ann would move under any conditions. But would he be able to support the family?—a troubling question at a difficult time. "Alfred Kazin to dinner, tonight," Sylvia Plath wrote in a March 10 journal entry. "He's broken, somehow embittered & unhappy; greying, his resonance diminished. Lovable still." Working as an instructor at Smith, married to the poet Ted Hughes, Plath could appreciate Kazin's situation—"his wife too a writer, another couple to speak to in the world." She was also alert to family matters—"how babies complicate life." But if Kazin seemed forlorn and diminished to Plath (who was not feeling particularly happy herself), he sounded a more resolute note in a letter to Hannah Arendt. "Looking forward without much fear to the future," he wrote in April about their move. "My whole inner freedom was being blasted by this job." In New York, he would be free and in the right frame of mind to write the book that had been "tormenting" him for some time—"on the presentness of present moments in American fiction (the unchartered country ahead)."[2]

Although it was forced on him, Kazin came to see his return to New York as a plunge back into life, "life as its broadest and keenest," as well as an opportunity to take his work in a new direction—one less preoccupied with the solitary, meditating self he associated with rural New England and more focused on "the presentness" of the present amid the noise and excitement of the city. He was also returning at a time when the present seemed on the verge of something new. The Eisenhower administration had two more years to go, but the worst of the "dark ages" seemed to have passed. Alger Hiss and HUAC were no longer in the headlines. Senator McCarthy had recently died, following his censure by the Senate. The anti-Communist paranoia of the late forties and early fifties had largely dissipated. There was talk of "détente"—nothing very definite, but enough to allow a critic freshly focused on the present to think that history was on the move again, that the world might be opening up a little. Perhaps there was room in it for an intellectual interested in something other than anti-Communism.

It turned out there was. Over the next several years Kazin would reach the peak of his influence as a writer/critic/intellectual, appearing regularly in the *Reporter* and the *Atlantic,* frequently in the *American Scholar,* the *New York Times Book Review, Commentary,* and the *Partisan Review*— with occasional visits to *Holiday* and one regretted appearance in *Playboy* —"it was stupid of me to write for them." He was invited to a private meeting with the secretary general of the United Nations and to a private lunch with the president of the United States. He was asked to join the first cultural delegation to the Soviet Union, and was "sent . . . for" by the state of Israel, all the while appearing on countless radio and television panels and speaking at more than a dozen colleges. In 1953, Randall Jarrell had explained (and complained) that the country had entered "an age of criticism." "There has never been an age in which so much good criticism has been written," or been so "astonishingly or appallingly influential." Its influence would continue into the late fifties and early sixties, with Kazin a major beneficiary and a major voice—one of the "go-to guys," remembers Theodore Solotaroff, the person one turned to for the latest on Saul Bellow and Bernard Malamud or for a sober assessment of recent literary enthusiasms and cultural trends. Kazin was "the ideal reviewer" for the period, Robert Alter recalled—not, perhaps as sporting and provocative as Leslie Fiedler, nor as politically in-touch as Irving Howe, but lucid, lively, and "sane."[3]

Kazin enjoyed his growing prominence—"I love my worldliness, my snobbery, my ease." But worldliness, influence, and proximity to power also posed risks (and temptations) to a critic trying to work out a satisfactory stance toward the contemporary scene. Would the public Kazin swamp the private Kazin? "It is not to favor the ideal self over the world, or the world over the self," he warned himself in May 1959, "but to bring the self back into the world as its natural home." The need to balance the self and the world (the writer and the world), to exist in both, but not to lose oneself in either, would be a subject much on Kazin's mind over the next several years, shaping his reflections on current fiction and culture, on politics and the role of the intellectual—as well as guiding his efforts to achieve a psychic or spiritual balance in his own life. Alfred looked to the shocks and changes of the public world (much as he looked to the intimacies, surprises, and eruptions of living with Ann) as a means of forcing him out of himself, out of the "private reveries" to which he knew he was dangerously prone—always "lost in this labyrinth of my own soliloquy." Yet, he did not want to lose touch with "the inwardness" he encountered every day in his journal, the inward voice of Alfred Kazin thinking, which, like Emerson's "man thinking," went its own way, made its own discoveries, refusing the circumscribed expertise of "the delegated intellect" as well as the compromises of public life. If he was happy to bid good-bye for the time being to nineteenth-century New England, "that old landscape of dreams and wonders," he was not prepared to relinquish the habits of thought of the Emersonian thinker-at-large, intent on his intellectual independence, working out things his own way—whatever the admitted risks of loneliness and self-preoccupation, "that cruel self-consciousness that I feel pressed over my brain like a vise every night."[4]

Alfred would not resolve the quarrel between the self and the world in articles or in his journal, where the "soliloquy" continued unabated—and certainly not in his dealings with Ann. He did, however, work his way toward a resolution (or compromise) of sorts in his next autobiography, *Starting Out in the Thirties* (1965), where, prompted by memory and the aesthetic demands of narrative, he merged the public and the private into a version of history, "personal history," that achieved its ends outside the rigors of "objective" scholarship. While the result might not have satisfied Oscar Cargill or those who preferred their history with footnotes, it pleased readers and reviewers immensely and remains one of Kazin's most popular and useful works.[5]

"The Alone Generation"

If you lived in New York in the late fifties, the Upper West Side was "the place to be," Ann Birstein wrote in her autobiography. The apartments, once the homes of the *alrightnik* crowd, now removing to midtown and Westchester, were affordable and spacious, if in need of some repair. For the array of (mostly Jewish) writers, intellectuals, and academics, many of them associated with Columbia University, now moving in, it seemed the ideal neighborhood in which to raise children and keep the conversation going. Daniel Bell, then at Columbia, remembered it as a sort of "intellectual kibbutz." Nathan Glazer, another neighbor, described it as "a bourgeois extension of Greenwich Village . . . an area to which intellectuals moved when they had children and a more stable life." For Birstein, recently decamped from WASP Amherst, it was an "extended Jewish family," the members borrowing each other's crockery, exchanging children's clothes, walking freely and unannounced in and out of each other's kitchens, parties, and lives. "We socialized easily and frequently—and haphazardly," remembered Irving Kristol, who lived on West End Avenue in the apartment building later occupied by Irving Howe. It was all rather "loose" with Columbia professors—Lionel Trilling, Richard Hofstadter, Meyer Schapiro, Fritz Stern, Daniel Bell—mixing (sometimes uneasily) with former Columbia students—Norman Podhoretz, Steven Marcus—and with visiting City College and *Partisan Review* intellectuals. There was even a shared "family" physician—Dr. Herman Tannenbaum, the Upper West Side's family doctor to Jewish intellectuals, who, it was alleged, was not above gossiping about the state of Podhoretz's hemorrhoids.[6]

Kazin was grateful (more or less) for the company and conversation, for the casual encounters as well as the parties and dinner engagements— though he could become impatient with the never-ending chatter and argument, everyone "chopping away." In *New York Jew* he would satirize the members of "the Upper West Side Hebrew Relief Association" as an acute but rather sour lot, chronically disillusioned with their radical past and the evils of Communism. He had additional blighting things to say about the Columbia contingent, who managed to assuage their disillusionment with "a certain intellectual contentment" attributable to their rising professional status. Kazin was not part of the Columbia community, and listening to Bell, Stern, and Hofstadter (who loved Columbia for its "society"), he could feel excluded and aggrieved—as well as embarrassed by his own resentment. "My lower-class immigrantish reverie for schools, for the university. Symbols of authority still to the Brownsville boy. How absurd. But see Danny Bell and Columbia."[7]

Still, he was glad to be back in the mix, and he if sometimes tired of the competitive personalities, he was also stimulated by good talk. Following an evening's conversation with Nathan Glazer, he came away impressed— "his comparative intellectual success is not accidental"—and inspired by his determination to write sociology as "contemporary history." Glazer was attempting to do in his field exactly what Kazin wanted to do in his—to write *"historie contemporaine, historie morale."* An evening with the more combative Lionel Abel could also be exciting and productive. "His intelligence was a real pressure on me. None of this relaxing with the dopes or the yahoos. We talked so well that he inspired me, and my whole idea of man as a future-seeking animal seemed clear to me." Even Irving Kristol, whom Kazin sometimes found "as appetizing as a stale fish," and whose politics he deplored, was a friendly, helpful neighbor—as well as a supportive editor (now at the *Reporter*), offering encouragement and constructive advice on Kazin's book plans.[8]

Alfred went to his share of parties and dinners. Ann loved to attend and to give parties, and she was an excellent and ready hostess—one area in which her husband had no complaint. She reveled in the company, the social excitement, and could (reportedly) turn out a wonderful meal, often impromptu, when he unexpectedly brought people home for a meal—a practice few wives would tolerate. Edmund Wilson recalled an "excellent little buffet supper" Ann provided on the spur of the moment when he, Paolo Milano, Max Kampleman, Ved Mehta, and Alfred unexpectedly arrived at 110 Riverside Drive after drinks at the Algonquin. Alfred, however, had only so much time for socializing. With no regular salary, he had to scramble. He had signed on to teach a course in the fall of 1958 at the New School titled "Novelists and Storytellers of Contemporary Experience: American Fiction since World War II," much of which he had to work up from scratch. He was also reviewing regularly for the *Reporter* and writing as many pieces as he could for whatever journals and magazines would pay him. Depending on the length, he received between two hundred and four hundred dollars for most pieces, which together with the fellowships was enough (barely) to support a family of three in minimal comfort in the post-*alrightnik* Upper West Side.[9]

Kazin found the work demanding and at times exhausting, but he also found it rewarding. "Yesterday, wrote the piece on Pound and the Freshmen, then read proof on the *Holiday* piece on New York, the *Harper's* piece on contemporary fiction. When I see from how many different memories, learning periods, the assembled sentences in an essay come, I am staggered and awed by the amount of training that goes into the actual race I run in a particular piece . . . before the race will be run again." He was also feeling increasingly confident of his critical skills and gratified by signs of his growing influence. His frequent appearance in the more prestigious and intellectually fashionable magazines and journals was turning him into a force to be reckoned with. Favorable mention by Kazin in the *Atlantic* or the *Reporter,* John Aldrich wrote in 1964, had become a necessary rite of passage in the making of a new writer's career. Kazin learned firsthand of his influence when he received a grateful word from writers whose books he had praised as well as from writers such as Bernard Malamud, Herbert Gold, and Vladimir Nabokov, who complained he had misread their latest. He was sometimes bemused by his influence—"O mighty Kazin, the critic, whom all authors supplicate for a good word (while mighty Kazin shivers in his boots)"—but took comfort (somewhat melodramatically) in the conviction that he knew what he was talking about. "To have this diagnostic power is to feel lonely, but it is an aloneness that is undescribably powerful and reassuring, for it starts with the fact that I know what I think."[10]

In May 1959, Kazin was asked to testify (with Malcolm Cowley) at a hearing on a charge by the Post Office Department that D. H. Lawrence's *Lady Chatterley's Lover* was an "obscene" novel and should not be distributed through the mails. Kazin testified that the novel was not obscene but rather a religious or spiritual novel that treated sex and sexual passion as something very real but also "very much as a symbol of man's need to fulfill himself religiously in the world." While he acknowledged, when pressed by the Post Office attorney, that sex was increasingly prevalent in contemporary writing and that certain parties may have been marketing books by appealing to "sexual interests," he argued that nothing was further from Lawrence's intentions. "His whole purpose is to make sex seem holy, beautiful, free. The last thing in the world he ever wants is to appeal to sexual interests in what I call the bad sense." Whether or not his and Cowley's arguments were decisive, the Post Office allowed the book to be shipped through the mail.[11]

Kazin was not through with the subject of Lawrence, sex, and its place in the culture. Shortly after the trial, Norman Mailer asked him to read a manuscript and possibly recommend it to his publisher, George Putnam. Kazin, who had reviewed *The Naked and the Dead* (unenthusiastically) and was familiar with *The Deer Park* and a number of Mailer's shorter pieces, read the manuscript of *The Time of Her Time* (eventually published in *Advertisements for Myself*) and recommended it to the publisher as "a powerful and significant piece of writing." He sent a more ambivalent note to the author. After acknowledging Mailer's considerable talent, Kazin told

him he found his "self-conscious" preoccupation with male sexual performance depressing and his determination to make sex the measure of everything alarming. "You are the Rabbi of screwing, the Talmudist of fucking,
the only writer in years who has managed to be so serious about sex as to
make it grim." Moreover, Mailer's apparent determination to abstract sex
from personal relationships had reduced it to a mere marker of "neurotic
self-esteem." "What an ultra bourgeois fondling of one's own face, one's
own thoughts, one's own prick—what coldness—in bed and out of bed and
toward the world in general!"[12]

After such a dressing-down, one might have expected Mailer either to
have written Kazin off or to have sought him out for a fight. Instead,
perhaps grateful for the recommendation, perhaps looking for an intellectual sparring partner, he invited him to lunch at the Plaza Hotel, where,
Kazin recalled, Mailer lectured him about the importance of sex and argued that sexual repression caused cancer—all the time oblivious to the
fashion show taking place in the same room with models in "sexy dresses"
circling their table. In fact, Kazin's quarrel with Mailer, as Mailer undoubtedly realized, was as much with the times as with himself—specifically, with
a culture in which sex was the latest form of irrationalism disengaged from
the world. His case for *Lady Chatterley's Lover* was that sex in Lawrence
meant love, love of another, love of the world. But sex, Kazin explained in a
piece following the trial, "Lady Chatterley in America," seemed increasingly to consist of a lonely yearning for sensation and (to judge from the
dress and manner of the youthful "Beat" culture) defiant expressions of
personal license. Watching a group of teenage boys with their earrings,
tight pants, and ducktails "swish" by him on the street, Kazin concluded
that Lawrence was neither pornographic nor risqué, but, by current standards, passé, hopelessly out-of-date. Like Keats and the other Romantics,
Lawrence believed in the "the holiness of the heart's affections." He also
believed that the heart's affections (including sexual passion) could change
things, unleash energies that would make for a better, less constrictive
world. By contrast, Mailer and his ilk seemed to think that sex was for
sensation ("cheap thrills") and showing-off ("performance")—"nothing
joyous or beyond-self in it at all."[13]

At one point during their Plaza lunch, Mailer, trying to stake out the
grounds of their disagreement, reportedly told Kazin: "You are a nine-

teenth century man, still close to your emotions, I'm mid-twentieth century, all assaulted and besieged and assailed." It was a shrewd observation.
In an important sense, the differences between them were generational—
not so much in years—Kazin was only seven years older—as in the age with
which each identified. Despite his determination to engage with "the presentness" of the present, Kazin often felt closer to times past (the nineteenth and early twentieth centuries) than he did to the present. "I am
beginning to feel that I belong, truly, to a passing generation," he had
written in 1951. That feeling had deepened throughout the decade, exacerbated in part by his marriage to Ann Birstein, twelve years his junior, who
was not above calling him in private and in public a grumpy, old pedant—a
"hopelessly distracted academic fossil." Reviewing and teaching recent
fiction, much of which he found disappointing, also suggested disturbing
generational differences.[14]

His complaint was not the lack of talent. Like everyone else, he savored
"the hilarious accurate cadences" with which J. D. Salinger mimicked the
conversations of jaded New Yorkers, as well as the "highly polished comedy"
in Truman Capote's depiction of upper Bohemian New York. He acknowledged "the obvious talent and guts" that marked nearly everything Mailer
wrote. But serious fiction demanded more than a comic sense and a flare for
dialogue, even more than "talent and guts." It demanded a probing curiosity
into the way the world worked. Unfortunately, the writers he was reading,
members of "the alone generation," as he called them, seemed determined
to close themselves (and their characters) off from a world that they considered too insensitive, boring, banal, or pointless to be worthy of serious
attention. For Kazin, the most egregious instances of this incurious, "know-
nothing" self-centeredness were to be found in the writings (and posturing)
of the Beats. Whatever his earlier interest in Jack Kerouac (never very
strong), he now saw his "deliberately churned up novels" together with the
Beat poetry of Peter Orlovsky and Allen Ginsberg as the essence of intellectual "sluttishness." Catering to a thrill-seeking army of "spoiled brats"
playing at poverty and "alienation," the Beats pretended to the Romantic-
Protestant spirit of rebellion only to empty it of serious content. Disgusted
with the media attention lavished on them and possibly chagrined at his
early support of Kerouac, whose *On the Road* became the "sacred" text of
the Beat phenomenon, Kazin warned serious readers against "allowing the

addict-quality of such books to stand for 'intensity' "—as if "carelessness" and "slovenliness" signaled some new order of authenticity.[15]

By the spring of 1959, he was losing all patience with current fiction. "I know what I think. I know what I believe, and I believe that much of contemporary lit. I read nowadays is bad," he wrote in a March journal entry—a conclusion he found dispiriting and socially awkward. "What to say . . . to my friends and would-be and very hostile friends like Herbert Gold or Harvey Swados, or Monroe Engel, or Ralph Ellison, that I think their works are poor to bad? I am surrounded by lovely and fascinating people, most of whose works seem insignificant to me, *c'est tout.*" Over the next few months, he would publish less-than-flattering remarks about the efforts of all of these writers (and friends). Such candor did not make his social life any easier—Gold was particularly incensed—but he felt he had little choice. "As a critic, all I have is my diagnostic power. My honesty and my gift for judgement are one."[16]

Kazin's interest in contemporary fiction would continue to ebb. By the early sixties, *The Twenties and After* had moved to the back burner, to be revived and published in 1973 as *Bright Book of Life.* His Guggenheim pledge to be "wholly in the service of contemporary fiction" had not reckoned with the direction that fiction was taking, nor with the proclivities of his own literary temperament. Having come of age when the "realist" novel was the prevailing fictional mode (and the main focus of his first book), Kazin rarely felt at home with a postwar fiction that eschewed social and historical realism for more narrowly private or "subjective" interests. He believed what he believed: the novel works best when "the individual and society are in constant and concrete relation with each other," when it acknowledges its close kinship with history, and when it is not embarrassed to present life in all "its beautiful and inexpressible materiality"—goals that did not strike him as a high priority among many postwar writers.[17]

But if Kazin deplored overall trends in contemporary fiction, he took some satisfaction in a development that was beginning to attract national attention—the emergence of Jewish-American fiction. Until the late fifties that emergence, or "breakthrough," as Leslie Fiedler called it in a 1958 essay, had been confined largely to the career of Saul Bellow. Kazin, who had been encouraging Bellow personally while supporting him with letters for Guggenheim grants, was pleased but hardly surprised when his friend broke onto the national stage with *The Adventures of Augie March* in 1953, to be followed in 1956 with *Seize the Day* and *Henderson, The Rain King* in 1959. Bellow, he later claimed, "was a man chosen by talent, like those Jewish virtuosos—Heifetz, Rubinstein, Milstein, Horowitz." Now Bellow was being joined by others. One of them, Bernard Malamud, a classmate of Kazin's at City College, had sought Kazin out in 1952 for assistance in getting his first novel, *The Natural,* published. Kazin recommended it to Harcourt (where he was an advisor) and escorted Malamud around to see the editors, who agreed to its publication. In 1958 he supported Malamud for a Guggenheim grant to finish the short-story collection *The Magic Barrel*—"I don't know of any American fiction writer of his generation whom I believe in more." He reviewed the book positively (with qualifications), and it went on to win the National Book Award. *"Please* read *The Magic Barrel!"* he wrote to Edmund Wilson in March 1959, who was studying Hebrew at the time. "It's a better guide to the Jews than the Hebrew language."[18]

In Norman Mailer, Kazin saw a very different kind of Jewish writer. Whereas Malamud typically depicted Jews as humble, ineffective, suffering, and virtuous—*schlemiels*—Mailer was uninterested in Jews per se, preferring to project himself (or fictive versions of himself) in poses that were the farthest thing from humble; these poses, Kazin would later argue, constitute the essence of Mailer's Jewishness. "Determined to leave all those centuries of Jewish tradition (and of Jewish losers) behind him, Mailer represents the unresting effort and overreaching of the individual Jewish writer who seeks to be nothing but an individual (and if possible, a hero)." After recommending *The Time of Her Time* for publication in 1958, Kazin reviewed it and other pieces collected in *Advertisements for Myself* in a 1959 essay, "How Good is Norman Mailer?" Kazin's answer—with due allowance for Mailer's "screaming self-consciousness"—"very, very good indeed."[19]

Another welcome discovery was Philip Roth. Kazin claimed that, after coming across Roth's "Defender of the Faith" in a recent *New Yorker* (rousing him from his usual *New Yorker* stupor), he "went around [for days] exhilarated by the change in the literary weather." When the story came out in the collection *Goodbye, Columbus* in the spring of 1959, he was excited all over again. Roth, a Jew, was writing of Jews not in a "grand collective," invoking "Jewish solidarity in the face of oppression," but as an "appeal to raw human nature" and an expression of the "bruised and angry and unassimilable self." Kazin touted the "tough-minded Mr. Roth" as a writer to be watched. "He is acidulous, unsparing, tender, yet more than anything he is *young*, he sees life with a fresh and funny eye." He and Roth would in time become friends—Roth sending him manuscripts for assessment (over which they often disagreed), Kazin consistently impressed by Roth's critical intelligence—"a sharp, logical analyst of character and motivation."[20]

Morris Dickstein would later cite Kazin (along with Irving Howe and Leslie Fiedler) as one of the "aggressive" champions of "the Jewish-American renaissance" of the late fifties, though Kazin was, in fact, less aggressive than others in championing Jewish-American writers as a group in the fifties. While Fiedler (*Midstream*) and Theodore Solotaroff (*Times Literary Supplement*) were announcing breakthroughs and describing the advance in terms of "calculated aggression followed by dramatic gains," Kazin was confining his public remarks to a few promising instances. Though gratified by the "gains," noting in a January 1958 journal entry "the immense cultural authority of all us Jewish writers and critics," he did not write publicly of a general breakthrough until his 1966 essay "The Jew as Modern Writer," by which time Jewish writers were not only in the cultural mainstream, they virtually defined it. In the late fifties and early sixties, however, it was individual writers, not the group, who had his public attention—writers who may have been Jews, but who were also part of the larger culture, part of "the alone generation," suffering the same self-absorption (Mailer), the same detachment from the world (Malamud's dreamlike characters), the same "excess of human possibility over social goals" (Bellow). Kazin was pleased with the emergence of these writers, but he saw no reason not to hold them to the standards he believed were fiction's reason for being—to tell about the world inside *and* outside ourselves, largely within the conventions of social realism—"to elicit and prove the world we share."[21]

Russia and Puerto Rico

In August 1959, Kazin joined Arthur Schlesinger Jr., Edward Weeks (editor at the *Atlantic Monthly*), and the playwright Paddy Chayefsky on a three-week State Department–sponsored visit to the Soviet Union. The invitation was another gratifying sign of his growing prominence, following a

June meeting with Dag Hammarskjöld at the United Nations. The secretary general, who knew Kazin's writing from the *Reporter* and had read of his testimony at the hearing over *Lady Chatterley's Lover,* had invited him to lunch at the United Nations to talk about Lawrence, American literature, and other matters. Kazin found it all very exciting. "I thought going up in the elevator that I had never experienced such a pure sensation of delight . . . the sense of being carried utterly into another world. The lunch was exquisite, the view from the 38th floor reminded me of Jesus being shown the mountains of the earth."[22]

The Russian trip was also a visit to another world, provoking many sensations, not all of them delightful. It was certainly an honor to be asked, and it came at an important moment. After Stalin's death in 1953 and Khrushchev's denunciation of the former leader in 1956, there had been glimmers of hope, intermittent and uncertain, of a lessening of tension between Russia and the West. But by the spring of 1959, Khrushchev had been making threatening noises about Berlin, and there was talk of expelling American troops from the American sector. The crisis passed, however, amid plans for a summit between Khrushchev and Eisenhower in September to be preceded by a "cultural exchange" of artists, writers, and scientists. Kazin's delegation was part of the exchange.

He did not know what to expect or how to feel. He had only recently learned that his mother was gravely ill with inoperable cancer, and he wondered whether he should be going at all. But she insisted that he go and hoped he might visit her old village on the Polish border. (This proved impossible.) He also worried about accommodations—"I am less disposed to discomfort than any writer that has ever lived"—and wondered whether Soviet officialdom had a file on him. In 1951, the *New York Times* had reviewed a book from the Soviet Union, titled *Contemporary American Literature*, in which Kazin was identified as a "criminal, treacherous Trotskyite literary agent." (T. S. Eliot and W. H. Auden appear as "worms that crawl and multiply in a grave amidst rot and decay.") In November 1958, he had broadcast on Radio Free Europe a tribute to Nobel Prize winner Boris Pasternak, whom the Soviets repeatedly denounced as a "traitor." But whatever they thought of him and whatever the accommodations, he could hardly pass up the chance. "I will hate it . . . but it will do me good to get jolted out of the comfort and refinements and sterilities of my usual existence."[23]

What he encountered did come as a jolt, but not wholly as a surprise. Russia had long been a subject of intense personal interest—a place of ancestral origins and legendary writers, a focus of radical hopes in the thirties, a totalitarian state since the war, which, if less brutally "Stalinist," remained dictatorial and repressive. Kazin went there apprehending the worst—"I will hate it"—but intensely curious and hoping for unexpected revelations. The worst, he soon discovered, was the programmed responses of the Russians delegated to convey the correct line on all subjects of interest to the American visitors—Boris Pasternak (not to be discussed), the absence of American newspapers (Why spread pornographic filth?), recent American fiction (Who has there been since Hemingway and Dreiser?), and so on. Kazin had expected boilerplate from the official speechifiers, but he was unnerved to find it among literary groups that should have known better. After his speech on contemporary American writing at the office of *Foreign Literature Today*, there was silence, then attack and more attack. Why was he prejudiced against the proletarian novel? Why did he undervalue social dramatists like Arthur Miller? Why had he abandoned Theodore Dreiser? When he explained that he was one of the few critics defending Dreiser, he was accused of ignoring Dreiser's essays—some of which he had edited! Arthur Schlesinger, who attended this and similar meetings, later concluded that "the last thing the Soviet Union cares about is a free exchange of ideas." Kazin agreed. Whether dismissing Pasternak or denouncing all American magazines as "filth," "they talked as if they were unable to absorb any new ideas whatever." It was "maddening."[24]

There were, however, surprises. One of the more interesting, at least for Kazin, whose parents, aunts, and uncles were from Russia and Eastern Europe, was the unexpected prominence of Jews. Not only had Jews survived World War II and the traditional anti-Semitism of Russians (and especially of Stalin), they had gained a certain predominance in contemporary Russian culture. In an essay published in *Harper's* following his return, "Among Russia's Jews," he noted their seeming ubiquity and usefulness, at least in literary circles. All of their interpreters were Jews, and virtually all the editors, translators, and technical personnel they met. The guide for their group, Georgy, was a Jew. The professors who had attacked him in the offices of *Foreign Literature Today* were Jewish; many of the writers he met in Moscow and Kiev (Samuil Marshak, Gregory Plotkin, Ilya Ehrenberg) were Jewish; and, of course, Boris Pasternak (whom he was not permitted to meet) was Jewish. Not all the Jews he met were writers or officially employed, however. At a marketplace in Tashkent, he encountered an elderly Jewish couple, the man with a magnificent long beard, the woman swathed in veils—a sight "I had dreamed of all my life . . . They could very well have been my grandparents." When Kazin spoke to them in Yiddish, they threw their arms around him and, much to the chagrin of Georgy, began to complain bitterly about their life during and after the war.[25]

There were other moments suggesting long-forgotten connections as though some ancestral unconscious were struggling to break through the programmed speeches of the guides and welcoming committees. "There is so much I recognize on sight, that bustling propriety in offices and hallways, the pillows piled high on my bed, the flash of golden teeth, those square (yet somehow round) females . . . Surely I was here in a former life." But the moment would yield to bewilderment and suspicion—feelings that crystallized in a strange occurrence in a Leningrad (St. Petersburg) hotel room. He had become friendly with one of the female guide interpreters, Natalia, who, unlike the prickly Georgy, was friendly and forthcoming. Kazin later described their relations as "easy." She talked freely about her physicist husband currently in prison, about the behavior of the present regime, even about Trotsky and the secret police. Their "easy terms," however, had not prepared him for the moment when, returning from the Hermitage together, she entered his hotel room and "made a solid straightforward Russian declaration of love for me"—followed immediately by Georgy's walking into the room without knocking. Had he been set up? He could not answer it then, nor could he twenty-five years later. "Remembering Maryam [Natalia] Salganick, the Russian guide of 1959. She was small, feisty, and in the years since I left her 'disconsolate' at the airport, she has become increasingly mysterious in my mind . . . What was M up to? And who was M?"[26]

Kazin hoped to write up his experiences immediately after returning to the States, but there were too many disparate impressions, too many unresolved feelings to sort through. The picture kept slipping out of focus. He eventually published three accounts of his trip, two on Russia's writers, one on its Jews, not including a section in *New York Jew*; but none satisfied him. He simply did not know enough. He would continue to read about Russia and would return for a second visit decades later. But the mystery remained. "Like my Russian-born parents, here I am nibbling at the edges of 'Holy Russia,'" he wrote from Moscow in May 1990. "Although I know much more through my reading than they did, in Russia we are all strangers together."[27]

Back in New York at the end of August, Kazin learned that his mother's condition had deteriorated and she could no longer talk. He was the more distressed that in a few weeks he was to take up duties at the University of Puerto Rico, where, through the good offices of Keith Botsford, an instructor in the English Department and friend of Saul Bellow's, he had obtained a teaching position for the fall semester. Kazin was not excited by the assignment, but the family badly needed the money. The situation was made more difficult by the July death of Rabbi Birstein. Ann, who had been close to her father, was still grieving when she and Kate accompanied Alfred to Puerto Rico in September. They had hoped that the Caribbean setting, beaches and the sun, would make their months there seem like a vacation. Instead, it was Amherst (and Nice) all over again, only worse—Alfred lecturing at the school to students even less enthusiastic than those at Amherst, and Ann taking care of a four-year-old—this time in "miserable housing" and "intolerable heat."[28]

Kazin returned to New York and was with his mother when she died on October 10. The death was expected, and although he had tried to prepare himself for it, it was still a shock. "Every thought of my mother," he wrote in his diary two weeks after her death, "is of an inexpressible poignancy—not sorrow so much as a clear note of amazed loss." He had long regarded his mother as the major influence on his life, far more than his "sweet but numb, silent and much defeated" father, who remained largely in the shadows. He attributed no small part of his ambition and energy, his almost desperate need "to win" (as well as his intelligence), to his mother. But he also credited her with his general fearfulness—his "lifelong sense of insecurity and even terror about everything"—as well as his guilt and nagging sense of inadequacy that he was always letting her down, "that I didn't do enough for her—her life was so miserable." He even traced his radical, rebellious temperament to his mother, or rather to his resentment of her authority—"the old tyrannical idea of God, as my mother in her authority personified it to me." However valid these different insights may have been, aided undoubtedly by many sessions with Janet Rioch, Gita Fagelman would remain a presence in her son's life, much as Birstein's father would be in hers. "And there we were," she said of their months in Puerto Rico, "Daddy's girl and Mama's boy, with a dark whistling wind behind us."[29]

Ann would later characterize the stay in Puerto Rico as a "disaster." The loss of parents undoubtedly had much to do with it. Neither she nor Alfred could turn to the other for support. Ann "is utterly incapable at this moment of giving me anything," he complained bitterly. Apparently, Puerto Rico did not offer much support either—at least not for the Kazins. For all its frustrations, Russia had been stimulating, stirring feelings of personal and historical association. By contrast, Puerto Rico was hideously irrelevant. "Tree frogs, crickets, chickens, wet heat, rusty swings, marshes, rice and beans . . . Sticky, sweetish smell. Oh Lord. What days." Nor were things much better at the university. He found little stimulation among the faculty, and the students were unresponsive. "I get nothing from them, and they must get little enough from me," he wrote to Josephine Herbst near the end of the semester. "You ought to see me teaching Emily Dickinson here. It would be hilarious if it weren't so ridiculous." As for their social life—the closet thing to an interesting occasion was the evening an acquaintance brought murderer Nathan Leopold (of Leopold and Loeb fame) over for dinner. He was out on parole but not allowed to leave Puerto Rico.[30]

Kazin would later publish his impressions of Puerto Rico in a *Commentary* article, portions of which were reprinted in the San Juan *Star*. The piece was stunningly rude and raised many hackles. Its general argument was sympathetic enough: that in their efforts to create an indigenous culture, Puerto Ricans had never been able to extricate themselves from the baleful influence of colonial powers—Spain and more recently the United States. But the tone and incidental comments were offensive. Kazin referred to Puerto Ricans as "lambs." He declared their "famous docility" to be "the apathy of tropical countries and . . . Step'n Fetchit sloth." They drive "as if they were on muleback; they drive *en familie,* arms perpetually hanging out of the car, talking and eating as if they were home." Brooks Atkinson in the *New York Times* called Kazin's attitude "contemptuous." Keith Botsford, who had been instrumental in bringing Kazin to the school and would bring Saul Bellow the following year (who very much enjoyed his stay), described it as "a blend of conceit and truculent provincialism."

Kazin, who possessed unusual talent for evoking the ambience of places with which he felt some personal connection, was at a loss when dealing with others that did not in some way move or excite him. Puerto Rico was an alien world—"a waste, a nothing," he told Herbst.[31]

"Big with the Jews"

Kazin returned to New York in mid-December, and the city never looked so good. Even routine social occasions seemed concentrated points of excitement. "Cocktail party. The juice of New York. The accumulated personal energy of these people (sex-power-position), standing together, an energy machine." He had other reasons to be excited. He had been appointed to the editorial board of the *American Scholar*, not just a prestigious position, but an opportunity to take the measure of certain cultural notables about whom he was curious—like Jacques Barzun: "terribly stiff and carefully well-mannered. Brown double-breasted suit like a Frenchman's. Very efficient mind, I guess, but carefulness of manner threw me off. Another handsome and white haired actor, like Lionel Trilling . . . O, so careful." He had also accepted a position as an editorial advisor to Readers Subscription, a high-brow book club founded by Trilling, Auden, and Barzun. (Kazin came on after Trilling left.) Irving Kristol had left his editorial position at the *Reporter* to head the service and edit its magazine, the *Griffin*. He hired Kazin to help him make choices for the book club and to write occasional pieces for the magazine. Kazin took this as another sign of improving conditions. Although still without a permanent teaching position and worried about money, he was increasingly convinced that things were going in the right direction. "The spiral is so definitely upward . . . the outlook is definitely good—no use pretending that it isn't."[32]

Contributing to his good mood was his growing interest in his next autobiographical venture. When he and Seymour Lawrence had signed their letter of agreement the summer of 1957, Lawrence had paid little attention to the autobiographical work, *The Love of Women*, listed among future projects. He was interested in Kazin, the literary critic, not the autobiographer, and astonishingly, he had not read *A Walker in the City*. He read it the following summer, after Kazin sent him a copy, and wrote back— very excited and now convinced that "there is more of you as a writer and as a human being in this [autobiographical] form of writing." Accordingly, he urged Kazin to devote "most of his time and energy" to his *Love of Women* book in the months ahead. He added in a "publisher's afterthought" that Kazin might also "want to think of doing a direct sequel to *A Walker*—namely your undergraduate days and life in New York during the thirties."[33]

In the months immediately following Lawrence's note, Kazin had been too busy working up his course for the New School and writing reviews to give much thought to the autobiography or to his "publisher's afterthought." By the spring of 1960, however, he was giving the project serious attention; and perhaps prompted by Lawrence's suggestion, he was rethinking how to proceed. No longer *The Love of Women,* the book would be called *The History of a Literary Radical* and would be divided into two sections—one on the thirties, "Starting Out in the Thirties," and another on the forties, "New York Jew." It would tell the hopes and struggles of Alfred Kazin, a youthful writer and radical from "darkest Brownsville," making his way in literary New York, complete with accounts of radical activity, encounters with other writers, and aroused personal expectations—"a romance, a tale of the rise of Alfred Kazin, from misery, poverty, and literary chastity to power, intelligence, sexuality, reputation, etc. . . . It's been a rise. It's all been a rise." The more he thought about it, the better it felt. He could incorporate ideas and portraits from the "orthodoxy book" while tapping into feelings that he knew from the writing of *Walker* would keep the juices flowing. "I want in my heart, obviously to be an initiate again, to write the story of youth, to look forward to everything," he wrote in a May journal entry. "Surely that is the excitement, again, of the new book—*starting out.*" It would be four years and many distractions later before *Starting Out in the Thirties* (1965) was finished. Kazin would continue to write reviews, take trips, give talks, and accept teaching assignments—to the frustration of his editor, who begged him to get on with the book. But he had to make a living, and there were too many other things that interested him, too many opportunities to pursue.[34]

One opportunity he felt he could not pass up came in the summer of 1960. "The Israelis have sent in a call for Kazin," he wrote to Josephine Herbst on August 1. "And we will then sweeten the Jewish pill with Greece and Paris." It was a time of unusual excitement in Israel. In May, Israeli agents had captured Adolf Eichmann in a suburb of Buenos Aires and brought him to Israel to stand trial for crimes against the Jewish people.

The boldness of the move had pushed Israel into the headlines and involved the country and Jews everywhere in a whirl of controversy and bouts of soul-searching. A few Jews (and many non-Jews) saw it as a violation of the principles and procedures set forth in the Nuremburg trials. Others feared a trial would promote the image of Jews as a vengeful Old Testament people; still others worried about the images projected of the Jew as victim. Whatever the worries, beyond question was the fact that Israel had made an audacious, dramatic move on the international stage, reminding the world of the evil perpetrated by the Nazis and of Israel's own right and power to deal with murderers of Jews.[35]

That Kazin would arrive in Israel at the same time the country was moving toward a trial of a chief architect of the Holocaust was not a coincidence. Israel had many reasons for bringing to justice a murderer of millions of Jews. The most urgent was to remind Jews everywhere that the persecution of the Jews had a long history, that pogroms and worse can break out anywhere, and that Israel was the only country where Jews could live assured of their physical safety. Prime minister David Ben-Gurion saw the Eichmann arrest and trial, in which the state would document in detail the horrors of the Holocaust, as an opportunity to garner fresh support for Israel and to encourage, indeed frighten, Jews everywhere, including those in America, to emigrate to Israel. The trial was not, however, the only means for persuading hesitant Jews to join the "in-gathering." Another was the use of special emissaries, those whose reputation and authority in their respective countries placed them in positions of influence to argue Israel's case to the people back home. Kazin was not long in Israel before discovering that this was why he had been sent for.

If that was the reason, he was a disappointing guest. When Yigael Yadin, the commander of the Israeli forces in the 1948 War of Independence, warned Kazin's group of the dangers of living outside of Israel, Kazin laughed aloud. Offended by his levity, other guests attempted to shout him down. "Until they became more and more insistent," he later wrote in his journal, "I hadn't realized American Jews were so much in danger, and the dear old U.S. of A so much on the rocks." Following the line laid down by Ben-Gurion, Yadin insisted that "it was impossible to be a Jew and not 'come back' to Israel." Kazin boisterously disagreed. He was more restrained in his meeting with Zalman Arrane, a former minister of education. Arrane also pleaded that American Jews send their children to Israel: "we were a brand he would save from the burning." Kazin, however, rejected the argument that Diaspora Jews had no future except in Israel. Such reasoning struck him as "dangerously short-sighted, since Israel is not likely to survive if the Jews do not survive elsewhere."[36]

But, if he was not persuaded by arguments that he settle in Israel, Kazin was not indifferent to the air of crisis precipitated by Eichmann's arrest. While he resented the use of Eichmann to frighten Jews into immigrating, he was impressed by the Israelis' determination to confront Jews and the rest of the world with the facts of the recent past. And Jews everywhere did face it. Heavy press coverage of the arrest and trial left them little choice. They faced facts many had hoped they never would have to face; they faced them, remembered them, wrote and argued about them. Silence and denial were no longer options. For many Jews (and others) the destruction of European Jewry, or the Holocaust, as it soon came to be called, became for the first time a distinct subject, an event that previously had been understood primarily as an expression of Nazi savagery and totalitarian terror. With the public acknowledgment and discussion came personal reflection —about the war, about lost family members, about the accidents of history that left some alive and millions of others dead, about Israel, about what it meant to be a survivor and a Jew.[37]

Kazin shared in the general heightening of Jewish consciousness. "Feel very Jewish these days. Eretz-Israel," he wrote in his journal shortly after his arrival. "One might indeed. For what is it I draw my basic values from if not from the Jews! . . . A forgotten passion. A burning necessity." "I have been seized, I have been pregnant with the Jews," he wrote while working up a piece on Eichmann for the *Reporter.* "The fascination of this subject, when I find myself in it again, is such that I feel as if I were big with the Jews, as if they occupied a space in me." But feeling big with the Jews did not signal new enthusiasm for Israel. Kazin had never been a Zionist and in the forties had rejected the arguments for a Jewish state—though he acknowledged in private that he had been "unable to read any newspaper articles [about its founding in 1948] without bursting into tears." Subsequently, he had paid little serious attention to Israel, beyond resenting what he saw as its growing nationalism and militancy. "The Jews are historically a chosen people," he wrote in 1953. They were chosen in history to "keep alive the memory of the divine source from which our lives come." But "Israel today is no longer a religion but a state. By every sign the state will be increasingly nationalistic, military, cynical, and in the fashion of states, hypocritical."[38]

Touring the country in 1960, listening to its officials talk about Israeli military prowess, point out its modern amenities (complete with a beatnik nightclub), and argue for immediate emigration, Kazin felt as spiritually distant as ever. Militarism, middle-class comforts, "normality" were not qualities he associated (or wanted to associate) with Jewishness. They were certainly not the qualities he associated with his parents—their poverty, their fears—nor with "artists and originals like Kafka," nor with "the gifted and extreme individualists who had never seen Israel and would never live here." The trip to Israel would lead to two essays reflecting his reservations —"At Ease in Zion" and "Eichmann and the New Israelis"—neither of which could have made Israeli officials very happy. In subsequent essays and in *New York Jew*, written after the 1967 war, he would express more sympathy toward the Israeli state and be less dismissive of its military. In 1960, he found something much closer to his ideas about Jews and Jewishness awaiting his return to New York—a copy of Elie Wiesel's *Night*.[39]

Wiesel's memoir of his experiences at Auschwitz and Buchenwald was first published in Yiddish in Argentina, as *Un di velt hot geshivgn* (*And the World Remained Silent*). In 1958, it was published in France as *La Nuit*. After being turned down by twenty publishers in the United States, Hill and Wang brought it out as *Night* in a limited edition in 1960. Kazin's October review in the *Reporter* gave it its first major notice in America. It was also Kazin's first substantive literary-critical engagement with the Holocaust. He and Ann Birstein had written an introduction to a 1959 edition of *The Works of Anne Frank*; but reflecting the spirit of the times (and the attitudes of Frank herself), they had placed less stress on her Jewishness and the Jewish victims of the Holocaust than on her humanity— "a separate and precious human spirit"—and her evident abilities as a "born novelist." *Night* was different. It told the story of a devout young Jew, who, having witnessed the destruction of his Jewish community in Romania and the murder of his family in the concentration camps, struggles with the meaning of his Jewish faith. After watching a youth strangle to death at the end of a rope in Auschwitz, the young Wiesel refuses to join the other Jewish prisoners chanting the traditional benediction, "Blessed be the name of the Eternal." This day I had ceased to plead; I was no longer capable of lamentation. On the contrary, I felt very strong. I was the accuser, God the accused." For Kazin, this act of rebellion was the spiritual center of the book. "The young Wiesel's embittered interrogation of Providence unites, as it were, the ever-human Job to the history of our Time; it recalls that peculiarly loving and scolding intimacy with God, which is the most powerful single element in the history of the Jews."[40]

Kazin's enthusiasm for *Night* led him to seek out its young author, then living in New York. For more than a decade, they saw each other frequently —had dinner together, appeared on the same panels, attended each other's talks. "Wiesel," he would later write, became "my Holocaust." He was not alone. In the sixties and seventies, as the Holocaust occupied an increasingly central place in the thoughts and feelings of American Jews, Wiesel, through his books, public statements, and appearances, emerged as its best-known survivor and most influential interpreter. Kazin, however, who professed a "horror of public piety," would grow increasingly disenchanted with Wiesel's public persona and "platform" manner. In a 1989 essay, he signaled his disillusionment by contrasting Wiesel's testimony with that of Primo Levi, whom he called "a far more trustworthy witness," provoking Wiesel to accuse Kazin of "lending credence to those who deny the Holocaust." In 1960, however, the book had made a deep impression, its depiction of the despairing Wiesel anguished and outraged by his sudden loss of faith—"the absolute emptiness of soul, the blackness of 'night' "—appealing powerfully to Kazin's sense of what it meant to be Jewish.[41]

"In Touch with Power"

In November 1960, Alfred rented "a studio" at 145 West Fourteenth Street. With the social traffic growing daily in their apartment and the constant tension with Ann—"each of us is so ambitious, so eager to get his way, to write *the* book"—he was finding it increasingly difficult to work at home. The socializing had grown particularly intense of late in preparation for Pearl and Daniel Bell's wedding. The ceremony took place in the Kazin apartment on December 20, an affair he (Bell) remembers as "thronged with New York Intellectuals." The studio was an escape from all that. It reminded Alfred of his old Pineapple Street apartment—"full of possibility." He went there virtually every day, occasionally to meet a girlfriend—the most recent, a "beauty" named "Rosalind"—but mostly to work. There was much to do. Kazin was concentrating more and more on the autobiography—"everything radiates from that and back to it." But he was also assembling a set of lectures on "the novel of society" in late nineteenth-century America. When delivering a talk at a conference of preparatory schoolmasters, he had run into R. P. Blackmur, who headed Princeton's Christian Gauss Seminar. The subject of the Gauss lectures had apparently been raised, and in the spring Blackmur sent him a formal invitation to deliver the lectures in the fall of 1961 (with a fifteen hundred dollar stipend). Kazin had long coveted the honor and was particularly pleased to be returning to a literature more to his taste than that of the alone generation.[42]

Another topic of pressing interest in the fall of 1960 was politics—presidential politics and the political intellectuals. Kazin had been asked to address the New England American Studies Conference at Tufts University the week before the election. Prompted, perhaps, by candidate John F. Kennedy's reputation as an "intellectual," Kazin chose to speak on "War and the American Intellectual." His message was that American writers and students of American studies, to a degree few were willing to admit, had a stake in the cold war and profited from its execution—in subvention funds for books and magazines, in sponsored lectureships in Europe and Asia, in support of American studies programs at home. Kazin did not disapprove of historians and literary people disseminating information and opinions about America at home and abroad. He had done a good deal of it himself. But he did object to the fact that many of them went about their work remaining staunchly oblivious to the war interests they were serving or dismissing all thoughts of complicity with a shrug of high-minded powerlessness. It's "tragic," but what can we do about it? Kazin understood why intellectuals might want to dissociate themselves from the war economy and the operations of the power state. But he also knew that at some level they were part of the machinery and that at a moment when intellectuality had become an issue in the political debate, they needed to be alert to the interests they were serving.[43]

A few days after the speech, the country elected a president who, if not an intellectual himself, was certainly popular with many intellectuals. Norman Mailer in a much discussed preelection piece, "Superman Comes to the Supermarket," had suggested that Kennedy just might be the "hero America needed, a hero central to his time," a hero who would among other things restore intellect and imagination to the nation's public life. Kazin's old friend Richard Rovere had written glowingly of Kennedy's "extraordinary political intelligence" in the *New Yorker*. Harvard historian Arthur Schlesinger had signed on as an advisor to the campaign, later serving as a special assistant to the president. Kazin, who had been as eager for a Kennedy win as many another "intellectual" tired of what Walter Lippmann had called the intellectual "vacancy" of the Eisenhower presidency, was relieved and pleased by the election. Perhaps, as Mailer had imagined in his piece, a brilliant new era was in the offing. If not the era of "the superman," then at least, as Schlesinger had more modestly imagined, a time for the "renewal of conviction, a new sense of national purpose." But Kazin was also uncertain and wary. Would the youngest president in U.S. history be up to the job? "Sick with worry about Pres. Jack," he wrote the day after his election. How would his intellectual interests and gifts (if he really had them) figure in his performance—beyond appointing Harvard academics to high positions? "He is essentially a tabula rasa," he wrote in a January 1961 journal entry; "the really interesting thing will be to see how he changes," how he will meet the test of office.[44]

The testing would come soon enough. On April 17, just three months in office, Kennedy authorized an ill-advised, poorly planned amphibious assault on Cuba at the Bay of Pigs that was quickly repelled by Fidel Castro. Of the fourteen hundred badly trained Cuban exiles who landed during the assault, about one hundred died and the rest were taken prisoner. Although a stunning defeat for the new president, the misadventure did not apparently hurt him with the American public; his popularity rose to its highest levels after a nationally televised speech in which he took full responsibility for the debacle. But it created deep unease and suspicion among many intellectuals who feared that Kennedy was captive to the very forces and psychology from which they had hoped an "intellectual" president would be free. Kennedy "is now the defender of the West *in extremis,* taking a 'tough' line," Kazin wrote in his journal. "Goldwater is pleased; [conservative columnist] David Lawrence is pleased. The *News* and *Mirror* are pleased. I am full of doubt and wonder."[45]

Kazin was sympathetic to Kennedy's situation—a man in the middle, "pushed and pulled" by powerful forces. But he was exasperated that his "intellectual" interests apparently extended no further than a respect for technical expertise. Noticeably missing from his administration was a coherent and detailed vision of what he intended for the country—beyond platitudes about "the new frontier" and bearing burdens. Lacking a "long view" or a "philosophical view," Kennedy, it seemed to Kazin at least, was vulnerable to shifting political and military pressures—as well as to his own enthusiasms, including hare-brained schemes like the Bay of Pigs invasion. This evident lack of intellectual coherence (and seriousness) would be the focus of Kazin's observations in "The President and Other Intellectuals," published in the fall issue of the *American Scholar*. How, he asked, is one to reconcile the "immoral," "impractical," and "down right stupid" Cuban invasion with the president's famously "intellectual" and "brilliantly" competent White House? What is the point of Kennedy's surrounding himself with notable academics and intellectuals, entertaining cultural stars in the East Room, if government policy is to be a mish-mash of hasty decisions, gut impulse, personal "recklessness," and ad hoc political calculation? "Where, then is the meaningful relation of intellectuals to power? Is it only to write memoranda, or to 'educate' the decisions that others make?" Is this what it means for intellect to be "in touch with power"? Kazin concluded that for Kennedy, intellectuals were largely a diversion and the most recent version of political showmanship, "irrelevant to the tragic issues [of the time] and contribut[ing] nothing to their solution." "To be an 'intellectual' is the latest style in American success, the mark of our manipulable society." Simply put, the intellectuals were being used.[46]

In May, while Kazin was working on his piece, Schlesinger told Kazin he thought he could arrange a meeting between him and the president in the summer. When the luncheon took place on August 1, the essay was largely finished. The conversation was lively and amicable. Schlesinger, who was present, recalled that the talk ranged from "Cooper and Malraux to Khrushchev and Chiang Kai-Shek." They also chatted about the role of the writer in society and about the "ultimately unsatisfying" quality of success "construed in individual terms." Kazin's notes indicate there was also discussion of the John Birch Society, the Lincoln bedroom, and F. Scott Fitzgerald as well as some "veiled hints at Cuba." After the meeting, Kazin made a few minor changes to his piece and sent it off—not without misgivings and uneasy dreams. "In my dream AMS Jr [Schlesinger] went to prison for criticizing some important personages. It was AK—and Oh, what a shame to be afraid."[47]

When the piece came out in the fall, Kennedy could not have been pleased, though reports on his reaction conflicted. Kazin said that he heard from two sources, Gore Vidal and Kennedy advisor Richard Goodwin, that the president was "outraged" and "furious." But Schlesinger said he merely laughed it off. "We wined him and dined him," he recalled Kennedy saying, "and talked about Hemingway and Dreiser with him, and I later told Jackie what a good time she missed, and then he went away and wrote that piece!" Kazin was not sent to prison, but neither was he invited to the state dinner for André Malraux the following April attended by many of the country's notable literati—a slight that, according to Birstein in her roman à clef, *The Last of the True Believers,* he took personally. In his chronicle of the Kennedy years, *A Thousand Days: John F. Kennedy in the White House,* Schlesinger, after noting that Kazin refused to be seduced by Kennedy's charm, used him to illustrate the divergent strains of liberal-leftist thought in America. One of these, the progressive "pragmatic" strain, presumably Schlesinger's own, "accepted the responsibilities of power," believing that practical results were better than idealistic gestures. The other, "utopian," strain, Kazin's, refused all complicity with power and "thereby risked irrelevance."[48]

Although Schlesinger's division of the left into pragmatists and utopians was too neat, it did accurately register Kazin's deep distrust of power and its seductive effect on intellectuals. In his own account of the Kennedy meeting in *New York Jew,* Kazin recalled that it was the aura and presumption of power that had most unnerved him about Kennedy and the White House intellectuals. Schlesinger, however, was incorrect to call Kazin a "utopian" who believed intellectuals should resist all connections with power. "When all is said and done," Kazin had written in his essay, "action *is* the natural sphere in a mind sane and hopeful, eager to revive the classic center of man's public activity. To real intellectuals, power means not Caesarism but right influence." If the Kennedy intellectuals were merely "educating" (acquiescing in) decisions made by others, like the Bay of Pigs, rather then influencing those decisions, they were not acting as genuine intellectuals or responsible citizens. "History will not absolve them that cheaply."[49]

But neither would history absolve them of *wrong* influence. The Bay of Pigs would be followed by "Operation Mongoose" (CIA sabotage in Cuba), an avoidable (and world-threatening) missile crisis in Cuba, a secret war in Laos, and deepening involvement in Vietnam. Kazin was certainly correct to warn intellectuals of the risks of being used, but what did he mean by "right influence"? Did he oppose the cold war stance of the Kennedy administration on which the Castro invasion was predicated? Castro, he noted in his essay, had "shown himself a cynical and dangerous ally of totalitarianism." Would the invasion have been "immoral" had it removed this "totalitarian" menace from the Caribbean? And how helpful was the term "totalitarian" in discriminating among the dangers in the world? In 1961, Kazin, like many intellectuals, was not prepared to answer unsettling questions about the reality of "totalitarianism," nor to calculate the price of countering it wherever it was said to appear. In the coming years, he would have little choice—and little satisfaction knowing that "the best and the brightest" were in on the decisions. It was not enough for intellect to be in touch with power.[50]

Contemporaries

Searching for an apartment in August 1957, Kazin had looked forward to his move to New York with a mix of dread and excited anticipation. Looking back in the fall of 1961, he had few doubts about the move. Although relations with Ann Birstein remained tempestuous, the marriage that had been doomed at Amherst was holding up—so far. He had certainly been very busy, but also productive—"October 13, 1956–October 13, 1961, the greatest period of my life," he exclaimed exultingly at the time. His reputation as a critic of literature, culture, and politics had continued to grow. In a city that, according to W. M. Frohock, "has something like a total monopoly upon criticism in America," where criticism and cultural commentary were read and argued over, Kazin seemed to be everywhere: publishing in prestigious magazines and journals, giving talks, appearing on panels, radio, and television. Birstein remembered that waiters and shopkeepers were beginning to recognize him. Kazin liked to tell of an encounter with a woman at a Broadway fruit stand. "Aren't you the famous critic?" the breathless shopper had rushed over to ask. To which he had modestly replied: "You mean

Lionel Trilling? No, I'm Alfred Kazin, the second most famous critic." He had as many college speaking engagements as he could handle—at Bowdoin, Northwestern, the University of New Hampshire, the University of Chicago, Goucher, Earlham, Princeton, Yale, and more. *Time* magazine had excerpted and discussed a talk he had given at Yale in May 1960, complete with a picture of Kazin, "all-round man of letters," denouncing the ascendancy of "psychological man" in the current theater and the "secret hunger for wickedness and bohemianism found in a rich, middle-class society."[51]

With his growing reputation had come more social opportunities—*American Scholar* editorial board dinners; dinner parties thrown by publishing entrepreneur Jason Epstein for the literary-intellectual trendsetters; the usual "cocktail party circuit" attended by publishers, agents, and literary hangers-on, all in an "enveloping mist of alcoholic cordiality"—affairs in preparation for which Kazin sternly counseled himself "to be quietly honest" and "not to solicit love"—though he would appreciate "a smiling recognition of what I have become." In addition there were the artist-celebrity shindigs, which he was pleased to attend, ogle, and ridicule:

> And last night we were at a soiree, a real soiree, honest, at the Frankfurters on Park Avenue. O Lawd, and it was all the Prof with his nose in the air, and he was there too, the Trilling. Mr. Frankfurter made conversation about Russia, and Mrs. Shaw, the press agent of the Museum of Modern Art, whom I would have liked to grab, but not make conversation with, talked about what Allen Dulles told her in Paris and there was a cute number, a Mrs Luytens or something, and there was all these painters, even great ones like Hans Hofmann and Bill de Kooning, and Tom Hess with his fish-like look of deprecating the group before it deprecated him. So it got so dull they put on music, and everyone stood around as if waiting to hear where he was expected to go. Ah, nuts, ah soiree, ah poo-poo-nuts. Such cultural lah-de-dah and self consciousness all over the place.

More rewarding were the intimate dinners at home to which Alfred and Ann invited their friends, including the columnist Murray Kempton and the noted translator Francis Steegmuller, both of whom, Ann once noted, helped to "leaven" the New York Jewish intellectual loaf. Alfred and Ann were especially fond of Steegmuller—and his fiancée, the Austrian writer Shirley Hazzard. Alfred had heard of Steegmuller in 1945 at the American military headquarters in Paris, where his fluency in French and Italian had made him a valuable asset to the Allies. Since then he had published a celebrated biography of Gustave Flaubert, translated *Madame Bovary*, written fiction under a pseudonym, and done travel pieces for the *New Yorker*. Slim, tall, and elegant, kindly and quietly witty with perfect manners, Steegmuller struck Alfred and Ann as the last word in urbane sophistication—a figure of intellectual grace out of a different era who had survived into "overheated New York," quietly coexisting with "Norman Mailer and other public declaimers who dominated the literary scene at the moment." Steegmuller endeared himself to Birstein forever, when at her request he translated her and Kazin's beloved "The Owl and the Pussycat" into French. And how to translate *pussycat*? Easy—"*La Poussiquette.*"[52]

Another indication of growing good fortune, evidence that the "spiral" continued upward, were broad hints from Jack Ludwig, a friend of Kazin and Saul Bellow and an official with the expanding New York State university system, that there might be a permanent position for Kazin in the English Department of the Stony Brook campus that was scheduled to open in 1962. The salary being discussed was twenty-five thousand dollars, a nice sum for the early sixties, and he could live in Manhattan. If everything worked out, he would begin in the fall of 1963. He had also learned he was to be offered the Gallagher visiting professorship at City College in the fall of 1962 and the Beckman visiting professorship at Berkeley in the winter of 1963. "Everyday, it seems to me, something new, something richer, not just in money but in quality of the opportunity it opens up. The booming society, with even a critic booming along with it." Kazin was, admittedly, a little uneasy about the Beckman—not so much about his chances of getting it, as about the process. He had recently written an effusive review of his friend Mark Schorer's biography of Sinclair Lewis—"stupendous in its completeness," "brilliantly just," the work of "an expert scholar and acute literary intelligence." Schorer was not only a friend; he was a professor at Berkeley with influence on the Beckman appointment, and Kazin did not feel right about the review. "Crawly sensation of guilt . . . my obvious effort to play ball with Schorer in the review." A reviewer who prided himself on his critical integrity, he felt he might have violated a code. "Unsatisfactory performance all around—but one can say to oneself, I did it for the following honest and calculated and human reason—I am not a saint."[53]

Kazin had yet another reason to be excited about the future. In the spring of 1962, Atlantic-Little, Brown would be bringing out *Contemporaries*. A collection of previously published essays going back to 1956, the book, he felt, would represent the full range of his critical interests while making a comprehensive statement about the present—"*Contemporaries:* an argument against the alone generation, against lostness as a cause, for a transcendent sense of public realism." Shortly before publication in April, Kazin wrote to Josephine Herbst that he was very happy with the collection, not least because he believed he had done himself justice. "For once, I feel good about a critical book of mine. I never have felt really satisfied about the other two [*On Native Grounds* and *The Inmost Leaf*]; but this one is true to so much of what I think. I don't feel misrepresented."[54]

The critics were also pleased. Albert Guerard (*New York Times Book Review*) praised it for its "unremitting moral seriousness," its "undeviating common sense," its "Arnoldian sanity"—as well as for the assurance with which Kazin wrote on an extraordinarily wide range of subjects. Lionel Abel in *Commentary* wrote that Kazin was "always intelligent" and "well informed" and that his judgments were more reliable than those of Edmund Wilson's. (Kazin had dedicated the book to Wilson.) He felt that Kazin's essays on Melville and Faulkner were themselves "beyond praise, as fine as anything in American criticism." Gay Wilson Allen (*Saturday Review*) believed that *Contemporaries*, more than any of his earlier books, showed just what kind of a critic Kazin was—"an expert in separating honesty from sham, pretense, meretriciousness." Kenneth Lynn (*Christian Science Monitor*) also praised the book but felt that Kazin was more convincing on canonical figures than on recent talent such as Norman Mailer and J. D. Salinger, whom he felt Kazin overrated. The only negative reviews, from Nelson Algren in the *Nation* and Joseph Heller in the *New Republic*, Kazin dismissed as sour grapes from writers unhappy with his treatment (or in Heller's case, nontreatment) of their books.[55]

He could not so easily dismiss criticism from the British reviews, the *Times Literary Supplement* and the *New Statesman*, as he in part agreed with them. They observed that Kazin, like other American critics, was unsure of his audience and thus at times uncertain at what level to pitch his remarks. Lacking an audience of peers, Kazin occasionally slipped into intellectual laziness and middle-browism—"teaching the great mass audience" with "glib" references to "society" and "experience." This struck a nerve. Kazin had himself written of the "mad department store quality" of

American magazines and complained that the country's intellectual life lacked "the authority of a common center." Thus, he felt "in a strange way glad" that the Brits had indicated the special difficulties facing the "literary intellectual" in America. Still, he could not but feel "snubbed, humiliated, outraged." The English had behaved in their usual "snotty" manner toward anyone not a member of the club.[56]

Kazin was right to be happy with *Contemporaries*. It showed he could write authoritatively, easily, and entertainingly on a range of different subjects—American and European literature; Freud and psychoanalysis; contemporary culture; the function and practice of criticism; politics and power; Russia, Israel, Eichmann. Reading through the collection, one has impressions, similar to those felt while reading in his journals, of a lively interest in a surprising number of subjects, complete with the intellectual-linguistic resources to write well on each of them. Learning in 1957 that the young French critic Roland Barthes had been given the freedom to write a regular column in *Lettres Nouvelle* on any subject he chose, Kazin remarked, "How I've longed to do this, to make this private notebook a public journal, to have the chance for regular articles in a single magazine." His wish had been at least partially granted in his arrangement with the *Reporter*, where, during a five-year period, he published more than sixty pieces, many republished in *Contemporaries*, on virtually any (literary) topic that interested him—pieces that demonstrate the seriousness of mind reviewers noted, as well as a restless, curious intelligence and an impulsive pleasure in personal expressiveness that one also finds in his journals. The book does make an argument, a number of them—"against the alone generation" and for the realist novel, against the temptations of power (for intellectuals), for the centrality of nontechnical criticism. It also reflects a critical temperament more at home with established nineteenth-century and prewar writers than with many contemporaries. Yet it is never dogmatic or narrow (except possibly on the Beats and their followers) and more ready than most of its reviewers to give credit when credit is due. The work of an informed, highly intelligent thinker about everything, *Contemporaries* was proof that serious criticism could still be written in the tradition of "the great American lay philosophy, the intellectual conscience and intellectual carry-all," whose passing Kazin had fearfully (and prematurely) predicted in *On Native Grounds*.[57]

"Like Nothing Any of Us Would See Again"

Perhaps the most gratifying response to *Contemporaries* came from the writer to whom the book was dedicated. In a series of letters, Edmund Wilson told Kazin how much he liked what he was reading and that he thought Kazin had finally produced something worthy of himself. Kazin's relations with Wilson, with whom he had frequently been compared since the publication of *On Native Grounds,* had never been easy. He had invested too much in Wilson, in the example of Wilson, as an inspiring literary enabler and admitted "father figure," for their relations to be comfortable and casual. "From the time I was a boy, his writing thrilled me," Kazin confided in his journal after a May 1956 meeting with Wilson at the Aaron's in Northampton. "I use the term advisedly—because of its virtuosity, its consummate proof of the art that could be brought to criticism." Determined to become a writer since he was a child, but "dumbfounded" that he had no talent for fiction or poetry, he had learned from Wilson one could be a critic *and* a "literary artist." Though Kazin knew he could never "meet him as a scholar, as the relentless student of all literatures and languages he so wonderfully is," he believed he shared with Wilson the right critical instincts. "Since I have always approached all literary and critical questions with the instinctive quick sympathy of the writer, not with the objectivity or heaviness of the critic, I suppose I found in E.W. the one solid proof that my own kindred literary personality was real."[58]

Kazin was well aware of how much he idealized Wilson and took it as a healthy sign that he could at times feel "gnawingly impatient with E.W.'s lacks." His blistering review of *Memoirs of Hecate County* had certainly shown impatience, as had his private and public complaint about Wilson's persistent "pessimism." He would take strong exception to Wilson's contention in the introduction to *Patriotic Gore* (his "single greatest work") that wars are pure power struggles—one sea slug trying to devour another sea slug. Such a view, he wrote Wilson, ignores politics and morality, perversely overlooks personal and historical differences, and "makes Hitler out to be no worse than Churchill." Wilson for his part seemed to have had difficulty forming a clear impression of Kazin. He had not liked *On Native Grounds,* thinking its diction vague and imprecise—imprecision, he warned Kazin more than once, was something he must guard against. Lewis Dabney,

Wilson's biographer, tells the story of Wilson, suffering from a bad cold and propped up in bed in the Plaza Hotel, reading something Kazin had brought him and then declaring in a stagy British accent, "It won't wash Alfie." He had, however, very much liked Kazin's introduction to the *Portable Blake,* and he thought well of *A Walker in the City*—though he had turned down Kazin's request in 1952 for a blurb, saying he never wrote blurbs. Since their first meeting in New York in 1943 when Wilson had announced his reservations about *On Native Grounds,* they had seen each other occasionally and exchanged a number of friendly notes. But, according to Wilson, it was not until a night of bar-hopping in Northampton in May 1957 that he had had his "first real talk with Alfred, who, though self-important, is shy and needs drinks to loosen him up." Wilson remembered it as a pleasant evening but felt that the author of *On Native Grounds* and *A Walker in the City* had yet to make his mark. "I hope that the time will come when he gets over his lack of confidence and comes out with something really important."[59]

He apparently felt Kazin was moving nearer the mark when he began reviewing for the *Reporter* in the late fifties. Wilson wrote him in the fall of 1959 to say how much he liked his recent pieces on John O'Hara and Arthur Schlesinger's book on FDR. He added that reading Kazin's pieces in the *Reporter* confirmed his belief that writers were better off working outside the pressures and conventions of the academy—a welcome statement of solidarity from another struggling freelancer. Wilson was even more complimentary when he began reading *Contemporaries.* He did not agree with everything, including Kazin's discussion of his own work; but he was impressed by the sustained high level of critical intelligence, particularly on political-cultural matters. "On Arthur [Schlesinger Jr.] you are perfect." An expert in assembling books from previously published essays, Wilson appreciated that "all the pieces gain weight [from] being massed together in this way." Moreover, "it makes it possible to take account of how far you have progressed since *On Native Grounds.* You are able to express yourself much better." Wilson's longtime admirer seemed finally to be hitting his stride.[60]

Pleased with Wilson's positive response to *Contemporaries,* Kazin was looking forward to the summer. For the first time in years the Wilsons would be in Wellfleet when the Kazin family was there. Not only would he have the chance to socialize with Wilson, he would be able to see how he fared in the charged social-intellectual environment of a Wellfleet summer. Kazin already thought of Wilson as a "character," a throwback to very different times. His reading of *Patriotic Gore* (1961), Wilson's magisterial treatment of the literature of the Civil War (which Kazin reviewed), had fixed "the great man" more firmly than ever in his imagination as America's preeminent man of letters, voracious student of languages, and "small town atheist and crank." It would be interesting to watch Wilson maneuver among the ever-growing crowd of writers, Harvard professors, and White House intellectuals congregated on the dunes in mid-August. In fact, as Kazin already suspected, Wilson would not maneuver. Amid the writers, intellectuals, and academics gathered on the beach and partying in the rented cabins and houses, Wilson, Kazin noted in a June journal entry, was simply and stolidly himself, looking and sounding "more dogged and firm-lipped [than] H[erbert] Hoover," while the world seemed to gather around him. "Edmund sits stiffly behind the table laden with drinks, stiffly shouting out his thoughts. Each [thought] a spoke of the wheel. He thinks. He thinks." While others hazard conversational gambits, drop names, and speculate in literary futures, "Wilson says exactly what he knows, and what he doesn't know, he doesn't say. The most meticulous honesty is always his resource."[61]

In *New York Jew,* Kazin would paint a loving and justly celebrated portrait of Wilson that begins with his arrival at the crowded Wellfleet beach "in a stained old Panama hat, the long dress shirt he wore everywhere . . . [and] brown Bermuda shorts that bulged with his capacious middle." Shouting out against waves, wind, and the surrounding human tumult, "his cane propped up in the sand like a sword," Wilson would launch immediately into his current "topic" of interest—the latest work by Sartre, his recent discoveries in Hungarian literature, the operations of the CIA in Cuba. "The formality of sentence structure even on the beach, like the aloofness of his manner . . . was like nothing any of us would ever see again. Ponderously shy, abrupt, exact, and exacting, he was matter-of-fact in a style of old-fashioned American hardness."[62]

Sitting uncomfortably on the beach populated by Harvard professors, Manhattan psychiatrists, and White House staffers, many of them "eager beavers . . . of recent immigrant stock," Wilson had "authority"—authority from his sound education in literature and languages, from his precision and competence as a writer, from his ancestral "class"—"the professional gentry of lawyers, preachers, educators, scientists, which from New England's clerical oligarchs had remained the sustaining class in American life." Dismissing objections to his recent views on the Kennedys with the "caustic smile he reserved for anxiously Americanized and patriotic Jewish intellectuals," Wilson was a reminder of how new *they* were to America—a reminder Kazin hardly needed of the ancestral differences separating him from his treasured American icon. "Edmund Wilson in his wonderful 'old' house on Route 6 in Wellfleet," he wrote in a September 1963 journal entry following a recent visit with Wilson. "Everything in this house passed down or acquired by someone who could recognize immediately its historical application to himself. By contrast, everything I own I have bought for myself or have had to decide its merit in relation to an entirely new situation. The critical factor in the life of the 'new man' who is the Jewish writer in this country is this lack of transition. Sometimes, like Oscar Handlin he will try to interpret all American history in terms of immigrants. But no one can tell me that Edmund Wilson feels like an immigrant's son." Wilson in his "wonderful 'old' house" in Wellfleet, in his study with its three desks (each dedicated to a different project), in his ancestral stone house in Talcottville studying languages, was as much a part of Kazin's discovery of America as the pictures in the American section of the Metropolitan Museum, the weathered brownstones of Brooklyn Heights, the authors he had read (and was now rereading) for his book on nineteenth-century America. Reading, knowing, describing Wilson was for this "eager beaver" a special privilege, a personal contact with history—"I can never think of him without becoming historical-minded"—a national treasure and living connection with the America Alfred Kazin was still striving to possess.[63]

Starting Out in the Thirties

On September 19, 1962, Kazin exited the IRT station at 137th Street and began "the same bloody exhausting walk up and down hills and streets" he had made thirty-one years earlier on his first day as a City College freshman. As the Gallagher Visiting Professor at City College, he was scheduled to teach an honors seminar in American literature. The fortresslike buildings at the top of the hill were as dark and forbidding as ever—the same echoing hallways, the long climb up three dimly lit flights of stairs, the sad-looking instructors shuttling silently about. But there was nothing sad and dreary about his students—"the sharpness, the tight little questions in the armed mind. Despite everything, the students have not changed at City"—except that some were female. It would prove an interesting semester, not least for returning Kazin to the world he was reimagining in his book, helping him recover faded memories and offering a fresh view of the protagonist. "Now I walk into class and sit listening to them [the students], I can see so much of myself, I can feel such unexpected tenderness for that boy I was."[64]

Kazin would come to feel very close to his students that semester. Unlike his bored, entitled Amherst students, these "kids," with their "coarse" accents and immigrant working-class backgrounds, "city intellectuals in my style," were interested and intense, grateful for the privilege of reading literature with their famous teacher. His enthusiasm would dim a little when he got their final papers. "They are all liberal, progressive, and . . . on the whole ready and able to use these same books as documents of their own point of view." But "could anything be shallower and more sterile than these same complaints about American society?" "They never seem to think a book can be argued with." His Amherst students, at least, held attitudes different from those of their teacher. Still, Kazin was grateful to these young "heroes." "Fine kids, wonderful kids—gracefully serious—Miss Gattuso, Miss Halpern, Mr. Koch. . . . I love them. They make me feel less lonely, less queer to myself in this time. I understand them." If they lacked the kind of intellectual independence he would have preferred in his students, they helped him look back on his own unhappy college years—"so many weary periods of doubting myself and disliking myself"—with fresh sympathy and less foreboding.[65]

In January 1963, Alfred and Ann left for Berkeley, where he would spend a semester as the Beckman Professor. After Amherst, Nice, and Puerto Rico, they were uneasy about assignments that took them out of New York. Berkeley, however, seemed safe. He knew a number of people on the faculty—Henry Nash Smith, Mark Schorer, and Paul Jacobs—and was eager to meet Alexander Meikeljohn, the former president of Amherst whose work he much admired. Ann had relatives in the area, and they would be taking trips into San Francisco as well as to Stanford and Los Angeles.

There would, as always, be moments of rancor and grief. Ann's difficulty finding a publisher for her third book, *The Sweet Birds of Gorham*, a novel based in part on her memories of Amherst, was a darkening cloud on the horizon for the duration of their stay. Alfred, who very much wanted to see the book published, "to see her gifts recognized," was nonetheless irritated and resentful that her "defeat and dreariness" were spoiling the fun. Still, compared with their other sojourns out of New York, Berkeley was relatively peaceful.[66]

As was the campus itself—though there were portents of things to come. On May 7, Kazin was among an overflow crowd listening to James Baldwin talk on race and racism in the university gymnasium. He thought that Baldwin, a friend, whose essays he had reviewed favorably, was very good, that he "had just the right tone." But it was the audience that most interested him. "If I ever saw the excitement of a public meeting, this was it," he wrote in his journal immediately after the speech. "The flow of feeling . . . was extraordinary—it was a perfect example of a crowd filling up the present and waiting to be fulfilled." He had been reading about the Freedom Riders and Martin Luther King's campaign in Birmingham, Alabama, and he had seen pictures of Bull Connor's deputies harassing blacks with dogs. The Berkeley audience was the closest he had come personally to the spirit that was soon to shake the country. "A moment in time—the present itching for the future."[67]

The Kazins returned to New York in the summer with brightened prospects. The "distinguished professorship" at Stony Brook had come through, beginning in the fall. He could live in New York and teach two days a week at the Stony Brook campus. The "long hard pull" was over—no longer the need to scramble for reviews and visiting professorships to pay the rent. Although Alfred would continue to write essays and reviews (less for the *Reporter* and more for the recently founded *New York Review of Books*), he was financially free to think longer term than the next article or speaking engagement. He and Ann were happy and relieved. So was Seymour Lawrence. "I urge you not to be deflected by lectures and assignments and what not else," he wrote Kazin. "It is not fair to the book which rightfully demands all your concern and devotion." Now there was less reason to be "deflected." He could finish the book.[68]

A major obstacle remained, however—how much to include. He had planned to write the book in two sections, the first part on the thirties, the second on the forties, which would include an account of his affair with Mary Lou Petersen. But every time he got to the part about the affair, he faltered. "I get sick of heart just thinking of the original incidents, connected still in my mind with so much suffering, so much fear. I can't break up that bone again for the book—I just can't." So what to do? The answer, which was becoming clearer the more he wrote his way into the proposed first part, was to let the thirties story stand on its own. "Starting Out in the Thirties" would not be part of a larger book; it would be an entire book—to be followed later by another on the war years and after. Kazin made the decision reluctantly, but, encouraged by his editor, he came to see that the thirties told a good story in their own right. When it appeared in 1965, *Starting Out in the Thirties* was not the work he had originally intended. "I can't look at the thing without seeing it as a fragment of the larger book of which it was the first part," he told Josephine Herbst on finishing it. But he was not complaining. "When I think of what else I might have done, I have to shrug my shoulders. I am glad of the book, it is a good book"[69]

It was a good book and a timely one. During the forties and much of the fifties, the radical thirties was not a subject that attracted many people in literary studies. Walter Rideout's *The Radical Novel in the United States* (1956)—a book on which Kazin submitted an unenthusiastic reader's report ("neither literary criticism nor social history") to Harvard University Press—was one of the few scholarly discussions of the radical writing of the period. Rideout's book was followed in 1960 by Daniel Aaron's *Writers on the Left*. Open-minded, "objective," and extraordinarily well-documented, *Writers on the Left* went a long way toward opening up the writing of the radical thirties to serious study—though thirties veteran William Phillips complained that Aaron's scholarly "objectivity" left the impression that, extracted from the intensities of the moment, there was something absurd and unreal—"the vulgarity and the idiocy"—about the issues and arguments that had convulsed a generation of writers and intellectuals. The special achievement of Kazin's nonscholarly, nonobjective *Starting Out in the Thirties* was precisely its *subjective* re-creation of that historical moment in radical New York—the feel of the times, as they registered on the consciousness of his young, ambitious, hopeful hero.[70]

"A stunning book," wrote Eliot Freemont-Smith of the *New York Times* when it was published in early October 1965, "perhaps the most evocative reminiscence of a vital corner of the nineteen-thirties we are likely to get." Theodore Solotaroff of the *Herald Tribune* agreed. By skillfully linking his impressions and responses to various characters and events, Kazin created a "montage of the movement of the age as lived experience," an experience "that kept being missed by the ideologues." Reviewers in the journals sounded the same theme. Instead of rehashing that era's sectarian debates, Kazin, according to Hilton Kramer in the *New Leader* and Richard Gilman in *Dissent*, conveyed better than anyone they knew "what it felt like" to live in those exciting and frightening times (Gilman). "Kazin's racy, headlong style is equally good at dealing with the books and people, and his fragmentary narrative strongest where he shows that he is responding with all their energies to the accelerating catastrophes of the prewar years."[71]

Kazin conveys what "it felt like" by linking his hero's radical hopes with his unfolding personal aspirations. We experience thirties New York by following closely and sympathetically the efforts of a young radical struggling for a foothold in the city's literary world—a young man convinced that his own advancing career and the rush of history are on the same side. Though we know his revolutionary hopes are doomed, we share in his aspirations, confident he will survive and thrive when history goes its own way. Kazin understood very well the point of Phillips's complaint. Considered "objectively," the debates of the thirties could seem remote and grotesquely irrelevant, and the thirties themselves strange and absurd—"the sour, hysterical, clownish, screeching 30s," he remarked in a 1961 journal entry. "What a *period* to identify with!" But he also understood that essential to the "truth" of those years was the experience of living through them. To follow his attractive, ambitious young idealist—making his way in literary New York, trekking back and forth between Brownsville and Manhattan, introducing himself to editors, meeting with writers and old revolutionaries, making friends with other young radicals, beginning his book, meeting his wife, all the while hoping for the revolution and registering the violent changes in the political-historical weather—is not only to relive the times; it is to acknowledge the truth of their excitement, their idealism, their desperate hopes, their tragic denouement. Told from the inside, history ("personal history") becomes plausible and compelling as shared experience. "My interest in this book," Kazin wrote in May 1964, "is in the period, in the forcing time, in the hardness of a time entirely political," But, he told Josephine Herbst, his deepest intention was to create "a human-scape—the setting of my loves and discoveries." Kazin's "humanscape" of thirties New York is an indispensable "inside" guide to our understanding of that troubled and exciting era.[72]

In the fall of 1964, as he was completing the manuscript, Kazin learned that Seymour Lawrence had been replaced as his editor at Atlantic-Little, Brown. Peter Davison, who had been Lawrence's deputy, was now in charge and would be handling his book and future writing projects. Kazin, who had benefited from Lawrence's encouragement and advice, was not alarmed, however. He had known Davison since 1950 when they both had worked for Harcourt, he as a literary scout, Davison as a junior editor. They had renewed their acquaintance in 1955 when Kazin was teaching at Smith. As his publisher's representative, Davison occasionally visited Northampton, where on one visit Kazin had introduced him to Sylvia Plath. Davison had had a brief affair with Plath, then later married Jane Truslow, who, like Plath, had also been a student in Kazin's writing seminar.

When it was clear he was taking over at Little, Brown, Davison wrote Kazin, regretting that their relationship was in arrears and stating that he was eager to renew it. Things got off to a good start when he read the manuscript. "I think it is marvelous," he wrote Kazin. "You evoke the period . . . with such eloquence! The free-for-all of ideas, the amazing social and intellectual mobility . . . an extraordinary mosaic." Davison was gen-uinely enthusiastic, but he may also have learned from Lawrence that Kazin needed strong support and encouragement. (Davison would later say he needed more than that; he needed constant "love."). He did, how-ever, offer a few suggestions in a later letter. One was to date each of the sections (e.g., Part I, 1934; Part II, 1935). It was sound advice that Kazin accepted. The chronological chapter headings, following one after the other, indicate that whatever the hopes of Kazin and his friends, it was history that was setting the rhythm, rushing events to their conclusion.[73]

Davison's other suggestion was to add a couple of pages after the "1940" concluding chapter that would look to the future. "The book now *stops*, it does not *end*." Kazin accepted this advice as well and sent off a brief "Epilogue: 1945," the last paragraphs of which describe a scene inside a Piccadilly newsreel theater where he had watched the prisoners, "sticks,"

moving about amid piles of bodies in the recently liberated Belsen concentration camp. He had cited the discovery of the Belsen camp in *Walker*
in connection with memories of his mother's kitchen. Here, it serves as a
point of historical demarcation, casting a darkening shadow back over the
innocent hopes of the previous decade, signaling the advent of a very
different era—the era that comes after. "The last sentences," Davison
wrote back appreciatively, "have the toll of a bell."[74]

CHAPTER NINE

The Writer in the World
Part 2
1963–1970

I want to be thoroughly engaged with the world.

—Alfred Kazin, Journal, December 29, 1965

S *tarting Out in the Thirties* was a deeply gratifying book for the fifty-year-old Kazin—the more so because it came as a surprise, an extra book he had not intended, and with it an opportunity for yet another installment of his autobiography. The reviews were good—very good, in fact, discounting the usual deprecating remarks from the "snotty" Brits. Responses from friends were also heartening. Edmund Wilson told him how much he had learned from it—though, naturally, he quibbled with factual points. Josephine Herbst, who knew the radical New York milieu of the thirties better than virtually anyone, liked it immensely. Most gratifying was the response of Richard Hofstadter. Although his old friend, appearing as "John," has only a minor part in the book, Felice Swados ("Harriet"), his wife at the time, plays a more central role and not a very flattering one. Kazin had worried about Hofstadter's reaction, but he had little to fear. Hofstadter thought it a highly intelligent and very moving book, felt that Kazin had been more than generous to himself and their acquaintances, and assured him of his abiding friendship and love. From Mary McCarthy, the subject of a very negative portrait, he heard nothing (at least not immediately), nor from Philip Rahv, whose portrait was not wholly flattering. Even the subject of his harshest criticism, William Canning, "Francis," a

"Holy Informer" who ratted on his colleagues at City College, refused to be offended. He told Kazin he thought he was "joshing" him in the portrait. All in all, a very satisfying response.[1]

Starting Out in the Thirties was gratifying for another reason. It proved Kazin could find in his personal past, in images, events, and feelings reconstructed from memory, a way of writing history, "personal history." Through the objectification of art, he could bring the public and the private into meaningful relation "to prove the world we share." An achieved literary fusion of private feeling and public event did not, however, signal any lessening of the chronic tension between Kazin's impulse toward self-reference and self-involvement—"the *me, me, me* in my writing"—and his need to engage the public world "out there," to test himself and his sanity against the restraints of the other—"always the other and the otherness of the world." In the forties and fifties, after the intense public consciousness of the thirties, "the forcing time," Kazin's preoccupation with self and self-consciousness had found a certain sanction in the existential and religious concerns of those years—the solitary walker-writer-Jew intent on his anguished creative-spiritual relations with a hostile or indifferent world. In the late fifties, as he grew weary of the alienated pleadings of "the alone generation," he had turned with fresh interest to the writer's role in the public world, the writer returned to history. By the late sixties, however, that role would once again prove difficult and problematic as he and other writers struggled to come to terms with the demands of another forcing time—"the hardness of a time entirely political."[2]

Like many "Old Left" veterans of the thirties, Kazin spent the late sixties in an anxious state of moral and political uncertainty. Profoundly unhappy with the government's prosecution of the war in Southeast Asia—the growing brutality (evident on the television news), the incompetence of its execution, the rising body count of Americans and Vietnamese, the intransigence of Lyndon Johnson—the Old Left were almost equally dismayed to find that those most opposed to the war, the students, brought to their protest a heterogeneous New Left "philosophy," appeared ignorant of or indifferent to the evils of totalitarianism, blithely equated liberal democracy with "liberal Fascism," countenanced the seizing of university buildings, and dismissed the counsel of their elders (particularly one time thirties radicals) as the maunderings of old men who had sold out their radical

ideals for position in a corrupt power structure, Kazin shared the concerns
of his contemporaries with the New Left's anti-intellectualism and totalitarian proclivities, but (more than most) he sympathized with and even
envied the students precisely because they rejected the passivity of their
elders and insisted on engaging the world in direct action to change it. "Life
consists in acts and actions, in performances and deeds," he wrote in 1967
after learning that his son, Michael, had been officially reprimanded for
barricading a Dow Chemical representative in a Harvard lecture hall. Kazin understood that one need not barricade classrooms or invade deans'
offices or even attend a protest rally to act, that thinking and writing were
also actions, and that critical thought and good writing could change things.
In 1959, he had written that literature "exercises its classic function" by
"providing ideas central to social policy and behavior." But, the times being
what they were, he could not but wonder whether thought and critical
commentary (and even literature) might also work as obstructions to acting. "Too much of what I live gets pissed away in all the attitudes of the
spectator. Oh the intellectuals, the Jewish intellectuals, the commentators
and scribes, the wisdom of non-doing."[3]

Alfred Kazin, thirties-radical-turned-professor, family man, father of a
college radical, would devote no small part of his attention during the late
sixties meditating on the attractions and dangers of the active life as opposed to the rewards and seductions of solitary reflection. He would worry
that the material comforts and predictable placidity of his middle-age,
middle-class life were shielding him from the excitements and risks of the
world outside the study and classroom. He would worry that his natural
caution, political uncertainty, and subjective preoccupations—"a self preoccupied with itself (in an effort to understand itself)"—were disabling his
will to act decisively. But he would also worry that public life was driving
out private life, that the war, the "over-organized" power of the state and
society, the politically inflamed atmosphere of the times were intimidating
writers, crowding out individual consciousness, and making rational delib-
eration (and good writing) virtually impossible. He would not resolve these
concerns, then or ever. One of the more important lessons of the sixties,
particularly the late sixties, was to suggest once again, more forcefully than
ever, the degree to which the solitary, ruminating self is inevitably and
irrevocably implicated in the events of the world out there.[4]

Distinguished Professor

Jack Ludwig, head of the English Department, had good reasons for bringing Kazin to the Stony Brook campus of the State University of New York. The university was eager to bring some instant star power to a school that was rising out of the empty fields and woods of northern Long Island to serve the bourgeoning population of Long Island baby boomers. An acclaimed writer-critic and literary "personality," Alfred Kazin was a recognized scholar of American literature and a connection with the larger, exciting world of literature and culture. Stony Brook offered in turn a good salary, a title—"distinguished professor"—and a schedule that allowed Kazin to live in Manhattan, spending only two days a week (Thursday and Friday) on campus. Since resigning from Amherst in 1957, he had been living from article to article, grant to grant, always on the lookout for the next visiting professorship. The Stony Brook offer left him feeling "as if a terrific burden had been lifted off my shoulders." It also enabled him to sign a lease for a spacious new apartment on West End Avenue. On October 30, the Kazins moved in and shortly thereafter celebrated with a party for some seventy people. "Our new apartment faces on the Hudson all around and the rest of the city, and is very exciting to live in," he wrote Josephine Herbst, who had not been able to attend. "New York is really fabulous when you feel yourself part of it, when you catch a hint of the imperial rhythms it has to offer. I walk out every day as if to embrace what my eyes have loved all day from the 16th floor."[5]

Financially secure and happily housed, Kazin quickly settled into a weekly rhythm of commuting and lecturing, holding regular office hours and attending faculty meetings. While not exactly "imperial," the rhythm of five days in New York and two days and a night at Stony Brook brought both order and variety to his life—the daily crush and excitement of New York alternating with leafy suburbs and solitary walks on the beach. Teaching at an expansion campus of the state university system was different from any of his earlier teaching experiences. The abrupt appearance and factorylike functionality of the campus—"building[s] that [have] nothing but corridors for students to walk in and teachers to listen to, offices that have nothing but desks and bookcases and files and pencils"—initially impressed him, suggesting the "terrible urgency" currently attached to higher education in

America. But they could also depress him—"the rolling mill of education, the grinding industrial process of education"—particularly when he chose to dwell, melodramatically, on the regularity of his life as professor-in-the-suburbs: "Middle aged boredom . . . suburban ennui, flatness, nullity, insignificance, doom."[6]

The students, nearly all of them from Long Island, were not consistently of the highest quality, and he sometimes wondered about the impression he, the high-powered New York intellectual, was making on them. "Why are these kids so numb, so sad sacky, so *low?*" he wrote to Herbst. "I feel (intellectually) like the old roué in the top-hat and white gloves taking out a neurotic young chorus girl: he laughs, he sports, he winks, and she talks about her mother." But he often found the teaching exciting and gratifying: "took the undergrad class through first part of 'Song of Myself,' then the graduate group through 'Tintern Abbey.' Was very good, if I say so myself—analyzed Wordsworth's command of the human heart better than I have ever done before." Much of the pleasure (and frustration) came from working closely with students. Unlike the lecturing he had done over the past five years—the Gauss lectures at Princeton, the Beckman lectures at Berkeley, his Monday night lectures at the New School—he now had to listen to students, talk with them, take them seriously—"not to instruct and guide and captivate all the time. Teaching must be a real discovery—not a critic's notebook." The daily encounter with students who seemed never to have read anything—"How, I keep asking myself, could they understand so little"—often exasperated him, but the rewards of patience and persistence could be very high: "Pamela Jacobs, that earnest but literal student in my American lit course, has blossomed out into one of these kids for whom Emerson-Thoreau-Melville-Whitman become a revelation, a transfiguring of the universe. This kind of revelatory power, that the Romantics can exercise is very moving to watch—the routine paper and exams smell with excitement, Great."[7]

Kazin regarded the faculty with a similar mix of pleasure, weariness, and frustration. Some he very much liked and respected. He never tired of talking with the young Americanist, Peter Shaw, about Henry Adams or listening to Judah Stampher on early English drama or on anything at all: "all that "boiling lava . . . always trying to match its energy to some great and surpassing object." He sought out the economist Robert Lekachman for his sophistication and wit—"he is so easy, civilized, and humorous," and the medievalist Peter Alexander for his sanity and common sense, "so manly-looking and Scottish and straight that one is surprised to see someone so burly . . . and manly-looking teaching literature." For the most part, however, he was unimpressed by his Stony Brook colleagues, who "were not intellectual in the least"—a feeling reinforced by the newness and rawness of the school itself as well as by his two-hour commute that reminded him weekly of the gap separating him from the charmed circle of writers and friends whose conversation he shared in New York. "Morning [at Stony Brook]; horribly depressed. The cold outside and the cold inside, the peculiar rawness and bareness of the atmosphere at Stony Brook. Last class—then drove fast in the piercing cold [to the] *American Scholar* dinner, which in anticipation excites me so much—John Hersey, Dr. Henry Murray, Dick Rovere, Dan [Bell], Dick Hofstadter, Barzun, etc. etc."[8]

There were no *American Scholar* dinners at Stony Brook, nor, in Kazin's opinion, much intellectual life. Instead, there were occasional visits by select luminaries, tribunes from the literary-scholarly world outside, to whom Kazin, in his role as "distinguished professor" was expected to play host. It was for the most part a pleasant duty, giving him the chance to meet and assess prominent figures—Northrop Frye, Frank Kermode, William Arrowsmith, Conor Cruise O'Brien, and Harold Bloom, among others. In the case of Kermode, the meeting would lead to a friendship; others, like Bloom, would leave him abashed. After dining with this "fascinatingly gifted" young scholar, Kazin felt "like I know nothing and have read nothing of the English romantics of whom I have prated so much. . . . By contrast with the Stony Brook brigade Bloom looks *big.* Extraordinary how that round, vaguely baby, Jewish, unworldly face imposes itself, takes hold."[9]

Kazin was at Stony Brook from 1963 to 1973. Despite a good salary and a prestigious position, one could not call them happy years. Too many things depressed him about the school, its "low prestige," its "sad sacky" students, its "mediocre" faculty. "I feel vaguely lowered to be here at all," he wrote in his journal in 1966. "I am bitter and angry at the mediocrity that is like a bad smell at SUNY. . . am intellectually lonely here." In truth, there were probably few colleges or universities where Kazin would have been happy. Academic life, academic manners, and academics as a group generally irritated and unnerved him. Not only did he despair of the academic temperament, he felt he could not compete in an arena where someone like Bloom was such an obvious champion. "Listening to him last night on Yeats and the Romantic Tradition, I realized that his interest is in literary history, and that he is a brilliant representative of an academician, which, as always, I am so out of that I can only suffer the exclusiveness, while I am on the academic spot." Although he had first made his mark writing literary history, Kazin knew from his efforts on *The Western Island* that he could not write the kind of "detached" scholarly work prized by academics, who value nothing as much as "the precious superiority of the uninvolved." If there was a mode of literary history that he wanted to write—and he did!—it was in the style of Edmund Wilson's *Patriotic Gore* ("EW's going at things exactly in his own way") or Van Wyck Brooks's evocative histories, which, whatever their lack of critical rigor, were the works of a "writer" not a "scientist" or "objective" commentator. Theirs, however, was not the kind of work much practiced or honored among academics; and, indeed, it was difficult to imagine either Brooks or Wilson settling comfortably into any university. Despite the comfort of a steady salary and the occasional rewards that came from discovering and encouraging talented students, Kazin often found it difficult to imagine himself where he was—a writer, lost amidst the professorate, "always trying to find my place."[10]

He did, however, have a place, a rather comfortable one—which presented him with another problem: how to reconcile his longtime yearning for position, power, and success with the rather "boring" fact that by the mid-sixties he had achieved a significant measure of each. Was not happiness a world to be hoped for rather than to be lived in? Just how keenly Kazin felt this need to be continually striving for the prize is evident in *A Walker in the City* and *Starting Out in the Thirties,* which derive much of their lyrical force from youthful yearning, passion, and hope. With the securing of a permanent "distinguished" university position, the challenge more than ever was boredom and security, "boredom with one's very success and power as opposed to the endless deprivation that *was* so dramatic in the past . . . The middle-aged man, distinguished professor, doctor of literature, blah, blah, blah . . . , he is bored, he is idle, he doesn't know what to do with himself half the time."[11]

Middle-aged, married fifteen years, with children, a comfortable home, a secure job—Alfred feared (with some reason) that he was losing touch with his deepest source of inspiration. He also feared he was losing touch with the world, the world of risk and danger and undisclosed opportunity outside the insulated enclaves of tenured professors. On a 1965 Christmas visit with the Aarons in Northampton, he walked about the town hoping to recapture some of the more positive feelings he had felt a decade earlier while teaching at Smith. Instead, he found himself recoiling at the sight of the expanding campuses of Smith, Amherst, and the University of Massachusetts, which like Stony Brook had been recently created to accommodate the exploding student population: "I feel utterly bored and desolate by all this soft academic mediocrity. . . . It is the boredom of feeling myself to be like so many of the others in the academic power plant . . . I want to be better, clearer, sharper, more proficient than ever, I want to be thoroughly engaged with the world." Alarmed that he was being drawn deeper into the maw of an insatiable educational machine that isolated him from the risky, adventurous world outside, Kazin yearned to break beyond the numbing routine (and material comfort?) of the ever-expanding modern academy, to get back to a world of youthful striving—"my old image of myself as struggle"—and as yet undefined horizons. It was a sentiment more felt than acted on, an indulgence of genius he could no longer afford—How would he pay Kate's tuition at the Dalton School and then at Smith? He would remain at Stony Brook for ten years, a lively if sometimes impatient teacher, an engrossing if often difficult colleague, an exciting, restive presence.[12]

"The Closeness Is the Crux"

The move into the spacious apartment on West End Avenue was as exciting for Ann Birstein as it was for her husband. She, too, was entranced by the view of the river and the city, and its space allowed her to host the large, freewheeling cocktail parties that she preferred to sit-down dinners. Alfred's salary enabled them to hire a maid for five days a week and to send Kate to the nearby Dalton School. Ann now had both the time and space to work regularly on her own writing. Expensive New York seemed at last to be opening to the possibilities that she and Alfred had hoped for when they left Amherst five years earlier. Happiness, however, marital happiness, remained as illusory as it had been in rural New England.

In *New York Jew*, Alfred attributes these difficulties in part to the fact that Ann was a novelist with "many selves" and that he, "hopelessly one self," was a critic, "forever perched on the judgment seat," unable to give her "the hearty unending approval" she demanded. There was some truth in this. Though he valued Ann's intelligence and her "modest" creative abilities, he never believed that she would become the "great" novelist she expected to become. Bitterly alert to the reservations of one of the country's most celebrated critics, Ann resented his lack of enthusiasm (and loyalty), attributing it to the fact that he was an "intellectual" lacking in novelistic sensibility. She had long harbored hostile feelings toward the "intellectuals" associated with the *Partisan Review,* who she believed lacked literary sensibility and treated her as a lightweight.[13]

Compounding their difficulties was the fact that Alfred was as demanding of Ann's constant and unqualified support as she was of his—mutual and seemingly absolute claims that led inevitably to frustration, anger, and deepening resentment. We are "clamorous with indignant demands on everything and everyone," he wrote after a particularly unpleasant evening with the family. "I think of the incessant tension between Ann and me, each of us demanding everything of the other and incapable of foregoing any of his demands on the other . . . We go at life like one of those monster children on television devouring cereal. We are manic with hunger. We feel deprived all the time." Alfred regretted his "insane sense of deprivation," his "sickening demand for love and protection." He agreed with Ann that he was too much "the mama's boy" and was abashed by his desperate need "for the reassurance of being loved, that is infantile to the point of insanity." Yet he felt helpless to help himself and equally helpless to satisfy Ann's need for reassurance, particularly when he felt he was not getting the kind of attention he believed he deserved. The result was an eruptive cycle of claim and counterclaim, shouting and imprecation, fed by a constantly aggrieved sense of want and injustice. Sometimes a trivial remark would trigger an explosion; sometimes the matter was (symbolically) more serious —as when the *New York Post* published an interview with Ann under the title "At Home with Mrs. Alfred Kazin." "The sight of this threw her into such a fierce depression that in the evening, not unnaturally, it made me mad . . . 'All my life,' wept Ann bitterly, 'It's been the same all my life.' Ann regards herself as 'suicidal,' as 'sick,' as a victim. . . . The hold the victim has on me! And yet I get furious when the same victim seems not to pay enough homage to *me*—when this sadness turns aggressive and resentful as I felt it did in the restaurant last night."[14]

Outbreaks in restaurants, at dinner parties, and during meetings with friends were hardly unusual. An evening out with the Kazins, a meeting for drinks at the Russian Tea Room, could lead anywhere, very often to embarrassed silence. " 'You deal in pain,' said Jerry Barondess [Alfred's physician and personal friend] wonderingly over the Peking Duck the other night as Ann and I disagreed with the usual violence—this time about Salinger." Alfred himself wondered about the pain and violence, his own and hers— the yelling, the spitting, the throwing of papers and books, the slamming of doors, the storming out of restaurants. Were they a form of revenge for his domineering temperament, or for his recurrent unfaithfulness? Were they an expression of the passion that Ann brought to everything, including making love, which always took on special intensity after a terrible fight? Following a row that began with supper and continued to three in the morning in a motel room with Ann screaming and cursing and Alfred putting his hand over her mouth to stop the people in the next room from beating on the walls—"after all this, she asked me to bed. We fucked, and in the morning made up for the whole weekend with the most delicious session we had in ages."[15]

Were the violence and pain inseparable from the ecstasy of lovemaking and the sweetness of reconciliation—a pattern of emotional highs and lows that suited Ann's extreme mood swings, and kept Alfred's attention? Or were they, as he frequently hypothesized, attributable to family and ethnic background? "What a neurotic set we all are—but in a particular East-European, poor Jewish style of personal aggrandizement. It is not so much our secret psychological 'motivations' that make us this way as it is our manners. There is no tradition of self-restraint, or true politeness and inquiry. We feel threatened in the darkest kind of way, and we are always trying to rise straight up from every possible frustration." Whether the extremes of his and Ann's behavior can be attributed to manic-depressive mood swings, retribution for suffered wrongs, a lack of proper breeding, or the residual terror of pogroms, the violence, anger, and pain were punishing and destructive for both of them—and undoubtedly for their daughter Kate! Ann would wake up morning after morning threatening suicide; Alfred would repeatedly contemplate hanging himself from the chandelier.

There seemed to be no way out: "The usual screaming. I complained about the dinner. Ann got furious and we were at each other hammer and tongs, as usual. So it goes—so I am—so it was—so I have been. Kazin the man forever fighting with women. No change—no peace—no comfort. It is New Years Eve and all blackness in my heart again; the old pattern."[16]

The obvious way out, of course, would have been separation and divorce —the option recommended earlier by Dr. Rioch and more recently by his present psychiatrist, Dr. William Marvin. Alfred acknowledged the wisdom of this advice: "Ann will not change; I will not change; nor will my dream of getting away from it all ever be realized." Yet he could not bear the thought of a third marriage collapsing and, most importantly, of losing Kate. The loss of Michael in his divorce from Carol had left scars, absences, and regrets from which he knew he would never recover. The thought of being left out of Kate's life the way he had been left out of Michael's was one he could not, would not, seriously contemplate. He also worried (with good reason) about the pathetic, self-pitying emotional state that a separation would likely bring on—living alone "in some miserable furnished room, where I can lie awake all night, feel sorry for myself to the end of time, and hope, unsuccessfully, to die." Each of his two earlier divorces had plunged him into depression and long periods of desperate loneliness that he did not want repeated.[17]

In fact, he remained convinced that what had brought him out of "his old hole of loneliness and despondency was Ann, from [19]50 on." It was she who had led him out of the darkness of his solitary, underground life into the shared world of others. "This was 'public' life, true life, lived not by the solitary will seeking to pierce through by intellectual effort alone, but by companionship and understanding, by love and dialogue." Though one could think of terms other than "companionship," "love," and "dialogue" to describe the nature of their relations, it was also true that "for all the hot depths and cold depths," Alfred remained fascinated, "enthralled" by Ann. In part, the fascination came from the shock value of the unexpected. Would even he have guessed that Ann would accuse him of serving on the Pulitzer committee for the sole purpose of denying her the prize? But it also came from his recognition that, more than anyone else he had known, Ann had the power to force him out of himself, to acknowledge the presence of another, that "the Heart of the World is people," other people.

"The truth is that with all the conflict and meanness, I owe my sense of this [otherness] to Ann, simply because I have never been so fully deeply involved with anyone else."[18]

Looking back to "the bookish solitudes and the self-occupying staleness" of the forties, Alfred remained grateful for the happiness and the exciting sense of connection with the world that Ann had then brought into his life. Although this early happiness had long since faded amid the resentment and anger of their troubled marriage, he continued to believe that Ann, through the sheer intensity of her will, her strident, hysterical demands, her determined insistence on her rights, brought a necessary and saving "corrective" to his own tendency to withdraw into an "inner dream." He occasionally reflected on what it would be like to drift off into a such a dream world, a "world without fault . . . a world of perfect contemplation and ease . . . in which nobody is allowed to be an egotist but I." He even wondered whether such a life might be practically possible with one of his mistresses, women who "are competent, confident, easy." "I have known several such women and had unforgettable satisfaction from them: Lou, Sylvia Marlowe, Celia, Vivienne, Jean Garrigue, Rose. They are women who make everything easy, who have this side of their nature as a gift." Indeed, his very latest mistress (another Sylvia) apparently asked nothing more from him than his own sexual pleasure: "Looking at her extraordinary lips, which I so gladly tell her are like the lips of a cunt (into which I would as gladly slip my prick as I have into her cunt), I think—how easy life would be if I had her all the time—if the rooted and easy love making I long for beyond anything else were there, for me with her!" But in his "heart of hearts," he knew this was impossible—that he needed the very resistance (and violence?) and emotional intensity and closeness that he expected and endured from Ann. She imposed herself. Instead of drifting off into his own dream world, he felt he was always being forced into hers. "The feeling I had about her one night in Paris, staring at her eyes revolving, stareless, meaningless (for me) in reflecting the inner depths of her constant dream, I thought to myself: I am subject to her dream! I am caught up in her dream!" "The closeness is the crux: I take every bit of the woman so seriously: as if my life depended on it, literally that." If life as a university professor all too often left Alfred feeling that he had been taken over by a routine as safe as it was predictable, life with Ann, life loving Ann, suffering

Ann, was never safe and never predictable: "to love Ann is like a prolonged journey into an interior that changes so sharply and (still!) unexpectedly, every rotating, shifting, bewildering part of the day. Still, how interested I am all the time!"[19]

"Growing Up in the Sixties": A Liberal's Dilemma

If Ann Birstein provided an internal, or familial, check on Kazin's yearning for "a world of perfect contemplation and ease," the times themselves provided a powerful external corrective. No decade in recent history has imposed itself so violently on the conscience and consciousness of the nation, or demonstrated more power to outrage and shock. A tumultuous time for all Americans, the sixties, particularly the late sixties, were uniquely disturbing to middle-class liberals, even more to liberal-left parents of children who, having assimilated the values of their fathers and mothers, carried them into the streets, onto the campuses, even to the steps of the Pentagon, and not infrequently turned them back on the very people from whom they had learned them. The young radicals' "rebellion," Kenneth Kenniston wrote at the time, "characteristically consisted in using against their parents the parents' own principles." Often stirring the rebellion were feelings of "angry outrage and betrayal upon discovering that the parents themselves did not practice the values they espoused." Kazin titled the chapter covering the sixties in *New York Jew* "Growing Up in the Sixties," and, as its unspecified reference suggests, the children were not the only ones suffering growing pains.[20]

Like many ex-radicals from the thirties, Kazin entered the sixties disgusted with eight years of Eisenhower's leadership and dismayed by his "disastrous record" on domestic issues, including his "sell-out to McCarthy" and his "opposition to Negro advance." Yet, he remained largely in agreement with a foreign and military policy (inherited in broad outline from Truman) whose defining mission was to contain Soviet expansionism and the spread of "totalitarian" Communism. Although he often complained about the "complacency" of "The New [anti-Communist] Liberalism" enunciated in Arthur Schlesinger's *The Vital Center*, Kazin subscribed (however restlessly) to its fundamental assumptions. He was both a staunch anti-Communist—a foe of the Soviet Union and Castro—and a political and intellectual liberal: "everything I hold dear," he wrote in 1958, "everything that moves my work at its best and that at its best becomes the content of my work, is embraced by the word 'liberalism'—or freedom by the full power of criticism." He was for social justice, expanded civil liberties, and increased support for the poor, as well as for intellectual openness and critical independence. At the same time, he believed, like most Americans (liberal and conservative), that the "totalitarian communism" of the Soviet Union represented a continuing danger to democracy and human freedom everywhere, a threat whose containment demanded constant vigilance and, when necessary, the use of force. Indeed, as a one-time thirties radical-Socialist, who had closely followed the betrayal of Socialist ideals by Stalin and the imposition of state tyranny in the Soviet Union and its satellites, Kazin felt an abiding and passionate resentment toward Russian Communism and the totalitarian state, the "intensity" of which, he acknowledged, might well seem a source of "wonder" to those, particularly "the young," who did not share his experience.[21]

The so-called "liberal consensus," combining anti-Communism with a commitment to liberal and progressive values, would not survive the sixties—at least not in recognizable form. The decade that began with a newly elected "liberal" president declaring that the United States must be prepared to go anywhere, pay any price, in defense of freedom and democracy would conclude with Republican and liberal scourge Richard Nixon in the White House, the country divided over a war that would not end, liberals angry and bewildered—wondering what had gone wrong, many of them lashing out at the kids, all of them troubled and conflicted. Kazin's response to events was in many ways typical—growing disenchantment and disgust with the war and the administration; resentment of the student radicals; guilt, shame, and uncertainty about what he was doing—and not doing. What was less typical was his willingness to acknowledge his confusion and his conflicted feelings. To follow Kazin through the politics of the late sixties is to get a glimpse of the chagrin, the shame, the bewilderment, and the anger, but also the reflective and self-critical openness of a liberal trying to be honest with himself about a historical, moral (and parental) predicament he self-admittedly did not understand. It was perhaps this honesty together with his newfound feelings of connection with his son that enabled him to emerge from the sixties still in possession of the liberal spirit that many of his contemporaries had lost.

The obvious starting point of Kazin's journey through the political sixties is his 1961 essay "The President and Other Intellectuals." An attack on the way intellectuals allowed themselves to be used by Kennedy in the pursuit of cold war policies (resulting in, among other things, the disastrous Bay of Pigs invasion), the essay would seem to have been a prescient warning of the dangers to come. Kazin was calling for the best and the brightest to think as independent-minded intellectuals, not as technocrats and implementers of established policy. But while the essay challenges intellectuals to protect their independence from the aura and temptations of power, and to question the policies and assumptions, even "the essential philosophy" of the administration, it does not indicate just what these policies and assumptions might be. Specifically, though Kazin calls the Bay of Pigs invasion "immoral" and "stupid," he does not challenge Kennedy or his intellectual entourage to rethink the cold war assumptions underlying the Cuban misadventure. Indeed, he emphatically links Castro's Cuba with the Soviet Union, calling Castro "a cynical and dangerous ally of totalitarianism"—and presumably just the kind of "dangerous" leader, only ninety strategic miles off America's coast, that a staunchly anti-Communist president might well want removed. What, then, is left for the Kennedy intellectuals to question—troop numbers? landing craft? reliability of information about counterinsurgency? And what made the failed invasion "immoral"? Would it have been immoral if it had succeeded? Kazin urges the kind of tough criticism and unprejudiced discussion of assumptions that liberals prize; but without a readiness to question ingrained habits of thought and political faith, the liberal ideal remains, at best, an ideal, and at worst, an accessory after the fact, the illusion of criticism.[22]

Little would happen over the next three years to lead Kazin to question any of his anti-Communist liberal assumptions. Indeed, the Soviet's resumption of nuclear testing, Khrushchev and Castro's decision to place missiles in Cuba, images of East German border guards shooting down citizens trying to escape to West Berlin, and mounting evidence that the Soviet Union was persecuting Jews and preventing them from moving to Israel—all reinforced his long-held resentment and hatred of Soviet rule and his disgust with those who would apologize for its crimes. "When I get and read the papers, I want to vomit," he wrote in August 1961. "The Princeton idiot, Erich Kahler, has a letter in the *Times* explaining that we should not look so hard at the Russians. Somehow, when one is faced by this enormous totalitarian pressure, some small voice cries out that maybe if we were nicer, maybe if we tried a different tack." He was also disgusted with the likes of C. Wright Mills, who, when confronted with Castro's jailing of dissidents, told his challengers to look at Little Rock—as though racism in the American South indicated a moral equivalence with "totalitarian" Cuba or Russia. There was no disputing the evils of racism and the readiness of U.S. politicians to exploit race for political gain. But the United States, unlike the Soviet Union, was susceptible to social and political change (even in matters of race) and to exertions on the part of its citizens for the implementation of constitutional rights—as developments in Arkansas and Alabama were beginning to demonstrate.[23]

In fact, Alfred Kazin, like most liberals in the early sixties, saw the emerging campaign for civil rights in the South as part of a defining (and redeeming) moral struggle for the nation—and an occasion to reaffirm their liberal convictions. During a 1961 radio broadcast, Kazin observed that in the centenary year of the Civil War, it was difficult to forget that the "presence of the Negro in American civilization . . . is the central fact about our moral history," a reminder of the "tension between what this country is ideally supposed to mean and what it actually has been." He followed the skirmishes and confrontations in the South, the Birmingham bus boycott, the Freedom Rides, the registration of black voters in Mississippi with mounting enthusiasm—but also with misgiving. Events were clearly on the move, he wrote to C. P. Snow, but "the Negroes are a minority and the majority is often too worried about its suddenly achieved status in comforts to risk anything." He looked to black writers like Ralph Ellison and especially James Baldwin for moral clarity and eloquence—yet he doubted that writers had much political effect. "Jimmy—not a politician, not a Negro leader but a writer." But by the fall of 1964, Congress, at President Johnson's urging, had passed the Civil Rights Act; and the following year, after the marches in Selma and the savage reactions by local authorities had alarmed and shamed the country, it passed the historic Voting Rights Act, changing the politics of the South forever. Kazin watched all this with growing excitement, convinced that the country was participating in a historic act of spiritual redemption. "Rain, rain and rain from Selma to Montgomery. A huddle of Americans, white and black, marching in the rain, while ladies sitting in lawn chairs on the side yell 'Nigger!' The US is trying on the idea of brotherhood, and it hurts like hell, and we will keep trying it. Selma is one of the great events in American history. It lights up our day. It is great, great, great. Religion as politics."[24]

The Selma march in 1965 and the terror exercised against the marchers (which riveted the attention and aroused the conscience of the public) marked for Kazin and many Americans the high moral-political moment of the sixties, a moment that brought together liberals, dissidents, "the kids," and people of good hope throughout the country. "Thank God for the kids, for the churches, for the outsiders, for the conscience bearers and the bearers of hope," Kazin wrote after listening to President Johnson's speech to Congress proposing the voting rights bill. Here at last was a cause and a result in which all people of goodwill could rejoice.[25]

But 1965 was a year of decision in another area as well—one where it would be more difficult to claim common cause with "the outsiders," with the kids, with people of conscience, and one that would mark the beginning of the end of the liberal consensus. On February 13, President Johnson ordered the start of a sustained bombing campaign against North Vietnam, "Operation Rolling Thunder," that would eventually result in the dropping on North Vietnam of three times the number of bombs that had been dropped by all sides during World War II. Three weeks after Johnson's order, on March 8, the Ninth Marine Expeditionary Brigade went ashore on the beaches north of Da Nang—the first American ground troops introduced into a war that would conclude with more than fifty-eight thousand Americans killed and hundreds of thousands of American casualties.

Kazin had watched the events leading up to the bombing with growing unease—the Gulf of Tonkin Resolution, the increasing number of "military advisors" in Vietnam, the desperate attempts to shore up unpopular regimes in Saigon. He wondered and worried about America's "power complex" and the smug confidence of its leaders and the cheering media. "*Time* is so happy, Johnson is so happy, [the country] assures itself that the most powerful nation believes in freedom." The misgiving would deepen as he grew more convinced that Johnson and his advisors were hypnotized by the limitless possibilities of American power and had let the cold war dominate all other national concerns. He was disgusted when Johnson sent a contingent of marines to take over the Dominican Republic in April, supposedly to prevent a Communist takeover; and in a May review of Christopher Lasch's *The New Radicalism,* he raised again the issue (raised in his 1960 speech "War and the Intellectuals") of the American intellectual's stake "in the perpetuation of the cold war." He made his first public protest of the Vietnam War in the summer issue of the *Partisan Review,* signing a letter with nine other writers, including Irving Howe, Steven Marcus, William Phillips, Norman Podhoretz, and Richard Poirier, that challenged the government's intervention in Vietnam and the Dominican Republic.[26]

In fact, it was not much of a challenge, as a number of later respondents pointed out. While straightforward in its condemnation of the Marine incursion in the Dominican Republic, the writers hedged their bets on Vietnam. "We do not think that the present or past policies of the United States in Vietnam are good ones, and we lament the increasing and often self-defeating military involvements which those policies require." But, they hastened to add, "we have not heard of any alternative policy . . . which would actually lead to a negotiated peace in Vietnam or promote the interests of the people of Southeast Asia." As for those questioning the present policy at "teach-ins" and in various petitions, "it is not unfair to ask that their criticism be based on more than the apolitical assumption that power politics, the Cold War, and Communists are merely American inventions." Nor was it unfair to ask "whether these critics think Asia will not go Communist . . . or whether they don't care." The writers concluded by saying that "obviously, the time has come for some new thinking."[27]

Published as the war began to take on a terrible life of its own, and images of burning villages and civilians were being spread by the American media, the letter indicated the kinds of problems ahead for those who were unhappy with American involvement in Vietnam but were unwilling to consider ending it. While clearly distressed by America's policy, the writers, as Norman Mailer noted, just as clearly supported it. "For after all somber dubiety, and every reservation . . . (they are liberals after all) . . . we are left back at the beginning—'we have not heard of any alternative policy which would actually lead to a negotiated peace in Vietnam.' " Though written in the language of "milk and milk of magnesia," Mailer added, the protest by the writers in the *Review* was not liberal at all, but as unthinkingly "radical" in its knee-jerk anti-Communism and its denunciation of critics as that of the most truculent Goldwater reactionary. As for the demand for new thinking—What new thinking? asked Harold Rosenberg. What new thinking is allowed by long habits of anti-Communism? "It is precisely the implications of the old anti-Communist formulas that need to be rethought." Although written and signed by "people of intelligence and good will," the letter "illustrates the danger of falling into grooves of thought, particularly when one is busy with other matters."[28]

Rosenberg's scorn for "new thinking" from those who refused to rethink cold war anti-Communist formulas recalls the difficulties inherent in Kazin's attack on the Kennedy intellectuals for not using their critical intelligence to challenge the Bay of Pigs invasion. Critical intelligence to what end? It is a question that Kazin would find increasingly difficult to avoid in the months ahead. What "responsible" critical stance could liberal intellectuals take toward a war they were convinced was an escalating disaster? And if responsible intellectuals with a lifetime of serious reflection on such matters could not work out positions essentially no different from the jingoistic hard right, who would? The kids? The wild-eyed radicals and campus crazies? And even if one did come up with a plausible solution—what should one do about it? Was "right thinking" enough?

In April 1966 with the war going badly, hundreds of thousands of new troops being called up, and no evidence that the bombing was affecting North Vietnam's behavior, Kazin joined twenty-three other writers for a protest trip to Washington, D.C. Calling themselves "the conscience of America," they delivered a petition that the United States halt the bombing and immediately seek a negotiated settlement to end the conflict—even if the outcome were to "bring unsatisfactory or problematic results for men who desire both peace and democracy." The writers held a press conference and then met privately with Vice President Hubert Humphrey. Humphrey, the longtime embodiment of American liberalism, was proving a profound disappointment to those who believed he would push Johnson for a rapid end to the war. Although he had first opposed widening the war (for which offense he had been "frozen out" of all White House discussion of its progress for a year), he had reclaimed his credibility with his boss when, after touring East Asia in early 1966, he returned to report that not only was the war winnable, it had to be won because the clear intent of the Communists was "to take over the governments of Asia by force." Nor would they be satisfied with Asia: "Saigon is as close to this ballroom tonight," he told his old friends at an April convention of Americans for Democratic Action, "as London was in 1940."[29]

Humphrey had been hearing from his aggrieved friends that he had violated his liberal principles, and he was probably prepared for more of the same when meeting the writers who spoke for "the conscience of America." Still, he was apparently shocked by the degree of bitterness from a group of writers and intellectuals whom he once would have considered allies. They accused him of betrayal, of double talk, of having no backbone, of meta-morphosing into a Johnson lackey. Kazin turned the confrontation distinctly personal when he told Humphrey he was suffering "from the Hemingway syndrome: you can never be tough enough, and you have to prove your mas-culinity." It was a literary below-the-belt that provoked a personal letter from Humphrey, saying he was saddened to be "selected for personal criti-cism on something which is a matter of government policy." Though Kazin had no illusions that the exchange would produce results, he was pleased that "we attacked (I especially) our great and immortal vice-president like anything." His frustration and anger *were* personal because America and the war were intensely personal matters for him, and because he saw in Humphrey the betrayal of the liberal ideals he wanted to believe in. There may also have been an element of self-projection and self-recrimination. He was, after all, attacking the vice president for views that he himself had held until very recently, that the United States had little choice but to take whatever measures necessary to prevent Southeast Asia from going to the Communists—a prospect he continued to find disquieting.[30]

The petition, which, in essence, called for an unconditional withdrawal from Vietnam, was an important step for Kazin. From this point, he consis-tently and forthrightly opposed the war. The question was, *how* to oppose it. He supported the teach-ins (which he once scorned) and "read-ins" in which he and other notable literati read material from their work as a protest against the war. He was unwilling, however, to support acts of civil disobedience and refused to be part of an effort at Stony Brook to withhold grades from the Selective Service boards. It was important to work within the system; "all one can do is to oppose this criminal war *politically* at the source and with so much passion." But what if working within the system didn't work? What if legitimate "political" activity not only failed to stop the war, which every week grew more insupportable, but stiffened the resolve of those prosecuting it? This, of course, was the question confronting all those passionately opposed to the war, both the middle aged liberals (a few of them ex-radicals) who insisted on the abiding values of democratic institutions and the need for a deliberative response, and the young and not-so-young radicals who argued that scruples about tactics were getting in the way of necessary action at a time when it was themselves, "the kids," who were asked to make the ultimate sacrifice. A middle-aged, one-time radical, with a decided fear of simplicities, Kazin was obviously a member of the first group; but he was also moved (and conflicted) by the arguments and example of the second group—"Thank God for the kids"—a sympathy derived in no small part from the fact that his son was one of them.[31]

Fathers and Sons

Kazin's relations with Michael had always been tentative and uncertain. Separated from his son at the time of his divorce from Carol, he had watched him grow up mostly from a distance. There were the weekly, sometimes biweekly, visits, spent often in Central Park, "watching the see-saw go up and the see-saw go down," and the occasional vacation visits at Wellfleet—but for the most part they lived very separate lives. Some years after the divorce, Carol had married Mario Salvadori, Alfred's one-time marriage counselor and a professor of civil engineering at Columbia, and moved to Englewood, New Jersey. Michael grew up in a cultured, comfortable, upper-middle-class suburban environment. The family made regular trips to Europe and particularly to Italy, where Mario had been born and educated and which Carol had always loved as a second home. (Alfred frequently said that the two great gifts Carol had given him were Michael and her love of Italy.) Watching his son mature from visit to visit, Alfred knew that he and Michael were losing something they would never recover, that "something [had] dropped out of *his* life forever." But he was also proud and happy with what he saw—among other things, the different ways the boy took after mother and father. To Carol he ascribed Michael's good looks and social manner—"the beautiful son, a beautiful mother . . . Carol's blue-black splendor in the social ease of her son." He credited the Kazin side with his more intellectual, competitive qualities, including Michael's rapid manner of speaking; "particularly eager to show that he is on the ball, that he has got it."[32]

Yet as pleased as he was with what he saw, he remained uneasy, alert to signs of disapproval, all the while baffled and shamed by his own wariness and discomfort. After a trying vacation visit with Michael in Wellfleet, Alfred felt that he had gotten his "walking papers." "It is important not to feel this vulnerable, as if every slight and rebuff threatens. God knows he does not love me very much." But after an April 1961 visit to Washington, D.C., where Arthur Schlesinger gave the family a personal tour of the White House, he wondered why he so often felt edgy around his son. "I must say whatever my own tensions and guilts and resentments about Michael, the boy is so good and sweet that I feel more than ever ashamed to be anything but gratuitously loving and good to him."[33]

Alfred's conflicted feelings toward his son would take on new definition and intensity when it came time for Michael to leave Englewood for college. Largely shut out of Michael's childhood, resentful of the influence he had never had, Kazin saw college as an opportunity to exert some constructive influence over his son's future. Irritated to learn that Mario Salvadori was taking Michael around Columbia, he jumped at the chance to accompany him on his interview visit to Harvard—a school at which Kazin had taught, had many friends, and with which he felt a personal connection. On the day of the visit, a heavy snow storm diverted their Boston flight to Providence. They rode a bus through driving snow, just making it to University Hall in time for Michael's appointment with the director of admissions. "The yard was thick with snow, and I hurried Michael along from Widener to the Chapel to the new Visual Arts building—so proud to show Michael Harvard and Harvard to Michael. We had drinks with Peter D[avison] at the Kaplans and dined with the [Ed] O'Connors. I felt so proud of my son, so astonished to see him grown up enough for an interview, 'even,' and when today, Tuesday, the 30th, I finally got him home to Englewood, I felt empty, but very proud, terrible at seeing him off again, but very pleased indeed that we had come this far." Just how far they had come is not clear, but, in Alfred's mind at least, they had made a connection that seemed to open a new stage in their relations. When he learned that Harvard had accepted Michael and that Michael had accepted Harvard, he was both exultant—"Glory be— Michael has been admitted to Harvard"—and anxious that he do well and not be intimidated. In the latter area, he felt that his son's strongly held radical views would see him through: "The poor guy seemed nervous before taking off with his mother," he wrote to Peter Davison, "but he's such a powerful arguer about Negro rights and such far-out causes that he may yet argue himself into deserved self-confidence on the subject [at] Harvard."[34]

As his father noted, Michael arrived at Harvard with strong political opinions, where they were quickly reinforced. His mother had a long interest in civil rights; his stepfather worked with inner-city youth on projects that instructed them in math and physics. As a freshman in high school, he had implored his mother (unsuccessfully) to let him participate in an all-night sit-in at the Englewood City Hall. In his junior year he had worked in the Washington office of Americans for Democratic Action. Once on campus, Michael joined the Young Democratic Yards Council, and by October he was working for Students for a Democratic Society (SDS) signing up people on a petition to get Robert McNamara to debate the editor of *Ramparts*. By March he had been elected to the executive committee of the Young Democrats of America, while also serving as a member of SDS and attending (when he could) meetings of the Young People's Socialist League, his father's old organization. Steven Kelman, a classmate with whom Michael argued politics, remembers how quickly Michael became a recognized political figure among the Harvard undergraduates—an achievement Kelman attributed not just to Michael's political energy. "He was strikingly handsome" and ambitious. He had plans to run for office and change the Democratic Party. Michael was a "very strange mixed bag—a playboy radical . . . conscious of his good looks," often "finish[ing] off arguments over immediate withdrawal from Vietnam or Black power by saying, 'I don't care, Kelman, I'm better looking than you.'" As Michael would later write, "By 1965, a young radical was something to be."[35]

In the spring of 1967, Michael resigned from the Young Dems (to devote full time to SDS) because of their refusal "to take a clear position of immediate and unconditional withdrawal of the American occupying army which is in Vietnam fighting the Vietnamese people." In October, he joined the "bloody" March on the Pentagon, returning to Harvard in time to participate in the barricading of a Dow Chemical representative in a lecture hall—for which Harvard officially admonished him. In the summer of 1968, he went to Chicago with other SDSers to protest the war at the Democratic National Convention, where he was gassed and beaten by Mayor Richard Daley's troops.[36]

Kazin followed Michael's activities with a mixture of pride, frustration, alarm, and moral chagrin. "I do like Michael's sense of outrage," he wrote after learning of the warning for barricading a representative of the company that manufactured the napalm used in Vietnam. But he also thought the gesture futile—"napalm gets manufactured just as much as ever and lands on Vietnamese peasants with the usual regularity"—an instance of the "typical existential radicalism of our day" that proposes no real solutions but expresses the middle-class individual's "anxiety and inner struggle." Like most thirties veterans who associated radical action with the working class's struggle for economic justice, Kazin found it difficult to credit middle-class radicalism, referring to it variously as "radical chic," "upper-class bohemianism," and now "existential radicalism." But neither was he prepared to dismiss outright the young activists who had contributed so much to the civil rights movement and now, outraged by American use of military power in Vietnam, wanted to do something about it—"to put their bodies on the line." In a 1964 *New York Review* essay on Rolf Hochhuth's play *The Deputy,* Kazin had written sternly of "the moral failure" of the Vatican to intercede with the Nazis on behalf of the Jews. He knew that acting or refusing to act can make a difference, a big difference. Were the intellectuals (he among them) too content to look on musingly from the sidelines? It is the difference, he told himself in his journal "between the revolutionaries and the commentators, between Christ and the Christians, between the young and the old, between the alive and the merely watchful . . . O the Trilling syndrome, the James syndrome, the beast that never sprang from the jungle."[37]

The entry reflects the general state of unease of many intellectuals, writers, and academics during the sixties—a wariness about joining the young in their increasingly confrontational protests and acts of civil disobedience and a shamed sense of moral-political impotence that they were not doing enough to stop a disastrous war. In a 1967 *New York Review* article, "On Resistance" (which Kazin much admired), reflecting on his participation in the march on the Pentagon, Noam Chomsky described the dilemma of those who "share my instinctive dislike of activism" but who found themselves moving toward a crisis of conscience demanding more active involvement in the antiwar movement. For Chomsky (and Kazin), the war had begun to move one's thoughts "from dissent to resistance," and increasingly to the kids who were leading the fight. "It is pitiful but true," Chomsky wrote, "that by an overwhelming margin it is the young who are crying out in horror at what we all see happening, the young who are being beaten when they stand their ground, and the young who have to decide whether to accept jail or exile, or fight in a hideous war." At the same time, Chomsky insisted on the need for the utmost thought and care before engaging in an act of civil disobedience. He noted that for some, certain acts will seem more justifiable than others, that any resort to violence as a tactic is bound to fail—"No one can compete with the Government in violence"—that each person has to make the decision for himself or herself at which point to resist the law, and that events are continually overriding the most considered plans for personal response.[38]

Chomsky impressed Kazin with his rational consideration of ends and means, but also for recognizing that decisions are based ultimately on a distinctively personal and often contradictory mix of moral feeling and ad hoc reflections that shifted with mood and event. Kazin noted in his journal that Rev. William Sloane Coffin of Yale and Dr. Benjamin Spock and Marcus Raskin had been indicted for counseling resistance to the draft and wondered: "Where am I in all this? It's true I don't believe in civil disobedience, but the Vietnam war is so sickening that anything is justified against it." But he also questioned that when "anyone can take the law into his own hands, where is the law for the rest of us?" He was sensitive to the force of "the good German" argument that arose in discussions of the Holocaust, but added that the argument only works if you draw a "parallel between Nazi Germany and Johnson's USA," a claim he found offensive. Nor, despite frequent remarks on the irresponsible power exerted by "the Big State, the Crusher," would he accede to the arguments of his son that "the U.S. and USSR were equally repugnant empires competing for dominance." Finally, he was dismayed by the hesitation toward which his conflicting moral concerns seemed always to lead: "Every day now, reading of the torture of the Vietnam people, I think with shame—why, oh why, don't we do something about that? Why are we content to remain beholders, intellectual critics. Why are we also so proud of 'thinking correctly' ad hoc rather than following out a definite line of thought, of principle."[39]

Like most teachers, Kazin was unsettled by the increasingly angry protests on college and university campuses. He found particularly frightening the action of the gun-toting militants who seized a building and intimidated the faculty at Cornell. But it was the war itself that stayed with him, crowding his consciousness, disturbing his dreams. During a 1968 visit to quiet, Catholic Villanova, where he had hoped to read and write and lecture far from the din of protests, he found himself distracted—"all the while the thing on my mind is the insanity of the war, the failure—moral failure, my failure to do enough by way of resistance and response." Back home, with the students in an uproar, as they were just outside his rented study on the Columbia University campus in 1968, intellectual and scholarly work could seem grotesquely beside the point—"the old fashioned bookish solitude as difficult for middle-aged scholars as it is for the young students." He agreed with his friend Richard Hofstadter, who in his 1968 Columbia commencement address (given at St. John the Divine Cathedral because the campus was too "bloody minded to accommodate the usual ceremony") warned of the university's vulnerability, suspended "between the external world, with all its corruption, and evils and cruelties, and the splendid world of our imagination"—though he (Kazin) also found it slightly comic "to see our generation the custodians of law and order."[40]

Although he often felt surges of resentment toward the massing, shouting, partying students—"having a field day of gleeful dishonesty"—he was far more incensed by the professors who were "running after the younger set," determined to be "with it" at any cost. He found particularly offensive the "action" staged by the activists at the 1968 Modern Language Association (MLA) Convention in New York to politicize "the world of [thought and] the imagination." He watched "with the greatest contempt" as "a bunch of overage SDS's broke up the American literature meetings" and massed in front of the stage while "old gray bald Henry Nash Smith" was framing his "weak" response to the troubles. Particularly revolting was the behavior of the recently elected president of the MLA, Louis Kampf, whose slogan was "To Hell With Culture" and who advised his followers to "Smear the Walls of Lincoln Center with Shit." While Kazin could usually summon a measure of sympathy for students who saw the war as a direct threat to their future, he had no patience with the "overage" types who, "weary with literature," got their kicks by "running after the angries and the motherfuckers and the revolutionary student brigade . . . in a vain effort to catch up with the young." They were betraying their trust as professors of literature—which, whatever the exigencies of the moment, preserves a space where politics is not everything, nuance and contradiction are possible, and slogans are no substitute for thought.[41]

Yet, even here, at "the dark and bloody crossroads where literature and

politics meet," Kazin was uncertain how far to press the matter, particularly
with the kids. Large questions were at stake. Did the "complexities" of
literature necessarily have the last word over political thought and action?
And did not literature, even great literature, sanction action on occasion,
even revolutionary action? One might be revolted by the show-boating
fecklessness of the MLA politicos, but what did the ever-thoughtful, sober,
patient counselors of the young have to offer—except more patience? Kazin,
typically, was of two minds. Responding to an August 1968 questionnaire
from the *Washington Post Book World* asking prominent educators whether
the current unrest was affecting their teaching plans for the fall, Kazin
announced he was making no changes. He would deliver, as planned, a
series of lectures on the *Iliad,* the Oedipus cycle of Sophocles, *The Brothers
Karamazov*—all of them sagas of human frailty, indicating humanity's tragic
incapacity to set the terms of its fate. But, while insisting on the sobering
truths in this literature, he acknowledged that the message would have little
appeal with students who "do not see why politics of vision and hope should
always be condemned to disillusionment and failure." Indeed, he wondered
(in this essay and another on George Orwell written during the same period)
whether a tragic view of the world, such as the one found in Sophocles or
Orwell, might not in important ways be disabling to the young—the young,
who in their hopefulness, their belief that they could change things, even in
their capacity for "brutal simplification," had become "a spearhead for
radical action" and "morally the most stimulating, restless, generous, and
disinterested social group in the country." Writing out of an age "haunted by
poverty and unemployment," and reflecting on the betrayals of the left and
the emergence of the totalitarian state, Orwell had turned political analysis
into a tragic literature that spoke to the wounded sensibilities of Kazin's
disenchanted generation. One found nothing comparable in the prose of
Mark Rudd or Abbie Hoffman; but if the New Left did not write interesting
prose, it "has the virtues of the affluent society that produced it; it is not
wedded to depression, social or personal, and in a society bursting with
abundance, it may practice austerity as a personal gesture again—one's own
thing—but admirably doesn't believe in poverty as a way of life or defeat as a
political habit."[42]

A decade earlier, Kazin had scorned the alienated poses of "the alone
generation," the pushing self-centeredness of youth as "a pressure group."

By the end of the sixties, he would not have disagreed with his earlier views that many youth were simply out for themselves and looking for a good time. Nor did he disagree with Irving Howe that the New Left valued "instinct" and "innocence" over reason, liberalism, and "civilization"; nor with Daniel Bell that it demonstrated an unhealthy "concern with violence and cruelty . . . a desire to make noise, an anti-cognitive and intellectual mood; an effort to erase the boundary between 'art' and 'life.'" He certainly did not take issue with Hofstadter's warning that the university must be protected from the radicals as the last redoubt of learning and free expression. In sum, he did not disagree that "the kids" posed a challenge to much that thoughtful, politically experienced people rightly cherished. He did, however, disagree that this was wholly a bad thing. The young radicals want to break things up, he wrote in a June 22, 1969, review of Stephen Spender's *The Year of the Young Rebels*, "to disturb all those who had made their peace with life." But did not the great Romantics—Emerson, Thoreau, Shelley, Whitman—also insist that "the past must no longer dominate," "that habits must not be allowed too much power"? If some saw a frightening strain of madness in the young radicals' behavior and slogans—"Imagination Is Revolution"—could they be sure that they would not have found the same strain in Blake? Initially reluctant to allow the young into the company of Blake, Whitman, and Lawrence, those who pleaded the holiness of the heart's affections, Kazin was no longer so certain. In a country of "all-sweeping corporatism and super-technology," a country devastated by an out-of-control war machine, was there not something to be said for the madness that names the madness? Could it be that the tigers of wrath are wiser than the horses of instruction?[43]

Perhaps because of his conflicted feelings on the subject, Kazin, unlike Howe, Bell, Hofstadter, Leslie Fiedler, and others, offered no definitive assessment nor ringing declamation on the young radicals or the "sixties sensibility." His preferred medium for commenting on these (and most other) controversial subjects was the book review, where he could raise questions without feeling obliged to answer them, try out or advance views indirectly in the idiom of critical (aesthetic) response without feeling the need to argue them systematically on their own merits. Two essay-reviews that attracted considerable attention at the time deserve mention: a front-page 1968 review in the *New York Times Book Review* of Norman Mailer's account of the 1967 march on the Pentagon, *The Armies of the Night,* and a 1970 piece in the *New York Review of Books* on Saul Bellow's *Mr. Sammler's Planet.*

Kazin had followed the careers of both writers closely, noting how their very different literary gifts and interests responded to and reflected the changing zeitgeist. Drawing on childhood memories, the experience of urban Jewish life, and traditional (mostly European) literary models for inspiration, Bellow had found American postwar conditions highly congenial to the development of his particular genius—a reflective, frequently nostalgic genius, which Kazin, in a deeply appreciative 1968 critical portrait, characterized as "vibrant with the moodiness of the Jew, the intellectual, the city man." By contrast, Mailer, after the success of *The Naked and the Dead,* had struggled with limited success to find a literary mode equal to his aggressive, restless intelligence that could convey with sufficient urgency his opposition to the bland, repressive, "totalitarian" forces he believed were perverting the country's culture. Searching for a radical "philosophy" that would support his artistic-revolutionary quest, he had flirted with Trotskyism, Reichianism, and French existentialism, finally cobbling together a "desperado" philosophy and style of his own based on an ethic of personal risk, hipster violence, and Laurentian sexuality. Unimpressed by Mailer's efforts to turn sex into ideology, but fascinated by his bravura performances as novelist, journalist, and self-publicist, Kazin had wondered whether Mailer, the "gifted rebel" and egotist par excellence, would ever find a subject and mode suitable to his remarkable intelligence and unstable talents. The publication of *The Armies of the Night* convinced him that he had.[44]

It also convinced (or reminded) him that troubled times can produce a significant literature—in this case a hybrid that Mailer called "History as a Novel, the Novel as History," but which might more appropriately be called "History as Autobiography, Autobiography as History," a generic mix for which Kazin had considerable sympathy. In *Armies,* Kazin sees Mailer "crack[ing] open the hard nut of American authority at the center" and exposing "the bad conscience that now afflicts so many Americans." He has done this by creating a literary-political *Song of Myself* that pits the full range of his personality—actor, clown, self-publicist, fierce literary competitor, even "the nice Jewish boy from Brooklyn"—against the hard, blank, impersonal forces of the state, embodied in the Pentagon. Mailer brings all of himself and much of America with him to Washington—though the psychedelic mix on the Mall might well have given Whitman pause.[45]

Kazin is much amused by Mailer's clownish, bull-dog competitiveness in *Armies* and by the social commentary and snobbishness by which he keeps himself at a distance from the other marchers. But he is also impressed by Mailer's readiness to move beyond his snobberies, to celebrate the differences and the commonality of purpose of the American types represented. The kids attracted Mailer's special attention. Like Kazin, he did not know what to make of them. They irritated—"cocky, knowledgeable, and quick to mock the generations over thirty." Some seemed simply mad, believing "in LSD, in witches, in tribal knowledge, in orgy and revolution." Yet at the deepest level, he understood that the day belonged to them, that it was their story, their adventure, their "bloodyings," their "rite of passage." Accordingly, it is on those few hundred "spoiled children of a dead de-animalized middle class," who had spent the long night in the field fronting the Pentagon, waiting for arrest and for more beatings, that Mailer closes his narrative and concentrates the final thrust of his protest. One might resent the cockiness of the young, wonder at their sanity, but Mailer (and Kazin, who notes that the women took the worst of the beatings) is inclined neither to belittle their courage nor dismiss the shaming, disturbing force of their opposition. It was the young, Mailer notes, who were in the trenches, who formed the first line of resistance to "this obscene war . . . the worst war the nation has ever been in."[46]

There is neither shame nor bad conscience in *Mr. Sammler's Planet*—at least not in the consciousness of the protagonist. An account of two days in the life of Artur Sammler, an elderly Holocaust survivor with Oxonian connections, living on Manhattan's Upper West Side, Bellow's novel is also set in the sixties—but the sixties viewed from a perspective that found only cause for physical revulsion and moral declamation in the appearance, behavior, values, and odors of "the children of joy." While Mailer discovers that he has something to learn from the example of the sons and daughters of the American middle class, Mr. Sammler (whose fate and consciousness are the only ones seriously considered in the novel) discovers that he has nothing to learn and nothing to say to them. He had tried on occasion, but they had proved hopeless—"hairy, dirty, without style, levelers, ignorant . . .

poor kids . . . resolved to stink together in defiance of a corrupt tradition built on neurosis and falsehood." Bellow's novel is about more than the kids. Women, blacks, the Upper West Side, Hannah Arendt, modernism, and modern life itself are all at some point subjected to Sammler's withering scorn. It is, however, Sammler's generational resentment toward all aspects of the 1960s that establishes the acrid, intolerant tone of the book—and provokes the most hostile critical response that Kazin had made (or would make) to Bellow's fiction.[47]

Kazin's complaint is attitudinal and aesthetic. Sammler is not only insufferable, he is the only person with a voice in the novel, which, Kazin insists, is indistinguishable from Bellow's. Kazin notes that from *Dangling Man* to *Mr. Sammler's Planet,* Bellow's protagonists "are generally the voices of his own intellectual evolution" and that Bellow has always found vehicles—diaries, letters to politicians and philosophers, arias to the reader in *Augie March*—to voice his thinking while also objectifying it in the thought performances of his protagonists. In *Sammler,* however, Kazin sees the distinction between writer and hero collapsing in a work that is so full of uncontested attitudes and opinions that in the end one can only assume that Sammler is Bellow and the book a "didactic" editorial on the issues of the day. Bellow has yielded to the confrontational ethos of the times and written "a normal political novel of our day, didactic to a fault. With his stern sense of justice Bellow wants to right the balance after so much evil. God lives."[48]

The review brought a personal rebuke from Bellow. He did not like the review, he told his old friend, adding spitefully that he "didn't dislike it more than any other piece of yours." While granting Kazin the right to say what he liked about his book, Bellow accused him of crossing the line between criticism and "slander." "What offended me was that you were not reviewing my novel, you were saying that its author was a wickedly deluded lunatic." How, he asked, did Kazin know that he and Sammler were the same? Bellow had a point—though he himself would later concede that *Sammler* was less a novel than "a dramatic essay wrung out of me by the crazy Sixties." Familiar with Bellow's personal views on the issues raised in the book, including especially "Saul and his hatred of the young," Kazin had jumped the gap between author and protagonist and responded to the book as an unmodulated cri de coeur against the times. He may also have welcomed the chance to express his long-felt resentment of what he perceived as Bellow's snubs and "coldness" toward himself. "One can admire the man's (Sammler's) intellectual austerity and yet be amazed that Bellow's hero should be so intelligent about everything except his relations with other human beings." Kazin's criticism had always had a strong "personal" element to it, based on his belief that he could directly engage the personality of the writer, "read the mind behind each book." When the writer was a friend whose views were familiar to him, the temptation to respond to the mind behind the book would have been very strong indeed.[49]

But Kazin was responding to more than Bellow in his review. He was reacting to the absolute value placed on *right thinking* by those of his generation who had outlived their earlier radicalism and felt justified, indeed, honor-bound, to take a most uncompromising stand against the wrong thinking of others, particularly the young. To be sure, those who had suffered the shocks of Stalinism and struggled to absorb the horrors of the Holocaust had something to tell the brash young men and women seizing the campus buildings. But was it necessary to take such an assertive stand on one's bitter experience, to turn adult wisdom into a weapon against youthful error? "They are all such specialists," these members of the Old Left, Kazin wrote after a particularly depressing evening with the Kristols, Diana Trilling, Arnold Beichman, James Wechsler, and Theodore Draper, "such knowers on a limited scale, such professors impaled on their own bitterness." Sure they are right; "they have to be right . . . The world can go to hell, but they are *right*." Mr. Sammler is also right; he has lived through the Holocaust, and he knows. And for Kazin, that is the problem: "The unsatisfactory thing about Mr. Sammler is that he is always right while most other people are wrong—sinfully so." Nor was right thinking confined to friends and colleagues. Confronted by the jargon-spouting, Mao-intoxicated young, Kazin thinks he, too, is right and that the young radicals' (and Michael's) romantic infatuation with Castro, with the Vietcong, with totalitarian regimes of any stripe, are wrong. But how to prevent right thinking from discrediting youthful idealism? And, how to keep the heat of righteous indignation from wilting the few tentative sprouts of a relationship with his son? Were there not more important things than being right?[50]

It was a question Alfred asked himself repeatedly as he followed Michael's intensifying political activity in the late sixties. In *New York Jew* he recalls a Harvard visit in the spring of 1968. He had been interested in the display of Hebrew grammars and dictionaries at the Widener Library and remembers the historical suggestiveness they held for him of the ancient world of their Hebrew fathers. "I rejoiced in the yellowing pages. . . . These Hebrew letters surrounded me as the deepest part of my history." Michael, however, had little time for Hebrew fathers, including his own. "The sons were out to get the fathers—especially if the fathers had been 'radicals' during a certain ancient Depression." Michael and his friends were for "action" and were "clear" about everything, seeing "all justice and truth in the Vietcong." Yet, he acknowledges, Michael ("Tim") and his friends were "also part of my history"—history in the making. They were the ones being drafted "to save Vietnam for democracy" by the policymaking of their elders—by Johnson, Dean Rusk, Robert McNamara, by Walt Rostow, "owl-glassed, with his sheaf of position papers, briefing papers, scenarios, game plans," confident that a few thousand more bombs on Hanoi, a few thousand or hundred thousand more young men would assure victory. History and politics may have been more complicated than SDS's bright, clear rhetoric of revolution; what was not complicated was the identity of those being asked to risk everything for the politics of the fathers.[51]

A journal entry of January 1969, which Kazin titled "Fathers and Sons" after Turgenev's novel about the rebellious youth of mid-nineteenth-century Russia, offers an inside look at his effort to gain perspective on his quarrels with Michael:

> On this fine Saturday, enter Michael, in two shades of corduroy, brown boots, moustache. We had lunch at Nocital, a Mexican joint on West 46th, and as usual, when the four of us [Kazin, Michael, Ann, and Kate] get together, we make the place jump with the violence of our arguments. Michael, who later on was all suave honey with Daniel Bell when the Bells came over after lunch, jumps at me like a bull, and I jump at him with quieter but even more intense feeling, then Ann jumps in, and Katey, and the four of us are hollering and quoting and what-not like drunken peasants at an Irish wake. The amount of violence that is set up between Ann and me is always *something*, but when Michael introduces his conversation-by-political-slogan, my reaction to him is one of violent disapproval. And yet, I ask myself, what is it that makes these political dogmas the occasion of so much heat. Because they are the symbols . . . We want to remain idealists and faithful souls of one kind or another, and politics is the way we reproach or approve each other. Michael seems to think

> that I have betrayed the leftist directions of my youth; I on my part think that
> the socialist thing, one way or another, betrayed *my* idealism. It's no good my
> trying to say this to him. I care only for art and literature! Of course I don't.
> The real question behind all the heat: where do you find truth. Truth as all-
> operative from one set of principles, one perspective? Michael's SDS line
> irritates me as much because it is always colliding with the truth as because it is
> so abstract and sometimes downright false. Yet compare Michael talking about
> Cuba with so much love because workers in a factory worked all night and all
> day to supply food to the North Vietnamese with the margarine-faced Prof. Dr.
> Rostow, who in his interview with the *New York Times* today (January 5) says
> with the ridiculous worldliness of the high diplomatic world: "Cuba is a nui-
> sance, dangerous still, but manageable."

The arguments may have been furious and the misunderstanding and feelings of personal grievance painful. Still, father and son had found something significant to talk about, and if Alfred found Michael's ideological
abstractions infuriating, he could not but be impressed by his idealism and
his feelings for the Cuban workers.[52]

Later in the spring of 1969, an article in the *Wall Street Journal,* titled
"Angry Young Man," offered a more public, much toned-down glimpse
into the family quarrel. Under the subtitle "Eminent Critic's Son Works for
a Violent Upheaval," the article describes Michael, a co-chairman of Harvard's SDS chapter, leading three hundred undergraduates through a police line to the door of President Nathan Pusey's mansion on which he
nailed (with a knife) a list of demands, including the abolition of ROTC on
the campus. This "flamboyant gesture," noted the newspaper, marked the
beginning of the "siege of Harvard"—an "action" that would result in the
occupation of University Hall, the forceful expulsion of deans, a police raid,
the arrest of more than one hundred Harvard students, a student strike,
and eventually the expulsion of sixteen students (not Michael)—and the
elimination of ROTC from the Harvard campus. Though a leader of the
more moderate faction of Harvard's SDS, which opposed the seizing of
buildings, Michael was an attractive radical figure to profile, not least because the "fiery revolutionary" was the son of the famous writer and thirties
radical Alfred Kazin, who was eager to support his son's idealism whatever
his reservations about his philosophy and tactics. "I don't always agree with
Mike," he told the newspaper, "but I admire him very, very much. I feel his

goals are very humane ones. I think he has the good of society at heart, which is better than thinking of money all your life or of killing Vietnamese people. I just think he is a great guy—he's one of those Americans who's not thinking about himself. He's an idealist."[53]

Kazin's remarks were not merely for the public's (and Michael's) eyes. Though he took strong exception to his son's simplistic rhetoric, so reminiscent of the worst of the thirties—"The establishment just won't give up its power and wealth voluntarily—it has to be taken away from them, by force. It's quite simple"—entries in his journals indicate that he continued to respect Michael's sincerity and selflessness. They also indicate his alarm when, at the end of his junior year, Michael decided to leave Harvard (temporarily) to join a commune in Portland, Oregon, where he hoped to organize workers. In part, he envied Michael's youth and freedom—"Here is Michael, so free of his parents, so [free] from 'obligations'—not yet 22, yet free of that old slavery. And here I am, at 54, still chained to these obligations [and to] the mad alley cat I am married to." More often, he worried about Michael's future and the lack of direction in his life: "Had dinner with Michael at the Tien-Tsin restaurant 125th street under the high girders of the E. He was coughing, he was pale, he was unshaven, and I was trying with all my might and main (a): to show that I 'sympathize' with his goals (b): that I was concerned about his leaving school again and drifting about, as he had done increasingly. But it was no use. He goes his way, he goes, he goes, and I watch him with my heart sore . . . He is and will be a sacrifice . . . a human missile, taking no thought for himself . . . I could insult and outrage him by calling him a rentier, a parasite, etc. But it is stupid and untrue. He is a sacrifice. . . . He wants to be a piece of the action."[54]

Kazin sympathized. He also understood the impulse to act. A few days after writing the above entry, he spoke to a crowd of eight hundred mostly editorial workers at an end-the-war rally in Dag Hammarskjöld Plaza. Delivered as a protest against the war, the speech was motivated as much by regret and anger at the divisions the war was creating in the country. Titled "Our Flag" and later published in the *New York Review*, the speech noted that the war had divided the country as nothing else in recent memory and that the symbol of that division had become the flag, which the super-patriots flaunted as proof of their patriotism and the treachery of all those who did not wear flags. "Love America or leave it. Hippie, long-haired nut, peace freak, Red slime, free-talking bastard, shut up, get off the streets, disappear. You don't wear a flag, I wear a flag. I wear it to show you don't, and if you ask me, then you're the enemy of my flag, my country and my God." Thus Kazin interpreted the flags worn on the hard hats of the crane workers in downtown Manhattan and the flag decals on the car windows of much of America's "silent majority." At a time of extreme division between the working class and the "intellectual class," between college administrators and students, between fathers and sons, Kazin understood (perhaps better than most) that what was needed was self-restraint, forbearance, a recognition of what one shared with others below the level of ideological dispute.[55]

Over time, father and son discovered they had much in common. In his own account of their relations (also called "Fathers and Sons"), written long after he had graduated from Harvard, completed a Ph.D. in history at Stanford, and become a professor at American University, Michael observed how they began sidling closer toward each other during the Reagan years as his father took up arms against the neoconservatives and he (Michael) gave up his dreams of revolution "and began to appreciate the merits of social democracy." But in Alfred's mind, they had been moving slowly toward each other for some time. Though they continued throughout the seventies to argue heatedly on the phone, in letters, and whenever they saw each other, he sensed their talks were becoming less acrimonious, that despite disagreeing on virtually everything—liberalism, American imperialism, Israel—they were also groping toward some personal understanding not unmixed "with a good deal of forgiving tenderness." Perhaps it was wishful thinking on Kazin's part, or growing pride in Michael's success, or familial superstition—Kazin liked to invoke the "mystic ties of family." Whatever their disagreements and occasional agreements, they kept talking. By the end of the sixties, they were in each others lives and thoughts in a way neither could have anticipated in former times.[56]

Bright Book of Life: Making Sense of the World

Kazin's remark in the spring of 1968 that times were as difficult for the solitary writer as for the students was no idle thought. Amid the demonstrations, the bouts with Michael, the endless agonizing over the war, Kazin was, as always, struggling with a book. And, as always, he was finding it difficult to settle on a subject. In 1961, unhappy with the direction of contemporary fiction, he had put aside the study of *The Twenties and After* and used the Gauss lectures to explore the possibilities of a book on the literature of society in the late nineteenth century. He had expanded on this topic in his 1963 Beckman lectures at Berkeley, adding writers from earlier in the nineteenth century. However, his plans to turn these lectures into a book were soon overtaken by his decision to finish *Starting Out in the Thirties*. In early 1965, with that book nearly completed, he returned to his study of nineteenth-century literature. After receiving an enthusiastic letter from Peter Davison about an essay on Henry Adams he had recently published in the *New York Review*, he notified Davison, who was anxious for a book of literary criticism from Kazin, that he intended the Adams essay to be the first in a book that "is actually written, or exists in preliminary form," titled *The Imagination of Society*. Davison would wait nearly eight years for a book of criticism from Kazin. When it finally appeared in 1973, *The Imagination of Society* had turned into *Bright Book of Life*, a study of twentieth-century American fiction—the original topic of his 1958 Guggenheim project, *The Twenties and After*. In the meantime, Kazin had received a second Rockefeller grant and a fourth Guggenheim award (he and Rene Wellek were the only applicants at the time to have been awarded four Guggenheims).[57]

Kazin's difficulties with his "actually written" book were hardly new. Since the publication of *On Native Grounds*, he had failed to produce a sustained piece of critical-historical prose longer than his fifty-five-page introduction to the Blake anthology—this despite a steady stream of titles, proposals, outlines, possible chapters, long bouts of worrying, and harsh self-criticism. The problem was an old one: intellectual restlessness and wavering intentions. He had plans for many books and did not know which book he wanted to write first—a book on himself and the Jews, titled *My People;* a small book on Edmund Wilson; a book based on his journals and the vocation of the writer, to be titled *Writing in the Dark;* a study of literature and power in America; a book on H. G. Wells; a book on religion and prophetic writings in America—all this in addition to the third volume of his autobiography. Emerson once wrote that "the very naming of a subject by a man of genius is the beginning of insight." Genius or not, Kazin seemed to be better at naming than finishing. Books are completed one at a time, and Kazin was typically interested in too many subjects and projects at once to give any one of them the single-minded attention needed for completion.[58]

He was also hampered by an "impatient" critical temperament more suited to essays and reviews than to book writing. "My tendency as writer and critic [is] to dwell on the 'high-points' of a text, the emotional peaks, the 'isolated beauties' instead of the *argument* of a book," he acknowledged while struggling with his book. "My weakness as a literary scholar and as a writer is to opt for the creative moment" rather than sustained careful discussion. "High points," "isolated beauties," "the creative moment" are the stuff of short essays, reviews, and introductions, another favorite Kazin mode. Ongoing argument, close reading, the careful weighing of evidence are the work of books—work that Kazin in his impatience found himself hard-pressed to sustain.[59]

Peter Davison knew of his friend's distractibility and short attention span in the writing of literary criticism. From his predecessor at the *Atlantic*, Seymour Lawrence, he had learned of Kazin's difficulties completing assignments. But he also valued his critical abilities; and judging from their experience on *Starting Out in the Thirties*, he was confident that with enough patience and prodding, he could tease an excellent effort out of Kazin. Thus he was prepared to see the book metamorphose over the course of a year from *The Imagination of Society* into *Novelists and Story Tellers of American Society*, then back into *The Imagination of Society*, then into *The Gathering of the Forces*—each title change bringing with it new themes and new writers. He was even prepared to see Kazin revert back to the subject and title of his unfinished fifties book, *The Western Island*, and happily wrote in support of Kazin's (successful) bid for a Rockefeller grant (to be spent in Bellagio, Italy) that was to bring it to conclusion.

He was less prepared to learn that instead of using his Rockefeller grant to finish *The Western Island*, or *The Imagination of Society*, Kazin had used it to work up a series of lectures on contemporary fiction—given as the Ewing lectures at UCLA in the fall of 1969—that he now wanted to turn into *Bright Book of Life*. Stifling any irritation he may have felt, Davison, after seeing some of the chapters, could only wish Kazin well, allowing himself the most restrained of entreaties: "I do hope you can avoid magazine reviews and concentrate on our book." Wanting Kazin to stick to the job at hand, Davison and his editorial assistant at the *Atlantic*, Peggy Yntema, who understood that Kazin responded to and demanded constant encouragement, inundated him with praise and repeated expressions of deepest interest. "Your first four chapters are really quite amazing. As Peggy says, no one else could possibly have written them, but what's more I can imagine no one else writing more interestingly about the subject." "I think this is certain to be one of the very best books we've ever published; certainly one of the most thrilling for me." The strategy apparently worked. Despite interruptions for reviews and lecturing engagements, as well as family arrangements surrounding his father's death in 1970, Kazin finished *Bright Book of Life: American Novelists and Storytellers from Hemingway to Mailer* in August 1972—while teaching summer school at the University of Michigan.[60]

After the extravagant praise of his editors, Kazin must have found the book's reception disappointing. "It *will* win the National Book Award when it comes out," Kazin had written his friend Stanley Burnshaw about the book in August 1971. "The Atlantic Monthly Press is rapturous over it and I am also so full of it, excited, that I know it will be at least interesting." Some of the reviews were positive and some merely polite. It was the negative ones, however, that were most deeply felt and convincingly argued. The most positive reviews (for a change) came from the British reviewers. V. S. Pritchett called the book an ideal survey for "the foreign reader" and noted that Kazin had "read everything worth reading from Hemingway onwards" and managed to convey "the essence" of his writers in the manner of "a catholic and discursive commentator, who makes excellent asides." Philip French in the *New Statesman* and the reviewer for the *Times Literary Supplement* were also impressed by Kazin's easy, discursive manner. *Bright Book of Life* is written in the entertaining, urbane style of "the new journalism"—"breathless, hurried, determined to sparkle at all costs"—an approach perfectly suited to the material under discussion.[61]

But where the British saw urbanity and easy intelligence, a number of American reviewers saw blandness, temperamental bias, and intellectual laziness. Writing in the *New Republic*, Richard Poirier accused Kazin of lacking the necessary sympathy for his subject. *Bright Book of Life* shows what happens when "Your Accommodated Commonsensical Critic" tries to come to terms with a literature, "which is, if bright at all, lit by flashes of stylistic violence, systematic disorder and apocalyptic vision." Kazin's "breezy," "on-the-run" conventionality betrays a sensibility lacking any appreciation for "the wonderful, zany, and powerful impulses at work in modern literature." Jack Richardson in *Commentary* and Alvin Rosenfeld in *Midstream* also noted Kazin's lack of sympathy for much of the literature he discussed and faulted him for not explaining the grounds for his distaste and for failing to examine the historical conditions out of which such fiction arose. Roger Sale in the *New York Review* was particularly severe. He found the book "terribly disappointing, not dull, but enervating, self-defeating" and objected strongly to the "all too obviously arranged chapters: 'The Secret of the South,' 'The Decline of War,' 'Professional Observer,' 'The Earthly City of the Jews,' 'Cassandras,'" which hold little interest for Kazin beyond serving as convenient categories in which to dump different writers. Both Sale and Richardson suggested (insightfully) that Kazin failed to make the adjustment between reviewer and literary historian and had come up with a hybrid that falls awkwardly between both stools.[62]

The reviews could hardly have pleased Kazin, particularly those in such prominent journals as the *New York Review of Books* and the *New Republic*, but he did little complaining. He may have felt that some of the criticism was justified. He admitted to Peggy Yntema that he was "thin" on the women and had to drag himself though the absurdists. He had expected the charge that too much of the book had the mark of old reviews strung together. (Much of the material *was* excerpted from previous reviews.) He knew that he had not produced another breakthrough like *On Native Grounds* and that he would inevitably be measured by that standard. He also understood that in challenging the direction of much contemporary fiction he was sailing against the wind in a way that would offend many "advanced critics" (like Poirier), who were making careers of explaining and promoting it. *Bright Book of Life* was a minority report, an uneven and often a grumpy one, occupying uncertain ground between the omnibus critical survey and literary history. But it was also a strongly felt personal statement compelled by Kazin's long-standing and very real unhappiness with the direction of contemporary fiction. He had a case to make (not unlike the one in *Contemporaries*), a case he made more through attitude and assumption than analysis, but a case all the same.[63]

The novel, he agrees with D. H. Lawrence, is "the bright book of life" because of its capacity to represent and celebrate life in the fullness of its variety and complexity. But since World War II, Kazin argues, American fiction has suffered a drastic narrowing of interest in the shared social-political-historical world and, more recently, a repudiation (or at the least a debilitating distrust) of the representative and enlightening powers that have been the source of its strength. Thus, Kurt Vonnegut in his introductory chapter to *Slaughterhouse-Five* despairs of writing anything more significant about the bombing of Dresden than the sound of a bird, "Poo-teet-weet," and shifts immediately into science fiction peopled by extrater-restrials and a cartoonlike hero who can only shrug "so it goes" at the disturbing events in twentieth-century history. Truman Capote in his "non-fiction novel" *In Cold Blood* buries us in facts about the murder of the Clutters by a couple of ex-convicts—but the facts tell us nothing. "There is no 'sense' to the crime." We are confronted by the impenetrability of public event and private motive. "Irony more than truth is the motif of such fact books." Susan Sontag in her essays argues that we live "in an era of perma-nent apocalypse" in which "art must tend toward anti-art; the elimination of the 'subject' . . . the substitution of chance for intention." She then "improvises" novels that exist as "illustrations of an argument" in which character, event, and causality are dismissed as irrelevant to the more interesting philosophical matters at hand. "We do not experience a novel: we experience [Sontag's] readiness to see what she can think of next." Vonnegut, Capote, and Sontag are obviously very different writers pursu-ing very different interests; yet, in Kazin's view, they share with each other and many of their contemporaries the same radically reduced conception of the possibilities of their art. Instead of regarding the novel as a historic means for engaging the public world, for discovering that "life within us that ties us to what is out there," they have used their moral intelligence and novelistic skill to reinforce our sense that the outside world is "mad," "insane," "absurd," "sick," or simply not worth bothering about. Instead of "succeed[ing] to the sacred office of the historian" (a favorite phrase from Henry James), the novelist has become a cheerleader for an indulgent subjectivism which holds that "there cannot be anything but our own sa-cred consciousness," that "everything outside is *hell*."[64]

Bright Book of Life is not an unrelieved diatribe against the state of recent fiction. Kazin finds genuine value in such favorites as Flannery O'Connor and Saul Bellow. He is excited by the appearance of new writers like Walker Percy, Joan Didion, and Joyce Carol Oates. But the exceptions prove the rule. As a "bright book of life," the novel is an ideal that has not been met. That Kazin had written more than three hundred pages about material in which he took such little pleasure is undoubtedly what prompted Roger Sale's complaint that the book is "self-defeating" and Richard Poirier's that Kazin lacked the sensibility to enjoy the "zany" qualities of recent fiction. Poirier was right. A self-admitted "cultural conservative," whose novelistic ideal remained the realist novel of the nineteenth century, Kazin had never felt comfortable with the formal and stylistic experimentation associated with the avant-garde, whether in the "pyrotechnical display" of Dos Passos's *U.S.A;* the "arbitrary," "obsessive exaggeration" of Faulkner's style in *Absalom! Absalom!;* or the "twisting, howling, stumbling murk" of *Finnegans Wake*—"a language so convulsed, meaning so emptied, there is nothing." He was no less impatient with what Morris Dickstein and others have called the "new modernism" of the fifties and sixties. Though he understood that genius, particularly American genius, did not always, or even typically, do its most notable work in conventional modes, he had never developed much taste (or tolerance) for the fantastic and eccentric, particularly when they preempted the historical and social, or challenged "reality" conceived in the old-fashioned sense of empirically perceived circumstance. "The other day, reading Nabokov's Gogol, I found myself getting jittery, just as I did when reading the complete Lolita," he had written in 1959; "I cannot read an utterly idiosyncratic and farcical, eccentric mind like Nabokov without some slight sense of hysteria." Though he makes a valiant effort to find qualities in writers with whom he had little temperamental affinity, including Nabokov and even the "porno-Sade" work of William Burroughs, Kazin was working too obviously and painfully against the grain.[65]

There is, however, another matter to consider in assessing Kazin's response to American fiction since 1945—the Vietnam War. The war hangs like a menacing cloud over the book, intruding into the portraits, darkening judgment, adding to the idiom of lament. "Watching the war [on television] death steals into my soul on faint, almost imperceptible wings," he would later recall, bringing with it guilt and an oppressive sense of futility. The war had eaten into the nation's conscious and unconscious life; and Kazin, reading the minds behind the books, felt and responded to it in the anxieties of his writers, in "the sense of fright, of something deeply wrong" that impressed and disturbed him in the astringent prose of Joan Didion, in the cartoonish nihilism of Vonnegut, in the vulnerability of Oates's doomed characters, "a world in which our own people, and not just peasants in Vietnam get 'wasted.'" He understands the vulnerability, the fear, the outrage, and the sense of impotence, but he also believes that writers, precisely because they are writers, must somehow keep their heads, not yield to the "madness" and "nihilism," but rather exert some necessary moral resistance against the forces of chaos and despair.[66]

This was a lot to ask, particularly in the late sixties and early seventies, but it was hardly the first time Kazin had looked to writers for reassurance during a period of crisis. In *On Native Grounds,* he had found the same acquiescence in the "panic and extremism," as well as the same "fatal division" between the private and the public; between the self-obsessed interiority of a Wolfe or a Faulkner and the grimly uncomprehended public facts of the documentarist, unwilling or unable to go beyond his or her material. There was, of course, a difference. However frightened and uncomprehending, the writers in *On Native Grounds* were contributors to "an authentic literature of democracy," from a country at war against tyranny; while many of the novelists in *Bright Book of Life* spoke from a nation bitterly divided, at war with itself. In the former, Kazin could believe that even a writer's most private fantasies contributed to the nation's public life; in the latter, he could believe in no such thing. Indeed, confronted by "the unprecedented and dominating power" of the United States and its prosecution of a never-ending, pointless, unwinnable war in Southeast Asia, he found it increasingly difficult to think of the public realm as anything more than the insane, mechanistic workings of the "power state" beside which the writer was as impotent and irrelevant as his novelists feared. Kazin, was, in other words, searching among his writers for a source of moral reassurance in which he no longer had much faith but which he could not bear to renounce. In *Starting Out in the Thirties,* he had looked fondly back to a time when he believed that "salvation would come by the word, the long awaited and fatefully exact word that only the true writer would speak." By the early seventies, that belief was barely a memory of a hope, replaced by the suspicion that whatever salvation literature might bring, it would come as a private pleasure in a world where writers spoke the fatefully exact word to amuse themselves and the few with the time to listen.[67]

CHAPTER TEN

New York Jew
1970–1978

New York. . . . the book of my life.

—Alfred Kazin, *New York Jew*

Change and change and change . . . moving fast, always so fast, that "success" becomes a joke.

—Alfred Kazin, Journal, June 25, 1975

The grim, even despairing, mood that hangs over much of *Bright Book of Life* undoubtedly owed a great deal to Kazin's feelings of helplessness and outrage before the specter of the never-ending Vietnam conflict. But there may have been more personal reasons for the book's darkening mood. Kazin was losing some of his closest friends. On December 28, 1969, Josephine Herbst had died of cancer in New York Hospital. He had been with her the day before and knew the end was near, her "hot, dying hands, just like the hands of BB [Berel Birstein] and GK [Gita Kazin] ten years ago this year." An indispensable friend in the months after his 1950 separation from Carol, "Josie" had remained a loyal "comrade" and confidant. "I have never known in my life any other writer who was so solid, so joyous, so giving, who was able to take so many difficulties in her stride," he had written in a memorial piece for the *New York Review*.[1]

There would soon be other deaths. If the sixties saw the emergence of a brash new generation, Michael's generation, the seventies seemed increasingly to mark the passing of Kazin's own—not completely, but enough to make him feel he was surviving into a very different world. "Now it is a different journey, the landscape is almost unrecognizable at times," he wrote in a 1975 journal entry reflecting on the changes in his life. Personal loss, "absent friends," were part of that changed landscape; but so was the immediate landscape in which he lived, the "great, rich city of New York." The city was changing—in disturbing ways. He knew it from the reports of impending fiscal crises, from the growing fear in the streets, from the smell of smoke in the air, from the screaming headlines in the tabloids: the " 'Last Days' of New York!" "New York is just a failure." Had "the promised city" promised too much?[2]

Had America promised too much? The civil rights movement, political activism, and the "Great Society" programs had certainly raised the expectations (and demands) of women, blacks, and other minorities in the 1960s —even as the Vietnam War, the sometimes violent protests, the emergence of a "counterculture," and the backlash against the so-called rights revolution fractured the country into hostile camps. Responding to these expectations and conflicts in a period of declining financial resources and political retrenchment would be a major challenge of the 1970s, a decade referred to variously as an "Age of Limits," a "Time of Conflict," an "Era of Decline." The cities, with their growing concentrations of poor and minority populations, their narrowing tax bases, rising crime rates, and contentious politics, bore much of the brunt of these developments, and none more than New York City, known for its generous social services and welcoming attitude to new arrivals. How was Kazin's "world city of freedom, openness, hope" to cope with such changes?—one of many disturbing questions he would take up in New York Jew (1978), the next installment of his autobiography and his most extended account of his long, intimate, arousing, and frequently troubling relationship with New York City.[3]

Like Starting Out in the Thirties, New York Jew is a success story of Alfred Kazin and his generation. It would tell of "the golden age of the Jews—the Age of our Success," he wrote in a 1968 journal entry. "Write about Bellow and Trilling and Mrs. Trilling—about Jerome Wiesner and how many others who have 'made it'—Robert Brustein, Jules Feiffer, Byran Dorbell, Harry Levin, Irving Ribner, Edward Saveth, Bernard Malamud, Mailer, Barbara Solomon." But, written over a period of unending marital difficulty and increasingly uneasy reflections about mortality and the curve of his career, New York Jew is also a story of losses and failures—of close friends, dead and forgotten, of Jews who never made it, anonymous Jews, parents, grand-parents, those left behind. Even "the successes," those who had "made it," including Ann Birstein and himself, saw failure always threatening—their competitiveness, their desperate need to succeed, their bitterness and an-ger: all anxious responses to the deprivations of the past and continuing fear—"the old Jewish nightmares of annihilation played out at the bar of the Russian Tea Room." Intractable family troubles, recurrent reflections on the Holocaust, and the increasingly ominous conditions of New York are never far from the surface of *New York Jew*, nor from Kazin's often mordant reflections on his life and the unsettling changes of the 1970s. A decade for tallying up successes as well as measuring costs, the seventies were a difficult period for Kazin—the personal losses and unhappiness at home only partly offset by the honors and recognitions that came with an advancing career.[4]

The Century

One of those recognitions arrived in the spring of 1969, when Kazin was inducted into New York's Century Club, an "Association" of writers, artists, intellectuals, doctors, and other professionals housed in a West Forty-third Street mansion between Fifth and Sixth avenues. Of the various honors and awards he had received in the recent past, including his 1965 induction into the National Institute of Arts and Letters, the invitation to join the "Century" was the one he most valued. Established in 1847, the "Associa-tion," declared its founders, was for "gentlemen of any occupation pro-vided their breadth of interest and moral qualities and imagination made them sympathetic, stimulating and congenial companions to the society of authors and artists." Intellectual and creative achievement rather than fam-ily caste had always been the criteria for entry, and unlike other New York clubs, it had long welcomed Jews. "There's a club down on 43rd that chooses its members mentally," a member of the competing Union Club had once remarked. "Now isn't that a hell of a way to run a club?" Over the years it had proved to be a successful way, numbering among its members Albert Bierstadt, William Cullen Bryant, Frederick Church, and the archi-tect Henry Hobson Richardson, as well as fifteen presidents and three chief justices of the Supreme Court. Cleveland Amory, an expert on New York's and the nation's upper social circles, called the Century Association "probably the most interesting of New York's clubs and easily the most distinguished from a Who's Who if not from a *Celebrity Register* point of view." Mark Twain once referred to it as "the most unspeakably respectable club" in the United States.[5]

A writer who sought out the company of other writers and artists, Kazin had had an interest in the Century since Henry Steele Commager had first invited him there in 1945 to discuss *On Native Grounds*. The Century accepted very few young men, however. "They are all over a hundred there," a member of the Knickerbocker Club had once remarked. "That's why they call it the Century Association." It would be some years before Kazin was asked to join. Indeed, when told by Centurian Peter Davison in 1968 that he was going to nominate him, he said he was grateful but that his "case had been hanging on for so long, I think I'm prepared to forget it." Perhaps he was not the clubbable type. Davison's effort may have been what was needed; Kazin (age fifty-four) was inducted the next year.[6]

Once in, he was enchanted. "The Century kills me. Like another world when you get in. I love the old floor and portraits." He also liked the company (most of the time) and the convenience of having a distinguished place to meet friends and invite interesting people for drinks and conversation. He was often amused by the self-importance and extreme good manners of the members—"At the Century, all voices so nicely modulated. . . . We are all 'notables.' We are Important and Influential People, we gravely exchange courtesies like ambassadors." He also, like the Knickerbocker man, was conscious of the age of the members—a fact with special resonance during the Vietnam War days. "Monthly dinner of the Century Club. Never trust anybody over 77! Hundreds of gray hairs in black evening coats, self-consciously listening to old Dean Acheson defaming the youth as carriers of violence, defending Rhodesia and South Africa—Acheson being charming, lordly, the state secretary still, architect of our foreign policy. Oh Lord, save us from these successes." Still, Kazin loved the place, gray hairs and all, much as he loved Yaddo, another door into an older, more polite America. "The bust of G. Washington at the head of the stairs. The mellow old landscapes. The old men have this look of being weathered in the service of coming here to lunch. The whole thing so preposterously an act of old-fashioned gentility, servility, the behavior of gentlemen, that past the outside door [onto Forty-third Street] you have to catch your breath."[7]

For a Brownsville Jew, writing about growing up in New York, participating in "the incessant American struggle for status and achievement," the Century was an indispensable point of arrival and connection in this city of connections—"At the Century—crossroads of the New York 'powers.'" It was also a relief from the clamorous, rapidly changing city outside—the "nicely modulated" voices in the carpeted dining room, far from the "Puerto Rican voices" echoing in the street outside his West End apartment. There were no abrasive voices in the Century. Everything was "muted, respectable, repressed looking. 'Would you want to find yourself dining some night with Bella Abzug?'" (Women were not admitted until 1988.) Kazin makes no reference to the Century in *New York Jew*, but he does describe the marble staircases, the old pictures, the long oak tables of the New York Public Library, where he had worked on his first book and sensed in the mammoth reading rooms with their vaulted ceilings "the powerful amenity [he] craved for his own life." Now, in his mid-fifties, surveying "the mellow landscapes" and old portraits in the Century (built, like the library, in the late nineteenth century), he found himself surrounded by the amenities he had long yearned for. Here was a corner of New York, old New York, seemingly impervious to change, a sanctuary of civility (and rather elderly men) protected from the noise and rancors of a city—"the bazaar of the squashed"—that Kazin continued to care for, found endlessly novel and exciting, but often unnerving and tiring to live in.[8]

"See Jew and Think Jew All the Time"

The last week of June 1970, Kazin boarded a plane for Frankfurt, Germany, the first leg of a group pilgrimage that would take him to Bergen-Belsen, the site of the former concentration camp, then on to Jerusalem and a conference with writers and Israeli government officials. Organized and paid for by Josef Rosensaft, a Belsen survivor and wealthy art collector, the journey would be Kazin's first to a concentration camp site. He had seen the gruesome pictures coming out of Belsen when it was liberated by Allied troops in 1945, but those images seen in the Piccadilly newsreel theater were little in evidence in 1970. The buildings and barbed wire had been replaced by well-kept grassy plots. Instead of the "sticks" in prison garb seen in the film, there were now survivors returning in the rain to commemorate the dead. Kazin did not need physical reminders to explain the purpose of the pilgrimage. "The whole experience," he wrote in his journal, the visit to Belsen followed by the trip to Jerusalem, "has been to screen us individually as Jews, to put the 'Jewish' experience at the center of our consciousness, to make us see Jew and think Jew all the time." Emil Fackenheim, one of the pilgrims, described the purpose more expansively. The trip, he wrote in "Bergen-Belsen to Jerusalem," was an opportunity "to affirm our Jewishness" through a recognition of the "unique" nature of the Holocaust and in "celebration of Israel as testimony to the Jewish people's determination to survive." Acknowledging the significance of both events and "the connection" between them was to move beyond "universalism" to a new "religious" understanding of Jewishness independent of the "definitions and sufferance of others."[9]

The Holocaust, Israel, and the "sufferance" of the Gentile world were topics to which Kazin had already devoted some attention—though without Fackenheim's certainty of their meaning. After his first visit in 1960, he had applauded Israel's determination to face the horrors of the Holocaust (in the Eichmann trial) but had resented the effort to frighten Jews to immigrate. In his 1964 essay on Rolf Hochhuth's play *The Deputy,* he had addressed directly "the definitions and sufferance of others"—specifically the Nazis' success in defining Europe's Jews as victims whom non-Jews, "others" (the Poles, the Germans, even the Allies and the pope), were arguably willing to see sacrificed. "How could you identify with people who had suffered so much . . . ? Suffering can make people disgusting. The people whose martyrdom was called an 'extermination' . . . make them not objects of compassion, but a disease to stay away from." The logic of this disturbing insight suggests that the surest answer to victimization (and the revulsion it provokes) was precisely the kind of political self-confidence and military prowess that compelled respect for Israel (and for Jews) but that had always made Kazin deeply uneasy.[10]

He had showed less than his usual amount of uneasiness in a 1967 *Harper's* essay, "In Israel: After the Triumph," describing his trip to Israel following the Six-Day War. The war had been a terrifying experience for Jews everywhere. As the Arab armies massed on Israel's borders and Arab spokesmen threatened to wipe Israel off the map and throw Israelis "into the sea," it seemed to many that a second Holocaust might be at hand. The terror turned quickly to jubilation (with some lingering dread) when it was learned that in six days the Israeli military had not only defeated the Egyptian military but secured the entire city of Jerusalem and much of the West Bank. The effect on Kazin and Jews everywhere was galvanizing. "I go to bed thinking, we are not as fit for the killing as we were—we can be proud," he wrote in a June journal entry. "Every time I think of what might had happened to the Jews of Israel if the Arabs had won, I find it easier to accept the audacity and toughness of the present Israeli position . . . When I think of Mama dying under that picture of Herzl, of the touching faith of the Jews in redemption, their only redemption, through Israel, I feel an inexpressible pride in our ability to live, to fight it through, to *live*." The same pride is evident in the *Harper's* essay. Describing his visit to the Wailing Wall, Gaza, the Suez Canal, and the Golan Heights, the essay is ebullient and expansive, full of the confidence and pride the Israelis felt in their recent triumph. Although Kazin continued to be wary of the "militant patriotism" that excited many Israelis and did not share in the belief that Israel (after the Holocaust) was "the great symbol of Jewish redemption"— which, according to historians Arthur Hertzberg and Jacob Neusner was becoming "the religion" of many American Jews—he kept his misgivings well in check. In 1967, joy, solidarity, and celebration were the order of the day. "The war made many of us Jews again."[11]

Back in Israel after the Belsen visit in 1970, his mood had shifted. Now he felt "the Jewish obsession . . . without a lifting of the heart." Partly the problem was personal. "I associate so much pain, lunacy, and outrage with so many Jews I have recently suffered—not just Ann, but the madly ambitious [George] Steiner, who has plots like in Shakespeare and is so full of his life, every moment at the moment, that I can hear the pistons madly clacking in his brain." Partly, it was the jarring discrepancy he felt, had always felt, between the spiritual yearnings of Jewish writers like himself and the "official" positions and political "matter of factness" of the Israeli politicians. He noted the contrast between Golda Meir and Elie Wiesel at a Jerusalem conference following the Belsen visit—Wiesel's soliloquy "teetering on the edge of incommunicable profundities," Meir's tense, abrupt *"wir wollen das alles uberleben"* ("we want to get beyond all of that [the Holocaust]." How, he asked himself, was one to reconcile this "long[ing] for transcendence" with "the hard political urgencies" of this "grimly functional society"? It was an old question that not only went to the spiritual-political significance of Israel but to the loyalties of the Diaspora Jew and to the insights and independence of the individual writer. In "Bergen-Belsen to Jerusalem," Fackenheim argued that Jews who do not "run away" from their Jewishness no longer need worry about such questions. The Holocaust, Israel, and the Six-Day War had put "an end to all Jewish 'identity crises' forever after." Kazin was not so sure. He had no intention of running away from his Jewishness, but neither was he convinced that Israel answered the question of what it meant to be a Jew. That, he believed, was up to the individual Jew. " 'A Jew is someone who is conscious of being a Jew,' " he quoted his favorite Israeli prime minister, Moshe Sharrett. "And it is consciousness that determines economics and politics."[12]

Kazin would return to Israel one more time, in November 1973, to report on the aftermath of the Yom Kippur War for the *Atlantic.* Unlike the Six-Day War, this conflict, while eventually successful, cost many Israeli lives and left Jews everywhere shaken and insecure. Arab enmity, it seemed, would never end, and the world appeared not to care. As Kazin toured the battlefields, interviewed writers, and listened to officials, the song at the top of the Israeli chart was "The Whole World Is against Us." "We are just waking up from our dream," one Israeli told him. "Everything's just normal again. The whole world hates Jews and always will." The experience left Kazin anxious about Israel's security and baffled by the postwar politics of blame. He had no answers. He looked up the young Israeli writer A. B. Yehoshua, who argued that it was necessary to meet the Palestinians halfway and to give up the territories. But Kazin offered no advice. He titled the *Atlantic* article "What Do We Do Now? What? What?" If he had been asked for his opinion, it would have been for Israelis to move beyond the rhetoric of victimization and recrimination, to rejoice in their country and themselves. "I would have shouted with all my might: Brothers! Friends! LIVE!"[13]

Kazin would find less and less cause for rejoicing in the years ahead as Israeli politics shifted decisively to the right. He deplored the expansionist politics of the Likud, "[Menachem] Begin and Co," which he felt was turning Israel into a "pariah state, an occupier, super militarized." The brutality of the war in Lebanon appalled him as he believed it did "other Jews not Zionistically inclined." There were even moments when he thought (with whatever seriousness) of writing a book on the demoraliza-

tion of Israel. Yet he continued to care for the country and to worry about
its future. He sought out and kept in touch with Israeli writer-friends,
Amos Elon, Yehoshua, Yaron Ezrahi, inviting them to dinner at the Century when they were in town, prodding them with questions. Israel would
remain "one of the great enigmas of history," evoking feelings of pride,
protectiveness, and righteous anger, a country to which Kazin would repeatedly return in thought, if not in person, whose history and people and
very existence continued to move him almost in spite of himself.[14]

"The Death God"

Returning from the Belsen-Israel pilgrimage in mid-July 1970, Kazin went
directly to the Menorah Home for the Aged in Brooklyn to see his father. In
December, Gedahlia "Charles" Kazin had suffered a stroke that had left
him aphasic and crippled in one leg. His son had been pleased to find him a
place in an Orthodox nursing home—"I do like the sedateness of the Orthodox"—where there were other immigrant Jews of his father's generation. The social advantages had meant little to his father, however. He was
unhappy to be there and had thrown his first meal up against the wall. He
made no effort to converse with the other men and refused to join in their
pinochle games. He lay mostly silent on his bed, sometimes wooping,
sometimes mindlessly reiterating the Hebrew word *Lefkenuschuh* (before
Thy face), an invocation from a children's prayer. A symptom of his aphasia,
the repeated term meant nothing to him and provoked derisive comments
from his fellow companions and the staff. Kazin was not surprised to find
his father miserable and very much alone. He had always been a "loner,"
self-preoccupied and silent, preferring to sit by himself, usually by an exit
where he could make a quick escape to the streets—"a great man for
walking about instead of talking, for walking alone." Kazin thought of him
as the original "walker in the city" and had often worried about the traits
they shared, particularly the penchant for self-preoccupation and self-pity
—"the habit of loneliness." "One looks for one's father—one looks—one
looks and one realizes I *am* my father." In fact, he was different from his
father in significant ways and much more like his mother—energetic, resourceful, endlessly worried, always thinking ahead, and despite (or perhaps because of) his "habit of loneliness", compulsively sociable—when it

NEW YORK JEW 303

suited his mood. He was proud of one quality he shared with his father . . . his good looks.[15]

On September 23, 1970, Gedahlia Kazin died in the nursing home. "My old man will no longer prowl the boardwalk, my old man, the most solitary man in creation unable ever to communicate his loneliness." Since his mother's death in 1959, Kazin had been a dutiful son, calling his father frequently on the phone, bringing him into the city for family affairs, taking him to the movies—all the while feeling frustrated and guilty that he seemed never able to reach a man whose "reclusive, ungiving" habits made simple conversation an ordeal. He retained a few positive memories of him re-counted in a portrait in *New York Jew*—the story of his sojourn "out West" working for the Union Pacific Railroad; his devotion to the American Social-ist Eugene Debs; father and son trips to the old *Forward* Building on East Broadway; an occasional visit to Lewisohn Stadium, where they sat in silence on the concrete seats, listening to Brahms, Beethoven, Tchaikovsky. Kazin remembered his father as a "sweet man," but weak, ineffective, and "defeated" in a household dominated by his strong, resourceful wife. Kazin had long believed his own difficulties with women (especially wives) were attributable to this imbalance, turning him into the primary target of his mother's attention, a "mama's boy." (He also believed it was responsible for his "lifelong fantasies of making it with married women"—not competing with his father, "Freudian style," but somehow making up for him, "displac-ing the husband, even humiliating him in front of me as I make love to his wife.") Relegated to the background in the two previous autobiographies, Charles plays a more important role in *New York Jew* by virtue, ironically, of his personal insignificance—a reminder of the "failed," largely forgotten, immigrant Jewish fathers whom their successful sons had left behind. "I made my father up in the image of the dispossessed, the excluded, the oppressed working class, until neither of us was young any more and Jews were no longer in the working class."[16]

Charles Kazin's death would quickly be followed by others. On October 24, Kazin learned that his friend from the thirties and forties, Ben Selig-man, had died the day before of heart failure. Although they had drifted apart as Seligman, a noted labor economist, took jobs in Washington, D.C., and later at the University of Massachusetts, he was for twenty years Ka-zin's closest friend—"Herschel" in *Starting Out in the Thirties*, a committed Marxist with an exegetical passion for T. S. Eliot and James Joyce. On the same day, Kazin learned that Richard Hofstadter had died of leukemia at Mount Sinai Hospital in Manhattan. Though deeply upsetting, the news was not wholly a surprise. Hofstadter had been diagnosed with leukemia in November 1969 but had been showing signs of failing health for some time. After a conversation in April 1968, Kazin had written in his journal that his old friend looked "scared," that he had "the angry look of a sick man"—adding that his "intelligence is an extraordinary grace and makes up for everything. Amazingly adroit, elegant mind." Hofstadter's health had continued to deteriorate, and Kazin found visits increasingly painful, in part because his friend, who had been something of a hypochondriac during much of his life, now refused to acknowledge the gravity of his condition. (David Brown, Hofstadter's biographer, writes that two months *after* he had been diagnosed with incurable leukemia, Hofstadter had signed a contract with Alfred Knopf for a "big American history" that he anticipated would take him eighteen years to finish.) On his last hospital visit, Alfred remembered Hofstadter's talking as always with "great intelligence" and gesturing toward the manuscript at his bedside that everyone else knew would never be completed.[17]

Hofstadter's death was a serious loss. He and Kazin had been close friends in the thirties, each recognizing in the other the qualities of sensibility and intelligence that would mark their future careers. After receiving his Ph.D. from Columbia in 1942, Hofstadter had accepted an assistant professorship at the University of Maryland before returning to Columbia in 1946. Throughout this period the two had exchanged letters about their lives and work—including a long, enthusiastic, not wholly uncritical, letter from Hofstadter about *On Native Grounds*. They had resumed their friendship when Hofstadter had returned to New York, meeting socially (often at Thanksgiving dinners) as well as on professional occasions such as *American Scholar* editorial board meetings. Their friendship meant a great deal to Kazin. "I have never known another man who meant so much to me," he would later write. He was "the only man I ever loved." It is unclear just how much Kazin meant to Hofstadter, however. Michael Kazin has remarked that his father considered Dick "his best friend, but Dick was perhaps no one's best friend." Kazin seemed to have sensed this himself, or, more precisely, sensed that the Richard Hofstadter he had known from

Montague Street, from ping-pong, and from conversations in the Public
Library reading room, the "early emotional, nostalgic friend" of the thirties, was not quite the same person as the brilliantly successful professor at
Columbia. "The historian Richard Hofstadter was something so entirely
different—[that] over and over—since his death I have been trying to ac-
custom myself to the duality (or the single Dick Hofstadter behind the
duality)."[18]

This "duality" did not prevent Kazin from writing an eloquent personal
tribute to his friend for the *American Scholar,* on whose editorial board they
had both served. He described their first meeting in Brooklyn Heights, his
talent for telling stories "funnier than any jokesmith," the pleasure of listening to him talk "about *anything,*" his charm, his "unbreakable dignity," his
"lucid intellectual humor," his old-fashioned gift for writing narrative history, his keen literary sense, and the simple privilege of knowing him and
being in his company. "He was so important a part of my life that it will
always be natural to look for his face, to expect his voice." Kazin was very
good at commemorative pieces (a skill not dissimilar from his gift for literary
portraiture) and in future years would be called on to write and deliver a
number. None, however, would be more obviously heartfelt than this quiet
statement of reminiscence, professional praise, and personal loss.[19]

Hofstadter's death left a void, deepening the feelings of loss after the
deaths of Josephine Herbst, his father, and Ben Seligman. But the onslaught was not over. On October 31, Kazin's friend, confidant, and "metaphysical psychologist" Heinrich Bluecher died. "In these weeks I have lost
Papa, Dick, Heinrich. I think to myself: where have they gone?" Absence
and loss, he was coming to feel, were his portion. There was no stopping the
losses; one could only record them—"the only release is to get it all down"—
in his journal and in the next volume of his autobiography he was planning.
He could make them part of the story and even take strength in the telling
—"Dick [Hofstadter] in the first chapter—carrying me along by his reserved intelligence and sophistication." There would be more losses, Mark
Van Doren and Edmund Wilson in 1972—"our great tree is fallen"—Hannah Arendt in 1975. "The death God suddenly walks into the distracted,
sodden New York Party! And life suddenly becomes a book." Whatever else
it might be, *New York Jew* was also going to be a work of "commemoration,
remembrance, fealty to the past."[20]

"Homecoming"

One effect of these losses was to increase Kazin's interest in rediscovering, remembering, and preserving his connections with his past, specifically his New York past, his city of connections—"New York is my connection. In New York I make my connections"—where the past kept reemerging and which would constitute the setting and subject of his next memoir. Not that he felt he had to remain there all the time. He continued to travel and give talks around the country. "I am lecturing at the U. of Toronto March 5–7," he wrote to Peggy Yntema at the *Atlantic* in February 1973; "at York College (New York), end of February, am addressing a big teachers thing on Long Island March 23, will be at the University of Wisconsin in April, then at the U of Indiana, then for two weeks at the U of Iowa." He also participated in the occasional intellectual junket where notables in their fields are paid handsomely to assemble and exchange big ideas about large subjects. The *New York Times* reported on one at the University of Texas (April 1972), convened to discuss "Problems in the 21st Century," at which "the soft literate moralisms of Alfred Kazin . . . clashed with the steely statistical analyses" of Herman Kahn, a policy analyst at the RAND Corporation. The participants (paid twenty-five hundred dollars each for appearing) could not agree on the terms for discussion, much less on the important issues. The composer Aaron Copland had to ask what GDP referred to. Kazin, who admitted to not knowing what was meant by "a factor of two," confided at the end that he was "a nonbeliever in symposiums."[21]

In the fall of 1972, he turned to a subject on which he felt he could speak with more competence. *New York Magazine* had invited him to do an essay on his life in New York City, under the promising title "Nightmares, Dreams and Lusts of a New Yorker." The article never appeared; instead, Kazin submitted a piece to the *New York Review* titled "New York Jew," which was published in December. Composed in part from journal entries, it said little about his dreams and lusts and focused rather on incidents and news stories that provoked memories of his life in New York, Jewish New York—his neighbor's difficulties with his devalued Brownsville properties; a tour of devastated Brownsville with an old Amherst student, now a New York detective, his impressions of Norman Mailer at a cocktail party; an account of his meeting with Josef Rosensaft, the Belsen survivor, and with

Isaac Bashevis Singer. Restating its Jewish theme, the piece concluded with a copy of the 1944 letter of Shmuel Ziegelboym on the destruction of Poland's Jews. Kazin sent Peter Davison the piece, said he was not sure where he was going with it, but hoped it would lead toward the eventual publication of a book based on his journals. Such a book, he believed, would reveal levels of personal associations and interconnections that described his life in the city—the city with its myriad connections to his past, "the city [where] everyone touches everyone else."[22]

One place where everyone seemed to touch everyone else was in court. In early January 1973, Kazin was summoned to jury duty. He had been summoned before but had never been chosen. This time he was "determined" to be selected and even tried to conceal from the court the fact that he was a teacher, which he feared would disqualify him in the eyes of the prosecutor. When he slurred over his answers about his profession, the judge told him to speak up and then asked why the hesitation. "Has teaching fallen to so low an estate that our teachers are now ashamed to admit that they are teachers?" Kazin's fears proved unfounded, and he was selected for the jury. He had journalistic motives for wanting to be chosen; he saw an opportunity to write up yet another experience about the life of a New Yorker, and he was soon negotiating with *Playboy* about a piece—eventually published as "Memoir of a Jurist" in the *Village Voice*. But he was also genuinely curious about the experience, particularly the New York personalities involved—the defendant (a policeman who had taken bribes and perjured himself); the "flamboyant" Jewish judge; the district and defense attorneys; the other jurors, one of whom was Elia Kazan, the director. Kazin knew Kazan from his work in the Group Theatre in the thirties; he occasionally got his mail and had once been contacted by a professor of theater, requesting the director's script for *A Streetcar Named Desire*. Now he had the chance to watch the famous man in action—constantly taking notes, ever watchful, "super alert to every little drama in front of him." At the end of deliberations, when it looked like the defendant might escape all charges, Kazan (with Kazin's help) secured a conviction. It was, Kazin concluded his article, "a Big Experience." It was also a New York experience. Sitting next to Kazan in the jury box, running into his Amherst detective student on the steps to the courthouse, meeting another former student in the courtroom—all confirmed Kazin's sense of New York as the point of connections and reconnections. "All connected . . . all plugging yourself in here and there."[23]

His contacts and connections with the city would intensify (and diversify) significantly in the fall of 1973. He had been appointed Visiting Distinguished Professor at Hunter College for the 1973–1974 school year, an appointment that would become permanent the following year. The long-sought faculty position in New York City had finally materialized. No more weekly commutes and stay-overs on Long Island; no more shady streets and walks on the beach. The contrast with Stony Brook was dramatic. Stony Brook was the suburbs; its students were mostly middle class, many of them children of parents who had attended a branch of the City University of New York (CUNY) before relocating to Long Island. "Hunter is a city. Mass scene. Everybody pops up, sooner or later. So the teaching business— passing on your experience—becomes more real than ever." In fact, Hunter and the CUNY system generally were more than a city; they were New York City. With students from more than one hundred nations speaking more than one hundred languages, CUNY was a city unto itself, one of the most ethnically and culturally diverse universities in the world.[24]

Kazin found the change bracing and challenging. What common knowledge or shared values could he assume from such a student body? How to explain to the girl from the West Indies Yeats's eschatological musings in "Sailing to Byzantium"? How to persuade a recent immigrant from Honduras that Faulkner's *Absalom! Absalom!* contains something relevant to his life? In one of his very few essays on teaching, "The Happy Hour," Kazin described the experience of teaching Eliot's *The Waste Land* to a mixed group of students during the happy hour at Hunter—"Elsie the brown-faced refugee from 'mainland China,'" "Dominic from Staten Island," Myra who taught English in a Bronx High School, "the black lady who comes to class all the way from Paterson, New Jersey." Excepting Myra, everyone was afraid of poetry. "With little Latin and less Greek, no real knowledge of history, no foreign languages to speak of, my students have to grope their way to knowledge. A great poet makes them feel uneducated." Yet they seemed moved by Eliot's poem. It was full of unfamiliar images, of languages not their own, of feelings dimly recognized. But reading *The Waste Land* on Lexington during the Happy Hour, or "The Cocktail Hour" in a classroom "so noisy it could as well meet on the street outside," in a city at least as chaotic, tense, and vaguely ominous as London, could be an exciting experience. "The poem works on us as some irresistible discord—a succession of fragments that becomes a mysterious striving within ourselves to eliminate fragmentation, to reach the unity we also despair of. There is a chorus of different voices in ourselves: that is the life of the poem." New York may be chaotic, threatening, alien—"Who are these hooded hordes swarming?" But it was also a way into the poem, perhaps the best way—and the poem, a meaningful way to find some order (and tradition) in the chaos, the "heap of broken images" that is the city.[25]

While there were many rewarding moments at Hunter, there were also moments of doubt and frustration. "It has taken me all this time to realize what a bad, impatient teacher I am. I had supposed I was talking to intellectuals," Kazin complained after one class. "It turns out that I have been talking to . . . patients, people with serious diseases of the intellect . . . We are dealing with an extreme case of fright." Kazin was not the only teacher disturbed by the performance of many CUNY students. Academic standards were a matter of general concern in the CUNY community during the early seventies. In 1970, after intense negotiation between the state and various political and ethnic groups within the city, CUNY had adopted an open-admissions policy guaranteeing all graduating high school seniors within New York's boroughs entrance into one of the CUNY colleges. The decision came partly as a consequence of pressure from underrepresented minorities (mostly blacks and Puerto Ricans) at a time of intense national activism. But it was also favored by many administrators, faculty, and grateful former students, committed to the 1849 mission of the university that education be for "the whole people," not just "the privileged few." The open-admissions policy had led to the enrollment of many students who were ill-prepared for college-level classes, who might well have regarded the study of poetry and of many subjects with "an extreme case of fright."[26]

Whatever his frustrations with the students, Kazin was grateful to be back. Asked to address the 1974 Hunter Honors Convocation, he titled his talk "A Homecoming" and praised the students for their "intellectual seriousness." He noted that as a graduate of City College in the 1930s, he knew something of "the handicaps" facing the Hunter students, not least "the daily slavery" of the subway. He was also aware of the differences between then and now, the astonishing mix of students, "everybody pops up," the cacophony in the classroom—"a whole pandemonium of building and sky noises that come between you and the delicate little poem" being read to the class. It was great to be back, but he was back to a very different school from the one he had attended, one that was changing as fast as the city.[27]

"A Sort of Autobiographical Book"

On January 31, 1974, Kazin wrote Peter Davison describing his intentions for his next "personal history," which he was determined to get back to and which he now called *You Must Change Your Life*. He would take up his story in 1942 after the publication of *On Native Grounds*, carry it through the war and his second marriage, and conclude with the writing of *A Walker in the City* in 1950. Like his other personal histories, he assured Davison, it would describe "the historic *in* the personal and the personal in the historic" through "the working out of a particular moment." That "moment might be called 'The Coming of the Jews'—i.e., the decisive entry of Jewish writers and intellectuals into American culture." Kazin added that he was also working on "a volume of my diaries on New York and the New York scene in our own day" and had already published a sample piece in the *New York Review*. Davison had read the piece, recognized its potential, and believed that a book written in the same vein would find an enthusiastic reception. After consulting with his associates at Little, Brown, he offered Kazin a contract for forty thousand dollars, twenty thousand each for *You Must Change Your Life* and *New York Jew*. Kazin initially agreed, but in March, he told Davison that he had decided to combine the two books, bringing the narrative timeline of *You Must Change Your Life* up to the present, calling the single composite book *New York Jew*.[28]

Davison welcomed the news. He had worried that *You Must Change Your Life*, the story of a love affair and a "fall," might be "a bit literary." He also thought *New York Jew* would be "a more saleable item" than *You Must Change Your Life*. The new project, he told his associates, would be "a sort of autobiographical book," drawing on Kazin's gift for nostalgic evocation. "Situated in the present and reaching into the past," it would include portraits of noted contemporary intellectuals and would "be focused . . . on New York . . . as the literary center, particularly of the Jewish literary experience." Little, Brown offered Kazin twenty-five thousand dollars for the completed book. Unhappy to see the forty thousand dollars shrink to twenty-five, Kazin began talking to Robert Gottlieb, president of Alfred Knopf, and within the month had signed with Knopf for thirty-five thousand dollars. Davison was "rankled" to see Kazin go to another firm—though he was determined that it not end their friendship. "I understand, I understand," he wrote when Kazin later gave his reasons—the lack of trust shown him by the "money men" at Little, Brown and the fact that he "needed money for very pressing personal reasons." "Mr. G [Gottlieb] is a good publisher," Davison told Kazin, "but he is not 'the author's friend,' as you once described Max Perkins. I think the book is going to be majestic and wonderful." Nor did Kazin want to break off relations with Davison, a longtime friend and a connection to the *Atlantic,* which, he told his one-time editor, he "need[ed] as an outlet for my critical stuff." "Believe me our 'separation' is not one I enjoy or expect to profit by."[29]

There was another consideration behind Kazin's decision to combine both books. By linking the two narratives, he would be able to create a more inclusive, dynamic picture of the changing life and character of New York City over time—the Greenwich Village of the wartime forties, the booming midtown of the postwar years, the growing generational and racial conflicts of the sixties, the "apocalyptic" uncertainties of New York in the seventies, a period of increasing alarm about the city's future during which much of the book was written.

There was cause for alarm—though the warning signs had been visible for years. In the fifties and sixties, middle-class New Yorkers (many of them Jews) had begun leaving the city for the suburbs, replaced in large part by unskilled blacks, Puerto Ricans, and other minorities, many of whom depended heavily on the city for social services. The demographic shift had accelerated during the late sixties and seventies, further eroding the tax base, while the demand for social services continued to grow. The shift was hardly unique to New York. The exodus of middle-class, tax-paying citizens to the suburbs was a national phenomenon, as was the growing concentration of poor minorities in the inner city. Pundits and politicians repeatedly cited the growing "urban crisis" as one of the most serious challenges facing the country. Because of its size, its enormous economic importance to the country, and its symbolic status as the nation's first city, New York was frequently in the news—an emblem of the desperate straits of the nation's cities. New York was also one of the most vulnerable, in large part because of its generous social services and the huge influx of very poor immigrants from Mexico, the Caribbean, and Central America. In the early seventies, at a time when the city could not pay interest on its debt, it was supporting more than one million welfare clients, spending more than twice per capita on its people than did any other U.S. city. Meanwhile, crime was on the rise: muggings—"100 muggings a day"—murder, arson. By 1976, deliberately set fires in the South Bronx had turned once thriving neighborhoods into charred ruins. In 1976 alone, the Fire Department recorded more than thirty-five thousand fires. With the smoke and smell of charred wood drifting over the Upper West Side, Kazin's thoughts turned eschatological. "People in trouble—a city in trouble . . . I seen the first and I now see de last," he quoted (roughly) from *The Sound and the Fury.* "I see the sequence whole—the plot has arrived on the verge of the last act."[30]

The smell of smoke was the least of Kazin's concerns. One of the more generous (and expensive) services provided by the city was free tuition at an excellent university with a highly paid faculty. CUNY's budget had been growing rapidly, advancing from $67 million in 1960–1961 to $327 million in 1970–1971, the initial year of open admissions. By 1975, it was approaching $650 million. As New York's financial crisis deepened in 1975–1976 and the city began laying off police officers, firefighters, and hospital workers by the thousands, it was clear that CUNY was in for some draconian cuts. Fearing he had just joined a sinking ship, Kazin began sending out job enquiries—to MIT, Boston College, Stanford. "As I needn't tell you," he wrote to Peter Davison in December 1975, "the situation in New York is as bad as it can be and is likely to get worse. I am on a super-committee elected by the faculty and already know more than I want to know." The "super-committee" consisted of four professors elected by the CUNY combined faculties to make proposals on steps the university might take to deal with the crisis. Their proposal, delivered in February 1976 to the Board of Higher Education, was that the university charge tuition, restrict admission to the top 20 percent of high school graduates, and close a number of the community colleges. The proposal provoked stiff resistance among parts of the city population and was not adopted. On May 28, 1976, during final exams, City University was forced to close its doors.[31]

It reopened in the fall after laying off many employees, canceling many programs, and closing some campuses. Kazin did not lose his job, and the city would slowly begin to get its financial house in order. But the landscape had changed. Kazin's "promised city" was now "the embattled city." Although its skyline, energy, mass, and volume could still rekindle "the old NY feeling," that feeling had lost much of its resilience and swagger. Devastated Brownsville and the smoldering Bronx were more than ever part of Kazin's New York, as were the "dementia, hatred, and blind suffering" he witnessed daily in the streets and the subway. They are also present in *New York Jew,* among the many jarring reminders that this success story about "the coming of the Jews" was playing itself out in an environment marked by many broken promises and failures.[32]

There is another way in which *New York Jew* (both the book and its defiant title) reflected the changes in the city (and in the country). Begun in the late sixties during what has been called the "rights revolution," the book was completed in the 1970s, the "decade of the ethnics," or "the unmeltable ethnics," a time when a variety of minority groups—such as blacks, Hispanics, women, American Indians, and Asian Americans—were competing with increasing success for recognition in the national culture. Teaching at culturally diverse Hunter and alert as ever to the shifts in zeitgeist, Kazin understood what was happening. To write as a New York Jew was to join a growing chorus of diverse voices, each insisting on its difference, its special story. Kazin had told parts of that story before. "My autobiography will always be most deeply the autobiography of a Jew," he had written in 1960 while working on *Starting Out in the Thirties.* That work, however, and *Walker* were written as Jewish writers were beginning to make their mark on the national consciousness, a time when Kazin felt his generation very much in the ascendancy. By the seventies, things were not so clear. To write about "the golden age of the Jews—the Age of our Success," was to sound a new, elegiac note while the competing voices grew louder and louder, "the most marvelous cacophony" singing away "in the cultural pond." Not that Jewish writers and intellectuals had fallen on hard times or were at risk of being marginalized. There was still little reason to doubt "the immense cultural authority of all us Jewish writers and critics," as Kazin had put it in 1958. But neither was there the special excitement of a "breakthrough," the exhilaration of being lifted by a rising tide of unexpected triumphs. *New York Jew* is a long look back, a summing up, an expression of pride and defiance, as well as some bitterness and regret, a chance to get it all on the record in what Kazin had assured Peter Davison was to be his last autobiography.[33]

He managed to put a good deal on the record—three marriages; four decades of living in New York; extended visits and teaching assignments in Europe, Russia, Israel, and New England; friendships and associations with dozens of interesting and accomplished people; additional portraits of family members. Kazin clearly hoped that the variety of his interests, acquaintances, and experiences, living "directly *and* symbolically in the storm centers of the twentieth century," would compensate for the loss in formal and tonal integrity he had achieved in his two previous autobiographies with their restricted venues and time frames. To a degree the strategy worked. *New York Jew* is a lively, highly entertaining personal account of the wartime forties, the booming fifties, the revolutionary sixties, and the ominous seventies. It also contains an impressive gallery of portraits widely praised by reviewers (including those who thought them unfair) as "vivid," "unforgettable," "masterly."[34]

Kazin, as noted, had a fine talent for literary portraiture, and in *New York Jew*, his largest canvas, he made generous use of his gift. Some of the portraits (of Saul Bellow, Edmund Wilson, and Hannah Arendt) are major efforts, others are very brief, but virtually all of them show an expert's eye for telling detail: Delmore Schwartz's "squalid box of a room on Greenwich Street . . . that only practice in disaster could have discovered"; Henry Luce's "ferociously oversize eyebrows that looked as if they had been planted and watered to intimidate subordinates"; Edmund Wilson's "round bald head and that hoarse, heavily breathing voice box coming out of the red face of an overfed fox-hunting squire"; Lionel Trilling, "his distinguished white hair over a handsome face that seemed to be furrowed, hooded, closed up in constant thought."[35]

"Autobiography," Kazin wrote in his journal while working on *Starting Out in the Thirties*, "deals with the delights of 'personality,' rather than character-in-action, in 'portraits' rather than in *plot*." But portraits can be more than portraits, he later wrote of *New York Jew*. They can also be "characters," "relationships [in] this non-fiction novel." "Now we put this 'classicist' [Hannah Arendt], this believer in permanent values, up against

Bellow, who resented being told anything about Faulkner by a Kraut, against Goodman, who shocked her by leaving a mound of peanut shells around him, by Mary McCarthy, who, after trying to insult her at Rahv's house, became her frenzied acolyte." If this sort of thing is the material of "the higher gossip," as one reviewer complained (one could say the same of Henry James's "situations"), it is material Kazin put to good use—using attributes of one character to indicate contrasting qualities of another; highlighting points of significance in writers where personality, appearance, and career coalesce in sharp relief. More than a gallery of still lifes, the resulting "characters" provide entrée to a complex, dynamic intellectual-cultural milieu that retains much of the texture and intensity of a life "lived . . . among brilliant intellectuals."[36]

But an autobiography is more than a series of portraits or "characters," however good; and there are serious problems with *New York Jew* as autobiography—problems that carry over in some measure to the portraits. "As I can testify," Kazin wrote in an essay published the same year as *New York Jew,* autobiography, or "personal history," is "directly an effort to find salvation, to make one's own experience come out right." In the two earlier autobiographies, Kazin found salvation, or a measure of salvation, in the hope and idealism of an aspiring young writer that carried him beyond the poverty and constriction of Brownsville and the disappointments of history. "Salvation would come by the word." In *New York Jew*, that future is mostly in the past and, it seems, so are hopes for salvation. Having achieved a measure of success, Kazin no longer believed in it with the old urgency, nor in the happiness it was supposed to bring. Indeed, his story leaves the impression that for this New York Jew in "the golden age of the Jews," much of the earlier hope and excitement, the yearning and struggle for advancement, had dissipated or turned sour, draining away that contagious sense of expectation that had been essential to the charm and achievement of the two earlier narratives. "It ought to be a success story," Mark Krupnick complained, "but it is almost unrelieved lamentation."[37]

It is in some sense an old story—American success at the expense of spiritual heritage. "I can never forget the days of my misery," exclaimed David Levinsky, the protagonist of Abraham Cahan's novel, *The Rise of David Levinsky*, who paid for his material success in America with the loss of his Yeshiva past and his religious faith. "I cannot escape from my old self.

My past and present do not comport well." Kazin, the successful native from Jewish Brownsville, has a similar problem in *New York Jew*. He cannot return to his past (certainly not to devastated Brownsville), yet he feels that he has left an essential part of himself and that past (innocence, hope, idealism, struggle) behind. The problem is compounded by the fact that his "rise" (and that of his generation) coincided with the destruction of Europe's Jews. How to enjoy "the best of times" in the shadow of the worst of times? What can success, the enjoyment of success, possibly mean in a world where such a horror is permitted? Kazin makes no effort to answer such questions, questions that might have been helpfully elucidated, if not resolved, in a discussion of "survivor guilt," a subject he mentions and then dismissively drops. Instead, seemingly trapped in the clutches of that guilt, he repeatedly brings in the Holocaust and the historic suffering of the Jews as the defining event of the times and the measure of moral seriousness and a final check on the possibilities for happiness. "Nothing else was serious. Murder had become the first political principle. We had to recognize the abyss on whose edge we lived."[38]

The result is an autobiography combining the Horatio Alger story with a dark Jewish allegory, a morality play in which the history of Jewish persecution sets the terms for assessing behavior and character. Kazin's account of his affairs and marriages describe the moralized pattern. The affair with Mary Lou Petersen breaks up his marriage with Asya, destroys the "old invisible connections" that had tied him to family, and plunges him into bouts of loneliness and paroxysms of guilt: "I was as bad as any Nazi." His next marriage is a "businesslike" affair to a wealthy non-Jewish Jew, "Louise" (Carol Bookman). Dismissed as a "visceral infatuation," its dissolution enabled him to return to Jewish Brooklyn. Once there, closer to his Jewish roots, he wrote *A Walker in the City* and soon fell in love with "Beth" (Ann Birstein), a rabbi's daughter, who proves to be as intensely, agonizingly, and violently Jewish as himself. At this point the allegory turns toward tragedy, their turbulent marriage an emblematic reenactment of Jewish history. "Family! The dismemberment and torture of the Jewish family was a too familiar fear in our house. The further we got away from the Holocaust in time, the more it took up residence right on New York's West Side. . . . This we had in common; this we knew: for Jews the war had never ended."[39]

It is hard to know how to take this. Did Alfred honestly think his relations with Ann were driven by dark, destructive impulses out of the Jewish past? That their life together was possessed by history's demons? Journal entries about their marriage indicate that he often did, with frequent references to "ancestral nightmares," to historical forces erupting amid the daily routine, to "history seething . . . history in movement . . . history working on you." He also wondered (as noted earlier) about the "East-European, poor Jewish style of personal aggrandizement." "We feel threatened in the darkest kind of way, and we are always trying to rise straight up from every possible frustration." It is very likely that by citing the historical and sociological sources of his and Ann's difficulties, Alfred sought to account for, to find some larger reason for, the apparently hopeless nature of their situation, as though their continuing misery was in some way historically fated—"the same quarrels, the same slammed doors, the same tirades," the same "sickly futile arguments of which this marriage is now darkly composed." In the fall of 1974, suicidal and suffering from nervous exhaustion, Ann was admitted to the Payne Whitney psychiatric clinic for observation, only to return home to the same cycle of unhappiness. "I listen to her, I listen to her—there is nothing to be done—there is nothing to say any longer."[40]

One can understand why Alfred would want to find a larger historical meaning in their daily strife, something that might explain, or at least lend some significance, even a little dignity, to their terrible fights and endless unhappiness. But he also knew there were other less portentous sources of their difficulties—competing ambitions, exacerbated, he felt, by Ann's increasing interest in feminist politics—"Never yield to a mere man! So fuck you—but good!"—petty selfishness in their daily habits, and a string of adulterous affairs on his part, some of which Ann knew about, others she suspected, and which, he noted in a 1967 entry, he had no intention of ending—"Thank God for Carol and Carla and Rose and Jean, for Celia and Elsie and Sylvia and Rosalind, for Alice and Vivienne—for the other Sylvia, for Lou, Lou, Lou! Quite a party, but it's not yet over . . ." The party continued into the seventies, now largely with a married former student that concluded only with Kazin's involvement with Judith Dunford in the late seventies.[41]

Autobiographers are under no obligation to tell all about their love lives and marriages. "Don't be so eager to confess," Kazin had written while working on an early draft. "It's none of their fucking business. The secrets that I bear in my heart are my business." But, as more than one reader complained, he tells just enough to suggest concealment and evasion. He then compounds the problem by looking to a level of historical causation, "the historic in the personal," that takes too little account of precisely those personal matters—habits of inconsideration and selfishness, lack of self-control and forbearance, willfulness, recurrent acts of infidelity—that are the stuff of failed marriages and of Kazin's in particular.[42]

While Afred Kazin is the central figure in the rather grim Jewish allegory played out in *New York Jew,* various other Jewish "characters" appear as foils and exemplary instances, those who embrace and those who run from their Jewishness. Carol Bookman ("Louise") is hardly a Jew at all—"There are some Jews for whom the Jews don't exist." Saul Bellow is emphatically a Jew. "I believed in him as a novelist because, like his strength in being a Jew, *this* was his sealed treasure undamaged by his many anxieties." Lionel Trilling, by contrast, whose portrait is pointedly juxtaposed against Bellow's, has sloughed off his Jewishness and spent his life "quietly defending himself from the many things he left behind." While Bellow was direct and unpretentious, Trilling, who reportedly told Kazin, when he was editing the *New Republic,* that he wanted no assignment that did not "promote my reputation," was self-consciously elegant—"I had never encountered a Jewish intellectual so conscious of social position, so full of adopted finery in his conversation. 'I should scarcely have believed that.' "[43]

Kazin's lengthy portrait of Trilling, another non-Jewish Jew—"to be a Jew and yet not be Jewish"—is clever, mocking, and backed by years of festering resentment—for snubs, for excluding Kazin from social occasions, for keeping him out of Columbia. Not surprisingly, it provoked an outcry from Trilling's admirers, who accused Kazin of libeling the memory of an honorable man. (Trilling died in 1972.) Robert Langbaum, essentially accusing Kazin of slander, claimed that Trilling's alleged remark about his reputation would have been wholly out of character. Robert Penn Warren, in a letter to the *New York Times Book Review,* declared that after years of friendship with Trilling he had never seen any of the qualities Kazin described. The same issue included a letter calling Kazin's portrait "a grotesque misrepresentation of the truth"; it was signed by nineteen distinguished scholars and writers, a number of them Kazin's friends, including Meyer Abrams, Frank

Kermode, Arthur Schlesinger Jr., Barbara Probst Solomon, and Howard Mumford Jones. Kazin, who had expected some fallout from the Trilling portrait, was stunned by its ferocity. "I feel humiliated, devastated, etc, by this onslaught against me. . . . I knew that the Columbia acolytes would organize this demonstration against me, but I did not suspect that so many 'old friends' would join in."[44]

But he had no regrets. "There is not a single line about Trilling I would take away from the book or apologize for." He understood that the portrait was a literary creation—"the pompously respectable professor is a character in *my* imagination of society, not a person to argue with—the Jew's dream of literary England, of surpassing his servile state by culture . . . Jews as snobs, Jews as climbers." He also acknowledged the personal animus behind the portrait, his resentment of Trilling's discomfort with Jews, like himself, who were " 'too Jewish,' too full of my lower-class experience." "And what has it been all these years?" he asked himself in 1968. "Trilling cannot stand my temperament—he cannot stand the ghetto Jew in me—he cannot stand my vitality. L.T., the would-be gentleman—the little gentleman." "The simple secret of it all—social ambition and shame of the 'lower class' or too intense Jew." Kazin had been working on the Trilling portrait since the mid-sixties, determined to use his art to settle old scores, consciously mining his "inner resentments [for] the possibilities of literary use."[45]

Much as Kazin uses Bellow as a foil for Trilling, he uses the Trillings (Lionel and Diana) as a foil to introduce Hannah Arendt. After quoting from Diana Trilling's rather smug account of a "gathering of the pleasant professional sort" that occurred in their Claremont apartment, where everyone except W. H. Auden was dressed in "proper suits," Kazin describes the gatherings that occurred in Arendt's living room, not on Claremont Avenue, but in a rundown, "dark, shadowy" Morningside Drive apartment, "secured by two locks and a pole," where the recent refugee from Hitler's Europe took in a boarder to make ends meet. If the Trilling get-together reflected "a certain intellectual contentment" and "middle-class claustrophobia," the Arendt gathering reflected intellectual and moral intensity. Where the former suggested a comfortable and professional adjustment to "the abyss created in modern culture . . . by the extermination of the Jews," the latter indicated the persistent seriousness with which Arendt pursued her thinking on the sources of that disaster—interrupted only by the bor-

der's long walk down the hall and the flushing of the toilet. Unlike Lionel
Trilling, who managed "to be a Jew and yet not be Jewish," Hannah Arendt
was a "blazing Jew, working round the clock for Jewish Cultural Reconstruction from a little office in Columbus Circle."[46]

Arendt died in 1975, and Kazin's extended portrait sums up thirty years
of reflections on her life, personality, and influence. Their friendship,
which began so excitingly in the forties, had begun to wane by the middle
and late 1950s. After the disastrous ceremony at the Institute of Arts and
Letters in 1954, when Arendt had ordered Ann Birstein to the balcony,
Birstein had refused to see her socially and eventually demanded the same
from her husband. He had continued to see her, however, sneaking away to
have "tea with Heinrich and Hannah—my forbidden pleasures." He understood that Arendt could be insufferably arrogant, and he sometimes resented the "disciple" role that he felt he needed to play around her. "Hannah certainly blots out the other person, and you have to submit to her final
authority or break away." But convinced that her imperious manner was
inseparable from the originality and "self-dependence" of her genius, he
was prepared to indulge her presumptions, her "crushing authoritativeness
in relation to others," as Birstein was not. "What a visionary you are!" he
wrote her after reading and reviewing (in a 1961 issue of *Harper's*) her
collection of essays, *Between Past and Future*. "I realized with fresh plea
sure . . . how privileged I am to have known you. I think that of all the
people I have ever known, you have been the staunchest in thought, the
freest from conventional faithlessness."[47]

Two years later, in October 1963, Kazin found (or stumbled into) an
opportunity to show his regard publicly. The previous December, Arendt
had sent him a manuscript copy of *Eichmann in Jerusalem*, her reflections
on the Eichmann trial, subtitled "A Report on the Banality of Evil," in
which she accused (or seemed to accuse) Jewish leaders of collaborating
with the Nazis in the killing of the Jews. He read it and was impressed—
initially. "'The banality of evil,' the banality of it all," he noted in a journal
entry, "the fearful ominousness and incomprehension in a horrid sense the
insignificance of so much killing—as of the fearful selfishness and 'respectability' of so many Jews' behavior." He would soon discover that his was a
minority opinion, however. The publication in the spring (1964) of *Eichmann in Jerusalem* in a series of five articles in the *New Yorker*, followed

immediately by the book, ignited a firestorm of criticism. Perhaps out of "long suppressed grief," as Irving Howe later put it, or guilt for not responding earlier to the Holocaust, many New York intellectuals turned on Arendt and her book, accusing her of insensitivity to the suffering of the Jewish victims and slander of their leaders. Norman Podhoretz, in one of the more moderate responses, accused her of brilliant "perversity." Lionel Abel said that Adolf Eichmann "comes off much better in her book than do his victims." Irving Howe wrote that Gentiles reading Arendt's essays in the *New Yorker* would "learn" that had "the Jews not 'cooperated' with the Nazis," fewer would have been killed. Arendt was in Europe when the storm broke. "Many phone calls are flooding in for you," Heinrich Bluecher wrote her, "you should be glad you are not here."[48]

Feeling the issue needed further airing, Howe organized a public forum in early October at the Woodstock Hotel, where people were invited to share their views. More than three hundred packed into the room, and the tension was high. Lionel Abel and Marie Syrkin, a Zionist official, spoke against Arendt's book; Daniel Bell and the historian Raul Hilberg tried to represent Arendt's views. (Although in the city at the time, she did not attend.) The meeting was tumultuous, with many in the audience, including Holocaust survivors, joining in the attack. Vladka Meed, a hero from the Warsaw ghetto uprising, denounced Arendt's views in Yiddish as Howe translated for the audience. As the meeting wound down, Kazin, who had entered the hall late, walked to the podium and, according to Theodore Solotaroff, who was in the room, remarked: " 'That's enough, Irving. This disgraceful piling on has got to stop.' Something like that." Kazin then said a few things about "the distinction of her thought and the complexity of the book and walked out."[49]

Though Kazin would later be complimented for his courage, he took little satisfaction in his performance. He had walked over to the hotel with Stuart Hughes after an *American Scholar* dinner, and "under the influence of two quick martinis" had "intervened in a way that makes me feel like an utter fool." "I was so irritated with Irving Howe's attack on Hannah," he wrote in a journal entry at the time, "that I triggered, absolutely gushed out like a cut artery." He was particularly irritated that Howe and Abel, who, he felt, had never shown much interest in the Jews or their destruction, were now all afire in indignation at Arendt, who had long been preoccupied with

Jewish matters. He did not regret having spoken up but thought he had expressed himself badly. "I feel ashamed at having been so obviously confused. I was defending Hannah personally." His confusion may have come from the two martinis, but it may also have come from second thoughts about the book. He told Stanley Plastrik a year later that he did not "like the way in which HA's thesis expresses itself," that it showed an "involuntary haughtiness toward people who were in a bind." He also complained that its "total effect is to turn the disaster into a philosophical case, an idealistic abstraction." But he added, "this doesn't permit us to say that she blames the Jews for not resisting. She never brought this question up."[50]

Although their friendship had lapsed some years before her death, Kazin remembered Arendt as his most valued European "instructor," and while the friendship lasted, the most insistent and devoted of friends. "I had never met a woman so reflective, yet so eager and gifted for friendship." Learning of her death on December 4, 1975, his first reaction was that he "had been struck from behind," followed by the "overwhelming thought that the serious people are gone, have gone, are going one by one."[51]

Most of the portraits in *New York Jew* are of writers and public figures. But, following the pattern of the two earlier autobiographies, Kazin reserves space for family members—an imaginary sketch of his grandfather, Abraham, who died in his twenties, his body flung into an unmarked grave, and an extended portrait of his orphaned father, who died unnoticed, silent in the Brooklyn nursing home, as isolated in death as he was in life. In a book on "the golden age of the Jews," the portraits of his father and grandfather look back to beginnings, mark the changes over two generations, and suggest the familial source of Kazin's Jewish consciousness—"somewhere I had come to believe that Jew and my family were identical." They also indicate one of his reasons for writing the book. "Jews are supposed to bear witness," he explains in "Words," the book's first chapter, "to give meaning to their historic existence as Jews, to lift the curse of the word 'Jew' and turn it into a blessing." Kazin saw himself bearing witness in these portraits—rescuing from obscurity those who lacked the words to speak for themselves. "What breaks my heart is how little they mean to anyone," he had written of his family and old Brownsville friends in a 1957 journal entry. "Their lives are utterly wrapped in silence. If I were not here writing, as I always do . . . what would it all come to? . . . The dark street—and suddenly it's nothing. The dying fall, the voice unheard, the deadness of the dead."

Composing portraits of parents and grandparents, he was shining a light once again into the darkened street, completing the family picture he had begun in *A Walker in the City*—a picture just visible amid the glittering Jewish "successes," reaffirming "the old invisible connections" to family and past, "those great dark years instilled in me before I was born." In this area, if in few others, Kazin's book does achieve a measure of "salvation."[52]

The publication of *New York Jew* in early May 1978 created a stir. A front-page essay, "Literary Ids and Egos," in the *New York Times Book Review* by Mordecai Richler hinted at a succès de scandale: a behind-the-scenes look into New York's cultural salons exposing the literati for "the self-serving rascals" they are. Alfred Kazin, "the somewhat bruised survivor of literary and marital wars," dishes the dirt on Saul Bellow, Henry Luce, Lionel Trilling, and other greats and near-greats with "illuminating anecdotes" describing behavior "unacceptable at a children's party." Though disgusted with "the shallowness and smartyness" of the Richler review, Kazin was not unhappy with the publicity and was pleased to appear on the *Dick Cavett Show*, where the interest, presumably, was less about his spiritual journey than about the unruly behavior of the writer-celebrities he had known.[53]

The reviews that followed in the journals were more serious, but also more critical. Virtually everyone found the book entertaining and informative about an important aspect of the nation's culture. Most praised the portraits. But they also expressed bewilderment about the narrator. Robert Alter (*Commentary*), who thought it the most interesting of Kazin's autobiographies, said that he would have done better to keep himself and his personal life out of it. Others (Earl Rovit, the *Nation;* Philip French, the *New Statesman*) complained that Kazin, who had every reason to rejoice in his life and career, represented himself as too much the "beaten man" and eternal sufferer. Mark Krupnick, who had recently published a biography of Lionel Trilling, described the book as "a work of wounded vanity." "Kazin, the avenger," he wrote in *Salmagundi,* "has a lot of scores to settle with 'refined' Jews whose very existence he appears to have experienced as a slight." John Lahr (*Harper's*), in what Kazin called "one of the most abusive reviews I've ever had," declared *New York Jew* the creation of a cultural "con man" and "symptomatic of an attenuated modern America where hype is fast replacing history."[54]

Although surprised by the "onslaught" from the Trilling "acolytes," and disappointed that the reviewers were "all for my writer-characters" with "barely a crumb for me," Kazin took most of the criticism in stride. Indeed, he did not wholly disagree with it. "The truth is that I cannot bear to look at *New York Jew*," he wrote a year after its publication. "It all seems to me such a series of reactions to (a series of 'provoking' people, Ann being last in the series and somehow the sum of them all) . . . I look at the book now and wail to myself, where am I, where is my mind, my strong and immortal self? Like the 'Jewish tragedy,' the war in which this book was born— reaction to, flight from, complaint against, instead of some sweet, strong, solitary affirmation—or as old Walt says, 'assurances.' "[55]

CHAPTER ELEVEN

A New Life
1978–1984

Neue Liebe, neues Leben.

—Goethe

I feel like Ulysses transported in his sleep," Alfred Kazin wrote in his notebook in May 1978. "Something mysterious happened this year; something decisive beyond words, clearing up my life, putting familiar things in unfamiliar places and making the unfamiliar more and more *intimate.*" He had reason to feel something had happened. It had been a year of change and a culmination of earlier changes that would bring more changes. Of course, people in their sixties (Kazin would be sixty-two in June) do not make wholly new lives for themselves. And for someone forever reliving, rethinking, rewriting the past, a new life inevitably entailed negotiating with the old. A good deal of renegotiation and reconsideration had already taken place in the writing of *New York Jew.* A similar process was under way with his next book, *An American Procession,* which he finished in the summer of 1983. Begun well before the much-postponed *New York Jew,* it too represented a final (and not wholly satisfactory) working out of a project long delayed by difficulties and diversions. Kazin would later describe this period, which began in California, the land of "God's second chance," as the start of a "new life," one he had not dared to hope for. But it could just as well be described as a period of relief—relief that the past was not conclusive, that one could move beyond the unfinished and the seemingly intractable. That there was a price for moving on, in unresolved difficulties and hurt feelings, would become apparent in time; but it was a price that he was more than willing to pay.[1]

California

If some mysterious and decisive things happened in 1977–1978, they were not unprepared for. Kazin had set the stage for change. Earlier in the year, he had applied for and received a grant from the National Endowment for the Humanities that would free him from teaching to work on his book on nineteenth-century American literature. He had also applied for and accepted a position as Senior Fellow at the Center for Advanced Studies in Behavioral Sciences at Stanford University for the 1977–1978 school year. For the following academic year he had accepted the William White visiting professorship at Notre Dame. Beyond that he was unsure. He had expressed some interest in an endowed chair at Stanford, but he was not at this point prepared to relinquish his position at CUNY. In anticipation of these changes, he and Ann Birstein had decided to give up their apartment on West End Avenue, to put books and furniture in storage. If and when they did return to the city, they would look into something smaller, possibly on the East Side. With Kate no longer at home, they did not need such a large apartment. And they both had grown weary of the dirt and disorder of the Upper West Side.

Not all the changes in Kazin's immediate future were planned, however though he later wondered whether God might have been in on the plotting. On April 30, 1977, he had received a phone call from a Judith Dunford, asking if she could return a picture from Kazin's friend Francis Steegmuller. Kazin had bought the picture, painted by Bea Stein, Steegmuller's former wife, but had returned it when she died, thinking that Steegmuller might want it as a remembrance. When he later learned that instead of keeping the picture Steegmuller had passed it on to Bea Stein's nephew, he asked for it back. The nephew agreed, but en route to Kazin's apartment, the nephew's car had broken down—opposite the Citicorp office of Judith Dunford, an old acquaintance from Yale, whom he asked to return the picture. Kazin remembered the call:

> just a little nervous but with the most charming voice in the world. . . . Could she just possibly bring the picture over to me. . . . Could she? Would she?
> Yes, there is a God.[2]

The actual meeting would be a delayed a few days, however, as Dunford put herself through a brief refresher course on Kazin's writings. In 1954, she had heard him lecture in Northampton on the sorry state of contemporary fiction. The lecture and the lecturer had made a powerful impression. An English major on scholarship at Mount Holyoke, Judith Dunford, née Schwartz, a graduate of the Bronx High School of Science, remembers being "swept away," "overwhelmed," by the brilliant, handsome lecturer. Returning the painting meant a chance to meet the man whose image had remained vividly in her imagination for more than twenty years. After her refresher course, she arrived at Kazin's with the painting. The meeting went well—she, recounting the Smith lecture, he, charmed by the evident intelligence, wit, and manner of this longtime admirer. The meeting led to more meetings, as they came quickly to realize that they had more in common than literary interests.[3]

At another time, the meeting with Judith might have led nowhere or perhaps to another transitory affair. Alfred, however, in plotting his open-ended future, was looking for more than an escape from New York. Relations with Ann had been reaching new lows. Periods of open hostility no longer led to the intense reconciliations of the past, but to resentful silence, fresh hostilities, and occasional bouts of physical violence on both sides. Alfred had given up hope that the situation would change and felt shamed by what the continuing hostilities were doing to him. "Why and how did I sacrifice my dignity like this? Why and how did I allow myself to become this bawling, brawling contestant—where and how did I slip back like this?" But neither of them was yet willing to end the marriage. They had invested too much in it—too many years, too much hope, too much passion, even too much anger. Perhaps what was needed was a change, a period of separation in new circumstances—something that would end the daily battles and give them time and space to reflect on what they meant to each other, whether the marriage was worth salvaging—and, in Alfred's case, whether Judith might have some answers. Getting away from New York for an extended period might be the solution, or the first step toward a solution. Ann could remain behind in New York for a time, then, if she chose, join him in California, which was, after all, a land of fresh starts. Would she be willing to join him in South Bend, Indiana, the following year? That was another question to be answered when the time came.[4]

In early August, Alfred left by himself for Stanford, happily vague about the future—with Ann, without Ann, with or without Judith. For the moment, he enjoyed the luxury of not having to decide. Did not the allure of California lie in its suggestion of the possible? Kazin had always been attracted to California. Addressing Hillel groups, he sometimes referred to it as "Israel without Arabs." "The dryness and dustiness of the place seemed to say that life was wide open. Everything was possible." But if the California prospect of an open-ended future was exhilarating, it did not suggest a frame of mind conducive to the hard work and commitment necessary to save a troubled marriage. That Alfred and Judith were soon exchanging letters regularly showed even less determination to make the marriage work.[5]

Ann joined her husband in the middle of September, somewhat to his surprise: "But Ann again! My perpetually angry wife." And for a time, a very short time, it seemed things might work out. Alfred remembers being astonished by her arrival, which, combined with the "beauty and convenience" of their apartment made him wonder whether a new life might just be possible for them in California. But within a few days, the old battles resumed, and with them "a dreariness and grief beyond description. . . . I have absolutely nowhere to go. I am numb." Literally speaking, he did have somewhere to go. He (unlike Ann) could climb the hill every day to his office at the center to work on his next article for *Esquire* (with which he had recently negotiated a year's contract), read for his book, talk to interesting people in the corridors, go to lectures, participate in the seminars. "The intellectual heat of the place is mounting at a dizzying pace," he wrote to Judith, "lectures, seminars all over the place on language-bound and language-optional, social biology, independent variables, etc. I listen with open mouth and occasionally understand what is said . . . It is exciting to put together political 'scientists' with (God save the mark) Cornell medicos, smart ass young lawyers." What most impressed him (for the moment) was the "objectivity" that he saw in the attitude of his colleagues—a "professional rationality" that seemed the farthest thing from the oppressive "subjectivity" that awaited him back home. "How wonderful it is to let the mind do its own thing."[6]

Ann had fewer resources, fewer places to go. She was unsure of just why she had come to California, but suspected it was partly out of fear that her husband had found a new lover and that this one "means trouble." Now that she was there, she could only watch as he went off daily to his "prestigious paradise on the hill," leaving her "behind in the lowlands without any reason for being." She felt that she was back in Amherst. Unhappy with this arrangement, Ann insisted to officials at the center that she, too, be given an office where she could work on *her* book—a request that was soon granted but that did little to relieve her unhappiness. Meanwhile, life in the apartment was becoming unbearable. The screams and shouts were disturbing the neighbors and alarming the landlord. Alfred reported to Judith that one evening in late October Ann created a "big suicide drama that ended up with the police in our bedroom demanding that I commit her or 'accept the responsibility.'" In a later letter he wrote that "the domestic news has been so bad, so far-out, so full of cops and possible ambulances and screams in the middle of the night and now two psychiatrists, that I have learned to hold my peace, am no longer fighting." Ann recalled things differently: "Alfred was shouting and carrying on so loudly that complaints from the neighbors caused our landlord to ask him to leave our apartment." Regardless of who was making the most noise, he moved into a motel room.[7]

In early December, Kazin flew (alone) to New York. There he attended a luncheon of the National Institute; had pictures taken for the cover of *New York Jew;* talked with his editor, Robert Gottlieb, about his nineteenth-century book; and ate meals with his daughter, Kate, just in from Cornell, where she was pursuing a Ph.D. in English. He stayed in his flat on Fourteenth Street and saw a good deal of Judith. On December 11, while walking on Sixth Avenue, he slipped and fell on an icy sidewalk, breaking his left shoulder. The break was serious and required two successive operations and a week's stay in St. Vincent's Hospital. Judith joked that with his left arm out of commissioner, Alfred had "finally become a right-winger!"[8]

When he returned to California the second week of January, it was to live alone. Ann remained in their old apartment, and he moved into an apartment complex on Oak Creek Drive—complete with a whirlpool for his sore shoulder. He felt like a survivor, "the field littered with corpses." With no plan for resolving their differences, he and Ann remained in a holding pattern. This ended on February 7, when, showing up at an arranged meeting at his apartment, she declared the marriage over with a resounding kick to the door and a loud "Drop dead!" Ann would stay on at Stanford for another month before returning to New York. Her immediate situation was difficult and frightening. She had not lived alone since her student days in Paris. She had no job, no apartment, and little experience dealing with money, taxes, and apartments. "There I was, a good Jewish girl, member of a huge family, rabbi's daughter," estranged wife of an "eminent literary critic in the center of an eminent literary circle, now outside any circle at all." She did in time find an apartment and reach a financial settlement with Alfred, while picking up jobs at City College and Barnard teaching creative writing. She would not remarry.[9]

In the years after his and Ann's separation and divorce, Alfred would occasionally reflect on the "terrible turbulence" in her behavior that seemed to culminate in a paroxysm of self-destruction during the year in California. One scene in particular held him. Several nights after the "Drop dead" message, he had been awakened by a call from a friend saying that Ann had just been in an accident. He rushed to the site and found her car smashed into an abutment and Ann drunk, standing outside the car—"the black cop smiling thinly at me." "What was it about California, God's second chance," he wondered, "that drove her more into herself instead of giving her a sudden sense of space and the great wild openness that I saw [and felt] careening along Route 1, gyrating, floating and flying? The 'new life' in the West (the new land for us old city bodies) turned out to be a form of death." This obtuse reflection, celebrating the California myth of new beginnings, indicates how little Alfred understood (or would let himself understand) the pressures under which Ann was then living and how their daily battles of wills had led to such desperate behavior. Where he had seen California opening to a "new life" that might well include Judith, Ann had seen her life with Alfred closing in—for the last time. She had felt threatened before, particularly by his many infidelities, and had responded dramatically, angrily, out of an intensity of helpless feeling that he had found disturbing, but also "dazzling" and "irresistible"—"the girl who is either on your neck or at your feet—the girl whose powerlessness has been such a power over me." But by the fall of 1977, Ann's helplessness was losing its power to move him. Exhausted by the intensity of her "implacable subjectivity," and seeing in Judith a possible way out of this enervating emotional cycle, he had not only grown resistant to his wife's increasingly desperate cries for help, but had come to regard them as evidence of the need to free himself once and for all from their hold on him. It was not California that drove Ann into herself but the terrible logic of their imploding relationship.[10]

Ann's departure, whatever fear and pain it caused her, brought Alfred

considerable relief. Her presence at the center had been a source of awkwardness and embarrassment. Never loath to express her feelings in public
and often in graphic and startling ways, she had made it clear from the
outset that she would not tolerate treatment that placed her in a position
second to her husband—or to men generally. With Ann back in New York,
Alfred could enter somewhat more easily into the social-intellectual life of
the community. But if he was more comfortable socially, he was increasingly impatient intellectually. The "professionalism" and "objectivity" that
had originally attracted him (as a respite to Ann's subjectivity) struck him
now as a form of power politics played by specialists. "Knowledge is power
here," he wrote in his journal. "Specialization is even more power; pride in
knowing how much smarter you are than the others is the final power." He
would later complain to the center's directors that he had often felt intellectually lonely at the meetings and presentations. He was, he explained, "an
old fashioned 'intellectual' interested in many things at once . . . apt to
make connections, to guess at them, positively to 'see' them without elaborate formal evidence on every point." Though initially impressed by the
"abstractions" of the scientists and social scientists, he now found their
presentations "disappointing, timid, overspecialised, and even, unwittingly
condescending." In contrast, he found the discussions at meals and informal gatherings lively and exciting. And he was not above boasting to Judith
Dunford that, given his brazen readiness to talk on all subjects, making
connections at will, his public presentations were received with enthusiasm
and obvious relief.[11]

What most interested Kazin about the center at this point were the
fellows with whom he had developed personal and intellectual relations.
Two were in literature: Houston Baker, a rising star in African-American
studies, and Sacvan Bercovitch, an authority on Puritan writing. Another
fellow with whom he had developed a relationship was the famous pedi-
atric hematologist, Louis Diamond. One surprising discovery was Ruth
Bader Ginsburg from the Columbia Law School, "who looks like a 19th
century Jewish maiden in a tintype, but is studiously solemn and boring."
Initially put off by her prim appearance and manners, he came to appreciate (as others would later) her implacable resistance to arguments of the
brilliant right-wing lawyers. "Ruth Bader Ginsburg sits delicately eating
her salad and expressing displeasure? outrage? boredom? You would never

know anything just looking at a face." When at one point she opened up to Kazin at a "bagel breakfast," he listened with surprised, half-ironic admiration. "Turns out she is quite a revolutionary: the woman's movement is the *only* one that . . . is likely to change anything just now."[12]

The friendship made at the center that meant the most to Kazin was with Yaron Ezrahi. A young lecturer at the Hebrew University in Jerusalem, Ezrahi was both a sophisticated political theorist and a rising spokesman for the Israeli liberal left. He shared many of Kazin's reservations about Israeli nationalism and militarism, as well as his ambivalence about the goals and consequences of Zionism. Kazin, who sometimes felt an apostate among Israelis for his uncertain attitude about Israel, was gratified to find his uncertainties shared by a respected Israeli political scientist. However, it was autobiography and journal keeping that formed the most frequent topic of conversation between them. Ezrahi saw in autobiography's insistence on the centrality of the self a value largely missing from the consciousness of a nation such as Israel formed under the pressure of repeated historical crises. In his quasi-autobiographical book on Israeli politics, *Rubber Bullets,* he argues that a belief in the intrinsic worth of the self, fostered by autobiography, can be a healthy corrective to the collectivist thinking of Israelis; and he credits Kazin for disclosing how autobiography can be used to critique contemporary society. The two men would stay in touch until Kazin's death in 1998, Ezrahi offering inside observations on tendencies in Israeli politics, and Kazin, his reflections on the political mood in America.[13]

In early May, Kazin returned to New York for a short visit to mark the publication of *New York Jew.* Promotional activities included an appearance on the *Dick Cavett Show* and a book signing—"old cousins, young cousins . . . a reunion of people I never knew before." The most difficult part of the trip was a weekend visit to Ithaca to discuss his and Ann's separation with his daughter and to tell her about Judith. Kate knew of her parents' separation. She and her father had talked over the escalating difficulties in the marriage when he was in New York in December, and they had exchanged phone calls and letters since. Still, Alfred was anxious. He worried about her response to "the unraveling of everything in our lives." The phone conversations had not relieved his concern. "I could not help noticing," he remarked after one call, that "her voice is pitched terribly high . . . a lot of tension there! But she has an understanding and loving heart. I feel much sustained. I still have a family." The visit, however, was not reassuring.[14]

Kate remembers being bewildered by it. "It was like he came on some mission, but I didn't know what the mission was." He talked about Ann and what would become of her. He finally mentioned Judith, and very quickly the conversation became awkward and tense. "Well, she's wonderful," Kate recalls him saying, "and she keeps me from straying off the reservation." This struck Kate as an odd way of putting it. After all, the relationship with Judith *was* straying off the reservation. And did he really expect her to sanction his philandering? "There was this man saying, basically, I can't keep my trousers zipped, and wanting his daughter to . . . I don't know what." Alfred's account also indicates that the meeting (or mission) was not very satisfying. Indeed, the entire trip to Cornell depressed him—Kate's "stony independence" and the "claustrophobia" of the rural campus, suggesting what he faced at "Our Lady at South Bend."[15]

That he was depressed by Kate's "stony" response was not surprising. Kate had known for a long time, as long as she could remember, that her parents' marriage was chronically troubled. She recalls that while still a child she became convinced that "these two people should not be living together." She had witnessed the verbal abuse—they "would say anything to each other"—and had seen and heard it escalate into physical abuse. She also understood that matters had become worse since she had gone to college and graduate school. But if Kate had witnessed much over the years, she had rarely complained. Kazin often regarded her as the strangely peaceful center of an ongoing family war. At one point when relations seemed to be unraveling, he had credited her with being the "seamstress of the family [like his mother] who sooner or later sews everything into a pattern on the thread of herself." She had always excelled academically. Indeed, she seemed to fulfill in every way the high hopes her parents cherished for her—not only attending Smith, but writing her honors thesis on George Herbert, her father's favorite poet from his undergraduate days. In sum, Kate was talented, accomplished, and had shown every sign of having "an understanding and loving heart"; she seemed to want nothing more than happiness for her battling parents. That she now seemed unwilling to sanction their separation and Alfred's apparent decision to build a new life with Judith was unsettling. Not only did it not augur well for the future, it raised troubling questions about the long-term consequences of his and Ann's behavior. Perhaps the past was not so easily left in the past. It seemed a new life might entail some unexpected costs.[16]

Kazin returned to Stanford after his week in New York anxious and upset. The reviews of *New York Jew* had not been what he had wanted, and he worried there would be worse to come. (The "onslaught" from the Trilling "acolytes" would not arrive until June.) The incident with Kate had been deeply unnerving. He had hoped desperately that she would approve of his relationship with Judith Dunford, and she clearly had not. Finally, there was the nagging question of how far along he was on his book—the reason for his tenure at the center and for receiving an NEH grant. He was more determined than ever to write it. In March, Knopf had offered him a contract for the completed manuscript on terms similar to those for *New York Jew* (thirty-five thousand dollars). But the completion date seemed farther off than ever. In a July 5 statement of progress to the center, Kazin wrote that the scope of the book had expanded significantly since he arrived, that he would need several years to finish. Journal entries at the time proliferate with fresh plans and ideas: "The key to RWE is . . ." "I can finally see what this is about . . ." "The agonizing question behind the book . . . " What they do not indicate is much progress in the actual writing. There would be time for that in "claustrophobic" South Bend.[17]

Alfred left Stanford at the end of July, returning to New York and his Fourteenth Street flat. He had been phoning Judith every day since his May return, and she had flown to California during his last days there. He had come to depend heavily on her. Indeed, considering his terror of loneliness, one doubts he would have been prepared for the final break with Ann had Judith not been there to offer comfort and hope for the future. For the moment, however, that future remained murky.

Eighteen years his junior, married with three children, Judith was also trapped in an unhappy marriage. She had wanted out of the marriage with Nelson Dunford for some time—with or without Alfred Kazin. By the summer of 1978, she was searching for a suitable apartment. She was also looking to Alfred for some kind of commitment. He, however, was uncertain—about himself, not about Judith. Judith seemed in every way the ideal lover and companion. After the collapse of his marriage with Carol, Alfred had determined never to involve himself in a serious relationship with someone uninterested in writing. He told Ann more than once that he couldn't love her unless she was a writer, and he repeated the same to Judith. Judith was both a writer and an ardent reader. (Alfred complained unfairly that Ann was the only writer he knew who never read anything.) After graduating with honors from Mount Holyoke in 1955, Judith had entered Yale's English graduate program but had dropped out to marry and raise three children. She had retained her literary interests, however, writing reviews and essays for *Newsday* and even ghost-writing a novel (under a pseudonym). Alfred was constantly amazed at the breadth of her reading, her critical insight and retentiveness. Yet, for all her evident intelligence, she remained incurably "modest" and unassuming. Compared with the ambitious, ever competitive Ann, who reportedly said that she had published more than her husband if you removed the quotations from his books, Judith was "so non-pushing" as to be "a truly religious lesson" to him.[18]

Like Alfred Kazin, Judith (Schwartz) Dunford was the child of immigrant Jews. Her father, Ignatz (Harry) Schwartz, immigrated from the Hungarian-Romanian border in 1923 and settled in the "fur" area of the Bronx, where he had worked as a "cutter." Her mother, Hedvig Kurzbart, came from Silesia. Born August 23, 1933, Judith grew up in the East Bronx, a twenty-minute walk from the Bronx Zoo at Southern Boulevard and 174th Street. She remembers family life as warm, happy, and supportive—though she sometimes felt she was living in the shadow of her brilliant older brother, Jacob, who became a mathematics professor at New York University. Unlike Alfred's parents, both of Judith's parents spoke and wrote fluent English (her mother had taught English in Silesia); they were also more integrated into American life than his. Alfred jokingly called his and Judith's a "mixed marriage"—she from the relatively upscale blue-collar East Bronx, he from "darkest Brownsville." Judith attended the prestigious Bronx School of Science and in 1950 was awarded a scholarship to attend Mount Holyoke—after members of the Mount Holyoke awards committee visited their third-floor walk-up apartment to check on her financial "need." She graduated from Mount Holyoke in 1955, Phi Beta Kappa, magna cum laude, and winner of the senior essay prize. Kazin liked to refer to her and Emily Dickinson (also a star pupil at Mount Holyoke) as fellow alumnae, his "Mount Holyoke girls," and to her occasional shyness and sense of propriety as "Dickinson redivus: Mt. Holyoke to the letter."[19]

Whatever genteel characteristics he felt Judith shared with Emily Dick-

inson, Alfred had no reservations about her emotional and sexual warmth.
He, however, was uncertain about himself and anxious that Judith was
anticipating too much too soon. Earlier in the year when the separation
with Ann appeared inevitable and Judith was enquiring about the future,
he wrote that his feelings were much too unsettled to make any long-term
plans or to look for a way out of his year at Notre Dame. He noted his
"wavering moods," his "anxiety" about committing himself to a close relationship. By the summer he was surer than ever that Judith would be a part
of his future. Still, he insisted on taking things slowly. He had made mis-
takes in the past and was determined not to make them again. Fortunately,
he had other commitments that deferred difficult decisions to the future
and gave him a chance to think, to gain perspective on his new life. In
August he embarked (by himself) on a two-week lecture tour in the Far
East, a trip that took him to Japan, Singapore, and New Zealand. Immediately on his return, he flew to South Bend, Indiana.[20]

"How the hell could you live there?" Kazin's friend Lucy Dawidowicz
had asked when she learned he would be spending a year at Notre Dame.
Kazin had worried about this himself. Stuck in the middle of the Indiana
cornfields, South Bend seemed even more isolated ("claustrophobic") than
Cornell in Ithaca, New York. He was not unhappy, however. He had accepted the White professorship when he desperately needed a break from
Ann (whom he was virtually certain would not join him in South Bend). He
now saw it as a valuable respite from all immediate emotional commitments and an opportunity to make progress on his book—a spiritual and
emotional retreat within the monastery walls. "I just want to be alone
forever and do my work," he had written to Judith from Stanford, exasperated that he was spending so much time and energy dealing with Ann. "I do
like things to be peaceful, the peaceable kingdom." At Notre Dame, he had
all three—time, solitude, and peace. The fact that his apartment faced a
graveyard made the solitude and quiet palpable. "I not only live next to the
cemetery, but life here is so quiet and oh so private! That I sometimes feel I
am living in it."[21]

Kazin did take frequent trips away from South Bend. In October, he
lectured on Isaac Bashevis Singer in Montreal. He attended a lunch and
conference at the University of Chicago with James E. Miller, Wayne
Booth, and Richard Stern. In January he participated in an "executive

seminar" on American literature and history in Washington, D.C., and in April, he delivered the Joseph Warren Beach Memorial Lecture at the University of Minnesota, preceded by an exhilarating discussion with some students—"marvelous students . . . reminded me of that farm boy, Hansen, in my Whitman seminar in 1946 at Minneapolis." Less exhilarating was a lunch in Evanston, Illinois, with Joseph Epstein, the editor of the *American Scholar*. Kazin was unhappy with the rightward direction that Epstein was taking the magazine on whose editorial board he had once served. He expressed his misgivings about the magazine and about Epstein's friend, Hilton Kramer. Kazin described the meeting as "boring"; Epstein remembers it as thoroughly unpleasant. It was a prelude of things to come.[22]

In May, Kazin met Saul Bellow for lunch at the Chicago Arts Club. Hearing that his estranged friend was teaching only seventy miles away, Bellow thought it might be nice if they could move beyond the acrimony that had risen out of Kazin's review of *Mr. Sammler's Planet*. Bellow had broken off relations after the review, and a hurt Kazin had made matters worse when he accused Bellow of not being able to take the slightest criticism and of using the review to throw over a long friendship. "When, oh when, will this monstrous self-love, manic protectiveness, whatever it is, have an end? I don't miss our friendship, hysterical as you were in ending it," he wrote to Bellow in 1974. "But I do resent these insults, and I am grieved by their human stupidity, for in point of fact, no critic has done your work more honor or has written about you with more sympathetic understanding." Reluctant to let the relationship die on that note, Bellow suggested that there might be "something or other to talk about" that would not open old wounds. That he had recently won the Nobel Prize for literature seemed to offer a subject sufficiently interesting and elevated to avoid the traps and sinkholes of past troubles. And indeed, the lunch in Chicago went well: "Saul, quiet, very cordial, elegant and precise in his speech and manner. Struck by the difference that the years do *not* make. Sad in a reserved kind of way. Puts things unmistakably without emphasis. The waiters all bowing to him. O Mr. Bellow. I asked him what Stockholm was like. He quoted Gregory—'I know St. Peters is the largest thing of its kind but I want to get out of it.'" "I do understand his difficulty in enlarging himself all the way. And I guess the whole quarter of a million, or whatever it is, went to *her* lawyers." (Bellow was recently divorced.) If there was no returning to the easy intimacy of their youthful years, they could, at least, be civil with each other.[23]

In mid-August, his stint at Notre Dame finished, Alfred returned to New York, dividing his time between his Fourteenth Street flat and Judith's apartment on Columbus Avenue. In January 1980, he gave up the flat—a signal event. He had been renting it since the early sixties, and it had become an important part of his life—a place for play as well as work. Ann remembers it from one of her rare visits as squalid. She could not imagine how he worked there. But it had served Kazin's purposes. He would later remember it in his dreams—a room that was "truly 'my own,'" a room where "I used to meet little —— and Gracious Case and how many other ladies." To give *that* up did, indeed, indicate the start of a new life. He wept when he moved out: "It is hard for me to give up *anything*."[24]

"In New York I Live My Own Life Over and Over"

Alfred would later look back somewhat mistily on his return to New York in the summer of 1979. He was "finding life new and calling it blessed." What made it new, of course, was Judith, "neue Liebe, neues Leben." With Judith, he could see the city with fresh eyes, make adjustments, overlook old disgusts and outrages. He had left New York in the summer of 1977, determined never again to live on the Upper West Side. On this, he and Ann had had no quarrel. They were done with the dirt, the reeling drunks, the carnage of the battered and fallen, the perpetual aura of threat. Now, two years later, after picking his way among the prostrate bodies and over-turned garbage cans on upper Broadway, he was home again, not in the sprawling suite of rooms he and Ann had on West End Avenue but in a cramped one-bedroom apartment on Columbus Avenue. "Lovers cannot choose the site of the romance."[25]

After the graveside watch in South Bend, the move back to the city had been a shock. "Bang, bang, bang," he wrote on his return. "I already feel poisoned by the fumes everywhere and tired of the enemy faces." Judith, however, made everything different. After a day of teaching, Alfred could return home to easy conversation with someone who wanted to listen and talk, not fight. And he could go out and be reminded once again what a strange, wonderful place New York was. In what other American city, he asked in a 1981 commencement address at the City University Graduate Center, would you find a crowd queuing up on a cold Sunday morning for a five-hour German film on Mozart's childhood? Where else, he asked privately in his journal, would you find such types in the audience—"Crazy old people, marooned in their loneliness on Sunday." One "weirdy" behind Judith asked for some of her candy. In fact, the New York to which Kazin returned in the summer of '78 was both new and old—the new, forever leading back to the old, to walks, neighborhoods, buildings, as well as to friends, enemies, friends-turned-enemies. "In New York, I live my own life over and over." The old, in turn, kept turning into the new. A familiar street opens onto a vista of Central Park never noticed before and notably enhanced by "the beauty of the young girl most unconsciously arching her back as she walks." A class on Henry Adams comes suddenly to life. "Nothing like these left-over young New York intellectuals for getting into the heart of the intellectual mystery." After South Bend, the Graduate Center, so much a part of Kazin's past life, could seem a brave new world all over again, an "extraordinary concentration of higher learning . . . surrounded by refugees from every tyranny on earth," he remarked in the commencement address.[26]

One effect of this movement between the old and the new, each leading to the other, was to throw the past and the future into new and startling relief—a recurrent experience provoked in large part by his new life with Judith. But there were other changes to similar effect. On August 24, 1980, Alfred attended the wedding of Michael Kazin and Beth Horowitz.

After his tumultuous junior year (1968–1969), Michael had dropped out of Harvard. With the war escalating, continuing with his studies seemed out of the question. In the summer of 1969, he joined the Weathermen faction of SDS but pulled out in the fall, thinking that "this so called 'National Action,' or 'Days of Rage'" could well prove "suicidal." Though he largely agreed with the SDS analysis of the situation, "if you could call it that," he was not ready to die, which seemed an increasing likely possibility for the more militant Weathermen. He continued to write propaganda for SDS, including a booklet that was handed out on the streets of Boston titled "Red Army Marches on Chicago," but he no longer considered himself one of the cadre. After a brief expedition to Cuba to cut sugarcane with the workers, he moved to Portland, Oregon, where, like many other dis-

affected radicals, he joined a commune. In the winter of 1970, he returned
to Harvard and resumed his political activism, this time against a think tank
established by Henry Kissinger to involve faculty and graduate students in
State Department and Pentagon policy planning. The action led to his
being officially "severed" from the university for a year. In the winter of
1972, he returned once again, took courses in Marxism, radicalism, Socialism, and society—"You could do pretty much what you wanted to do"—and
graduated in the spring with a degree in social studies.[27]

Back in Portland, he enrolled in Portland State University to pursue a
master's degree in history, but he was uncertain about the future. "I still
saw myself primarily as an activist or organizer, a revolutionary. I didn't
want to forestall the possibility of things getting hot and heavy again."
While pursuing his degree, he worked as a short-order cook and ran a tape
library. Partly, he needed the money; partly, he believed it was better to be
a worker than to be an intellectual—though he found the work boring.
After receiving an M.A. in 1975, he moved to San Francisco, where he
wrote for and edited two radical newspapers, *In These Times* and the
Socialist Review. But he was increasingly convinced that he wanted a Ph.D.
and in 1977 was accepted by Stanford to pursue a doctorate in history.
There, he met Beth Horowitz, a pre-med student from Hillsdale, New
Jersey, only a few miles from Tenafly, where Michael had grown up.[28]

Michael and his father had kept in touch during these years—through
phone calls, letters, and an occasional visit. Relations between them remained unsettled, however. On one visit to Portland, Alfred had grumbled
over Michael's living arrangements, complaining, much to his son's irritation, that his companions were "losers." Yet he had sat at the kitchen table
and read straight through Michael's recently completed master's thesis and
declared it not at all bad. He was, in fact, delighted that Michael could
write good prose; and, indeed, writing would prove to be one area where
father and son could safely meet. Michael respected his father's literary
achievement, and Alfred was thrilled that his son had obvious writing ability. He was also happy to see him resuming his studies. Politics would
remain a sticking point between them until well into the 1980s, though
even here, father and son were discovering more grounds for agreement.
By the wedding day, Alfred found much to admire in his son—and his
future daughter-in-law. "Michael and Beth Horowitz Kazin . . . Dr. Beth

Kazin [she was now working for her M.D.]. Very happy in my son and daughter-in-law to be. Gazed long and loving at my beautiful son and thought: well done!"[29]

The marriage of one's child, especially the first one, can be wrenching. For someone as acutely sensitive to change as Kazin, it was overwhelming and revelatory. "What a milestone Mike's marriage signifies to me—I feel as if I had been lurched ahead to a point on life's horizon which I never expected to go." The ceremony and reception were on the Horowitz estate in New Jersey (Beth's father was a successful financial planner). Kazin remembers it as a splendid affair marked by that "air of hard won prosperity that is the real laurel wreath hanging over a Jewish wedding." Fearing that Judith's presence might prove awkward, he had attended with Lucy Dawidowicz. Ann, who was fond of Michael, was also present, as were her brother and sister—all invited by Alfred. "I needed a family," he told Kate. Walking down the aisle with Michael and Carol, observing (for the first time) Mario Salvadori playing the role of father, ever conscious of Ann's presence, Alfred was swept by "a spectrum of feelings." One of the sharper impressions, then and later, while looking over wedding photos, was "the gap between the familiar and the faded"—so many familiar faces now receding into the past, Ann's the most vivid. "That pleasing smile! That handsome face! What a good looking girl in what a pretty dress"—but seen across a widening divide. "She is all there, but not with me . . . Not in my heart . . . No Siree." After seven and a half hours, Alfred left for home, relieved his son had made such a happy choice, reassured that his past with Ann had lost its hold on him, and desperately glad to get back to Judith. Ann rode home crying in the backseat of the Bells' car.[30]

The wedding was an important milestone, marking a new stage in Alfred's relations with his son and confirming his emotional release from Ann. But it came with an anxious awareness of how much of his life was slipping behind him. He had been recording and lamenting dead friends for some time. *New York Jew* was in part a memorial, and he had begun to contemplate another book, *Absent Friends,* that would serve as both a tribute to the dead and a gallery of "ex-friends," those with whom he had broken or had broken with him. The book would not get written, but Kazin continued to keep track of the lost and missing, the betrayers and the betrayed: "Absent Friends! The dead (Hofstadter, Schorer, Leslie Farber). The rene-

gades to the extreme right (Allan Weinstein, Lucy D[awidowicz], Norman
Podhoretz, etc.). Types he [Kazin] never liked, like Leslie Fiedler, Capote,
Vidal. Old wives and sweethearts/Asya . . . Haughty betrayers—Steeg-
muller . . . Bureaucrats: Barzun, Kappy Kaplan . . . Police officials (Arnold
Beichman). Celebrities—never in his orbit—Updike, Schlesinger. People
he has mocked and betrayed: Leon Edel, the sculptress. Actors playing the
Holocaust circuit: Wiesel. Actress playing lit—Sontag." The list was a work
in progress, under constant revision. Particularly missed were old radicals,
Richard Rovere (died in 1979), one of the last of his thirties friends; Harold
Rosenberg (died in 1978): his "kind of slashing critical intellect will seem
unnecessary, as that kind of criticism (of everything) disappears"; his great
Aunt Nechama, whose radical and atheistic views had excited him as a
child. He delivered the eulogy at her "godless" funeral also in 1979.[31]

Like family members going through old family albums, Kazin went over
and over the names at his desk, in his dreams, and lying awake "in the
infamous watches of the night." He was not simply clinging to the past; he
was constantly tracking the changes—so many changes—Ann, Judith, Kate,
Michael. And there was yet another change, this one self-initiated. In the
spring of 1981, after two years of renting weekend and summer cottages in
Southampton, he made a bid (later accepted) on an "ancient house" in
Roxbury, Connecticut, owned by the writer Maureen Howard and Mark
Probst (brother of his and Ann's old friend, Barbara Probst Solomon).
Kazin had never owned property, and the prospect excited and frightened
him. "I can't drive a nail in without breaking everything in sight," he told
Michael at the time, and those familiar with his domestic efforts agreed. A
bigger worry was the mortgage. Earlier in the year he had sold a collection
of his journals, correspondence, and manuscripts to the Berg Collection of
the New York Public Library for thirty thousand dollars. This provided the
down payment. On July 8, 1981, he and Ann were divorced, entitling her to
fourteen hundred dollars a month in alimony payments. Alimony and the
mortgage would have to come from salary, royalties, and speaking fees. Ann
recalls a panicky (and futile) call from Alfred at the time. Would she help
him out with the purchase? He was, he said, the only writer he knew
without a country house.[32]

On August 18, 1981, Alfred Kazin, age sixty-six, became the proud owner
of an 1870 house in historic Roxbury, Connecticut, and his feelings were

mixed. He was unsure whether he had a character suited for responsible homeownership. "There will be so much time, money, energy, and above all self-control expected from this unruly and incompetent house owner." Yet he was pleased he had taken the plunge. He found Roxbury and its environs beautiful and trusted that he would have the "calmness, proportion, sense" to make it all work out. In the end it was Judith who made it work. Alfred was useless with tools and hopeless at any outside chores more complicated than shoveling snow or mowing the lawn. Arriving one cold February night from New York, they found the pipes burst, the kitchen awash in water and ice, the toilets unworkable. Alfred took to his bed with "the tremors"—"It was such a shock!"—leaving Judith to get help and clean up the mess. Later, he was abashed by his behavior. "Such a delicate organization, this Kazin! Everything must be just so, and on time, or otherwise we play Proust!"[33]

While acknowledging that playing Proust in an 1870 farmhouse was not "the most manageable of roles," he did relish the image of himself as writer-homeowner on "Kazin Acres" and amused himself with precedents —Thoreau's hut, Van Wyck Brooks on his "grand corner central house in Bridgewater," Hawthorne in the Old Manse, Mark Twain in the gabled mansion in Hartford, William Dean Howells on Beacon Street, Edmund Wilson in his "Old Stone House," Henry Adams across from the White House—and, when disaster strikes, Henry Sutpen in his broken-down southern mansion in *Absalom! Absalom!* He also liked the fact that there were writers in the vicinity with whom he and Judith could socialize: the playwright Peter Gurney and his wife; Barbara Ungeheuer and her husband, Friedel, who wrote on economics for *Time;* William Styron, whom they saw occasionally; and Arthur Miller, whom Kazin met regularly at the dump and who liked to preside over feasts on his four-hundred-acre estate: "my favorite millionaire . . . I like Arthur, have always liked him, for being so plain and doggedly honest—for being so businesslike, which helps explain why I like plays about business—and corruption."[34]

Kazin had many reasons for purchasing the house, including literary-historical precedent. None, however, was more important than his need for respite from New York City. To live in the city and write about it, he needed to keep from feeling engulfed by it and from succumbing to "the sheer animal dislike" that one felt for the other in the daily crush. The Roxbury house, eighty miles from Manhattan, provided the necessary relief. It would also keep him in touch with a "natural" America to which he was strongly attracted. He had only to walk to a nearby overlook of the Shepaug River to be moved by the beauty and harmony of the scene. "Connecticut Pastoral"—"What is it that makes rocks—water—trees, the enveloping greenness—such constituents of each other? Why does everything seem right?" The appeal of the pastoral has always been its vision of rural peace and its fresh perspective on life's essentials obscured by the entanglements and diversions of the city (or the court). Roxbury provided Kazin with a retreat from the city and a vantage point from which to assess the progress of his new life, yet another marker on his long journey out of Brownsville.[35]

But even rural peace couldn't protect him from the inevitabilities of aging. On a cold night in February 1982, while walking home from the movies, Alfred complained of trouble breathing. Judith called his doctor, who insisted he go straight to the hospital. Shortly after his arrival, he suffered a heart attack. The next morning he underwent a double bypass operation that kept him in the hospital for a month. If Michael's marriage lurched Alfred ahead "to a point on life's horizon," a heart attack at age sixty-seven brought that horizon perilously close, close enough to concentrate the mind on unfinished business. The most pressing business was his unfinished book, *An American Procession*. Less than a week after the operation, he was writing notes (in bed) on ways to get his "procession" back on track. He had already settled on a theme, one that correlated with his advancing age—the limits that intransigent reality posed to the Emersonian dream of total freedom. Now, that reality was turning more implacable than ever. "Death always in my mind. And always the ridiculous wasteful angst of trying to control it."[36]

The other business on Alfred's mind was the status of his relations with Judith. Would he remarry, and if so, when? He and Ann had been divorced in July 1981. Judith's divorce, which took place a year later, had been more difficult. Nelson Dunford did not want a divorce and refused to discuss the subject. When the summons for him to appear in court was served, he made a violent scene, and police had to be called. Nor would he accept the legal proceedings as final. For months afterward, he sent Judith letters and called repeatedly on the phone demanding her back.

But the obstacles were not only legal. After the failure and misery of his third marriage, Alfred had determined he would never remarry. He had no doubts about Judith, and he was sure of his own feelings. But he had been sure of his feelings before. Was there something about marriage that poisoned his relations with women? "No doubt about it," he had confessed in *New York Jew*, "I was not good at this marriage business." He felt that what he had with Judith was a piece of "incredible luck," but he worried that he might not "be clever enough to sustain it." Lying awake at night, he divided his time between planning "the next chapter of the Procession" and testing his "earnest will not to marry." By the spring of 1983, he had made up his mind, and on April 22, he proposed. The wedding took place May 21 in Roxbury on the terrace of the house of Judith's friend, Elinor Arneson, overlooking a waterfall on Jack Brook. A female justice of the peace officiated, wearing a corsage and bedroom slippers. Attending were two of Judith's children, Hillary and Jonathan, and (much to Alfred's relief) his daughter Kate, sporting a fedora. Once the wedding was over, Alfred could only wonder about his hesitation. "Lord, Lord, what happiness, excitement, sharing, interest, curiosity unlimited in being married to Judith. I dragged my feet so long—dragged it right into this kitchen on a rainy holiday morning—suddenly wishing that I had met her 60 years ago." Alfred would never regret his decision; nor, if the journals are any indication, would he ever be unfaithful to Judith.[37]

An American Procession

In deciding to buy a house and remarry, Kazin was near to consummating the changes that had been occurring in his life since he had sent his application to the Stanford Center early in 1977. What remained of this adventure into a new life was completing the project that had been his nominal reason for applying—his much rethought, rewritten, and retitled chronicle of American writers from Emerson to Fitzgerald. He had been at it in one form or another for nearly forty years. "The book was conceived when I finished *On Native Grounds*," Kazin explained in 1980 to Eric Glaberson, who was planning to write a dissertation on Irving Howe and Kazin. It is "my most ambitious book," and, he warned, any assessment of his career would have to wait until it appeared. Kazin submitted the finished manuscript of *An American Procession* in the summer of 1983. It appeared the following March.[38]

Although long expected and widely reviewed, the reception was disappointing. By and large, reviewers were respectful. Kazin was a venerable figure in American letters, and people wanted to give the benefit of the doubt to a book that represented his most substantial work of literary criticism since *On Native Grounds*. But with some notable exceptions (Morris Dickstein in *New York Magazine*, Richard Howard in the *New Republic*, and Mark Schechner in the *Nation*), reviewers were less than enthusiastic. *An American Procession* quickly disappeared over the horizon, leaving its author surprised, disappointed, and wanting "to laugh at all the expectations I had built up." What went wrong? How could a book so long planned and meditated on sink with barely a ripple? Did it deserve better, and should Kazin have been surprised?[39]

In some ways, he should not have been. *An American Procession* advanced no new ideas about American literature. It did not contribute to ongoing discussions about the character of American writing or about the achievement of individual writers. With the exception of a brief attack on Hugh Kenner and some slighting references to the theories of Harold Bloom (unnamed), Kazin mentions no current critical authorities. Nor does he acknowledge the continuing debate about the changing literary canon. Whereas *On Native Grounds* contained portraits of more than one hundred American writers, Kazin limits his "procession" to two dozen canonical male figures, none of them minorities, and one woman, Emily Dickinson. The book was reviewed perfunctorily in a handful of critical-scholarly journals, but provoked little serious response. It is difficult to imagine its being assigned in a course or seminar dedicated to the contemporary study of American literature.

Yet, *An American Procession* represents a sustained effort by one of the country's preeminent critics to come to terms with writers he had spent a lifetime teaching and studying. That it should arouse so little interest among the professionals may suggest, as Kazin believed, that academics were more interested in each other's views than they were in the literature itself. But it also suggests the risks incurred when a critic relies wholly on his own personal impressions and reflections. *An American Procession* is a very personal work. Kazin keeps other critics out to get more of himself in. He insists on being alone with his writers—one-on-one, writer-to-writer, taking their measure according to his lights, his experiences, his prejudices. "I must make them my characters," he wrote excitedly after discussing progress on the book with Kate, "but only if I really cut them to size." In the hands of a critic who is also a "writer," such a possessive attitude can bring an intensity of response that is both startling and exciting—D. H. Lawrence on Whitman, Melville on Hawthorne, Dr. Johnson on Shakespeare. The intent is to record that "shock of recognition," which, according to Melville, marks one writer's response to another's genius. When responding to a writer with whom he feels a special connection—Emerson in his journals, Whitman on the Civil War, Dreiser on the American city—Kazin does create a quality of personal recognition that is both arousing and reassuring. But when responding to a writer with whom he is out of sympathy— "rich and bossy" Edith Wharton, "fat little" W. D. Howells, the "snob" Henry James—the effect of this "cutting to size" can be very irritating, particularly if delivered casually without argument or apparent recognition of the writer's achievement. Morris Dickstein has referred to the intensely personal quality of Kazin's readings in *Procession* as "phenomenological" rather than "formal," a preoccupation with "the grain of the wood," rather than "the finished object." It is a helpful distinction. Kazin is less concerned with the shape of the literary work than with probing its author's idiosyncratic genius—an interest that can lead to memorable characterizations of a writer's distinguishing talent but also to intemperate (and annoying) displays of personal pique.[40]

But *An American Procession* purports to be more than a series of personal encounters with American writers. It is a literary history (of sorts) with a story to tell; and it is here that Kazin runs into his most serious difficulties, partly because the story reads too much like a rambling lament and partly because he has thrown too much into the mix. The subject of his story, we learn in the preface, is "the literary century that began with Emerson's *Nature* (1836) [and] closed (but not entirely) when the free spirit of the moderns was dissipated by war, depression, political ideology, academicism, 'post-modernism.'" His subject, in other words, is a story of decline, of the loss of "the free spirit" that began with Emerson and largely, "though not entirely," exhausted itself amid the intellectual waste and political horrors of the twentieth century—not the most inviting introduction to the four-hundred-page procession to follow. And, indeed, a sense of historical (and personal) despair hovers over much of the book. Writers are introduced on their deathbeds or at the fag end of their careers. The initial exuberance of

an Emerson or a Thoreau is quickly throttled by a reminder of disillusionments to come, while the spirit of Henry Adams, invoked throughout for his
conviction that "the modern world was meaningless, insane, out of control,"
becomes the touchstone of the bitter wisdom with which the twentieth
century, the "terrible" century, "the pitiless century," "the ghastly century,"
has learned to assess the nineteenth "century of hope."[41]

Not all is gloom and doom, however. If the mood tends to be disenchanted, a number of the portraits, though painted in somber tones, can be
arresting. One of the more successful is of Herman Melville, living out his
last years in New York City, working as a customs inspector on the docks,
retiring to his desk in the evening to write poetry. The chapter is written in
a distinctly minor key—the once hopeful novelist and friend of Hawthorne,
now anonymous and forgotten in "the frantic busyness of New York." Yet
Kazin, recounting the novelist's "heroically" expressive achievements
against the backdrop of a failed career and long obscurity, finds cause for
celebration in Melville's determination to keep on, to work out in verse
what he had earlier wrestled with in prose. In the 1940s and 1950s, Kazin
had repeatedly turned to Melville for his celebration of the writer's unfolding creative potential, his "inmost leaf." In the 1980s, he turns again to his
fellow New Yorker, this time for the resilience of the aging thinker-writer
forced to accept life's limits but unwilling to let his endlessly "seeking"
mind rest. "When I read Melville," Kazin told an interviewer in 1978, "I
feel restored by tragedy"—a sentiment clearly evident in this fine portrait.[42]

An American Procession contains other excellent portraits. The account
of Dreiser in his later years working on *An American Tragedy* is as impressive as anything Kazin had written on that writer. (Kazin simply could not
write badly about Dreiser.) Whitman is described movingly in his last days,
putting together his latter-day testaments of the Civil War. Fitzgerald is
honored for having faced the disillusionments and brutalities of the twentieth century without turning hard, bitter, and reactionary, as other modernists had. Taken together, these portraits and a few others might have
constituted an interesting study of the temperament and skills that enabled
some writers (rather than others) to confront limits and defeats through
reserves of spiritual strength and the gift of expression—"the triumph of a
prisoner over his cell, a desperado over his philosophy." Kazin, however, is
unwilling to give up his book's historical scope or to place restrictions on
what to include. Thus we have chapters and sections of chapters on *The*

Narrative of Arthur Gordon Pym, Tom Sawyer, The Red Badge of Courage, U.S.A., Hemingway's debt to painting, *The Golden Bowl, The Sound and the Fury,* and more—writers and works whose only common quality is that Kazin had once written an essay about or an introduction on them.[43]

In the book's acknowledgments he gives notice that he has drawn heavily on past work. He does not indicate how heavily (more than two-thirds of the book had been previously published), nor the difficulties of refurbishing. "I have been so long at the book that I am not quite sure what the whole book looks like, what makes it hang together," he admitted while reworking a Hawthorne essay. "But I have to trust to my sometimes 'unconscious' line in these things." In October 1982, two months before submitting the manuscript, he wrote, "My procession is walking ahead of me, is sometimes out of my sight, is definitely not in my control!" Kazin would never gain control over his book, a fact evident in awkward (or nonexistent) transitions between sections and chapters, in sudden shifts of tone, in repeated information (we are told three times that Dreiser's mother was a Mennonite), and in the absence of a coherent argument elucidating its overarching theme of historical and creative decline.[44]

Inevitably, *An American Procession* invited comparison with *On Native Grounds.* Although a few reviewers saw it complementing his earlier work, most saw a serious falling off. Kenneth Lynn compared it unfavorably not to *On Native Grounds* but to Vernon Parrington's *Main Currents in American Thought,* which, unlike Kazin's *Procession,* benefits from a "grand historical design." It is a pointed comparison, as *On Native Grounds* is itself modeled closely on Parrington's work. What Lynn does not say (but must have known) is that the progressive formula, followed by Parrington and Charles Beard in the 1920s, had long outlived its usefulness for the writing of American political and literary history. Kazin understood this. He also understood that the writing of narrative literary history on any model had become extraordinarily difficult and that it would have been impossible to repeat his earlier performance. When writing *On Native Grounds,* he observed in a 1995 preface, "I felt what I have never felt since 1945—that the age was wholly with me, that I was appealing to 'the spirit of the age,' I was writing literary *history,* a genre long abandoned by critics and now suspect (history can no longer be characterized and summed up as confidently as it was in the 30s and early 40s by the young man who wrote this book). This means that I saw connections everywhere between history and literature—between the populism of the 1890s and the realism of Howells, Dreiser and Wharton." Kazin did not feel that the age was with him in the writing of *An American Procession* or that history provided a model or structure that could support his discussion and judgments. Lacking such support, he had struggled for years to put together a book that would continue the effort that had succeeded so well in *On Native Grounds*. As late as 1981, he was writing to Michael that he had yet to arrive at an "organization putting the enormous [amount of] material into historical relief, which [would have] its own form of drama." He never found the organizational scheme and opted instead for "a series of closeups" (portraits), acknowledging that "it cannot on the present scheme, be an 'historical work.' "[45]

An American Procession was a book Kazin had long promised himself (and his publishers). It concluded more than two decades of planning, rethinking, starts, and restarts. It gave him a chance to express once again his anguish over the fate of "the century of hope" and to revisit writers who meant a great deal to him. It was also an opportunity (at least in his own mind) to strike a blow against the academics, "my long sought vindication as a critic—a critic outside the fashionable university opinion." In what sense it was to be a vindication is hard to say—beyond the fact that it ignored the academics and that he could do without them. They, for their part, largely ignored the book, which hardly surprised Kazin. He was, however, surprised by the other reviews—as well as disappointed and bitter. He scoffed at the "empty" notices that were merely polite and accused Robert Silvers at the *New York Review* of being "malicious" in giving the book to a reviewer, Denis Donoghue, not on Kazin's "wavelength"—continuing a pattern of assigning his books to reviewers who Silvers should have known would be unfavorable. He was (justifiably) incensed by Kenneth Lynn's mean-spirited review, in which Lynn complained that Kazin was once again "getting things wrong." But the anguish and anger were short-lived. By July, Alfred was bored with all the "hooplah" over the book and happy to turn to new things. *An American Procession* was in many ways an old thing—the project of an earlier life, now relinquished, like his years with Ann, to the past. He would return in later works to a number of the *Procession* writers—he was not about to relinquish *them*—but no longer under the compulsion to write literary history, to discover an order in which he no longer believed.[46]

CHAPTER TWELVE

Politics

Politics is how we live, how we are forced to live.

—Alfred Kazin, "Not One of Us," *New York Review of Books,* June 14, 1984

You can no more keep out of politics than you can keep out of the frost.

—Ralph Waldo Emerson, Journal, 1862

Although the reviews of *An American Procession* did not make Kazin happy, they were for the most part well mannered, discriminating, and considerate of his long career in American letters—with two notable exceptions, Kenneth Lynn's in *Commentary* and Lionel Abel's in the *New Criterion.* Both Lynn and Abel, who had praised Kazin's earlier work—"beyond praise, as fine as anything in American criticism" (Abel)— not only denounced *An American Procession,* they dismissed Kazin as an indifferent critic and an overrated writer. He should not have been surprised. A year earlier, the *New Criterion* had published a lengthy attack on him, also by Lynn, marking the republication of *On Native Grounds* on its fortieth anniversary. Why mount a double-column, seven-page polemic against a forty-year-old book? The surprising answer to someone familiar with Kazin's career is—politics. In March 1983, Kazin had thrust himself very publicly into the political line of fire with an incendiary piece in the *New York Review of Books* titled "Saving My Soul at the Plaza," an account of a conference held at New York's Plaza Hotel in February.[1]

The conference was organized by a group calling itself the Committee for the Free World, and its mission, expressed in the "Opening Statement" by Midge Decter (Norman Podhoretz's wife and an old friend of Kazin's), was to "speak out" against "those writers and artists and thinkers" who had demonstrated "principled ingratitude" to the country and "unremitting hostility to American society." In the keynote speech, Hilton Kramer, editor of the *New Criterion,* accused American writers and intellectuals of falling back into old habits of estrangement from America. Other speeches chastised them for attacking capitalism and warned that universities were increasingly under the influence of "New Left" professors who were luring their brightest students into radical environmentalism (Robert Nisbet) and radical "populist history" (Gertrude Himmelfarb). Norman Podhoretz, editor of *Commentary,* concluded the conference by objecting to the "objectivity" of the press, praising those present for their partisanship, and taking credit for publicizing the ideas that contributed toward Ronald Reagan's election as president. In his spirited polemic, Kazin denounced the conference and its participants, ridiculed their self-importance, while noting their close connection with powerful corporate interests.[2]

The article brought Kazin more fan mail than any other piece of journalism he had written or would write—mostly from people relieved and grateful for what he had done. But it also exposed him to some angry members of the committee and their "neoconservative" sympathizers, who with knives sharpened waited for the right moment to counterattack. The republication of *On Native Grounds* in 1983 provided one occasion; another was the appearance of *An American Procession* a year later. There would be more.

Kazin did not enjoy political confrontation. He had, he said, "learned long ago to stay private and unpolitical, not to fight City Hall, much less the IRS." He even called himself a "political coward." "I never claimed any particular virtue or originality for my political ideas," he told Eric Glaberson. "I do not see myself as one of those 'armed intellectuals.' It is not my mind, not my style, not in the least." Yet he had entered the arena with a host of armed intellectuals who he knew were ready to pounce. Why? And why now? The 1980 election of Reagan was the most immediate reason. The Plaza speakers were speaking for the party in power. But the pressure had been building for more than a decade as Kazin watched one-time radicals and progressives (many of them friends) turn away from the commitments of their liberal past. He had spoken out at various times in the seventies on "the racism, poverty and neglect and degradation to be witnessed in the streets of America," but he had refrained from direct, personal attacks. By 1982, it was evident to Kazin that the "Reagan Revolution" was not just redressing imbalances that might have occurred in the 1960s; it was taking the country sharply to the right, pursuing provocative policies abroad and threatening liberal programs that had taken decades to achieve. That Reagan and the Republican Congress were being cheered on by ex-radicals (supported by corporate money), who had taken it upon themselves to scold as "anti-American" those writers who did not share their "neoconservative" enthusiasms, was enough to tempt the most cowardly liberal into the fray. One did not need original ideas about politics to raise one's voice.[3]

"This Age of Woman"

It would later be said that the 1970s had prepared for the conservative resurgence of the 1980s, that Reagan's election was a culmination of tendencies that had been gathering momentum in the political culture for a decade. At the time, things were not so clear. The seventies lacked "distinctive historical flavor," complained Irving Howe, who was currently working on his autobiography. The Nixon-Agnew victories in 1968 and 1972 suggested a swing to the right, but Agnew's liberal-baiting rhetoric notwithstanding, Nixon governed more or less from the center, establishing affirmative action guidelines, creating the Environmental Protection Agency, even proposing a negative income tax for poor families. Gerald Ford, who assumed the presidency in 1974, was more conservative. However, he was soon replaced in 1976 by Jimmy Carter, who, like Nixon, governed largely as a centrist. But if the political scene in the seventies often seemed amorphous and indeterminate, it was clear to many on the liberal left that the sixties and the Vietnam War had changed things, that old alliances had cracked, that the mutual interests of liberals were no longer that mutual, and that the right was well positioned for dramatic gains.[4]

In his 1970 antiwar speech in Dag Hammarskjöld Plaza, delivered a few days after flag-waving, hard-hatted workers had beaten up protesting students at a New York rally, Kazin had noted in dismay that the war had become a "class matter"—the working class versus the intellectual class—and that the flag had become a means "to divide our people, to start fights, to end conversation." Over the next several years, Kazin would see more division, faction, and hostility among erstwhile friends and allies, much of which could be traced back to the war and the sixties, all of which he believed benefited the forces of reaction. "The 60s were the shattering time," he wrote in 1976. "The old faith was destroyed." Like many an Old Leftist, he had been dismayed and disgusted by the New Left both for its simplistic vulgarities and for the divisions it created among the electorate. He had no doubt that the irresponsible excesses of the young radicals had helped elect Nixon in 1968, and he was equally severe on "the kids" for the debacle over George McGovern in 1972. Though he voted (with misgivings) for McGovern, he admitted to a certain schadenfreude in the magnitude of his loss. "The truth is, god damn it, that I am impressed by McGovern's defeat—impressed by the futility and arrogance of minority righteousness. The intellectual left, the young left, cannot win—they can only force domination over others." The student left would dissolve rapidly with the winding down of the war, the idealism and passion of headier times dissipating in communes or in the "complacent acquiescence" of the new yuppie generation. Some of the activist energy did survive the war, however, in the social movements—feminist, gay and lesbian, black nationalist, Mexican American—defending the rights and advancing the cultural identities of groups long ignored by or spurned in American society. Kazin regarded the emergence of these groups with a mix of restrained enthusiasm, political resentment, and personal alarm.[5]

Well aware that women and minorities had suffered discrimination, that they had shared unequally in the country's opportunities and rewards, Kazin sympathized in principle with their circumstances and supported the efforts to rectify historical wrongs. He approved of the affirmative action regulations passed by the Nixon administration; and when Sidney Hook in 1974 formed the Committee on Academic Nondiscrimination to protest federal affirmative action in hiring and in the academy, Kazin signed and circulated a petition (along with Irving Howe and Arthur Schlesinger) countering the aims of Hook's committee. He shared the views of the other signatories that there has been "historic massive discrimination against women" in the academy and that the hiring of women and minorities need not lead to the hiring of less qualified applicants. Washington should press forward with its affirmative action policies.[6]

But if Kazin recognized the need to right historical wrongs in hiring practices and to insist on equal pay for equal work, he was generally unsympathetic with the promotional and ideological claims of the women's movement, which he tended to dismiss as an indulgence of ambitious, middle-class women. Nor was he particularly concerned that women were denied admission to men's social gatherings—like the Century Association. He was certainly not about to join Robert Lekachman, who left the Association because women were not admitted as members. "Of all the many injustices and ordeals that every day rack me in the U.S. this is not one of them," Kazin wrote in his journal. In the fifties and sixties Kazin had ridiculed the efforts of Norman Mailer and Allen Ginsberg to incorporate sex into politics, to formulate an ideology of sex, "sexology." With the advent of the women's movement (as well as that for gays and lesbians) in the seventies, he saw "sexology" reappearing in a new, more combative form as "gender politics," a "pressure group" that was not about to be laughed off—though he was prepared to use ridicule.[7]

There were some obvious personal sources for his animus. In her autobiography, Ann Birstein describes the arrival of the women's movement in the late sixties and seventies as a godsend—"It was saving my life, or at least my sanity." Long frustrated in her efforts to work out equitable domestic arrangements with her husband and unhappy at being forced to write and publish in his shadow, Ann saw the women's movement as a vindication of her complaints and a source of emotional and political support. She was no longer alone. Alfred saw things differently, however, and quickly came to resent her new militancy. He often felt Ann was not so much arguing with him as participating in a counteroffensive against an implacable enemy with the full backing of ideological soul mates. Personal differences were historical wrongs to be avenged. It was a matter of honor. He was now "a symbol"—to be fought relentlessly as part of the cause. In the early years of their troubled marriage, Alfred had admired Ann's rebelliousness, while acknowledging (to himself) that he would not have put up with the demands he was making on her. By the mid-seventies, that admiration had long faded. Ann had become "my perpetually angry wife," her attacks on him the screams of a "feminist hyaena." There was, he believed, no arguing, no reasoning with ideologues.[8]

It would have been surprising if some of this feeling had not carried over into Kazin's reflections on the women's movement; and, indeed, his reviews and commentary in which sexual politics are an issue show little forbearance or rhetorical restraint. The first of these, "The Writer as Sexual Show-off," a discussion of the sexual politics of Norman Mailer, Gore Vidal, and Erica Jong, appeared in *New York* magazine in June 1975. Jaunty and witty on the surface (befitting its venue), it is serious enough in intention. Kazin, who found Mailer's conflation of sex and ideology implausible, nonetheless treats him as a serious writer to be contrasted with the unserious Vidal and Jong, who, he says, use sex as a form of literary and political special pleading. Vidal and Jong not only write out of anger and resentment (Vidal against homophobes, Jong against chauvinist men), they take their anger as a badge of solidarity with their fellows and a sign of literary merit—"the sexual elite is the creative elite. The braver you are in print, the better writer." Kazin forcefully disagreed. He expresses bewilderment that Henry Miller (and John Updike!) found anything of value in Jong's writing and calls *Fear of Flying* and Jong's latest collection of poems "vulgar," exploitive, and pornographic. "There hasn't been so much public exploitation of a woman's parts, a woman's fantasies, a woman's 'chemistry,' a woman's idlest daydreams, since cosmetic ads were invented."[9]

Kazin returned to the subject of sexual politics two years later after signing a contract with the men's magazine *Esquire* to write a monthly piece ($1,250 per column) on subjects of cultural and political interest. One interest for Kazin and presumably for *Esquire*'s mostly male readers, uneasy about the women's movement, was feminist politics and female writers. In his view, the two had little relation to each other. Accomplished writers, he argued in separate articles on Elsa Morante, Virginia Woolf, and Gertrude Stein, owe their reputation to their distinctive talents and their appreciation of human differences, not to membership in a group or adherence to an ideological line. Recent middle-class champions of women (and gay) writing, however, seemed to think that literary excellence derived from agreement on a common enemy—heterosexual men. "The bitterness is monumental but too often expresses itself as uninformed sociology and shrill pamphleteering even when it pretends to be literature."[10]

Kazin claimed that his intent in these pieces was to argue that "women are not all alike," that talent transcends group and ideology, and that women do themselves a disservice by surrendering judgment to "pressure groups." But the rhetoric undermines its high-mindedness. With phrases like "the troopers of the movement," "authoritarian intimidation," "shrill pamphleteering," the *Esquire* essays recall the ideological name-calling of the thirties and the lingering resentments of the sixties. Self-admittedly obsessed with "extremism" in any form, Kazin tended to focus on the more provocative statements of the women's movement and to react with extreme characterizations and judgments of his own. Not only were the feminists middle-class discontents; they, together with the more militant blacks, were responsible for the Reagan phenomenon. "If liberal America is dead or dying," he wrote in a 1984 journal entry, "the culprit is liberal America—the feminist separatists, the black separatists," all pushing their own agendas, all oblivious to practical politics and the common good.[11]

There was another source of the exasperation in these and other essays on literary politics in "this Age of Woman"—Kazin's painful recognition that cultural issues were moving away from him. Though he had always quarreled with the zeitgeist, he also knew that for most of his career he had been its beneficiary. When *On Native Grounds* appeared in 1942, he became an important figure in the American studies movement that would expand rapidly in the decades after World War II. *A Walker in the City* (1951) had in turn presaged the surging interest in Jewish-American writing in the 1950s and 1960s of which Kazin had been a leading interpreter. "Definitely, it was now the thing to be Jewish," he had written in his 1966 introduction to a *Commentary* miscellany. In the mid-seventies, it was still good to be Jewish, but it was also good to be a woman, a homosexual, an African American, a Hispanic, an American Indian. Looking through the literary journals, observing student interests and campus politics, Kazin understood (or thought he understood) what was happening. " 'The woman's movement,' " he wrote in 1976, "insofar as it is a minority movement, resembles all other minority movements; pushy, seeking all possible support in the 'movement.' The Jewish movement is exactly the same sociological and political phenomenon except for the intuition of a transcendental truth that was worked into its still mysterious sense of closeness." Kazin found little transcendental in the new movements. What he found instead was politics—"sexual politics," "minority politics," "academic politics"—a world of "grievance" and contention that left him feeling "out of it—unnoticed, unwanted, on the shelf."[12]

In no area were these "movements" more pervasive and militant than in the universities, especially university English departments. Noting the changes in the curriculum, overhearing conversations in the elevators, looking into the forums attended by students and young faculty, Kazin wondered whether any common ground was left on which an old-fashioned "humanist" like himself could contribute to the conversation. "Tribal" interests seemed to be replacing the shared interests that he felt were the special province of the literary experience. Equally discouraging was the bourgeoning interest in theory—theory that seemed particularly intent on denying the status, even the existence, of the author. Kazin had long objected to "the pretentiously 'scientific'" vocabulary of the New Criticism, which he felt tended to reduce literature to "strategies" and "problems" to be solved by academics with the right kind of "professional" training. Such practices, he had argued in 1942, divorced literature from the shared world of human intercourse and turned the writer into "a kind of machine that did its work in poetry." Recent theories, even more "technical," turned the literary work into a "text," and the text into a nexus of other texts—a "site" to be deconstructed and excavated and into which the author finally disappeared—a "projection" of the reader, an "author function," a "fold in history," an illusion for the gullible. A critic who took pride in his ability "to read the mind behind each book" might well have felt sidelined by repeated pronouncements on "the death of the author."[13]

But if Kazin sometimes felt that he was being placed "on the shelf," he did not rest there comfortably. A frequently quoted cultural figure and sought-after spokesman in American letters, he seized the available opportunities—an address to the patrons of the New York Public Library, a keynote speech at a University of Oklahoma symposium, a commencement address at the CUNY Graduate Center, an interview in *Newsweek*, a commemorative essay for the fiftieth anniversary edition of the *Partisan Review*, a Phi Beta Kappa address at Harvard—to fight back, to make his case against what he saw as the worst of the current cultural-academic trends and to restate what he saw as literature's continuing value as a special and invaluable form of communication between people. Kazin acknowledged that he was a "cultural conservative," even, he admitted half-jokingly to Dennis Wrong, a literary "reactionary"; but he was also an unabashed critical rhapsodist or enthusiast who refused to apologize for the uninstructed joy he took in responding to a new or established work or in discovering a new writer, whatever the academic enthusiasms and political strictures of the moment. "The weakness of literary studies these days," he announced to an audience of graduating doctoral students "is abstractness, factionalism, ideologizing, intellectual group think." Featured as the spokesman for the "humanist" point of view in a 1981 *Newsweek* article on deconstruction, Kazin is cited for his insistence on literature's relevance to the entire human community and for his accusation that for all their pretensions, many of these new New Critics "can't even write English."[14]

Alfred's irritation with critical tendencies was also evident in his classes. He had always been a temperamental teacher, and recent trends made him more mercurial than ever. A good class could still leave him happy and gratified, even if he felt he was bucking the trends. A bad class, and there were a number, left him impatient and irritable—"Hunter illiterates, stupid high school teachers, drive me crazy. I'm a danger to myself and everybody else in this terrible mood." Daniel Born recalls Kazin's response to a student who asked whether a Faulkner character was a "Christ figure." "You must be a high-school teacher!" he snorted in reply. She never again raised her hand. He preferred seminars at the Graduate Center, where he felt reasonably confident that the students would be literate. His typical teaching method in seminars was to collect cards from the students at the beginning of class on which they had written questions covering the assignment. He then took up what he felt were the more interesting questions. "He could be quite blunt and even devastating," Mary Beth McMahon remembers. "Your question deeply saddens me," was one of his more alarming responses. He had been known to throw things at students, including a Bible—"using the canon as a cannon." He was openly contemptuous of the theoretical and political concerns that engaged other professors and many students, but he could be mesmerizing when discussing the distinctive vision and biographical details of a writer. He had a special "gift for closeness with a writer," an "intuitive grasp" of what a writer was doing. There was no denying that "he was difficult," but he could also be riveting, "both riveting and terrifying."[15]

He could also be an unsettling presence on dissertation committees, sometimes bullying, at other times surprisingly sympathetic. Lyon Evans, a doctoral candidate, recalls the traumatic afternoon when, after asking Kazin to be on his Melville dissertation committee, Kazin told him that his ideas on *Billy Budd* were "preposterous." In a manner that was "witheringly caustic, imperious, patronizing, and oddly plaintive (he gestured more than once at the photo of Melville above his desk) [he] directed at me the same rhetorical firepower he had unloaded on more formidable antagonists in the pages of *Partisan Review* and *Commentary.*" Then, "without warning," possibly out of respect for the way Evans stuck to his guns, "he became kindly, conciliatory, almost apologetic for his previous aggressiveness." In the end, not only did Kazin agree to be the outside reader on his dissertation, "he became solicitous, fatherly, even tender." McMahon, who also did a dissertation with him, remembers him as "the Jewish mother" she never had.[16]

In 1982, Kazin was presented with the James Branch Hubbell Award given by the Modern Language Association to a critic-scholar whose "total range . . . of scholarly and critical work has been a major influence on the way members of the American Literature Section of MLA think and read and write and teach." James Cox, the president of the MLA at the time, added a personal note to the official letter, writing to Kazin, "Your life in American letters exemplifies courage of conviction, humane learning, and critical intelligence—of the highest order." Like all awards for lifetime achievement, the Hubbell prize was bittersweet. It was nice to be recognized—even by an organization that Kazin had often ridiculed. At the same time, the recognition carried with it more than a whiff of antiquarian respect. He was becoming a monument, an éminence grise, important for work done in the past and less a factor for what was going forward in the present. (Kazin complained in private that he had to "pay" for the award by sitting through papers on Emerson "that would not have told the visitor from Mars even that E was an American of the 19th century." He also had to sit next to "that creep and fag [Richard] Poirier," who had attacked *Bright Book of Life* in the *New Republic* and who "continues to write as if he were masticating on old rhetorical distinctions taught him 20 thousand leagues under the sea by old Ted Baird at Amherst.")[17]

"The Toughness, Inflexibility, Absolute Rottenness of These Ex-Comrades"

One of Kazin's complaints against the women's movement and the ethnic "separatists" was that they were a distraction from the deeper economic-political forces at work in society. While various groups struggled for recognition, the economic conditions for many Americans in the 1970s, particularly the poorest among them, were turning increasingly dire. The engine of rapid economic growth that began with World War II and had supported the expansion of the welfare state seemed to be sputtering out. Various commentators noted that the standard of living, which had been rising for thirty years, had begun to turn downward, while the liberal hopes for a more economically equitable society, which had accompanied the years of expansion, were, in the opinion of Kazin and many other liberals, yielding to a narrowing concern with economic individualism, corporate profit, "the bottom line."[18]

For a city dweller accustomed to walking the streets (and riding the subways), the increasingly desperate conditions of the urban poor and the growing inattention to the public welfare was a painful daily experience. While he claimed no special expertise in tracking shifts in social and fiscal policy, Kazin was sensitive to what he saw happening around him and seized the appropriate opportunities to have his say. The most significant of these was an invitation from the *New Republic* to contribute an article to its July 3, 1976, bicentennial edition. Titled "Every Man His Own Revolution: 1776 and American Egotism," the piece might well have been called an anti–Declaration of Independence. Instead of celebrating the virtues of individual liberty, Kazin argues that our "secular religion [of] the free individual" has become a "menace to the public good. . . . In the name of the free individual hundreds and thousands of Americans live neglected and despised, they die unobserved like leaves falling off a tree." What does America have to offer the world on the eve of its two-hundredth birthday? —personal rapacity, arrogant nationalism, indifference to the general welfare. Intended as a rebuke to the self-congratulatory patriotism evoked by the bicentennial celebrations, "Everyman" recalls some of the harsher anticapitalist progressive rhetoric of the late nineteenth and early twentieth centuries. In a separate essay, Kazin wrote that American society is now more "peculiarly concerned with exploitation and savagely defensive of ['the cash nexus'] than the 19th century society attacked by Karl Marx."[19]

Kazin's feelings of dismay and alarm would intensify with the election of Ronald Reagan in 1980, which also brought in a Republican Senate and narrowed the Democratic margin in the House to five votes. The subtle and not-so-subtle economic and ideological changes that Kazin and others had sensed in the seventies had turned into an irrefutable historical event. The old Democratic liberal coalition now seemed truly dead, with consequences liberals could only imagine. Kazin was shocked by the election and appalled by its implications for the future. "By the time Reagan is out," he wrote in his journal after the election, "the Right, even the Extreme Right, will have been institutionalized beyond revoking for another generation."[20]

He was equally appalled and disgusted, though hardly surprised, by the gleeful responses of some old friends, one-time "comrades" of the liberal left, now Reagan supporters. Over the years Kazin had watched with interest as members of his generation had drifted away from their radical beginnings to become *"converts"* to America and ardent defenders of a political-economic system they had once hoped to vanquish. In *New York Jew,* he describes "the ex-radical intellectuals" as "total *arrivistes* and accommodating in their thinking." Happy with the advantages they enjoyed in America and ferocious in their hatred of the Soviet Union, they were largely oblivious to "what was really going on at home—especially in their native streets of New York." He remembered Irving Kristol telling him portentously that he was "turning right" in the late fifties. In the late sixties he had noted that Kristol and his brother-in-law, Daniel Bell, were busy editing a new magazine, the *Public Interest,* whose purpose was to show the overreaching and inefficiencies of the Great Society social programs that were helping America's poor. He had followed Norman Podhoretz's shift to the right as *Commentary* editor—with attacks against blacks, against kids, and against liberal Democrats and support for a more aggressive military posture. So it did not surprise him to find general rejoicing among the "new conservatives" or "neo-cons" in Reagan's election (Bell voted for Carter) and to discover Podhoretz—"the brutal little mind of Norman Podhoretz!" —taking partial credit for it. "If the grip of the conventional wisdom and leftist orthodoxies in the world of ideas had not been loosened by the criticisms of the new-conservatives," Podhoretz announced, "Ronald Reagan would in all probability have been unable to win over the traditional Democratic constituencies."[21]

Disgusted with the gloating of his former comrades—"these little ideological cretins"—Kazin groused in his journals and waited for an opportunity to pounce. He got his chance in a June 1981 *New Republic* review of

Prisoner without a Name, Cell without a Number by the Argentine publisher Jacobo Timerman. Timerman had been imprisoned, tortured, and
subjected to anti-Semitic abuse for thirty months by the Argentine military
for publishing the names of "the disappeared." When his book describing
his ordeal appeared in the spring of 1981, Anthony Lewis and John Leonard
had used it to argue in the *New York Times* against the Reagan administration's support of Argentina's authoritarian military regime, which they felt
was run by Fascists and anti-Semitic thugs. Irving Kristol had then denounced the book in the *Wall Street Journal* and portrayed Timerman as an
unreliable, rather shady figure, while defending the administration's close
relations with the anti-Communist Argentine regime. Kazin was outraged.
"It was not enough," he wrote in his piece, "for Timerman to have electrodes
applied to his private parts; he must also be attacked in the *Wall Street
Journal* by Irving Kristol." He accused Kristol and other "right wing" Jews in
America of turning a deaf ear to the cries of Timerman and Argentinian Jews
being tortured in front of their families. What, Kazin asked, are we to make
of "the right wing salesmen" in the American-Jewish community denouncing Timerman while making excuses for the horrors occurring in Argentina?
The implications were clear and disturbing. Has history not provided
enough instances of Jews sacrificing other Jews in their desire to play ball
with brutal anti-Semitic regimes?[22]

The Timerman affair nicely suited Kazin's polemical purposes—embarrassing the neoconservative Jews with the story of a Jew tortured for coura-
geously speaking out against the brutality and anti-Semitism of an authoritarian regime favored by the Reagan administration. He seized another
opportunity to "play Swift," as he put it, when, in early January 1983, Robert
Silvers of the *New York Review* offered him eight hundred dollars to cover
the conference to be convened February 12–13 by the neoconservative
Committee for the Free World at the Plaza Hotel. "The Plaza piece will have
a smashing end," Kazin told himself as he contemplated the possibilities.
"Andropov in the Kremlin is shaking in his boots because of the power of
anti-Communism displayed by Midge [Decter] and friends."[23]

"Saving My Soul at the Plaza" is a broad-brush attack on the pretensions
of the Committee for the Free World and the interlocking "right-wing"
corporations and associations that supported it and various "right-wing"
journals. It is also an expression of personal resentment and outrage. In his

book on the neoconservatives, Peter Steinfels observed that no emotion directed at them was as intense, powerful, and "destructive" as the sense of betrayal. "Political opponents are honorable men; former allies are something else. Anger clouds judgment; embitterment destroys reflection." Whether or not feelings of betrayal clouded Kazin's judgment (and how could they not?), they contributed mightily to his resentment of the neoconservatives. "How far Irving Kristol . . . has come from the streets of Williamsburg [and] a Trotskyite alcove at City College." One would never know from his high-brow pretensions as editor of the New Criterion, named after T. S. Eliot's the Criterion, that "Hilton Kramer, is descended from 'the inconceivable alien' [the Jew]." How could "the wretchedness on the streets of New York" not disturb Norman Podhoretz, "who had grown up in the Brownsville section of Brooklyn"? "It is undoubtedly true," Kazin concludes, reflecting on the move from "Ellis Island to the Age of Power" evident in the Plaza ballroom—"We live in a time of many reversals."[24]

One of the polemical advantages the neoconservatives felt they had over traditional conservatives was their intimate experience with the liberal left. Unlike William Buckley and the National Review people, they knew the liberal left firsthand, knew their sensibilities and arguments; they had once shared them and could skewer their former comrades from the inside. Battle-tested from their days in the City College alcoves, they came armed with information, polemical savvy, ingrained habits of ruthlessness. What was fascinating (and delicious to some) about "Saving My Soul" was that it was so patently an inside job on the neoconservatives. Kazin knew these people; he had grown up with them, socialized with them, knew their weaknesses and vanities; and he was prepared to be as ruthless and personal as they were. "As I read about how you made Midge [Decter] and Normie [Podhoretz] and Gertrude [Himmelfarb] and Irving [Kristol] and Jean [Kirkpatrick] lose their virginity at the Waldorf [sic], I kept yelling out loud, listen to this, listen to that," wrote New York Times cultural critic Herbert Mitgang in a private note to Kazin. "You hung them by their own cut balls, laughingly, beautifully. And I couldn't help thinking what my grandmother used to say to us kids A gezunt af dien keppele [good health to you]."[25]

Kudos came from others. Elizabeth Hardwick said that Kazin had "hit the brass helmets and two-ton breastplates with [his] five little stones and played on the harp at the same time." Irving Howe congratulated him for a "smashing" piece. Philip Roth told him that the opening paragraph "will live forever in the annals of mockery." Anthony Lewis declared the whole thing "glorious." The targets chose not to confront him directly, though Joseph Epstein, the editor of the *American Scholar,* noted with some pride that he was now a "hate" figure for both Gore Vidal and Alfred Kazin. They either ignored him or waited for the opportunity to trash his reputation as a writer. Kenneth Lynn and Lionel Abel, who had once praised Kazin's work, soon went after him in *Commentary* and the *New Criterion* as well as in letters to the *New York Times Book Review.* It was straight party line, as Mark Shechner noted at the time, and they took no prisoners.[26]

While Kazin found it unpleasant to be the subject of public abuse, it was better than looking on impotently from the sidelines. Initially, the Reagan ascendancy had brought back old habits of self-recrimination. To be "just an observer, a bloody book reviewer . . . this mere looking-on, is becoming a disease." The Timerman and Plaza pieces had helped salve his bad liberal conscience; they did not, however, allay his rage and indignation. In the summer of 1983, after finishing the revisions of *An American Procession,* Kazin began preparing something unusual for him, a political speech. He called it "The Strange Death of Liberal America" and delivered it in the Great Hall of the Cooper Union on October 20, 1983.[27]

The Great Hall has a rich history. In 1860, Abraham Lincoln delivered his famous "Cooper Union Speech" there, outlining his views restricting the spread of slavery in the free states. The Fabians had addressed curious audiences there in the 1880s and 1890s. In 1909, the young textile worker Clara Lemlich, protesting conditions at the Triangle Shirtwaist Factory, delivered a speech (in Yiddish) in the Great Hall that had led to a general (and successful) strike against the entire shirtwaist industry. As a child, Kazin had accompanied his father to the Great Hall to hear speeches by Socialists and labor organizers. He may have had these precedents in mind. "I had seen myself in fantasy committing a great political act, making myself 'famous' overnight, reversing the reactionary course of things." The intent of the speech was to raise the alarm over the profound historical changes that the Reagan revolution was bringing about in American politics and attitudes—changes aimed at the heart of "liberal America . . . the still idealistic America of its greatest writers and public spirits, of its reformers, libertarians, eccentrics and insurgents." Kazin detailed Reagan's cuts to social programs, his tax cuts for the wealthy, his accelerated defense spending and saber-rattling. He then extended the attack to the growing number of "ex-liberal" intellectuals who had lined up behind Reagan.[28]

Passionate and rambling, the speech provoked little interest and left Kazin wondering why others seemed not to share his sense of alarm. Was he perhaps making "too much of the right wing administration, the right wing intellectuals, and the arms build up?" Whatever the response and his second thoughts, it was an important speech for him to make. Coming nearly forty years after World War II had destroyed the radical dreams and shaken the progressive liberal hopes that had fired his imagination in the thirties, the Cooper Union speech showed a new willingness on Kazin's part to defend that earlier liberalism in all its alleged "innocence" and "naivete." During the fifties, he had watched ruefully as Lionel Trilling, Richard Hofstadter, Leslie Fiedler, and others had "chastened" and disciplined American liberalism—to the point at which liberalism itself seemed discredited. While acknowledging the failure of liberals to anticipate the horrors of the twentieth-century "power state," he had resented the accusations of "sentimentality," "simplicity," "innocence" that the "new liberals" directed against the country's liberal traditions. Indeed, he suspected that the new liberalism, or new "realism," was in part a disguise for self-aggrandizing assertions of power and growing middle-class complacency that came with one's improved prospects in the world. Now, with Reagan waging class warfare against the poor and the neoconservatives (many of them old "new liberals") warning once again of liberalism's "weakness within," Kazin was determined to fight for liberalism with no apologies, to fight, not by making excuses for America's "innocent" liberal past, but by celebrating it, by keeping "faith in a future based on images of the past." The Reagan election, Michael Kazin would later write, had turned his father into "a fighting liberal again."[29]

Kazin had few illusions about his influence, especially after the Cooper Union speech. Still, he took what opportunities he had to make his case—a speech on George Orwell at a 1984 Library of Congress symposium in which he went after the neocons for trying to expropriate Orwell; an essay on Mencken, whose iconoclastic views he saw as a corrective to that of the neoconservative "super-patriots"; a review of a book on the nineteenth-century American utopians, whose moral vision he contrasted with the current ideology of greed; a 1985 speech celebrating *Partisan Review's* fiftieth anniversary in which he denounced the Reagan administration's policy toward South Africa. Even a brief statement solicited by the *New York Times* on his Brooklyn childhood could serve the cause. Growing up in Brownsville, he wrote, offered a view of American life that made him suspicious of those "neoconservative" Jews of his generation who are so "proud of their connections with power. Brooklyn gave me a lasting sense of the kind of powerlessness and suffering that are endemic in our society." Kazin doubted he could do much to curb the influence of the neocons, but he felt he had to try. "The toughness, the inflexibility, the absolute rotten-ness of these ex-comrades," he wrote in his journal the day before Reagan's certain reelection. "You have to fight them hard, but they are in power, and after tomorrow's Election Day, God help us all! They will be nastier to deal with than ever."[30]

Breaking Ranks, Mending Fences

As the response to the Plaza piece indicates, Kazin's political turn had personal as well as public repercussions. Politics had always been a strongly felt personal matter with the members of his generation, the basis of relationships that could quickly sour with shifts in the political weather. In a pair of books, appropriately titled *Breaking Ranks* and *Ex-Friends*, Norman Podhoretz has described how political changes of heart among the New York intellectual "family" had often led to the fraying of personal relations. But he also marveled at the intensity of personal feeling that political differences could sometimes provoke—and in none more than his one-time friend Alfred Kazin. He "became almost dementedly hostile, even obsessed," Podhoretz wrote. "I thought sometimes that Alfred was 'crazy'—even thought that I had driven him crazy." Demented or prin-cipled (or both), Kazin did come to view both Podhoretz and Irving Kristol with a kind of moral loathing, not so much for their regrettable conserva-tive politics, but because he saw them as the worst of betrayers. Having grown up among the poor and the weak, they had, in his view, decided that their real interests lay with the rich and the powerful, and, unforgivably, against the poor and the weak.[31]

Politics was also affecting his off-again, on-again relations with Saul Bellow. Although Bellow refused to be grouped with the neoconservatives, he was sympathetic to many of their views and let his name be used on the stationery for the Committee for the Free World. Kazin chided him for this in the occasional friendly note but did not press the issue with a friend who easily took offense. His restraint collapsed, however, at a joint seventieth birthday party organized for the two of them (Kazin was born June 5, 1915; Bellow, June 10, 1915) by Gerald Freund, a mutual friend and former director of the MacArthur Fund. They had not met since their amicable dinner in Chicago, and in the spirit of the birthday occasion, each made an effort to keep things friendly. But political differences kept emerging— over Israel (Kazin hated Begin and the Likud), over Leon Wieseltier's articles in the *New Republic*, over Spain. Bellow claimed that Franco had at least saved the Jews. Kazin was outraged, but Bellow stood his ground. "I was a Trotskyite and you were writing for Luce!" he retorted. When Kazin complained that the *New York Times* was taking an increasingly conservative line on Israel, Bellow blew up. "How can you call a paper conservative that publishes Anthony Lewis?" Bellow left shortly thereafter without saying good-bye.[32]

It was, Kazin recalled, "a bad evening." Instead of reminding two old friends of how much they had shared since meeting in the offices of the *New Republic* forty-three years earlier, the party had turned into a bitter political quarrel, bringing to the surface old resentments. Reflecting on the affair afterward, Kazin admitted to being as impressed as ever by Bellow's intellectual adroitness and "his gift of the apposite quotation"; at the same time, he was filled with an "absolute loathing of the self approval in which he [Bellow] sits encased like a cat in a milk bath." That such "conceit" should be allying itself with "power types" and "the voices of privilege" was insufferable—though Kazin acknowledged that it was not always possible to draw a clear line between comrades and ex-comrades. "Karl Shapiro, Alfred Kazin, Saul Bellow, Bernard Malamud. [We] wear white on white shirts like Jewish dentists or brokers . . . and some of us have had as many wives as Henry VIII and as many mistresses as Dracula or Jack Kennedy . . . but o my! how our social opinions reflect our top lofty incomes, and what excuses we do find [for ourselves,] we who once had no trouble execrating everyone in power." Typically, Kazin's harshest criticisms of others owed no small amount of their acuity and passion to his ongoing critique of himself.[33]

The social consequences of Kazin's heightened political interests were not all negative. If his new militancy damaged relations with some longtime acquaintances, it opened (if only in a limited way) possibilities with others —such as Irving Howe. Though they had known each other for years, appeared on the same panels, met frequently at parties, and shared roughly the same political sympathies, the two men had never become friends. Howe's ill-conceived 1948 attack in the *Partisan Review* on Kazin for leading Europe's "future commissars" at the Salzburg Seminar in singing the *Internationale* had started things off badly. Howe's close association with Rahv and the *Partisan Review* over the years had done little to relieve Kazin's wariness, and frequent meetings on literary panels and Ph.D. orals at CUNY had not brought them much closer. Kazin took little interest in Howe's *Dissent*, which he told Dennis Wrong was "the dullest magazine in the world," and he was appalled that Howe in *A World of our Fathers* would critique *A Walker in the City* as a less-than-accurate representation of tenement life. Nor was he pleased that so many people saw them as a kind of intellectual couple. "By putting me side by side . . . with Irving Howe," he warned Eric Glaberson, "you are creating a stock figure that bears no resemblance to me." In an address he gave at a memorial service honoring Howe after his death in 1993, Kazin told the story of his falling over an obstacle one night at Brandeis, which Howe, following close behind, fell over as well. "He got up very disgruntled. 'God damn it, Alfred,' he muttered, 'why must we always have the same experiences!' This was a line all too familiar to me, one I had long detested in the mouths of other people, and now that the man himself had said it, I happily retorted— 'Irving, I assure you, we don't!' "[34]

In fact, Kazin acknowledged that many of their experiences *were* similar —both of them grew up in Yiddish-speaking homes; they both graduated from City College; they both began as freelance critics during the Depression and became university professors (without doctorates) teaching English at CUNY. He also acknowledged (in a 1997 interview with Gerald Sorin) that he saw many of the same problems that Howe saw. "I still do— the poverty, the greed, the materialism, the complacency of intellectuals. But Irving had 'solutions'"; Kazin added, "I had no solutions." Howe said much the same thing in 1988: "Kazin and I are often lumped together, but we are very different. I am a socialist activist, Kazin was more the individualist romantic. He also wrote more rhapsodically than I did. I am drier. Still we were often on the same 'side.' Often against the same things, even if not always or even often, *for* the same things." They were very much against the same things in the 1980s, and Howe was pleased to welcome Kazin into the political fray. He complimented him on his Plaza piece as well as on his Cooper Union speech, which he hoped Kazin would revise for publication in *Dissent* (Kazin did not). He made a number of friendly overtures in person and in correspondence, attempting to sort out differences they had had in the past. When Kazin's heart attack in 1982 kept him in the hospital for several weeks, Howe stepped in and taught his classes. Though he never really warmed to Howe—"Mr. Irving Howe, a bigger klutz that ever. No manners, no grace, just a head like a pot belly"—Kazin did appreciate the effort he was making and in 1987 submitted his first piece to *Dissent*. Titled "They Made It," it is a four-square personal attack on the neocons and "the new brutality" that their writing had brought to political journalism.[35]

By far, the most important coming together of minds accompanying Alfred's new liberal militancy was between him and his son, Michael. Michael remembers 1980 as the year he and his father began "sidling . . . to the same side of the barricades" after years of political tension. Reagan's election, which alarmed both father and son, was the catalyst. "Send me stuff you publish," he wrote Michael in March 1981; "it delights my awakening, I mean reawakening, rebelliousness. . . . I was planning to go down to my grave as a virtuous anti-Communist, but your California man is driving me back to some very old feelings." Michael was a Ph.D. candidate in history at Stanford at the time and still writing for and editing the *Socialist Review*. In that journal's lead editorial analyzing the implications of the 1980 Reagan victory, Michael described the conditions that would soon bring Old Left father and New Left son together: "the right is in power"; the New Deal is in retreat; "statist liberalism" is off the table; "the least visible and most defenseless" are in the hands of the "apostles of meanness and fear." Though Alfred had little faith in his son's hopes for a new "populist ideology" that would include Socialists and divergent strands of the liberal left, he took satisfaction in knowing they agreed on both the meaning and the gravity of what had happened. Liberal America was under furious attack. The rise of the right had united them against a common foe.[36]

Kazin continued to challenge Michael's radical views during the 1980s, particularly those arguing that the United States and the USSR were "equally repugnant empires." He strongly disputed Michael's easy assumption that Socialism offered the best answer to every nation's problem. "You ought to think about . . . concrete situations in themselves," Kazin wrote him. "What continued *dumbness* on your part not to recognize that each country, each situation, has its historical past, its specific traditions. All I want is to keep non-Russian cultures from going too Russian!" And he enjoyed calling him "comrade" on the phone, or concluding letters with remarks such as, "Any chance of your coming out here before you Seize Power?" But he knew that they were on the same side, and he wanted Michael to know it. "I have written a bitter article, satiric and personal, about the Neo-Conservative conference at the Plaza for the *NY Review;* and, while it may not yet get published, the editor is worried it is 'too strong.' So you see that, despite my being *ideologically* null and void, I am not entirely hopeless." For a while they thought of doing an anthology of labor writings together.[37]

Daniel Bell believes it would be a mistake to underestimate Michael's influence on his father's politics, that Alfred very much wanted his son's approval and that his new political militancy might be attributable in some part to Michael's radicalism. "Michael was his *Kaddish*." He is undoubtedly right. Having watched Michael grow up from a distance, Kazin yearned for connections with his son, even when they were most at odds in the sixties. That he tried to keep an open mind toward "the kids" throughout that decade may be attributable in part to his pride in Michael's idealism and "guts"—however much he disagreed with his views on America, liberalism, the Soviet Union, and the Vietcong. Michael's radicalism and idealism appealed to that same youthful spirit of rebellion that Kazin celebrated in *Starting Out in the Thirties,* those "very old feelings" that would never lose their hold over the older man's imagination. To discover in Michael something of his youthful, radical self, and increasingly, his writer-self, was a deep source of satisfaction. These were not, however, reasons to accept his New Left Socialism. In fact, it was Michael who did most of the "sidling" in the 1980s. Without abandoning his Socialist dreams, he no longer called for the wholesale overthrow of the system, but rather sought out those movements and traditions in the American past that spoke most directly to his own radical sympathies. It was a family trait—like father, like son. Michael's first book would be on the labor unions, and his next on the American populist tradition, the same tradition that had prompted his father's excited early reading for *On Native Grounds*. "I came to admire his brand of patriotism," Michael would recall about his father in the 1980s: "tough minded, eternally wary of kitsch and platitudes but deeply in love with America—its land, its personalities, its language, its ideals."[38]

"We Are All Here"

It was, in fact, his patriotism, his lifelong fascination with and love of America, that made the accusations of the neoconservatives so appalling to Kazin—or, as he put it, with ironic restraint, so "endearingly comic." He knew the country, its literature, its landscape, its people, its regions, its small towns and college campuses in ways none of them would think of claiming. If he was critical, he was critical as an anxious, often exasperated, lover. Irving Kristol recalled a conversation in which Arthur Schlesinger Jr. (who also knew America) told Kristol: "You know, you're very bright and all that, but you don't really understand American politics. You don't understand what America is like." Kristol agreed. "He [Schlesinger] was right. But of course, we [New York intellectuals] didn't believe him. We had read all the right books, you see." Kazin doubted that Kristol and his neoconservative friends had read the books, much less made the effort to understand America—even as they lectured liberals like himself for being "ungrateful" to America, for displaying "unremitting hostility" to American society. He believed, had long believed, that the ex-radicals turned "super-patriots" were motivated not by their knowledge or love of America, but by a long-time ideological passion against the Soviet Union and by the satisfactions that came from siding with the wealthy and the powerful. "These people do not believe in America per se, but support it vis-à-vis Russia, or *faute de mieux*." They "show not the slightest interest in the common pleasures of American life, no feeling whatever for the different American regions, for indigenous American characteristics and personalities." And "of course they show no interest in American domestic life and civil strife, the devastation currently visited on so many farmers and factory workers in the Middle West . . . the ever-boiling race hatred, the dominating force of greed." What does interest them, has always interested them, is "America-as-ideology, the very latest."[39]

As if in response to the complaints of the neoconservatives, Kazin published three books on America and American literature in the 1980s, all concerned with the hope and promise of America—even as he saw that promise being betrayed. The first, *An American Procession,* is, as already described, an extended examination of the romantic, hopeful impulse in nineteenth-century American writing as seen from the unillusioned perspective of the "ghastly" twentieth century. The two that follow, *A Writer's America: Landscape in Literature* (1988) and *Our New York* (1989), are less ambitious—though they, too, reflect Kazin's concern with the fate of "innocent" idealism and democratic hope in the contemporary "fallen" world. Unfortunately, neither book adds much to what he had already published, and neither attracted serious critical attention. There are passages in *A Writer's America,* specifically the discussion of William Bartram's *Travels* and Francis Parkman's *Oregon Trail,* that recall that "fresh instant delight" that Kazin had felt when he had discovered Constance Rourke's book on Audubon back in 1942 and had begun to see himself as a "student of American landscape and culture." Otherwise, *A Writer's America,* which was handsomely produced, with reproductions of paintings and photographs, reads like an illustrated coffee-table book of American writers, a "picture book," as one reviewer dismissively put it.[40]

Our New York, a collaborative effort with the photographer David Finn, a fellow Brownsville native, adds a few items to Kazin's biography—most notably his childhood trips with his father to the old *Forward* Building and the "bazaar of the lower East Side"—but little else to his earlier portraits of the city. Moreover, the political angers and personal discouragement that creep into the book (together with the uninspired photographs) have the effect of making New York seem like a lost cause, its best days behind it. Only in the last section, "Post-script: We Are All Here," describing his experiences with New York's taxi drivers, does Kazin succeed in recapturing some of the excitement and historical significance of the city. Coming from every corner of the globe, the taxi drivers, "messengers, the peculiar links of the city to the world," are reminders of what New York had been to his parents and to millions of other immigrants—"planet Earth's still-favorite shore of refuge, first port of call." In this hopeful spirit, he concludes an otherwise rather dour book with some favorite quotations from native New Yorker Walt Whitman, who said of his *Leaves of Grass* ("a work

inconceivable except by a New Yorker"): "If anything can justify my revolutionary attempts and utterance it is such *ensemble*—like a great city to
modern civilization & a whole combined clustering paradoxical unity, a
man, a woman." If anyone could help Kazin recover his original excitement
with New York, its "endless contradictions" and "the incessant play of
human differences," it was Whitman.[41]

Kazin's final remarks on Whitman and New York—"the wildest, zaniest
experiment ever open to democracy on such a scale"—sound a note often
missing in his recent reflections on trends in American politics, the notion
of an exciting, all-inclusive public life in which politics is an essential part of
the conversation. One of the great "truths" he claimed to have learned
from Hannah Arendt in the fifties and sixties is that politics is not "that
which divides us," but rather "the common element of our humanity, the
public element." "May it not be," Kazin asked himself in 1962, "that so
much which divides us just now springs from our inability to believe what
does unite us?" The fracturing of the "liberal consensus" in the seventies
and eighties into competing, hostile camps—students and workers, Old and
New Left, minorities and entrenched majorities, old liberals and neoconservatives—had made it more difficult than ever to believe in a common
interest or to find value in "the other side." Given the political angers of the
late sixties and the disappointments of the following years, it was perhaps
inevitable that Kazin would find himself speaking bitterly of "the troopers
of the [women's] movement, the "pushy[ness]" of minority movements,
"the absolute rottenness" of his Reaganite "ex-comrades." Like most
Americans, Kazin could lose sight of the whole paradoxical *"ensemble,"*
particularly when he sensed that others were making their own too urgent
claims of possession, insisting too forcefully on *their* America. In less partisan times, he might well have granted that Irving Kristol's America was
not wholly anathema to Alfred Kazin's—democratic capitalism had in fact
conferred extraordinary benefits on generations of Americans, including
descendants of working-class Jews. But having decided (not without reason) to "fight them hard," he had little inclination to seek out common
ground, or even to keep the debate civil. As a "fighting liberal" he had
discovered unexpected sources of energy in indignation and outrage un-
available to a mere "observer, a bloody book reviewer." He had even gained
some new friends. But the fight had also deepened his anger and resent-

ment. He had assailed the "separatists" and "enragés" for ignoring and denying America's common ground; he had attacked Podhoretz for proclaiming that all truth resided in partisanship. But had he not been playing the same game—and with people more skilled and practiced than himself? By the late 1980s, Kazin was beginning to wonder whether he was cut out for the political fight after all. He would continue to speak out, but politics would become less of a defining concern. He had other pressing issues on his mind.[42]

CHAPTER THIRTEEN
"The End of Things"
1984–1998

So much thought these days, suddenly, given to the end of things, the end of a
season, the end, the end. . . . How brief it has all been, how sudden, how much it
contracts now. The river, the eternal river rushing on, but rushing us into eternity.

—Alfred Kazin, Journal, March 21, 1987

Kazin's foray into politics in the early 1980s brought a measure of
satisfaction. He was no longer watching from the sidelines. He was
taking his outrage public. Yet, in the end, he did not find political
confrontation very gratifying, partly because he felt that the political situation in the country was hopeless, partly because politics failed to address
deeper sources of worry and grievance. Kazin's political writing typically
conveyed feelings of exasperation, even despair, that extended beyond politics to the deteriorating streets of New York, to the direction of academic
literary study, and, increasingly, to the narrowing conditions of his own life.
Was his political outrage, he wondered, simply the "personal bitterness" of
"an old man" angry at "being thought redundant"? A recurrent feature of
much of Kazin's best writing had been the evocation and celebration of
hope and expectant beginnings. By the mid-1980s, youthful hopes were for
Kazin a memory of a memory. A survivor of a heart attack and bypass
surgery, and increasingly worried about his health—he seemed to break a
new bone every year—he found himself thinking more and more about
endings, often anxiously and bitterly but also with new attention to priori-
ties—to his work, to family and a narrowing circle of friends, and to those increasingly urgent questions of faith and doubt raised by his favorite writers.[1]

For someone who had always regarded his life as a struggle, and frequently a lonely, insecure, and unhappy one, the prospect of seeing that
struggle wind down might be expected to bring a small sense of relief or at
least some relaxation from the daily grind. Kazin never gave it much serious
thought. On particularly difficult days, he might quote lines to himself from
Keats on being "half in love with easeful death" or ceasing "on the midnight
with no pain," or from Robert Frost's "Stopping by the Woods on a Snowy
Evening"; but, he quickly asked himself, if "the woods are lovely, dark and
deep," "how would I know if I bury myself there?" And he had many
promises to keep—to publishers, to editors, to himself. Keeping them
would be painful and exhausting. Not keeping them, not to keep working,
was unthinkable. "It is the forward movement that saves me," he had
written in 1983, thinking of the long struggle ahead: it is the lectures, the
articles, the books, "the need to write x and to review y, that keeps me
going, literally." Anything less than a full effort would be "a helpless lurch
toward death."[2]

Moreover, with retirement looming and the list of "absent" and "ex-
friends" lengthening, working—that is, writing—was becoming the one
reliable constant in his life (excepting Judith Dunford). Though he made a
few new friends in his later years, Kazin worried about a constricting social
life that left him increasingly on his own, talking to himself in his journal,
while pushing ahead incessantly with his work—"What else is there? I have
no life these days except in work." Indeed, much of his sustained work in
these last years seemed to grow out of his deepening sense of isolation and
his desire to pursue religious needs not unconnected with solitude. "Why
in the world was I condemned to so much isolation, why as always are there
so few friends?" he asked himself in 1989 as he was starting on his "religion
book." He had no ready answers, but he had little doubt about the connection between his loneliness and his intensifying religious interest. "The
lonely man imagines God," he explained, adding a favorite quote from
Alfred North Whitehead, "Religion is what we do with our solitariness." He
would publish three books in the 1990s—*Writing Was Everything* (1994),
A Lifetime Burning in Every Moment (1996), and *God and the American
Writer* (1997)—all of them meditations on solitude, literature, and belief,
and all of them written with a view toward the end: "the absolute loneliness, anonymity, of the experience—so limited to you alone that it can seem

unreal as well as unbearable." While "starting out" was unquestionably Kazin's surest, most consistently radiant muse, "the end of things" proved an unexpected source of inspiration—not least because he remained convinced to the very end that in the struggle of the solitary consciousness against nothingness, words were, indeed, the last hope for salvation, that "writing was everything."[3]

"How Long Can This Last?"

On November 15, 1984, Alfred wrote Michael an out-of-sorts postelection letter. He had, he said, expected Reagan's reelection. "A society based more and more on nothing but the good life deserves its replica." He was, however, disgusted by the "Mondale fiasco" and the behavior of "the left, the near left, the far left, the liberals! Bah!" He complained that Michael's friends at the *Nation* had lost touch with everyone in America except Gus Hall, head of the American Communist Party, and that his own friends at the *New Republic* were pushing a seventieth anniversary issue with Henry Kissinger, Irving Kristol, and Warren Beatty as "lead stars." He concluded on a personal note. Reagan was planning substantial domestic cuts, and his own Medicare benefits had already been reduced. "Meanwhile, my retirement is approaching, my petty pension looms up like a nightmare, and all the richies we are trying to enlist to keep me at it (the Graduate Center) seem very shy, very! Oh well, I am sure I can lean on my family."[4]

In June 1985, Alfred would be seventy years old, the mandatory retirement age. Because he had started "regular" teaching late in life, his pension would be less then a third of his present salary, and he was worried. Manhattan was expensive, he had a mortgage for a "mansion" in Connecticut, and he had health concerns. He hoped the Graduate Center would come up with funds that would enable him to teach individual seminars for a few more years—which it did. But he was not taking any chances. He had already agreed to deliver a series of lectures at Drew University in the winter of 1985 for ten thousand dollars. He was negotiating with New York University to do a course there in the fall, and he continued to line up speaking engagements: a speech at the Grolier Club on Sinclair Lewis in February, lectures at Brandeis and Boston universities in March, more lectures in Salamanca, Spain, in June.

The pace did not slacken after the official August retirement. "In the last eight days," he wrote in an October journal entry, "I have written over 30 pages [of a] first draft of the Pound lecture for Alabama, 'Teacher,' for Louis Rubin's Algonquin Press book, the Yaddo memoir for the group of memoirs they are putting out there, and this morning hope to get on with the last chapter of the book [A Writer's America]. Slightly breathless, for this week has included two classes at N.Y.U., the usual seminar at City Graduate Center. I am so pent up that I find it hard to sleep except on those now all-too-frequent nights when I take Halcion, and often strain to catch my breath as I walk. The steps going up the exits at the 96th St. subway are hard. Yet I pound away, all this steady work . . . sometimes makes me uneasy . . . how long can this last?"[5]

It would last quite a while. Kazin had always been a "scrambler"—Judith Dunford's term. Now, the need to scramble was more urgent. He had been in this situation before, the freelancer looking out for the next visiting professorship, applying for grants and fellowships, lining up speaking engagements and review assignments, "piling it up, item by item, adding it up, making things come out neat and right"—except that he was now in his seventies with the future closing in. In the thirteen years from his official retirement until his death June 5, 1998, Kazin published five books, more than fifty articles, reviews, and introductions; taught dozens of courses; lectured in Spain, Amsterdam, Copenhagen, Berlin, and Salzburg—all the while applying for new positions and grants. After a 1990 visit to the Hospital for Special Surgery, where he received gold injections for arthritis, he remarked that he was not "fit for all the misery" ahead of him. Yet he thanked God for that "very impatience [which] is keeping me alive and taking me forward. Full of work, work."[6]

Kazin was modestly successful in finding visiting professorships. In the spring of 1988, he served as Howard A. Newman Professor of American Civilization at Cornell. In the fall of 1989, he taught a seminar on Emily Dickinson at Barnard; and in the spring of 1990, he gave a series of seven lectures as the Heritage Professor of Artistic and Social Criticism at George Mason University. He had mixed results applying for grants. He had already received four Guggenheim fellowships and was not encouraged by the director, Gordon Ray, to apply for another. Nor did Ray think there was much chance of his getting a Mellon Foundation grant. Kazin had some hope for one of the recently established MacArthur grants and asked recipients Irving Howe and Robert Coles whether they would support him. They explained that past recipients could not make recommendations for MacArthur fellowships and that the process of nomination and selection was rather mysterious. Kazin might have arrived at the same conclusion when the MacArthur people contacted him for an opinion about the worthiness of his longtime nemesis, Diana Trilling. He had more success with the New York Foundation for the Arts, which offered him grants of thirty-two thousand dollars in 1991, 1992, and 1993 for the completion of a book on his journals and another on religion.

His most consistent source of income in his postretirement years, besides his pension and social security, was book reviewing and the occasional essay —reliable standbys since the early thirties. The *New York Times Book Review*, the *New York Review of Books*, and the *New Republic* remained his primary outlets, though he also published in *Diversion: A Magazine for Doctors in their Leisure Time,* in *Travel,* in *Christianity Today,* in the *New York Observer* (founded in 1989), and in the *Forward.* In 1992, *Forbes* paid him seventy-five hundred dollars for a short essay on "the human side of business." The editors did not much like the piece, which criticized the Reagan administration, but were happy enough with his remarks on the current cultural decline. The array of subjects on which he wrote reviews and essays had narrowed some. Though he ventured occasionally into contemporary fiction (by Gore Vidal, John Updike, E. L. Doctorow, and Richard Ford), he wrote primarily on figures and subjects that had long interested him (Bellow, Dreiser, Dickinson, nineteenth-century American history, William Blake) or that he would be discussing in forthcoming books.[7]

Knowing that he was moving closer to "the end of things," Kazin was also determined to have a last say on certain issues of longstanding concern. One of these was Ezra Pound. He had written on Pound before in *New York Jew,* in *An American Procession,* and in a 1956 essay in which he stated that "any man of good will *must* be divided about Pound." His intention in this final contribution on Pound, "The Fascination and Terror of Ezra Pound" (*New York Review,* March 1986), was to remind people of Pound the Fascist and unsettle the consensus among academics that Pound's Fascism, while regrettable, was incidental to his achievement and no longer a central concern. Far from being an aberration, Kazin argued, Pound's Fascism, his passion for authority, his disgust with ordinary people, his gut hatred of the Jews were inseparable from his "genius." The cruelty of Fascism and hatred of the Jews were essential elements in his poetry and cannot be shrugged away in judging his work. He also faulted Pound for promoting the more offensive features of literary modernism—its self-preening avant-gardism, its antidemocratic authoritarianism, its arrogant, ahistorical revaluation of the literary past. Despite the overreaching of the "curators" of "the museum of modern literature," "modernism," Kazin argued "is not our only tradition."[8]

The Pound essay provoked responses both in support of Kazin's attack (Kay Boyle and Al Alvarez) and in defense of Pound (Allen Ginsberg and Princeton professor Theodore Weiss). But it is doubtful it did much to shift opinion about Pound. By the late eighties the Pound wars were over. Few needed to be reminded of Pound's anti-Semitism or told that "modernism" was not our only tradition. The bitter fights over Pound had entered the culture and the anthologies; and that is precisely what troubled Kazin—as though the injury and hurt of Pound's pronouncements could be filed away with other scholarly notations. Like the searing images of the Holocaust never far from consciousness—"the dates of the Holocaust living in me"— Kazin's case against Pound was a case for historical remembrance, for keeping the wound open, for refusing to let the pain be numbed, catalogued, forgotten.[9]

He describes a different kind of wound in a 1986 New Republic essay on writers and the Spanish Civil War. Titled "The Wound That Will Not Heal," it, too, is an essay of historical remembrance, an effort to keep the painful past alive. It is also a counterattack against those (mostly neoconservative) revisionists out to discredit all progressive ideals ever held by the American left. The war had been a chronic sore spot with Kazin (and others) since the thirties. He had returned to it repeatedly in reviews, essays, and portraits as well as in Starting Out in the Thirties, where he tried to recapture something of the desperate hope and idealism that had fired the imagination of writers in support of the Republic. What had made the war so difficult for radicals like himself was that in supporting the Republic against Franco and the forces of Fascism, they were also joining sides with the Stalinists, an unpalatable but understandable choice at the time. "Fascism was still the major threat to peace." Over time historians would document how pervasive, cynical, and corrupting the Stalinist influence had been in the failed struggle for Spain, raising painful questions for those who had supported participation. Had they made the wrong choice? Was their idealism misplaced? Were they dupes or worse?[10]

For an answer (or answers) Kazin turned in his 1986 essay to the writers who had gone to Spain during the war: George Orwell, André Malraux, Georges Bernanos, John Dos Passos, Simone Weil, and Ernest Hemingway. Writers, he believed, were better able than historians to capture and preserve the feelings of the moment—the hope and idealism as well as the bitterness, anger, and uncertainty. In *Homage to Catalonia*, Orwell had attacked the cynicism and dishonesty of the Stalinists and called Spain a political "disaster," while insisting that it was "one I do not wish I had missed" and that had left him "with not less but more belief in the decency of human beings." It is this intensity and complexity of feeling, Kazin argued, that are too often missing in the histories and commentaries on the war. Two months later, as if to illustrate his point, Ronald Radosh, citing recent histories, attacked Kazin and his writers for naivete and bad faith— had they "looked closer they could have discerned the truth at the time."[11]

Radosh's response (in the *New Criterion*) demonstrated precisely why Kazin felt his own piece had been necessary. It also indicated the need for the kind of "personal history" that traditional history too frequently leaves out. Radosh could cite authority after authority on the Stalinist domination of the war, the ineptitude of the anarchists, the brutalities committed by both sides—the general folly of it all. What he was unable (or unwilling) to do was to understand the depth of feeling, the hopes and feelings of betrayal, of those involved. Determined to show up the errors of the past, he missed (and dismissed) the experience of those who had actually lived through it. "I called my piece "The Wound That Will Not Heal," and it hasn't . . . it never will," Kazin wrote following the rebuke by Radosh. "Spain is deep in my heart, truly a sacred memory, for all the bitterness I feel equally about Stalin-Russia's tortures." "What I am feeling most [after reading Radosh and *New Republic* publisher Martin Peretz, who joined in the scolding] is a cultural lag in extremis," evident in "the forgetfulness of people" content to know the past, not through its lived-in moment-to-moment uncertainty, but with the safety of hindsight enforced by the ideological certainties of the present. Like "The Fascination and Terror of Ezra

Pound," "The Wound That Will Not Heal" was an attempt by Kazin to place on the record the still unsettled anguish of a generation.[12]

Family, Friends, and Ex-Friends

In 1988, father and son, who had been "sidling" toward each other politically for a decade, achieved a new level of understanding when Alfred accepted Michael's invitation to deliver an address at a banquet celebrating the founding of the magazine *Tikkun*. (Michael was its book editor.) Founded in 1986, partly as a counterweight to the neoconservative *Commentary*, *Tikkun* was an effort by young Jews of Michael's generation, many of them former members of the New Left, to repair relations between American Jews (and Judaism) and liberal left thinking and causes. Essential to that reparation—*tikkun olam* means to mend or repair the world—was reaching out to sympathetic members of the Old Left—among them Alfred Kazin and Irving Howe, both of whom addressed the gathering.

Calling his piece "The Cry for Justice," Kazin described the influence of his mother's "Orthodoxy" and his father's "orthodox socialism" on his life-long commitment to justice both for the Jews (especially poor Jews) and for humanity at large. Justice, he noted, is an admittedly idealistic commitment, especially when juxtaposed against the "grimly realistic" values of the Reagan administration and its unabashed celebration of "greed" and "selfishness." He was not prepared to say what "justice" was, and he doubted that there was any such thing as "eternal justice," but he did know from his daily experiences on the New York streets how injustice and suffering cried out for redress—much as the evictions of families onto the Brownsville streets in the thirties cried out to his indignant mother and the neighbors. The question that disturbed him now, watching the support among official Jewish groups for the Reagan-Bush administrations, was whether Jews, so long the victims of persecution, could any longer hear that cry.[13]

It would be an exaggeration to conclude from Kazin's remarks and from his (and Howe's) prominent place at the banquet that *Tikkun* had succeeded in merging the thirties and the sixties generations of Jewish writers and intellectuals. "We speak as a different generation of Jews," *Tikkun*'s editor, Michael Lerner, wrote in the journal's founding editorial. "We do not feel ourselves outside of this [American] reality" in the way the Jews of

Depression and World War II America felt. Nonetheless, the two groups shared important interests and convictions, which in a period of conservative resurgence could at least bring them into closer relation. "To mend, repair and transform the world" meant, among other things, repairing relations between fathers and sons—something Michael and his father were already working hard to achieve.[14]

Indeed, Alfred's improving relations with Michael were one of the happier developments of his later years. Not that all things had been resolved between them. Despite their "sidling" moves toward each other, Kazin was often impatient with Michael's continued radical sympathies, particularly when they reminded him of the painful past. "I had much to endure in Michael's 'revolutionary' period, which seemed to last forever and whose traces can still be found in the suburban professor, home-owner, father." But politics, particularly Michael's historical interest in American politics, was also a point of connection. Kazin was pleased that Michael had written his dissertation (and first book) on trade union power in the "progressive" era. He was equally proud when Michael obtained a position (and tenure) as a labor historian at American University in Washington. He worried, however, New York intellectual that he was, that Michael might be tempted to overspecialize. "Is there any chance, now that your book is practically done," he wrote in 1985, that "you shift to a slightly *wider* people, not forgetting labor?" "I don't know what I can say to convince you," he wrote more emphatically a few years later, "that stirring as all this labor history is, you might broaden your interests a little." In fact, Michael's interests were already fairly broad, evident in dozens of reviews and essays he wrote for a variety of journals on politics, populism, and American history generally. His next book, *The Populist Persuasion: An American History* (1995), a study of American populism and its rhetoric, indicated that he could write narrative history on topics other than labor. His father could not have been happier, "a brilliant book"—though he warned Michael to be careful to "avoid the thousand and one clichés" that mark our "corporate culture."[15]

A more intractable difficulty was the irrecoverable past and Alfred's longtime yearning for the kind of father-son intimacy he had never had with his own father and had largely missed with Michael. "I want to keep remaking the past until it becomes a different affair of father and son—a father who lived with his son, saw him grow up, had some effect on his upbringing." It is a gulf he knew would never be filled—at times "a wide yawning space," at other times, simply a "vacancy" eclipsed by the sheer miracle of Michael's existence—"a constant astonishment to me." In one poignant letter, he told Michael that he had "always hoped you would call me Dad or Father, but since that seems beyond you except at certain enchanted moments, by all means stick to 'AK.' 'Alfred' is out!" Having largely missed Michael's childhood years, Alfred often found himself thinking of his son more as a brother, a younger brother to be sure, but now that "we are intellectually the same age, so to speak," a "spiritual brother." Son or brother, Michael was for his father increasingly a figure of "continuity," of the persistence of family and tradition—"Avraham ben Gedahlia, and now Michael ben Avraham." And the tradition continued. On the eve of Rosh Hashanah 1987, Michael called to tell Alfred he was to be a grandfather. "You can't get away from the ancientness and obstinacy at once. Jews as a family," rejoiced the grandfather to be. "Whatever else, a family. The brethren. Right in there, ineluctably, with the eternal *mispocha* [family] . . . you can't help feeling a bit grateful."[16]

In his last years Kazin would have many reasons to be grateful for Michael and his growing family. The birth of Daniel on May 18, 1988, would be followed by that of Maia Rebecca Kazin on June 2, 1991. Alfred was a welcome and frequent visitor in Michael's and Beth's home in Chevy Chase; and while he was sometimes frustrated that his son and daughter-in-law, now teaching at the George Washington School of Medicine, seemed preoccupied with work and their immediate family, he took comfort in the steadiness of their lives and the pleasantness of the surroundings. "In the morning, this morning, up before everyone, I eat in their extraordinarily beautiful kitchen and looked at Suburbia. . . . and dreamed that I too could get out of NY."[17]

Steadiness was not the word he would use for the rhythm of Kate's life—or of their relations after his separation from Ann Birstein. He had been unnerved by Kate's initial response to his involvement with Judith Dunford. He was relieved that Kate had attended the marriage in 1983, but he also recognized that it had created difficulties, that Kate now felt less a part of his life and resented the displacement. In the often bitter exchanges that occurred between them, Alfred inevitably found himself justifying his decision on the basis of his new happiness with Judith. But his pleading with

Kate, as he frequently did, that she must understand how much he loved and depended on Judith (rather than her mother) was not persuasive. It also raised troubling questions about the many problems that had plagued his and Ann's marriage, the anger, screaming, and violence, and how they might have affected Kate. Watching his daughter explode with anger at some remark of his, Alfred was torn between self-justification and guilt— "all that bad chemistry between Ann and me [had gotten] into Kate's veins and arteries."[18]

Another point of contention was Kate's career. Kazin had prized her literary gifts since she was a child. Her success at Smith, where she graduated with high honors in English and won prizes for her poetry, confirmed his faith in her talents. Though he had misgivings about her going on for a doctorate, which he feared might stifle her creative instincts, he was pleased to see her gain entrance into Cornell's prestigious Ph.D. program and then obtain an academic appointment in 1981 at the University of Iowa. When four years later he learned that she was contemplating law school, he was stunned. Why throw over a promising career teaching literature to go into something wholly new? What did she think she was doing? Nor was it only the changes in her career plans that unnerved him. He also worried about the changes in her mood and temperament, often in rapid succession—"incredible variations from immaturity to infernal intelligence," the alternating highs and lows (not unlike her mother's or his own), and "most startling of all, the way she will suddenly cast a cold eye as neutral as a crocodile's sizing you up." As anxious about the future and security of his children as his mother had been about his own, Kazin feared that Kate lacked the emotional stability to make her way in the world; and he continued to worry that "her turbulent life with Mama and Papa contributed to her decidedly marginal way of thinking and perhaps of living."[19]

The changes and the worries would continue. In 1986 Kate left Iowa for the University of Pennsylvania Law School. Upon graduation in 1989, she took a job at a Washington law firm, followed by a position in the U.S. Department of Labor Civil Rights Division, where among other duties, she worked on speeches for Labor Secretary Robert Reich. Then in 1995, to her father's consternation, she decided on another change. "Kate is definitely set on moving to Israel," Kazin wrote to Michael (who was then on a Fulbright in Holland), "and is so defiant about the whole biz and not needing money from me that I am sad beyond words." Not only was she throwing over another promising career, she was moving to Begin's and Sharon's Israel. Her father was in despair. He felt that he might never see her again, and he continued to worry that her uncertain and mercurial temperament precluded the kind of order and happiness he wanted for his daughter. Still, he could not help but admire her nerve. "You have to hand it to Kate," he wrote Michael. "No one I know has such guts for changing profession—and now countries." A month later, he wrote that he was "getting excited about Kate's '*aliyah*' to Israel and am rounding up all possible friends in Israel to help her out."[20]

Alfred's relations with Kate never recovered from the breakup of his marriage to Ann. There was too much to overlook—too many unresolved problems between himself and Ann, too much resentment from Kate about his divorce and remarriage, too much accumulated guilt. At any moment, conversation between father and daughter could turn into a "minefield," "one triphammer effect after another." Even long-distance calls from Israel ended in shouting matches with his hanging up the phone. The explosions of anger and painful awkwardnesses would have mattered less had he cared less. "I am afraid to death to say what is in store for her. She is such an eternal waif." For all Kate's obvious intelligence and strength of will, her father saw something frighteningly provisional and willful about her life and personality that unnerved him—something that resisted all his (Jewish mother's?) efforts to direct and secure her future. "She goes her own way in everything and is sometimes a pain in the neck," he wrote to Israeli friends who had helped her. "I never know what she will do next and where she will turn next. But she is very dear to me." For her part, Kate deeply regretted the strained relations with her father, particularly in his later years when he seemed to become more "difficult" than ever and his "dense defensiveness" even more dense. "A brilliant student of his own loneliness," she wrote in a later memorial, he seemed increasingly and "heartbreakingly unreachable." Yet she recognized his anxious love and concern, which, however clumsily expressed, revealed "a desperate longing to connect, a wish for you that was impossible to resist."[21]

Changes were also happening in Alfred's social life outside the family. The divorce had shifted the basis of earlier social arrangements, leaving him unsure about how to deal with his and Ann's mutual friends. Though socially adept and an engaging conversationalist, Judith had not been part of Alfred's earlier life. It was not easy for her to pick up the interwoven threads in her husband's past. His reminiscing with old friends could leave her feeling awkward and isolated, and Alfred was anxious not to subject her to social situations in which she felt ill at ease. There was also the problem of space. Instead of the suite of rooms he and Ann had occupied on West End Avenue, he and Judith lived in a cramped one-bedroom apartment that could at best accommodate two guests crammed between the table and the sofa and the books piled everywhere. It is hard to entertain in a closet.

But Kazin was not particularly interested in entertaining old friends and acquaintances under any conditions. Relations with many of them had not been the same since the publication of *New York Jew* in 1978. The hostile response of so many "old friends" to his portrait of Lionel Trilling had left him feeling "humiliated" and wondering what friends he had left. Would Meyer Abrams still want to talk to him? Had Frank Kermode written him off? Kermode assured him that they were still friends, but Alfred was uncertain. Since his first visits to an analyst in the forties he had been hearing of his "deficiency in 'interpersonal relations.' " He knew he could be "difficult," that he was "not easily likeable." He was all too aware of his "famous aggressiveness and resentfulness." He was known to be "testy" and irritable, and he was not surprised to hear gossip about his becoming so angry with Cynthia Ozick at a party that he had seized his coat and stomped out of *his own apartment!* He had long worried about his lack of social skills, and advancing age had done little to change things for the better. A lengthening backlog of slights and offences, grudges and resentments, made encounters with longtime acquaintances awkward and painful. And he was less and less willing to make the effort. "I feel sort of marvelously desolate, hung up in outer space, 'out of it.' "[22]

Still, the growing isolation was upsetting, and he anguished over the breaks. One particular unhappy break was with Francis Steegmuller. Steegmuller and his wife Shirley Hazzard had always been great favorites of Alfred and Ann. Whether visiting them in their art-filled apartment on East Sixty-sixth Street or in their house overlooking the bay in Capri, Italy, or reading Steegmuller's commentary on Flaubert or Cocteau, Kazin had always been impressed by his talent, humor, and taste. Like Edmund Wilson, another "old-style man-of-letters," Steegmuller seemed to come from an earlier literary era, bringing with him a social-cultural ambience that Alfred and Ann found exciting—and flattering. "The Steegmullers had this gift of turning their dinner guests into replicas of *their* social graces." Yet, he could never suppress the feeling that they did not wholly approve of him, a lower-order upstart tolerated by "the salon keepers, the dinner-party givers, great picture owners." He had kept such feelings in check during the years with Ann, but he began to chafe under their "infernally snotty" eyes as their marriage fell apart. When the marriage ended, Kazin broke off relations. He agonized over the break, thinking he might well be overreacting: "No doubt there is still a lot of self-conscious proletarian youth in me." But he had come to resent Steegmuller's "snubs and little faggy airs of distaste," those small but cumulative insults to his sensibility that demanded some final squaring of accounts. Besides, he would rather be the one to take the initiative. "I have made more breaks with the gentry than they have with me," he had written in 1982. "67 years and I haven't changed a bit . . . and I must accept that unexpected view of my own assertiveness and even harshness."23

Of course, Kazin broke with others besides the gentry. If he resented being "snotted" by the likes of Steegmuller (and Malcolm Cowley and John Chamberlain), he also resented the behavior of those from his own background who were willing to do whatever was necessary in their push for personal advancement, including the repudiation of their early ideals. The ferocity of his attack on Norman Podhoretz, Irving Kristol, Lionel Abel, and other old friends and acquaintances in his 1987 *Dissent* piece, "They Made It," left little room for reconciliation—even had Kazin wanted it. He was also, reportedly, not above snubbing old friends when they met in public, which, according to Kristol, he frequently did to his wife Gertrude Himmelfarb, a colleague of Kazin's at the Graduate Center. Known for his relaxed, easy manner with both political friends and opponents, Kristol learned to keep his distance. "Alfred was a temperamental porcupine, to put it bluntly. One approached with caution." Podhoretz, who in 1986 sent Kazin an unanswered note asking whether they could be friends once more, thought he had simply "gone off the deep end." Lying awake at night, Kazin sometimes worried about his anger and growing isolation from so many "ex-friends." There were moments when he felt "ashamed of roiling so much in these disaffections, of feeling so 'apart' from certain people." He was not about to change, however. He had "decided to take a stronger line"—even if it left him "hung up in outer space."[24]

The loss of old friends was somewhat salved by the gain of a few new ones. One was the novelist Philip Roth. Kazin had first heard of Roth in 1959 when he had read and written a highly favorable review of *Goodbye, Columbus* and some of Roth's short stories for the *Reporter.* He and Roth had become acquainted at Wellfleet in the summer of 1962 and later at Yaddo, but they didn't become friends until the 1980s when Roth bought a house in Cornwell Bridge, thirty miles from Kazin's place in Roxbury. They visited each other in Connecticut and met occasionally in the city for dinner. The friendship was not close, but it was satisfying to both of them. Kazin was fascinated by Roth's "shrewdness," his "savage, suspicious, witty" intelligence. He enjoyed watching his "clever, sharp, sharp" mind at work, which seemed to be summed up in "his pointy nose and pointy instrumentalist personality." (He also enjoyed the company of Roth's companion, the actress Claire Bloom.) Roth, in turn, admired Kazin as a serious critic with a lively intelligence, sometimes sending him unpublished manuscripts for his comments. He also liked his pugnacity, a trait that seemed to becoming more and more apparent. He called him a "fellow pugilist."[25]

Philip Roth was one of the livelier figures in Kazin's social-intellectual circle in Roxbury—which, he acknowledged, was not all that lively or intellectual. To be sure, one might run into Arthur Miller at the dump or the art critic John Russell at the market. At the occasional cocktail party, Kazin might find himself talking to Susan Cheever, Erica Jong (!), John Styron, the actor Richard Widmark, and if he was lucky, "the adorable beautiful Barbara Ungeheuer, in a red dress"—all very pleasant, but hardly comparable with the Wellfleet gatherings of twenty years past. "Intellectuals there were intellectuals," Kazin reminisced. "Roxbury is lovely, but the intellectual company is, how shall I put it, all money. There's nobody here except people with money." There was money in Wellfleet, too: money, influence, power—emanating straight out of the Kennedy and Johnson White House. But there were also Edmund Wilson, who never had any money, and Richard Hofstadter and Daniel Aaron and Stuart Hughes and Arthur Schlesinger, the Washington brain trust, and half the Harvard faculty. The competition could get intense. One had to be on one's mettle. Roxbury had other amenities, not insignificant to a man in his seventies—a quiet room in which he could write (a rarity in Wellfleet), a view from the kitchen to the surrounding woods and fields, a walk to Mine Hill overlooking the Shepaug River. "The view is so beautifully archaic and 'old America' that, every time I step off [route] 67 to look at it, I draw a deep breath in perfect satisfaction. I could never get tired looking at that 'clearing.' "[26]

Kazin had some new friends in the city as well, or more accurately, two old acquaintances with whom he had recently developed a closer relationship—Saul Steinberg and Anatole Broyard. Kazin had known Steinberg since the late forties when they were both working for the New Yorker, Kazin as book reviewer, Steinberg as cartoonist. They had become friends in the 1980s, drawn together in part by their age—Steinberg was a year older than Kazin—and their long, fascinated relationship with New York City. That Steinberg was a European Jew was also a recommendation. Like Edgar Wind, Hannah Arendt, Paolo Milano, and Erich Heller, Steinberg was another link with European culture from before the war, another "displaced" European always seeing the country from the alert but slightly detached perspective of the outsider. Born in Romania, Steinberg had studied philosophy at the University of Bucharest and in 1940 received a doctorate from the Reggio Politecnico in Milan. With the sponsorship of the New Yorker he emigrated to the United States in 1942, and after nearly forty years of living in New York and working for the New Yorker, he was for Kazin "all European still."[27]

Their relationship was not exactly easy. Steinberg could be intimidating. "He takes you in, studies you, speaks in a slow reflective tone which seems to swallow you up!" Conversation tended to be in one direction and could become tense with concentrated insight. "S.S. is oracular, deliberate in the smallest things." Dinner chez Steinberg could leave one slightly breathless —"brilliant, dazzling, every word positively an original perception." The intellectual pressure relaxed a little when the two tried out some violin duets. Amateurish brashness was more the order here than brilliance. Playing duets broke down barriers and had long been for Kazin a kind of Jewish bonding. Steinberg was a happy, unexpected discovery at a time when "staleness, elsewhere and everywhere and otherwise, absolutely confound[ed]" him. His "world city," it seemed, still had some "buried treasure" left.[28]

Anatole Broyard was another recent discovery. In fact, it was Broyard who contacted Kazin in the spring of 1988 to ask whether he would look at a few chapters of a memoir he was writing of Greenwich Village during the war years. Kazin knew Broyard vaguely from the forties and more recently from his work as an editor of the *New York Times Book Review,* and he did not trust him—partly because he was an editor of the *Book Review,* and he distrusted all journal editors. But he was also was put off by Broyard's manner. He seemed "too utterly quick and debonair" when they ran into each other on the street or at the Forty-third Street subway exit at Times Square—debonair and strangely "truculent." Kazin could not place him and remained wary—until he read the chapters of the memoir. Broyard had evoked the atmosphere of those "expectant" Greenwich Village years in a way that made them live again. Kazin encouraged him, supported him for a Guggenheim, "hectored" him to finish his memoir, and over the course of several months found him to be "a most open friend." On September 3, 1989, Broyard told Kazin he had prostate cancer. He died in November 1990, the book unfinished. Kazin wrote a memorial piece for the *Times Book Review* lamenting his death and the unfinished book, which would be published posthumously and unfinished in 1993 with the title *Kafka Was the Rage.*[29]

Kazin's latter-day encounter and friendship with Broyard would stay with him—"so strange to make real connections with anyone, these solitary days"—a connection renewed in memory whenever he heard of the death of another friend or figure from the Greenwich Village years: Seymour Krim, Paolo Milano, and art historian and critic Meyer Schapiro, a favorite figure from the New School. "Meyer Schapiro dead at 91. The attentiveness Schapiro inspired as he beautifully stood there thinking out loud, weaving his mind around the painting being shown on the screen. Those gloriously expectant days, right after the war. Anatole Broyard caught the atmosphere of the time in his memoir, *Kafka Was the Rage.* On the roof of the New School with a girl, the madly learned Schapiro addressed me on the subject of *Belgian surrealists!*" Socially and intellectually, if not politically, the forties had also been a time of "starting out," a moment when, in Broyard's words, there was "a sense of coming back to life," and, not surprisingly, a moment that Kazin in his seventies recalled with the same nostalgia and yearning he had earlier recalled the hopeful thirties. If the thirties had been a time when history seemed swept up in one grand unfolding idea, the postwar forties, "those intoxicatingly unsettled years right after the war," had been a time of intense new interests and fresh starts—a moment when the intellectual life had seemed terribly important and one's future as open-ended as the country's.[30]

With so many of his own generation turning into absent friends or ex-friends, Kazin took some consolation in the friendships he had developed with a few younger people—colleagues, journalists, and a few students—who shared his interests and did not make him feel too conscious of his age. One new friend he particularly valued was Morris Dickstein, a colleague at the Graduate Center. Dickstein had long admired Kazin's work and, after some initial awkwardness, found him an approachable, even eager friend—and a marvelous raconteur, his conversation, "full of humor, sarcasm, vivid recollection, and quick intelligence." Kazin in turn was impressed by Dickstein, not least for his interest in his "elders" and his fund of local information. A " very nice fellow, he is also into all available gossip. The Columbia Connection—with so much of literary NY as well as Columbia itself, and its past great men." He was also fond of Louis Menand, another colleague, who had an office next door at the Graduate Center. Menand was witty, well informed, and a great audience. He loved listening to Kazin on the personalities he had known, and "he knew everybody." He could go on and on with anecdotes full of truly "wicked" characterizations. Menand acknowledged that Kazin was "a grumpy guy," but not with him. Menand, who wrote regularly for the *New Yorker*, felt that the strongest tie between them was the fact that they were both "writers." Kazin was much "more comfortable around writers and journalists than academic types."[31]

Kazin also sought to establish friendly relations with young journalists outside the university. In part, he was simply looking after his business interests, as in his relations with Leon Wieseltier, book editor of the *New Republic*. Kazin valued the magazine as an outlet and wanted to be on good terms with the literary editor. (He self-censored more than one harsh letter to Wieseltier objecting to an editorial decision.) Yet he genuinely liked Wieseltier, badgered him to look him up when he was in New York, and was always happy to meet him for lunch when he was in Washington. He was especially pleased when Wieseltier brought along his *New Republic* colleague Hendrick Hertzberg. Kazin had known Hertzberg's parents in the forties—"Rick has Hazel's rabbit-like cuteness and Sidney's gentleness"—

and in recent years had been happy to renew the family connection. "Nice lunch in WA yesterday with Rick Hertzberg and Leon Wieseltier," he wrote in his journal. "Leon the prankster and punster looking (as he says) like George Washington in a circumambulating mop of white hair (and him not 40 yet). Weird. But the talk was fast and good and full of gossip, and I was so moved by being with friends again."[32]

Students were another source of friendship—though differences in age and experience could make connections difficult. Lecturing at various schools around the country, Kazin often felt he was from a different planet. "You find yourself talking to kids as if you were blowing smoke rings at them. Just awful, becoming an old age phony like our President." Recognizing the gulf between them, he was the more touched when a group of students and former students at the Graduate Center and Barnard proposed that they meet occasionally for dinner to socialize and talk about American literature. Mary Beth McMahon remembers his being exhilarated by the "salon-like" arrangement, which she and the others, including Carol Saltus, Margaret Thompson, and Elizabeth Thompson, found "wonderfully informative and loose." Kazin, for his part, was flattered and pleased. "They are my claque, they love me, feel attuned to me, want to know how to evade the spreading tide of theory." It was all very "touching and a little poignant," and he felt "warmed and gratified for their love."[00]

If facing a room full of students could make Kazin feel old and irrelevant, gatherings of those his own age did not make him feel much better—or younger. Nowhere was he more aware of the ravages of old age than in meetings of the National Institute and the American Academy. After delivering a eulogy for James T. Farrell at the National Institute in 1980 (eulogies were standard fare at the meetings), Kazin could only wonder at the "tedious embarrassing evening." "What bores these immortals are . . . no one under 58 in sight." To be sure, the meetings provided the opportunity to see old acquaintances, friends, and ex-friends, but for Kazin, the rewards were negligible—"So much old age, creaking senility and self importance at the American Institute," he remarked after a December 1982 meeting. In November 1989, he was inducted into the American Academy of Arts and Sciences, whose membership, unlike that of the National Institute and the American Academy of Arts and Letters, is limited to less than one hundred. A new member is admitted only when another dies. Kazin was elected to fill the seat of the recently deceased Malcolm Cowley. But if the company was more select (and older still) than its "sister" academy, it was even more deadly. "As Groucho would say, I wouldn't belong to any club that had me as a member. . . . I have Cowley's seat, who succeeded Van Wyck Brooks. I am the fourth (Seat 43) after Edwin Blashfield, Brooks, Cowley! Each of whom seem[s] to have lasted in the seat a very long time." Kazin found the induction ceremony comical—"the solemnity of it all"—which became truly "laughable" when "the big discussion came up whether or not to abolish the whole thing."[34]

For all his impatience and boredom at meetings of the "immortals" and the "elect," with their inevitable reminders of time passed and passing, Kazin was not indifferent to the honor of belonging to a select company. Throughout the eighties, he had encouraged Henry Steele Commager to support his membership in the American Academy of Arts and Sciences. To be "elevated" to the rank of the immortals was, after all, to play out the role and narrative of "the rise of Alfred Kazin." "For the Jew making his way up from the ranks," he had written in a 1966 journal entry, "the drama of society, the drama of *place,* is overpowering." And if he was often amused and sometimes irritated by the pervading aura of self-importance among the "elect," he remained as fascinated as ever by the social skills and manners on display—whether in the consistently genial deportment of John Kenneth Galbraith or "the limitless amount of social cheeriness Shirley [Hazzard] can get out of (for instance) the fact that Francis's [Steegmuller] cane had lost its rubber bottom." None among the select, however, fascinated like Arthur Schlesinger Jr.[35]

Kazin and Schlesinger had known each other a long time; and despite Kazin's suspiciousness of intellectuals close to power, they had enjoyed remarkably good relations—no small achievement among Kazin's long-term acquaintants. In part, this may have been a result of their moving in different social circles. Kazin grouped Schlesinger among those intellectual "celebrities" not in his orbit, so questions of rivalry never arose. Another reason was Kazin's genuine respect for Schlesinger's intellectual and social skills—"the perfect courtier. Intelligence of the most flexible [kind]. Manner (public) absolutely flawless. Never at a loss." Though sometimes annoyed with what he believed was Schlesinger's liberties with the truth, Kazin was constantly amazed by the way correct social manner could de-fuse even his irritation. "AMS Jr. greeted me as he appeared on the 15th floor. Expressed 'concern' about my illness [arthritis]. Arthur always blunts my exasperation with him by being the perfect gent." At a dinner party Schlesinger had no match:

> As usual, Arthur Schlesinger stole the show [Kazin remarks after a Century dinner in honor of Daniel Aaron]. At least for me. His knowledge of American "society," his very quick mind, and above all his experience at such dinners make him fascinating. Despite the troubles we have had, I have to confess that Arthur (and I am not forgetting what a fibber he can be when it comes to his authority figures) is the nearest thing to a Howells with Adams-like intelligence and political emotion that we have. I am always amazed by his familiarity with the current fiction as well as the various notables whom [he is] in touch with. Arthur has been everywhere and knows everybody, and I have to say, with some ruefulness, has the sharpness that comes with social experience. My mulish solitariness these days certainly has its limits.

If this passage testifies to Schlesinger's singular skills, it also testifies to Kazin's capacity for honest appreciation and painful candor.[36]

One honor that Alfred accepted without reservation during this period (despite the elderly company) was a request from the Union of Soviet Writers that he and Judith join Schlesinger, Elizabeth Hardwick, Louis Auchincloss, David Halberstam, and Harrison Salisbury on a trip to Russia in May 1990. Although he had largely lost interest in traveling abroad by the nineties, this was not an opportunity to pass up. "One of the many reasons I would hate to die in the next thrilling ominous decade," he wrote on October 23, 1989, five months after Mikhail Gorbachev had announced that he would not stop democratic reforms in the satellite states of the USSR: "I would have to miss the thrilling developments and the Big Quake that may erupt politically in old Stalin land." Within weeks (November 9), the Berlin Wall had fallen and the Soviet Union, already in a state of economic and political confusion under Gorbachev's policies of perestroika and glasnost, seemed to be moving haltingly, blunderingly, but inexorably, away from its Marxist-Leninist totalitarian past.[37]

In Moscow, Kazin saw a country "in limbo," caught between the heavy officialdom that he had found so oppressive in his 1959 visit and a "hidden" Moscow that seemed to be coming out of hiding. There were still the "official huge blocks of Stalinist crash housing," but there were also the "dark sooty monasteries and churches," pointed out by the hosts from the Union of Soviet Writers, "where every wall is lined up and down with precious, opulently colored icons. . . . God is back!" The group attended the usual panel discussions with the Soviet cultural representatives plumping for their country's literature, but now well aware of the changes that were coming—one of the topics: "Social Changes in the Modern World and Their Influence on Morals." There were the same delays and confusion. But what most impressed Kazin was the mystery of what they were seeing and where it was all going. At a time when so much in the world and in his life could seem stale and routine, Russia, of all places, was awakening unexpected new hope. History on the move again. Some things had not changed, however; he was refused permission to visit Minsk, the place of his father's origins.[38]

"So Now We Must Work Harder Than Ever"

In July 1991, Kazin learned that he had prostate cancer and that it might have metastasized. He was scheduled for forty sessions of radiation treatments, which, it was hoped, would drive the cancer into permanent remission. His immediate response was to refocus. "So now we must work harder than ever. That old joke about the coming of a terrible flood that would wipe everything away, and the Rabbi said, 'We have just a few weeks in which to learn to live under water.'" Working even harder meant finishing two long-planned projects, a book based on his journals and one on religion and the American writer. But it also meant looking after his finances. His special seminar arrangement with the Graduate Center came to an end in 1989. "No [more] special treatment for this old man at the only place that ever gave me special treatment." He was able to make up some of the differences with grants from the New York Humanities Council, and he continued to write reviews, give speeches, and look for visiting professorships.[39]

For some time, he and Judith had hoped to move out of their one-bedroom apartment on Columbus Avenue. There was just too little space to live and work, and the misery and sense of threat that confronted them on the streets had become a daily ordeal—though Alfred could not but be amused on returning from a Connecticut weekend by the contrast between the "nonchalant but unmistakably propertied Roxberies in their casual summer shirts and shorts" and the heterogeneous scene greeting him on upper Broadway—"every possible color of skin, decrepitude, eccentricity . . . A mob united only by the streets they walk in." But health problems— arthritis, a persistent ulcer, phlebitis in the leg, a heart condition with recurrent chest pains, and now cancer—made moving out of the question. He did not have the will or the energy. He would remain one of the heterogeneous mob. What strength he had must be directed to work. The unusually hot New York summer together with the daily radiation treat- ments quickly turned July and August into a "season of hell," and the fall was not much better. Still, he managed to write a review-essay on nineteenth- century British and American culture for the *New Republic,* an essay on Henry Roth for the *New York Review,* and a review of Josephine Herbst's memoirs for the *New York Times Book Review.* He also gave a reading from his journals at the Jewish Museum, delivered a paper on Melville at the Melville Centenary Symposium at UCLA, and another on William James at the Graduate Center. The latter he felt had been "a great success."[40]

The project that most excited him during this period was a book based on his journals. Kazin had been thinking of such a book for much of his adult life and had come to see it in recent years as a spiritual obligation. "I owe it to my own soul to get something like the core of the Journal published in my lifetime," he wrote William Cain in 1992. Writing in the journals was where he felt closest to himself emotionally and intellectually, where he could indulge his astonishing fluency without fear of censure. After *New York Jew* in 1978, a book of his journals seemed the obvious way to con- tinue publishing autobiography. But the difficulties were daunting. What would be his principle of selecting from tens of thousands of entries going back to the early thirties? Did he even want to read through thousands of pages to make the selections? How to strike a balance between the the- matic concerns that make the journal a significant intellectual-spiritual enterprise and the spontaneity, "the fragments and sputtering and inter- ruptedness" that makes for exciting journal reading where anything might pop up? And what about libel? Some of the choicer entries were about living people, wives, mistresses—to say nothing of his own angers, petti- ness, and depressions. "The fact is that the journals scare even me when I look them over—so much longing, so much resentment, so many names to worry about even if they don't sue me." Having transcribed so much of himself into his journals, often at low points and in moments of crisis, how much of the offending material could he remove and retain "the raw materials" of his life, the inimitable flavor of "interruptedness" and unexpected discovery?[41]

In June 1985, he had had a long talk with his Knopf editor, Robert Gottlieb, but came away discouraged. Gottlieb had no answers; the project seemed too vague, and the problems intractable. He continued to wrestle with the subject over the next several years, even hiring an assistant, Carol Saltus, to help him go through the massive amount of material. But the closest he came to a satisfying solution was a title, *A Lifetime Burning in Every Moment,* and a possible theme. Taken from Eliot's *Four Quartets,* the title suggested both "the moment to moment life, the impulse and waywardness" of daily living, as well as the religious significance of that Augustinian "moment" when "time past, time present, time future [becomes] instantaneous with the present." While this sounded good, it did not provide a method of selection and organization, and by the spring of 1991, he had decided on a different title, *Jews: Experience of a Lifetime.* He would begin in the present, look back to a few signal events in his earlier life, and focus primarily on his new life with Judith following the 1978 publication of *New York Jew.* The title would have audience appeal and allow him flexibility as well as a means for selection. It may also have helped him sell the project to HarperCollins, with whom he had contracted for a book based on his journals to be "simply called JEWS."[42]

In the fall of 1993, the *New Yorker* agreed to publish a piece excerpted from the journals also called "Jews." It appeared in March with a headnote stating that "these recollections come from the journals of a lifetime." The note is vague enough about the status of the undated journal entries to leave Kazin free to rewrite and reorder them as he wished—which he did. The strongest part is the opening description of his visits to the radiation treatment center, where mostly aging Jewish men wait in line "for the machine that is going to postpone our death." Kazin fills in a few more gaps from his Brownsville past and offers up a number of unflattering portraits of notable Jews he has known—Zero Mostel, Harold Bloom, Jerzy Kozinsky, Saul Bellow. After praising Bellow for asking the right questions in his novels, he recalls the failed party at Gerald Freund's home and accuses his old friend of joining the ranks of the "Big Conservatives" at the University of Chicago, of turning his back on his working-class past, and of cultural ethnocentrism. "My heart sank when I heard that Bellow once said, 'Who is the Tolstoy of the Zulus? The Proust of the Papuans? I'd be glad to read him.' "[43]

Accompanied by a photograph portrait by Richard Avedon of the author looking frail, meditative, and bewildered, the *New Yorker* piece brought sympathetic notes from many old friends and acquaintances, some of whom had not known of his cancer diagnosis. Saul Bellow was not among them. A month before "Jews" appeared, he had sent Kazin a friendly note wishing him the best. It would be his last. Bellow, who had a degree in anthropology, had been stung by the flood of accusations that had followed his reported remarks about the "Proust of the Papuans." To discover that his old friend was prepared to go public with a private political quarrel and to join the chorus against his alleged cultural bigotry was the last straw. Faltering for years, the off-again, on-again friendship was finally over.

In the fall of 1993, Kazin interrupted work on his "journal-book" to write out a set of three talks about his life as a reader and writer to be delivered the following spring at Harvard as the William E. Massey Lectures in the History of American Civilization. Excepting City University, Harvard was the institution where he had the most longstanding connections. He had been giving lectures there since the early fifties, including a semester's stint as visiting lecturer in 1954, and most recently (1987), the Phi Beta Kappa address—"Where Would Emerson Find His Scholar Now?" His son was a Harvard graduate, his brother-in-law, Daniel Bell, the Henry Ford Professor of Sociology. Many of his friends were on the faculty, including William Alfred, Monroe Engel, Sacvan Bercovitch, and his longtime colleague and collaborator from Smith, Daniel Aaron. And there were other friends in the Boston-Cambridge area, including Peter Davison, Judge Kaplan, and, of course, his sister, Pearl, all of whom could be expected to attend his talks. Kazin was pleased by the honor, pleased for the chance to reminisce and discuss his life as a reader-writer among old friends, and pleased to say a few things about the state of contemporary criticism.

Delivered on May 9, 10, and 11, the three talks (later published by Harvard University Press as *Writing Was Everything*) recall writers, works, and reading experiences that Kazin considered critical to his education— reading *Oliver Twist,* for example, when sick in bed as a child; discovering Albert Camus's *The Stranger* in a postwar period of "human defeat and shame"; encountering Czeslaw Milosz's spiritual concerns in a postmodern world of fractured interests and "contented nihilism." (*Reading Was Everything* would have been a more accurate title.) By organizing his talks around writers of special moment to him, Kazin challenged the current academic practice of "discounting" writers by suspending them in a cloud of "hermeneutic suspicion" or denying them their distinctive voice and individual existence. Instead of critiquing these destructive and deconstructive tendencies in a systematic way, he offered himself as an example of the "private reader" who has been inspired and changed by writers, a number of whom—Melville, Dickinson, Kafka, Weil, Milosz—were of particular interest to him at this stage in his life for their reflections on questions of religious belief. *Writing Was Everything*, as Mark Krupnick and Paul Berman correctly noted in their reviews of the published book, is a personal retrospective that derives its sense of urgency from immediate spiritual needs.[44]

Despite mounting concerns over his health, Kazin had accepted an Annenberg Fellowship to teach at Brown University in the fall of 1994. He was responsible for one course and had chosen for his subject material he would be discussing in *God and the American Writer*. It would be his last semester of teaching and, as it turned out, not a very pleasant one. Health was part of the problem. Although the prostate cancer appeared to have gone into remission, he felt increasingly weak and under the weather. In a letter to Dr. Win Beck of the Harvard Medical School, who had written him about a recent article, he wrote that the radiation treatment had created a small fracture at the base of his spine, that he suffered from insomnia and was taking enough medicine to make a "pharmacy rich." Besides two medications for the prostate, "I take Midamor, Folic Acid, Methotrexate, Calan and Capoten and wear a Nitro dur patch (I had a double bypass some eleven yrs ago), Prilosec, Nytrin, Prednisone. Wow!" Recurrent fatigue and worries about his health might have bothered him less had Judith been with him in Providence. She, however, was working in New York. They saw each other on most weekends, but the traveling had become a genuine hardship.[45]

Nor was Kazin happy with the teaching. He had looked forward to bright, enthusiastic students consistent with Brown's reputation as a highly selective university. Instead, he wrote to Martha Nussbaum, he found them "appallingly unread and unwilling to read beyond assignments." His course, "God and Man in American Writing," was a subject that he cared deeply about. But he despaired of creating much excitement among his students, who complained about the reading and seemed unable to grasp its historical significance. One student astounded him by asking whether Lincoln's Second Inaugural Address, in which the president stated that "God has his own purposes," was not a violation of the First Amendment. The unpreparedness of Brown students together with the university's wholly elective curriculum left Kazin "dumbfounded as to what passes for education" among the "best" colleges in the country. He would look for no more visiting professorships.[46]

Alfred was relieved to get back to New York—New York with Judith. New York itself was as bad as ever. "The subway havoc and horrors—guy openly masturbating while a crowd screaming with laughter cheered him on." Judith made the difference. "Only Judith could make a bus trip from 96th to 14th on Second Avenue pure joy. . . . I thought I was weary to death of NY—death in the soul, etc., but not when I walk or ride with Judith." But even Judith could not solve his physical ailments or the weakness that seemed to gain on him daily. That HarperCollins was clamoring for a final draft of his journal book while chapters of God and the American Writer remained unwritten only heightened feelings of anxious helplessness—as well as his insomnia. In August 1995, he was hospitalized for a perforated ulcer. Lying on his back night after night without sleep, he thought about "the yearning of the sick man for freedom." But he also reminded himself, with a smile, of the words spoken by Richard Hofstadter before his death: "I never had any trouble with my will." He was back at work in September, but the strain of illness and age was taking its toll.[47]

There were, to be sure, compensations for hard work and longevity. In May, the Graduate Center had held a day-long symposium in Kazin's honor. Organized by Morris Dickstein and Mary Beth McMahon, the symposium featured speeches on "The American Experience" by students, friends, and colleagues, including Louis Menand, Daniel Aaron, Sean Wilentz, Leon Wieseltier, and New York Times columnist Anthony Lewis. Michael Kazin also gave a talk in which he described the course of his relations with his father, his father's lifelong love affair with America, and his passion for good writing. Later published in Dissent, "Fathers and Sons" was a tribute to make any father proud. For Kazin, who had worried long about his relations with Michael, it was the latest sign of their reconciliation and confirmation of what he already knew—"Michael's amazing goodness in so many situations."[48]

Kazin learned of another tribute in the fall of 1995. He was to be the first recipient of the one-hundred-thousand-dollar Truman Capote Lifetime Achievement Award in Literary Criticism. Presented at a ceremony at the Metronome Restaurant on January 8, 1996, the award, given in memory of Newton Arvin, had its ironies. Neither Capote nor Arvin enjoyed particularly good relations with the recipient. Alfred knew Capote and even called him a "friend," though it was Ann Birstein and Pearl whom Capote counted among his friends. Whatever friendship existed between the two men collapsed in 1973 when Kazin chastised Capote for a "Nazi-pogrom" mentality in complaining about a "Jewish mafia" in New York cultural circles. Capote was hurt by Kazin's charge but continued to insist on the Jewish influence, and the breach had never healed. A mentor and lover of Capote, Arvin might also have been surprised to learn that the award in his name had gone to a critic whom he had long resented for attacking his friend, Granville Hicks, in *On Native Grounds*. Kazin, who believed that Arvin had blackballed him at Smith, could not but enjoy the irony of being the first recipient of an award from two ex-friends who in all likelihood would have been appalled by the decision of the awards committee. "This is a dream come true," he remarked at the party. "The last time I was famous was at Truman Capote's Black and White Ball," referring to Capote's celebrated masked ball held at the Plaza Hotel in 1966.[49]

The Capote award came as a happy surprise at a time when there was little else to be happy about. Alfred's arthritis had returned, more crippling and painful than ever. In early February, Judith was admitted to the hospital for a week with an embolism in her leg, leaving him to fend for himself with his four-post walker. On February 18, he learned that Kate was moving to Israel. "I feel as if I had been socked in the head," he complained after a futile discussion with her on the phone. "I am dismayed by Kate's move," he wrote Michael. "At my age and in my debility [I] will probably not see her after she leaves." He was also discouraged by his struggles with his "God book." He was making headway but feared the chapters were coming out "pretty safe and flat."[50]

In May, his journal book appeared under its original title, *A Lifetime*

Burning in Every Moment—along with reviews. Though not bad, they hardly matched his expectations for this long-planned, much-worried-over project. One (quite legitimate) complaint was that the book was not really a compilation of journal entries but a quasi-reminiscence created out of the heavy revision of selected (and undated) journal entries. Kazin had attempted to deflect the charge of misleading readers with the subtitle "From the Journals of Alfred Kazin: Selected and Edited by the Author," assuming that "edit" means the author can rewrite and reorder entries as he pleases. But such an assumption is inconsistent with the usual understanding of a journal—a collection of dated entries written without the advantage of hindsight. *Lifetime* is not a book of "untouched candid shots" of a writer's life but a self-portrait Kazin chose to present to the world in 1996.[51]

Another complaint was that the portrait itself is dispiriting, that Kazin comes across as "irritable," "petulant," and despairing of life in general. "The progressive melancholy of these journal entries is distressing," wrote Edward Rothstein in the *New York Times Book Review*. A "desolate air" hangs over the pages, agreed Christopher Lehmann-Haupt, marked by "intermittent cries of despair." *Lifetime* is certainly disenchanted, particularly when compared with the radiant hopefulness of Kazin's first two autobiographies. But it is a very different kind of book. Though it contains like them accounts of memorable events in his life (including a taxi ride with Jacqueline Onassis) and numerous portraits (some of them quite vivid) of various personalities he has known, *Lifetime* is in the end a work of brooding spiritual reflection and yearning, or, as he says at various points, a kind of "prayer." "In the middle of the night, the terrible middle of the night, I writhe sleepless in a bed that is like a raft in a devouring ocean. As I have all my life when I feel myself up against the ropes, I pray to a God who cannot be very real, since he seems to be only a word, a name, a hope, a reach. Yet I pray; it is suffocating to be so bound up in oneself, a tangle of longings, useless memories, and violent recriminations. I pray to get beyond myself, to indicate to this believing unbeliever that there is a territory beyond this bundle tied up so angrily in the night. I pray to be relieved of so much 'self.' I ask to be 'extended.'"[52]

Not all of Kazin's "prayers" are so despairing. He is also grateful—for Judith, for being a Jew, for Italy, for Michael, for books, for the joys of reading and writing. "Gratitude," he had written in 1950, is essential to religion, "gratitude [for] that which is always *given* us." But as Kazin moved into his eighties, gratitude slipped into despair. "I don't mean unhappiness," he told an interviewer a few months before his death. "I mean despair. Despair is when you come to realize you don't have enough, that you need something else. . . . Whatever religious impulse I have, and I don't know what it is, has despair behind it." Whether one wants to read about such despair depends on one's taste and mood. Some reviewers clearly did not. Others, like Marshall Berman and Robert Alter, felt differently. For Alter, always one of Kazin's more thoughtful, sympathetic readers, *Lifetime* was a lonely, "transcendental" meditation in the tradition of Blake, Dickinson, Melville, and Kafka. The book demonstrates the ways in which "writing and reading and writing about reading can serve the most serious spiritual ends." It also indicates why Kazin, "this post-traditional Jew," remained "a kind of hidden stranger among his New York intellectual peers"—a characterization Kazin would strongly have seconded.[53]

In October 1996, Kazin turned in the manuscript of *God and the American Writer* to Harry Ford, his new editor at Knopf. He told Ford in September that he thought it his "best work in literary studies "and hoped that it would be published early in 1997, as he dreaded "the idea of posthumous publication." He also wrote Ford that he was working on a new book that might interest Knopf, *In Praise of the Diaspora,* which would show how Jewish intellects "benefitted from pluralistic societies since the seventeenth century." He still had plans for *Absent Friends,* and he told Daniel Aaron in January that he would like to do a longish piece titled "Melville Pursued by His Addicts" for a new collection of essays. Meanwhile, he was encouraging an editor at Harcourt to begin work on a *Kazin Reader,* which would include some previously published pieces as well as selections from his journals. Finally, there was *Jews: The Marriage of Heaven and Hell,* a book he had been thinking about for some time that was to draw on his long fascination with the extreme contradictions in Jewish experience. None of these projects had reached the initial planning stage. Indeed, it is likely that the prospect of their completion was less important to Kazin, now that he had finished *Lifetime* and the "God book," than the need to be engaged, as always, on a number of projects—anything less than a full effort signaling a "helpless lurch toward death." Besides, what was there to do but write? "I have nothing else to do," he told an interviewer in October 1997, shortly after *God and the American Writer* had been published. "Life would be too boring without it.'"[54]

He was certainly not bored by the critical response to his "God book" (published in late October 1997), which received better notices than any of his works since *Starting Out in the Thirties* (1965). Undoubtedly, the positive reviews were in some measure a tribute to the author's sixty-year career, but the consensus regarding the book's strengths (and weaknesses) indicates that the enthusiasm was genuine, that the qualities discovered by different readers were real. To appreciate those qualities it was necessary to recognize the kind of book Kazin had written—a collection of loosely linked, appreciative, often rhapsodic essays on the religious imagination of certain American writers. "I am interested not in the artist's professions of belief but in the imagination he brings to his tale of religion in human affairs." This open-ended statement allowed Kazin the freedom to respond to writers as the spirit moved him without the need to advance a thesis or sustain an argument. A book of "many epiphanies," wrote Todd Gitlin in the *Chicago Tribune,* "there is not another critic alive who is capable of such luminous, frequently startling sentences." "At his best," said Andrew Delbanco in the *New Republic,* "Kazin has the zeal of an artist possessed, rather than the caution of a strenuous critic." Kazin, wrote Paul Berman (*New York Times Book Review*), "interweaves his own emotional responses with quotations from one writer and another to produce an especially lyrical prose-poetry, which follows a logic all its own." Even the academics were impressed. *American Literature* called the book "well researched and deeply engaging." David Reynolds in the *Journal of American History* agreed: "a bold and engaging series of essays" containing the "seasoned insights of a critic who himself is something of a cultural institution." Kazin seemed to have made his peace with the academy at last.[55]

"We thank thee, Father, for these strange minds that enamor us against thee." The epigraph from Emily Dickinson is exactly the right opening for a book that concentrates on the American writer's enquiring, solitary, uneasy relations with God. It is also an expression of gratitude in a book where gratitude is pervasive. In *An American Procession,* Kazin often appeared to be resisting, even at times resenting, his writers, as if he felt the need (he told Kate at the time) to "cut them to size." The present book leaves a very different impression. While Kazin clearly prefers certain writers over others, his attitude is deferential, even, as he says in the afterword, "loving." No longer presences to be resisted, "my characters"—he still calls them that—are now kindred spirits speaking in an idiom at times all but indistinguishable from his own about religious matters that had long preoccupied him (and them): God as "a property of the human mind"; religion as a vision (in Alfred North Whitehead's words) "of something which stands beyond, behind and within, the passing flux of immediate things"; belief as "the most secret of personal confessions"; the nineteenth century as the last age of faith. Kazin's critical ventriloquism on these and other spiritual matters can be unnerving, but also, as one reviewer noted, "positively thrilling." Reciting, celebrating, interpreting, he explains his writers (and himself) to all who care to listen—"rhapsodizing out of his heart and soul," as he said of Emerson, "communing with himself in order to address his audience." Such close identification with one's subject poses risks. More than one reviewer wondered where Kazin left off and his writers began. Sanford Pinsker asked whether Kazin were not "at bottom, writing about himself." He was—but in a form that allowed him to celebrate from the inside, as it were, the qualities and "words" for which he had long valued these writers. *God and the American Writer* is an unabashed work of love, enthusiasm, and gratitude, testimony that Kazin's sixty-year effort to possess American literature was concluding where it began, with that literature's possessing him.[56]

The reviewers were not the only ones who liked the book. Kazin was overjoyed. "Life is strange at the moment reading reviews and letters about *God and the American Writer*," he wrote to his old Harvard student, Edward Hoagland. "I am so pleased, for once, with a book of mine, and in this instance, one that at last speaks for my own soul, heart and predicament in America." "The book is the best thing I've ever done," he told a reporter from the *Jerusalem Report*. He had originally been pleased with *Bright Book of Life, New York Jew,* and *American Procession,* but the reviews had rattled him. Was he on his way out? He kept thinking of Melville, forgotten, "dwelling somewhere in New York." Kazin was hardly forgotten. The Truman Capote award was only the most visible (and lucrative) of the many awards and notices of recognition he had received of late, among them the Lifetime Achievement Award offered by *Present Tense,* a journal published by the American Jewish Committee (1990); the Literary Lions Award

(1990), presented by the New York Public Library; the Lifetime Achievement Award from the National Book Critics Circle; and the Author's Guild Foundation Award for Distinguished Service to the Writing Community. Awards, of course, are one thing, but did people still want to hear what he had to say? In the case of *God and the American Writer*, it seems many did.[57]

The reviews came at a good time. Kazin was feeling weaker by the day, and he was worried. Had the cancer come back? "Aches and pains half the night," he wrote in late December 1997. "What will the actual dying, if I am fully aware, be like?" That his book, which had been nominated for a National Book Critics Circle Award, had found an appreciative audience was a deep source of satisfaction. It was also encouragement (though he hardly needed it) to keep working, chasing down review assignments and planning for the next book. He was busy doing reviews, he told a *Newsday* interviewer at the time; he needed them to live on. He also needed to stay active, to continue working as always—"piling it up." Between October 1997 and his death on June 5, 1998, Kazin published five essays in the *New York Review of Books*, three essays and reviews in the *New York Times*, and two essays and a poem in the *New Republic*. In addition, he reworked an address he had given in May 1997 at the Metropolitan Museum of Art for spring publication in the *American Scholar*—which to his delight had recently been taken away from Joseph Epstein and handed over to Anne Fadiman, the daughter of his old friend from the forties, Clifton Fadiman.[58]

The most remarkable fact about these last pieces is their freshness of response. Kazin in his eighties could still get as excited by the appearance of a new writer—Charles Frazier for *Cold Mountain*, for instance—as he could get irritated by the failings, the "Jewish jingoism," of the more established David Mamet. Judith Dunford reports that to the end he never lost "the rapturous sense of possibility" when first opening a book. Three of the pieces are tributes: to Murray Kempton—"my only radical friend from the 1930s who never sold out"; V. S. Pritchett, "the soundest, least partisan and least proprietary of critics"; and Varian Fry, an old friend from *New Republic* days, who, as head of the Emergency Rescue Committee in Marseilles during World War II, had helped two thousand people (including Marc Chagall and Hannah Arendt) escape Hitler's clutches. The longer pieces, as sharp and engaged as the best of his early reviews, are on Bernard Malamud and Isaac Bashevis Singer, writers he had reviewed before and was pleased to reassess in preparation for his proposed book, *Jews: The Marriage of Heaven and Hell.*[59]

It is difficult to say how seriously Kazin saw this project—whether as an actual book to be written or a fascinating subject to be endlessly explored. He thought it likely that his own published work, tracing and retracing the rise of Alfred Kazin, had already "exceeded the natural possibilities" of his contribution on the subject of the Jews. He even wondered whether his preoccupation with *Jews* reflected "some longing, still, to be back home with the people surrounding me in my childhood." His journals and correspondence give no indication of a plan for the book. They do indicate a desire, in the limited time he had left, to reflect further on a subject that engaged him years earlier—the tension between the Jew as victim and the Jew as Freud's "conquistador." "I have long been fascinated with the contrast in the Biblical story of Joseph between the pit and his triumph in Egypt," he wrote an Israeli friend late in 1997. "So many incredible successes in the world of thought (to say nothing of finance) and so much ignominy, persecution and murder." "My favorite notion of the Jew in history," he had written a few years earlier, reflecting on the career of the physicist Léo Szilárd, is the " high and low, the first man and the last, the nearest to God (he thinks) and the pariah, the 'prophet and the bounder' (Proust), the most creative and the most abject, the most 'in' and the most 'out.'" Kazin did not suggest where these contradictions and paradoxes might lead except to further contradictions. Indeed, it may be that reflecting on the permutations of the central enigma itself, "the triumph and the agony of the Jew," was stimulating enough—a "riddle" to articulate, not to solve.[60]

Contemplating the paradoxical extremes of Jewish history had the additional advantage of allowing Kazin to stay close to the Jewish experience in his remaining time without having to deal with questions of religious observance and belief. "I am truly a modern, secular Jew," he had written in 1996. "Emotionally, I am entirely loyal to the Jews and all memory of them. Intellectually, I cannot see that Jewish orthodoxy has contributed anything to human thought [beyond] a summons to prayer, ritual and obedience." Kazin was no more observant in his last months than he had ever been. Much as he might have wished otherwise, the synagogue with its routine collective responses, its usual "boredom" and "lack of inner truth," meant little to him. And he remained as adamantly resistant to the Jewish religious establishment as ever. "I love being Jewish, but I pursue my own way in these things," he told Dan Cryer from *Newsday.* "I'm an Emersonian and always have been." He acknowledged that such spiritual self-reliance could bring on bouts of "intellectual homelessness," that it narrowed his religious and communal options and even raised questions about his relations with God. "Can one really worship the Jewish God privately?" he had once asked himself. Jewish history tells of "hidden Jews [in Nazi Poland], but even they prayed together in the attics, cellars and the sewers of occupied Warsaw." He chose to pray alone (as he had walked alone)—often lying awake at night, lonely, frightened, beseeching. Eschewing public worship, he knew that he was missing an important part of the Jewish experience, but felt he had little choice in such matters. "I just am what I am," he told the reporter from the *Jerusalem Report,* who pressed him on the subject. "I have my own feelings."[61]

One afternoon in the middle of March 1998, Alfred complained to Judith that he had a backache. When she told him that of course he had a backache, that he needed to get out of his desk chair and walk around a little, he replied that it didn't feel "like that kind of a backache." Judith remembers thinking she knew immediately what it was, and a biopsy confirmed the worst: the cancer had metastasized to the bones. The oncologist was not hopeful; nonetheless, he recommended another regimen of radiation treatments. But the radiation had no apparent effect, and in May, Alfred, now terribly frail, was admitted to the hospital—a stay that lasted three weeks.[62]

While there (and later at home), he received a string of visitors—colleagues and friends from the Graduate Center; former students, including Michael Shaenen from the Amherst years; Dr. Tony Dajer, a recent friend of both Alfred and Judith; and David Bell, Philip Roth, and Morris Dickstein, to name but a few. Dickstein remembers being impressed by Kazin's lucidity till virtually the end. On his last visit, Kazin was reading a Vietnam memoir, discussing its qualities, and trying to work out the exact chronology of events. He still needed to get a book straight in his head.[63]

One of the visitors was Jonathan Rosen, the cultural editor of the *Forward,* where Kazin had recently published some pieces. Rosen was another of the younger generation of journalists with whom Alfred had become friendly in his later years. He had called Rosen in 1991 to ask whether the *Forward* would be interested in a piece he had done on Isaac Bashevis Singer (it was). Shortly afterward they had met and would meet intermittently on occasion over the years, one such occasion being Kazin's eighty-first birthday party. Kazin was glad to see the young Rosen bringing his talent and youthful enthusiasm to the venerable publication his father had read, much as he was to see Anne Fadiman injecting fresh editorial life into the equally venerable *American Scholar*. If he sometimes felt disillusioned with various members of his own generation, he believed there were reasons for hope among the brighter lights of the younger set.

Kazin returned home the last week of May. On June 5, the morning of his eighty-third birthday, he died, surrounded by his books and members of his family—Judith, Michael, Beth, and Kate, who had returned from Israel to be with him. The funeral, at the Riverside Memorial Chapel on Amsterdam Avenue, was a private service attended by the immediate family, including Daniel and Pearl Bell. Alfred had not wanted a religious service. Rather than a rabbi reading prayers, members of the family read favorite pieces they felt appropriate and passages from his works. His eight-year-old granddaughter, Maia, read "The Owl and the Pussycat," which Alfred, only half-jokingly, thought the greatest love poem in English. Judith read Robert Burns's "John Anderson, My Jo," and Kate read Kaddish, the Jewish prayer for the dead, in Hebrew. Afterward, the only nonfamily member present, Philip Roth, told Judith it was the best funeral he had ever attended.

On a sunny June morning, little more than a year after the funeral, about the time observant Jews would have unveiled a headstone, Judith, accompanied by Michael and Alfred's devoted student Mary Beth McMahon, carried a small box of Alfred's ashes onto the Brooklyn Bridge. After taking turns reading from the section on the Brooklyn Bridge in *A Walker in the City* and after Judith read Kaddish, they dropped the small box of ashes into the river—"halfway from each shore, Brownsville on the right, 'Beyond' on the left. Then it went down. Just where he wanted to be."[64]

Notes

ABBREVIATIONS

People, periodicals, and other works and collections cited frequently are identified by the following abbreviations and short titles.

AK. Alfred Kazin
AM. Atlantic Monthly
AS. American Scholar
Beinecke. Beinecke Rare Book and Manuscript Library, Yale University
Berg. Berg Collection, New York Public Library
EW. Edmund Wilson
HA. Hannah Arendt
JD. Judith Dunford
JH. Josephine Herbst
MK. Michael Kazin
NR. New Republic
NYHTB. New York Herald Tribune: Books
NYRB. New York Review of Books
NYT. New York Times
NYTBR. New York Times Book Review
PR. Partisan Review
PD. Peter Davison
SR. Saturday Review of Literature
TLS. Times Literary Supplement

Books by Alfred Kazin

BBL. Bright Book of Life: American Novelists and Storytellers (Boston: Little, Brown, 1973).
Blake. The Portable Blake, selected and arranged with an introduction by Alfred Kazin (New York: Viking Press, 1946).
Contemporaries. Contemporaries (Boston: Little, Brown, 1962).

Contemporaries (82). *Contemporaries: From the 19th Century to the Present* (New York: Horizon Press, 1982).

God. God and the American Writer (New York: Alfred A. Knopf, 1997).

Leaf. The Inmost Leaf: A Selection of Essays (New York: Harcourt Brace Jovanovich, 1955).

Lifetime. A Lifetime Burning in Every Moment: From the Journals of Alfred Kazin, Selected and Edited by the Author (New York: HarperCollins, 1996).

NYJ. New York Jew (New York: Alfred A. Knopf, 1978).

ONG. On Native Grounds: An Interpretation of Modern Prose Literature (New York: Reynal and Hitchcock, 1942).

ONY. Our New York: A Personal Vision in Words and Photographs. Text by Alfred Kazin, photographs by David Finn (New York: Harper and Row, 1989).

Procession. An American Procession (New York: Alfred A. Knopf, 1984).

Thirties. Starting Out in the Thirties (Boston: Little, Brown, 1965).

Walker. A Walker in the City (New York: Harcourt, Brace, 1951).

Writer's America. A Writer's America: Landscape in Literature (New York: Alfred A. Knopf, 1988).

Writing. Writing Was Everything (Cambridge: Harvard University Press, 1995).

Frequently Cited Essays by Alfred Kazin

When Alfred Kazin's reviews and essays have been collected, they are cited from the books, where they are more accessible.

"Desperate." "Desperate to Write," in *Contemporary Authors: Autobiography Series*, Vol. 7, ed. Mark Zadrony (Detroit, MI: Gale Research, 1988), 85–96.

"Jew as Modern." "The Jew as Modern Writer," *Commentary* (April 1966): 37–41.

"New York Jew." "New York Jew," in *Creators and Disturbers: Reminiscences by Jewish Intellectuals of New York* (New York: Columbia University Press, 1982), 194–209.

"The Past." "The Past Breaks Out," in *Inventing the Truth: The Art and Craft of Memoir*, ed. William Zinsser (Boston: Houghton Mifflin, 1987), 79–100.

"Under Forty." "Under Forty: A Symposium on American Literature and the Younger Generation of American Jews," *Contemporary Jewish Record* (February 1944): 3–36.

Manuscripts

Unless otherwise noted, references to Alfred Kazin's journals, correspondence, speeches, and personal papers are to the Alfred Kazin Papers held in the Berg Collection of the New York Public Library. All journal references are dated and preceded by "J."

The cited papers and correspondence of Edmund Wilson and Josephine Herbst are held in the Beinecke Rare Book and Manuscript Library, Yale University.

Other manuscript collections are identified in full in the notes.

Frequently Cited Collections of Letters

Letters on Literature. Edmund Wilson, *Letters on Literature and Politics: 1912–1972*, ed. Elena Wilson (New York: Farrar, Straus, and Giroux, 1977).

Within Four Walls. Within Four Walls: The Correspondence between Hannah Arendt and Heinrich Bluecher: 1936–1968, ed. Lotte Kohler (New York: Harcourt, 1996).

CHAPTER 1. BROWNSVILLE

1. *Walker,* 8, 10; AK, "Jews," *New Yorker* (March 7, 1994): 72; *Walker,* 11.

2. Orville Prescott, "Books of the Times," *NYT* (October 30, 1942): 17.

3. J6/8/62; AK to PD, January 31, 1974, Davison Papers, Berg; J1/4/60; J10/3/49; "New York Jew," 203; J9/24/44.

4. J4/12/66; AK to author, May 4, 1986; "New York Jew," 203; "The Past," 93.

5. Louis Finkelstein, Preface, *Brownsville: The Birth and Passion of a Jewish Community in New York,* Alter F. Landesman (New York: Bloch Publishing, 1971), vii; "New York Jew," 195; *Walker,* 58, 43.

6. *NYJ,* 9; AK, "Jews," 68.

7. J1/2/91; AK, "Jews," 64; *Walker,* 60; *Thirties,* 45.

8. *Walker,* 38.

9. AK, "Jews," 71.

10. *Walker,* 67–68; "New York Jew," 196; *Walker,* 67.

11. Interview with AK, July 12, 1985; J5/15/84.

12. AK, "Memoir: The Sweet Nechama," *Present Tense* (September/October 1989): 45; J6/8/66; J3/14/76.

13. AK, "The Cry for Justice," *Tikkun* (May/June 1998): 77; *Walker,* 46; *ONY,* 88–90; "Jews," 68.

14. Arthur Hertzberg, *The Jews in America* (New York: Simon and Schuster, 1989), 198; Hapgood quoted in Irving Howe, *World of Our Fathers* (New York: Simon and Schuster, 1976), 253; "Desperate," 86; "New York Jew," 195.

15. AK, "The Sweet Nechama," 45–48.

16. Interview with Daniel Bell, October 16, 2003.

17. *Walker,* 62.

18. AK, "Jews," 71; Howe, *World,* 272; *Walker,* 17.

19. *Walker,* 18; Norman Podhoretz, *Making It* (New York: Harper Colophon Books, 1967), 9; AK, "Jews," 69.

20. *Walker,* 18–23.

21. William Poster, "'Twas a Dark Night in Brownsville," *Commentary* (May 1950): 459; Samuel Tennenbaum, "Brownsville's Age of Learning," *Commentary* (May 1949): 175.

22. *Walker,* 21–23; J8/30/44.

23. Wellborn Hampton, Alfred Kazin Obituary, *NYT* (June 6, 1998): 13; "Desperate," 87; Pearl Bell to author, April 2001; Poster, "'Twas a Dark Night," 463.

24. Irving Howe, *A Margin of Hope* (New York: Harcourt Brace Jovanovich, 1982): 12–14; Joseph Dornan, *Arguing the World: The New York Intellectuals in Their Own Words* (Chicago: University of Chicago Press, 2001), 33–39.

25. *Lifetime,* 339.

26. *Walker,* 23; *Lifetime* 339; floppy disk "From Old Files," Berg; *Walker,* 120, 172; interview with Daniel Bell, October 16, 2003; *Lifetime,* 339.

27. *Walker,* 150–152.

28. "New York Jew," 206, 203; J6/11/91; J10/17/84; *Walker,* 9, 11.

29. *Walker,* 40, 172, 95, 22, 27.

30. Podhoretz, *Making It,* 20; *Walker,* 95.

31. AK, "The Useful Critic," *AM* (December 1985): 73.

CHAPTER 2. THE THIRTIES: STARTING OUT

1. AK, "Teachers—Two Particular Teachers," in *An Apple for My Teacher,* ed. Louis D. Rubin Jr. (Chapel Hill, NC: Algonquin Books, 1987), 29.

2. AK, "Writers in the Radical Years," *NYTBR* (March 23, 1980): 7.

3. *Thirties,* 86.

4. J9/18/33; J3/16/60; Irving Howe in Joseph Dorman, *Arguing the World* (Chicago: University of Chicago Press, 2001), 81.

5. *Thirties,* 4; Sidney Hook, *Out of Step: An Unquiet Life in the 20th Century* (New York: Harper and Row, 1987), 155; *Thirties,* 86.

6. J9/19/62; AK to author, May 11, 1986; Alexander Bloom, *Prodigal Sons: The New York Intellectuals and Their World* (New York: Oxford University Press, 1986), 36.

7. Irving Howe, *A Margin of Hope: An Intellectual Autobiography* (New York: Harcourt Brace Jovanovich, 1982), 64–69; Irving Kristol, "Memoirs of a Trotskyist," *New York Times Magazine* (January 23, 1977), 50.

8. AK, "Teachers," 33; J1/14/97.

9. J12/17/91; Howe, *Margin,* 61.

10. AK to Mr. Phelps, April 28, 1994, cc. Berg; AK to author, September 1, 1987; AK to Eric Glaberson, April 29, 1980, cc. Berg; AK to Daniel Bell, January 1, 1992, cc. Berg.

11. AK, "Teachers," 32, 38.

12. J7/29/57; J1/14/59.

13. Howe, *Margin,* 63; AK, "Teachers," 34.

14. AK, "Teachers," 38; *Walker,* 100; Dorman, *Arguing,* 43.

15. AK, "Teachers," 38–39, 43; Bird Stair, Guggenheim Report on AK, January 2, 1940; AK, "Teachers," 39.

16. *Thirties,* 7, 10.

17. AK, "The Bitter Thirties," *AM* (May 1962): 84; "To Be a Critic," in *Contemporaries* (82), 13; Howe, *World,* 599; Joseph Freeman, *An American Testament: A Narrative of Rebels and Romantics* (New York: Farrar and Rinehart, 1936), 28; *Thirties,* 10.

18. "New York Jew," 207; *Thirties,* 10.

19. *Thirties,* 30, 49–50, 46–47.

20. *Thirties,* 15; "New York Jew," 197; J1/2/62; Leslie Fiedler, "The Breakthrough," *Midstream* (Winter 1958): 13; Irving Howe, "The New York Intellectuals," in *The Decline of the New* (New York: Harcourt Brace, 1970), 216, 220.

21. Malcolm Cowley, *The Dream of the Golden Mountains* (New York: Viking, 1980), 265; Malcolm Cowley to AK, May 18, 1962, Cowley Papers, Newberry Library, Chicago; *Thirties,* 17; AK, "The Bitter Thirties," 84. After Cowley's complaint, Kazin would remove the remarks about his showing off his literary connections in front of the reviewers. *Thirties,* 11; AK to Malcolm Cowley, May 6, 1962, Cowley Papers, Newberry Library, Chicago; J8/16/86.

22. *Thirties,* 54; Daniel Aaron, *Writers on the Left* (1961; repr., New York: Columbia University Press, 1992), 322.

23. *Thirties,* 66–67.

24. Hook, *Out of Step,* 155; AK to author, May 11, 1986; J6/30/62; J2/26/62; AK, "The Eloquence of Failure," *Reporter* (May 13, 1964): 59.

25. Richard Kluger, *The Paper: The Life and Death of the New York Herald Tribune* (New York: Alfred A. Knopf, 1986), 324; Irita Van Doren, Guggenheim Report on AK, December 26, 1939; J12/12/84; AK to Irita Van Doren, July 7, 1940, cc. Berg.

26. AK to author, March 10, 1992.

27. AK, review of *A Time to Remember* by Leanne Zugsmith, *NYTBR* (September 13, 1936): 5.

28. *Thirties,* 12–13.

29. AK, "All Quiet on the Home Front," *NYHTB* (April 25, 1937): 5; *NYJ,* 8.

30. AK, review of *James Joyce* by Herbert Gorman, *NYHTB* (February 18, 1940): 5; AK, review of *Finnegans Wake* by James Joyce, *NYHTB* (May 21, 1939): 4.

31. J5/20/64; J3/7/75; "Writing for Magazines," in *Contemporaries,* 474.

CHAPTER 3. THE THIRTIES: *ON NATIVE GROUNDS*

1. AK interview with Alexander Bloom, *Prodigal Sons* (New York: Oxford University Press, 1986), 33–34.

2. David Kennedy, *Freedom from Fear: The American People in Depression and War* (New York: Oxford University Press, 1999), 218.

3. *Thirties,* 83.

4. J1/11/73.

5. *Thirties,* 142, 94.

6. Ibid., 98–99; AK, "Richard Hofstadter, 1916–1970," *AS* (Summer 1971): 397.

7. *Lifetime,* 13; *Thirties,* 100; *NYJ,* 60.

8. Susan Stout Baker, *Radical Beginnings: Richard Hofstadter and the 1930s* (Westport, CT: Greenwood Press, 1985), 81; William Keylo, 1972, interview with AK on Richard Hofstadter, *Columbia Oral History,* Oral History Research Office, Columbia University, 801 Butler Library, 4; *Thirties,* 85, 138.

9. *Thirties,* 83, 19; Keylo, *Oral History,* 7.

10. Quoted in Baker, *Radical Beginnings,* 89–90; *Thirties,* 85, 137, 85.

11. Sidney Hook, *Out of Step: An Unquiet Life in the 20th Century* (New York: Harper and Row, 1987), 155–156.

12. AK to author, September 1, 1987; J8/5/34; *Thirties,* 6, 4; J2/19/42.

13. AK to MK, January 16, 1982; J9/3/42; EW, "What I Believe," *Nation* (January 27, 1932): 98; Sidney Hook, "Why I Am a Communist," *Modern Monthly* (April 1934): 143; Malcolm Cowley to AK, May 18, 1962, Cowley Papers, Newberry Library, Chicago; AK to Eric Glaberson, April 29, 1980.

14. AK to Matthew Josephson, November 25, 1967, Matthew Josephson Papers, Beinecke; J6/24/38; J9/12/33; AK to author, September 1, 1987.

15. J3/5/71.

16. AK to author, February 1, 1985; *Thirties,* 49.

17. J10/22/58; J11/18/55.

18. AK to author, April 9, 1991; AK, *Edward Gibbon, Literary Critic,* master's thesis, Columbia University, New York, 53, 109.

19. AK to author, April 9, 1991; AK, *Edward Gibbon,* 25.

20. Robert Silvers, "Alfred Kazin: The Critic as Creator," interview with AK, *Horizon* (July 1962), 99; "Desperate," 90; Kermit Vanderbilt, *American Literature and the Academy* (Philadelphia: University of Pennsylvania Press, 1989), 152; J3/15/88; J7/31/80.

21. AK, Preface to the Fiftieth Anniversary Edition, *On Native Grounds* (New York: Harcourt Brace, 1995), xii.

22. *Thirties,* 132.

23. Ibid., 133; J12/3/38; *Lifetime,* 9.

24. *Thirties,* 144; AK to Richard Rovere, August 22, 1940, Richard Rovere Collection, State Historical Society of Wisconsin, Madison.

25. Richard Rovere, *Final Reports* (Middletown, CT: Wesleyan University Press, 1984), 70–71.

26. *Thirties,* 153; AK, Guggenheim Grant Application, March 28, 1939; Bertram Wolfe, "America's Coming of Age," *Communist* (November 1927): 461–462; *Thirties,* 134.

27. *NYJ,* 4; AK, "To Room 315, With Love," *NYTBR* (April 30, 1972): 42; *Thirties,* 135.

28. *NYJ,* 4–8.

29. AK to author, March 25, 1992; *NYJ,* 14.

30. *Thirties,* 139.

31. Ibid.

32. Ibid., 153; *Nation* (September 1, 1940): 283.

33. *Lifetime,* 15; *ONG,* x.

34. AK, Letter of Application to the John Guggenheim Memorial Foundation, Summer–Fall 1939.

35. AK, Guggenheim application, 1939; Vernon Louis Parrington, *The Beginnings of Critical Realism in America: 1860–1920* (New York: Harcourt, Brace, 1930), xxi, xxv; Lionel Trilling, "Parrington, Mr. Smith and Reality," *PR* (January–February 1940): 24–40; *ONG,* 163–164.

36. AK, Preface to the Fiftieth Anniversary Edition, xx.

37. F. O. Matthiessen, "Criticism and Fiction," *Journal of the History of Ideas* (June 1943): 368–373; R. W. B. Lewis, "Contemporary American Literature," *American Literary Scholarship* (1963): 204; Robert Alter, "The Education of Alfred Kazin," *Commentary* (June 1958): 44; Morris Dickstein, *Double Agent: The Critic and Society* (New York: Oxford University Press, 1992), 152.

38. Silvers, "Alfred Kazin," 99; *NYJ,* 7; Walt Whitman, *Complete Poetry and Prose,* ed. James E. Miller Jr. (Boston: Houghton Mifflin, 1959), 487, 456; *NYJ,* 385.

39. *ONG,* ix, 33.

40. Ibid., 90.

41. Ibid., 341, 312, 314, 352.

42. Ibid., 34, 371, 372; AK, "Flies in the Mid-West Kitchen," *NYHTB* (March 5, 1939): 7; *ONG,* 387, 386, 385, 379.

43. AK to Malcolm Cowley, May 6, 1962, Cowley Papers, Newberry Library, Chicago; AK, "We Are No Longer Innocent," address to the students of Goucher College, April 1962, typescript, Berg.

44. *ONG,* 400, xi.

45. Gordon Haight, "Our Prose Writers," *Yale Review* (March 1943): 620–622; William York Tindall, "Literary Signposts," *American Mercury* 56 (1943): 114–115; Robert Spiller, "Our Prose Writers," *American Literature* (March 1943): 303–305; Howard Mumford Jones, "Literary History and Literary Plenty," *SR* (October 31, 1942): 5–6; Matthiessen, "Criticism and Fiction," 368–373; Lionel Trilling, "Four Decades of American Prose," *Nation* (November 7, 1942): 483–484; Irving Howe, a.k.a. Rote Fahne, "A New Literary Critic," *New International* (March 1943): 91; Cleanth Brooks, "Mr. Kazin's America," *Sewanee Review* 54 (1943): 52–61.

46. Mark Van Doren to AK, November 11, 1942; Mark Van Doren to AK, November 12, 42; Trilling, "Four Decades," 483.

47. *ONG,* 504, 487–489; *Thirties,* 137.

48. Orville Prescott, "Books of the Times," *NYT* (October 30, 1942): 17; Oscar Cargill to Reynal and Hitchcock, September 14, 1942; Irwin Edman, "Discovery of America by Its Own Writers," *NYHTB* (November 1, 1942): 1–2; Trilling, "Four Decades," 484; Jones, "Literary History," 5–6.

49. Brooks, "Mr. Kazin's America," 52–61; *ONG,* 421; Granville Hicks, "The Ground Alfred Kazin Stands On," *Antioch Review* (March 1943): 21–31; Isadore Schneider, "The Safe Squat," *New Masses* (February 9, 1943): 24; F. W. Dupee, "The Native Critic," *PR* (March–April, 1943): 24–26; AK to Ms. Barrett, November 5, 1982, cc. Berg; AK to author, February 2, 1986; Haight, "Our Prose Writers," 621.

50. *NYJ,* 3, 30; Henry Commager to AK, January 3, 1945; Carl Becker to AK, May 4, 1943, in *What Is the Good of History: Selected Letters of Carl L. Becker 1900–194,* ed. Michael Kammen (Ithaca, NY: Cornell University Press, 1973), 300–301; Henry Miller to AK, n.d.; Harold Laski to Curtice Hitchcock, December 24, 1943.

51. *ONG,* 458; Allen Tate to AK, December 19, 1942.

52. "Desperate," 92; *Thirties,* 158; F. O. Matthiessen, *American Renaissance: Art and*

Expression in the Age of Emerson and Whitman (New York: Oxford University Press, 1941), vii; *ONG*, 163–164.

53. Amy Kaplan, *The Social Construction of American Realism* (Chicago: University of Chicago Press, 1988), 2–8; Daniel H. Borus, *Howells, James, and Norris in the Mass Market* (Chapel Hill: University of North Carolina Press, 1989), 182–189; William Stott, *Documentary Expression and Thirties America* (New York: Oxford University Press, 1973), 3; Warren Susman, *Culture as History* (New York: Pantheon, 1984), 303; *Thirties*, 12–13; Alan M. Wald, "In Retrospect: *On Native Grounds*," *Reviews in American History* (1992): 276–288.

54. Quoted in Philip Gleason, "World War II and the Development of American Studies," *American Quarterly* (1985): 348; see also Philip Gleason, "Americans All: World War II and the Shaping of American Identity," *Review of Politics* (1981): 503–504; Arthur Hertzberg, *The Jews in America* (New York: Simon and Schuster, 1989), 302.

55. J2/28/42.

CHAPTER 4. THE BREAK

1. *NYJ*, 3–4.
2. J9/16/89.
3. J1/27/42; J10/27/42; J1/27/42; *Lifetime*, 15.
4. J2/8/42.
5. *NYJ*, 53; see Morris Dickstein, "I'm Interested in Everything!" *AS* (Winter 1999): 13–22, on the connection between Blake and Kazin's "furious hunger for experience." William Blake, "The Marriage of Heaven and Hell," in *Blake*, 251; *NYJ*, 97.
6. *NYJ*, 20–22.
7. Ibid., 38–43; J9/3/42.
8. *Lifetime*, 6; J4/30/92.
9. John Cheever, Preface, *Six Decades at Yaddo*, private publication, 1986, to commemorate Yaddo's sixtieth anniversary; AK, ibid., 25.
10. *ONG*, 421; J6/12–30/42.
11. J6/12–30/42; J6/19/68.
12. AK, "Edmund Wilson's Role as Critic," *NYHTB* (August 31, 1941): 2; *ONG*, 447–448.
13. *NYJ*, 67; J9/19/61; J4/14/62.
14. *NYJ*, 23; AK, "Delmore Schwartz, 1913–1966," *Chicago Tribune: Book Week* (October 9, 1966): 1; *NYJ*, 24; James Atlas, *Delmore Schwartz: The Life of an American Poet* (New York: Farrar, Straus, and Giroux, 1977), 199.
15. *NYJ*, 25, 48.
16. Irving Howe, *A Margin of Hope* (New York: Harcourt Brace Jovanovich, 1982), 133; J6/19/62; *NYJ*, 52.
17. *NYJ*, 48, 42; Janet Richards, *Common Soldiers* (San Francisco: Archer Press, 1979), 109; James Atlas, *Bellow: A Biography* (New York: Random House, 2000), 28; *NYJ*, 41.
18. Atlas, *Bellow*, 83.
19. AK, "Midtown and the Village," *Harper's* (January 1961): 86.
20. J7/20/63; J6/9/66.
21. J7/20/62; AK, "Delmore Schwartz," 17; Seymour Krim, *Views of a Nearsighted Cannoneer* (New York: Dutton, 1968), 16–18.
22. "Jew as Modern," 40; *NYJ*, 23.
23. Editorial Statement, *PR* (December 1937): 3; interview with Daniel Bell, October 16, 2003; J9/17/41; *ONY*, 150.
24. J3/29/85; *ONY*, 150.

25. H. Stuart Hughes, *The Sea Change: The Migration of Social Thought, 1930–1965* (New York: Harper and Row, 1975), 1.

26. *Writing,* 83.

27. J9/5/85; J4/2/88.

28. J5/27/43.

29. J5/27/43; *NYJ,* 54–56.

30. AK to author, May 11, 1986.

31. *NYJ,* 73; AK to Clive James, December 6, 1996, cc. Berg; *NYJ,* 72.

32. *NYJ,* 87; "All that most maddens and torments; all that stirs up the lees of things; all truth with malice in it; all that cracks the sinews and cakes the brain; all the subtle demonisms of life and thought; all evil, to crazy Ahab, was visibly personified, and made practically assailable in Moby-Dick. He piled on the whale's white hump the sum of all the general rage and hate felt by his whole race from Adam down; and then, as if his chest had been a mortar, he burst his hot heart's shell upon it." Herman Melville, *Moby-Dick* (New York: W. W. Norton, 1967), 160; *NYJ,* 72.

33. AK to Dr. Win S. Beck, June 17, 1994, cc. Berg; J6/5/90; J1/27/64.

34. *NYJ,* 81.

35. Ibid., 89, 88, 97.

36. Ibid., 89; J8/30/44; *NYJ,* 96; J4/3/44.

37. *Lifetime,* 52; Janet Rioch, "The Transference Phenomenon in Psychoanalytic Theory," *Psychiatry* (1943): 147–156; AK to author, February 23, 1991.

38. J8/30/44; J9/25/44; AK to author, February 23, 1991.

39. *Lifetime,* 51; *NYJ,* 53; AK in Peter Manso, *Mailer: His Life and Times* (New York: Simon and Schuster, 1985), 217; J11/28/43; J5/28/58; *NYJ,* 96.

40. AK, "In Every Voice, in Every Ban," *NR* (January 10, 1944): 44–46.

41. Ibid.

42. Daniel Bell to AK, n.d.; Lewis Mumford to AK, January 14, 1944; Archibald MacLeish to AK, n.d.; Saul Bellow to AK, n.d.

43. AK, "No More Wailing Wall," *NYHTB* (January 10, 1937); J9/9/42; J5/27/43.

44. AK, "Under Forty," 3–36.

45. Ibid., 9–12.

46. *NYJ,* 258, 196.

47. AK to Richard Rovere, July 8, 1944, Richard Rovere Collection, State Historical Society of Wisconsin, Madison.

48. J2/48/42; *Blake,* 6, 44; J6/17/43.

49. *NYJ,* 103, 102.

50. J2/24/62; *NYJ,* 101; J6/24/64; J11/19/59.

51. J8/30/44.

52. Martin Duberman, *Black Mountain: An Exploration in Community* (New York: Dutton, 1972), 222–223; J9/28/44.

53. J12/18/44; J11/8/44; *Lifetime,* 31; Duberman, *Black Mountain,* 223; AK, "Have You Seen the Folk?" *NR* (February 5, 1945): 172–173.

54. *NYJ,* 121.

55. Ibid., 129.

56. Ibid., 122, 125.

57. Ibid., 127; AK, *The Education of Soldiers,* submitted to the Rockefeller Foundation, 1945, 33, typescript copy, Berg.

58. *NYJ,* 128; J1/12/60; *Lifetime,* 41; J4/8/45; *Lifetime,* 41.

59. *NYJ,* 139; J5/3/45; J3/12/45.

60. *Lifetime,* 39; J5/21/78; J1/12/60.

61. *Writing*, 77.

62. J7/13/45.

63. *Writing*, 83, 84 (quoting Camus), 86.

64. Maureen Waller, *London 1945: Life in the Debris of War* (London: St. Martins, 2004), 343; AK, *Education of Soldiers*, 81, 26.

65. *NYJ*, 146–147.

66. Ibid., 141; *Thirties*, 166.

CHAPTER 5. AFTER THE APOCALYPSE

1. *NYJ*, 149; quoted in William H. Chafe, *The Unfinished Journey: America Since World War II* (New York: Oxford University Press, 1986), 30, 67; J3/4/96; J3/22/46.

2. J2/10/47; J2/17/47.

3. Mark Schechner, *After the Revolution: Studies in the Contemporary Jewish Imagination* (Bloomington: Indiana University Press, 1987), 4; Irving Howe, *A Margin of Hope: An Intellectual Biography* (New York: Harcourt Brace Jovanovich, 1982), 133; J2/10/47; *Lifetime*, 15.

4. *NYJ*, 152, 150; J2/10/47; J4/3/51; *Lifetime*, 52.

5. J6/28/84; AK interview with author, January 6, 1985; *NYJ*, 19.

6. *NYJ*, 152–153.

7. AK, "A Devout Russian Iconoclast," *NYTBR* (January 6, 1946): 1, 14, 16; Arthur Schlesinger Jr., *The Cycles of American History* (New York: Houghton Mifflin, 1986), 19; J5/31/43.

8. J10/3/46; J3/22/46.

9. J6/20/46; AK, "Letter from America," July 6, 1946, typescript.

10. AK, "*Le Misanthrope*," *PR* (Summer 1946): 375–381.

11. AK to EW, June 9, 1950, Beinecke.

12. J10/7/46; AK, 1946 Guggenheim Application for *The Western Island*.

13. *Lifetime*, 54; AK to Van Wyck Brooks, January 3, 1949; AK to Allen Tate, February 4, 1947, Allen Tate Papers, Princeton University Archives, Princeton, NJ.

14. J2/27/47.

15. Anatole Broyard, *Kafka Was the Rage: A Greenwich Village Memoir* (New York: Random House, 1993): 15; "Kafka," in *Leaf*, 145; *Blake*, 22–23, 27; "Kafka," 145, 146, 142.

16. *Lifetime*, 105–106; HA to AK, April 10, 1947; *Lifetime*, 109.

17. J2/27/47; J3/16/47; J3/8/47.

18. J5/29/84; J2/20/51; J1/17/57; J9/17/42; J6/30/49; J11/15/51; J11/30/93.

19. J11/27/49; J7/8/57; interview with MK, September 26, 2003.

20. Moses Rischin, *The Promised City: New York Jews 1870–1914* (Cambridge: Harvard University Press, 1962), 97; *Lifetime*, 63; *Thirties*, 4.

21. J6/2/47; *Lifetime*, 62; J6/5/47.

22. J6/11/47.

23. Quoted in Frances Stonor Saunders, *The Cultural Cold War* (New York: New Press, 1999), 25.

24. "From an Italian Diary," in *Leaf*, 165–166.

25. Ibid.

26. J6/26/47; J6/16/47; J6/24/47.

27. *NYJ*, 166; AK, "Salzburg: Seminar in the Ruins," *Commentary* (July 1948): 58.

28. Margaret Mead, "The Salzburg Seminar in American Civilization," available at http://www.salzburgseminar.org; F. O. Matthiessen, *From the Heart of Europe* (New York: Oxford University Press, 1948), 28; Mead, "Salzburg Seminar."

29. J7/31/47; AK, "Salzburg," 58; Kenneth Lynn, "Teaching: F. O. Matthiessen," *AS* (Winter 1976–1977), 93.

30. J8/13/47.

31. J9/1/47.

32. J9/29/47; AK, *The Open Street* (New York: Reynal and Hitchcock, 1948), 7.

33. J9/3/47; J12/17/47; *Lifetime*, 99; *NYJ*, 81.

34. *NYJ*, 164; J10/29/47.

35. J5/13/48.

36. J12/17/47; J1/9/48.

37. J1/28/48; J12/21/47.

38. F. O. Matthiessen to AK, February 3, 1948; AK to author, April 16, 1997; Saul Bellow to AK, May 2, 1948.

39. J3/14/48

40. EW to AK, May 12, 1950; Ben Yagoda, *About Town: The New Yorker and the World It Made* (New York: Scribner's, 2000), 297.

41. *Lifetime*, 103; J6/20/48; *Lifetime*, 111.

42. J5/13/48; J6/24/48; Matthiessen, *From the Heart*, 143–144.

43. Irving Howe, "The Sentimental Fellow-Traveling of F. O. Matthiessen," *PR* (October 1948): 1125; quoted in William L. O'Neill, *A Better World: The Great Schism: Stalinism and the American Intellectuals* (New York: Simon and Schuster, 1982), 179.

44. AK to *PR*, October 7, 1948; Irving Howe, "L'affaire Matthiessen," *PR* (November 1948): 1256.

45. AK's remarks to Matthiessen are quoted by Matthiessen in a letter to AK, November 7, 1948; AK to Matthiessen, November 9, 1948, photocopy from George Abbot White, keeper of the Matthiessen Room, Eliot House, Harvard University, Cambridge.

46. Quoted in David Caute, *The Great Fear: The Anti-Communist Purge under Truman and Eisenhower* (New York: Simon and Schuster, 1978), 27; quoted in Chafe, *Unfinished Journey*, 101.

47. Michael Wreszin, *A Rebel in Defense of Tradition: The Life and Politics of Dwight MacDonald* (New York: Simon and Schuster, 1994), 132; J11/20/46.

48. "Europe-America Groups," copy in Kazin Papers, Berg.

49. Carol Brightman, *Writing Dangerously: Mary McCarthy and Her World* (New York: Clarkson Potter, 1992), 307; J5/17/48; J6/24/48; "Old Revolutionists," in *Contemporaries*, 401; Dwight MacDonald, "I Choose the West," speech delivered in 1952, in *Politics Past: Essays in Political Criticism* (New York: Viking, 1957), 197.

50. J7/22/48.

51. Thomas Mann to AK, November 5, 1948.

52. Jack Kerouac, *Windblown World: The Journals of Jack Kerouac 1947–1954*, ed. Douglas Brinkley (New York: Viking, 2004), 161, 172; Jack Kerouac to AK; February 20, 1951, in *Jack Kerouac: Selected Letters 1940–1956*, ed. Ann Charters (New York: Viking, 1995), 312; Jack Kerouac to AK, October 27, 1954, in *Selected Letters*, 450; "Psychoanalysis and Literary Culture Today," in *Contemporaries*, 365.

53. *NYJ*, 182; AK to Richard Chase, January 4, 1950, Richard Chase Correspondence, Rare Book and Manuscript Library, Columbia University, New York; J2/20/49.

54. J5/19/48; J2/17/47; "The Past," 88; J2/24/49.

55. J10/11/49; J5/8/49.

56. "Under Forty," 11; "Jew as Modern," 39.

57. Isaac Rosenfeld, "Terror Beyond Evil," in *An Age of Enormity: Life and Writing in the Forties and Fifties*, ed. Theodore Solotaroff (New York: World Publishing, 1962), 198; Irving Howe, quoted in Alexander Bloom, *Prodigal Sons: The New York Intellectuals and Their*

World (New York: Oxford University Press, 1986), 140; Howe, "The Lost Young Intellectual," *Commentary* (October 1946): 361–367; Daniel Bell, "A Parable of Alienation, *Jewish Frontier* (November 1946): 12–14.

58. Elliot E. Cohen, "An Act of Affirmation," *Commentary* (November 1945): 2; Cohen, "Jewish Culture in America," *Commentary* (May 1947): 417, 414; Cohen, "The Intellectuals and the Jewish Community," *Commentary* (July 1949): 29.

59. *Lifetime,* 104.

60. Leslie Fiedler, "What Can We Do about Fagin?: The Jew-Villain in Western Literature," *Commentary* (April 1949): 416.

61. "The Jewish Writer and the English Literary Tradition: A Symposium: Part II," *Commentary* (October 1949): 367–368.

62. Bloom, *Prodigal Sons,* 149; J10/13/49.

63. J2/28/42; "To Be a Writer," in *Contemporaries* (82), 4.

64. AK to James Kutcher, December 20, 1953, records of the Kutcher Civil Rights Committee, State Historical Society of Wisconsin, Madison.

65. Ian Hamilton, *Robert Lowell: A Biography* (New York: Random House, 1982), 145; Wreszin, *Rebel,* 223.

66. Quoted in Wreszin, *Rebel,* 223; quoted in O'Neil, *Better World,* 290–291; *NYJ,* 205.

67. AK interview with Neil Jumanville, in Jumanville, *Critical Crossings: The New York Intellectuals in Postwar America* (Berkeley: University of California Press, 1991), 29–30.

68. Richard Chase, *Herman Melville: A Critical Study* (New York: Macmillan, 1949), v–viii; "Melville as Scripture," in *Leaf,* 198.

69. Lionel Trilling, "Reality in America," in *The Liberal Imagination: Essays on Literature and Society* (New York: Viking, 1950), 10, 18; Arthur Schlesinger, *The Vital Center: The Politics of Freedom* (Boston: Houghton Mifflin, 1949), xx, 39.

70. Robert Silvers, "Alfred Kazin: The Critic as Creator," interview with AK, *Horizon* (July 1962): 100; J12/10/45; "Kafka," in *Leaf,* 143; "Melville as Scripture," 201; J4/2/27.

71. *NYJ,* 142; quoted in Eric Goldman, *The Crucial Decade and After: America, 1945–60* (New York: Random House, 1960), 142.

72. AK to Saul Levitas, April, 19, 1950, cc. Berg.

CHAPTER 6. *A WALKER IN THE CITY*

1. J9/22/49; J9/20/49.

2. AK to JH, May 24, 1950, Beinecke; "The Past," 88; Alvin Rosenfeld, "Inventing the Jew: Note on Jewish Autobiography," in *The American Autobiography: A Collection of Critical Essays,* ed. Albert E. Stone (Englewood Cliffs, NJ: Prentice Hall, 1981), 140; Abraham Sachar, *A History of the Jews in America* (New York: Alfred A. Knopf, 1992), 413.

3. J11/8/49; Eleanor Langer, *Josephine Herbst* (Boston: Little, Brown, 1984), 277–278.

4. J11/8/49; J4/23/92; Jean Garrigue to AK, n.d.

5. *ONG,* 387; AK to JH, January 7, 1950, Beinecke; Langer, *Josephine Herbst,* 302; AK, "Josephine Herbst (1897–1969)," *NYRB* (March 17, 1969): 19.

6. J12/9/49; AK to JH, January 7, 1950, Beinecke.

7. AK to JH, February 14, 1950; J2/10/50; J2/12/50.

8. *NYJ,* 195–199.

9. Ibid., 198; Elizabeth Young-Bruehl, *Hannah Arendt: For the Love of the World* (New Haven, CT: Yale University Press, 1982), 268; David Laskin, *Partisans: Marriage, Politics and Betrayals among the New York Intellectuals* (New York: Simon and Schuster, 2000), 159–160; *Lifetime,* 107.

10. *Within Four Walls,* 138; *NYJ,* 200; J2/12/50; J2/27/50; *Within Four Walls,* 139.

11. *Within Four Walls,* 139, 110, 201, 113; *NYJ,* 197.

12. AK to JH, February 25, 1950, Beinecke; J9/8/50; AK to JH, February 22, 1950, Beinecke.

13. J3/11/50; J3/18/50; AK to JH, n.d., Beinecke.

14. J9/25/50; *Lifetime,* 126; AK to JH, n.d. (same as undated letter in note 13), Beinecke; AK, "Josephine Herbst (1897–1969)," 20.

15. AK to JH, May 24, 1950, Beinecke.

16. Ibid.; AK to JH, June 18, 1950, Beinecke; AK to JH, July 15, 1950, Beinecke.

17. AK review of *Low Company* by Daniel Fuchs, *NYHTB* (February 13, 1937): 10; Saul Bellow, "From the Life of Augie March," *PR* (October 1949): 1077; Elliot Cohen, Foreword, *Commentary on the American Scene: Portraits of Jewish Life in America* (New York: Alfred A. Knopf, 1953), xx.

18. AK to JH, June 18,1950, Beinecke; AK to JH, May 24, 1950, Beinecke.

19. EW to AK, May 12, 1950; AK to EW, June 9, 1950, Beinecke; EW to AK, June 10, 1950.

20. AK to JH, July 22, 1950, Beinecke; J1/16/68.

21. AK to JH, July 29, 1950, Beinecke.

22. J9/3/50; J9/23/50; J9/25/50.

23. *Lifetime,* 135; Ann Birstein, *What I Saw at the Fair* (New York: Welcome Rain Press, 2002), 106–107.

24. Birstein, *Fair,* 111–112.

25. Ibid., 119.

26. J2/15/51.

27. "The Past," 93–94, 89; *Walker,* 8; "The Past," 94.

28. *Walker,* 5, 103, 173; "Under Forty," 10; "The Past," 89.

29. Leslie Fiedler, "The City and the Writer," *PR* (March–April 1952): 238–241; *Walker,* 71.

30. *Walker,* 175–176.

31. AK, "Autobiography as Narrative," *Michigan Quarterly Review* (Fall 1964): 21 ff. J3/8/67.

32. AK to JH, November 16, 1951, Beinecke; J5/23/49; Irwin Edman, "Urban Landscape with Figures," *NYTBR* (October 28, 1951): 1; Charles Rolo, "Readers Choice," *AM* (January 1952): 89; Brendan Gill, "Two Self Portraits," *New Yorker* (November 17, 1951): 178; Fiedler, "The City and the Writer," 240.

33. Oscar Handlin, "In Crowded Streets," *SR* (November 17, 1951): 14; David Daiches, "Brownsville Idyll," *Commentary* (December 1951): 605; Morris Freedman, "The Jewish Artist as a Young American," *Chicago Jewish* Forum (Spring 1952): 212–214; *Walker,* 161, 159, 162.

34. Lewis Mumford to AK, October 20, 1951; Van Wyck Brooks to AK, November 20, 1954.

35. Marshall Sklare interview with D. Venkateswarlu in *Jewish-American Writers and Intellectual Life in America* (New Delhi: Prestige Books, 1993), 105–106, 117; AK to M. Sperber, February 20, 1955, cc. Berg; AK to Eric Glaberson, April 29, 1980, cc. Berg.

36. Theodore Solotaroff, "Hard Times and Great Expectations," *New York Herald Tribune: Book Week* (October 10, 1965): 5.

CHAPTER 7. LIVING IN THE FIFTIES

1. J5/11/51; *Lifetime,* 114; J6/20/51; J2/3/51.

2. Ann Birstein, *What I Saw at the Fair* (New York: Welcome Rain Press, 2002), 126; *NYJ,* 213.

3. J11/7/51.

4. Birstein, *Fair*, 128.

5. Quoted in James T. Patterson, *Grand Expectations: The United States, 1945–1974* (New York: Oxford University Press, 1996), 367; J6/28/55; J6/27/55.

6. J6/6/51; *Lifetime*, 142.

7. Birstein, *Fair*, 133; AK, "Carrying the Word Abroad," *American Studies International* (April 1988): 64; AK to HA, July 16, 1951, Arendt Papers, Library of Congress, Washington, D.C.

8. J9/27/51.

9. *NYJ*, 196; J10/8/50; J10/5/51; J10/29/51; AK, "Woman in Dark Times," *NYRB* (June 24, 1982): 9; J10/26/51.

10. J11/4/51; J1/1/52; J1/28/52.

11. J1/2/52.

12. J1/2/52; "The Gift," in *Leaf*, 212.

13. AK, "Carrying," 63.

14. Birstein, *Fair*, 144; HA to Heinrich Bluecher, April 11, 1952, *Within Four Walls*, 153; HA to Heinrich Bluecher, April 24, 1952, ibid., 161.

15. Ann Birstein, "When the Wind Blew," *Summer Situations* (New York: Coward, McCann and Geoghagan, 1972), 148; Diana Trilling, *The Beginning of the Journey* (New York: Harcourt Brace, 1993), 305.

16. HA to Heinrich Bluecher, April 22, 1952, *Within Four Walls*, 162; "*Gastprofessor für Amerikanistik*," in *Contemporaries*, 308; J7/4/52; "*Gastprofessor*," 310; *NYJ*, 219; J7/5/52.

17. Birstein, *Fair*, 145–146; J6/26/52; HA to Heinrich Bluecher, August 1, 1952, *Within Four Walls*, 213.

18. *NYJ*, 221; J7/10/52; *NYJ*, 221–222; AK, "Carrying," 64.

19. Marcus Cunliffe, "Backward Glances," *American Studies* 14, 1 (1979): 91–92.

20. *Lifetime*, 141; J7/10/52.

21. J8/13/47; AK to Bernard Malamud, September 22, 1952, Malamud Papers, Harry Ransome Humanities Center, University of Texas, Austin.

22. Birstein, *Fair*, 121, 122; J3/10/59; HA to Mary McCarthy, May 18, 1960, *Between Friends: The Correspondence of Hannah Arendt and Mary McCarthy 1949–1975*, ed. Carol Brightman (New York: Harcourt Brace, 1995), 76.

23. Birstein, *Fair*, 117

24. *Lifetime*, 138.

25. J10/6/52; AK to EW, October 13, 1952, Beinecke; AK to Henry Moe, December 4, 1952, Guggenheim Foundation, New York; AK to Morton Zabel, December 16, 1952, Zabel Papers, Newberry Library, Chicago.

26. J9/8/52; clipping in Kazin Papers; J12/30/52; AK to Irving Mansfield, December 31, 1952, cc. Berg; J11/28/54.

27. AK, Introduction, *The Stature of Theodore Dreiser*, ed. Alfred Kazin and Charles Shapiro (Bloomington: Indiana University Press, 1955), 10, 12.

28. Lionel Trilling, *The Liberal Imagination* (New York: Viking, 1950), 10–21; AK, *Stature*, 10.

29. AK to Irving Kristol, May 7, 1953.

30. J3/14/53; AK to JH, April 23, 1953, Beinecke.

31. David Laskin, *Partisans* (New York: Simon and Schuster, 2000), 28; Trilling, *Beginning*, 330; J6/10/53; J6/1/64.

32. J5/1/53; "The Writer and the University," in *Leaf*, 242–252.

33. J9/25/53; J10/7/53; J10/14/53; Birstein, *Fair*, 157.

34. Harry Levin to AK, January 12, 1978; J2/6/92.

35. J8/16/54.

36. Birstein, *Fair*, 161, 162; J1/18/64.

37. EW, *The Fifties: From the Notebooks and Diaries of the Period*, ed. Leon Edel (New York: Farrar, Straus, and Giroux, 1986), 267; Mary McCarthy to HA, August 10, 1954, *Between Friends*, 20.

38. AK to EW, September 18, 1954, Beinecke; Sylvia Plath, "The Neilson Professor," *Smith Alumni Quarterly* (Fall 1954): 2; J9/17/54; J6/20/55; J9/22/54; Rachel Mellinger, "American Studies Programs in Colleges," *Mademoiselle* (December 1954): 115.

39. AK, "The Age of Harmlessness," speech delivered at Mount Holyoke, October 11, 1954; JD, "Remembering Alfred Kazin," *AS* (Winter 1999): 33.

40. J11/27/54.

41. J11/20/54; J11/9/54; *NYJ*, 234.

42. J11/29/54; Jack Kerouac to AK, October 27, 1954, *Jack Kerouac: Selected Letters 1940–1956*, ed. Ann Charters (New York: Viking, 1995), 449.

43. J11/28/54.

44. J6/22/55.

45. AK to Henry Nash Smith, January 3, 1955, Henry Nash Smith Papers, Bancroft Library, University of California at Berkeley.

46. AK to HA, March 18, 1955, Arendt Papers, Library of Congress, Washington, D.C.

47. "College Sponsors Symposium about Novel at Mid-Century," *Sophian* (March 8, 1955): 1, 3, 4; Birstein, *Fair*, 165.

48. AK, "Postscript, 1955," *On Native Grounds* (New York: Doubleday Anchor Books, 1955), 410–411.

49. J6/27/55; "The Solitude of Paul Rosenfeld," in *Leaf*, 156; J6/19/55; J7/23/57; J6/27/55.

950. "The Uses of Experience," in *Contemporaries*, 397; Leslie Fiedler, *An End to Innocence: Essays on Culture and Politics* (Boston: Beacon Press, 1952), 70; "Solitude of Paul Rosenfeld," 156.

51. AK, "The Uses," 397–400; J10/15/55.

52. J8/19/56; J12/7/51; J7/8/55; J7/23/57; J10/15/55.

53. J0/0/55; *Writer's America*, 100–103.

54. AK to author, May 11, 1986; J11/4/66; Jackson Bryer to author, August 29, 2003; Peter Schrag, *Out of Place in America* (New York: Random House, 1970), 6; J3/12/56.

55. J9/2/55; *Lifetime*, 157; J2/23/55; "Writer and the University," 150; J12/18/55.

56. J3/5/56; interview with Daniel Aaron at Harvard University, July 7, 1989; J1/17/57; *NYJ*, 232.

57. J9/23/55; Birstein, *Fair*, 171; J10/11/55.

58. Ben Yagoda, *About Town: The New Yorker and the World It Made* (New York: Scribner, 2000), 297; AK to Seymour Lawrence, October 20, 1955, Seymour Lawrence Correspondence, University of Mississippi Library, Oxford.

59. J5/5/56.

60. J7/25/56; Birstein, *Fair*, 173.

61. J9/15/56; J10/29/56; J9/16/56; J9/27/56; J1/23/57.

62. J12/n.d./55; J9/23/57.

63. AK to Henry Moe, December 4, 1952, AK file, Guggenheim Foundation, New York; J10/6/54.

64. J12/27/54; J9/27/56; J6/29/57.

65. J1/20/57; *Lifetime*, 157.

66. Alfred Kazin and Daniel Aaron, eds., *Emerson: A Modern Anthology* (Boston: Houghton Mifflin, 1958), 7–13; J6/27/65.

67. "Alfred Kazin: The Critic as Creator," interview with Robert Silvers, *Horizon* (July 1962): 100; Philip Rahv to AK, March 14, 1957; "The Stillness in *Light in August*," in *Contemporaries*, 130–149.

68. J2/26/42; J4/2/57.

69. AK to Seymour Lawrence, May 21, 1957.

70. J10/6/52.

71. *Lifetime*, 162; J7/13/57; Birstein, "Love among the Dunes," *Summer Situations*, 17–18, 37, 54, 17; *Lifetime*, 162; J9/19/57.

72. J9/6/57; *NYJ*, 234; J9/9/57.

73. J9/23/55; J8/11/57; J1/27/57.

74. Leo Marx, "Kazin and the Religion of Art," *NR* (November 28, 1955): 18–19; Hans Meyerhoff, "A Critic's Point of View," *PR* (Spring 1956): 278–283; J7/23/57; J6/27/55.

75. AK, Application to the Guggenheim Memorial Foundation, January 10, 1958.

76. J8/11/57; Walt Whitman, *Democratic Vistas*, in *Complete Poetry and Selected Prose*, ed. James E. Miller Jr. (Boston: Houghton Mifflin, 1959), 411, 476.

CHAPTER 8. THE WRITER IN THE WORLD: PART 1

1. AK to JH, November 29, 1958, Beinecke; Oscar Cargill, "The Role of the Critic," *College English* (December 1958): 105–110; Cargill, reader's report to Reynal and Hitchcock on *ONG*, September 14, 1942.

2. J1/1/58; Sylvia Plath, March 10, 1958, *The Unabridged Journals of Sylvia Plath: 1950–1962*, ed. Karen V. Kukil (New York: Anchor Books, 2000), 347; AK to HA, April 21, 1958, Arendt Papers, Library of Congress, Washington, D.C.

3. J8/7/62; Randall Jarrell, "The Age of Criticism," *Poetry and the Age* (London: Faber and Faber, 1955), 71–72; Theodore Solotaroff, Introduction, *Alfred Kazin's America* (New York: HarperCollins, 2003), xxxii; Robert Alter, "The Education of Alfred Kazin," *Commentary* (June 1978): 47.

4. J1/2/59; J5/2/59; J12/10/62; J10/1/56; J8/8/63.

5. J1/21/58.

6. Ann Birstein, *What I Saw at the Fair* (New York: Welcome Rain Press, 2002), 175; interview with Daniel Bell, October 17, 2003; Nathan Glazer email to author, June 17, 2002; Irving Kristol to author, June 20, 2002.

7. J6/1/1962; *NYJ*, 185, 194; J8/30/61.

8. J6/20/61; J10/18/61; J7/24/59.

9. EW, *The Sixties: The Last Journal 1960–1972*, ed. Lewis Dabney (New York: Farrar, Straus, and Giroux, 1993), 94.

10. J7/27/1959; John Aldrich, "The Price of Being Taken Seriously," in *Time to Murder and Create: The Contemporary Novel in Crisis* (New York: David McKay, 1966), 65; J8/26/60; J3/5/59.

11. "The Trial of *Lady Chatterley's Lover*," *New York Post* (May 28, 1959): 24.

12. AK to George Putnam and Sons, May 21, 1959, cc. Berg; AK to Norman Mailer, May 21, 1959, cc. Berg.

13. *Lifetime*, 172; "Lady Chatterley in America," in *Contemporaries*, 105; AK to Norman Mailer, May 21, 1959, cc. Berg.

14. J6/11/59; J12/7/51.

15. "J. D. Salinger: 'Everybody's Favorite,'" in *Contemporaries*, 237; "Truman Capote and 'The Army of Wrongness,'" in *Contemporaries*, 251; "How Good Is Norman Mailer?" in *Contemporaries*, 249; "The Alone Generation," in *Contemporaries*, 209–210.

16. J3/5/59.

17. "J. D. Salinger,", 239; "Bernard Malamud: The Magic and the Dread," in *Contemporaries*, 207.

18. Leslie Fiedler, "The Breakthrough: The American Jewish Novel and the Fictional

Image of the Jew," *Midstream* (Winter 1958): 15–35; *NYJ*, 42; AK to Guggenheim Committee on Bernard Malamud, 1958; AK to EW, March 16, 1959, Beinecke.

19. *BBL*, 157; "How Good," in *Contemporaries*, 250.

20. "Tough-minded Mr. Roth," in *Contemporaries*, 258–260; J7/28/65.

21. Morris Dickstein, *Gates of Eden: American Culture in the Sixties* (New York: Basic Books, 1977), 30; Theodore Solotaroff, "A Vocal Group: The Jewish Part in American Letters," *TLS* (November 6, 1959):35–36; "Jew as Modern," 41; "The Alone Generation," 211, 217.

22. J6/17/59.

23. J6/29/59; Marc Slonim, "'American Writers Are as Good as Dead,'" *NYTBR* (October 14, 1951): 28; J6/29/59.

24. Arthur Schlesinger Jr., *The Politics of Hope* (Boston: Houghton Mifflin, 1963), 277; AK, "Meeting Russian Writers," typescript of speech, n.d.

25. AK, "Among Russian Jews," *Harper's* (May 1961): 135.

26. AK, "From a Russian Diary," in *Contemporaries*, 327–328; *NYJ*, 271–272; J4/2/85.

27. J4/24/90.

28. Birstein, *Fair*, 180.

29. J10/25/59; AK to author, March 16, 1962; J3/17/60; J4/17/59; J1/3/64; J7/26/57; Birstein, *Fair*, 181.

30. Interview with Ann Birstein, January 1, 1990; J10/2/59; J9/6/59; AK to JH, November 20, 1959, Beinecke.

31. "In Puerto Rico," in *Contemporaries*, 315–316; Brooks Atkinson, "Critic at Large," *NYT* (April, 20, 1962): 22; Keith Botsford, "On Puerto Rico," *Commentary* (May 1960): 430; AK to JH, November 20, 1959, Beinecke.

32. J1/18/60; J1/16/60; J1/16/60.

33. Seymour Lawrence to AK, August 15, 1958.

34. J11/6/64; J5/13/60.

35. AK to JH, August 1, 1960, Beinecke.

36. *Lifetime*, 171; "At Ease in Zion," in *Contemporaries*, 330; "Eichmann and the New Israelis," in *Contemporaries*, 447.

37. On the importance of the Eichmann trial in identifying "a distinct thing called 'The Holocaust,'" see Peter Novick, *The Holocaust in American Life* (New York: Houghton Mifflin, 1999): 127–144.

38. J8/3/60; J3/30/61; J5/15/48; J10/25/53.

39. "At Ease," 343.

40. AK and Ann Birstein, eds., Introduction, *The Works of Anne Frank* (Garden City, NY: Doubleday, 1959), 9–10; Elie Wiesel, *Night* (1960; repr., New York: Bantam Books, 1982), 65; "The Least of These," in *Contemporaries*, 298.

41. AK, "My Debt to Elie Wiesel and Primo Levi," in *Testimony: Contemporary Writers Make the Holocaust Personal*, ed. David Rosenberg (New York: Times Books, 1989), 120, 118; Elie Wiesel, *All Rivers Run to the Sea: Memoirs* (New York: Random House, 1995), 336; Wiesel, "My Debt," 120.

42. J11/10/60; Daniel Bell to author, 2003 [n.d.]; J11/7/60; J3/13/61.

43. AK, "War and the American Intellectual," typescript.

44. Quoted in "The President and Other Intellectuals," in *Contemporaries*, 450, 448; Arthur Schlesinger Jr., "The New Mood in Politics," *Esquire* (January 1960), reprinted in *The Sixties*, ed. Gerald Howard (New York: Washington Square Press, 1982), 45; J11/10/60; J1/28/61.

45. J3/21/61.

46. J4/21/61; J6/17/61; "The President," 462–463, 458, 465.

47. Arthur Schlesinger Jr., *A Thousand Days: John Kennedy in the White House* (Boston: Houghton Mifflin, 1965), 681–682; J8/1/61; J8/12/61.

48. *NYJ*, 253; Schlesinger, *A Thousand Days*, 682; Ann Birstein, *The Last of the True Believers* (New York: W. W. Norton, 1988), 202.

49. "The President," 458–459, 463.

50. Ibid., 463.

51. W. M. Frohock, "It's Hard to See beyond the Hudson," *NYTBR* (June 24, 1962): 1; J10/21/61; *Time* (June 6, 1960): 67.

52. J11/19/61; J11/16/61; J5/1/61; Birstein, *Fair*, 183; AK, 1994 Steegmuller Memorial, typescript.

53. J10/2/61; AK, "Poor Old Red," *Reporter* (November 9, 1961): 63; J10/18/61.

54. J9/12/61; AK to JH, April, 27, 1962, Beinecke.

55. Albert Guerard, "The World Is One the Writer Must Not Scorn but Love," *NYTBR* (April 22, 1962): 6, 8; Lionel Abel, "Alfred Kazin, Essayist," *Commentary* (November 1962): 457–460; Gay Wilson Allen, "The Artistry of a Thinker," *SR* (May 5, 1962): 21; Kenneth Lynn, "Kazin," *Christian Science Monitor* (April 26, 1962): 11.

56. Dan Jacobson, "Teach Yourself Literature," *New Statesman* (February 8, 1963): 209; "Middle of the Road," *TLS* (May 10, 1963): 342; J11/26/61; J5/24/63.

57. J9/28/57; *ONG*, 400–401.

58. J5/21/56.

59. J5/21/56; Lewis M. Dabney, *Edmund Wilson: A Life in Literature* (New York: Farrar, Straus, and Giroux), 287; EW, *The Fifties: From the Notebooks and Diaries of the Period,* ed. Leon Edel (New York: Farrar, Straus, and Giroux, 1986): 417.

60. EW to AK, March 31, 1962, *Letters on Literature*, 626–627; EW to AK, April 13, 1962, ibid., 627.

61. J9/19/61; J6/6/62; J6/30/62; J7/9/62.

62. *NYJ*, 236–242.

63. Ibid., 238, 243; J9/8/63; J6/12/72.

64. J9/19/62; J10/4/62

65. J11/27/62; J1/10/63; J11/27/62; J10/4/62.

66. J4/18/63.

67. J5/7/63.

68. Seymour Lawrence to AK, December, 27, 1961.

69. J12/12/62; AK to JH, September 8, 1965, Beinecke; J4/21/65.

70. AK to Thomas Wilson, Harvard University Press, August 19, 1954, cc. Berg; William Phillips, "What Happened in the 30's," in *A Sense of the Present* (New York: Chilmark Press, 1967), 17.

71. Eliot Freemont-Smith, "At the Heart of Things," *NYT* (October 11, 1965): 37; Theodore Solotaroff, "Hard Times and Great Expectations," *New York Herald Tribune: Book Week* (October 10, 1965): 5; Richard Gilman, "A View of How It Was," *Dissent* (May–June 1966): 325; Hilton Kramer, "The Age of the Intellectuals," *New Leader* (September 27, 1965): 23.

72. J5/30/61; J5/23/64; AK to JH, September 8, 1965, Beinecke.

73. PD to AK, December 14, 1964; PD to AK, January 18, 1965; interview with PD, April 12, 2002.

74. *Thirties*, 166; PD to AK, January 30, 1965.

CHAPTER 9. THE WRITER IN THE WORLD: PART 2

1. EW to AK, 1965, *Letters on Literature*, 200; Richard Hofstadter to AK, September 13, 1965.

2. "The Alone Generation," in *Contemporaries,* 217; J9/12/63; J12/27/65; J5/23/64; J11/22/67.

3. J11/22/67; "The Function of Criticism Today," in *Contemporaries,* 505.

4. J7/30/63; J4/16/65.

5. J12/25/63; AK to JH, February 8, 1964, Beinecke.

6. J9/26/63; J1/21/65; J12/25/63.

7. AK to JH, February 8, 1964, Beinecke; J11/11/65; J10/17/63; J1/27/68.

8. J7/19/68; J9/8/67; J11/11/65; J2/4/72; J1/15/65.

9. J3/31/65.

10. J9/30/66; J4/2/65; J9/19/61; J8/15/60.

11. J1/27/62; J6/12/64.

12. J12/29/65; J8/9/63.

13. *NYJ,* 257; J2/11/68.

14. J5/5/64; J11/22/70; "At Home with Mrs. Alfred Kazin," *New York Post* (May 14, 1966): 51; J5/14/66.

15. J5/20/70; J7/26/65.

16. J5/5/64; J12/31/65.

17. Interview with AK, October 4, 1986; J6/24/64; J1/9/65.

18. J7/23/1963; J6/12/73; J11/12/72.

19. J11/12/72; J6/3/55; J10/26/58; J1/23/68; J5/14/66; J3/20/72.

20. Kenneth Kenniston, *Young Radicals: Notes on Committed Youth* (New York: Harcourt Brace and World, 1968), 85.

21. AK, "The Sweet Music of Dwight D. Eisenhower," *NYRB* (November 14, 1963): 1–3; *Leaf,* 200; J2/7/58; J12/7/67.

22. "The President and Other Intellectuals," in *Contemporaries,* 463.

23. J8/18/61; J5/12/61.

24. Transcript of 1961 discussion on the negro in American culture broadcast over WABI-FM in New York, published as "The Negro in American Culture," in *The Black American Writer,* Vol. 1: Fiction, ed. C. W. E. Bigsby (Deland, FL: Everett Edwards, 1969): 79–107; AK to C. P. Snow, April 29, 1964, C. P. Snow Correspondence, Harry Ransome Humanities Research Center, University of Texas, Austin; J5/7/63; J3/24/65.

25. J3/15/65.

26. J6/23/64; AK, "Radicals and Intellectuals," *NYRB* (May 20, 1965): 34.

27. "On Vietnam and the Dominican Republic," *PR* (Summer 1965): 397–398.

28. "On Vietnam," *PR* (Fall 1965): 638, 651–655.

29. AK to EW, including Antiwar Statement, n.d., Beinecke; Carl Stolberg, *Hubert Humphrey: A Biography* (New York: W. W. Norton, 1984), 292–294.

30. John W. Finney, "24 Writers Urge New Steps for Vietnam Peace," *NYT* (April 27, 1966): 6; Hubert Humphrey to AK, May 4, 1966; J4/26/66.

31. J6/20/66; J3/15/65.

32. J2/12/60; *NYJ,* 207; J9/25/61; J10/14/61.

33. J4/17/61; J6/27/61.

34. J3/29/65; AK to PD, September 17, 1966, Davison Papers, Berg.

35. Steven Kelman, *Push Comes to Shove: The Escalation of Student Protest* (Boston: Houghton Mifflin, 1970), 66; MK, review of *Fugitive Days* by William Ayres, *American Prospect,* September 24–October 8, 2001.

36. Kelman, *Push Comes to Shove,* 71.

37. J11/14/67; AK, "The Vicar of Christ," *NYRB* (March 19, 1964): 1; J10/22/67.

38. Noam Chomsky, "On Resistance," *NYRB* (December 7, 1967): 4–12.

39. J1/7/68; J1/23/68; J12/9/67; MK, "Fathers and Sons," *Dissent* (Fall 1998): 103; J2/7/68.

40. J3/4/68; *NYJ,* 259; Richard Hofstadter, "The 214th Columbia University Address," *AS* (Autumn 1968): 585; J9/6/68.

41. J4/28/68; AK, "Professors Are Too Sophisticated," *SR* (May 22, 1971): 26; J12/27/68; J12/27/68; *NYJ*, 263.

42. Lionel Trilling, "Reality in America," *The Liberal Imagination* (New York: Viking, 1950): 11; AK, "Book Learning and Barricades," *Washington Post Book World* (August 4, 1968): 4; AK, review of *The Collected Essays, Journalism and Letters of George Orwell*, *Washington Post Book World* (October 27, 1968): 3.

43. AK, "Youth as a Pressure Group," in *Contemporaries*, 438; Irving Howe, *Decline of the New* (New York: Harcourt Brace, 1970): 53; Daniel Bell, *The Cultural Contradictions of Capitalism* (New York: Basic Books, 1976), 121; AK, "At Young People's Rebellions," *Washington Post Book World* (June 22, 1969): 3.

44. AK, "Bellow's Purgatory," *NYRB* (March 28, 1968): 32–36; AK, "How Good Is Norman Mailer?" in *Contemporaries*, 246–250.

45. AK, "The Trouble He's Seen," *NYTBR* (May 5, 1968): 1–2.

46. Norman Mailer, *Armies of the Night* (New York: New American Library, 1968): 91, 103, 311; AK, "The Trouble," 2.

47. Saul Bellow, *Mr. Sammler's Planet* (1970; repr., New York: Penguin Books, 1977): 33, 36–37.

48. AK, "Though He Slay Me," *NYRB* (December 3, 1970): 3–4.

49. Saul Bellow to AK, n.d.; James Atlas, *Bellow: A Biography* (New York: Random House, 2000), 392; J4/15/67; AK, "Though He Slay Me," 3; *NYJ*, 8.

50. J4/20/69; AK, "Though He Slay Me," 3.

51. *NYJ*, 260–261.

52. J1/4/69.

53. The complete title reads "Angry Young Man: Mike Kazin Finds Outlet for Revolutionary Ideas in Harvard SDS Group: Eminent Critic's Son Works for Violent Upheaval, Also Gets Honors Grades: No Pity for Stricken Dean" by William M. Carley, *Wall Street Journal* (May 5, 1969): 1.

54. Ibid., 1; J5/8/70; J5/19/70.

55. AK, "Our Flag," *NYRB* (July 2, 1970): 3.

56. MK, "Fathers and Sons," 102–105; J12/18/73; J9/23/70.

57. AK to PD, January 5, 1965, Davison Papers, Berg.

58. Ralph Waldo Emerson, journal entry, October 3, 1837, *Emerson in His Journals*, ed. Joel Porte (Cambridge: Harvard University Press, 1982), 169.

59. J5/14/64.

60. PD to AK, July 30, 1971, Davison Papers, Berg; interview with PD, April 12, 2002; PD to AK, July 13, 1971, Davison Papers, Berg; Ester "Peggy" Yntema to AK, July 26, 1971, Davison Papers, Berg.

61. AK to Stanley Burnshaw, August 2, 1971, Burnshaw Papers, Harry Ransome Humanities Research Center, University of Texas, Austin; V. S. Pritchett, "*Bright Book of Life*," *NYTBR* (May 20, 1973): 3, 30; Philip French, "Thirty Years On," *New Statesman* (March 18, 1974): 364–365; "Reconsidering the Lost and Later Generations," *TLS* (June 14, 1974): 634.

62. Richard Poirier, "Opposing the Wonderful, Zany and Powerful," *NR* (May 19, 1973): 25–28; Jack Richardson, "The Working Critic," *Commentary* (November 1973): 64–66; Alvin H. Rosenfeld, "Alfred Kazin and the Condition of Criticism Today," *Midstream* (November 1973): 68–73; Roger Sale, "Wrestling with Fiction," *NYRB* (March 21, 1974).

63. AK to Ester "Peggy" Yntema, July 26, 1972, Davison Papers, Berg.

64. *BBL*, 87–88, 219, 180–181, 184, 288, 270.

65. *ONG*, 353, 461; AK, "The Strange Dream World of James Joyce," *NYHTB* (May 2, 1939): 4; Morris Dickstein, *Gates of Eden: American Culture in the Sixties* (New York: Basic Books, 1976): 232.

66. *NYJ,* 266; *BBL,* 205.

67. *ONG,* 489, 29; AK, "History as LBJ," *NYRB* (December 1, 1966): 3; *Thirties,* 5.

CHAPTER 10. NEW YORK JEW

1. J2/27/68; AK, "Josephine Herbst (1897–1969)," *NYRB* (March 27, 1969): 19.

2. J10/18/75; J9/1/74; *NYJ,* 291, 295.

3. James T. Patterson, *Restless Giant: The United States from Watergate to Bush v. Gore* (New York: Oxford University Press, 2005), 10; *NYJ,* 59.

4. J11/19/68; *NYJ,* 234, 257.

5. E. Digby Baltzell, *The Protestant Establishment: Aristocracy and Caste in America* (New Haven, CT: Yale University Press, 1964), 372; Cleveland Amory, *Who Killed Society?* (New York: Harper and Brothers, 1960), 203, 214; Mark Twain, quoted in Christopher Gray, "Streetscapes: The Century Association Clubhouse; Richardson's Lost Work Discovered," *NYT,* Real Estate section (December 11, 1988): 1.

6. Amory, *Society,* 201; AK to PD, December 7, 1968, Davison Papers, Berg.

7. J6/19/69; J10/25/74; J5/7/70; J12/22/70.

8. J7/11/65; J5/16/73; J10/25/74; J6/3/71; *NYJ,* 7; J11/5/72.

9. J7/2/70; Emil Fackenheim, *The Jewish Return into History: Reflections in the Age of Auschwitz and a New Jerusalem* (New York: Schocken Books, 1978), 129–143.

10. AK, "The Vicar of Christ," *NYRB* (March 19, 1964): 1.

11. J6/22/67; Arthur Hertzberg, *The Jews in America: Four Centuries of an Uneasy Encounter: A History* (New York: Simon and Schuster, 1989), 375; Neusner, *Death and Birth of Judaism* (New York: Basic Books, 1987), 268; AK, "In Israel after the Triumph," *Harper's* (November 1967): 77, 83, 74.

12. J7/1/70; *NYJ,* 285; J7/10/70; Fackenheim, *Jewish Return,* 138; J8/27/61.

13. AK, "What Do We Do Now? What? What?" *AM* (April 1974): 72, 77.

14. J3/7/87; J2/19/89; AK, "In Israel," 77.

15. J2/19/70; *NYJ,* 289; J2/7/65; J1/16/65.

16. J9/23/70; *NYJ,* 12; AK to author, March 3, 1992; J3/22/88; *NYJ,* 12.

17. J4/12/68; David S. Brown, *Richard Hofstadter: An Intellectual Biography* (Chicago: University of Chicago Press, 2006), 229; AK interview, Richard Hofstadter Memoir, Columbia Oral History Project, Columbia University, New York, May 1, 1972.

18. AK to author, March 25, 1992; MK quoted in Brown, *Richard Hofstadter,* 166; J11/22/70.

19. AK, "Richard Hofstadter (1916–1970), *AS* (Summer 1971): 387–401.

20. J11/4/70; J5/5/75; J6/12/72; J10/17/75; J3/18/74; J3/8/74.

21. J1/11/73; AK to Peggy Yntema, February 2, 1973, Davison Papers, Berg; *NYT* (April 10, 1972): 11.

22. AK to PD, December 17, 1972, Davison Papers, Berg; AK, "New York Jew," *NYRB* (December 14, 1972); J12/7/72.

23. AK, "Memoirs of a Juror," *Village Voice* (April 14, 1975): 32–34, 36; J1/11/73.

24. J10/1/74.

25. AK, "The Happy Hour," *Esquire* (October 1980): 70–73, reprinted in *Contemporaries* (82), 175–186.

26. J10/22/75; David E. Lavin, Richard D. Alba, Richard A. Silberstein, *Right Versus Privilege: The Open-Admissions Experiment at the City University of New York* (New York: Free Press, 1981), 2.

27. AK, "A Homecoming," address to the Hunter Honors Convocation, April 29, 1974, typescript.

28. AK to PD, January 31, 1974, Davison Papers, Berg; PD to J. R. Williams, in-house memo, March 19, 1974, Davison Papers, Berg.

29. PD to J. R. Williams, in-house memo, March 19, 1974, Davison Papers, Berg; PD to AK, March 2, 1976; PD to AK, April 12, 1977; AK to PD, May 19, 1975, Davison Papers, Berg.

30. George Lankevich and Howard B. Furer, *A Brief History of New York City* (New York: Associated Faculty Press, 1984), 281–311; J9/23/72; J5/18/76.

31. AK to PD, December 12, 1975, Davison Papers, Berg.

32. J5/20/76; J9/24/76; J9/4/76.

33. Michael Novak, *The Rise of the Unmeltable Ethnics* (New York: Macmillan, 1971); J1/4/60; J1/19/68; J10/26/70; J1/21/58.

34. AK, "The Self as History," in *Contemporaries* (82), 422; George Stade, review of *New York Jew*, *NR* (May 20, 1978): 30; Robert Langbaum, "Return of the Native," *TLS* (November 19, 1978): 1313.

35. *NYJ*, 24, 54–55, 67, 43.

36. J1/27/64; J8/24/69; J11/28/76; Mark Krupnick, "An American Life," *Salmagundi* (1979): 200; *NYJ*, 42.

37. AK, "The Self as History," 416; *Thirties*, 5; Krupnick, "American Life," 199.

38. Abraham Cahan, *The Rise of David Levinsky* (New York: Harper and Brothers, 1917), 530; *NYJ*, 195.

39. *NYJ*, 97, 96, 152, 258.

40. J10/25/75; J5/5/64; J8/9/73; J1/13/76; J10/2/76.

41. J4/20/72; J11/8/66.

42. J7/30/62.

43. *NYJ*, 143, 42, 43.

44. Ibid., 44; Langbaum, "Return," 1313; Robert Penn Warren, "New York Jew," *NYTBR* (June 25, 1978): 56; the complete list of those signing the joint letter in the *Book Review* of the same date are M. H. Abrams, Quentin Anderson, Eric Bentley, Morton Bloomfield, Frank Kermode, Leslie Fiedler, Charles Frankel, Richard Howard, Howard Mumford Jones, Stanley Kauffmann, Steven Marcus, Robert K. Merton, Edward Said, Arthur Schlesinger Jr., Fritz Stern, Barbara Probst Solomon, Aileen Ward, Michael Wood, and Paul Zweig; J6/16/78.

45. J6/26/68; J3/5/66; *NYJ*, 46; J10/20/68; J12/17/61; J3/5/66.

46. *NYJ*, 193–196.

47. J4/13/61; J1/18/64; AK to HA, September 13, 1961, Arendt Papers, Library of Congress, Washington, D.C.

48. J12/22/62; Irving Howe, "Mid-Century Turning Point: An Intellectual Memoir," *Midstream* (June–July 1975): 25; Norman Podhoretz, "Hannah Arendt on Eichmann," *Commentary* (September 1963): 201–208; Lionel Abel, "The Aesthetics of Evil," *PR* (Summer 1963): 219; Irving Howe, "The New Yorker and Hannah Arendt," *Commentary* (October 1963): 319; Heinrich Bluecher to HA, mid-March 1963, *Within Four Walls,* 386.

49. See Gerald Sorin, *Irving Howe: A Life of Passionate Dissent* (New York: New York University Press, 2002), 195–198, for a recent account of what took place at the gathering. Theodore Solotaroff, *Alfred Kazin's America* (New York: HarperCollins, 2003), xxxvii.

50. J10/19/63; AK to Stanley Plastrik, March 7, 1964.

51. J10/21/63; *NYJ*, 196; J12/4/75.

52. J7/2/70; *NYJ*, 28; J10/8/57; *NYJ*, 97, 8.

53. Mordecai Richler, "Literary Ids and Egos," *NYTBR* (May 7, 1958): 38–39; J5/6/78.

54. Robert Alter, "The Education of Alfred Kazin," *Commentary* (June 1978): 44–51; Earl Rovit, "The Darkroom Album," *Nation* (April 22, 1978): 480; Philip French, "Lonely

Heart," *New Statesman* (September 8, 1978): 302–303; Krupnick, "American Life," 198; J8/18/84; John Lahr, "The Critic as Cultural Confidence Man," *Harper's* (July 1978): 88.

55. J5/3/78; J6/20/79.

CHAPTER 11. A NEW LIFE

1. J5/13/78; J4/3/91.
2. *Lifetime*, 184.
3. Interview with JD, October 23, 1998.
4. J2/27/77.
5. J6/30/90.
6. J9/12/77; J9/18/77; AK to JD, October 13, 1977; AK to JD, September 29, 1977; AK to JD, October 13, 1997.
7. Ann Birstein, *What I Saw at the Fair* (New York: Welcome Rain Press, 2002), 230.
8. *Lifetime*, 186.
9. J1/9/78; J2/7/78; Birstein, *Fair*, 233.
10. J11/20/79; J8/3/91; J4/16/80.
11. J3/13/78; undated evaluation of Fellowship Year 1977–1978 at the Stanford Center, cc. Berg.
12. AK to JD, February 19, 1978; J1/?/78.
13. Yaron Ezrahi, *Rubber Bullets: Power and Consciousness in Modern Israel* (New York: Farrar, Straus, and Giroux, 1997), 298.
14. J3/25/78.
15. Interview with Cathrael Kazin, October 12, 2003; J5/6/78.
16. Interview with Cathrael Kazin, October 12, 2003; J10/26/65.
17. J6/18/77; J5/27/78; J7/17/78.
18. J6/20/92.
19. AK to JD, March 27, 1978.
20. J1/28/30.
21. Lucy Dawidowicz to AK, September 14, 1977; AK to JD, October 22, 1977; J9/27/78.
22. J4/12/78; J6/5/79; phone interview with Joseph Epstein, March 23, 2003.
23. AK to Saul Bellow, March 27, 1974, cc. Berg; Saul Bellow to AK, November 1978 [n.d.]; J5/8/79.
24. J3/2/87; J1/31/80.
25. J3/21/88; AK, "A Walker in the City Again," *New York Magazine* (January 19, 1987): 32.
26. J8/21/79; AK, "Looking for the American Mind," Commencement Address, in *News* of the Graduate School and University Center, City University of New York, June 4, 1981, 5; J12/15/80; AK, "A Walker," 35; J8/21/79; J3/11/80; AK, "Looking," 5.
27. Phone interview with MK, September 26, 2003.
28. Ibid.
29. Ibid; J2/30/79.
30. J8/24/80; Birstein, *Fair*, 241; J8/27/80; Birstein, *Fair*, 241.
31. J8/31/80; J10/16/82; J7/14/78; J12/2/79.
32. J10/16/82; AK to MK, May 29, 1981, author's copy; Birstein, *Fair*, 250.
33. J8/18/81; J2/19/83.
34. J2/19/83; J12/12/81; J10/25/81; J8/23/82; J9/3/84; J8/23/82.
35. J11/13/82; J9/3/82.
36. J4/10/82
37. *NYJ*, 234; J1/21/82; J8/5/82; J5/30/83.
38. AK to Eric Glaberson, April 29, 1980, cc. Berg; J5/9/84. Despite Kazin's protestations,

Glaberson did complete the dissertation: *Historical Humanism in the Work of Two New York Intellectuals* (October 1982).

39. J5/9/84.

40. J11/11/81; *Procession,* 156, 187, 223; Morris Dickstein, review of *An American Procession, New York Magazine* (June 4, 1984): 77.

41. *Procession,* xiii; 10, 21, 373, 365, 6.

42. Ibid., 155, 146; "Work Habits of a Writer and Teacher," AK interview with Jane Forman, *Composition and Writing* (1978): 28.

43. *Procession,* 157.

44. J4/15/82; J10/12/82.

45. Kenneth Lynn, "Getting Things Wrong," *Commentary* (July 1984): 72; AK, Preface to the Fiftieth Anniversary Edition, *On Native Grounds* (New York: Harcourt Brace, 1995), xii; AK to MK, May 29, 1981, author's copy; J12/22/81.

46. J4/14/81; J5/9/84; AK to Robert Silvers, June 27, 1984, cc. Berg; Lynn, "Getting Things Wrong," 72; J6/27/84.

CHAPTER 12. POLITICS

1. Lionel Abel, "Alfred Kazin, Essayist," *Commentary* (November 1962): 457–460; Kenneth Lynn, "Act One," *New Criterion* (May 1983): 72–79; AK, "Saving My Soul at the Plaza," *NYRB* (March 31, 1983): 38–42.

2. *Our Country and Our Culture: A Conference of the Committee of the Free World* (New York: Orwell Press, 1983): 2, 43, 47, 109; J1/9/82.

3. AK, "Confessions of an Armchair Thrill Seeker: A Slightly Unorthodox View of Spy Stories," *Diversions: For Physicians at Leisure* (July 1980): 59; AK to Eric Glaberson, April 29, 1980, cc. Berg; AK, "Every Man His Own Revolution," *NR* (July 3, 1967): 23.

4. Irving Howe, *A Margin of Hope: An Intellectual Biography* (New York: Harcourt Brace Jovanovich, 1982), 328.

5. AK, "Our Flag," *NYRB* (July 2, 1970): 3; J5/28/76; J11/9/72; Irving Howe, *The Critical Point: On Literature and Culture* (New York: Horizon Press, 1973): 10.

6. "New Group Backs Hiring Guidelines," *NYT* (February 27, 1975): 12.

7. J12/9/83.

8. Ann Birstein, *What I Saw at the Fair* (New York: Welcome Rain Press, 2002), 218; J6/12/77; J6/1/78.

9. AK, "The Writer as Sexual Showoff," *New York* (June 9, 1975): 36–40.

10. AK, "Women Are Not All Alike," *Esquire* (June 1977): 50.

11. Ibid., 50; J4/25/84.

12. "The Jew as Modern," 41; AK, "Women Are Not All Alike," 50; J3/14/76; AK, "We See from the Periphery, Not the Center: Reflections on Literature in an Age of Crisis," *World Literature Today* (Spring 1977): 188–189.

13. AK, "We See from the Periphery," 187; *ONG,* 436–437; Michel Foucault, "What Is an Author?" in *The Foucault Reader,* ed. Paul Rabinow (New York: Pantheon, 1984); Roland Barthes, "The Death of the Author," *Modern Criticism and Theory,* ed. David Lodge (New York: Longman, 1988), 101–120; *NYJ,* 8.

14. AK to Dennis Wrong, October 28, 1980, cc. Berg; AK, "Looking for the American Mind," Commencement Address, in *News,* of the Graduate School and University Center, City University of New York, June 4, 1981; Kenneth L. Woodward, "A New Look at Lit Crit," *Newsweek* (June 22, 1981): 80–83.

15. J11/23/82; phone interview with Daniel Born, April, 25, 2003; phone interview with Mary Beth McMahon, April 17, 2005; Born interview; McMahon interview.

16. Lyon Evans, "In Memoriam," *New England Quarterly* (September 1998): 478–479; McMahon interview.

17. James Cox to AK, July 20, 1982, for award to be given December 28, 1982, in Los Angeles; J1/4/83.

18. One of the books that Kazin read on the changing economic conditions in the late 1970s and early 1980s was Thomas Byrne Edsall, *The New Politics of Inequality* (New York: W. W. Norton, 1984), which tracks the shift in economic and political power toward the wealthiest Americans.

19. AK, "Every Man His Own Revolution," *NR* (July 3, 1976): 21; AK, "We See from the Periphery," 189.

20. J4/24/81.

21. *NYJ*, 190–191; J7/28/79.

22. J7/28/79; Irving Kristol, "The Timerman Affair," *Wall Street Journal* (May 29, 1981): 24; AK, "The Solitude of Timerman," *NR* (June 20, 1981): 32–34.

23. J1/21/83.

24. Peter Steinfels, *The Neoconservatives: The Men Who Are Changing America's Politics* (New York: Simon and Schuster, 1979), 22; AK, "Saving My Soul at the Plaza," *NYRB* (March 31, 1983): 2, 4, 8, 2.

25. Herbert Mitgang to AK, March 10, 1983.

26. Elizabeth Hardwick to AK, March 25, 1983; Irving Howe to AK, March 11, 1983; Philip Roth to AK, March 22, 1983; Anthony Lewis to AK, March 10, 1983; Joseph Epstein, ("Aristides"), "Let Us Now Praise Knuckleheads," *AS* (Autumn 1983): 446; Mark Schechner, "Rhapsody in Red, White and Blue," *Nation* (June 23, 1984): 759.

27. J2/5/82.

28. J10/20/83; AK, "The Strange Death of Liberal America," typescript, Berg.

29. AK, "The Strange Death"; MK, "Fathers and Sons," *Dissent* (Fall 1998): 102.

30. AK, Orwell speech, "Not One of Us," *NYRB* (June 14, 1984): 13–18; AK, "Mencken's Ghost," *NR* (October 22, 1984): 32–37; AK, "Alternative America," *NYTBR* (April 24, 1983): 9, 27; AK, "Brooklyn: Borough of Writers," *NYTBR* (May 8, 1983): 12; J11/5/84.

31. Norman Podhoretz, *Breaking Ranks: A Political Memoir* (New York: Harper and Row, 1979); Norman Podhoretz, *Ex-Friends* (New York: The Free Press, 1999); Podhoretz email to author, August 23, 2006; telephone interview with Podhoretz, May 13, 2002.

32. *Lifetime*, 329; James Atlas, *Bellow: A Biography* (New York: Random House, 2000): 517–519.

33. J5/29/85; J5/27/85.

34. AK to Dennis Wrong, October 28, 1970, cc. Berg; AK to Eric Glaberson, April 29, 1980, cc. Berg; Gerald Sorin, *Irving Howe: A Life of Passionate Dissent* (New York: New York University Press, 2002), 138–139.

35. Sorin, *Irving Howe,*, 139; J2/1/84; AK, "They Made It," *Dissent* (Fall 1987): 612–617.

36. MK, "Fathers and Sons," 102; MK, "Editorial: The Right's Victory and Our Response," *Socialist Review* (January–February 1981): 7–8.

37. MK, "Fathers and Sons," 103; AK to MK, December 19, 1980, author's copy; MK, "Fathers and Sons," 103; AK to MK, February 26, 1983, author's copy.

38. Interview with Daniel Bell, October 17, 2003; MK, "Fathers and Sons," 103.

39. AK, "They Made It," 615; Joseph Dorman, *Arguing the World: The New York Intellectuals in Their Own Words* (Chicago: University of Chicago Press, 2001), 94; AK, "The Ideology of Experience," undated speech; AK, "They Made It," 615.

40. J2/24/42; Thomas H. Pauly, "Picture Book," *American Quarterly* (September 1989): 558–562.

41. *ONY,* 218–220.

42. J2/9/62.

CHAPTER 13. "THE END OF THINGS"

1. J10/30/92.

2. J1/10/94; J3/9/83.

3. J5/27/89; J1/10/94; J3/9/83.

4. AK to MK, November 15, 1984, author's copy.

5. J10/5/85.

6. J9/12/84; J2/28/90.

7. Casper W. Wineberger, "Seventy-Five Years Ago," *Forbes* (September 14, 1992): 41.

8. "The Youngest Man Who Ever Was," in *Contemporaries,* 114; AK, "The Fascination and Terror of Ezra Pound," *NYRB* (March 13, 1986).

9. J3/7/88.

10. AK, "The Wound That Will Not Heal," *NR* (August 5, 1986): 39–41; *Thirties,* 137.

11. AK, "The Wound," 39–41; Ronald Radosh, " 'But Today the Struggle': Spain and the Intellectuals," *New Criterion* (October 1986): 15.

12. J10/26/87.

13. AK, "The Cry for Justice," *Tikkun* (May–June 1989): 77–80.

14. Michael Lerner, "Tikkun: To Mend, Repair and Transform the World," *Tikkun* (1986): 8.

15. J6/24/89; AK to MK, April 30, 1985, author's copy; AK to MK, September 12, 1987, author's copy; AK to Jane [no last name], November 7, 1994, cc. Berg; AK to MK, September 12, 1987, author's copy.

16. J8/9/84; AK to MK, March 3, 25, 1996, author's copies; J6/29/85; J9/25/87.

17. J3/3/90.

18. J6/30/88.

19. J9/17/84.

20. AK to MK, February 19, 1996, author's copy; AK to MK, March 25, 1996, author's copy.

21. J7/11/83; J11/25/90; AK to Shimson [no last name], February 10, 1997, cc. Berg; Cathrael Kazin, "Memories of My Father," *Paris Review* (Winter 1998): 232–235.

22. *Lifetime,* 52; J8/16/86; J11/13/83; J8/16/86; Morris Dickstein, "Remembering Alfred Kazin," *AS* (Winter 1999): 19; J5/20/82.

23. J8/15/84; J4/17/77; J8/16/86; J6/17/82.

24. J5/12/82; Irving Kristol to author, June 2, 2002; Weissberg, "Norman Podhoretz Was Here: Profiles of New York Intellectuals," *New York* (January 30, 1995): 14; J6/29/83.

25. J9/28/69; J7/4/83; Philip Roth to AK, October 28, 1983.

26. J8/23/82; J11/29/86; J6/17/91.

27. J8/14/80.

28. J5/1/75; J1/16/87; J12/19/89; *NYJ,* 60.

29. AK, "Anatole Broyard, 1920–90," *NYTBR* (November 24, 1990).

30. J4/3/90; J3/4/96; Anatole Broyard, *Kafka Was the Rage: A Greenwich Village Memoir* (New York: Random House, 1993), vii; J3/2/88.

31. J1/10/87; Dickstein, "Remembering Alfred Kazin," 19; phone interview with Louis Menand, May 29, 2003.

32. J5/8/85; J3/24/90.

33. J10/12/84; phone interview with Mary Beth McMahon, April 17, 2003; J3/14/87.

34. J1/24/80; J12/3/82; J12/1/89.

35. J8/26/66; J1/19/94.

36. J5/20/84; J5/28/82; J4/2/85.

37. J10/23/89.

38. *Lifetime*, 272.

39. J2/4/89; J5/29/91.

40. J3/13/91, J3/24/90; J12/7/91.

41. AK to William Cain, August 13, 1992, cc. Berg; J5/26/85; J7/27/89.

42. J11/11/87; J1/28/88; AK to Arthur Hertzberg, June 23, 1993, cc. Berg.

43. AK, "Jews," *New Yorker* (March 7, 1994): 62–73.

44. *Writing*, 87, 151, 5; Mark Krupnick, "Soul-Searching: The Best Memoir Yet from a Unique Literary Intellectual, Alfred Kazin," *Chicago Tribune Books* (October 22, 1995): 8, Zone C; Paul Berman, "You Must Remember This," *New Yorker* (December 1995): 140.

45. AK to Dr. Win Beck, June 17, 1994, cc. Berg.

46. AK to Martha Nussbaum, October 31, 1994, cc. Berg; AK to Jane [no surname], November 11, 1994, cc. Berg.

47. J3/9/95; J1/23/95; J9/30/95; J9/23/95.

48. J1/28/90.

49. Truman Capote to AK, May 4, 1973; Matthew Flamm, "Kazin Cited at Capote's Kind of Bash," *Newsday* (January 11, 1996).

50. J2/18/96; AK to MK, February 19, 1996, author's copy; J5/22/96.

51. Robert Alter, "A Believer in the City," *NR* (August 12, 1996): 35.

52. Edward Rothstein, "Standing His Ground," *NYTBR* (May 23, 1996): 14; Christopher Lehmann-Haupt, "Thinking of Great Men, Trying to Know God," *NYT* (May 16, 1996); *Lifetime*, 243.

53. AK, "Religion and the Intellectuals," *PR* (March 1950): 232–236; Kim Echlin, "In Search of God: Alfred Kazin Examines the Roots of American Religious Tradition," *Ottawa Citizen* (November 23, 1997): E4; Robert Alter, "A Believer in the City," *NR* (August 12, 1996): 35–36.

54. AK to Harry Ford, September 19, 1996, cc. Berg; AK to Harry Ford, January 2, 1997, cc. Berg; AK to Daniel Aaron, December 18, 1996, cc. Berg; AK to Mr. Bernard, January 8, 1997, cc. Berg; Dan Cryer, "Talking with Alfred Kazin," *Newsday* (October 26, 1997): B11.

55. *God*, 14; Todd Gitlin, "Spiritually Challenged: Alfred Kazin's Study of American Writers and Their Working Relationship with God," *Chicago Tribune Books* (November 16, 1997): 4; Andrew Delbanco, "Divine Criticism," *NR* (November 10, 1997): 48–49; Paul Berman, "The Searchers," *NYTBR* (October 12, 1997): 7; Bonnie Gaarden, review of *God and the American Writer, American Literature* (1998): 671–672; David Reynolds, Review of *God and the American Writer, Journal of American History* (December 1998): 1046–1047. Not everyone in the academy was happy with the book. Peter Rawlings in a review in the *Modern Language Review* 94.4 (1999): 1084, found it a "deeply unsatisfying book," faulting it for its "non-reflexive, untheorized approach."

56. *God*, 258, 15, 175, 236; Berman, "The Searchers," 7; *God*, 42; Sanford Pinsker, "The American Writer's Search for God," *Tikkun*, Vol. 14, no. 6: 78–79.

57. AK to Edward Hoagland, November 2, 1997, cc. Berg; Jeremy Eichler, "A Literary Lion in Winter," *Jerusalem Report* (February 19, 1998): 48.

58. J12/23/97.

59. AK, "The Long Voyage Home," *NYRB* (November 20, 1997); AK, "Oy Gevalt!" *NR* (November 3, 1997): 36–37; JD, "Notes from Mrs. K.," *AS* (Winter 1999): 33–36; AK, "Missing Murray Kempton," *NYTBR* (November 30, 1997): 35; AK, "Witness to the Century," *NYTBR* (November 23, 1997): 9; AK, "Homage to Varian Fry," *NR* (February 9, 1999): 27–30; AK, "A Single Jew," *NYRB* (October 9, 1997); AK, "Laughter in the Dark," *NYRB* (April 23, 1998): 4–5.

60. J7/5/97; J8/20/97; AK to Shimson [no last name], February 10, 1997, cc. Berg; J2/2/88; J7/20/97.

61. J4/14/96; J3/11/97; Cryer, "Talking with Alfred Kazin," B11; J3/1/96; Eichler, "A Literary Lion," 49.

62. JD email to author, September 14, 2004.

63. Morris Dickstein, "I'm Interested in Everything!" AS (Winter 1999): 13–22.

64. JD, "Crossing to the Great Beyond via the Brooklyn Bridge," NYT (July 23, 1999): B41.

Index